EDUCATING EXCEPTIONAL CHILDREN

Seventh Edition

Editor

Karen L. Freiberg
University of Maryland, Baltimore

Dr. Karen Freiberg has an interdisciplinary educational and
employment background in nursing, education, and
developmental psychology. She received her B.S. from the
State University of New York at Plattsburgh, her M.S. from
Cornell University, and her Ph.D. from Syracuse University.
She has worked as a school nurse, a pediatric nurse, a
public health nurse for the Navajo Indians, an associate
project director for a child development clinic, a researcher
in several areas of child development, and a university
professor. She is the author of an award-winning textbook,
Human Development: A Life-Span Approach, which is now
in its third edition. She is currently on the faculty at the
University of Maryland, Baltimore County.

Cover illustration by Mike Eagle

A Annual Editions E
A Library of Information from the Public Press

The Dushkin Publishing Group, Inc.
Sluice Dock, Guilford, Connecticut 06437

The Annual Editions Series

Annual Editions is a series of over 60 volumes designed to provide the reader with convenient, low-cost access to a wide range of current, carefully selected articles from some of the most important magazines, newspapers, and journals published today. Annual Editions are updated on an annual basis through a continuous monitoring of over 300 periodical sources. All Annual Editions have a number of features designed to make them particularly useful, including topic guides, annotated tables of contents, unit overviews, and indexes. For the teacher using Annual Editions in the classroom, an Instructor's Resource Guide with test questions is available for each volume.

VOLUMES AVAILABLE

Africa
Aging
American Foreign Policy
American Government
American History, Pre-Civil War
American History, Post-Civil War
Anthropology
Biology
Business Ethics
Canadian Politics
Child Growth and Development
China
Commonwealth of Independent States
Comparative Politics
Computers in Education
Computers in Business
Computers in Society
Criminal Justice
Drugs, Society, and Behavior
Dying, Death, and Bereavement
Early Childhood Education
Economics
Educating Exceptional Children
Education
Educational Psychology
Environment
Geography
Global Issues
Health
Human Development
Human Resources
Human Sexuality
India and South Asia

International Business
Japan and the Pacific Rim
Latin America
Life Management
Macroeconomics
Management
Marketing
Marriage and Family
Mass Media
Microeconomics
Middle East and the Islamic World
Money and Banking
Multicultural Education
Nutrition
Personal Growth and Behavior
Physical Anthropology
Psychology
Public Administration
Race and Ethnic Relations
Social Problems
Sociology
State and Local Government
Third World
Urban Society
Violence and Terrorism
Western Civilization, Pre-Reformation
Western Civilization, Post-Reformation
Western Europe
World History, Pre-Modern
World History, Modern
World Politics

Library of Congress Cataloging in Publication Data
Main entry under title: Annual editions: Educating exceptional children. 7/E.
   1. Exceptional children—Education—United States—Periodicals. 2. Educational innovations—United States—Periodicals. I. Freiberg, Karen, *comp.* II. Title: Educating exceptional children.
ISBN 1–56134–255–6   371.9'05   76–644171

Seventh Edition

Manufactured in the United States of America

Printed on Recycled Paper

Editors/ Advisory Board

To the Reader

In publishing ANNUAL EDITIONS we recognize the enormous role played by the magazines, newspapers, and journals of the *public press* in providing current, first-rate educational information in a broad spectrum of interest areas. Within the articles, the best scientists, practitioners, researchers, and commentators draw issues into new perspective as accepted theories and viewpoints are called into account by new events, recent discoveries change old facts, and fresh debate breaks out over important controversies.

Many of the articles resulting from this enormous editorial effort are appropriate for students, researchers, and professionals seeking accurate, current material to help bridge the gap between principles and theories and the real world. These articles, however, become more useful for study when those of lasting value are carefully *collected, organized, indexed,* and *reproduced* in a *low-cost format*, which provides easy and permanent access when the material is needed. That is the role played by *Annual Editions*. Under the direction of each volume's *Editor*, who is an expert in the subject area, and with the guidance of an *Advisory Board*, we seek each year to provide in each *ANNUAL EDITION* a current, well-balanced, carefully selected collection of the best of the public press for your study and enjoyment. We think you'll find this volume useful, and we hope you'll take a moment to let us know what you think.

Special education and regular education are gradually combining their bodies of specialized knowledge and their functions in our public schools. Is this a helpful union? Federal legislation, supported by many court cases, has mandated the least restrictive environment for the education of every child with a special need. The new laws have given entrance to an inclusionary form of education and have given exit to countless institutions, special schools, and special classes. Regular education teachers must learn how to address the special needs of every child with an exceptional condition mainstreamed into their classes. Special education teachers must learn how to provide support services and consultations to regular education teachers to help them meet the needs of every child in their class, including those without disabilities. Special educators still work with students with special needs in some situations (e.g., pull-out time in resource rooms, some remaining special classes) but the Regular Education Initiative (REI) is actively changing the face of American education.

This anthology includes many articles that can provide assistance to both special and regular education teachers as they adjust to the advent of inclusionary classes. Not all administrators, teachers, consultants, psychologists, social workers, therapists, speech/language pathologists, other allied professionals, nor even parents, support the concept of mainstreaming children with disabilities or differences into regular education classes. In the selection of articles for this anthology, considerable attention was given to the readers' need for information on new laws and court decisions that are changing American education. Considerable attention has also been given to people's reactions to changes. Some of the selections in this new edition of *Annual Editions: Educating Exceptional Children* are personal experiences of teachers in the field who are struggling to accept inclusionary education.

The education of children with exceptionalities has also expanded to include services to persons with special needs from time of diagnosis (birth, if applicable) throughout their life span. PL 99-457 mandates comprehensive multidisciplinary services for infants and toddlers and their families. PL 101-476 requires schools to provide transition services and follow-up to all students with disabilities. These two pieces of legislation have brought many new persons into the process of assessing, planning programs, educating, providing supportive services, evaluating, and assisting with transitional services. Teachers need to work cooperatively with families and all professional and support persons concerned with the education of each child with an exceptionality.

Two new units to address the special requirements mandated by PL 99-457 and PL 101-476 have been added to this anthology. Unit 2 addresses transition concerns and unit 4 addresses the provision of special services to infants and toddlers with disabilities.

Units 5 through 12 concern the special needs of children who fit into one of the broad categories of exceptionality. Articles in these sections were selected to assure that the reader understands the uniqueness of every child. While we can group children together in terms of the nature of their area of difference (such as learning disabled, mentally retarded, emotionally disturbed), we can never understand each child simply by the label applied to the area of exceptionality. The exceptional child has his or her own degree of "difference," and it is in a constant state of flux. This degree of difference also varies with maturation and environmental input. A good teacher, adequate resources, a strong support system, and responsive and demanding parents can increase the abilities of each child.

To improve future editions of this anthology, the editor and advisory board would like comments, suggestions, and constructive criticisms from you, the reader. You are encouraged to use the article rating form on the last page of this book.

Good luck in using this information to make your own life, and the life of every person with whom you work, a little easier and a lot more rewarding.

Karen Freiberg

Karen Freiberg
Editor

Contents

Unit 1

The Regular Education Initiative

Three articles examine the status of the regular education initiative and services provided for exceptional students in mainstream classes.

Unit 2

Transition Concerns

Two articles examine the problems and issues regarding transitions within school or from school to the community and work force.

To the Reader — iv
Topic Guide — 2
Overview — 4

1. **Outcomes Are for Special Educators Too,** James E. Ysseldyke, Martha L. Thurlow, and James G. Shriner, *Teaching Exceptional Children,* Fall 1992. — 6

   The *Regular Education Initiative* (REI) has reduced isolated classrooms for *special education services.* Teachers in integrated settings must deliver outcomes-based education for all students, including those with exceptionalities. The future will see less tracking, less norm-referenced testing, and more *individualized education programs.*

2. **Severely Disabled Children: Who Pays?** Martha M. McCarthy, *Phi Delta Kappan,* September 1991. — 20

   Several litigations involving the education of students who need *special education services* in *regularized education classes,* as per the provisions of *PL 94-142,* are presented in this article. Congress appropriates little money for these services. State and local agencies cannot always pay for appropriate education in the *least restrictive environment* and also provide an *individualized education plan* for severely disabled children.

3. **Instructional Principles: Behind Computerized Instruction for Students With Exceptionalities,** Edward L. Vockell and Thomas Mihail, *Teaching Exceptional Children,* Spring 1993. — 26

   Should *special education services* include the use of *computers?* Their effectiveness in *regularized education* is determined by specific instructional strategies employed. This article presents the theoretical principles that educators should know before adding computerized lessons to an *individualized education program.*

Overview — 30

4. **EASE: Exit Assistance for Special Educators—Helping Students Make the Transition,** Nancy L. George and Timothy J. Lewis, *Teaching Exceptional Children,* Winter 1991. — 32

   Special education programs are being phased out as more exceptional children are entering *regularized education* classes in compliance with *PL 94-142.* This article describes how teachers can assess the *least restrictive environment* and the special student to make the exit *transition* smooth, positive, and successful.

5. **Transition: Old Wine in New Bottles,** Andrew S. Halpern, *Exceptional Children,* December 1991/January 1992. — 37

   Andrew Halpern examines the reforms in delivery of *special education services* and the development of policies that affect these changes. The current needs and concerns of the *transition* movement are outlined.

The concepts in bold italics are developed in the article. For further expansion please refer to the Topic Guide and the Index.

Unit 3

Inclusionary Education: Peer Interactions

Four articles present strategies for establishing positive interactions between students with and without special needs.

Overview   46

6. **Public Schools Welcome Students With Disabilities as**   48
   Full Members, Linda Davern and Roberta Schnorr,
   Children Today, Volume 20, 1991.

   Linda Davern and Roberta Schnorr detail some of the positive
   effects of including all students in *regular education.* The article
   includes feedback from teachers, parents, and classmates about
   inclusive classes. A sample of an *individualized education plan*
   and a day in the life of a student with special needs adds interest.

7. **Encouraging Peer Supports and Friendships,** William   54
   Stainback, Susan Stainback, and Amy Wilkinson, *Teaching
   Exceptional Children,* Winter 1992.

   *Interactions between students with and without special
   needs* can be promoted by sensitive teachers. This article suggests strategies for promoting informal peer supports and friendships. Such interactions may not be luxuries but rather
   necessities.

8. **Culturally Sensitive Instructional Practices for African-**   60
   American Learners With Disabilities, Mary E. Franklin,
   Exceptional Children, October/November 1992.

   Culture and language affect the delivery of *special education
   services.* The author suggests culturally sensitive practices to
   educate African-American students with disabilities and to encourage *interactions between students with and without
   special needs.*

9. **Disability Simulation for Regular Education Students,**   68
   Mark J. Hallenbeck and Darlene McMaster, *Teaching Exceptional Children,* Spring 1991.

   Volunteer students adopted simulated disabilities for a day, and
   they later talked about their experiences and reactions in an
   assembly program. The exercise fostered understanding of the
   *interaction between students with and without special
   needs.*

Unit 4

Early Childhood Special Education

Three articles discuss the implementation of PL 99-457, the provision of special services to infants and preschoolers with disabilities.

Overview   72

10. **Mainstreaming During the Early Childhood Years,**   74
    Christine L. Salisbury, *Exceptional Children,* October/No-
    vember 1991.

    Christine Salisbury describes an outcomes-based process for
    making decisions about providing *special education services*
    for young children. It is a challenge to follow *PL 99-457* guidelines
    and to include *interactions between children with and with-
    out special needs* in a *regularized education* setting at the
    early childhood level.

11. **Children With Disabilities Who Use Assistive Technol-**   82
    ogy: Ethical Considerations, Loreta Holder-Brown and
    Howard P. Parette, Jr., *Young Children,* September 1992.

    An amendment to *PL 99-457* identifies *computers and other
    assistive technologies* as specific *special education services*
    to be provided in *early childhood.* This article defines assistive
    technology and discusses its selection and appropriateness.

12. **Play for All Children: The Toy Library Solution,** Sara C.   87
    Jackson, Linda Robey, Martha Watjus, and Elizabeth Chad-
    wick, *Childhood Education,* Fall 1991.

    PL 99-457 mandates an *Individualized Family Service Plan*
    (IFSP) for infants and toddlers with special needs. Toy libraries are
    consistent with this mandate for family involvement. Play is
    central to the development of exceptional young children in *early
    childhood special education.*

Children With Learning Disabilities

Four selections address the assessment and special needs of students with learning disabilities.

Overview   92

13. **The Masks Students Wear,** Sally L. Smith, *Instructor,* April 1989.   94

   Learning disabled adults disclose ways they hid their disorders while in school. Knowing their "masks" can alert educators to look for and *assess* similar children with LD problems today. The author includes descriptions of the *effects of the disorder on the learning and development* of several famous adults.

14. **Examining the Instructional Contexts of Students With Learning Disabilities,** Janis A. Bulgren and Judith J. Carta, *Exceptional Children,* December 1992/January 1993.   98

   Do students with *learning disabilities* who make the *transition* from special education classes to *regularized education* have enhanced academic experiences or suffer losses? This article reports on 10 years of studies on the *assessment* of different classes and different teacher and student behaviors.

15. **Adapting Textbooks for Children With Learning Disabilities in Mainstreamed Classrooms,** Ruth Lyn Meese, *Teaching Exceptional Children,* Spring 1992.   106

   Many students with *learning disabilities* can be helped to comprehend textbook materials with small changes in instructional procedures. Strategies to maintain reading involvement are presented in this article. Special education teachers can help regular classroom teachers master skills necessary for the *transition* to mainstreamed classrooms.

16. **Teaching Study Skills to Students With Mild Handicaps: The Role of the Classroom Teacher,** Karen Decker, Susan Spector, and Stan Shaw, *The Clearing House,* May/June 1992.   109

   Learning disabled students, especially those in secondary school, may experience academic difficulties when placed in the *least restrictive environment* of the regular classroom. Teaching them study skills can enhance their learning.

Children With Mental Retardation

Three articles discuss concerns and strategies for providing optimal educational programs for students with mental retardation.

Overview   114

17. **Teaching Basic Concepts to Students Who Are Educable Mentally Handicapped,** R. Brett Nelson, Jack A. Cummings, and Heidi Boltman, *Teaching Exceptional Children,* Winter 1991.   116

   Special education programs would be more beneficial to children who are *mentally retarded* if they focused on systematically teaching basic concepts. General guidelines are presented for the application of concept education.

18. **Sex Education for Students With High-Incidence Special Needs,** Greg M. Romaneck and Robert Kuehl, *Teaching Exceptional Children,* Fall 1992.   119

   Students with *mental retardation* have the same sexual drives as normal intelligence students, but they have less knowledge. They are vulnerable to exploitation and pathology. This article suggests strategies for sex education that consider *assessment* of needs and *individualized education plans* for appropriate curriculum.

19. **The Task Demonstration Model: A Concurrent Model for Teaching Groups of Students With Severe Disabilities,** Kathryn G. Karsh and Alan C. Repp, *Exceptional Children,* September 1992.   122

   Since the implementation of *PL 94-142* and mainstreamed classrooms, students with *mental retardation* seldom have one-to-one teaching. This article presents an effective model for group teaching that holds students' attention, increases their correct responses, and reduces the need for teacher prompts.

The concepts in bold italics are developed in the article. For further expansion please refer to the Topic Guide and the Index.

Children With Special Gifts and Talents

Three articles examine the need for special services for gifted and talented students, assessment of giftedness, and ways to teach these students.

Children With Emotional and Behavioral Problems

Four articles discuss the regular education initiative and ways to teach emotionally and behaviorally disordered students in mainstream classes.

Overview   134
20. **Turning On the Bright Lights,** Jeff Meade, *Teacher Maga-*   136
    zine, February 1991.
    The debate over education of the *gifted and talented* reflects the
    larger conflict in education—equity vs. excellence. Is it fair to give
    special treatment to some children and not to others? This article
    examines both sides of the question.
21. **Poor and Minority Students Can Be Gifted, Too!** Mary   142
    M. Frasier, *Educational Leadership,* March 1989.
    Assessment of gifted and talented children that relies on
    narrow nomination and screening methods can miss poor and
    minority gifted students. Behavioral traits and a broadened con-
    cept of giftedness based on new definitions of intelligence can
    improve *testing and labeling.*
22. **Serious Play in the Classroom,** Selma Wassermann,   145
    Childhood Education, Spring 1992.
    This article looks at the *effect of creative play on learning and*
    development in such famous *gifted and talented* "tinkerers" as
    the Wright brothers, Thomas Edison, and Nobel Laureate Richard
    Feynman. Selma Wassermann describes how play can be a
    beneficial addition to any educational curriculum.

Overview   152
23. **Do Public Schools Have an Obligation to Serve Trou-**   154
    bled Children and Youth? C. Michael Nelson, Robert B.
    Rutherford, Jr., David B. Center, and Hill M. Walker,
    Exceptional Children, March/April 1991.
    PL 94-142 and its amendments *PL 99-457* exclude socially
    maladjusted children from special services unless they are also
    emotionally disturbed. The authors of this article argue that
    socially maladjusted children need *assessment* for emotional
    problems and appropriate *individualized education programs.*
24. **Suicide and Depression: Special Education's Respon-**   163
    sibility, Eleanor Guetzloe, *Teaching Exceptional Children,*
    Summer 1988.
    Severe *emotional and behavioral disorders* are the most preva-
    lent condition associated with suicide and depression. This article
    focuses on educators' responsibilities in providing suicide preven-
    tion programs in schools. It discusses *assessment* and interven-
    tion, and suggests a preventative curriculum.
25. **Values Clarification for Students With Emotional Dis-**   167
    abilities, Brian J. Abrams, *Teaching Exceptional Children,*
    Spring 1992.
    Assessment of each *emotionally and behaviorally disordered*
    student's awareness and values clarity, and affective education
    that matches each student's needs, can result in more prosocial
    interactions between students with and without disabilities.
    The author describes how to get started in values clarification.
26. **Working With Disturbed Adolescents,** Stanley C. Dia-   171
    mond, *The Clearing House,* March/April 1991.
    Placing *emotionally disturbed and behaviorally disordered*
    adolescents in a regular classroom to provide a *least restrictive*
    environment can stress teachers to their limits. This article
    presents several suggestions on what teachers can do when
    there seems to be little that can be done to help them.

The concepts in bold italics are developed in the article. For further expansion please refer to the Topic Guide and the Index.

Unit 9

Children With Communication Disorders

Four selections discuss disorders of communication and suggest ways in which adults can assist student's learning and development in speech and language.

Overview 174

27. **Preschool Classroom Environments That Promote Communication,** Michaelene M. Ostrosky and Ann P. Kaiser, *Teaching Exceptional Children,* Summer 1991. 176
Communication disorders such as speech delays or language delays develop when the environment does not require language or reinforce it. This article suggests techniques that work to promote language in *early childhood special education.*

28. **Do You See What I Mean? Body Language in Classroom Interactions,** Mary M. Banbury and Constance R. Hebert, *Teaching Exceptional Children,* Winter 1992. 180
This article details nonverbal behaviors that serve as *communications* in place of speech/language. Teachers can learn to communicate with body positions, eyes, gestures, and body movements, and they can learn to *assess* these behaviors in their students.

29. **See Me, Help Me,** Edward G. Carr and V. Mark Durand, *Psychology Today,* November 1987. 184
In some children, bizarre behavior is a means of communication with negative *effects on learning and development.* The authors discuss studies demonstrating that teaching such *communication disordered* children normal ways of communicating will reduce their bizarre behaviors. The speech instruction can be provided in the school setting with the assistance of the teacher.

30. **Using a Picture Task Analysis to Teach Students With Multiple Disabilities,** Wynelle H. Roberson, Jane S. Gravel, Gregory C. Valcante, and Ralph G. Maurer, *Teaching Exceptional Children,* Summer 1992. 187
The use of pictures to augment speech and language in children with *communication disorders* is common. This article describes a picture task analysis approach that enables students to learn meaningful skills that might otherwise be beyond their grasp.

Unit 10

Children With Hearing Impairments

Three articles examine due process for the provision of special services for the hearing impaired and strategies for teaching hearing impaired children in regular education classes.

Overview 190

31. **The Establishment Clause as Antiremedy,** Steven Huefner, *Phi Delta Kappan,* September 1991. 192
PL 94-142 guarantees children with disabilities appropriate education even if they attend private schools. The establishment clause requires scrutiny of public aid to private institutions to prevent "establishment of religion." This article asks, "Should an interpreter be denied a *hearing-impaired* student because the student attends a parochial school?"

32. **Reducing Ethnocentrism,** David S. Martin, *Teaching Exceptional Children,* Fall 1987. 197
If teachers believe that positive *interaction between the children with and without special needs* can lead to a better world, they must employ techniques to reduce ethnocentrism. The author suggests several strategies that can help reduce the negative attitudes, misunderstandings, and miscommunications between hearing children and children with *hearing impairments* who interact in schools.

33. **Hearing for Success in the Classroom,** JoAnn C. Ireland, Denise Wray, and Carol Flexer, *Teaching Exceptional Children,* Winter 1988. 200
Hearing impaired children in regular classrooms need the *technological aid* of frequency modulation (FM) auditory trainers. These units reduce background noise and improve speech intelligibility. The sound source (the teacher) wears a microphone and the student wears a receiver.

The concepts in bold italics are developed in the article. For further expansion please refer to the Topic Guide and the Index.

Unit 11

Children With Visual Impairments

Three selections discuss the special needs of visually impaired and blind children from infancy through secondary school.

Unit 12

Children With Physical or Health Impairments

Four articles examine the educational implications of medical treatments and physical impairments on children.

Overview   202

34. **The Parent and Toddler Training Project for Visually Impaired and Blind Multihandicapped Children,** B. Klein, V. B. Van Hasselt, M. Trefelner, D. J. Sandstrom, and P. Brandt-Snyder, *Journal of Visual Impairment & Blindness,* February 1988.   204

This article describes an *early childhood special education* program for newborn to 3-year-old children with *visual impairments.* The program describes how to increase the social responsiveness of infants, develop more adequate parenting skills, and initiate treatment approaches to reduce the *effect of the disorder on learning and development.*

35. **Appropriate Education for Visually Handicapped Students,** Geraldine T. Scholl, *Teaching Exceptional Children,* Winter 1987.   210

Geraldine Scholl addresses *individualized educational programs* (IEPs) for children whose only special education needs are those that accompany a *visual impairment.* Modified *assessment,* creative placement, and appropriate IEPs utilizing *computers and other technological aids* can help overcome barriers to learning.

36. **Efficacy of Low Vision Services for Visually Impaired Children,** H. W. Hofstetter, *Journal of Visual Impairment & Blindness,* January 1991.   214

Children with *visual impairments* from all grades were screened to determine their need for, and use of, low vision *technological aids.* A majority needed more low vision services than they were receiving. The fact that students qualify for *special educational service* does not guarantee that they will seek it.

Overview   218

37. **Medical Treatment and Educational Problems in Children,** Nettie R. Bartel and S. Kenneth Thurman, *Phi Delta Kappan,* September 1992.   220

The nature and treatment of three fairly common *physical and health impairments* of childhood are discussed: cancer, low birth weight and prematurity, and the "medically fragile." After presenting these problems, the implications for appropriate educational services are discussed.

38. **Physical Abuse: Are Children With Disabilities at Greater Risk?** Thomas J. Zirpoli, *Intervention in School and Clinic,* September 1990.   224

The title question is answered "depending on other variables." Children with *physical and health impairments* and children with *emotional and behavioral disorders* are more frequently victims of physical abuse. Most parents cope well with *disability demands,* but those who do not need appropriate supports from clinics, schools, and community groups.

The concepts in bold italics are developed in the article. For further expansion please refer to the Topic Guide and the Index.

39. **Integrating Elementary Students With Multiple Disabilities Into Supported Regular Classes,** Susan Hamre-Nietupski, Jennifer McDonald, and John Nietupski, *Teaching Exceptional Children,* Spring 1992. 230

The **regularized education initiative** advocates placing children with **physical and health impairments** and other multiple disabilities into regular classes. This article gives challenges and solutions for accomplishing this with supportive services at the elementary school level.

40. **Designing an Integrated Program for Learners With Severe Disabilities,** Jennifer York and Terri Vandercook, *Teaching Exceptional Children,* Winter 1991. 234

Placing children with severe **physical impairments** in the **least restrictive environment** requires that educators use the classroom environment to teach social competencies in addition to subject-area curriculum. This article presents several suggestions for **individualized education programs.**

Index 241
Article Review Form 244
Article Rating Form 245

The concepts in bold italics are developed in the article. For further expansion please refer to the Topic Guide and the Index.

Topic Guide

This topic guide suggests how the selections in this book relate to topics of traditional concern to students and professionals involved with educating exceptional children. It is very useful in locating articles that relate to each other for reading and research. The guide is arranged alphabetically according to topic. Articles may, of course, treat topics that do not appear in the topic guide. In turn, entries in the topic guide do not necessarily constitute a comprehensive listing of all the contents of each selection.

TOPIC AREA	KNOWLEDGE (These articles provide information about a handicap or about a special education concept.)	ATTITUDES (These articles contain personal experiences of exceptional persons or discussions about changing children's attitudes toward a handicap.)	TEACHING (These articles contain practical suggestions about how to apply special education principles to the teaching of exceptional children.)
Assessment	14. Examining the Instructional Contexts of Students 18. Sex Education for Students 21. Poor and Minority Students Can Be Gifted Too!	13. Masks Students Wear 23. Do Public Schools Have an Obligation?	24. Suicide and Depression 25. Values Clarification 28. Do You See What I Mean? 35. Appropriate Education for Visually Handicapped Students
Communication Disorders	27. Preschool Classroom Environments That Promote Communication 29. See Me, Help Me	30. Using a Picture Task Analysis to Teach Students	28. Do You See What I Mean?
Computers and Other Technological Aids	33. Hearing for Success in the Classroom 36. Efficacy of Low Vision Services	11. Children With Disabilities Who Use Assistive Technology 35. Appropriate Education for Visually Handicapped Students	3. Instructional Principles 15. Adapting Textbooks for Children With Learning Disabilities
Due Process PL 94-142	2. Severely Disabled Children: Who Pays? 31. Establishment Clause as Antiremedy	23. Do Public Schools Have an Obligation?	4. EASE: Helping Students Make the Transition 19. Task Demonstration Model
Due Process PL 99-457	10. Mainstreaming During the Early Childhood Years	23. Do Public Schools Have an Obligation?	12. Play for All Children
Early Childhood Special Education	11. Children With Disabilities Who Use Assistive Technology	10. Mainstreaming During the Early Childhood Years 34. Parent and Toddler Training Project	12. Play for All Children 27. Preschool Classroom Environments
Effect of Disorder on Learning	22. Serious Play in the Classroom	13. Masks Students Wear 29. See Me, Help Me	34. Parent and Toddler Training Project
Emotional and Behavioral Disorders	24. Suicide and Depression 26. Working With Disturbed Adolescents	23. Do Public Schools Have an Obligation? 38. Physical Abuse	25. Values Clarification
Gifted and Talented	20. Turning on the Bright Lights	21. Poor and Minority Students Can Be Gifted Too!	22. Serious Play in the Classroom
Hearing Impairment	31. Establishment Clause as Antiremedy	32. Reducing Ethnocentrism	33. Hearing for Success in the Classroom
Individualized Education Program (IEPs) and Individualized Family Service Plans (IFSPs)	2. Severely Disabled Children: Who Pays? 18. Sex Education for Students 35. Appropriate Education for Visually Handicapped Students	1. Outcomes Are for Special Educators Too 6. Public Schools Welcome Students With Disabilities 23. Do Public Schools Have an Obligation?	3. Instructional Principles 12. Play for All Children 40. Designing an Integrated Program for Learners
Inclusionary Education: Interaction of Children With and Without Special Needs	10. Mainstreaming During the Early Childhood Years 25. Values Clarification	7. Encouraging Peer Supports and Friendships 9. Disability Simulation for Regular Education Students 32. Reducing Ethnocentrism	8. Culturally Sensitive Instructional Practices
Learning Disabilities	14. Examining the Instructional Contexts of Students		15. Adapting Textbooks for Children With Learning Disabilities 16. Teaching Study Skills
Least Restrictive Environment	26. Working With Disturbed Adolescents	2. Severely Disabled Children: Who Pays? 4. EASE: Helping Students Make the Transition	16. Teaching Study Skills 40. Designing an Integrated Program for Learners

TOPIC AREA	KNOWLEDGE (These articles provide information about a handicap or about a special education concept.)	ATTITUDES (These articles contain personal experiences of exceptional persons or discussions about changing children's attitudes toward a handicap.)	TEACHING (These articles contain practical suggestions about how to apply special education principles to the teaching of exceptional children.)
Mental Retardation	18. Sex Education for Students 19. Task Demonstration Model		17. Teaching Basic Concepts
Physical and Health Impairments	37. Medical Treatment and Educational Problems in Children	38. Physical Abuse	39. Integrating Elementary Students With Multiple Disabilities 40. Designing an Integrated Program for Learners
Regularized Education Initiative	2. Severely Disabled Children: Who Pays? 4. EASE: Helping Students Make the Transition 10. Mainstreaming During the Early Childhood Years	1. Outcomes Are for Special Educators Too 6. Public Schools Welcome Students With Disabilities	3. Instructional Principles 14. Examining the Instructional Contexts of Students 39. Integrating Elementary Students With Multiple Disabilities
Special Education Services	2. Severely Disabled Children: Who Pays? 5. Transition: Old Wine in New Bottles 10. Mainstreaming During the Early Childhood Years 36. Efficacy of Low Vision Services	4. EASE: Helping Students Make the Transition 11. Children With Disabilities Who Use Assistive Technology	1. Outcomes Are for Special Educators Too 3. Instructional Principles 8. Culturally Sensitive Instructional Practices 17. Teaching Basic Concepts
Testing and Labeling			21. Poor and Minority Students Can Be Gifted Too!
Transition	5. Transition: Old Wine in New Bottles	14. Examining the Instructional Contexts of Students	4. EASE: Helping Students Make the Transition 15. Adapting Textbooks for Children With Learning Disabilities
Visual Impairments	35. Appropriate Education for Visually Handicapped Students 36. Efficacy of Low Vision Services		34. Parent and Toddler Training Project

The Regular Education Initiative

Special education for students with conditions of exceptionality was once a very different job from regular education of students free of major exceptionalities. The lines of demarcation between special educators and regular educators have been greatly diminished by recent legislation and by the Regular Education Initiative (REI) called for by special educators.

The Education for All Handicapped Children Act (Public Law 94-142), passed in 1975, had four major provisions. It guaranteed the availability of free special education to children with exceptionalities who required it, it assured that decisions about special education would be fair and appropriate in a least restrictive environment (the mainstream concept), it required clear management procedures for special education at all levels, and it provided federal funds to supplement the costs of state and local governments' special education programs.

The provision for fair and appropriate education, as defined by PL 94-142, did not mandate mainstreaming—not every disabled child must be educated in a regular classroom. Furthermore, the law did not abolish any particular educational settings, even within residential institutions. However, a policy of deinstitutionalization was written between the lines. PL 94-142 required that all children be educated in a least restrictive setting.

Further laws, most notably PL 99-457, the Amendment to the Education for All Handicapped Children Act (which extended its benefits to infants and toddlers), and PL 101-476, the Individuals With Disabilities Education Act (IDEA), reaffirmed the rights of people with disabilities to be educated in the least restrictive environment.

In 1986, the assistant secretary for the Office of Special Education of the Department of Education proposed that regular educators take over the responsibility of educating exceptional children in regular classrooms (the REI). Special educators could then serve as consultants and provide support services for regular educators. There would be one educational system with shared responsibility rather than two separate systems (regular education and special education). The Regular Education Initiative is currently being tested in some schools on a trial basis. Self-contained part- and full-time special classes and resource rooms for pull-out special education have been terminated. In these schools, special educators are working as consultants and supportive counselors rather than as teachers of children with special needs. There are both pros and cons emerging from these early trials of the REI.

Until recently, most regular education teachers had very little, if any, preparation for special education in their college or university teaching curriculum. Therefore, they have had to enroll in courses in special education, and/or do a great deal of reading on their own, to prepare for special education. Many of them have been very frustrated and dissatisfied with the challenges of inclusionary education and the mainstreaming of students with exceptional conditions into their classrooms. The REI has resulted in some incorrect labeling, some inappropriate programming, and many additional expenses. Some parents have fought to get their children with special needs out of mainstream classrooms and back into more restrictive special programs. Educators, administrators, parents, and other support service personnel have had difficulty working together to resolve problems, obey laws, and make regular education a happier situation for everyone concerned.

On the positive side, REI has furthered the cause of integration of U.S. schools. The movement has generated some very innovative service delivery systems. Many students both with and without conditions of exceptionality have expressed their preference for inclusionary education. The academic progress of some students with exceptional conditions has improved. However, not every child with a disability benefits from mainstreaming.

The question of the efficacy of mainstreaming has been debated since its inception. A public education agency must "show cause" if and when a child is moved from regular education to a more restrictive educational setting. The school must provide a written statement describing the extent to which the child will be able to participate in regular education programs. Parochial and private schools must afford the same rights and protections of PL 94-142 to children who are placed there by public agencies. However, if a parent, rather than an educational agency, places the child in private school, the rights may be surrendered. Fair and appropriate education requires an annual comprehensive educational assessment of every exceptional child, and it must be in the form of a written, individualized education program (IEP). Any special education services such as resource room pull-out, part-time special class, or full-time special class must be justified.

The REI is not law. Mainstreaming is not law. The least restrictive environment in which appropriate education can take place is the law. The settings in which education of children with disabilities are most appropriate have yet to be determined.

The first article in this unit discusses the need for special education teachers to be involved in outcomes-

based education and the assessment of outcomes for children with disabilities. The second article addresses the financial state of education in the United States. Deinstitutionalization, mainstreaming, and inclusionary education have stretched school budgets to their limits in most states. Will there be a backlash against children with special needs? If so, who will pay for the education of children with the most severe disabilities? The third article discusses computerized instruction for students with exceptionalities. The REI, mainstreaming, and inclusionary education have brought computers out of resource rooms and/or special education rooms and brought them into regular classrooms. The authors discuss ways to use computer software to provide an appropriate education for students with exceptionalities in regular classrooms.

Looking Ahead: Challenge Questions

Is education becoming more outcomes-oriented? Who will assess the educational outcomes of students with disabilities in regular education classes?

Who will pay for the special education services required by so many severely disabled children in public schools?

Are computers capable of providing the most appropriate education for students with exceptionalities in regular education classes?

Outcomes Are for Special Educators Too

A thermos bottle keeps things hot and cold, but how does it know?

James E. Ysseldyke
Martha L. Thurlow
James G. Shriner

James E. Ysseldyke *(CEC Chapter #367) is Director;* **Martha L. Thurlow** *(CEC Chapter #367) is Assistant Director; and* **James G. Shriner** *(CEC Chapter #405) is Senior Researcher, National Center on Educational Outcomes, College of Education, University of Minnesota, Minneapolis.*

It is September now, and everything about your classroom looks promising. You have a new mathematics curriculum and new materials for the first time in several years. The bulletin board has taken shape nicely. They even painted your walls over the summer. All in all, you feel great. This year you really will get a lot done. There is nothing to hold you back from having your best year ever!

Just one question: How are you going to know how you did as your last student walks, runs, or rolls out the classroom door in June? If you are stuck for an answer, you had better get unstuck in a hurry. Your students and their parents, your principal, the school board, the state legislature, Congress, and the president all want to know what you have accomplished over the 9 months of the school year.

Results?

Don't be frightened. Welcome to the newest system of educational accountability, sometimes called an *outcomes-oriented model* of education. It is possible, if not probable, that at the end of the year you will not be asked what classes you taught, what instructional programs you used, how many students you taught full time or part time, how many students you were able to integrate into general education settings, or how many collaborative teaching efforts you took part in. Instead, you will be asked to explain only one thing: *the results of*

what you did. Did your students make progress toward established standards and goals?

You may ask, "What standards and goals?" Already there are published, approved, even mandated outcomes for students. Some of these are national (e.g., National Education Goals; Curriculum and Evaluation Standards of the National Council of Teachers of Mathematics); state (e.g., Utah's Core Curriculum; Maine's Common Core of Learning); district (e.g., Waynesboro, PA, Mathematics Program Goals and Objectives; Aurora, CO, High Success Outcomes); and classroom level (Ms. Skinner's plan for math).

Special Educators Take Note

Outcomes and standards are important concepts for special educators to consider. Even though most position papers and calls for standards by policy groups, legislatures, and government agencies contain language that is inclusive of all students, few of their actions follow through on the inclusive rhetoric. Anderson (1992) has suggested that most, if not all, current reform-oriented activities are geared toward only 90% of students in U.S. schools because they do *not* consider students who have exceptionalities. In his view, the 10% of the school population with disabilities is simply overlooked in most reform activities.

It is imperative that special education professionals and advocates understand what is being discussed and how outcomes and accountability assessments are taking shape throughout the educational system, from the national level to the level of individual student program plans and evaluation. This article discusses what the term *outcomes* encompasses at different levels and provides descriptions of current and proposed strategies for assessing the educational outcomes of students with disabilities. "Windows" written by people working within each level highlight some of the ways outcomes activities are affecting professionals in the field.

Education remains grounded in the critical student-teacher interaction. As a teacher, you are the primary partner in this interaction, and you must recognize and understand the larger issues that affect student-teacher relationships. You must be aware of the outcomes issues with which you will be involved as the next century approaches, because you will play a part in decisions about the role that special education takes in outcomes initiatives and reform. A good place to start is with definitions of some of the key terms.

Learning the Words

The National Center on Educational Outcomes (NCEO) defines an *outcome* as the result of interactions between in-

Figure 1.
Most Recent Version of NCEO Outcomes Model

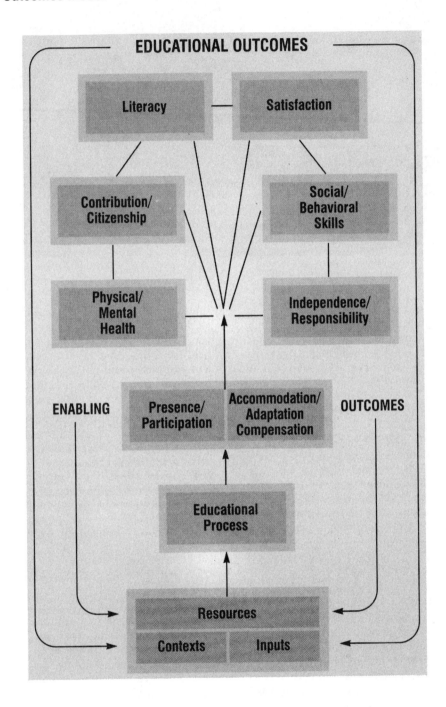

questions. Now, however, we expect increasing emphasis on the *outcomes* of schooling.

At the NCEO we are working with state directors of special education, teachers, parents, and others such as policy groups and local school administrators to develop a model of important educational outcomes for students with disabilities. The latest version of this model, which is still in the process of development, is shown in Figure 1. Currently, the model includes two kinds of outcomes—*enabling outcomes* and *educational outcomes*. Even though these terms may not be the best, the underlying assumption is that we must identify outcomes for *all* students, regardless of their individual characteristics, and that for some students, outcomes that enable them to participate meaningfully in the educational experience (e.g., learning braille or learning to communicate through the use of signs) must precede other educational outcomes such as reading or getting a job.

Outcomes-based education (OBE) is a system that seeks to define, design, deliver, and document instruction and assessment in terms of intended outcomes (Evans, 1992; King & Evans, 1991). Outcomes often are broken down into mastery outcomes (minimal competencies) and developmental outcomes (more complex and integrated products).

The outcomes-oriented approach is taking hold rapidly, and outcomes are being defined just as quickly. It is important to understand how this approach gained its popularity. Even more, you need to know about the ways in which the need for information about how students are doing in and out of school will affect you, your students, your school, your state, and the country as a whole.

There are several OBE models. Two of the better known are the Outcomes Driven Developmental Model (ODDM) (Champlin, 1991) and the High Success Network (HSN) Strategic Design Model (Spady, 1992). These models are both based on the belief that future-oriented outcomes should be the starting point of educational decision making. Goals (desired exit outcomes) must be set before any decisions about instructional implementation are made. Assessments of student progress toward outcomes must be conducted in real-life situations, rather than through tests that do

dividuals and schooling experiences. Most people recognize that outcomes include skills, knowledge, and attitudes. Outcomes are different from inputs, processes, and contexts, all of which teachers are used to being asked about at year's end. For example, "How many students in your class were on free lunch?" and "How many computers did you have available for your students?"

are *input* questions. "What spelling curriculum did you find useful for your class?" and "Did you use cooperative learning?" are *process* questions. "Where did most of your students receive reading instruction?" and "How many teacher assaults occurred in your school?" are *context* questions. Historically, special educators have been collecting data to answer these kinds of not reflect the real-life outcome goals. The curriculum becomes secondary in importance to the outcomes, in contrast to the current approach in most schools in which the curriculum determines the outcomes.

OBE is not new. Its advocates argue that it came about in response to a desire on the part of parents and educators to know the extent to which they are preparing students to participate effectively in and contribute to an adult community. Special education teachers argue that it has been around for a long time, especially as reflected in the notion of specifying annual goals and short-term objectives. Nearly half a century ago, Tyler (1949) stressed the importance of teaching to objectives related to life areas.

What *is* new is the strong impetus for districts and states to adopt OBE as policy. Recently, for example, Pennsylvania decided to replace existing graduation criteria with OBE goals and objectives. Whether this move is good or bad remains to be seen. The state does not yet have an assessment system to ascertain the extent to which students are making progress toward OBE goals. Other states (e.g., Kentucky) are accelerating efforts in the same direction and have begun to develop outcomes-based accountability assessments. Another thing that is new is the impetus to transform schools as a vital part of OBE. What began as a goal of mastery learning has progressed to the discussion of transformational OBE, which is focused on transforming schools and achieving broad outcomes such as "Students will be collaborative workers."

Standards are statements of criteria against which comparisons can be made. These are often value statements about what is important, and they are sometimes established for the purpose of changing an existing situation. The National Council of Teachers of Mathematics (NCTM) has published *Curriculum and Evaluation Standards for School Mathematics* (NCTM, 1989). The *Standards* are intended to reshape the discipline of mathematics education with respect to the skills, knowledge, and attitudes students will need in order to be fully prepared for life. For example, one of the NCTM standards states that students should develop and apply problem solving strategies to solve a wide variety of problems. This can be translated into a more specific

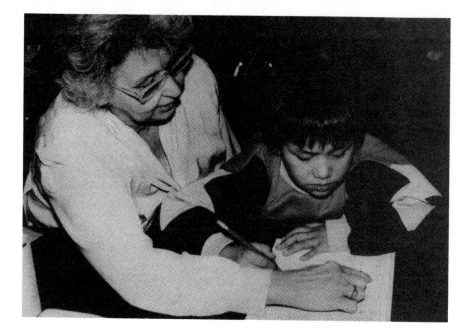

"essential learner outcome," as Minnesota has done in the outcome "Students should be able to solve consumer problems including budgets and taxes" (Minnesota Department of Education, 1991).

As new standards are prepared, new assessment strategies are needed to measure progress. Groups such as NCTM and the National Council on Educational Standards and Testing have also called for nontraditional approaches to assessment such as portfolio and performance measures, which are sometimes called *authentic assessments*. Wiggins (1989) defined authentic assessments as those that are "contextualized, complex intellectual challenges, not fragmented and static bits or tasks" (p. 711).

With the terms defined, it is now important to ask about the implications of these concepts for the education of students with disabilities at all levels of the educational system. In the end, all viewpoints relate to the questions directed to the teacher at the end of the year: *What have you accomplished with your students? How do you know?*

Outcomes at the National Level

National interest in the outcomes of education has been heightened since the publication of *A Nation at Risk* (National Commission on Excellence in

Education, 1983). The report warned the public that the U.S. educational system was failing to meet many of its widely held expectations and that achievement and progress could not be taken for granted. Continued evidence of the failure of U.S. schools to produce students with adequate skills eventually led the state governors and the Bush administration to propose the following six national education goals for improved school and student performance: "America 2000" is a national agenda that has been proposed to help our nation meet these six national education goals (see Sindelar, Watanabe, McCray, & Hornsby, 1992):

Goal 1: By the year 2000, all children in America will start school ready to learn.

Goal 2: By the year 2000, the high school graduation rate will increase to at least 90 percent.

Goal 3: By the year 2000, American students will leave grades four, eight, and twelve having demonstrated competency in challenging subject matter...; and every school in America will ensure that all students learn to use their minds well, so they may be prepared for responsible citizenship, further learning, and productive employment in our modern economy.

Goal 4: By the year 2000, U.S. students will be first in the world in science and mathematics achievement.

Goal 5: By the year 2000, every adult

American will be literate and will possess the knowledge and skills necessary to compete in a global economy and exercise the rights and responsibilities of citizenship.

Goal 6: By the year 2000, every school in America will be free of drugs and violence and will offer a disciplined environment conducive to learning. (National Education Goals Panel, 1991)

With the National Education Goals established, the need for information about the performance of students has become more important at the national level. Reasons for collecting data are often framed in relation to these goals, and progress toward them must be documented through national data collection efforts. Assessments that yield information about the overall performance of the educational system help to gauge improvements and deficiencies on a broad scale (Elliott, 1989). There may be specific areas of concern that are targeted for evaluation. For example, the federal government may seek specific information about student performance in mathematics and science. Test results may (and often do) show deficiencies in these subjects, indicating a need for more concerted educational efforts. National data collection helps the U.S. Department of Education make funding allocations and plans for programs to improve teacher preparation, instructional design, and service delivery.

Assessment

A current method of collecting national information for policymakers is the National Assessment of Educational Progress (NAEP), which consists of content area assessments in most subject areas. These are given to samples of students in grades 4, 8, and 12 every 2 years. Results provide an overall picture of current performance at different grade levels and an idea of the trends in academic achievement over time. Beginning in 1988, NAEP reading and mathematics tests were used to make state-by-state comparisons of student achievement.

Assessments such as NAEP raise several issues concerning outcomes for students with disabilities. For example, NAEP is restricted to academic achievement. For many students (not just those with disabilities), a broader conceptualization of educational outcomes is needed. (Figure 1 provided one conceptual model that has more outcomes than those traditionally encompassed by the content areas included in NAEP.) Another issue relates to the representativeness of the sample of students who participate in the NAEP system. NCEO has estimated that approximately one third to one half of all school-age students with disabilities are excluded from NAEP assessments (McGrew, Thurlow, Shriner, & Spiegel, 1992). Furthermore, the proportion of students who are excluded varies widely from state to state (Rothman, 1992). Thus, since current national data do not accurately reflect the achievement of the entire school-age population, caution must be used in drawing conclusions about student performance based on NAEP data. The true national picture, inclusive of *all* students, is probably different from the one NAEP describes. This national database provides no information about the performance of students with disabilities.

Standards

The NCTM (1989) *Standards* address the perceived need for increased performance levels of U.S. students. They establish a broad framework to guide reform in school mathematics, outlining both process and content standards. For example, the new standards ask that students (1) learn to value mathematics; (2) become confident in their ability to do mathematics; (3) become mathematical problem solvers; (4) learn to communicate mathematically; and (5) learn to reason mathematically (NCTM, 1989, p. 5).

The process standards stress higher-order thinking skills. NCTM advocates that the process standards be given increased emphasis because the current mathematics curriculum is narrow in scope and fails to foster mathematical insight, reasoning, and problem solving. Cawley, Baker-Kroczynski, and Urban (1992), in a discussion of mathematics education for students with disabilities, agreed with NCTM and added that special education has been stressing "rote learning of computational routines and memorization of basic facts" (p. 41). They argued that although these skills touch on the NCTM content standards, they have limited applicability to real-life situations.

In addition to the curriculum standards, NCTM includes standards for the evaluation of school mathematics that outline how outcomes assessment in mathematics should be conducted. NCTM strongly recommends that multiple sources of information (including written, oral, and demonstration assessments) be used in making evaluation decisions and that problem situations take a more realistic and holistic view of mathematics. These points reflect OBE's emphasis on real-life outcome goals. In special education, most assessments of student performance are criterion-referenced, objective tests rather than open-ended, authentic demonstrations of multiple skills.

What does all of this mean for the future of education for students with disabilities? For one thing, it means that national attention to standards and outcomes is currently moving *away from* the established system of special educa-

tion. Moreover, there is no indication that much serious attention is being given to how such proposals and initiatives affect students with disabilities. Therefore, special educators must take matters into their own hands to ensure that the education of students with disabilities remains a topic of the national standards and outcomes discussions (see Sindelar et al., 1992). Judy Schrag, Director of the Office of Special Education Programs, describes current national perspectives regarding the need for outcomes information on students with disabilities.

An example of special education addressing an outcomes-related issue at the national level is the testimony of The Council for Exceptional Children (CEC) delivered to the House Subcommittee on Elementary, Secondary, and Vocational Education in March, 1992, regarding standards and outcomes assessment. In the testimony several major points were made, including concerns that:

(a) The setting of standards is arbitrary—there is no empirical evidence that can tell us what students should know and when they should know it.

(b) There is no policy which requires groups that set standards to consider students with diverse needs.

(c) If standards are developed in core subject areas only, a narrowing of the curriculum could occur; students with special needs (gifted and disabled) need the challenge of subjects outside the core curriculum.

(d) If the purpose of any proposed national assessment system is to help the nation track progress toward meeting standards, *all* students must be included, even if they require modification of test administration procedures. (CEC, 1992)

Outcomes at the State Level

State education agencies also are becoming increasingly involved in efforts to assess the performance of students in ways that help policymakers form decisions regarding school programs. States need such information for some of the same reasons as the federal government; they must evaluate and fund many different programs. Many states also compare individual school districts, using assessment data as one piece of information in that process. These comparisons often yield the decision-making data for funding allocations.

All states have some sort of accountability system in place, and most of them include large-scale statewide testing programs. NCEO interviewed state directors of special education or their designees in the 50 state and 9 additional education agencies (e.g., American Samoa, Bureau of Indian Affairs) regarding their current and proposed activities for measuring educational outcomes for students with disabilities. The interviews, which asked about state-level information only, produced several major findings.

- States collect volumes of information on students with disabilities. However, most of it is related to placement and program data, *not* student outcomes information.
- State-level outcomes information is generated most often from general education assessments in which students with mild disabilities may participate, but the extent to which they participate is uncertain.
- Even when students with disabilities do take part in assessments, their data often are not reported; these data are deleted at some point after the testing.
- Most states have guidelines on who may be excluded from assessments and how to make testing accommodations for students with disabilities, but these guidelines are implemented at the local level with very little consistency.

A NATIONAL PERSPECTIVE

Judy A. Schrag *Director, Office of Special Education Programs,*
U.S. Department of Education, Washington, DC

Tremendous changes are being proposed for U.S. education, changes that reflect systemic reforms. Those who advocate education reform have been focusing on several questions, including the following:

- What do we want students to know and be able to do?
- What kinds of learning experiences produce these outcomes?
- What does it take to transform schools into places where student outcomes are enhanced?
- How will we know if we are successful? What kinds of accountability are needed to ensure a positive relationship between our services and interventions and student outcomes and other desired results?

From a federal perspective, it is critical for special education to be an integral part of current reforms. Restructured schools in all states must ensure improved outcomes for *all* students, including those with disabilities and other special needs.

The Office of Special Education Programs (OSEP) currently is supporting a number of efforts such as centers, research projects, and focus groups to address educational reform issues relating to students with disabilities. These efforts are in recognition of the many complex issues related to the evaluation and refinement of special education within the context of reform and a student outcomes framework. Currently, special education has a procedural focus, with emphasis on carrying out a set of procedures such as child find, multidisciplinary identification and assessment, procedural protections and safeguards, individualized education program (IEP) development and implementation, annual review, and parent involvement. We assume that these procedures result in effective educational programs and identified student outcomes.

However, data from the National Longitudinal Transition Study reveal that many of the desired student outcomes are not being realized. It is incumbent on us as special educators to view special education as a means to reach improved student outcomes rather than as an end in itself. Our procedural focus must allow for continued program evolution and change in areas such as assessment, service delivery, relationships among and between educational programs, roles among school personnel at all levels of government, curriculum and instruction, and accountability.

We need to work with administrators in our school districts and communities so that we can be active participants in discussions and activities related to school restructuring. We all have rich contributions to make to school reform. At the national level, we are interested in special educators' ideas about a number of complex questions that will require our collaborative efforts in the coming year:

- In what ways can a program that is based on a detailed set of procedures allow for systemic change?
- Are there alternative accountability models at the local, state, and federal levels that focus more specifically on student outcomes?
- How can we ensure that students with disabilities will be included in existing and emerging national and state data collection programs as well as "report cards" on the progress of students and the effectiveness of various programs?
- How can special education be a more integral and coordinated component of a unified educational system that works with social and health services to meet the needs of a diverse and changing population of students?
- As special education continues to evolve within the context of reform, how can we change our current mindsets and make needed transformational changes while at the same time continuing to protect the rights of students with disabilities and their parents?

- Most states want to examine educational outcomes more closely but have only limited resources to do so.
- Several states are exploring ways in which information from IEPs can be adapted to provide state-level outcomes accountability information.

Assessment

Because states are required to collect considerable data on students with disabilities, it would be reasonable to think that a strong outcomes database exists. This is not the case. Most information is on the processes and contexts (what Judy Schrag calls the *procedural focus*) of special education. For example, states are required to document the *level* of participation in general education of students with special needs, and about half of the states collect some sort of participation information beyond what is required. States also must document the *status* of students when they exit school (e.g., graduate, drop out, or age out), and about one third of the states collect additional information on the reasons for dropping out. These databases, particularly those that contain information extending federal reporting requirements, actually reflect certain school outcomes and might easily be improved to provide even better outcomes data on students with disabilities.

States *do* collect considerable academic achievement information, most often through large-scale general education efforts (see Shriner, Bruininks, Deno, McGrew, Thurlow, & Ysseldyke, 1991). All but one state and one educational agency report that students with disabilities participate in state-level achievement assessments. However, only 33 states can identify special education students in their data sets. The reasons for this discrepancy are many, but there are two major issues: inclusion/exclusion rules and test accommodations.

First, it is unclear how many students with disabilities actually take part in the testing programs. Estimates from states in which students are reported to participate range from 2% to 100%. Although most state departments of education have developed inclusion criteria, decisions are usually left to local school personnel, who implement the criteria in different ways. Often, the decision to include or exclude a student depends on the "stakes" associated with the assessment. If, for example, a particular school will get increased funding from the state for demonstrating better than average performance, local decisionmakers may be likely to exclude students with disabilities from assessments. On the other hand, if a particular school will receive supplemental funding based on lower performance, more students with disabilities may be included, thus raising the probability of lower overall scores (DeStefano & Metzer, 1991).

Exclusion can occur at times other than during the actual testing. For example, the tests of students with disabilities may be physically separated or coded in such a way that the scores of these students are not included in the data summaries. When this happens, state reports do not include the total population tested. Even when tests of students with disabilities *are* scored, results sometimes are not reported. This means that states may have more information on the achievement outcomes of students with disabilities than is being used.

A second major issue related to achievement outcomes is concern over the necessary accommodations and modifications for testing students with disabilities. Forty-two states allow some types of accommodations. These can be grouped into four major categories: alternate presentation modes, alternate response modes, flexibility of time limits, and flexibility of test settings. Braille or large-print versions of assessments are common modifications. The accommodations themselves are not the cause for concern to state personnel. Rather, their concern is with the extent to which such accommodations are used appropriately and their potential impact on test scores and results. These are technical concerns that sometimes result in decisions to avoid or exclude data summaries of students with disabilities.

These issues are important because special education units rarely conduct their own achievement assessments. Through increased communication and collaboration among state-level units, it might be possible to produce a tremendous expansion of the data available on how students with disabilities are faring in the educational system.

One outcomes area in which special education has already focused a great deal of attention is the postschool status of former students. Over half of the states have some information on the postschool experiences of students educated in special education programs. Often special education and vocational education combine their efforts in follow-up studies, and in some states the special education unit and a university research program cooperate on information-gathering projects. Postschool data often focus on the individual's level of employment, wages, marital status, living arrangements, and citizenship activities. These types of data are easily understood by the general public, so many states are seeking ways to expand their follow-up efforts. People want to know how students are doing in the "real world," and postschool assessments and studies such as the National Longitudinal Transition Study mentioned by Judy Schrag provide some idea of what happens to former students.

Standards

States also are developing new standards and outcomes goals for students. Some states are adopting new graduation standards and eliminating systems that require students to take a specific number and kind of courses. For example, Minnesota has identified a series of learner outcomes that students must achieve before they can leave school as successful completers. Other states are focusing on setting standards at the school level. In Kentucky, individual schools will be required to demonstrate an acceptable level of student performance as measured by newly developed accountability assessments. These assessments will be much like the NAEP tests and will include multiple-choice, open-ended, and performance tasks. Students with disabilities are expected to be fully included in the accountability assessments. Schools that exceed the acceptable performance level by a certain amount will be rewarded financially for their efforts. Schools that fail to meet their acceptable levels will be required to develop school improvement plans, and the professionals in these schools will be placed on probation. In addition, a "Kentucky Distinguished Educator" will be assigned to each of the schools to assist with the school's improvement plan. Nancy LaCount, Program Manager in the Kentucky Division of Special Learning Needs, describes what the switch to an outcomes focus has meant for special education in her state.

Outcomes at the District Level

School districts often make the decision to change to an outcomes focus. In Aurora, Colorado, for example, school district personnel have specified a vision for their school district that articulates intended exit outcomes for all students. The district has specified outcomes in five broad domains: Students are to complete school as self-directed learners, collaborative workers, complex thinkers, community contributors, and quality producers. Education is designed to focus on these outcomes, and the activities in all schools are outcomes driven toward these district goals.

Johnson City Central School District in Johnson City, New York, is another district that has taken a district-based outcomes approach. Johnson City employs the Outcomes Driven Developmental Model (ODDM), in which instruction is directed toward desired student exit behaviors in five areas: self-esteem, high cognitive functioning, self-directed learning, concern for others, and process skills (e.g., problem solving, communication, decision making, accountability, and group process).

Some districts have identified outcomes for different groups of students. For example, in the Traverse Bay, Michigan, Intermediate Unit Option II program, the curriculum is designed especially to meet the needs of students "who are not likely to pursue a college degree and are likely to enter the workplace soon after graduation from high school" (Traverse Bay Area Intermediate Unit Division of Special Education, 1991, p. 2).

In other districts, a focus on outcomes is starting as a joint effort of general and special education. Kaaren Allen, Special Education Curriculum Coordinator in the Albuquerque Public Schools, describes the process her school district has followed in identifying school district outcomes for all students.

In some districts, the implementation of an outcomes approach is based on a directive from the state. A state may decide, for example, to adopt an outcomes-based education approach but leave it to individual districts to decide on specific outcomes. These outcomes may then be used to evaluate the success of the individual district in educating its students.

A STATE PERSPECTIVE

Nancy LaCount *Program Manager, Student-Centered Programs,*
Kentucky Department of Education, Frankfort, Kentucky

The Kentucky Education Reform Act (KERA) of 1990 is transforming education for all students in Kentucky and providing an opportunity to design a single educational system rather than a dual system of general education and special education. KERA embraces three assumptions that have significant implications for students with disabilities:

- All children can learn, and at relatively high levels.
- Technology exists to facilitate student success.
- What children and youth learn should be approximately the same across the Commonwealth. How, by whom, and when can and should change to meet individual differences.

The state has established 6 learning goals that have been framed into 75 valued outcomes. Individuals representing students with disabilities have been participants throughout this effort and will continue to be a part of the reform process as it evolves.

Since KERA establishes an inclusive system for all children, Kentucky has focused efforts on answering questions about how to effectively include all students with disabilities in all components of KERA and not on how to create exemptions or exclusions. All valued outcomes have been reviewed for application to students with disabilities and a curriculum framework that has been developed that will be distributed to local school districts in final form by July 1993. Special educators also have participated in policymaking related to the assessment system. Sample perfor-

mance tasks are being created to help us study any implications for students with disabilities. We are raising preliminary evaluation questions to be answered through the Kentucky Instructional Results Information System (KIRIS). We have provided professional development sessions on the implications of the valued outcomes and KIRIS for students with disabilities.

Procedures for inclusion of students with disabilities have been established based on recommendations from the Disabilities and Diversity Committee. The policy states that all students with disabilities will participate in the KIRIS assessment program and will be counted in school building accountability. It also states that "adaptations may include changes in administration of the assessment and/or recording student responses that are consistent with the instructional strategies identified on the student's [IEP]. Adaptations shall not inappropriately impact content to be measured" (Kentucky Department of Education, 1992, p. 3). The policy also includes provision for postponement of inclusion of students with significant disabilities who meet eligibility criteria for an alternate portfolio assessment system. It is anticipated that only 1% to 2% of the student population will meet this criterion. The alternative portfolio assessment will be developed during the next year for implementation in 1993. The design of the portfolio system is proceeding; it is guided by eight principles that reflect a theme of inclusion of students with disabilities in a single educational system.

While there continue to be challenges as we proceed with our reform agenda in Kentucky, we have learned a great deal already. We have embraced the philosophy that all children can learn and that it is our responsibility to create school climates that are supportive of all children. This is essential in creating a system of inclusion. We have also learned that policies for establishing outcomes and assessment systems should not create disincentives for including students with disabilities. Special education must be part of reform and restructuring efforts and must evaluate itself in light of these efforts. Specific implications for students with disabilities are that (a) expectations for these students must be high, but appropriately designed and measured and (b) learning must move to the level of application of knowledge and skills in real-life situations and not remain at attainment of isolated skills. Students should demonstrate the attainment of outcomes through performance and the creation of products. Still, enabling outcomes that are viewed as skills unique to students with disabilities will continue to be the supports for attainment of self-sufficiency and lifelong learning. Individualized education programs need to be reviewed in relation to outcomes-based education to create compatible systems while protecting the rights of the individual.

Kentucky Department of Education (January, 1992). *Procedures for inclusion of students in KIRIS.* (Program Advisory No. 92-OAAS-004). Frankfort, KY: Author.

Or, the state may define the outcomes but expect individual districts to meet them in whatever way they deem best, although the outcomes still would be used to evaluate and compare districts. In some instances, this might be done by comparing district data to overall state data.

Outcomes at the Building/Classroom Level

Efforts to reform education by focusing on outcomes should have their greatest impact at the level of the individual

classroom. It would be interesting to know how instruction in a classroom implementing an outcomes-based approach might differ from traditional approaches to instruction. The building principal might say that the OBE approach being used in the school is one in which all instruction is based on out-

A District Perspective

Kaaren Allen *Special Education Curriculum Coordinator,*
Albuquerque Public Schools, New Mexico

Outcomes and outcomes-based education (OBE) have been favorite topics to share with colleagues recently. From the district perspective, a possible change toward a balance of results (outcomes) and compliance (process) is viewed as good news. The development of outcomes, or desired results of education, promises to provide the direction we need to develop and modify curriculum for students in special education classes.

Our district has received information about OBE from William Spady. His Transformational OBE model seem particularly well-suited to the needs of students in special education. Transformational OBE clarifies the basic aim we have for our students: to be successful in integrated school and community environments.

Professionals in the district have pointed out important Transformational OBE premises that fit with special education's philosophy. For example,

1. The life-skill/social-skill/literacy emphasis has long been a part of the special education curriculum.
2. District outcomes can unite general and special educators in working collaboratively toward common goals for all students.
3. The focus on fewer and more relevant outcomes (outcomes of significance) provides an organization and rationale for content and teaching strategy while reducing the pressure to "cover the curriculum."

The Albuquerque Public Schools are just beginning to gather and disseminate information about OBE. These are exciting times. The advantages of OBE will be maximized if general and special education work in partnership to develop outcomes. We must keep several issues and questions in mind as we move forward:

1. How does the move toward OBE take shape in a large district (89,000 students) already involved in restructuring and faced with budgetary shortfalls?
2. What will happen to the curriculum for students in special educa-

tion in the process of moving to common goals for all?
3. How should outcomes initiatives be coordinated as more and more stakeholders in public education become acquainted with the language and philosophy of OBE?

For this district and state, OBE makes a great deal of sense, and some changes are already being made. The state has replaced grade-level competencies with "Standards for the Pursuit of Excellence," a broad vision of general outcomes and essential competencies for each subject area. A few schools are beginning to use aspects of OBE to guide the restructuring of curriculum and use of resources. At the district level, we have had our first general education/special education meeting of the mathematics, art, and music curriculum committees to develop outcomes that will be used to formulate program evaluation questions.

OBE will become an increasingly important part of our system as outcomes that are backed by appropriate demonstrations of competency are articulated. In my opinion, OBE makes sense as a way of doing the business of education. I'm sure that OBE is here to stay.

comes and designed in such a way that all students will achieve the outcomes. The system is based on an approach suggested by Spady that is, in Spady's words, "success based." It directly implies that bell-curve thinking, quotas, and comparative grading distributions and standard systems have to be abandoned in favor of what is widely known as "criterion-based systems" (Spady, 1992, p. 16). This is the heart of "transformational OBE"; it reflects the kinds of questions raised by Kaaren Allen.

In observing an OBE school and its classrooms, you might notice that the focus is on mastery learning, with each student being taught and retaught without specific regard to the time constraints (e.g., schedule, class periods, curricular units) that typically characterize instruction. Students of different ages are learning side by side, and there is little competition among them. Norm-referenced tests are not used; they have been replaced by objective-referenced measures developed by teachers in the district. Much of what you see looks a lot like good special education in practice.

In designing the instruction they will use in their classrooms, OBE teachers first consider what conditions will look like in the future lives of their learners and then derive exit outcomes to meet those conditions. They develop performance indicators in order to monitor pupil performance. They design learning experiences and instructional strategies that will move their pupils toward accomplishment of outcomes.

An example of how this practice has taken shape is provided by Kim Martinson, Special Education Coordinator, Apple Valley, Minnesota. Ms. Martinson describes what teachers must consider on a day-to-day basis within an OBE system and presents several key issues related specifically to students with special needs.

The fact that a teacher adopts an outcomes-based approach does not necessarily ensure that it will be adopted well. The most commonly observed practice—one that is an inadequate and poor implementation of OBE—is when teachers teach a unit very quickly, test their students, and then divide them into two groups: those who have mastered the material and those who have not. The teachers move the mastery group on to the next instructional unit and reteach those who did not master the lesson on the first attempt. After reteaching, students are again assessed, and those who have not yet mastered the unit are taught it again. In essence, the practice consists of doing the same thing over and over until students "get it right." The practice reveals a failure to recognize that teachers might need to use different approaches to reteach skills or concepts and that it might take an incredibly long time for some students to attain mastery. In short, the

A Building Perspective

Kim Martinson *Special Education Coordinator,*
Apple Valley High School, Apple Valley, Minnesota

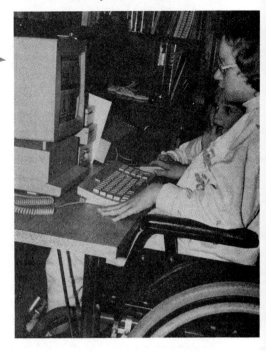

While the State of Minnesota has slowly taken on competency-based education in a politically correct manner, Independent School District 196 (Apple Valley, MN) has embraced OBE with open arms. We have revised competencies, determined indicators, rewritten and aligned curriculum, redesigned assessment, attempted to restructure the school day, and planned for an outcomes-based graduation in the year 2000.

As a teacher of secondary-level students with learning disabilities, I have collaborated often in co-teaching situations in mainstream classrooms. During the past year, I have also been able to take advantage of many opportunities through conferences, workshops, and reading to become immersed in the ideas of the current "gurus" of education reform. Each espouses a newly designed, perfect program with high expectations and revolutionary ideas sure to cure all of education's woes.

Apple Valley High School has encouraged teachers to make those "paradigm shifts," applying the principles and belief systems of outcomes-based instruction. The consequences of change already are becoming apparent, and the experimentation with OBE has unearthed a multitude of concerns and problems. In relation to many students with disabilities and students currently at risk in our educational system, we have opened Pandora's box, and what we are finding is unsettling and thought provoking.

One set of flaws relates to school structure (instructional hours, the trimester system, grades, attendance policies, and curriculum). The current school day does not allow for expanded learning opportunities or the extra time needed to reteach or relearn information. Students who are struggling with content need more time than others and different instruction to learn the same material. The failure to change the school day is a major stumbling block to the success of outcomes-based instruction.

The ineffectiveness of some teachers and their teaching strategies has also become apparent. We need to examine what the most successful teachers are doing in order to gather techniques, methods, and strategies for all teachers to learn. Even though teachers are espousing the values related to OBE, that does not guarantee that they are using the correct techniques and hold the necessary attitudes to provide successful learning experiences for all students.

Our initial reaction as professionals often has been to blame students for their lack of study skills, their inability to understand the system, their ability to undermine the system, their lack of concern, and their immaturity. With OBE, we have uncovered weaknesses in all students. Teachers are slowly recognizing the true range of abilities in their classrooms. They are realizing that they do have different learners whose needs must be met in different ways—a daunting discovery.

As special educators, we need to use the power of the child study team and the IEP to provide successful academic experiences for our students. We need to be partners with our colleagues in the educational transformations taking place so we can be strong advocates for our students.

test-teach-test-reteach-test method is not good OBE.

An illustration of better practice in classroom-level OBE is when a teacher decides at the outset of instruction specifically which outcomes pupils will demonstrate at the end of instruction. The teacher then tailors all instructional efforts to teach to the primary outcomes. But, as Kim Martinson advises, teachers should not overlook the power of child study teams and the IEP

to define successful academic experiences leading to these outcomes.

None of this is meant to imply that all outcomes-directed instruction occurs in traditional classroom settings. The most appropriate type of instruction and the best setting for it are determined by its intended outcomes. Marcia Pavkovich is a teacher consultant for students with visual impairments in Flint, Michigan. She teaches students who are blind how to cook. She does this by specifying an overall terminal outcome (the student will cook), task-analyzing the outcome into component parts, and working through parents to teach students the component parts.

Ideally, OBE will be implemented throughout a school building, not just by individual teachers. Spady (1992) described OBE as being evidenced when all of the school's programs and instructional efforts are focused and organized around clearly defined outcomes that all students are to demonstrate when they leave school. The extent to which this can be made to happen remains a question. Gary Harold, Principal, and Karen Maples, Special Education Teacher, at Swift Middle School in Quarryville, Pennsylvania, address some of the issues faced at the school building and classroom levels. Their state, you will recall, has recently opted to change the graduation requirements for students to outcomes-based criteria. Their "window" reflects some of their initial

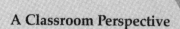

 ## Perspectives on the Future

Gary Harold, *Principal, and* **Karen Maples**, *Teacher, Swift Middle School, Quarryville, Pennsylvania*

A Building Perspective

Pennsylvania has proposed the following outcomes areas for all students: communications; mathematics; science and technology; environment and technology; citizenship; appreciating and understanding others; arts and humanities; career education and work; wellness and fitness; and personal, family, and community living. Each area will have four to nine subsections and accompanying performance criteria called *benchmarks*. Students will be assessed for performance relative to these benchmarks in classroom settings.

From my perspective as a principal, I do not anticipate major problems in converting to this system. However, I can foresee some of the proposed outcomes being met by resistance from some members of the community. For example, "appreciating and understanding others" and "personal, family, and community living" may concern conservative religious and social groups even though these outcomes areas are not significantly different from the existing curricular framework in the state.

The IEP will continue to be the focus for students with disabilities in my school. Student IEPs will incorporate the elements of the outcomes requirements that are deemed appropriate. Parents will decide whether or not to remove their children from the outcomes (benchmark) assessments; the option to do so is left open to them. Local assessments will be determined at the district level, as will the conse-

quences for students who do not achieve established benchmark performance.

As we begin to move in response to these outcomes-based initiatives and proposed assessments, there are two key issues that arise. First, interpreting and codifying the desired outcomes from the local school board into measurable outcomes for students is not an easy task. Appropriate assessments such as performance measures and portfolios require additional teacher training and community education. The authentic assessment rubric is not the traditional system with which most of us are familiar. It will be important to ensure that teachers, students, and parents are able to communicate effectively about performance levels that are measured in this way.

Second, the outcomes initiative has been launched on many fronts simultaneously in what appears to be a plan that has a basis in organizational logic. Even at this early date, public concern and pressure have caused a shift in some areas from centralized to decentralized decisionmaking, with more power resting in local school districts. Also, depending on population demographics, a particular outcome may be accepted or even heralded in one district, yet be the focus of protest in another. Local agencies and administrators will have to deal with these issues and decide whether to support the outcomes drive or lobby for the status quo at the expense of the initiative. In Pennsylvania, it is simply too early to tell what is going to happen.

A Classroom Perspective

As a special education teacher at the middle school level, I feel that a shift from the present educational requirements to an outcomes-based approach could have positive effects on students who are enrolled in learning support classes. By concentrating on outcomes rather than on earning a designated number of credits, we will be able to restructure the curriculum so that students can achieve mastery of the desired skills. This change will be advantageous for students with disabilities because they will not be required to retain volumes of factual information. Instead of receiving instruction from a curriculum that is parallel to the regular curriculum, these students will be taught according to the learning outcomes that are specified on their IEPs. As a student masters each learning outcome, the demonstration of that skill should be documented and concentration shifted to another outcome.

Teachers will be able to assess their students on the required skills and will not have to test them on the recall of facts in specific content areas. This shift may prove beneficial not only for students with disabilities, but also for students who are low achievers or are poorly motivated. I believe that all graduates will be better able to function in all areas of our society and better prepared for the world of work. Adults in our society must be capable of dealing with varied situations, and I believe that the outcomes-based program will prepare students, including those with disabilities, to do exactly that.

thoughts about what OBE means to them.

Sometimes the implementation of an outcomes model by teachers is directed through the state rather than the district. A good example is what is happening in Michigan, where outcomes have been (and continue to be) identified for each category of disability. In some instances, different outcomes are specified

for different levels of severity. Thus, Michigan has specified outcomes for students with educable mental impairments in seven domains: academics, social competence, community integration, personal growth, health and fitness, vocational integration, and domestic living skills. Outcomes specified for students with learning disabilities include basic academics, language

and communication, self-esteem and social integration, and personal efficiency and productivity.

When states encourage teachers to measure progress on state-identified outcomes, there must be sufficient training for those who are expected to implement the process. Frances F. Loose, Director of the Outcomes Training Project in Michigan, describes how spe-

MICHIGAN OUTCOMES TRAINING PROJECT

Frances F. Loose *Director, Howel, Michigan*

The Outcomes Training Project prepares special education personnel to use the Program Outcomes Guides that have been developed for 12 disability categories. One aspect of the state and federally sponsored training focuses on transforming the category-specific broad outcomes into useful individual learner objectives. The transformation is a three-step process.

First, participants are guided through a learner profile addressing the broad outcomes for the population with which they work. There are different numbers of listed outcomes for each of the categories (e.g., learning disabilities has 11, educable mental impairments has 19). Each participant rates one learner's current performance on each outcome relative to the learner's general education peers. Ratings are on a continuum from "emerging skill" to "strong skill." In this way, the learner's overall performance at a given point in time is profiled.

Next, participants refine the learner profile for one of the broad outcomes by completing part of the supplemental performance assessment. This provides a more detailed picture of learner progress toward the selected outcome. The procedure results in a completed learner profile that allows for a visual representation of the individual's strengths and weaknesses by charting the percentage of items related to each broad outcome.

Finally, participants are trained in the step-by-step transformation of outcomes into narrowed goals for educational plans. Based on the learner's present level of performance relative to the broad outcome, instructional objectives are written in terms that facilitate measurement of progress toward a particular goal (i.e., incorporating observable behaviors).

The Outcomes Training Project also assists staff by sharing ideas for useful alternative assessment and planning procedures. One example is the McGill Action Planning System (MAPS), a strategy useful for learners with multiple impairments. The MAPS is used in conjunction with the profiles developed earlier to ensure a comprehensive view of the learner's strengths and needs.

Through follow-up training, special education personnel are encouraged to implement the outcomes through IEPs and local curriculum enhancement projects.

cial education personnel in Michigan determine what instruction is necessary for students to reach specific outcomes.

The Parents' Perspective

What do parents think about the recent emphasis on outcomes, particularly as they consider its implications for their child with a disability? One viewpoint is presented by Patricia McGill-Smith, parent and Executive Director of the National Parent Network on

Disabilities, who makes it clear that parents must be proactive in bringing about changes in the educational system.

Implications and Considerations

As we read about outcomes, ODDM, OBE, and success for all and look at current practice with these models in educational settings, we believe that what we are reading about and observing is good special education in practice. Those of you who have been using an objective-referenced or curriculum-based assessment approach in your teaching will recognize much that is familiar. In fact, it is often argued that OBE is actually mastery learning with a new name.

One implication of using an outcomes-based education approach is that special educators will be integrated increasingly into the mainstream of education, with the same pressures to show results coming from business people, politicians, parents, and others. Another implication is that reform activities taking place now will have an impact on the future of special education, the standards to which it is held, and the ways in which it is evaluated. Action now by special education professionals will help to make the outcomes acceptable to special educators.

Spady (1992) identified the following seven classroom implications of using OBE:

1. Decisions, results, and programs will no longer be defined by and limited to specific time blocks and calendar dates. Things will simply be less time-based than they now are. Students of different ages will learn side-by-side in more flexible delivery systems than we have seen in most schools.

2. Grading and credentialing will be much more criterion-based and will focus on what students can eventually learn to do well rather than on how well they do the first time they encounter something. Averaging systems and comparative grading will disappear as the concept of culminating achievement takes hold.

3. There will be a much greater emphasis on collaborative models of student learning and much less interstudent competition for grades and credentials. The "success for all" principles of OBE will prevail because they are so powerful and so badly needed.

4. Traditional curriculum structures will, in fact, be modified significantly as the system develops the capacity to respond to differences in student needs and learning rates while at the same time helping them accomplish high level outcomes of significance. Not all "courses" will be nine months in length, nor will "passing" require that a given amount of time be spent attending a particular class.

5. Teachers will be much more focused on the learning capabilities of their students and far less on covering a given amount of curriculum in a given time block. At the same time, textbooks will be replaced by intended outcomes of significance as the driving force in

CAN'T GET ON THE TRAIN WITHOUT A TICKET

Patricia McGill-Smith *Executive Director, National Parent Network on Disabilities, Washington, DC*

With the enactment of Public Law 94-142 (the Education for All Handicapped Children Act, renamed the Individuals with Disabilities Education Act [IDEA]), parents of children with disabilities felt their children had, at last, gained a shot at a free, appropriate education. At the time when the educational rights of children with disabilities had the attention of most special educators, the public education system as a whole was being scrutinized and criticized in a series of national studies. In the 1980s, most study findings suggested that public education was ineffectual. Outcomes data supported the gut feeling that public education needed to be reformed and pushed reform movements past emotion-laden argument to reason-based discussion and action. For parents of children in regular education, this push to find out where education needed to go based on clearly defined outcomes data was good news.

Parents of children with disabilities now need to take the same step that public education as a whole was forced to take during the past 5 years. It is time that, as parents and advocates, we begin asking, "Where's the beef?" Would we accept only a teacher's *opinion* that our child was not succeeding in the placement for which we had fought? Probably not. My guess is that we would want objective information demonstrating how the IEP was going. Can we accept any less on a national basis? It is time we got a handle on the *national IEP.* Only solid outcomes data can provide a picture of the effectiveness of the special education system. If we are going to have a positive impact on the reforms of the 1990s, we need outcomes data to drive local, state, and federal policy. As with an individual IEP, we need outcomes data that (a) characterize educational experiences; (b) reflect how students with disabilities feel about themselves and their experiences; and (c) indicate what influence education has on students' quality of life after leaving school.

Parents must define the outcomes they feel are important to their children in terms that can be measured. It is not good enough to say that we want our children fully included. We must spell out the positive outcomes we expect from full inclusion. We must spell out the necessary characteristics of successful transitions, including the transition to employment. We must require objective measures of the impact of special education in terms of life-long outcomes for our children. We should do this by taking a strong interest in determining the *interim* outcomes that lead to those that are longer term. It is important to recognize what it takes to reach more distant goals. Finally, we must identify the experiences that lead to those outcomes and measure those experiences objectively to ensure that anticipated outcomes are achieved.

Reforms such as those embodied in the goals of "America 2000" are like a train leaving a station. Parents of children with disabilities are on the right platform, but we need tickets to get on the train. Outcomes data that help us evaluate reforms based on what works for our children are the tickets we need.

curriculum design and delivery, rather than the other way around.

6. Curriculum tracking will disappear, and all instruction will ultimately focus on higher level learning and competencies for all students. The instructional methods and materials used in gifted and talented programs will be accessible to all students.

7. There will be far less reliance on norm-referenced standardized tests as indicators of either stu-

dent or teacher accomplishment. Districts will custom-design criterion-based assessment measures that directly operationalize the outcomes they define as most significant. No national or state assessment system will ever be adequate for measuring all of the authentic outcomes of significance that local districts will want to foster. (p. 18)

Beyond these is the implication that the educational system will no longer consist of isolated classrooms, but rather will reflect an integrated effort of students, parents, teachers, administrators, community members, business people, and politicians. An increasing number of people are seeing the need for all of society to be involved in its greatest economic investment for the future—the education of its children.

So now you know what is coming. Teachers will face two important questions as the end of the current year approaches: What are the outcomes of schooling? and How will I measure the progress or lack of progress my students make toward those outcomes? In the long run, most of you will not answer these questions in isolation. Input will be provided from many sources. Still, for the short term you will have to form your own answers to show that what you are doing as a teacher fits within some outcomes framework. Framing an answer is much easier when you know the questions in advance. We hope that we have provided you with some indication of what the questions are likely to be, their origin, and their development. Have a nice year!

References

Anderson, R. J. (1992). Educational reform: Does it all add up? *TEACHING Exceptional Children, 24*(2), 4.

Cawley, J. F., Baker-Kroczynski, S., & Urban, A. (1992). Seeking excellence in mathematics education for students with disabilities. *TEACHING Exceptional Children, 24*(2), 40-43.

Champlin, J. R. (1991). Taking stock and moving on. *Journal of the National Center for Outcome Based Education, 1*(1), 5-8.

The Council for Exceptional Children. (1992). *Statement prepared for testimony before the House Subcommittee on Elementary, Secondary, and Vocational Education.* Reston, VA: Author.

DeStefano, L., & Metzer, D. (1991). High stakes testing and students with handicaps: An analysis of issues and policies. In R. E. Stake (Ed.), *Advances in program evaluation: Vol 1A. Using assessment policy to reform education* (pp. 281-302). Greenwich, CT: JAI Press.

Elliott, E. J. (1989). *Testimony before the Committee on Governmental Affairs.* Washington, DC: Subcommittee on Governmental Information and Regulation.

Evans, K. M. (1992). *An outcome-based primer.* Minneapolis: University of Minnesota, Center for Applied Research in Educational Improvements.

King, J. A., & Evans, K. M. (1991). Can we achieve outcome-based education? *Educational Leadership, 49*(2), 73-75.

McGrew, K. S., Thurlow, M. L., Shriner, J. G., & Spiegel, A. N. (1992). *Inclusion of students with disabilities in national and state data collection programs* (Technical Report No. 2). Minneapolis: University of Minnesota, National Center on Educational Outcomes.

Minnesota Department of Education. (1991). *Model learner outcomes for mathematics education.* St. Paul: Author.

National Commission on Excellence in Education. (1983). *A nation at risk: The imperative for educational reform.* Washington, DC: U.S. Government Printing Office.

National Council of Teachers of Mathematics. (1989). *Curriculum and evaluation standards for school mathematics.* Reston, VA: Author.

National Education Goals Panel. (1991). *The national education goals report: Building a nation of learners.* Washington, DC: U.S. Government Printing Office.

Rothman, R. (March, 1992). Experts urge caution in expanding state-level NAEP. *Education Week, 11*(25), 18.

Shriner, J. G., Bruininks, R. H., Deno, S. L., McGrew, K. S., Thurlow, M. L., & Ysseldyke, J. E. (1991). *State practices in the assessment of outcomes for students with disabilities* (Technical Report No. 1). Minneapolis: University of Minnesota, National Center on Educational Outcomes.

Sindelar, P. T., Watanabe, A. K., McCray, A. D., & Hornsby, P. J. (1992). Special educator's role in literacy and educational reform. *TEACHING Exceptional Children, 24*(3), 38-40.

Spady, W. G. (1992). It's time to take a close look at outcome-based education. *Communiqué, 20*(6), 16-18.

Traverse Bay Area Intermediate Unit Division of Special Education. (1991). *Option II: Curriculum guide. Secondary graduation requirements.* Traverse City, MI: Traverse Bay Area Intermediate School District, Special Education Department.

Tyler, R. W. (1949). *Basic principles of curriculum and instruction: Syllabus for education 360.* Chicago: University of Chicago Press.

Wiggins, G. (1989). A true test: Toward more authentic and equitable assessment. *Phi Delta Kappan, 70,* 703-713.

Preparation of this paper was supported in part by a Cooperative Agreement (H159C00004) with the U.S. Department of Education, Office of Special Education Programs. Opinions or points of view do not necessarily represent those of the U.S. Department of Education or the Offices within it.

Severely Disabled Children: Who Pays?

MARTHA M. McCARTHY

MARTHA M. McCARTHY (Indiana University Chapter) is a professor of education and co-director of the Indiana Education Policy Center, Indiana University, Bloomington.

In the absence of coordinated policies with well-defined responsibilities across agencies, the stage is being set for a backlash against federal mandates regarding the education of individuals with disabilities, Ms. McCarthy warns.

IN 1989 THE U.S. Supreme Court declined to review a significant decision in which the First Circuit Court of Appeals interpreted federal law as requiring school districts to provide educational services for *every* handicapped child regardless of the severity of the child's disabilities.[1] The appellate ruling in *Timothy W.* v. *Rochester, New Hampshire, School District* applies as precedent only in Maine, Massachusetts, New Hampshire, Rhode Island, and Puerto Rico. Nonetheless, this decision has received national attention and has sparked lively debate regarding what constitutes "education" and whether public schools currently are being required to support some services that are beyond their competence and fiscal capacity. This article provides an overview of legal developments pertaining to the educational needs of severely disabled children, an analysis of the *Timothy W.*

Illustration by Sally Eckman Roberts.

case, and a brief discussion of its implications.[2]

BACKGROUND

The past decade has witnessed a steady stream of litigation involving the rights of children with disabilities. Although school litigation in general leveled off during the 1980s, the number of cases involving handicapped students increased dramatically, representing more than 40% of the decade's cases involving students' rights and 30% of all school litigation by 1988.[3] A large portion of these cases dealt with severely disabled students, despite the fact that only a very small percentage of the 4.7 million children with disabilities is classified as severely or profoundly disabled.[4]

Almost all of these cases have been brought under the Education for All Handicapped Children Act (EHA) of 1975, which in 1990 became the Individuals with Disabilities Education Act.[5] This is a federal funding law stipulating that all children with disabilities must be identified and provided a free appropriate education as a prerequisite to states' participating in the federal assistance program.[6] Currently all states receive federal funds under this law. Congress authorized the federal share of excess costs for special education services (expenses incurred beyond the amount spent on nonhandicapped students) gradually to increase to a cap of 40% by fiscal year 1981. However, congressional appropriations have been far below this level, not yet exceeding 12% of such excess costs. Thus state and local education agencies have borne the major burden of providing appropriate services for children with disabilities.

Under this act, children with disabilities are entitled to special education and related services (e.g., transportation, physical therapy) necessary for them to benefit from special education. Central components of the act are the requirements that individualized education programs (IEPs) be designed for all children with disabilities and that such children be educated in the least restrictive environment (i.e., with nonhandicapped children where possible). The act also guarantees parents extensive procedural rights in the evaluation and placement of their children with disabilities, and such children are entitled to private placements if appropriate public programs are not available.

Prior to the *Timothy W.* decision, most legal controversies brought under the EHA focused on the *types* of educational programs and related services that must be supported by school districts, rather than on *whether* specific children with disabilities were entitled to educational services. In the initial wave of EHA litigation, the courts were unsympathetic when school districts claimed "lack of funds" as the rationale for denying appropriate programs for specific children with disabilities.[7] For example, in 1979 a California federal district court noted that severely disabled students "could place a significant burden on the resources of our public school systems, but Congress has determined that it is worth the price to develop the potential of the handicapped."[8] Children with severe disabilities have often been placed in year-round residential facilities, and most courts have held the home school districts responsible for the costs even though such placements have been made for a combination of custodial and educational reasons.[9] While the courts have acknowledged that school districts can enter into agreements with other state agencies to share the costs of providing services for these children,[10] such cost-sharing has not often occurred.

For example, in 1981 the Third Circuit Court of Appeals held that a Delaware school district was obligated to support a residential placement, including noneducational costs, for a severely disabled child.[11] The court noted that the child's combination of physical and mental handicaps necessitated a high level of consistency in programming and warranted a residential placement. Recognizing that the EHA specifically assigned public schools the responsibility for children with disabilities, the appellate court concluded that the school district was fiscally obligated to support services to address the child's needs — social and emotional as well as educational.

In most cases courts have applied an expanded definition of *education* that includes self-sufficiency and even some degree of self-care (e.g., toilet training and dressing and feeding oneself have been considered to be appropriate educational goals).[12] Accordingly, the responsibility for programs to attain these goals has been placed on the public schools. For example, in 1983 the First Circuit Court of Appeals ruled that a severely retarded child who needed round-the-clock training and reinforcement to make any educational progress was entitled to a residential program under the EHA.[13] Rejecting the school district's contention that the child's residential needs were cus-

> ## Courts have applied an expanded definition of *education* that includes self-sufficiency.

todial rather than educational, the court adopted a broad definition of education and declared that minimum educational benefits could not be obtained in a day program.

The following year the Sixth Circuit Court of Appeals held that a teenager who was seriously emotionally disturbed was entitled to placement in a long-term residential treatment facility. The court noted that cost considerations are relevant only when choosing among several options, all of which are considered appropriate to meet the child's needs.[14] Subsequently, in *Parks* v. *Pavkovic* the Seventh Circuit Court of Appeals struck down an Illinois law requiring parents to pay up to $100 a month for their handicapped child's living expenses in private facilities where the placement was based on the child's developmental disabilities.[15] The court rejected the contention that, if the child would have to live in an institution anyway (regardless of any efforts to educate the child), those living expenses are not caused by educational needs and should not be assessed against the education agency.

More recently, the Supreme Court declined to review a decision in which the 11th Circuit Court of Appeals held that a Georgia school district was required to pay for a residential program for an autistic child until age 21 if the child continued to need constant educational supervision in order to make progress.[16] The court further ordered the school district to reimburse the child's parents more than $42,000 for expenses that they had incurred in supporting residential placements in Tokyo and Boston. Although troubled by the fact that the parents had selected residential centers so far away from their home, the court concluded from the evidence (including itemized statements of the costs incurred in the private programs) that the parents deserved reimbursement because the school district had failed to propose an appropriate placement for the child.[17]

However, there are limitations on the responsibilities of public school districts under federal law. While school districts are required to provide related services necessary for children to benefit from special education, they are not obligated to provide *medical* services except for diagnostic and evaluative purposes.[18] The judiciary has interpreted medical services as those that must be provided by a physician or require constant monitoring by health-care professionals.[19] The Ninth Circuit Court of Appeals recently held that parents' placement of their child in an acute-care psychiatric hospital was primarily for medical rather than for educational reasons; thus the school district was not financially responsible for the placement. Among the factors that the court considered in reaching this decision were the intensity of the therapeutic program (six hours of psychotherapy a day), the development of the child's IEP by medical rather than educational personnel, and the fact that the hospital was not accredited as an educational institution.[20]

Courts have also not required school districts to support residential placements when less expensive programs are deemed appropriate for specific children with disabilities. For example, the Fourth Circuit Court of Appeals rejected a parental request for continuation of a profoundly retarded child's 24-hour residential care, concluding that the school district's proposed day program for the child constituted an appropriate placement under the EHA.[21] Similarly, the 10th Circuit Court of Appeals recognized that the EHA does not entitle children to residential placements that will maximize their potential. The court found appropriate a school district's proposed program of one-on-one instruction and counseling for

a child with multiple disabilities, even though a private placement might be superior.[22] Other courts have noted that, if two programs are considered suitable for a child, it would seem reasonable to select the less expensive program because excessive spending on one child can deprive other children with disabilities.[23]

In the 1985 *Parks* case, when the Seventh Circuit Court of Appeals invalidated the Illinois law requiring parents to contribute to the living expenses of their developmentally disabled children placed in private facilities, the court commented that the most severely disabled children may be beyond the public school's responsibility. The court declared that, "if the child is so far handicapped as to be unconscious, and is thus wholly uneducable, he falls outside the protection of the [EHA] even though his handicap is more rather than less severe than that of children protected by the Act."[24] The court further recognized that "it can be argued that the limited funds allocated for the education of the handicapped could be employed more productively on a child likely to make real educational progress . . . than on one too severely retarded to benefit much at all." While the appeals court at least hinted that public schools may not be required to serve some profoundly disabled children, this contention was not addressed directly until the federal district court rendered its opinion in *Timothy W.* v. *Rochester, New Hampshire, School District.*

LITIGATIVE HISTORY OF *TIMOTHY W.*

The controversy in *Timothy W.* centered on the school district's obligation to provide services for a child who suffered from severe spasticity, brain damage, joint contractures, seizure disorder, and other profound disabilities. He made virtually no sounds and was nonambulatory, quadriplegic, and cortically blind. The hearing officer had ruled that the child qualified for special education, noting that all handicapped children are entitled to an IEP, regardless of the severity of their handicapping conditions. He reasoned that "inquiry as to whether a child might benefit from special education is no longer relevant."[25]

The federal district court judge, however, disagreed. The judge concluded that, if a child is incapable of cognitive learning, he or she is *not* entitled to an IEP under the EHA. The court relied in part on a 1982 decision in *Hendrick Hud-*

son Central School District v. *Rowley* in which the Supreme Court had reasoned that children with disabilities were not entitled to programs that would maximize their potential, but rather to a floor of basic opportunity consisting of personalized instruction and support services "designed to provide educational benefit."[26] The New Hampshire judge interpreted the Supreme Court's emphasis on "educational benefit" as meaning that students incapable of benefiting from instruction are not entitled to IEPs. The judge declared: "It logically follows that a handicapped child who . . . does not have learning capacity was not intended to receive special education under the [EHA]. Surely, Congress would not legislate futility?"

The judge found support for this reasoning in *Parks*, discussed above, in which the Seventh Circuit Court of Appeals indicated that children incapable of learning (e.g., comatose) would not be entitled to IEPs under the EHA. The judge concluded that both the EHA and New Hampshire law required this threshold determination regarding whether a specific child can benefit from special education.

In making this determination, the judge relied on expert testimony with regard to Timothy's capabilities. Various medical and teaching personnel presented divergent opinions as to Timothy's ability to benefit from education. Some testimony indicated that Timothy was operating at the brainstem level and would never be able to care for himself or acquire academic skills. Other expert testimony, however, indicated that Timothy could benefit from an IEP carefully tailored to very limited goals involving basic survival.

After reviewing the extensive testimony, the judge reached the "regrettable conclusion" that Timothy's potential for learning seemed nonexistent. Noting that Timothy's activities were passive (with little, if any, purposeful movement), the judge reasoned that the greatest service that society can provide for Timothy is to alleviate his pain and suffering "and provide him a comfortable and secure living environment."[27]

The judge agreed with the school district that the EHA covers children who "require" special education and can benefit from educational services. Concluding that the school district was not obligated to provide special education services for Timothy, the district's motion for summary judgment was granted. The judge did note, however, that Timothy must be evaluated regularly for developmental signs indicating a capability to benefit from special education.

The First Circuit Court of Appeals, reversing the lower court's decision, relied on the wording of the EHA that entitles *all* children with disabilities to educational services. The court concluded that the language of the EHA could not be more unequivocal, in that the provision of services for severely disabled children who have not been served adequately is a specified priority of the EHA.[28] In essence, a "zero-reject policy" is central to the act. The court declared that "ability to benefit" is not a prerequisite to the provision of educational services.

> THE COURT RULED THAT "ABILITY TO BENEFIT" IS NOT A PREREQUISITE TO THE PROVISION OF SERVICES.

The appeals court reviewed the legislative history of the EHA and related case law in reaching its conclusion that education for the severely disabled under the act is to be defined broadly: "The district court's conclusion that education must be measured by the acquirement of traditional 'cognitive skills' has no basis whatsoever in the 14 years of case law since the passage of the Act."[29] The appellate court observed that other federal courts consistently have held that education under the act encompasses a wide spectrum of training, including the most basic life skills for some children.

Finding the district court's reliance on *Rowley* misguided, the appeals court noted that *Rowley* dealt with the level of services the school district was obligated to support for a child with a hearing disability and not with whether specific handicapped children were entitled to *any* services. The appeals court declared that "nowhere" in *Rowley* did the Supreme Court suggest that the basic floor of educational opportunity that must be provided for the handicapped "contains a trap door for the severely handicapped."[30] According to the appellate court, the only question the school district must consider

is what constitutes an appropriate IEP for Timothy, and this cannot be interpreted as *no* educational program at all.

In the school district's petition for the appellate court to rehear the case, the district faulted the court for not applying the EHA's definition of handicapped children (i.e., those who "require" special education).[31] Contending that the appellate court erred by holding that Timothy's program may consist solely or primarily of related services, the district asserted that the EHA deals with education and "is not a national health insurance statute."[32] The school district further questioned how there can be an objective legal standard for determining the level of services that the school district must provide when a child is incapable of benefiting from special education: "While the Court of Appeals asserts that *Rowley* was not intended to be a 'trap door,' its opinion turns *Rowley* into an elevator with no top floor."[33]

IMPLICATIONS

Groups that advocate on behalf of individuals with disabilities, including the Association for Retarded Children, the Disability Rights Education and Defense Fund, and the Council for Exceptional Children, cheered the *Timothy W.* ruling as reaffirming the "zero-reject" philosophy in that school districts cannot deny services because of the severity of a child's disabilities. Frank Laski, who filed a friend-of-the-court brief on behalf of the Association for Persons with Severe Handicaps, asserted: "If anybody thought there was any basis for excluding any kid, this puts an end to it."[34] The Justice Department had also urged the appellate court to reverse the district court's decision, arguing that it is not the role of federal courts to set a threshold under the EHA that excludes certain children with severe disabilities.[35]

However, the American Association of School Administrators and the National School Boards Association (NSBA) have contended that the appellate court's ruling sweeps too broadly and places unrealistic fiscal obligations on already strained education budgets. August Steinhilber, general counsel for the NSBA, has claimed that small school districts simply do not have $100,000 a year to spend on custodial care for a single child.[36] Gerald Zelin, attorney for the Rochester School District, has agreed with Steinhilber that, under *Timothy W.*, school districts could be held responsible for children in comas.[37] Indeed, Zelin has asserted that "the ruling could expose school districts around the country to tremendous costs for programs that would have minimal impact."[38] Moreover, Raymond Yeagley, superintendent of the Rochester (New Hampshire) School District, has indicated that the district must realign its educational priorities as a result of the *Timothy W.* decision. He also has voiced his concern that other students will suffer because of the appellate court's failure to place any financial limits on the school district's obligations to serve the severely disabled.[39]

The issue of program costs seems to be cropping up more often in recent special education cases than it did in the late 1970s and early 1980s. Given the federal government's failure to appropriate the promised level of funds under the EHA, state and local education agencies are questioning the justification for placing additional stress on local education budgets to support residential placements — primarily custodial in nature — for children with severe disabilities. At what point is the educational aspect of a severely disabled child's placement so minimal that the school district should not bear total responsibility? Is it an appropriate expenditure of school funds to pay for round-the-clock residential care for one severely disabled child, when such funds would support instructional services for a number of less severely disabled children? Sentiment is growing in educational and political forums that mandates to support custodial services are diverting funds from the educational mission of schools.

If the First Circuit Court of Appeals had affirmed the lower court's ruling, some problems for school districts might have been alleviated, but others would have been created. Even if public schools were relieved of the financial responsibility for placements made primarily for noneducational reasons, sensitive issues would still have to be addressed. The appeals court surely realized that it would be opening a Pandora's box if it ruled that children considered incapable of learning would not be entitled to educational services. How much cognitive ability would a child have to possess to deserve an IEP? Who would make this determination? Moreover, the "Solomon-like task" of separating educational and noneducational needs would have to be confronted.[40]

Rather than focus on whether specific children are educable and thus entitled to

free appropriate public education to be provided handicapped children."[42]

However, only a few states have enacted policies clearly delineating responsibilities across agencies. James Rosenfeld recently observed that school districts "have not been able to secure the cost-sharing anticipated by the EHA as other providers, also operating under stringent fiscal limitations, have backed away from serving handicapped children. Most of the education agencies have received little support from either their own states or the federal government in obtaining this financial help."[43] Comprehensive policies for youth are clearly needed, and

that arbitrarily excluded students from public schools and denied them other publicly supported services. While education agencies sorely need relief, we must ensure that children with disabilities are not hurt in the process.

> ## ONLY A FEW STATES HAVE ENACTED POLICIES CLEARLY DELINEATING RESPONSIBILITIES ACROSS AGENCIES.

services under the federal law, perhaps the more important issue is *which* government agencies should care for children with severe disabilities. Neither the Rochester School District nor professional education associations supporting the district's position claimed that Timothy should be denied publicly supported services to help him achieve whatever level of self-care he could. The controversy arose over whether it was the school district's responsibility to provide such services.

Much current attention is focused on developing policies that address children's health and welfare needs as well as their educational needs.[41] Congress actually attempted to do this in the EHA by centralizing supervisory authority for children with disabilities in the public schools, which were expected to enter into agreements with other social service agencies to support some programs. Recognizing that other agencies were not participating as it intended, in 1986 Congress amended the EHA to stipulate that, although state education agencies are responsible for ensuring that the [EHA] requirements are carried out, this "shall not be construed to limit the responsibility" of other agencies in "providing or paying for some or all of the costs of a

public school districts are the logical co-ordinating agencies. But for such policies to be effective, responsibilities must be shared by service providers.

The *Timothy W.* litigation has raised significant policy questions regarding the scope of public school districts' obligations to serve severely disabled children and the role that other social service agencies should play in this regard. Volatile debate in legislative forums over who must pay for services for these children seems inevitable. The contention that some profoundly disabled children are beyond the school district's jurisdiction — which would not have been voiced a decade ago — is gaining support among professional education associations. In the absence of coordinated policies with well-defined responsibilities across agencies, the stage is being set for a backlash against federal mandates regarding the education of individuals with disabilities.[44]

If Congress and state legislatures should reduce the public school's obligations without making other provisions for the severely disabled to receive appropriate care, this would be an unfortunate development indeed. Such action could result in an erosion of the gains made under the EHA and a reversion to practices

1. *Timothy W.* v. *Rochester, New Hampshire, School Dist.*, 875 F.2d 954 (1st Cir. 1989), *cert. denied*, 110 S. Ct. 519 (1989).
2. This article builds in part on Martha McCarthy, "The Public School's Responsibility to Serve Severely Disabled Children," *Education Law Reporter*, vol. 49, 1988, pp. 453-67.
3. Perry Zirkel has reported that court decisions concerning children with disabilities increased more than 600% from the 1970s to the 1980s. Perry Zirkel, "Litigation Forecast," *American School Board Journal*, December 1990, p. 16.
4. *Timothy W.* v. *Rochester, New Hampshire, School Dist.*, Petition for Rehearing, Appeal No. 88-1847 (1st Cir.), 8 June 1989, p. 5.
5. Throughout this article I will refer to this law as the EHA because the decisions discussed were rendered prior to the change in the law's name and because the substantive provisions of the law are largely unchanged.
6. 20 U.S.C. Section 1401 *et seq.*
7. See *Battle* v. *Commonwealth of Pennsylvania*, 629 F.2d 269 (3d Cir. 1980), *cert. denied*, 452 U.S. 968 (1981); *Lora* v. *Board of Educ.*, 456 F. Supp. 1211 (E.D.N.Y. 1978), *remanded*, 623 F.2d 248 (2d Cir. 1980), *on remand*, 587 F. Supp. 1572 (E.D.N.Y. 1984); *Frederick* v. *Thomas*, 419 F. Supp. 960 (E.D. Pa. 1976), *aff'd*, 557 F.2d 373 (3d Cir. 1977); *Mahoney* v. *Administrative School Dist. No. 1*, 601 P.2d 826 (Ore. Ct. App. 1979); and *Mills* v. *Board of Educ.*, 348 F. Supp. 866 (D.D.C. 1972).
8. *Boxall* v. *Sequoia Union High School Dist.*, 464 F. Supp. 1104, 1114 (N.D. Cal. 1979).
9. See *North* v. *District of Columbia Bd. of Educ.*, 471 F. Supp. 136 (D.D.C. 1979); *In re "A" Family*, 602 P.2d 157 (Mont. 1979); and text with notes, 11-17.
10. See *Mattie T.* v. *Holladay*, 522 F. Supp. 72 (N.D. Miss. 1981); and *Smith* v. *Cumberland School Committee*, 415 A.2d 168 (R.I. 1980).
11. *Kruelle* v. *New Castle County School Dist.*, 642 F.2d 687 (3d Cir. 1981).
12. See *Battle* v. *Commonwealth of Pennsylvania. . .* ; and Peter D. Roos, "Litigation: A Necessary Tool for Educational Reform," *Phi Delta Kappan*, February 1983, pp. 417-19.
13. *Abrahamson* v. *Hershman*, 701 F.2d 223 (1st Cir. 1983).
14. *Clevenger* v. *Oak Ridge School Bd.*, 744 F.2d 514 (6th Cir. 1984). See also *David D.* v. *Dartmouth School Committee*, 775 F.2d 411 (1st Cir. 1985), *cert. denied*, 475 U.S. 1140 (1986); *Board of Educ.* v. *Diamond*, 808 F.2d 987 (3d Cir. 1986); and *Vander Malle* v. *Ambach*, 667 F. Supp. 1015 (S.D.N.Y. 1987).
15. 753 F.2d 1397 (7th Cir. 1985), *cert. denied*, 474 U.S. 919 (1985).
16. *Drew P.* v. *Clarke County School Dist.*, 877 F.2d 927 (11th Cir. 1989), *cert. denied*, 110 S. Ct. 1510 (1990). But see *Matta* v. *Board of Educ.-Indian Hill Exempted Village Schools*, 731 F. Supp. 253 (S.D. Ohio 1990), in which the parents were denied reimbursement for placing their autistic child in the same Japanese school because an appropriate local placement was available.
17. See *Burlington School Comm.* v. *Department of Educ.*, 471 U.S. 359 (1985), in which the Su-

preme Court ruled that parents who have unilaterally placed their child in a private program can obtain reimbursement if it is ultimately determined that the school district's proposed program was not appropriate for the child.

18. Under the EHA, related services are defined as "transportation, and such developmental, corrective, and other supportive services (including speech pathology and audiology, psychological services, physical and occupational therapy, recreation, and medical and counseling services, except that such medical services shall be for diagnostic and evaluation purposes only" (20 U.S.C. Section 1401[17]). The 1990 amendments added "rehabilitation counseling and social work services" to this list of related services.

19. See *Irving Indep. School Dist.* v. *Tatro*, 468 U.S. 883 (1984); and *Detsel* v. *Board of Educ. of the Auburn Enlarged City School Dist.*, 820 F.2d 587 (2d Cir. 1987), *cert. denied*, 484 U.S. 981 (1987).

20. *Clovis Unified School Dist.* v. *California Office of Administrative Hearings*, 903 F.2d 635 (9th Cir. 1990). See also *Guempel* v. *State*, 387 A.2d 399 (N.J. Super., Law Div., 1978), in which the New Jersey court held that custodial care of subtrainable children does not qualify as education and school districts are not obligated to incur maintenance costs that are not based on educational needs. But see *Taylor* v. *Honig*, 910 F.2d 627 (9th Cir. 1990), in which the school district was held financially responsible for placement of a child in a residential facility that operated as a school *and* a psychiatric hospital. This placement was found to be primarily for educational reasons.

21. *Matthews* v. *Davis*, 742 F.2d 825, 830 (4th Cir. 1984). See also *Kerkam* v. *Superintendent, D.C. Public Schools*, 931 F.2d 84 (D.C. Cir. 1991), in which the appeals court held that an extended-day program offered by the school district satisfied the EHA, even if the severely retarded student could

have made more educational progress at a residential facility; *Burke County Bd. of Educ.* v. *Denton*, 895 F.2d 973 (4th Cir. 1990), in which an autistic student who had made educational progress in a day program was not entitled to in-home rehabilitative services; and *Abrahamson* v. *Hershman*, cited above, in which the court noted that "Congress did not intend to burden local school committees with providing all social services to all handicapped children" (228).

22. *Cain* v. *Yukon Public Schools*, 775 F.2d 15, 21 (10th Cir. 1985). See also *Martin* v. *School Bd. of Prince George County*, 348 S.E.2d 857 (Va. Ct. App. 1986); and *Hendry County School Bd.* v. *Kujawski*, 498 So. 2d 566 (Fla. Dist. Ct. App. 1986).

23. See *Thomas* v. *Cincinnati Bd. of Educ.*, 918 F.2d 618 (6th Cir. 1990); *Roncker* v. *Walter*, 700 F.2d 1058 (6th Cir. 1983), *cert. denied*, 464 U.S. 864 (1983); and *Nelson* v. *Southfield Public Schools*, 384 N.W.2d 423 (Mich. Ct. App. 1986).

24. *Parks* v. *Pavkovic* at 1405.

25. *Timothy W.* v. *Rochester School Dist.*, No. C-84-733-L (D.N.H. 1988), slip opinion at 4.

26. Ibid., slip opinion at 9, citing *Board of Educ. of the Hendrick Hudson Central School Dist.* v. *Rowley*, 458 U.S. 176, 188-189 (1982).

27. Ibid., slip opinion at 22.

28. *Timothy W.* v. *Rochester, New Hampshire, School Dist.*, 875 F.2d 954, 960 (1st Cir. 1989).

29. Ibid. at 970.

30. Ibid. at 971.

31. *Timothy W.* v. *Rochester, New Hampshire, School Dist.*, Petition for Rehearing, Appeal No. 88-1847 (1st Cir.), 8 June 1989, p. 2.

32. Ibid. at 9-10.

33. Ibid. at 7.

34. Frank Laski, quoted in Debra Viadero, "All Handicapped Must Be Served, Court Concludes," *Education Week*, 7 June 1989, p. 1.

35. "Feds Urge Reversal of Opinion Labeling Student Unable to Benefit from Education," *Education Daily*, 17 October 1988, pp. 3-4.

36. "Court Upholds Educating All Handicapped Children," *Education Week*, 7 June 1989, p. 9; and "Court Won't Touch Ruling Requiring Education for Severely Disabled," *Education Daily*, 28 November 1989, p. 1.

37. "No Child Too Handicapped for Special Education, Appeals Court Rules," *Education Daily*, 1 June 1989, p. 4.

38. Gerald Zelin, quoted in "Court Rules Schools Must Take All Disabled," *New York Times*, 28 May 1989, Sect. 1, p. 27.

39. Personal correspondence with Raymond Yeagley, 26 May 1989.

40. *North* v. *District of Columbia Bd. of Educ.*, 471 F. Supp. 136, 141 (D.D.C. 1979).

41. See *Conditions of Children in California* (Berkeley, Calif.: Policy Analysis for California Education, 1989); "Let's Form a National Children's Policy," *School Board News*, 6 March 1990, p. 2; and Deborah Cohen, "C.D.F. Focusing on How Schools Are Serving Children," *Education Week*, 14 March 1990, p. 6.

42. 20 U.S.C. Section 1412(6). In addition, the 1988 amendments to the Medicare law prohibit the Health Care Financing Administration from denying Medicaid reimbursement to schools simply because a service is part of a handicapped child's IEP. Medicare Catastrophic Coverage Act, P.L. 100-360, Section 411, amending 42 U.S.C., Section 1396b. However, the distinction between medical and educational needs of specific children remains ambiguous.

43. S. James Rosenfeld, "Role of Schools for Handicapped Children at Issue," *Education Week*, 8 February 1989, p. 32.

44. See Perry Zirkel, " 'Backlash' Threatens Special Education," *Education Week*, 1 August 1990. p. 64.

INSTRUCTIONAL PRINCIPLES

Behind Computerized Instruction for Students with Exceptionalities

A critical problem in the application of computers to special education is that computerized education is often undertaken without any theoretical framework. Teachers often tell their students to run software simply because it is "good," it is related to the subject matter, or the students seem to like it, without relating this use to any theoretical principles or specific instructional strategies. This is ironic, because in recent years there has been a considerable growth in solid research demonstrating the effectiveness of specific instructional strategies.

This article describes several principles of instruction that are well validated by educational research and suggests guidelines for integrating use of the computer with these principles. The principles can be applied to all learners, not just to students with special needs, and they pertain to all grade levels. Many are simply verifications of common sense. The key point is that research indicates that instruction will be more effective to the extent that these principles are put into practice.

Table 1 summarizes the principles of instruction, which are discussed more completely in Vockell and Schwartz (1992). The focus here is on showing how use of the computer can fit in with six of the significant principles derived from educational research.

EDWARD L. VOCKELL
THOMAS MIHAIL

Edward L. Vockell is Professor of Education; and Thomas Mihail (CEC Chapter #771) is Associate Professor of Special Education, Purdue University Calumet, Hammond, Indiana.

A special thank you to Kathy Dziadon and her students and tutors at Scott Middle School, Hammond, Indiana.

■ Direct Instruction

INSTRUCTIONAL PRINCIPLE:

When teachers explain exactly what students are expected to learn and demonstrate the steps needed to accomplish a particular academic task, students learn more.

Direct instruction is one of the most broadly applicable principles in special education. The key point of direct instruction is that it is fallacious to assume that students will develop insights on their own. Rather, direct instruction takes learners through the steps of learning systematically, helping them see both the purpose and the result of each step. The basic components of direct instruction are as follows:

1. Setting clear goals for students and making sure they understand these goals.
2. Presenting a sequence of well-organized assignments.
3. Giving students clear, concise explanations and illustrations of the subject and subject matter.
4. Asking frequent questions to see whether or not students understand the work.
5. Giving students frequent opportunities to practice what they have learned.

Direct instruction is one of the activities that computers perform especially well. For example, a program designed to teach students how to regroup numbers when adding and subtracting might state its objective, provide a tutorial upon request, and then provide numerous opportunities for practice with immediate feedback. Teachers can use almost any good computer program as a component of effective direct instruction even if the program itself does not incorporate all the features of direct instruction. For example, a teacher can clearly point out the objective of a unit of instruction, supply the computer program, indicate the connection between the objective and the program, and then monitor the students' use of the program as necessary.

From *Teaching Exceptional Children*, Vol. 25, No. 3, Spring 1993, pp. 38-43. Copyright © 1993 by The Council for Exceptional Children. Reprinted by permission.

■ Mastery Learning

INSTRUCTIONAL PRINCIPLE:

Given enough time and help, about 95% of the learners in any group can come to a complete mastery of the designated instructional objectives.

While it can be employed with all learners, mastery learning is particularly applicable for learners with disabilities. When mastery learning is successful, high standards are articulated and students receive ample time and help to meet these standards.

Two problems often arise with mastery learning. First, grouping and scheduling may become difficult. It is easier for a teacher to require people to work at a constant pace and complete tasks at a predictable rate than to permit wide variations in activities within a class. Second, while learners who need more instructional time to succeed spend extra time on minimum competency standards, the relatively faster learners may be forced to wait when they could be progressing to higher levels of achievement. These problems are overcome by providing individualized attention, setting high but attainable standards, and making additional materials available for learners who master objectives more quickly than others.

Computers can aid mastery learning in the following three ways:

1. Many students need additional time and individualized practice with feedback to meet objectives. Computer programs can often provide opportunities to study at the times and pace suited to the individual's needs.
2. Additional programs can be made available for students who master objectives quickly. These can either provide more intense study of the same objectives, allow the student to move on to higher objectives, or integrate the objectives covered in the unit with other objectives.
3. Computerized gradebooks and other recordkeeping programs can help teachers keep track of student performance.

For special education resource teach-ers, mastery learning has often been a special challenge because their students are integrated into regular classrooms. Resource teachers must help students attain mastery in classes and in subject matter over which they exercise no direct control. The three guidelines just presented can be especially valuable in helping resource teachers take advantage of the benefits of computers under these circumstances—either by using computers when they work with students or by showing other teachers how to use computers more effectively to help students attain mastery.

■ Overlearning and Automaticity

INSTRUCTIONAL PRINCIPLE:

With many skills and concepts, it is important to continue studying and applying them well beyond the point of initial mastery.

Just as computers can help students achieve mastery learning, they can help them practice skills well beyond the point of initial mastery until they become overlearned or automatic. The reality is that there are numerous skills that must be practiced in spite of the fact that students "already know them." Indeed, maintenance and generalization continue to be the premier issues facing special educators in measuring the success of intervention. Teachers have long recognized the value of varying modes of presentation to engage the learner and increase attending, discrimination, association, and memory skills; transfer of learning to new settings; expression of ideas; and incidental learning. By selecting computer software that provides repeated practice in different contexts and through different formats, students can achieve this necessary repetition without the stultifying monotony that might otherwise occur.

■ Cooperative Learning

INSTRUCTIONAL PRINCIPLE:

Many students learn better in a cooperative environment (where the success of

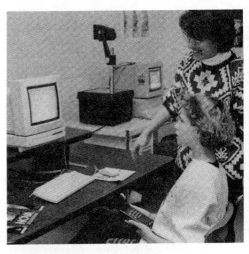

Frequent and systematic monitoring helps identify strengths and weaknesses in learning.

one student contributes to the success of the entire group) than in a highly competitive environment (where the success of one student requires that someone else be unsuccessful) or an individualistic environment (where students are unconcerned about the performance of others). In addition, cooperative environments often lead to acceptance of outsiders into a group and enhanced self-concept among students who would feel inadequate in a more competitive environment.

Excellent discussions of cooperative learning can be found in such sources as Slavin and colleagues (1985) and Johnson and Johnson (1987). Cooperative learning often overlaps with peer tutoring (see Table 1), but this is not always the case. Both cooperative learning and peer tutoring have proved effective in special education. It is easy to employ these principles at the computer. For example, many simulations work best when a group works together at the terminal and students discuss possible strategies before choosing one by consensus.

There are few instances in which it is essential to have individual students working alone at computer terminals. If students are going to work together at computers, it is a relatively simple step to give them cooperative guidelines to make the learning experience more effective. On the other hand, it is important to note that *some* guidelines may be

Table 1: Summary of Major Instructional Principles and Guidelines for Using the Computer

Principle: Direct Instruction
Summary: If teachers describe objectives and demonstrate exact steps, students can master specific skills more efficiently.
Guidelines:
1. Use programs that specify exact steps and teach them clearly and specifically.
2. Show the relationship of computer programs to steps in the direct teaching process.

Principle: Mastery Learning
Summary: Given enough time, nearly all learners can master objectives.
Guidelines:
1. Use programs that provide extra help and practice toward reaching objectives.
2. Use programs to stimulate and enrich students who reach objectives early.
3. Use recordkeeping programs to keep track of student performance.

Principle: Overlearning and Automaticity
Summary: To become automatic, skills must be practiced and reinforced beyond the point of initial mastery.
Guidelines:
1. Use computer programs to provide self-paced, individualized practice.
2. Use computer programs that provide gamelike practice for skills that require much repeated practice.
3. Use computer programs that provide varied approaches to practicing the same activity.

Principle: Memorization Skills
Summary: Recall of factual information is a useful skill that enhances learning at all levels.
Guidelines:
1. Use computer programs to provide repeated practice and facilitate memorization.
2. Use programs designed to develop memory skills.

Principle: Peer Tutoring
Summary: Both tutor and pupil can benefit from properly structured peer tutoring.
Guidelines:
1. Have students work in groups at computers.
2. Use programs that are structured to help tutors provide instruction, prompts, and feedback.
3. Teach students to give feedback, prompts, and instruction at computers.

Principle: Cooperative Learning
Summary: Helping one another is often more productive than competing for score rewards.
Guidelines:
1. Have students work in groups at computers.
2. Use programs that promote cooperation.
3. Provide guidelines for cooperative roles at computers.

Principle: Monitoring Student Progress
Summary: Close monitoring of student progress enables students, teachers, and parents to identify strengths and weaknesses of learners.
Guidelines:
1. Use programs that have management systems to monitor student progress.
2. Use recordkeeping programs.
3. Use computers to communicate feedback.

Principle: Student Misconceptions
Summary: Identifying misconceptions helps develop an understanding of topics.
Guidelines:
1. Use programs to diagnose misconceptions.
2. Use programs to teach correct understanding of misunderstood concepts.

Principle: Prerequisite Knowledge and Skills
Summary: Knowledge is usually hierarchical; lower-level skills must be learned before higher-level skills can be mastered.
Guidelines:
1. Use programs to assess prerequisite knowledge and skills.
2. Use programs to teach missing prerequisite skills.

Principle: Immediate Feedback
Summary: Feedback usually works best if it comes quickly after a response.
Guidelines:
1. Use programs that provide immediate feedback.
2. Use programs that provide clear corrective feedback.

Principle: Parental Involvement
Summary: Parents should be informed about their children's progress and assist in helping them learn.
Guidelines:
1. Use computers to communicate with parents about educational activities and progress.
2. Exploit home computers.

Principle: Learning Styles
Summary: Learners vary in preference for modes and styles of learning.
Guidelines:
1. Use programs that appeal to students' preferred learning styles.
2. Use programs that supplement the teachers' weaker teaching style.
3. Use programs that call upon students to employ a variety of learning styles.

Principle: Classroom Management
Summary: Effective classroom management provides more time for instruction.
Guidelines:
1. Use the computer as a tool to improve classroom management.
2. Use programs that have a management component.

Principle: Teacher Questions
Summary: If teachers ask higher-order questions and wait for students to answer, higher-level learning is likely to occur.
Guidelines:
1. Select programs that ask higher-level questions.
2. Use programs that individualize the pace of instruction, since wait time is likely to be better than with traditional instruction.

Principle: Study Skills
Summary: Effective study skills can be taught, and these almost always enhance learning.
Guidelines:
1. Teach students to use the computer as a tool to manage and assist learning.
2. Use programs that teach thinking skills.
3. Teach generalization of thinking and study skills across subject areas.

Principle: Homework
Summary: When homework is well planned by teachers, completed by students, and related to class, learning improves.
Guidelines:
1. Assign homework for home computers.
2. Have students do preparatory work off the computer as homework.

Principle: Writing Instruction
Summary: Writing should be taught as a recursive process of brainstorming, composing, revising, and editing.
Guidelines:
1. Use word processors for composition.
2. Use programs that prompt writing skills.
3. Teach students to use grammar and spelling checkers effectively.

Principle: Early Writing
Summary: Even very young children should be encouraged to write stories.
Guidelines:
1. Use simple word processing programs.
2. Use programs that combine graphics with writing.
3. Use graphics programs to stimulate creativity.

Principle: Learning Mathematics
Summary: Concrete experience helps students understand and master abstract principles.
Guidelines:
1. Match programs to children's level of cognitive development.
2. Use programs that provide concrete demonstrations with clear graphics.

Principle: Phonics
Summary: Instruction in phonics helps students to "break the code" and develop generalized word attack skills.
Guideline:
1. Use programs that combine sound with visual graphics to teach the sight/sound relationships of reading.

Principle: Reading Comprehension
Summary: Students often learn better if reading lessons are preceded by preparatory materials and followed by questions and activities.
Guidelines:
1. Use programs that have pre- and postactivities to accompany them.
2. Use computer programs before or after traditional reading materials.

Principle: Science Experiments
Summary: Students learn science best if they can do concrete experiments to see science in action.
Guidelines:
1. Use computer simulations.
2. Use tutorial and drill programs with concrete graphics.
3. Use database and word processing programs to manage and report noncomputerized science experiments.
4. Use science interface equipment to manage and analyze science experiments.

necessary to stimulate effective cooperative learning at the computer. It is not always safe to assume that cooperative learning will flow smoothly simply because two or more students are seated together at the computer. Without guidelines, students may instead work individualistically (concerned only about themselves) or competitively (concerned about doing better than others) at the computer, and such strategies may frustrate rather than enhance learning.

■ Monitoring Student Progress

INSTRUCTIONAL PRINCIPLE:

Frequent and systematic monitoring of students' progress helps students, parents, teachers, administrators, and policy makers identify strengths and weaknesses in learning and instruction. This often leads to improved student performance.

This principle provides the major rationale underlying the requirement for individualized education programs (IEPs) for students with exceptionalities. Computers can help monitor student progress. For example, many programs track the progress of the students running them. The teacher is able to check at convenient times to determine whether or not the students are making adequate progress. The teacher can confer with students individually to reinforce success, stimulate additional thought, or provide additional instruction as needed.

Teachers can use spreadsheet or database programs to record information about students. They can also use mailmerge options with word processing programs to generate individualized feedback for students, parents, or other teachers from the databases in which they have sorted information.

■ Learning Styles

INSTRUCTIONAL PRINCIPLE:

Children differ in their preferred styles of learning. Many children seem to learn much more

effectively when they are able to use one particular learning style than when they are forced to employ a nonpreferred learning style.

One of the major strengths of the computer is that it can present the same information in many different ways. A student who likes or needs an exciting, rapid-fire drill can often find one on the computer. That student's best friend might prefer a calm, slow-paced mode of presentation, and there is often a computer program to accommodate that child's learning style as well.

Distractibility is a common characteristic of the learning styles of students with mental retardation and learning disabilities. Attending behaviors are measurably increased when learning activities are unique, pertinent, and interesting. Colorful, attractive, and enjoyable presentations and materials are more likely to help students to learn than less attractive presentations. Computers can employ these basic strategies for reducing distractions and compelling students to be directly involved in learning.

When learning styles are a critical factor, there is no need to insist that all students run the same computer program. It may be better to make available several programs designed to teach the same objectives and let students choose the programs that suit them best.

Serious conflicts sometimes arise when a teacher employs a teaching style that is not compatible with a student's learning style. The computer may offer a way out of this dilemma. A wise teacher may be able to find supplementary programs that teach through a delivery method other than his or her own. When a student has a problem, the teacher can analyze the situation to determine whether the difficulty is really with the subject matter or with the mode of presentation. If the problem is with the delivery, then a computer program that calls upon a different learning style may solve the problem more effectively than a repeated explanation that is mismatched to the student's style.

Conclusion

The computer promotes learning most effectively when it makes a specific con-

Computers offer students access to preferred learning styles.

tribution to the implementation of a specific instructional strategy. Sometimes the principles discussed in this article will be applied by designers of instructional software. For example, a program might be written to provide effective, personalized feedback; include a management system to facilitate mastery learning; or enable the instructor to monitor student progress more easily. At other times, the principles will be applied by teachers using the software in the classroom. Examples of this application are when teachers encourage small groups to use a computer program according to the principles of cooperative learning or when they select a software package that is particularly suited to the learning style of an individual student. By being aware of and applying these principles, teachers can use computers as valuable tools to enhance learning among children with exceptionalities.

References

Johnson, D. W., & Johnson, R. T. (1987). *Learning together and alone: Cooperative, competitive, and individualistic learning.* Englewood Cliffs, NJ: Prentice Hall.

Slavin, R. E., Sharan, S., Kagan, S., Hertz-Lazarowitz, R., Webb, C., & Schmuck, R. (Eds.). (1985). *Learning to cooperate, cooperating to learn.* New York: Plenum.

Vockell, E. L., & Schwartz, E. (1992). *The computer in the classroom* (2nd ed.). Santa Cruz, CA: McGraw Hill.

Transition Concerns

Recent legislation has mandated that teachers involved in the education of children with exceptional conditions not only provide appropriate classroom instruction, but also provide transition services for them. PL 101-476, the Individuals with Disabilities Education Act (IDEA), requires schools to provide transition services from the world of school to the world of work and community (called vertical transitions). PL 99-457, the Amendment to the Education for All Handicapped Children Act, requires preschool and early elementary school teachers to provide transition services for young children from early childhood special education to public school education (called horizontal transitions). Transition services should also be provided for children with exceptionalities moving from regular education classes to part-time or full-time special education classes and for students moving from part-time or full-time special education classes to regular education classes. Children with disabilities may also require some assistance in making the transition from primary school to middle school, from middle school to high school, and perhaps from high school to some post-secondary education (e.g., technical school, college). All of the transitions involving functional curriculum to deal with changes within the school setting are called horizontal transitions.

All transitions involve life changes. Transitions are not easily accomplished even by adults in excellent physical and mental health! We should not expect them to be easy for children with disabilities. Transitions require planning, extra effort, and a commitment to completing the process. All transitions, whether horizontal or vertical, should be approached with input from all involved, assessment of needs, individualized planning, assistance to accomplish the change, and follow-up to assure that the transition continues to work.

Vertical transitions from the world of school to the world of work and community should be anticipated very early in the life of children with disabilities. Their individualized education programs (IEPs) should reflect a concern with post-school life as early as elementary school. By middle school and high school, children with disabilities should have an individualized transition plan (ITP) as well as, or a part of, their IEP.

The vertical ITPs (for post-school life) students with disabilities should focus on a broad array of living skills, not just future employment. Many questions need to be asked. What are the aptitudes of the student? What are the leisure interests? What kind of family and community support will this student have? Where will this student live as an adult? How will this student travel, work, and interact within the community? The ITP should be individualized enough to address the specific requirements of the student, yet flexible enough to be altered as the life situations and/or interests of the student change. Even though the ITP should be updated annually, it should be longitudinal in nature, planning for the future. Parents and experts from the child's area of disability should be involved in its formulation.

Three components that shall be considered in planning smooth transitions for children with disabilities from the world of school to the worlds of work and community are employment, living arrangements, and community involvement. Most children with disabilities need systematic instruction and a functional curriculum to help them cope with their special requirements in these three areas.

Employment preparation begins with an assessment of the interests and capabilities of each child with a disability. A child with a handicap should be allowed to explore many possible avenues of future employment and make some informed choices. Options and preparation should be commensurate with the reality of the capabilities of the student. Most students have more abilities than people think. There is a wide range of employment available to adults with disabilities, from work in a sheltered workshop, to supportive employment with mentors, coaches, and counseling, to independent employment in real jobs. Preparation for employment may range from the functional curriculum of the school, to vocational education, vocational rehabilitation or adult education; to technical or trade school; to college or university. Most employees with disabilities also have some on-the-job training. PL 101-476 (IDEA) mandates that employers with 15 or more employees hire qualified persons with disabilities and make reasonable modifications of the job structure or job requirements to meet the needs of the employee with the handicap.

Living arrangements for persons leaving school and

entering the world of work and community should be commensurate with their capabilities. They may range from group homes, to family or foster homes, to an apartment with a live-in-aide, to independent living in a home or apartment. School curriculum should include lessons on independent living such as meal preparation and clean up; home deliveries (e.g., mail) and pick-ups (e.g., trash); using money and paying bills; and making modifications to assure that doors, toilets, sink, appliances, etc., are accessible.

The preparation of students with disabilities for community involvement is an important part of transitional planning. Students who know how to drive or use public transportation, who can read maps and schedules, and who know how to use money are accepted by community members and make better adjustments to community living. Students should be taught social conventions (greetings, conversation skills, manners), grooming and clothing styles, access to medical care, and other interpersonal behaviors that will enhance their self-efficacy and self-esteem. When transitions from school to community go awry, it is more frequently from a lack of social living skills than from a lack of work skills. While much has recently been done to improve life transitions of persons with disabilities, much is left to be done.

The first article in this unit addresses horizontal transitions from special education to regular education classes. The authors describe ways to make transitions smooth, positive and successful. The second article addresses vertical transitions from school to work and community. Andrew Halpern discusses the current needs and concerns of the transition movement.

Looking Ahead: Challenge Questions

What can be done to ease the transition of exceptional children from more restrictive and protective special education classrooms to less restrictive and protective regular education classes? How much and what kind of exit assistance is desirable?

What are the current problems and issues regarding transition from the world of school to the worlds of work and community?

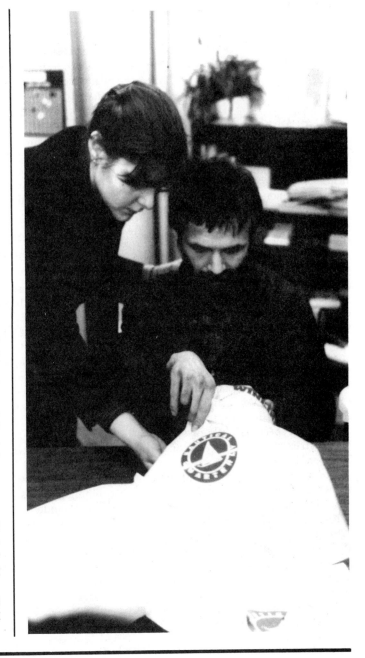

EASE: Exit Assistance for Special Educators—Helping Students Make the Transition

Nancy L. George
Timothy J. Lewis

Nancy L. George *(CEC Chapter #375) is Research Associate, Division of Teacher Education, and* **Timothy J. Lewis** *(CEC Chapter #375) is Instructor, Special Education, University of Oregon, Eugene.*

O ne of the greatest challenges facing special education teachers today is the development of strategies to help students with handicaps move from special education classrooms into less restrictive settings (Hundert, 1982). Although school districts have spent much time and effort in developing formalized procedures for student entry into special education, less attention has been given to developing procedures to determine when a student is no longer in need of special education services (Grosenick, George, & George, 1988; Salend & Viglianti, 1982). Consequently, teachers are often left on their own to make important decisions about the exit process. Without guidance for planning student exit and reintegration activities, many teachers may be hesitant to move students out of special education and into less restrictive settings (Laycock & Tonelson, 1985).

The professional literature widely acknowledges the need for clearly defined procedures for preparing both students (Grosenick, 1971; Hundert, 1982; Salend, 1984) and receiving teachers (Salend, 1984; White, 1980) for mainstreaming. Research suggests that the success of mainstreaming depends on the quality of communication and support between special and regular educators (Cantrell & Cantrell, 1976; Salend & Hanke, 1981). However, specific steps that special ed-

ucation teachers can initiate to implement a smooth transition from special to regular education have been lacking in the literature.

This article describes a four-phase process for reintegrating students into the mainstream. The process allows special education teachers to make data-based decisions about a student's readiness to move to a less restrictive setting and provides for a positive, fluid transition.

PHASE 1 Long-Range Planning

Ideally, planning for a student's exit from special education begins at the student's initial individualized education program (IEP) meeting. The first priority in developing the student's IEP is to formulate goals and objectives that address the reasons for the student's placement into special education. However, long-term educational goals can be developed at this meeting by thinking ahead to the types of behavioral, social, and academic skills the student will need to succeed in the mainstream. As a starting point, teachers may want to examine the curriculum guide, discipline policy, and/or student handbook from the student's home school to gain a better understanding of the social and academic demands of that setting. Input can also be solicited from the regular education teacher during the initial IEP meeting. Informal conversations and observations of regular education settings can provide further information on expectations for mainstreamed students.

The special education teacher should target these academic and behavioral competencies as long-range student goals—the standards or criteria by which the student will be judged ready to exit special education. A recapitulation of the needed competencies at all annual IEP reviews and other pupil progress meetings can serve as benchmarks for validating the student's progress and will remind all participants of the goal for the student's eventual exit from the special education program.

Time spent in long-range planning will allow special education teachers to develop behavioral and academic programs based on realistic and appropriate goals for students. In teaching the competencies needed to succeed in the mainstream, teachers should include strategies that promote the generalization of new skills to other settings (Epps, Thompson, & Lane, 1985; Stokes & Baer, 1977; Walker & Buckley, 1972). Grouping goals to create clusters of skills that promote success in the mainstream, targeting the skill areas necessary for reintegration, and programming for generalization of skills will provide a comprehensive plan that addresses specific student needs.

PHASE 2 Pre-Exit Activities

When the student begins to achieve targeted IEP goals, the focus shifts to equipping the student with the necessary skills to succeed in the new, less restrictive setting. To assist the teacher in preparing the student to meet the demands of the mainstream, the pre-exit phase is broken down into three steps.

Step 1: Assessing the Less Restrictive Setting

One goal of mainstreaming is to enable students to deal with different classroom routines and varying teacher styles and expectations as they move to less restrictive settings. Without an examination of mainstream settings, teachers may find it difficult to make decisions about whether or not students have the skills to succeed in less structured settings. To assist teachers in examining settings to which a student may return, a Classroom Inventory Checklist (CIC) is shown in Figure 1.

Two forms of field reviews were used in drafting the CIC. First, higher education professionals involved in special education teacher training were asked to provide feedback regarding the thoroughness of the checklist in evaluating classroom environments and the inclusion of variables known to be important for generalization. Next, feedback was sought from five special education teachers regarding the clarity of the CIC's format and its practicality and usefulness in programming for student generalization in a less restrictive setting. The overall response to the instrument was positive, and the CIC was revised based on suggestions made by the reviewers.

Use of the CIC allows the special education teacher to systematically examine key elements of the new setting, including the teacher's instructional method, curriculum materials used, how the student is evaluated, and the routines and policies of the classroom. By examining these features, the special education teacher can gain a better understanding of the academic and behavioral demands that will be placed on the student. Multiple observations should be made in each prospective setting so that the information collected represents an accurate sampling of the classroom routines and the teacher's expectations for performance.

Teachers may not be able to observe every new setting that their students enter, particularly at the secondary level, where students may be mainstreamed in several different classes. However, the need for assessment of less restrictive settings was supported strongly by the special education teachers and teacher trainers who reviewed the CIC. In cases

Figure 1
Classroom Inventory Checklist (CIC)

Teacher: _____ Grade: _____ Date: _____

Subject/Activity: _____

Observer: _____

Directions: Several observations should be made at different times and over different days and activities. It may be useful to develop a summary observation listing occurrences throughout the school day and situation-specific activities based on all the observations that have been made. In addition, the observer may wish to interview the teacher briefly to complete the inventory when all the information cannot be gained through observation. For questions 1 through 7, check all that apply or estimate percentage of time.

1. How is the room arranged?
   ☐ desks   ☐ study carrels   ☐ tables
   Notes:

2. What materials are used in the classroom?
   ☐ blackboard   ☐ textbooks   ☐ audiovisuals   ☐ workbooks
   ☐ worksheets   ☐ activity centers   ☐ games
   Notes:

3. What instructional format is used in the classroom?
   ☐ team teaching   ☐ independent activities   ☐ peer tutoring
   ☐ lecture/whole group   ☐ individualized instruction   ☐ small group
   Notes:

4. At what grade levels (or series/texts) are the students working?
   ☐ mathematics   ☐ reading   ☐ language arts
   Notes:

5. What other personnel are there in the classroom?
   ☐ teaching assistants   ☐ peer tutors   ☐ volunteers   ☐ no other personnel
   Notes:

6. How is student progress assessed?
   ☐ tests/quizzes   ☐ attendance   ☐ assignments   ☐ class participation
   Notes:

7. How does the classroom teacher manage student behavior?
   ☐ reinforcement (tangible/verbal)
   ☐ response cost (loss of recess, free time, etc.)
   ☐ use of school discipline procedures (List those procedures the teacher feels are important.)
   Notes:

8. What personal responsibilities does the student have? (e.g., assignments due by certain time, in seat before bell rings, assignments can be taken home vs. assignments must be completed in class.)

9. What are the daily routines in the classroom? (e.g., lunch at 11:20, PE on Thursdays only.)

10. What behaviors does the teacher like? (List behaviors the teacher emphasizes as important.)

11. What are the behaviors the teacher dislikes? (List behaviors the teacher disapproves or punishes.)

2. TRANSITION CONCERNS

where direct observation is not feasible, the special education teacher may want to meet informally with the receiving teacher to discuss specific classroom expectations and important routines. In other instances, receiving teachers may be asked to complete the checklist on their own. Although data collection takes time, information gained from examining less restrictive settings is crucial for the development of meaningful transition plans.

Step 2: Approximating New Placement Routines in the Special Class Setting

The information gathered from classroom observations is used to approximate features of the less restrictive setting in the special education classroom. Often students appear to have the necessary academic and behavioral skills to move into a less restrictive placement but quickly meet with failure due to an inability to generalize what they have learned in the old setting (Lira & White, 1978; Stokes & Baer, 1977). By alerting the student to the new materials and classroom routines, the special education teacher can help prepare for a smoother transition to that setting. For example, in Teacher Smith's classroom, receiving credit for an assignment may be contingent on putting the assignment papers on the teacher's desk at the end of the day. While the former special education student might complete the assignment, he or she might not receive credit if the work is placed in a personal folder, as was customarily done in the special education classroom, instead of on the teacher's desk.

Special education teachers cannot be expected to prepare students for all the changes they will experience in a new setting; however, student difficulties due to the unfamiliar routines of the receiving teacher can be largely eliminated by approximating some of the routines before integration occurs.

Other considerations to take into account when approximating the future placement include gathering information on the classroom's physical organization, the curriculum materials, and the teacher's instructional methods. The special education teacher may want to model the receiving teacher's style of instruction (for example, whole class versus individual instruction) to provide practice and familiarity with a particular teaching style.

An equally important step to begin during this phase is the fading of any reinforcement systems used in the special education classroom to those occurring in the new placement. Typically, this involves moving from a point or token system to the use of praise or free time. In addition, the student may need to be taught to use self-management skills or to delay reinforcement by systematically increasing the amount of time before reinforcement is given in the special education setting (Rhode, Morgan, & Young,

1983; Turkewitz, O'Leary, & Ironsmith, 1975).

In many mainstream settings, teachers do not need to reinforce students often to maintain appropriate behavior. Students who are moving from a placement rich in reinforcers to a setting that uses reinforcers infrequently can be taught how to solicit reinforcement. By assessing teacher likes (e.g., raising hand, being on time to class) and dislikes (e.g., not being prepared with the proper materials, turning in assignments late), the special ed-

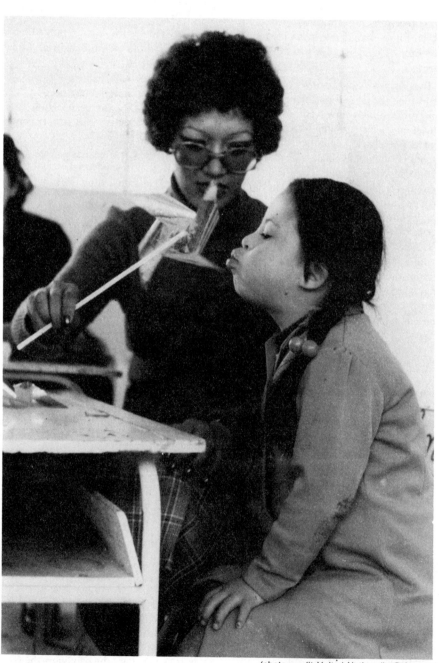

(photo credit United Nations/L. Solmssen)

Procedures for student entry into special education programs has been formalized over the years, but less attention has been given to developing procedures that determine when a student is no longer in need of special education services.

ucation teacher can identify the skills that are important for a returning student. Through social skills training or use of behavioral techniques, the special education teacher can teach the student to engage in behaviors the receiving teacher prefers. These competencies can be taught easily and may have a positive impact on the receiving teacher's impression of the student. This is particularly important when the receiving teacher is feeling reluctant or apprehensive about the new student.

Step 3: Assessing Student Readiness

The final step in the pre-exit phase involves assessing student readiness to move to a less restrictive setting. Just as the decision concerning a student's eligibility for special education must be supported by data, so should the decision about the student's exit. Demonstration of the student's accomplishment of IEP goals and ability to meet the demands of a less restrictive setting should be well documented. Current academic and behavioral skills should be compared to those required in the new setting as determined by information collected using the CIC:

- Is the student able to function without frequent reinforcement for appropriate behavior?
- Is the student at or near grade level in academic subjects?
- Can the student work independently for the required length of time as demanded in the new setting?

By comparing the progress the student has made in the current placement with information demonstrating the student's ability to succeed in the future placement, the special education teacher can reach a firm, data-based conclusion about the student's readiness to exit the program.

PHASE 3 The Transition

Once the data indicate that the student is ready to exit the current placement, the transition phase begins. In this phase, the focus shifts from preparing the student to preparing the staff and the student's parents for a change in placement.

The decision to move a student out of a special education placement should be made by a multidisciplinary team comprising special and general education personnel, parents, and the student. Prior to convening the team for discussion about the student's possible exit from special education, parent and student perceptions about reintegration should be considered fully. Parent and student understanding and support are essential for a smooth and successful transition into a new setting. Once they understand and agree with the need to move on from the present placement, the multidisciplinary team should meet to review student progress data and discuss placement options.

During the multidisciplinary team meeting, decisions should be made about what type of support services will be needed in the new setting. Timelines for a smooth transition should also be addressed. After preexit activities have been completed, transition may occur within weeks or over months, depending on the plans for reintegration and the readiness of both the student and the receiving personnel. The exit process might proceed more smoothly if one person on the team is designated as an exit coordinator. This person would be responsible for assigning the roles and responsibilities for team members. Typically the special education teacher coordinates the exit process; however it could be done by the counselor, the receiving teacher, the school administrator, or any other team member who is familiar with the student. This person is responsible for seeing that each of the tasks in the transition process is completed in a timely fashion.

PHASE 4 Follow-Up and Evaluation

Once the decision has been made to place the student into a less restrictive setting, team members should outline the specific procedures for student follow-up and evaluation. It is important to specify who is to be responsible for student follow-up and what types of follow-up data will be collected (e.g., behavioral performance data, reading and mathematics achievement, social interactions). Timelines for gathering student performance data also should be established. Ideally, information on the student's performance should be gathered at specified intervals to pro-

vide an accurate picture of the student's behavioral and academic progress in the new setting.

As a final step before placing the student into the mainstream, arrangements should be made to schedule consultative services for the receiving teacher. Consultation may occur routinely or on an as-needed basis, depending on the particular teacher and the particular situation. The important point to remember is that planning follow-up services prior to final placement will provide the receiving teacher with a ready source of support and can reduce the teacher's apprehension about receiving the student.

The information gathered on the student's performance in the new setting can be used to gauge student success and assess the overall effectiveness of the reintegration process. Teachers can use this information to pinpoint weaknesses in the exit process and improve the quality of future exit plans.

The EASE Checklist

The four phases of the exit process and accompanying questions are summarized in the Exit Assistance for Special Educators (EASE) checklist below.

Directions: Attach the checklist to the student's folder. Check off each question when the activity is completed. When all questions within a phase are answered positively, move on to the next phase.

Phase I: Long-Range Planning

- Do long-range goals address necessary skills to succeed in a mainstream setting?
- Do teaching strategies address and promote skill generalization to the mainstream setting?
- Are annual goals operationalized into long-range goals to promote student success in the mainstream? (Do goals build on one another to reach a terminal goal?)
- Do goals approximate the curriculum and behavioral demands of the mainstream setting?
- Are personnel from the mainstream setting involved in the IEP multidisciplinary team?

Phase II: Pre-Exit Activities

- Has the mainstream setting been assessed? (academic demands, behavioral demands)

2. TRANSITION CONCERNS

- Has current programming been matched to future placement? (academic-student progress data, behavioral-student progress data, criteria of new placement, student perceptions of readiness)

Phase III: Transition

- Have parent and student opinions been considered regarding possible change of placement?
- Has a multidisciplinary committee meeting been arranged to determine appropriate placement and possible support services for the student?
- Have timelines for reintegration been established?

Phase IV: Follow-Up and Evaluation

- Have arrangements been made for follow-up data collection and receiving teacher consultation in the new placement?
- Are follow-up data being collected?
- Is the mainstream setting teacher receiving consultative services?

This checklist can serve two purposes. First, it can serve as an overall guide for the special education teacher in planning exit procedures. Each phase is divided into key questions. Once all questions within a phase are answered positively, the next phase should be entered. Second, the checklist can be attached to each student's file, thereby following the student through his or her special education placement and serving as docu-mentation that the necessary steps for reintegration have been followed.

Summary

Preparing students with handicaps to function effectively in general education settings is a difficult and timeconsuming task. However, the establishment of well-defined exit plans ensures that students do not become "trapped" in special education. The four-phase process provides a framework for the fluid, positive, planned transition of students from special education classrooms to less restrictive settings. By following the steps outlined here, teachers at the initial IEP conference can begin to plan for the development of the competencies their students need to succeed in the mainstream.

References

Cantrell, R. P., & Cantrell, M. L. (1976). Preventive mainstreaming: Impact of a supportive services program on pupils. *Exceptional Children, 42,* 381–386.

Epps, S., Thompson, B. J., & Lane, M. P. (1985). *Procedures for incorporating generalization and maintenance programming into interventions for special education students.* Des Moines, IA: Iowa Department of Public Instruction.

Grosenick, J. K. (1971). Integration of exceptional children into regular classes: Research and procedure. *Focus on Exceptional Children, 3,* 1–8.

Grosenick, J. K., George, N. L., & George, M. P. (1988). The availability of program descriptions among programs for seriously emotionally disturbed students. *Behavioral Disorders, 13,* 108–115.

Hundert, J. (1982). Some considerations of planning the integration of handicapped children in the mainstream. *Jrnl. Lrng. Dis., 15,* 73–80.

Laycock, V. K., & Tonelson, S. W. (1985). Preparing emotionally disturbed adolescents for the mainstream: An analysis of current practices. *Programming for Adolescents with Behavioral Disorders, 2,* 63–73.

Lira, F. T., & White, M. J. (1978). Generalization of treatment effects: Preparing the resident for discharge. *Child Care Quarterly, 7,* 227–235.

Rhode, G., Morgan, D. P., & Young, K. R. (1983). Generalization and maintenance of treatment gains of behaviorally handicapped students from resource rooms to regular classrooms using self-evaluation procedures. *Journal of Applied Behavior Analysis, 16,* 171–188.

Salend, S. (1984). Factors contributing to the development of successful mainstreaming programs. *Exceptional Children, 50,* 409–416.

Salend, S. J., & Hanke, C. (1981). Successful mainstreaming: A form of communication. *Education Unlimited, 3,* 47–48.

Salend, S., & Viglianti, D. (1982). Preparing secondary students for the mainstream. *TEACHING Exceptional Children, 14,* 137–140.

Stokes, T. F., & Baer, D. M. (1977). An implicit technology of generalization. *Journal of Applied Behavior Analysis, 10,* 349–367.

Turkewitz, H., O'Leary, K. D., & Ironsmith, M. (1975). Generalization and maintenance of appropriate behavior through self-control. *Journal of Consulting and Clinical Psychology, 43,* 577–583.

Walker, H. M., & Buckley, N. K. (1972). Programming generalization and maintenance of treatment effects across time and across settings. *Journal of Applied Behavior Analysis, 5,* 209–224.

White, M. (1980). Classroom teacher report. *Strategies for planning and facilitating the reintegration of students with behavior disorders.* Des Moines, IA: Iowa Department of Public Instruction.

Transition: Old Wine in New Bottles

ABSTRACT: *The transition movement of the 1980s was preceded by two similar movements: (a) the career education movement in the 1970s and (b) the work/study movement in the 1960s. These three movements are described and compared to provide an historical context for understanding current problems and issues regarding transition. Some broad social issues, such as educational reform, are then examined to illustrate the potential influence of such issues on the future development of policy that will affect the transition movement.*

ANDREW S. HALPERN

ANDREW S. HALPERN (CEC Chapter #216) is a Professor in the Division of Teacher Education at the University of Oregon, Eugene.

One of my favorite books within the special education literature was written several years ago by Sandra Kaufman. Sandra is the mother of three children, one of whom, Nicole, is a daughter with mental retardation. During Nicole's childhood, Sandra and her husband Matt struggled, often unsuccessfully, to find ways of dealing with Nicole's problems. When Nicole was in her early 20s, however, and living in her own apartment, Sandra went back to school and became associated with the anthropological studies of mental retardation being conducted by Robert Edgerton. As part of her work in this area, Sandra decided that she would conduct a "field study" of her own daughter. A book eventually emerged out of this effort, which Sandra entitled *Retarded Isn't Stupid, Mom!* (Kaufman, 1988).

Although Nicole's story covers the full span of her life, the essence of Kaufman's book deals with Nicole's transition from adolescence into adulthood. This transition, as you might expect, was a struggle, not only for Nicole but for her parents and siblings as well. Although the hopes and aspirations of all concerned often remained high, there were times when the pathway had so many obstacles that the temptation to give up became almost insurmountable. In one particularly poignant example, Nicole burst into tears after attempting to buy a card for a friend's wedding shower. After purchasing the card, she discovered that it was worded in such a way for a man

to give to a woman. Nicole's despair was apparently very great as she contemplated one more piece of evidence of her self-perceived incompetence, which caused her to question her value as a human being.

Sandra recounted her own reaction to this incident through a conversation with Matt:

> "How does she take it?" I cried. "Everywhere she turns, the world screams at her that she's inadequate. She's barred from all the fun that [her brother and sister] enjoy. She's denied privileges they are given as a matter of course. She's excluded from the better paying, more interesting jobs. She's told she's too incompetent to have a baby. . . . She can't even buy a card in a store without being mortified. No wonder she's despondent."
>
> Matt stared out the front window.
>
> "And then," I continued, "we add to her problems. 'Go to work every day. Plan your time carefully. Eat right. Go to bed early. Clean your apartment. Budget your money. Use birth control.' That's what she hears from dawn to dusk. It's all so . . . rational, so middle class. Why does she have to live this way? Where is it written? Good God. She climbs mountains each day just to survive."
>
> Matt looked at me. "So what are you saying?"
>
> I shivered, "I guess I'm no longer sure I know what's best for her. There are many kinds of success. Maybe the best thing for her would be all-night sessions with friends, a baby or two, SSI for income. . . ."
>
> He was incredulous. "Could you really accept that? An aimless life in which each day is lived for itself?" (Kaufman, 1988, pp. 132-133)

From *Exceptional Children,* Vol. 58, No. 3, December/January 1992, pp. 202-211. Copyright © 1992 by The Council for Exceptional Children. Reprinted by permission.

Sandra Kaufman's anguished question about what's best for Nicole cuts to the heart of the transition movement for people with disabilities. Six years ago, Madeleine Will (1984a) defined a "new" federal initiative called "transition": "The transition from school to working life is an outcome-oriented process encompassing a broad array of services and experiences that lead to employment." A year later, I argued (Halpern, 1985) that the goals of transition should never be confined to employment, but should encompass all appropriate dimensions of adult adjustment and involvement in the community. Now, in the 1990s we no longer debate the appropriateness of a broader set of goals for transition. Instead, we have more appropriately turned our attention to the question of how to make transition work in our local communities. We have acknowledged that transition, from the perspective of families, is not only about services and social goals. From a phenomenological perspective, transition is better defined as "a period of *floundering* that occurs for at least the first several years after leaving school as adolescents attempt to assume a *variety* of adult roles in their communities."

A REVIEW OF HISTORICAL MOVEMENTS

The question of how to make transition work is complex and must be addressed at several levels, including policy development, program capacity development, and program implementation in local communities. The issues being addressed were obviously not invented in 1984, and we have experienced several broad social movements during the past three decades that have attempted to deal with these issues. Like old wine in new bottles, these issues have been addressed with varying levels of success by each new approach that has emerged to attack the old issues.

Cooperative Work/Study Programs

During the 1960s, a popular approach that emerged to address these issues was the work/study program, conducted cooperatively between the public schools and local offices of state rehabilitation agencies (Halpern, 1973; 1974; Kolstoe & Frey, 1965). The general goal of these programs was to create an integrated academic, social, and vocational curriculum, accompanied by appropriate work experience, that was designed to prepare students with mild disabilities for eventual community adjustment. The administration of these programs was generally structured by *formal* cooperative agreements between the schools and the rehabilitation agency.

The centerpiece of each cooperative agreement involved the assignment of a portion of each teacher's day (usually one half) to the role and duties of a work coordinator. This, in turn, led to

a significant increase in the number of students who participated in work placements as part of their high-school program. The formal relationship between a local school and the vocational rehabilitation agency also facilitated the efficient referral of students to become clients of the rehabilitation agency, which in turn eased the transition of students from school to the adult community.

Despite the tremendous growth and prosperity of this program during the 1960s, it basically died during the 1970s, primarily as a consequence of two intrinsic flaws. The first of these flaws derived from the funding mechanism that was generally used to support the program. This funding mechanism involved certifying the teacher's time (and accompanying salary) spent being a work coordinator as "in-kind" state contribution of dollars to the rehabilitation agency's budget. Because the majority of the rehabilitation agency's budget comes from federal allocations, at a ratio of several federal dollars for each matching state dollar, this certification of an already existing expenditure (the teacher's salary) as "in-kind" matching dollars became a clever way of generating additional federal rehabilitation dollars at no real additional expense to the state.

There was a hitch, however, in the federal regulations governing the certification of in-kind dollars for matching purposes. According to these regulations, if a person's salary from another agency was certified as rehabilitation matching money, then the proportion of that person's time represented by the "certified" salary had to be *supervised* by a representative of the rehabilitation agency. As you can imagine, school principals were not thrilled by the prospect of somebody other than themselves supervising their teachers. Although "creative" ways were often improvised for fulfilling this supervision requirement, it frequently emerged as a point of contention in the day-to-day implementation of the work/study agreement.

A second problem emerged from the "similar benefits" requirement of the 1973 amendments to the vocational rehabilitation act. This requirement, in a nutshell, stipulates that the rehabilitation agency cannot pay for services that are the legitimate responsibility of some other agency. Since the schools were *not required* to provide work experiences to their special education students during the 1960s, the provision of this service could be construed as a *rehabilitation* service under the terms of the cooperative agreement, thereby providing a justification for the generation of federal matching rehabilitation dollars (so long as the supervision requirement was met). A dramatic change occurred, however, with the passage of Public Law 94-142 in 1975, which required that every child with a disability is entitled to "a free and *appropriate* public education." Interpreters of this new law determined that "work experience" could be construed as a component of an "appropriate" education during high school for many students with disabilities. Such an interpretation made it risky for the rehabilitation agency to purchase this service, because it might be regarded as the responsibility of the schools and would then be governed by the rules concerning similar benefits.

In combination with several other constraints, the supervision and similar benefits requirements of the rehabilitation legislation led to the near demise of the cooperative work/study program during the 1970s. The needs being addressed through the program, however, were still very much alive. A new movement came into being during this period of time called "career education," which held some promise for addressing the persistent needs. The old wine was about to receive a new bottle.

Career Education

Unlike the work/study movement, which focused on the delivery of services within a specific type of interagency agreement, the career education movement was much more general in its articulation and diffuse in its implementation. In fact, the initial impetus for career education did not even mention the needs of people with disabilities. The beginning of the career education movement is often identified as occurring in 1970, when Sidney Marland, then the Commissioner of Education, declared career education to be the top priority of the U.S. Office of Education. Almost immediately following this pronouncement, a federal initiative began to emerge, with the awarding of approximately $90 million in demonstration grants through funding structures that were already available under Parts C and D of the 1968 Vocational Education Act (Hoyt, 1982). Most of these grants were concerned with career education for the *general* population of students.

During the decade of the 1970s, the movement progressed in several directions, including increased federal visibility (although not accompanied by increased federal support), extension of the concept to include a clear focus on the needs of people with disabilities, and formal endorsement of the concept by The Council for Exceptional Children (CEC) (Brolin, 1983; Cegelka, 1979; Hoyt, 1982). Each of these trends is worthy of comment.

Federal visibility for the career education movement was clearly enhanced in 1974 when the Office of Career Education was established within the U.S. Office of Education. The legislative mandate for the movement was crystallized in 1977 with passage of P.L. 95-207, the Career Education Implementation Incentive Act. In addition to providing a general impetus to career ed-

ucation, this act also specifically mentioned people with disabilities as an appropriate target population for services that would be facilitated through the act.

In 1976, the Division of Career Development was approved as a 12th division of The Council for Exceptional Children. In 1978, CEC formally endorsed the concept of career education through the publication of a position paper on the topic. The significant involvement of this organization in the career education movement laid the foundation for preserving the movement in special education irrespective of federal involvement. Such a foundation was indeed needed in 1982, when P.L. 95-207 was repealed by Congress, consistent with a preplanned federal intent to use this legislation only as a source of "seed money" to nourish the development of the movement (Hoyt, 1982).

When one reflects on the accomplishments of the career education movement—and these accomplishments were many—it is interesting to observe that a commonly accepted definition of "career education" never did emerge. Definitions that emerged from the field ranged from a narrow focusing of goals on the preparation of students for paid employment to a much broader concern with all aspects of adult life. Attempting, perhaps, to mediate between these two positions, the policy adopted by CEC contains elements of both extremes:

> Career education is the totality of experiences through which one learns to live a meaningful, satisfying work life. Within the career education framework, work is conceptualized as conscious effort aimed at producing benefits for oneself and for others. Career education provides the opportunity for children to learn, in the least restrictive environment possible, the academic, daily living, personal-social and occupational knowledge and specific vocational work skills necessary for attaining their highest levels of economic, personal and social fulfillment. The individual can obtain this fulfillment through work (both paid and unpaid) and in a variety of other societal roles and personal life styles including his/her pursuits as a student, citizen, volunteer, family member, and participant in meaningful leisure time activities. (*Position Paper,* 1978).

In many ways, the career education movement can be viewed as an expansion of the work/study movement that preceded it. The work/study movement was fairly narrow in its goals, generally restricted to secondary education, largely focused on serving students with mild mental retardation, typically implemented in programs reserved for students with disabilities, and formally structured as an interagency collaboration. The career education movement was diffuse in its goals, oriented to both elementary and secondary education, available to students with and without disabilities, implemented in both regular and special education environments, and broadly structured as a general education movement. Both movements were spawned through opportunities presented by federal legislation and were nurtured largely through federal financial participation. The work/study movement died as an inadvertent consequence of federal legislation and regulation, and the career education movement was intentionally disowned as a federal initiative. Both predecessors left a legacy for the emergence of the transition movement in the 1980s.

Transition

Only 2 years after the repeal of the Career Education Implementation Incentive Act in 1982, a new federal transition initiative emerged on the scene (Will, 1984a) in the form of a "position paper" from the Office of Special Education and Rehabilitative Services (OSERS). The essence of this paper involved the articulation of a "transition model," which has come to be known as a "bridges" model. This model describes three types of services (bridges) that are needed to facilitate the transition from school to work.

The first bridge, labeled "transition without special services," refers to the use of *generic* services available to anyone in the community, even if special accommodations are necessary within these services for people with disabilities. Postsecondary education, such as that provided in a community college, is mentioned as a prime example of a generic service.

The second bridge, "transition with time-limited services," refers to *specialized,* short-term services where the presence of a disability is usually required to qualify a person for access to the service. Vocational rehabilitation is offered here as an example.

The third bridge has been labeled "transition with ongoing services." As the model developers point out, this bridge did *not* in 1984 represent a widely existing service delivery system. Exemplified by "supported employment," it was relatively new (Will, 1984a, 1984b) and had made its presence known primarily in demonstration projects that were themselves supported by federal grants and contracts. The rehabilitation amendments of 1986, however, identified supported employment as a *regular* program, paving the way for an increased funding level over time.

The target of the OSERS transition model, as I mentioned before, has been restricted to "employment." Perhaps anticipating some concern about the narrowness of this goal, the choice of employment is justified in words such as the following (Will, 1984a):

> This concern with employment does not indicate a lack of interest in other aspects of adult living. Success in social, personal, leisure, and other adult roles enhances opportunities

both to obtain employment and enjoy its benefits.(p. 1)

> The focus on employment as a central outcome of effective transition provides an objective measure of transition success. (p. 2)

What the author of this policy seemed to be suggesting was that the nonvocational dimensions of adult adjustment are significant and important only in so far as they contribute to the ultimate goal of employment. Whether or not one agrees with the restricting of transition goals to employment, the impact of this policy was swift and deep. Almost immediately following publication of the OSERS policy on transition (Will, 1984a), requests for "transition" proposals began to appear in a wide array of federal programs dealing with disability. This trend was enhanced through the introduction of transition and supported employment components into new legislation that pertained to people with disabilities. The newest amendments to P.L. 94-142, now called the "Individuals with Disabilities Education Act (P.L. 101-476), contain several important new initiatives in the area of transition, including the requirement that all IEPs address transition goals no later than the student's 16th birthday.

Comparison of the Three Movements

Because the transition movement is still in full force today, it is impossible to evaluate the impact of the movement from an historical perspective. Certain comparisons with the work/study and career education movements, however, allow us to examine the transition movement within the broader context of its antecedents.

The transition movement's early focus on employment was narrower than the stipulated goals of either the work/study or career education movements. All three movements acknowledged that the dimensions of adult adjustment extend beyond employment, but only the transition movement adopted a clearly restrictive position on this issue. The reason for this restrictive position was not a lack of appreciation for the complexity of adult adjustment. Rather, it was the sense of the policymakers that a more limited objective would be more feasible, fundable, and easier to evaluate than a program with multiple objectives.

In a similar "restrictive" vein, both the transition and work/study movements focused their efforts on the limited time span of high-school years through early adulthood, whereas the career education movement covered a much broader span of human development. On the other hand, the transition movement provides the broadest focus on the types of *adult* service agencies that need to be directly involved in the partnerships with the public schools in order to facilitate the movement from school to work.

CURRENT NEEDS AND CONCERNS

Where, then, do we stand after 30 years of programs that have been designed to prepare young people with disabilities for adult roles in their communities? A candid answer to this question is that we still have a long way to go. In the area of curriculum and instruction, we are still frequently deficient in *what* we teach, *how* we teach, and *where* we teach. Curriculum content still tends to focus too much on remedial academics and not enough on functional skills. Instructional design often ignores the issues of maintenance and generalization without which we have no reason to believe that the skills being taught in the classroom will be used in the community settings where they are relevant. The location of instruction is frequently in the school-based classroom, even though a community-based setting would often be more appropriate.

Other concerns, in addition to curriculum and instruction, leave us less than satisfied with the current state of affairs. Integration of high-school students with disabilities into the mainstream remains a cloudy issue, both with respect to its desirability and its implementation. Too many students drop out, and those who remain often receive a meaningless certificate of attendance rather than some form of useful diploma. Transition planning is often ineffective or even nonexistent. The array of adult services is insufficient to meet the needs of those who leave school, and parents or other relatives must often assume the lifelong role of case manager for their child or children with disabilities.

These unresolved issues and concerns can be addressed in several ways.

1. New policies can be developed to structure the ways that we think about needs and priorities.
2. The capacity to address unresolved issues and concerns can be enhanced through legislation, resource allocation, and careful planning for the development of new programs and services.
3. New programs and services can be implemented, evaluated, and refined in local communities, drawing on the policy-development and capacity-building efforts that provide a foundation for local activities.

All three levels of effort—policy development, capacity building, and the effective implementation of new programs—can be enhanced through the collection and dissemination of appropriate follow-along information that documents the experiences of students while in school, and the outcomes that they achieve after leaving school. All of these efforts to address the unresolved problems of transition must work in tandem if widespread impact is eventually to occur.

LOOKING TOWARD THE FUTURE

Each of these approaches to facilitating change is worthy of extended discussion and analysis. Much has also been written about these various approaches, particularly those that involve capacity building and new program implementation. Perhaps the area that is least often considered is the set of conditions that influence the development of policy. Nearly 20 years ago, when I was a relative newcomer to our profession, I had the good fortune to be invited by Michael Begab to a conference on the sociology of mental retardation. At this conference, the gifted sociologist Amitai Etzioni made an interesting observation about the relationship between "special interest" concerns, such as the field of disability, and the broader concerns of society as a whole. He admonished us to avoid myopia, lest we become so caught up in our narrow concerns that we neglect to understand and respond to the broad social problems and issues that exert great influence on our society as a whole. He used the metaphor of attempting to cross the ocean in a 16-foot wooden boat with a 10-horsepower motor. For such a voyage to have even a chance of being successful, one must move with the waves and not against them.

Relevant Social Issues

If Etzioni was correct in his thinking, to make significant headway with the problems of transition for young adults with disabilities, we must first understand the broad social issues that have an impact, or a potential impact, on our narrower set of concerns. As one way of addressing this purpose, I spent a 3-month period (March-May, 1990) doing a very informal study of "relevant social issues." My method involved carefully reading newspapers and news magazines and cutting out and collecting anything that seemed in any way relevant to me at the time. I eventually gathered several hundred clippings and did an informal content analysis of my collection, which yielded the following categories: educational reform, our current health care crisis, increasing levels of poverty in our children, the movement of our society toward increased ethnic diversity, and the growing social implications of financing and managing our federal budget deficit. I have chosen to discuss educational reform to illustrate the influence of the broad social context on policy development that pertains to transition for students with disabilities.

Educational Reform

Much has certainly been written and discussed on the topic of educational reform over many years. In collaboration with the National Governors Association, a recent framework for crystallizing at least some of the major concerns was provided by President Bush in his 1990 State of the Union message. As part of this message, he outlined his preference for six national goals to be met by the year 2000. These goals were then embellished 15 months later with a set of proposed strategies in a document entitled *America 2000: An Education Strategy* (Bush, 1991). The goals include the following:

1. Every American child must start school prepared to learn, sound in body and sound in mind.
2. The high-school graduate rate in the United States must increase to no less than 90%.
3. All students in Grades 4, 8, and 12 will be tested for progress in critical subjects.
4. American students must rank first in the world in achievement in mathematics and science.
5. Every adult must be a skilled, literate worker and citizen, able to compete in a global economy.
6. Every school must be drug free and offer a disciplined environment conducive to learning.

Many of these goals have either clear or potential relevance for the transition programs that are of concern to us. *We* are concerned about functional illiteracy, and approximately 20% of the *entire* adult American population is unable to perform basic math calculations or read at a rudimentary level of effectiveness. *We* are concerned about high-school dropouts, and approximately 30% of *all* American students drop out of school. The commonality of concerns is easy enough to identify, and the examples that emerged in the news clippings were quite numerous. Some seemed to have particularly important ramifications for our narrower set of interest. For example:

• Should vocational apprenticeship programs, such as those found in Germany, be developed as a strong and viable alternative to the college preparation programs that are the cornerstone of high schools in our country?

• Should the federal government get into the business of determining and measuring minimum education competencies?

• Can all students be educated together, or is some sort of tracking system desirable?

• Should schools be the instruments of social reform, or should they stick to the business of education?

• What should be the role of parents in dealing with the education of their children?

Vocational Apprentice Programs. Although vocational education programs in the United States have a long history of their own, some interesting aspects of the vocational apprentice program in Germany have received recent public attention from the national syndicated columnist, William Raspberry, who visited these programs, along with a contingent of educators from Indiana. He introduced this topic with his perceptions of the haphazard manner in which many American youngsters begin their work careers:

> Typically, they leave high school to look for work wherever they can find it—sometimes with help from family friends, sometimes going full time into jobs in which they worked part time during high school. Only after a succession of random jobs, it seems, do they stumble upon something with real career potential—a permanent job with clear prospects for advancement that pays enough to support a family. . . . The delayed transition to adulthood signals to the youngsters that, no matter what we say, there is little real relationship between what they learn in school and their ability to make their way in the world.

Raspberry then presented his viewpoint, which praised the potential of Germany's apprentice program to address these issues that he had raised. The essence of this program, as he reported it, involves a refocusing of the last 2 or 3 years of public education to include 3 or 4 days a week pursuing an on-the-job apprenticeship, with only 1 or 2 days a week in the classroom. There are 380 apprenticeable skills in Germany, and the minimum competencies are standardized across the country. Government regulates the standards, and employers have no obligation to participate in the program.

But the employers do, in fact, participate. They pay for the cost of training even though there is no obligation, or even expectation, that the apprentice will continue to work for the employer who provides the training. "Employers consider the training expenses an unremarkable investment in the competency of Germany's work force and, therefore, an investment in their own long-term survival." Many companies train far more people than they have any possibility of ever hiring. Raspberry speculated that the employers are motivated to participate because they have real control over *what* is taught and *how* skills are taught. As for the value of this approach, he asked rhetorically, "Who would you rather have teach your child a job: A master craftsman or a school teacher?"

The extended involvement of the business sector in the educational enterprise is a topic of intensifying discussion in our country, with many businesses expressing a strong interest in participating. As we continue to explore innovative ways for businesses to become integrally involved in the education of all students, new models and opportunities likely will emerge that provide good opportunities for students with disabilities. To continue with the imagery of Etzioni's metaphor, this may be a wave worth catching.

Federal Involvement in Minimum Competencies. The federal government has entered the business of education in many ways. P.L. 94-142 and the OSERS transition initiatives are obvious examples in our field. The minimum competency strand of educational reform, however, has begun to explore the limits of federal intervention in education.

In response to President Bush's goal of testing student achievement in Grades 4, 8, and 12, the National Assessment Governing Board (NAGB) voted in December 1989 to ask Congress for a substantial expansion of the National Assessment of Educational Progress (NAEP) test that it has been operating for the past 20 years. The purpose of this expansion would be to develop new and better tests to address the President's goal. Opposition to this proposal has been strong and from many sources including the National Congress of Parents and Teachers Association (PTA), the Council of Chief School Officers, the National Education Association, and the National Association of Secondary School Principals.

The voices of opposition present several arguments. The multiple-choice formats that tend to dominate standardized tests measure only certain kinds of learning that emphasize fact recall. Because there are no commonly accepted definitions of minimum competency, developing a single standardized form of assessment is impossible. If the outcomes of such assessment are used to distribute sanctions and rewards, schools will slavishly pursue good scores regardless of their educational relevance.

The NAGB, of course, has some arguments of its own. Without accountability, they assert, society has no way of evaluating educational outcomes. Furthermore if schools are allowed to develop their own assessments, they will tend to set easy standards that make their programs look good.

It is too early to predict the outcome of this controversy. The potential impact on transition programs for students with disabilities is also uncertain. If a national competency assessment program is strengthened, will this result in a raising of minimum competency standards and increased difficulty in earning a high-school diploma, thereby decreasing the number of special education students who can earn a diploma? On the other hand, would a good set of standardized measures help to provide a valid paradigm for evaluating the impact of instruction and distributing financial resources to education programs? The eventual outcome of this debate will most certainly affect transition programs for students with disabilities.

Tracking and Mainstreaming. The issue of student tracking is not new to the field of special education. The concept of educating students with disabilities in the least restrictive environment was a cornerstone of P.L. 94-142, and the mainstreaming movement and regular education initiative (REI) have emerged as attempts to embody this concept. As we all know, these attempts have not been uniformly supported within special education, with both the success and appropriateness of such efforts being challenged, especially at the secondary level.

Concerns about mainstreaming have also emerged from the perspective of regular education. Within this context, the issue is often expressed as a concern about the appropriateness of tracking systems for organizing classroom instruction. A recent opinion presented by the syndicated columnist, Paul Greenberg, (1990, April 22) provides a perspective on this issue. He stated:

> The latest fad in Educanto is to eliminate "tracking," the grouping of students by ability. Such an approach might make sense to simple laymen like you and me, but the educationists have just about decided that it's ineffective—not to say elitist, racist, fascist and possibly even old-fashioned. Can any more serious indictment be imagined? . . . The newest approach is to throw kids together regardless of ability or knowledge; it is assumed that the superior knowledge and skills of the sharpest will rub off on the the rest. Uh-huh. This is the kind of assumption that would make Pollyanna look like a hard-bitten cynic. . . . In the days of the one-room school house, older or brighter students often took charge of the younger ones, rather than being challenged by new material. It had its advantages, but not that many. Mainly it was a matter of necessity. . . . Are we, in the name of progress, headed back to that system? If so, you can be sure it'll be given some multisyllabic name (how does "cooperative learning" sound?) and hailed in educational journals as a great advance. Educanto marches on.

Greenberg's stinging sarcasm is hardly a careful or fair evaluation of tracking or mainstreaming, but it does represent an important public perception that needs to be addressed. The issue gets even cloudier when we consider the legal requirement that tracking, if it is done, must be nondiscriminatory. The basic concern that seems to be involved in this debate is how to achieve excellence in education for *all* students, while acknowledging that their needs, abilities, and educational goals are diverse. In any case, it seems almost certain that decisions concerning tracking and cooperative learning in regular education will spill over into decisions concerning mainstreaming and REI for students with disabilities.

Schools and Social Reform. One of the three columns written by Raspberry about the apprentice program in Germany raised an interesting companion issue about the role of schools as instruments of social reform. His beginning sense of this issue emerged from an awareness that amateur sports in Germany have no connection with educational institutions, which relieves the schools of any responsibility for such budget-draining items as sports stadiums, uniforms and equipment for athletes, bands and cheerleaders, buses to transport these people to events, and coaches' salaries. He also noticed that German schools did not tend to support any form of school transportation, lunchrooms, or most extracurricular activities. His conclusion?

> One of the reasons German youngsters seem more serious than ours is that German schools are more businesslike and career-oriented than ours. While there are exceptions, schools are for those who want to learn something and are not used as day care centers or personality enrichment programs.

Schools in the United States, of course, tend to move in a completely different direction. Good schools are often viewed as those that "do it all." School personnel are expected not only to teach, but also to transport, feed, coach, counsel, advise, and support student development in a myriad of extracurricular activities. Furthermore, schools are expected to play a major role in solving serious social problems, such as drug abuse, child abuse, poverty, health problems, and teen-age pregnancy.

For example, beginning in October 1990, a new federal law requires all teenage parents on welfare to enroll in a high-school completion program if they don't already have a diploma or a GED. Failure to comply will result in a dramatic reduction of welfare benefits. These high expectations for our schools to serve as a major agent of social change are likely to remain intact for a long time. As the debate concerning school responsibilities unfolds, each decision to maintain or expand these multifaceted responsibilities will have obvious fiscal and programmatic implications. At some point, both money and energy will run out. Programs for students with disabilities will have to compete for both resources.

Role of Parents. The role of schools as agents of social change cannot be separated from the role of parents. The relationship is almost symbiotic; a partnership is most desirable, but whatever the schools don't do will be foisted upon parents, and vice versa. What, then, is a proper delineation of responsibilities?

Public sentiment seems to place a majority of this responsibility upon the schools. Columnist Mike Royko (1990, April 16) takes issue with this sentiment through a dialogue with his fictitious blue collar philosopher, Slats Grobnik.

> "Where did President Bush find this dummy?" asked Slats Grobnik, looking up from his newspaper.

Oh, let's leave poor Dan Quayle alone.

> "I don't mean Quayle. It's this secretary of education."

Ah, you mean Lauro Cavazos.

> "Yea, whatever his name is. What a klutz."

That's a rather harsh appraisal. After all, the man is our nation's highest education official. Show some respect.

> "Yeah? Haven't you read what he said about high school dropouts?"

I know that it is considered a grave crisis, particularly among minority groups, so Bush has set up task forces to look into the problem.

> "Nah, I mean the latest. This guy Cavazos went to one of these task force meetings and talked about whose fault it is that so many Hispanic kids drop out of school."

I assume he blamed the school systems, as everyone does.

> "Yeah, he mentioned that. But he didn't stop there. He started talking like a looney. . . . He said that it's not just the schools that aren't doing their job, it's the parents of the dropouts."

I don't understand. Why are you calling him a dummy? You've been saying the same thing for years.

> "I know, but I'm not the secretary of education, or the president, or a mayor or any other politician or mucky-muck. So it's OK for me to say it. But this stiff don't seem to know that what he said is a big no-no."

But if he believes it to be true, and if you agree, why shouldn't he come out and say it?

> "You're as dumb as he is. I'll tell you why. Because this ain't the old days. We got a new set of rules now. When there is a problem—or a grave crisis, like they call it—you gotta blame society, or the government or the one I like the best—the failure of institutions. You never blame people. But what this guy went and did is blame people. And that's against the rules. So that's why he's a dummy. He don't know how to play the game."

Slats goes on to point out that politicians who don't play by the rules eventually lose their jobs.

Royko's blue collar philosopher may be on to something important here. If our needed educational reforms can only be accomplished with the assistance of parents, and if some parents want to abdicate this responsibility, and if policymakers are afraid or unable to confront the issue, many of the problems that currently bedevil the schools will remain unresolved. Students with disabilities, of course, will be caught up in the vortex of these unresolved problems, which must inevitably have an impact on the opportunities that are available within special education and transition programs, whether or not parents of students with disabilities are actively involved in these programs.

CONCLUSION

This short excursion in the area of educational reform, of course, is only one example of many general social concerns that set the parameters and conditions for the development of policy concerning transition programs in our field. A similar analysis of other concerns, such as the health care crisis in the United States, would undoubtedly yield other insights into policy issues that are likely to affect transition programs. The outcomes of policy development in these broader social issues will provide definite opportunities and limitations for structuring the changes that we are attempting to implement in our narrower field of concern.

Within this narrower field, we have already learned a great deal about how to improve program capacity and how to implement specific programs that take advantage of this capacity. Our literature is full of many fine examples of such efforts. From the perspective and influence of broad policy, however, the transition movement of the 1980s may or may not be the program of the 1990s that will emerge to address the needs of adolescents with disabilities as they prepare to move into adulthood. The transition movement, if it remains viable, should be responsive to the broad issues and concerns of our general society. If "transition" eventually disappears as a rallying call for programs, however, this should not be cause for alarm. Something new will undoubtedly take its place, because many of the underlying problems being experienced by adolescents and young adults with disabilities are likely to remain in need of further attention. If necessary, the old wine will find yet another new bottle.

REFERENCES

Brolin, D. (1983). Career education: Where do we go from here? *Career Development for Exceptional Individuals, 6,* 3-14.

Bush, G. (1991). *America 2000: An education strategy.* Washington, DC: U.S. Department of Education.

Cegelka, P. (1979). Career education. In M. Epstein & D. Cullinan (Eds.), *Special education for adolescents: Issues and perspectives* (pp. 155-184). Columbus, OH: Charles E. Merrill.

Greenberg, P. (1990, April 22). Latest "educationist" fad on the wrong track. *The Register-Guard* (Eugene, OR), p. 3C.

Halpern, A. (1973). General unemployment and vocational opportunities for EMR individuals. *American Journal of Mental Deficiency, 80,* 81-89.

Halpern, A. (1974). Work-study programs for the mentally retarded: An overview. In P. Browning (Ed.), *Mental retardation: Rehabilitation and counseling* (pp. 120-137). Springfield, IL: Charles C Thomas.

Halpern, A. (1985). Transition: A look at the foundations. *Exceptional Children, 51,* 479-486.

Hoyt, K. (1982). Career education: Beginning of the end, or a new beginning. *Career Development of Exceptional Individuals, 5,* 3-12.

Kaufman, S. (1988). *Retarded isn't stupid, Mom!* Baltimore: Paul H. Brookes.

Kolstoe, O., & Frey, R. (1965). *A high school work-study program for mentally sub-normal students.* Carbondale, IL: Southern Illinois University Press.

Position paper on career education. (1978). Reston, VA: The Council for Exceptional Children.

Royko, M. (1990, April 16). Education secretary takes a risk. *The Register-Guard* (Eugene, OR), p. 9A.

Will, M. (1984a). *OSERS programming for the transition of youth with disabilities: Bridges from school to working life.* Washington, DC: Office of Special Education and Rehabilitative Services, U.S. Department of Education.

Will, M. (1984b). *Supported employment for adults with severe disabilities: An OSERS program initiative.* Washington, DC: Office of Special Education and Rehabilitative Services, U.S. Department of Education.

This article is an edited version of a keynote address delivered on three different occasions: at a regional conference on transition in Seattle, Washington, June 4, 1990; at a state conference on transition in Auburn, Alabama, April 18, 1991; and at a national conference on transition in Sydney, Australia, June 27, 1991.

Manuscript received June 1990; revision accepted February 1991.

Inclusionary Education: Peer Interactions

The inclusion of students with conditions of exceptionality in the regular classroom was mandated by PL 94-142. Successful integration requires cooperation and camaraderie between children with, and children without, disabilities or differences. The type and degree of cooperation and friendships that develop are, to a large extent, determined by the classroom teacher. The teacher serves as a model for acceptance and empathetic understanding of the child (or children) with the exceptional condition(s). The teacher can plan activities that foster cooperation and provide discipline when events which suggest intolerance occur. The school administrators and supportive service personnel also have a role in supervising and encouraging positive inclusionary practices in mainstreamed schools.

The effectiveness of special educational services provided to exceptional children must be measured in terms of psychosocial benefits as well as academic achievements. The Regular Education Initiative (REI) theoretically provides psychosocial benefits by mainstreaming children with disabilities or differences with nondisabled peers. Such integration, in practice, can have problems as well as promise.

Teachers trained in special education have seen their roles shift from classroom supervision of children with disabilities to itinerant teaching, pull-out teaching in resource rooms, and/or consultation with regular classroom teachers. They must be creative to find ways to encourage positive interaction between children with and without disabilities in light of their new roles and responsibilities.

Teachers trained in regular education have had to enroll in special classes or self-educate in order to become informed about the methods and materials needed to provide appropriate education for their mainstreamed students with exceptionalities. Each year the placement of children with special needs varies. The regular education teacher must continually learn about new children with new disabilities and new special needs. As the teacher learns, he or she must also help the peers of the student with special needs learn. It is a challenge for any teacher to foster positive attitudes toward all the new children with disabilities mainstreamed in the regular classroom each year. The regular teacher may experience fears, frustrations, and decreased self-esteem without adequate support from special education consultants, administrators, and other support staff.

Administrators play an important role in the implementation of the regular education initiative. As students with special needs are integrated into regular education classrooms, the school administrators must help coordinate supportive services for both student and teachers. Positive attitude change and successful inclusionary education requires positive feelings on the part of both students and faculty. Administrators should focus on supervising and supporting teachers in transition as well as evaluating them. Administrators need to assure that compliance with PL 94-142 includes psychosocial benefits as well as technical services appropriate for each integrated child with special needs.

There are often only one or two children with exceptionalities in a regular education classroom. They may have to cope with the jeers and/or jealousy of nonhandicapped children as they get special materials or get pulled out of class for special work in a resource room. Nonhandicapped children may be frightened by children with disabilities mainstreamed into their classrooms. They may have heard negative comments about children who are "afflicted," "burdened," "crippled," "unfortunate," "victimized," or "sick." They do not know how to react to the mainstreamed children. They need special help to understand the exceptional conditions and to accept the disabilities without fear.

Inclusionary education and positive interactions between children with and without disabilities is not easy. However, daily contact with a child with a condition of exceptionality can enrich everyone. Each child with a disability (emphasis on ABILITY) brings strengths and important lessons to a classroom. Teachers, administrators, and students need to appreciate that exceptional children are more similar to, than different from, themselves. All persons can develop an empathetic understanding of the rewards and problems of each unique child's area of disability. This can be done without pity or fear when strategies are carefully preplanned and initiated.

A goal of the regular education initiative and inclusionary education is to help each student participate in, and enjoy, as many aspects of normal living as possible. When teachers, administrators, and peers challenge children with disabilities to do all they are capable of doing, this goal can be achieved. In the process of achieving, the child with a disability will gain in both independence and self-esteem. Positive regard for a child with an exceptionality is fostered when the child has a positive regard for him- or herself.

The first article about inclusionary education presents positive feedback from teachers, parents, and classmates of mainstreamed children with disabilities. It gives an upbeat "day-in-the-life-of-Jamal." It suggests that inclusive classes teach a very important lesson—valuing each other! The second article in this unit gives a number of strategies for building peer support in inclusive classes. Students with and without disabilities benefit from learning the skills of friendship. The third selection discusses the special needs of African-American students with disabilities. An awareness of differences in cognitive styles, interests, and cultural practices between African-American and Anglo-American students can improve their peer relationships. Recommendations are included for organizing teaching to accommodate all students. The fourth

article suggests a creative way to promote positive attitude change toward children with disabilities in older school-aged children. Typical children may be asked to simulate an atypical condition for a day. Such simulation can generate a tremendous amount of understanding and empathy that can then be reported to other students.

Looking Ahead: Challenge Questions

Do public schools welcome students with disabilities as full members?

How can teachers encourage peer support and friendships between students with and without disabilities?

What teaching methods are most compatible with the social structure and cognitive styles of African-American students with disabilities?

Does simulation of a handicap increase or decrease negative reactions to the handicap?

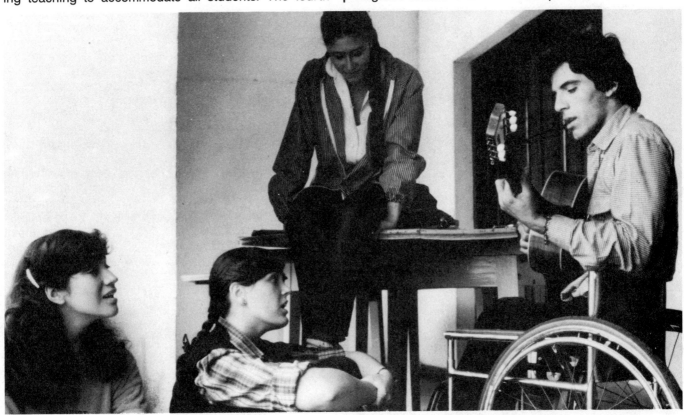

Public Schools Welcome Students with Disabilities as Full Members

Linda Davern and Roberta Schnorr

Linda Davern is the Coordinator of the Inclusive Education Project (a collaborative project between Syracuse University and the Syracuse City School District), Syracuse University, Division of Special Education and Rehabilitation, Syracuse, New York. Roberta Schnorr is a graduate associate with the Inclusive Education Project, and is currently involved in research related to the inclusion of secondary students.

A growing number of schools and districts across the United States and Canada are moving in the direction of welcoming all children—regardless of their learning, physical or emotional characteristics (including students with the most severe disabilities)—as full members of their school communities. Full membership means that children are based in regular classes and participate in a variety of learning activities with children without disabilities while pursuing individual goals appropriate to their success in the present and future. The parents of these children and the school staff involved in such efforts believe that "inclusion" is important for the general knowledge development of these children and young adults as well as the following:

● **Language/Communication Development.** If we expect students with special

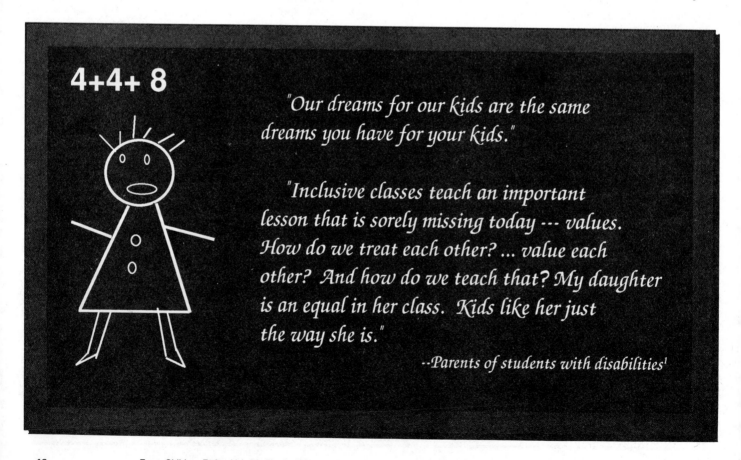

4+4+ 8

"Our dreams for our kids are the same dreams you have for your kids."

"Inclusive classes teach an important lesson that is sorely missing today --- values. How do we treat each other? ... value each other? And how do we teach that? My daughter is an equal in her class. Kids like her just the way she is."

--Parents of students with disabilities[1]

From *Children Today*, Vol. 20, No. 2, 1991, pp. 21-25. Reprinted by permission of *Children Today* and the authors.

needs to develop effective verbal language (or other forms of communication), these students need to be immersed in rich language environments with their nondisabled peers.

● **Social Skills Development.** A long term goal for our children is to live and work successfully in their communities. For children with disabilities, this same goal applies (although they may need additional support). The appropriate place for such preparation is regular classes and activities in schools. It is here that children can learn from each other. Every parent and teacher knows that children and young adults imitate each other. In order for students to develop the critical social skills which are vital for success in work and personal life, children and young adults need role models throughout their day and throughout their school years.

● **Building Friendships.** Friendship is very important in the life of a child or young adult. It is an integral part of their sense of well-being. In order to develop friendships, children need daily shared time and experiences with others their age. Schools can be a source of friendships that last a lifetime.

It is interesting to listen to what parents have to say about "inclusion" and their children:

"Now what has integration meant for my son Daniel?[2] Well first of all, Daniel likes sameness and familiarity. He has been able to walk in the exact same footsteps as his brother and sister, which is something I *never* imagined was possible when he was two years old. Both his older brother and sister went to [the same elementary, middle and high school] and it has been just lovely that Daniel has been able to follow the same pattern of schools. The development of language has been just tremendous because he has been surrounded by normal speech—bombarded with it six hours a day.

"What has integration meant to our family? First, it has made a big difference in how isolated and different and lonely and set apart we felt—because we really did feel that way when he was young.... I would say what is most important is that his school and work experiences combined have taught us as a family that Daniel is capable of leading a reasonably ordinary day-to-day life—like the rest of us.

When he was little it seemed impossible that he could lead a kind of 'regular life.' It has helped us feel hopeful and guardedly optimistic about his future."

How does the presence of students with special needs affect other students at school? The majority of students in our public schools learn very powerful lessons when students with special needs are separated from them. Since they do not get to know these students well, they often come to believe that these children and young adults are different and scary, and *should* be separated from them. When students with differences are not in their classrooms, these classrooms do not reflect society and do not adequately prepare our children for the future. If we want graduates who welcome others—regardless of their learning, physical or emotional characteristics—as neighbors, co-workers and friends, daily shared experience among students will be essential. As one parent expressed it:

"These [graduates] are going to be his job coaches; they may be the staff that work in the home where he lives. They're going to help him scrub his teeth, participate in selecting what he wears, and comfort him when he is ill— they'll be involved in very personal and intimate ways in his life. Some of them will be growing into positions of responsibility. They'll be running the program

he's in. Some of them are going to be moving into positions of bureaucracies ... they'll be directing policies that will determine the kinds of programs he's in. I think they will serve him better and be richer human beings *themselves* because they've had the opportunity of spending time with students like Daniel—because that was part of their normal school career."

How Are Individual Education Programs Carried Out in Regular Education Settings?

By law, each child and young adult who is identified by a school district as having a "handicapping condition" has an Individual Education Program (I.E.P.) developed by school staff and parents (and hopefully students). Schools which welcome all students as full members are finding ways for students to work on the individual goals which are important for them, while remaining with students without disabilities throughout the day. To show how teaching staff achieve this, we will present information on Jamal, a first grader.

In Jamal's first grade class there are two teachers. Six students with special needs are members of the class. One of the teachers is certified in special education and one is certified in both special and regular education. Schools and districts moving in this direction have worked out a variety of staffing arrangements to meet

Practice makes perfect with the help of a fellow musician.

the needs of students. Sometimes a consultant teacher will periodically meet with the regular class teacher to assist in planning for a student(s). In some situations, a teacher assistant will help in the classroom all or part of the day.

Jamal's teachers believe it is important to create an atmosphere where all children can learn actively, have fun doing it, and leave feeling good about themselves and others at the end of the day. These teachers are open to new approaches and are always changing and improving how they organize their classroom and activities.

Jamal has individualized goals on his education plan. A *sample* of some of the goals follows:

● indicating choices in a variety of situations;

● responding to greetings with a wave or a ''high five'' (he has no verbal speech);

● learning to tap people on the shoulder when he wants their attention;

● using a ''language board'' with pictures and a few words on it (for example, ''yes,'' ''no'');

● understanding an increasing number of gestures and ''signs'' (for example, ''now,'' ''later,'' ''more,'' ''finished'');

● attending to books and being able to turn the pages (it is unclear how much reading ability he has);

● using a picture schedule of activities for the day and moving towards the proper activity area when needed;

● handing a money pouch over to the lunch cashier when he gets his lunch;

● progressing with his toilet use skills;

● picking up and chewing his food; and

● other motor development goals, such as using his forefinger and thumb to grasp things, and sitting on the floor and getting up as needed.

Many of the goals above are considered ''functional skills''—that is, skills that are important in his day-to-day life. Opportunities to address these functional skills already exist in the daily routines of all students (e.g., taking care of personal belongings, taking off and putting on coats and hats, using the restroom, using the cafeteria and eating lunch). Jamal receives more focused instruction during these rou-

''How about right here?''—students enrich each other's work.

tines than most of his classmates who are independent in these activities.

In developing his daily schedule, his teachers and therapists have looked for all possible opportunities throughout the day to work on the goals mentioned above. Below is a schedule of a typical day:

8:30 Jamal arrives at school, greets his classmates (with help), and receives instruction unzipping the pack he carries back and forth to school, getting his lunch money out, and bringing his notebook to the teacher's desk. (His parents and teachers communicate daily through the use of a notebook.) Jamal and the other first graders have a few minutes to ''cruise'' the room. There are lots of books and activities around the room and it's a great time for kids to connect with each other.

8:45 The entire class divides up into partners who read books together for a few minutes. Jamal's partner brings two books over, and he picks one of the two by pointing to it. He will turn the pages while she reads aloud. She (or a teacher) may ask him to point to pictures. Since the class desks are placed in clusters of four, children spend a lot of time during the day talking and learning from each other in both formal and informal ways.

9:00 On some days, students are paired for ''class jobs.'' On this particular day,

Jamal and a partner will take the attendance cards and messages down to the office. These jobs teach all students to take responsibility for the smooth functioning of the classroom. After this, the whole class reviews the calendar and schedule for the day. At the same time, an adult or a student will help Jamal put his schedule pictures in the proper order for his day.

9:30 During a penmanship lesson, the students sit in groups of six. Jamal will pass out the papers to each child in his group as directed by the teacher. He is learning to associate their names and faces. He is also working on his ''grasping'' skills. Later, an adult will put two colors of crayons by him and ask him to pick up the blue one to color with. He is learning a lot about language in this and all class activities.

10:00 All students take a break for the bathroom and a drink at the water fountain at this time. Jamal will line up with the other children, but will need assistance and may take longer in the restroom.

10:15 There are a variety of activities during reading time. Sometimes children develop a class ''big book'' with a page about each of them. His teacher may write home to ask what Jamal's favorite TV show is, or what he likes to do with his family so that his page can be completed. Since his classmates are getting to know him so well, they can fill in some information like, "What's my favorite food?" He can use the "yes/no" section on his language board to tell them if they are right, and to answer questions about other reading stories.

11:15 Jamal needs to visit the nurse to receive his medication. An adult points to the picture of the nurse on his schedule to make the destination clear, and they walk together to the nurse's office. Afterwards, he returns to class, walks down to the lunchroom and sits with friends. An adult assists him with getting his lunch, paying the cashier and developing his eating skills.

12:00 All children are involved in Learning Centers—centers set up in the corners of the room with educational activities for individuals or small groups. Sometimes an occupational therapist will join a small group at a Learning Center to work with Jamal on specific skills. On other days, his teachers prepare a "cooperative learning" lesson.[3] The class is divided up into small groups which include students of different race and sex, as well as different learning and personality characteristics.

Group membership sometimes remains the same for several months so that the students develop a sense of group cohesion. Students learn positive interdependence by sharing goals and materials, and taking on different role assignments. Jamal is also given a role when these lessons occur, although the way he participates may look different from his peers (e.g., he uses a name "stamp" to sign his name, he gives members a "high five" to encourage them, instead of using words). One of the teachers provides support to him and his group.

12:55 Jamal joins his classmates for art, music, library or physical education class at this time. A variety of rich learning experiences occur in these classes.

1:30 Students usually have a math activity at this time. On some days, Jamal leaves the room for a session with a related service provider (e.g., speech therapy, physical therapy). On other days, his teachers develop ways to incorporate him into small group instruction. One day he works as a "checker" for his math group. The six children are using small cubes to solve number problems such as "eight minus four." After the children determine the answer, Jamal and his teacher will touch each block and count from one to four in order to "check" the answer. He is learn-

ing one-to-one correspondence through this activity.

2:00 Jamal begins to prepare for dismissal by getting his backpack off his hook and bringing it to his desk. He will put his notebook in the pack and re-zip it (with assistance). On this day, his class will join another class to have a sing-along. He will need to sit on the floor and get up after the singing is finished. He greatly enjoys the songs and often claps along. At dismissal, he walks with a partner and an adult to the bus.

It is clear that the "typical day" of this first grade offers many opportunities for Jamal to learn and grow.

What Happens When Students Get Older?

Shifting from "special" classes to inclusive programs is not limited to young children. In inclusive education programs, students with special needs continue to progress from grade to grade with their classmates. When they complete elementary school, students transition to middle, and later, high school with familiar classmates.

Students with disabilities in middle and high schools have individual schedules like other students. Teachers and parents help students select courses which will allow them to address their individual goals and interests. In some cases, an additional teacher or teacher assistant is assigned to a class that includes one or more students with significant needs in order to provide support or make adaptations in the curriculum. Some older students may receive instruction in functional skills in the community for one or more periods a day in addition to the regular classes they take (e.g., weekly instruction in a community workplace, learning to use the grocery store). Since the community is a rich environment for learning for any student, some teachers involve students without special needs in such instruction, and pose challenges to them related to *their* goals in school (e.g., applying math and health concepts in a grocery store).

Do Middle and High School Students Accept Classmates Who Have Disabilities?

Many students are both positive and supportive of their classmates who have disabilities. Many students who have been

in "inclusive" education classes in elementary school believe that students with disabilities should continue to be members of their classes.

"Before I came here, they were in all our classes in elementary school. They're people too, just like us.... They should be in more *[regular] classes here."*
—a middle school student who has a classmate with autism in one of his seventh grade classes[4]

Yet this kind of acceptance can also be heard among older students who have classmates with disabilities for the first time in middle or high school. A high school girl describes Terry, a classmate she met during her junior year. Terry had always been in special education classes prior to this year.

"She's real nice, you know. The way she used to walk in and yell 'hi' to everybody ... It's pretty good to have her in class. I was kind of helping her in the beginning. She sat at our table because her [wheel]chair didn't fit at the other ones. One time, I was helping her and she was helping me—you know how she does it. I think we were doing abstract or asymmetrical forms on paper. And she was having a fun time."

This student viewed her classmate as a "fun person." She didn't even mention Terry's disabilities. Terry is accompanied to class by a teacher or assistant for support in her work. Terry is a young woman who has severe physical disabilities and does not speak. This girl and other classmates describe her not as "handicapped," but as "outgoing, friendly, and fun."

What Do Students with Disabilities Learn in Regular Middle and Secondary School Classes?

Secondary students also have Individual Education Programs with specific goals determined. Students do not need to learn the same content at the same level as their classmates to benefit from attending regular classes. Many regular classes in middle and high school offer rich learning environments for modified academic and other related skills (e.g., communication and social skills)—as well as positive role models.

Dave is a middle school student who has autism. In his seventh grade social studies class, many of his individual goals were drawn from the same content as his classmates—although he is not expected to learn as many facts and details about American history as most of the other students. Participating in small group activities and listening to his teacher's presentations and class discussion contributed to his learning, particularly since his reading skills are different from most others in his class.

Dave was also enrolled in seventh grade math, but received individual instruction from a support teacher within the class. In addition to his math goals, much of what Dave learned in this class centered around staying "focused" and learning appropriate social behavior in group settings. The seventh grade math teacher commented on what Dave had learned by the end of the school year:

"His skills and behavior are much better than when he came in at the beginning of the school year ... In the very beginning of the school year when he came to class, I didn't think I was going to make it ... He would hit himself or he would make noises ... or he would get out of his seat and ask me something ... He would talk out loud instead of whispering ... His growth over this year has been phenomenal ... It is unbelievable that he is the same young man. He still demonstrates those behaviors ... He still has those days. But his productivity has tripled ... I mean he can sit through a class and

work ... Now, he can work through the distractions of the class. He can produce. There's a tremendous amount of improvement ...

"At the beginning of the year, I questioned whether he should be here ... But the interaction, the "feeling" part of the class, the knowledge of the need to function within a group, even if he's doing something totally different ... to be able to walk into a crowd and do what you need to do—I mean that's part of everyday living.... And I think that as educators, placing him in situations like this five different times a day can only help.... hopefully it will transfer into everyday functioning in groups and crowds—and being able to deal with other people."

One high school student, Sam, who had always been in special education classes, began taking a regular music class during his third year in high school. This young man lives in a state institution for people with developmental disabilities. He has extensive physical disabilities and appears to have intellectual disabilities. He does not have verbal speech. After his first year in a regular class, his teacher reported that he "is well-liked and has made a number of friendships." School is one of the few places this student has opportunities to make friends with people his age. One of his classmates, a sophomore, described the relationship:

"Sam hangs with us—me, Tom, Leon, Ted. And we like rap, and he raps ... He's pretty cool.... He's fun to be with ... And he knows what we're talking about ... Everybody wants Sam there. When he's not there, everyone's like, 'Where's Sam?'"

Sam's music teacher discussed the impact his presence had on other members of this high school class:

"If we learn to deal with it [disabilities] and associate with it, and identify with it, then it's much easier for us to cope.... There are kids that learned to love him and accept him that probably never had to deal with handicapped people at all. And just the environment itself—it changed. Learning to 'read' [his] sounds, be it good sounds or bad sounds, and people are willing to accept these forms of communication.... These things all had an impact."

Summary

As noted in a parent newsletter, the inclusion of children and young adults with disabilities with other students in our schools will result in "an ever widening circle of people who believe that disabilities are a part of life, that people with disabilities are a part of [our] natural environment who should not be isolated, and that people with disabilities can have a positive effect on non-disabled people and the general community."[5]

All students can benefit from regular

Making School Integration Work: Additional Resources

The following list of resources is geared for those interested in learning more about inclusive education:

D. Biklen, *Achieving the Complete School: Strategies for Effective Mainstreaming*, New York: Teachers College Press, 1985.

D. Biklen (Executive Producer), *Regular Lives* (Videotape), Washington, D.C.: State of the Art, Inc. (WETA, P.O. Box 2626, Washington, D.C. 20013), 1988.

J. Dobbins (Producer/Director), *Jenny's Story* (Videotape), Islington, Ontario: Integration Action Group (19 Rivercave Drive, MOB4Y8), 1987.

J. O'Brien, M. Forest, J. Snow and D. Hasbury, *How to Improve Schools by Welcom-*

ing Children with Special Needs into Regular Classrooms, The Centre for Integrated Education: Frontier College Press, 1989.

C. B. Schaffner and B. Buswell, *Opening Doors: Strategies for Including All Students in Regular Education*, Colorado Springs: Peak Parent Center, Inc. (6055 Lehman, Colorado Springs, Colorado 80918), 1991.

S. Stainback, W. Stainback and M. Forest (Eds.), *Educating All Students in the Mainstream of Regular Education*, Baltimore: Paul H. Brookes, 1989.

J. York, T. Vandercook, C. Macdonald, C. Heise-Neff, and E. Caughey, *Class Integration of Middle School Students with Severe Disabilities: Feedback from Teachers and Classmates*, Minneapolis: University of Minnesota, Institute on Community Integration, 1989.

class activities even though the individual goals for some may be quite different. Such efforts are not always easy to implement, and depend on adequate support for both students and school personnel—but the benefits for all students are substantial. As one regular education teacher noted:

"Above all, we want our kids to show concern for others, now and in their future days. Typical kids in integrated classrooms benefit because these goals are as much a part of their daily classroom experience as the 'academics.' In reality, I believe the academics are enhanced because of these goals."[6]

And this teacher observed:

"I believe that all kids have a right to be in inclusive classrooms—to be educated with their peers. When everybody in a class is considered equal, some very great things will happen."

———————

1. These and the two quotes from parents that follow are drawn from A. Ford, E. Erwin, L. Davern, R. Schnorr, D. Biklen and J. Black (Eds.), *Proceedings of the School Leaders' Institute on Inclusive Education*, Inclusive Education Project, Syracuse University and Syracuse City School District.

2. The names of students have been changed.

3. D.W. Johnson, R. Johnson, E. Holubec and P. Roy, *Circles of Learning*, Alexandria, Va.: The Association for Supervision and Curriculum Development, 1984.

4. These and the quotes that follow were gathered as part of a research project related to regular secondary classes which include students with disabilities.

5. P. Mosser and L. Sommerstein (Eds.), *Parent Network Connections: Parents Help Parents,* 3 (2), p. 1, Summer, 1989.

6. This and the following quote are taken from the *Proceedings of the School Leaders' Institute on Inclusive Education*, Inclusive Education Project, Syracuse University and Syracuse City School District.

Encouraging Peer Supports and Friendships

William Stainback
Susan Stainback
Amy Wilkinson

William Stainback *and* **Susan Stainback** *are Professors, College of Education, University of Northern Iowa, Cedar Falls.* **Amy Wilkinson** *is a general education teacher, Trenton, New Jersey School System.*

Photographs by Mark A. Regan.

Research has shown that one major problem many students with disabilities face as they are integrated into general education classes is rejection and isolation. They often have little peer support and few, if any, friends (Gottlieb & Leyser, 1981). Both educators and parents who have been involved extensively in integrated schools have noted that the major key to successful integration is the development of informal peer supports and friendships for isolated students (Forest, 1987; PEAK Parent Center, 1988; Strully, 1987; York & Vandercook, 1988). Some

professionals have gone so far as to state that peer support and friendships are not luxuries, but necessities (Grenot-Scheyer, Coots, & Falvey, 1990; Stainback & Stainback, 1987, 1988; Stocking, Arezzo, & Leavitt, 1980).

When a student enters a classroom, such unknowns as schedules, rules, routines, and student-teacher and student-student interaction patterns can be intimidating. Classmates can help the student get to know the new environment and make the student feel welcomed, accepted, and secure. In addition, peers can provide encouragement, understanding, and support during stressful times in educational and social activities. Thus, many teachers and parents are beginning to encourage the development of informal peer support and friendships for students who do not have friends in mainstream classes (Perske & Perske, 1988; Ruttiman &

Forest, 1987; Stainback & Stainback, 1987; Strully & Strully, 1985; Vandercook, Fleetham, Sinclair, & Tetlie, 1988).

This article suggests strategies for promoting such interactions. It is based on what classroom teachers have reported to be effective (Grenot-Scheyer et al, 1990; Forest, 1987; PEAK Parent Center, 1988) and a review of the research (Asher & Gottman, 1981; Epstein & Karweit, 1983; Gottlieb & Leyser, 1981; Oden & Asher, 1977; Rubin, 1980; Stainback & Stainback, 1987).

Supportive relationships and friendships may range from simple, short-term events such as saying hello in the hallway to more complex, long-term relationships. These relationships are highly individualistic, fluid, and dynamic; vary according to the chronological age of the participants; and are largely based on free choice and personal preference. They cannot be easily defined and programmed, and they certainly cannot be forced (Perske & Perske, 1988). However, this does not mean that they cannot be facilitated and encouraged by sensitive educators and parents (Stainback & Stainback, 1990; Stainback, Stainback, & Forest, 1989).

Strategies for Building Peer Support

Foster Proximity

Research has indicated that a critical variable in peer support and friendship development is proximity (Asher & Gottman, 1981). There are a number of things that can be done to provide a student who is isolated with opportunities to get to know classmates. One is to help the student become involved in extracurricular activities such as band, photography club, or pep rallies. Peer tutoring, buddy systems, and cooperative learning groups also can be useful. Sapon-Shevin (1990) and Gartner and Lipsky (1990) have outlined specific and practical ways to organize peer tutoring and cooperative learning activities that can lead to friendships. For example, a student without friends can be paired with one or two other classmates or "buddies" to carry the lunch money to the principal's office. Some teachers have been successful in pairing students without friends with popular students whom others tend to gravitate toward (Forest, 1987). This strategy has been used at the secondary (Strully, 1987) as well as the elementary level (Villa & Thousand, 1988). The isolated student becomes associated with the popular student through proximity, which can lead to interactions with a large number of other peers. Simply seating a new or isolated student close to a sensitive, outgoing, and accepting student might be helpful in some instances.

Another useful activity might be for every student in class to be paired with another class member whom he or she does not know well to write a paragraph, draw a picture, or report to the class about a positive characteristic of the classmate. Students of all ages can be paired to report on an event of shared interest such as a ball game or a concert.

School personnel also can encourage parents to provide opportunities in the community for their child to be around and interact with other students (Strully & Strully, 1985). A Scout troop that other class members participate in, swimming or horseback riding classes, neighborhood gatherings, playground time, or church youth activities can all be worthwhile opportunities to develop friendships. In addition, parents can invite their child's classmates to their home or on outings. Making an area of the home an enjoyable, safe, and hospitable "hangout" for after-school or weekend times can do much toward gaining acceptance for a student and promoting friendship. In some cases parents may have difficulty doing this because they are pressed for time, particularly when both parents work, there is only one parent, or they are experiencing hardships. When this is the case, it may be necessary for educators to collaborate with social workers and community groups such as Big Brothers or Sisters to foster opportunities for children to participate with their peers in community programs and activities.

Encourage Support and Friendship Development

There are a number of ways school personnel can encourage students to build peer relationships with one another. One way is to involve students in thinking about supportive relationships and friendships as a part of the curriculum.

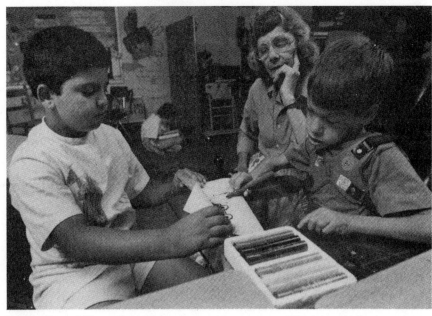

By observing social interactions, resource personnel can propose possible courses of action to encourage peer friendships.

The goal is to make students more aware of, sensitive and empathetic toward, and accepting of the needs of others. For instance, one topic in a health education class might be the support and caring needed by every person that can be provided by classmates and friends. Differences between paid helpers and friends in providing assistance also can be discussed.

When a new student enters a class, it is usually a particularly good time to have brainstorming sessions with the class members regarding what can be done to make the student feel welcome and secure. Helping students recognize how hard it is to come into a new class in which the other students already know one another might increase their sensitivity and encourage attempts to include the new student into their activities. This often leads to a number of peer support and friendship facilitation activities such as arranging for a welcoming committee of class members to call the new student at night and include him or her in out-of-school activities in the neighborhood.

A peer support committee of four or five students can be formed to make the classroom a supportive, accommodating, and positive learning environment. Its focus is to help *all* class members gain needed support and friends and experience success, rather than to determine how to solve a problem for a particular student. To accomplish this, the commit-

tee often is integrally involved in organizing buddy systems and establishing peer helpers and study partners. They also can brainstorm other ways to help foster classroom friendships and supports. The committee members not only have an opportunity to provide a valuable service, but also gain practice in problem solving and learn important social and civic responsibilities that can carry over into adulthood. All students, whether disabled or nondisabled, should participate on the committee at some time during the year.

Supportive relationships and friendships can also be fostered by involving class peers on a teacher and student assistance team such as the McGill action planning system (see Forest, 1987). Parents, teachers, administrators, specialists, and students are often included on the team. They brainstorm ideas of how educators and classmates can help a particular student entering the mainstream be made to feel welcomed, make friends, learn classroom routines and rules, and become an integral part of the classroom activities and programs. With the help of school personnel and the students on the team, often a circle of friends can be formed to make sure the student is included in school and nonschool activities and provided encouragement and support when needed. The reader is referred to the videotape, *With a Little Help from My Friends* (Forest & Flynn, 1988), O'Brien, Forest, Snow,

One way to encourage supportive relationships and friendships is to suggest that the students play together.

and Hasburg (1988), and Forest (1987) for specific and practical ways "circles of friends" can be formed. It should be emphasized that, as with the peer support committee, circles of friends should include students with and without disabilities and should be formed for any students who might benefit from them.

Another way to encourage supportive relationships and friendships is to verbally suggest to students that they work or play together. For instance, a teacher might say to a young student, "John, since you and Stephen are building houses with your blocks, why don't you work together to make a village that you can use for driving your cars and trucks around?" or to an older student, "Mary, since you and Theresa are both interested in the dress of the 18th century for your history project, you could work together gathering information and helping one another with your presentations."

Finally, it is important to reinforce students when they are exhibiting positive friendship and support behaviors (Stocking et al., 1980). When a student approaches an isolated peer and engages him or her in some activity, the teacher might say, "It is nice how Seth and Gene are working together" or "Since James, Alan, and Michael are playing so nicely together I will let them be first in line at lunch." For older students, it might be more appropriate to provide reinforcement in more subtle

ways, for example, letting them engage in a coveted activity such as looking at a new sports magazine. Letting students know that good things will happen when they include new or isolated peers into their group or activity will increase the chances that they will do it more often (Strain & Kerr, 1981).

Teach Peer Support and Friendship Skills

Students who lack friends can learn to display certain behaviors that will encourage others to be supportive and friendly toward them (Stainback & Stainback, 1987). All students should learn as many of these behaviors as they can.

Developing a Positive Interaction Style. A student's style of interaction and the behaviors exhibited during an interaction form the foundation for future friendship and support from others. Individuals who are positive, attentive, approving, encouraging, interested, and pleased to be a part of an interaction are more likely to receive support and be included in a group than individuals who talk about themselves excessively or behave in grumpy, annoyed, disinterested, or other negative ways (Trower, 1981). People generally like to be around and help others who approve of them, praise their acccomplishments, and show concern for their welfare. A student who wants to be

liked and supported by peers must also like and support others (Rubin, 1980).

Establishing Areas of Compatibility. Establishing what a student has in common with a peer can lead to friendship and support (Epstein & Karweit, 1983). Students without friends need to learn how to find out about other individuals and compare what is learned with their own interests, values, and experiences, asking questions such as "Where do you go to school?" or "Do you like sports?" They also need to learn how to communicate about such things as their favorite activities, hobbies, or school involvements.

Taking the Perspective of Others. Students who view friendships only in terms of what a friend can do for them are often unable to recognize the attitudes, feelings, and circumstances of others and do not say the kindest or most fitting thing (Selman, 1981). These students must learn to listen to others, put themselves in the other person's position, and evaluate the impact their behavior is having on others. This can enable them to exercise the tact and sensitivity needed to build supportive relationships and friendships with their peers (Stainback & Stainback, 1987).

Sharing and Providing Support. Special educators often go to great lengths to advocate for and provide assistance and help to students who are new, isolated, and without friends; however, such students are often provided little encouragement and few opportunities to reciprocate with their teachers and peers (Stainback & Stainback, 1987). To develop friendships and supportive peer relationships, students who lack friends must learn to share, comfort, help, and provide support to others, particularly in time of need (Bell, 1981; Berndt, 1986).

Building Trustworthiness and Loyalty. It is important for all students to develop a moral or ethical code to guide their behavior toward others (Hinde, 1979). Once friendship and supportive relationships begin to develop, loyalty and trustworthiness become necessary components if the relationship is to endure. These qualities often serve as testing functions to determine the limits or intensity of a relationship, particularly in close friendships.

Becoming Proficient at Conflict Resolution. The ability to deal effectively with conflicts is one of the most difficult skills for students to demonstrate (Stainback & Stainback, 1987). Conflict resolution requires a student to be able to make known and protect his or her own rights and needs while being sensitive to and respecting the rights and needs of peers (Stocking et al., 1980). Students who tend to lack friends often deal with conflicts in either an overly aggressive or submissive manner.

Learning Friendship Skills. Coaching is one approach that has been used successfully to teach friendship skills (Gottlieb & Leyser, 1981; Oden & Asher, 1977). Students are helped to gain an understanding of each of the positive peer support and friendship skills and then are encouraged to think of specific actions that could be taken to implement the general concepts in the context of real life activities.

After the students have been provided with ample opportunities to practice the skills they have learned in natural social interaction situations, they engage in review sessions with teachers to evaluate their success. An understanding of these skills can be fostered in such classes as social studies or health as content for themes, projects, class skits or role play. Discussions of friendship skills as they were practiced by students on the playground or in the classroom might be used as a focal point for general class discussions or individual counseling sessions about the value of supporting one another. See Stainback and Stainback (1987) for more specific information about how support and friendship skills can be facilitated.

Foster Respect for Individual Differences

Many teachers believe that social interactions and friendships tend to develop among students who understand and respect each others' differences and similarities (Stainback et al., 1989). There are a number of ways to foster this in the classroom. One is to infuse information about individual differences and similarities into existing reading materials, health and social studies classes, and extracurricular activities such as assembly programs, plays, school projects, service activities, and clubs.

A particularly good way to focus on similarities among students at the elementary school level is to have all students provide information about their families, pets, summer plans, daily chores, favorite celebrities, and vacations in special projects, themes, or presentations to be shared with the class. For older students, sports, teen idols, music, cars, pet peeves, or jobs may be more appropriate topics. This can help to foster an awareness among class members that students without friends often share their interests, characteristics, and concerns and have similar feelings, anxieties, dreams, and desires.

One way to note differences is to assign tasks based on the individual characteristics of the students, pointing out the differences of each student as assignments are made. Particular care must be exercised in seeing that the differences in *every* student are noted and recognizing the differences in a positive way. For instance, the teacher might say, "Judy, since you have good listening skills, would you listen for the timer to ring so we will know when our clay should come out of the oven?" "Jamie, you are tall, so would you please take responsibility for watering the plants on the top of the bookcase?" "Michael, since you have a lap tray on your wheelchair, will you take these books back to the library for us?" In the process of recognizing differences, teachers can point out the strengths and talents of each student in the class, which can facilitate friendship and support for all class members.

Provide a Positive Model

Possibly the most important thing a teacher can do to promote support and friendships among students is to be a good model. The teacher must communicate to students through his or her behavior that every student is an important and worthwhile member of the class. The teacher can also enlist the assistance of fellow teachers to interact positively with some of the students in the classroom. This is especially important at the secondary level due to complex scheduling arrangements and the number of teachers that students interact with. At all grade levels, care must be taken to assure that new or isolated students are included in friendly, supportive encounters with adults.

The notion that all students have something to offer and should be included can be pointed out by calling upon each student to contribute to the needs of the class. For example, students who are typically isolated can be asked, along with other students, to erase the chalkboard, carry lunch money to the

Some professionals have stated that peer support and friendships are not luxuries but necessities.

57

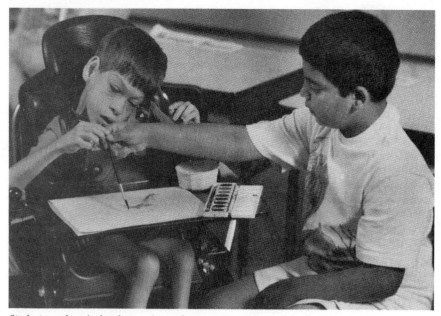

Students can be paired to draw a picture about a positive characteristic of a classmate.

principal's office, or contribute their talents to the class or school assemblies, student advisory committees, and bazaars.

In addition to modeling positive interactions with each student in the classroom, it is also important for the teacher to model positive support and friendship behaviors toward peers and colleagues by offering assistance, being courteous, and sharing with fellow teachers, parents, and other adults.

When Peer Support Does Not Work

Unfortunately, despite the best efforts of everyone involved, peer support is sometimes slow to develop or does not develop at all. While there are no foolproof ways to ensure that no student will be overlooked or rejected, there are several things to try when difficulties arise.

Sociometric assessment, informal or formal interviewing of students, and classroom observations can be conducted to ascertain who is being accepted or rejected and the reasons why. This might provide clues as to what can be done when some students continue to be overlooked or rejected. For example, if a student is being rejected because he or she never initiates social interactions, the student can be helped to learn how to do so (Strain & Kerr, 1981). If a student is being rejected because he or she is al-

ways complaining, school personnel and parents can work to help the student be more positive. It might be found that many students in mainstream classes hold stereotypic or negative attitudes toward certain students. School personnel can work to educate these students to be more accepting of and sensitive toward students with diverse backgrounds and characteristics. It should be noted that while acceptance of a student is not analogous to friendship, it is a necessary prerequisite to the development of friendships and informal supportive relationships. There are a number of books that provide clear and specific guidelines for designing sociometric assessments and structuring interviews and observations for use in the classroom and other school settings (e.g., Borg, 1981; Borg & Gall, 1979). Resource and consulting personnel with expertise in social interactions and behavior management can sometimes be called to observe in an effort to detect exactly what is happening and propose possible courses of action (Heron & Harris, 1987; Idol-Maestas, 1983)).

Conclusion

While it is important to help students who are new, isolated, or lonely make friends and gain the support of their peers, the value of these relationships should not be misinterpreted to imply that having lots of support and many

friends is always "good" and having few is always "bad" (Duck, 1983). For some students, having one or a few good friendships may be more satisfying than having a large number of friends, some who appear isolated may not be interested in developing friendships at all. Too often, particularly for students with disabilities, others try to help too much, to the detriment of learning opportunities. It is essential to respect the different social styles and needs of students, including the very real needs that some students have for privacy, solitude, and trying new skills on their own (Rubin, 1980).

It is also important to note that no student should be forced or cajoled into supporting or making friends with any other particular student or group of students. To a large extent, the people students choose to support and make friends with should be a matter of individual choice. Relationships that are based on something other than free choice and personal preference are unlikely to generalize and endure beyond the classroom setting (Allan, 1979).

References

Allan, G. (1979). *A sociology of friendship and kinship.* Boston: Allen & Unwin.

Asher, S., & Gottman, J. (Eds.). (1981). *The development of children's friendships.* Cambridge: Cambridge University Press.

Bell, R. (1981). *Worlds of friendship.* Beverly Hills, CA: Sage Publications.

Berndt, T. (1986). Sharing between friends: Contexts and consequences. In E. Mueller & C. Cooper (Eds.), *Process and outcome in peer relationships* (pp. 129–160). New York: Academic Press.

Borg, W. (1981). *Applying educational research.* New York: Longman.

Borg, W., & Gall, M. (1979). *Educational research.* New York: Longman.

Duck, S. (1983). *Friends for life.* New York: St. Martin's Press.

Epstein, J., & Karweit, N. (Eds.). (1983). *Friends in school.* New York: Academic Press.

Forest, M. (Ed.). (1987). *More education integration.* Downsview, Ontario: Roeher Institute.

Forest, M., & Flynn, G. (Directors). (1988). *With a Little Help from My Friends* (Videotape). Toronto: Center for Integrated Education.

Gartner, A. & Lipsky, D. (1990). Students as instructional agents. In W. Stainback & S. Stainback (Eds.), *Support networks for inclusive schools* (pp. 81–94). Baltimore: Paul H. Brookes.

Gottlieb, J., & Leyser, Y. (1981). Friendships between mentally retarded and nonretarded children. In S. Asher & J. Gottman (Eds.), *The development of children's friendships* (pp. 150–181). Cambridge: Cambridge University Press.

Grenot-Scheyer, M., Coots, J., & Falvey, M. (1990). Developing and fostering friendships. In M. Falvey (Ed.), *Community-based curriculum:*

Instructional strategies for students with severe handicaps (2nd ed.) (pp. 202–231). Baltimore: Paul H. Brookes.

Heron, T., & Harris, K. (1987). The educational consultant. Austin, TX: PRO-ED.

Hinde, R. (1979). Towards understanding relationships. New York: Academic Press.

Idol-Maestas, L. (1983). Special educator's consultation handbook. Austin, TX: PRO-ED.

O'Brien, J., Forest, M., Snow, J., & Hasburg, D. (1989). Action for inclusion. Toronto: Centre for Integrated Education.

Oden, S., & Asher, S. (1977). Coaching children in social skills for friendship making. Child Development, 48, 495–506.

PEAK Parent Center. (1988). Discover the possibilities. Colorado Springs, CO: Author.

Perske, R., & Perske, M. (1988). Friendship. Nashville, TN: Abington Press.

Rubin, Z. (1980). Children's friendships. Cambridge, MA: Harvard University Press.

Ruttiman, A., & Forest, M. (1987). With a little help from my friends. In M. Forest (Ed.), More education integration, (pp. 61–68). Downsview, Ontario: Roeher Institute.

Sapon-Shevin, M. (1990). Student support through cooperative learning. In W. Stainback & S. Stainback (Eds.), Support networks for inclusive schooling, (pp. 65–79). Baltimore: Paul H. Brookes.

Selman, R. (1981). The child as a friendship philosopher. In S. Asher & J. Gottman (Eds.), The development of children's friendships (pp. 242–272). Cambridge: Cambridge University Press.

Stainback, S., & Stainback, W. (1988). Educating students with severe disabilities. TEACHING Exceptional Children, 21, 16–19.

Stainback, S., Stainback, W., & Forest, M. (Eds.). (1989). Educating all students in the mainstream of regular education. Baltimore: Paul H. Brookes.

Stainback, W., & Stainback, S. (1987). Facilitating friendships. Education and Training of the Mentally Retarded, 22, 18–25.

Stainback, W., & Stainback, S. (1990). Support networks for inclosure schooling. Baltimore: Paul H. Brookes.

Stocking, S., Arezzo, D., & Leavitt, S. (1980). Helping kids make friends. Allen, TX: Argus.

Strain, P., & Kerr, M. (1981). Modifying children's social withdrawal: Issues in assessment and clinical intervention. In M. Hersen, R. Eisler, & P. Miller (Eds.), Progress in behavior modification (Vol. II) (pp. 171–196). New York: Academic Press.

Strully, J. (1987, October). What's really important in life anyway? Parents sharing the vision. Paper presented at the 14th Annual TASH Conference, Chicago.

Strully, J., & Strully, C. (1985). Friendship and our children. Journal of the Association for Persons with Severe Handicaps, 10, 224–227.

Trower, P. (1981). Social skill disorder. In S. Duck & R. Gilmore (Eds.), Personal relationships 3: Personal relationships in disorder (pp. 97–110). New York: Academic Press.

Vandercook, T., Fleetham, D., Sinclair, S., & Tetlie, R. (1988). Cath, Jess, Jules and Ames. A story of friendship. IMPACT, 1, 18–19.

Villa, R., & Thousand, J. (1988). Enhancing success in heterogeneous classrooms and schools: The power of partnership. Teacher education and special education, 11, 144–153.

York, J., & Vandercook, T. (1988). What's in an IEP? Writing objectives for an integrated education. IMPACT, 1, 16, 19.

Culturally Sensitive Instructional Practices for African-American Learners with Disabilities

ABSTRACT: This article discusses the cultural and educational needs of African-American learners with disabilities. Six theoretical assumptions establish some basic suppositions about culturally and linguistically diverse learners and effective instructional practices. A review of the literature describes African-American cultural practices, interests, and cognitive styles; highlights the attitudes, perceptions, and instructional practices of effective teachers of African-American students; and includes patterns of teacher-student and peer-group interactions that promote high academic achievement among African-American learners. Recommendations include organizing teaching, learning, and performance in ways that are compatible with the social structure of African-American students with disabilities.

MARY E. FRANKLIN
University of Cincinnati

MARY E. FRANKLIN (CEC #0011) is an Assistant Professor in the Department of Early Childhood and Special Education at the University of Cincinnati, Ohio.

American public schools have traditionally used a monolithic model of instruction, in which the organization of teaching, learning, and performance is compatible with the social structure of the dominant culture (Tharp, 1989). This traditional model, which is also adopted in the field of special education, emphasizes three patterns of cognitive functioning: (1) analysis of academic tasks, (2) the establishment of sequential learning objectives based on each task analysis, and (3) direct instruction of individual task components (Cummins, 1984). According to Tharp, teachers tend to expect that *all* students will learn based on these traditional patterns of cognitive functioning and instructional practices. The truth is, however, only learners whose cognitive functioning corresponds to these patterns are likely to succeed. Tharp and others (Cummins; Poplin, 1988) have asserted that many African-American, Hispanic, Native American, and Asian-American learners have difficulty with traditional patterns of cognitive functioning because the patterns ignore the impact culture has on language, learning, and thinking.

Despite the pervasive literature asserting that culture and language affect learning (Banks, 1981; Boykin, 1982; Hale-Benson, 1986; Hilliard, 1989; Piestrup, 1973; Tharp, 1989; Villegas, 1991), most special education teachers continue to plan instruction and activities based on their students' disabilities, with little consideration given to the diverse cultural and linguistic backgrounds of the students (Almanza & Mosley, 1980; Clark-Johnson, 1988; Cummins, 1984). In view of the disproportionate overrepresentation of culturally and linguistically diverse learners in special education classes, we cannot ignore the impact that culture and language have on learners' cognitive styles.

The goal of public education must be the same for *all,* that is, *to help students achieve their fullest potential.* The crucial question is, however, How can this task be best accomplished for African-American learners with disabilities? This article identifies effective teaching, learning, and performance strategies that are compatible with the social/cultural background of African-American learners (with or without disabilities). First, I examine six theoretical assumptions about culturally sensitive instructional practices. Second, I review the literature showing the relationship between affective, culturally sensitive instruc-

From *Exceptional Children,* Vol. 59, No. 2, October/November 1992, pp. 115-122. Copyright © 1992 by The Council for Exceptional Children. Reprinted by permission.

tional practices and high academic achievement among African-American learners. Last, I recommend ways to organize teaching, learning, and performance to be compatible with the social structure of African-American students with disabilities.

THEORETICAL ASSUMPTIONS

Educators must consider culture and language when they plan instruction and develop activities for students from diverse backgrounds. The following assumptions undergird recommendations for culturally sensitive instructional practices.

Assumption 1: Quality instruction should incorporate resources from the learner's environments outside the school parameters. The learner's immediate cultural environment is the home and the local community (Bronfenbrenner, 1979). In this environment, the learner interacts and develops language and interrelationship skills that may challenge the school culture.

Cultural-difference theory attributes the academic problems of culturally and linguistically diverse students to the discontinuity between home and school. Discontinuity exists in relation to differences in dialects (Piestrup, 1973) and in cognitive styles (Almanza & Mosley, 1980; Cummins, 1984) when the method of instruction is incompatible with the cognitive and interactive styles of culturally and linguistically diverse learners. The solution to cultural discontinuity between home and school is not necessarily having the school replicate every cultural condition of the home and community (Villegas, 1991), but rather requiring teachers to adapt and infuse cultural variables in their interactions with African-American learners and in their instructional practices.

*Assumption 2: Special education should **not** be the primary solution for African-American learners whose cognitive and behavioral patterns are incompatible with schools' monocultural instructional methods.* Chinn and Hughes (1988) reported that of all ethnic groups, African Americans were the most represented in special education programs, and African-American males were the most overrepresented in classes for students with behavior disorders and mental retardation. Traditional instructional methods tend to be unrelated to or incompatible with the experiences of culturally and linguistically diverse learners. Consequently, Tharp (1989) and others (Cummins, 1984; Poplin, 1988) found that many African-American, Hispanic, Native American, and Asian-American learners are much less successful in regular education programs than are white-American learners.

Assumption 3: African-American learners' dif-

ferences should not be perceived as genetic deficiencies but, rather, as sources of strength. The notion that minority learners' low achievement is due to genetic intelligence deficiencies has been disputed throughout the literature (e.g., Feuerstein, 1979; Mercer, 1973; Villegas, 1991). According to Sternberg (1983), there is great diversity in a culture's conception of intelligence. He explains: "People's personal experiences in various cultures almost invariably suggest that what is adaptive and 'intelligent' in one culture can be maladaptive and even 'unintelligent' in another culture" (p. 8). Thus, people's experiences within a culture formulate their definition of intelligence. Without an understanding of various cultures, well-meaning teachers may ignore cultural definitions that are peculiar to the learners' cultural backgrounds.

Assumption 4: Culturally sensitive teachers will identify and build on the learner's strengths and interests. Poplin's (1988) theory of constructivism/holism lends support to this assumption. This theory suggests that a learner's context for learning begins with what is currently known. Hence, special education teachers must develop a knowledge of learners' cultures and must design meaningful experiences around *what learners know* rather than *what learners do not know*.

Assumption 5: Language and dialectical differences are important cultural influences that affect communication and interaction between the teacher and learner (Piestrup, 1973; Poplin, 1988; Tharp, 1989). The required language in the school may differ from that used in the home—or may be the same (language) but differ in the way it is used (Villegas, 1991). Hence, language activities presented in the classroom may generate many different interpretations based on how the learner views the world. Teachers who lack cross-cultural sensitivity may view the responses of culturally and linguistically diverse learners as "wrong" and academically incompetent. The question then becomes, What use is prior experience to learners whose established ways of using language and making sense of the world are deemed unacceptable or prohibited by the classroom?

Assumption 6: Culturally sensitive instruction should be integrated with activities that provide learners opportunities to learn and practice new skills. The constructivist theory posits that learning is a process in which new meanings are created by the learner within the context of his or her current knowledge (Poplin, 1988). If a new experience is unrelated to a learner's developmental levels, interests, and problems, the learner will naturally reject and ignore the information. Teachers must understand the importance of

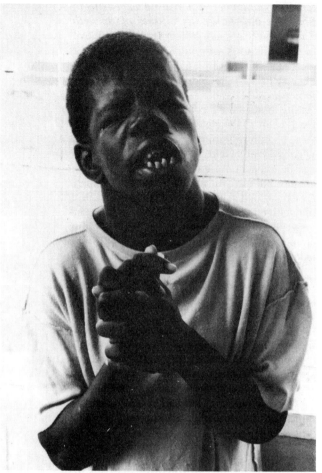

(Photo credit United Nations/S. Dimartini)

Handicapped African-American children need constant encouragement, recognition, warmth, and reassurance to continue participating in class activities.

knowing their learners' interests, hobbies, music, and so forth.

When learners are provided many opportunities to negotiate their cultural background, interests, and cognitive styles in the learning environment, they are more inclined to experience academic success. The following review of literature explores the cultural values and practices of African Americans, the effect these values and practices have on the cognitive and interactive styles of African-American learners, and the characteristics of effective teachers of African-American learners.

IMPACT OF AFRICAN-AMERICAN CULTURAL VALUES ON LEARNING AND INSTRUCTION

A review of 23 years of research shows *some* common cultural values of African Americans and the effect these values have on the learning and interactive styles of African-American learn-

ers. Further, an examination of teaching practices used with African-American students delineates certain teacher attitudes, perceptions, and interactive styles that have successfully facilitated continuity between the school and home and community environments.

African-American Child-Rearing Practices

In a study examining child-rearing practices of white families and African-American families, Young (1970) found that white children were more object-oriented, having available to them as infants numerous manipulative objects and discovery properties. Conversely, African-American children were person-oriented. As infants, they were held by their mothers or another family member most of the time, and few objects were given to them. When African-American infants reached for an object or felt a surface, their attention was immediately redirected to the person holding them, thereby reducing the value of material objects. Similarly, Lewis (1975) and Dougherty (1978) observed extensive interaction among African-American family members and infants involving touching, kissing, and holding the baby's hands.

Young (1970) observed other interactive techniques between African-American mothers and their children. For example, a "contest" style of speech was used between the mothers and children in which they "volleyed" rhythmically, and the children were taught to be assertive and to develop their individual styles. African-American mothers gave directions for household chores in a "call-and-response" pattern, an interactive style found in some African-American churches (Lein, 1975) and in some African-American music (Hale-Benson, 1986).

Other African-American values regarding child rearing included the value of strictness and the expectation that children assume responsibility early (Bartz & Levine, 1978). African-American parents also valued creative functioning in their children; that is, they were not immediately frustrated by their children's "typical" childhood behavior and encouraged its development (Greathouse, Gomez, & Wurster, 1988).

Engram (1982) found that African-American children were also socialized early regarding the realities of racism and poverty in society and told they must be twice as good if they were to succeed. In summary, researchers have found that child-rearing practices help form and shape the child's view of self and how he or she fits in the world. These practices also serve to establish the cognitive and interactive characteristics of learners.

Some Characteristics of African-American Learners

The emotional and social characteristics of African-American learners and their families have important implications for teacher-student relationships. Silverstein and Krate (1975) classified over half of the African-American students they studied as being "ambivalent." They explained that these students needed—and sought rather aggressively—teacher attention, nurturance, and acceptance. Students needed constant encouragement, recognition, warmth, and reassurance to continue participating in the class activities. However, when positive attention and affirmation were not given, students often became frustrated, angry, and disruptive.

Regarding African-American students' motivation and interests, Silberman (1970) reported that observers were struck by the liveliness and eagerness demonstrated by African-American learners in the early grades and by their passivity and apathy in the later grades. Lefevre (1966) reported that by the fifth grade, African-American students had become cynical and preoccupied with blatant attempts to confound the constrictions of the traditional instructional environment. Boykin (1982) explained that African-American learners were not inherently apathetic and cynical, but inherently eager and had become "turned off" by the nature of their school experiences. Many African-American children are exposed to high-energy, fast-paced home environments, where there is simultaneous variable stimulation (e.g., televisions and music playing simultaneously and people talking and moving in and about the home freely). Hence, low-energy, monolithic environments (as seen in many traditional school environments) are less stimulating.

In 1982, Boykin studied the effects of task variability on African-American and white students. Each learner's home stimulation level was assessed, based on the total number of adults and children in the home, total number of rooms in the home, and the total number of televisions, radios, and stereos. Findings indicated that African-American students experienced home environments higher in stimulation than did white students. Further, the difference in home environment was reflected in differential responsiveness to variability in task presentation format. African-American learners' performance was markedly better in the more varied condition than when there was less variability. White learners' performance was not affected by task variability.

Rohwer and Harris (1975) also studied task variability of African-American and white students—specifically, the effects of teaching prose by using multimedia variations. Again, the results indicated that the performance of African-American learners when using multimedia, especially oral plus visual media, was greater than when using single media. The performance of white learners generally was not affected when combined or single media were used.

Some Characteristics of Effective Teachers of African-American Learners

Teacher attitudes and perceptions both effect and moderate learners' academic achievement. According to Villegas (1991), an effective teacher has the ability to create meaningful and successful learning activities that take into consideration the learner's culture and background experiences.

Researchers examining teacher-student interactions found that affective-oriented teachers were more successful than task-oriented teachers in improving African-American students' academic achievement (Collins & Tamarkin, 1982; Cureton, 1978; Dillon, 1989; St. John, 1971). Affective-oriented teachers were described as being kind, optimistic, understanding, adaptable, and warm. They also were group conscious, cooperative, and sociocentric.

In a microethnographic study, Dillon (1989) found that effective teachers were "affective" and were successful in bridging home and school cultures. These teachers were able to create learning environments that were open and risk free; they planned and structured activities that met the interests and needs of the students.

Instructional planning should also incorporate small groups. According to Hale-Benson (1986), this practice provides African-American learners the human interaction they are familiar with in their families. Hale-Benson has encouraged teachers to incorporate peer- and cross-age grouping and cooperative learning groups in instructional planning.

Research on cooperative learning in the classroom showed that small, heterogeneous-ability groups working together on learning tasks and activities were particularly effective for African-American learners (Slavin & Madden, 1979; Slavin & Oickle, 1981). For example, Slavin and Oickle found that cooperative learning groups made significantly greater gains in academic achievement than did nonteam classes, largely because of the outstanding gains made by African-American learners.

Effective teachers also bridge African-American students' home and school cultures by using stimulus variety, greater verve, and verbal interaction. Piestrup (1973) identified varied techniques that were effective when teaching reading to African-American first graders who spoke a Black English dialect. Results revealed that when teachers used a culturally sensitive approach, African-American children demonstrated a high proficiency level. That is, the teacher spoke rhythmically, varied intonation, and engaged in verbal interplay with the learners. Similarly, Delpit (1988) observed a teacher successfully integrating today's learners' music (e.g., rap) into a lesson that included very complex science factors.

In summary, many African-American learners are reared in people-focused families and communities where human interaction and simultaneous stimulus variability are highly valued. Therefore, effective teachers of African-American students, with or without disabilities, will develop a repertoire of instructional practices that involve cultural aspects that are valued by these students and that will enhance their development. Teaching and learning should be compatible with the cultural characteristics of African-American learners with disabilities.

TEACHING AND LEARNING THAT IS COMPATIBLE WITH THE CULTURAL CHARACTERISTICS OF AFRICAN-AMERICAN LEARNERS WITH DISABILITIES

The literature reviewed previously suggests that the following instructional strategies are effective with African-American learners: task variability; culturally sensitive teacher-student interaction; and social learning in peer groups, cross-age groups, and cooperative learning groups. Researchers' findings, however, should be viewed not as rigid prescriptions, but as suggestions for guiding instructional decisions for African-American learners with disabilities. To be effective, educators must exercise their freedom to adapt instruction to meet the needs of local circumstances and individual students.

Stimulus Variability

Stimulus variability includes varying the format of instruction presentation and increasing the classroom energy. Many African-American students prefer a faster pace, with techniques that incorporate body movement.

Greater Verve and Rhythm. Variety in instruction provides the spirit and enthusiasm for learning. When instructional strategies facilitate stimulus variety, using combinations of oral, print, and visual media, African-American students perform better (Boykin, 1982; Rohwer & Harris, 1975). Instructional activities should include music, singing, and movement. For example, teachers can vary instructional activities to incorporate different media (e.g., film, filmstrip, transparencies, and pictures), instructional materials, and study locations. Teachers can also use multimedia test materials.

Verbal Interaction. Through verbal activities, teachers can encourage learners to treat the text

material orally. Motivation increases when teachers encourage the use of many expressive, creative activities (Collins & Tamarkin, 1982). Such activities could include rap (Delpit, 1988), choral reading (Collins & Tamarkin; Young, 1970), chants, and responsive reading (Piestrup, 1973).

Divergent Thinking. A method of problem solving, divergent thinking requires students to think in ways that differ from conventional thinking and problem solving (Boykin, 1982; Poplin, 1988). Teachers should provide experiences for students to explore various ways of arriving at a particular solution. These experiences include activities that require brainstorming, open-ended responses, and critical thinking. Learners need to practice making conjectures, gathering evidence, and building arguments to defend or refute their conjectures. The teacher's responsibility is to help students realize they have the power to make sense of a new question or problem situation. This can be accomplished by allowing students the opportunity to gather information about what they will study and to draw from information they already have in their cultural backgrounds. Teachers may also find it helpful to connect problems and activities to other subject areas of interest to the African-American learner (Boykin, 1982; Poplin, 1988; Tharp, 1989).

Teachers' Interactions With African-American Learners

Research reveals that interacting with African-American learners may require teachers to model affective behavior (e.g., affirming, giving positive reinforcements, etc.) (Collins & Tamarkin, 1982; Dillon, 1989; St. John, 1971).

Use of Dialect. Teachers may *at times* integrate aspects of the Black English dialect into their conversations with African-American learners, for example, "jive talkin'," which is based on African-American improvisation of the English language. This form of interaction should be used only by those educators who have established a rapport with learners; otherwise this form of interaction could be perceived as condescending. Teachers should inform African-American learners that although the Black English dialect is useful in their home and community environment, it is not accepted in all environments. Nevertheless, when the teacher uses the learner's dialect from time to time, the learner may be more inclined to engage in tasks he or she might otherwise reject (Collins & Tamarkin, 1982; Villegas, 1991).

Presenting Real-World Tasks. Teachers should include activities that are realistic to the African-American learners' cultural environment (i.e.,

(Photo credit United Nations/L. Solassen)

Educators must develop sensitivity, awareness, and insight into the needs of learners from diverse ethnic and cultural groups. African-American students with disabilities must be challenged and reenforced in their learning experience.

school, home, and community). Teachers should become familiar with African-American culture and integrate learners' real-life experiences in instructional materials, resources, and techniques (Boykin, 1982; Gay, 1978; Hale-Benson, 1986; Poplin, 1988; Tharp, 1989).

Including a People Focus. Person-to-person interaction is a learning-style preference of many African-American learners (Collins & Tamarkin, 1982; Cureton, 1978; Dillon, 1989; Dougherty, 1978; Young, 1970). This characteristic has implications for how teachers interact with African-American students with disabilities and how instruction is planned and implemented. As mentioned previously, for example, African-American students may benefit from small-group work (Cureton, 1978; Hale-Benson, 1986; Slavin & Oickle, 1981) and peer tutoring (Hale-Benson, 1986). Other examples include selecting reading textbooks and materials that include credible young people with whom African-American learners, of either gender, can relate (Franklin & Mickel, in press). Materials may emphasize the student's lifestyle, values, motives, speech, and mannerisms (see also Boy-

kin, 1982; Piestrup, 1973; Poplin, 1988; Tharp, 1989; Villegas, 1991). Teachers should also examine instructional materials carefully to ensure that the materials selected include African Americans, as well as other ethnic groups (Franklin & Mickel).

Grouping Patterns

Instructional activities for small groups can be organized to allow students to work together. This means that the room will not always be quiet, and some students may even be off task at times. Nevertheless, students need to have opportunities to work on problem situations together and to talk about ways of doing an activity or finding a solution to the problem. Further, this method gives students a chance to stimulate others' thinking and to realize that there may be many methods of accomplishing a task. Group activities also encourage social growth and cross-racial friendships.

Cooperative Learning. In this instructional strategy, students work together in teams. Specific methods include Student Team Learning, Jigsaw,

Group Investigation, and Learning Together (Slavin & Madden, 1979; Slavin & Oickle, 1981). Teachers divide the class into small, heterogeneous-ability groups in which each member is expected to contribute to an assigned task, and each group should work cooperatively on assigned, content-related tasks.

Peer/Cross-Age Grouping. In these groups, students of the same or different age work together informally. Learners in such groups may be working on different assignments (Hale-Benson, 1986).

Peer Tutoring. This person-to-person interaction fosters helping relationships between learners (Hale-Benson, 1986). In this technique, the teacher encourages learners to tutor each other and problem solve together as part of a small group (e.g., a cooperative group or peer or cross-age grouping).

To connect culturally with African-American learners' home and community, effective special education teachers may use stimulus variability, affective methods of interaction, and variable grouping patterns. Teachers must be especially mindful of these practices when they systematically plan successful learning experiences for African-American learners with disabilities. Although some of these instructional practices appear in the effective teaching literature, recognition and understanding of a learner's culture will expand the teacher's range of practices.

CONCLUSION

The Council for Exceptional Children (CEC, 1978) has strongly urged special educators to develop sensitivity, awareness, and insight into the needs of learners from diverse ethnic and cultural groups. As part of this initiative, this article has provided a review of the literature relating to African-American culture and its influence on the learner. This research has suggested culturally sensitive instructional practices, with specific suggestions for the instruction of African-American students with disabilities. The inclusion of these or similar practices in curriculum and instruction may enhance the learning experiences of African-American students with disabilities.

REFERENCES

Almanza, H. P., & Mosley, W. J. (1980). Curriculum adaptation and modifications for culturally diverse handicapped children. *Exceptional Children, 46,* 608-614.

Banks, J. A. (1981). *Multiethnic education: Theory and practice.* Boston: Allyn & Bacon.

Bartz, K., & Levine, E. (1978). Childrearing by Black parents: A description and comparison to Anglo and Chicano parents. *Journal of Marriage and the Family, 40,* 709-719.

Boykin, A. W. (1982). Task variability and the performance of Black and White children: Vervistic explorations. *Journal of Black Studies, 12*(4), 469-485.

Bronfenbrenner, U. (1979). *The ecology of human development.* Cambridge: Harvard University Press.

Chinn, P. C., & Hughes, S. (1988, October). Representation of ethnic minorities in special education for the mentally retarded and learning disabled. In L. Olion (Chair), *Reaching new horizons.* Symposium conducted at The Council for Exceptional Children Symposia on the Education of Culturally Diverse Exceptional Children, Denver.

Clark-Johnson, G. (1988). Special focus: Black children. *TEACHING Exceptional Children, 20*(4), 46-47.

Collins, M. & Tamarkin, C. (1982). *Marva Collins' way.* Los Angeles: Jeremy P. Tarcher.

Council for Exceptional Children. (1978). Minorities position policy statements. *Exceptional Children, 45,* 57-64.

Cummins, J. (1984). *Bilingual and special education: Issues in assessment and pedagogy.* San Diego: College-Hill Press.

Cureton, G. O. (1978). Using a Black learning style. *The Reading Teacher, 31,* 751-756.

Delpit, L. D. (1988). The silenced dialogue: Power and pedagogy in educating other people's children. *Harvard Educational Review, 58*(3), 280-297.

Dillon, D. R. (1989). Showing them that I want them to learn and that I care about who they are: A microethnography of the social organization of a secondary low-track English-reading classroom. *American Educational Research Journal, 26*(2), 227-259.

Dougherty, M. C. (1978). *Becoming a woman in rural Black culture.* Nashville, TN: Vanderbilt University Press.

Engram, E. (1982). *Science, myth, reality: The Black family in one-half century of research.* Westport, CT: Greenwood Press.

Feuerstein, R. (1979). *The dynamic assessment of retarded performers: The learning potential assessment device, theory, instruments and techniques.* Baltimore: University Park Press.

Franklin, M. E., & Mickel, V. (in press). Are publishers of reading textbooks for intermediate-students sensitive to the learning characteristics of African-American students. *SENGA: Sensitive to the Educational Needs of Growing Americans.*

Gay, G. (1978). Multicultural preparation and teacher effectiveness in desegregated schools. *Theory Into Practice, 11,* 149-156.

Greathouse, B., Gomez, R., & Wurster, S. (1988). An investigation of Black and Hispanic parents' locus of control, childbearing attitudes and practices and degree of involvement in Head Start. *Negro Educational Review, 39*(1-2), 4-17.

Hale-Benson, J. E. (1986). *Black children: Their roots, culture and learning styles.* Baltimore: Johns Hopkins University Press.

Hilliard, A. (1989). Teachers and cultural styles in a pluralistic society. *NEA Today, 7*(6), 65-69.

Lefevre, C. (1966). Inner city schools: As the children

see it. *Elementary School Journal, 7,* 8-15.

Lein, L. (1975). Black American migrant children: Their speech at home and school. *Council on Anthropology and Education Quarterly, 6,* 1-11.

Lewis, D. K. (1975). The Black family: Socialization and sex roles. *Phylon, 36,* 221-237.

Mercer, J. (1973). *Labeling the mentally retarded.* Berkeley, CA: The University of California Press.

Piestrup, A. (1973). *Black dialect interference and accommodation of reading instruction in first grade* (Monograph No. 4). Berkeley, CA: University of California, Language Behavior Research Laboratory.

Poplin, M. S. (1988). Holistic/constructivist principles of the teaching/learning process: Implications for the field of learning disabilities. *Journal of Learning Disabilities, 21*(7), 401-416.

Rohwer, W. D., & Harris, W. (1975). Media effects on prose learning in two populations of children. *Journal of Educational Psychology, 67,* 651-657.

Silberman, C. (1970). *Crisis in the classroom.* New York: Vintage Books.

Silverstein, B., & Krate, R. (1975). *Children of the dark ghetto: A developmental psychology.* New York: Praeger.

Slavin, R. E., & Madden, N. A. (1979). School practices that improve race relations. *American Educational Research Journal, 16,* 169-180.

Slavin R. E., & Oickle, E. (1981). Effects of cooperative learning teams on student achievement and race relations: Treatment by race interactions. *Sociology of Education, 54,* 174-180.

Sternberg, R. J. (1983). Criteria for intellectual skills training. *Educational Researcher, 12*(2), 6-12.

St. John, N. (1971). Thirty-six teachers: Their characteristics and outcomes for Black and White pupils. *American Educational Research Journal, 8,* 635-648.

Tharp, R. G. (1989). Psychocultural variables and constants: Effects on teaching and learning in schools. *American Psychologist, 44*(2), 349-359.

Villegas, A. M. (1991). *Culturally responsive pedagogy for the 1990s and beyond* (Trends and Issues Paper No. 6). Washington, DC: ERIC Clearinghouse on Teacher Education.

Young, V. H. (1970). Family and childhood in a southern Georgia community. *American Anthropologist, 72,* 269-288.

Preparation of this manuscript was supported in part by the Urban University Program of the Ohio Board of Regents.

DISABILITY SIMULATION

for Regular Education Students

Mark J. Hallenbeck
Darlene McMaster

Mark J. Hallenbeck *is a Resource Room Teacher and Special Education Coordinator, West Lyon School, Inwood, Iowa, and* **Darlene McMaster** *is a School Psychologist and Counselor, Marshall, Minnesota.*

Parents and educators are well aware that the attitude of nondisabled peers critically affects the success of students with disabilities (Dewar, 1982; Fiedler & Simpson, 1987; Riester & Bessette, 1986; Simpson, 1980). If students with special needs are to become truly productive and successful adults, educators must "concentrate on developing positive attitudes within our children, the adults of the next generation who will, in time, be the friend, neighbor, co-worker, or employer of a handicapped peer" (Dewar, 1982, p. 193).

In the fall of 1987, the parents of several students placed in our resource room suggested that the special education staff do something to educate regular education students about students with disabilities. The major goal would be to help dispel any distorted notions held by regular education students and to sensitize them to some of the problems faced by our students and by other people with disabilities.

Awareness programs frequently have incorporated simulation activities and guest speakers (Bookbinder, 1978; Dewar, 1982; Fox 1982; Martin & Cashdollar, 1980;

Riester & Bessette, 1986). The innovative "Kids on the Block" puppets are used widely in elementary programs as well.

The decision was made to present an assembly program to all students in grades 6 through 12. The program would focus on such varied disabling conditions as dyslexia, paralysis, vision impairment, hearing loss, and speech impairment. In order to make the experience more personal, members of the student body were involved as much as possible.

The program was to be spearheaded by a group of selected regular education students who were to spend an entire school day experiencing a simulated disability. These students were to share basic experiences and perceptions with the rest of the student body 2 days later at an assembly program. The assembly program was to feature guest speakers who had personal experience with disabilities. In addition, the audience was to take part in several simulation activities.

Student and Faculty Involvement

In order to foster "ownership" among the student body, it was left to the student council to choose the students who would adopt simulated disabilities for a day. Goals and procedures were outlined

to the student council, along with the traits a student must have to participate. Participants were to be responsible, articulate, sensitive, and self-assured. The student council was given 1 week to locate volunteers.

At the first meeting with the 14 volunteers, goals and procedures were discussed in detail. The volunteers learned of their key role in representing the student body and generating interest in the assembly program. Each volunteer identified the disability he or she would prefer to adopt. Participants were given permission slips for their parents to sign; this not only assured parental approval but also brought the project to the attention of the community. A faculty member was recruited to spend the day in a wheelchair to help generate faculty interest and to ensure that someone would stimulate discussion when the volunteers shared their thoughts at the assembly.

Equipment

Once the volunteers were matched with their disabilities, equipment was located for the simulation day. Wheelchairs were borrowed from a nearby school for children with physical disabilities and from a local equipment rental business.

For a simulated visual impairment,

ophthalmic eye patches were used. These are more comfortable than masks and are more effective in blocking out light. It is important to understand however, that few people who are classified as blind have no vision at all.

Foam rubber earplugs were used to simulate a hearing impairment. However, since these did not block out enough sound, padded earphones (borrowed from the industrial arts shop and a local auto body shop) were added.

The speech and language clinician coached one of the volunteers in effecting a stutter. The student was to spend part of an evening at the local shopping mall attempting to communicate with store-keepers, and a friend was to go along as an observer.

Procedures

The special education staff met with the volunteers during the week prior to the simulations to examine equipment. The volunteers also received the following instructions for the day of the simulations:

1. Line up reliable helpers, if necessary, to take notes, help with lunch, and assist in moving from class to class.
2. Take the simulation seriously; imagine that this is a permanent disability and not something that can be abandoned at the end of the day.
3. Do not give up the simulation unless it becomes unbearably uncomfortable; if that should happen, do not feel guilty about quitting. Realize, nevertheless, that a person with a genuine disability cannot simply drop the disability.
4. Do not fool around, and do not tolerate any fooling around.
5. Take mental or written notes during the day about memorable events, feelings, reactions of others, and ways in which compensation was made.

A meeting was arranged with the faculty during the week prior to the simulation to outline the goals of the program and discuss the procedures. A list of student volunteers and their disabilities was distributed. Teachers were asked to adjust their routines in whatever ways they felt necessary to accommodate the needs of the volunteers.

Simulation Day

On the morning of the simulation, the volunteers met one half hour before school to review procedures, receive encouragement, and "gear up." Students in wheelchairs tied their legs to their chairs with towels. They were also given the option of having their arms tied to the chair; only one student accepted.

The volunteers went about their business with sincerity and determination. One student in a wheelchair painted with her teeth in art class. Another, who was "visually impaired," did writing assignments and took part in a geography lesson by feeling a globe and answering her teacher's questions about countries and continents. Others competed in physical education class in their wheelchairs.

> ## "In the movies, it's funny to see a blind person walk, but in real life it's not so funny."
> *a student simulating a visual impairment*

After school, the volunteers met with the special education staff for a debriefing. They were all exhausted, and they attributed their fatigue to the added stress of their "disabilities." They completed a questionnaire that they would use for reference at the assembly program. As they wrote, they talked about their experiences and their reactions. Their reflections are best expressed in a few of their own comments.

Students Reactions

- Visually Impaired

  "I felt left alone and very tired."

  "I felt stupid trying to eat."

  "In the movies, it's funny to see a blind person walk, but in real life it's not so funny."

- Hearing Impaired

  "I felt alone when everyone around me was talking and I had to sit there alone."

- Physically Disabled

  "I thought it would be easy. It wasn't."

  "My friends treated me like I was helpless, like I was blind and deaf, too. One person even talked louder."

"I felt afraid thinking that this could really happen to me or to someone I know."

"I realize that handicapped people want to be independent, yet they want respect and guidance when they ask for it or need it."

"Handicapped people have 100 times the amount of stress of the average person because they have to find a way to overcome their disability."

Teachers' Reactions

The teachers reactions to having these "disabled" students in their classrooms reflected their concerns:

"I became very conscious of having someone in the room who was unable to perform some of the basic tasks we take for granted."

"I was having to constantly do things that would include her, such as typing assignments."

"I realized how very cluttered the room was when the student in the wheelchair arrived."

One teacher adapted to a "deaf" student by making more use of the blackboard during discussion. In another class, the teacher tried to anticipate problems while making assignments and worried that the "disabled" student might be hurt, that someone might tease her, or that she might be a burden to her helper.

Some teachers and students volunteered to write for the "disabled" students. They required more attention, and other students were forced to adjust to having less access to the teacher.

There was even an occasional light-hearted moment. The vocal music instructor, who was preparing his choir for an upcoming concert, told the volunteers to park their wheelchairs and climb onto the risers. A student who actually does use a wheelchair responded, "Sounds good to me!"

The Disability Awareness Assembly

The assembly program took place 2 days after the simulations. In order to involve the audience in the program right from the start, they were handed a printed message as they entered the auditorium. The words on the page were distorted, as they might appear to someone with severe dyslexia. After the audience puzzled over the message for several minutes, the decoded message was revealed. The audience was told that many of the students who are placed in the resource room have dyslexia and experience daily the kind of frustration they had just experienced.

The first speaker was a student at a nearby college who discussed his experiences as an individual with dyslexia. As a way of sharing a sense of his frustration with written expression, he involved the audience in another simulation. He asked them to fold a piece of paper in fourths, hold it against their foreheads, and try to write their names on the paper with the hand they do not normally write with. A chorus of groans and exclamations testified that he had made his point.

Another college student spoke next. As a young college student, he had been injured in an accident that left him paralyzed. Despite his disability, he lives a full life; he drives his own van and sings in a popular local rock band. He told the students that he does not like labels because a label relieves others of the responsibility to discover who the person with

---

"I realized how very cluttered the room was when the student in the wheelchair arrived."

a teacher

---

a disability really is. The label provides a ready-made definition. He explained that it is important to get to know the person with a disability as a *person* first and foremost.

The next speaker, an itinerant teacher of pupils who have hearing impairments, introduced himself while imitating the speech of a person with a hearing impairment, signing as he talked. After several minutes of this, he abruptly began talking normally. A collective gasp rose from the audience, and many whispered, "How did he do that?" He discussed the problems encountered by those with a "hidden disability" such as a hearing loss. He then administered an unfair spelling test, in which the audience attempted to spell words from a recording that was intentionally distorted to simulate a hearing

impairment. Predictably, most became frustrated and gave up quickly.

The final speaker was an occupational therapist with the local area education agency, who walks with crutches due to childhood polio. She offered the following advice on how to interact with a person who has a disability: Don't allow your uneasiness to cause you to ignore the person. Don't be afraid to ask about the disability, but be tactful. And don't be afraid of the person with a disability. She emphasized that individuals with disabilities want their independence and suggested that people should ask them whether or not they would like help and in what form.

The assembly closed with comments from the student and teacher volunteers, who shared their experiences of being "disabled." A good deal of spontaneous dialogue developed between the guest speakers and the volunteers, all of which was revealing to the audience.

Audience Reaction

The students in the audience were attentive and appreciative of the assembly. Several stayed after the program to talk privately with the guest speakers. Many wrote them letters. Excerpts from a few of those letters best express the impact of the assembly:

"Although I'll never be able to really understand what (dyslexia) is like, I'll now be more aware of people's feelings."

"I know what it's like to be in a tough spelling bee and it's your turn to spell a word and your mind goes blank, but to deal with something like this every day of your life is something I don't think I'd be able to handle."

"I think maybe I thought being in a wheelchair meant popping wheelies all of the time, but because of your speech, I now understand. Thanks."

"When I see people in wheelchairs I usually think they're helpless, but your speech made me feel different about them. Now I know they are people, too, and they deserve to have their rights just as much as we do."

"You worked with me in third grade in occupational therapy. I'm a freshman now, and schoolwork is not too bad. In sports I'm out for football, basketball, baseball, and golf. In golf I made the varsity team, and out of the five guys on the team, I'm the third man."

"My best friend is one of your students, and I never realized what she has to go through until I heard your tape. I notice that when I'm talking to her, she's always looking at my lips. I asked her about this, and she said that sometimes she can hear me and sometimes she can't, so she just reads my lips all the time so she doesn't miss anything I say. Thank you for showing me what she's going through so that I can be a better friend."

The following letter, written by a resource room student to the speaker with dyslexia, speaks volumes:

I realy [sic] liked your speech at the high school. I could relate to some of your problems like being dyslexic. I was diagnosed as having a reading & spelling problem in the 5th grade but before that I was in Chapter I reading. In the past four years I've goton alot better at reading but I'm still in 7th grade level of spelling.

"I got a lot of teazing from the other kids, exspeshaly aftere I got on the B & B+ honer roles this year. They say the only reason I was on the honer role was because I was in the Retard room.

"Before your speech most of the other kids had no idea what we did in the resource room. After your speech I had a few kids apologize for saying what they said about me before."

Conclusion

The results of the disability simulations and the assembly program were pleasing. Of course, a 1-day simulation does not provide a full understanding of what it means to have a disability. It does, however, offer a glimpse of the feelings and needs of people with disabilities. The exercise by itself also highlights the need for increased awareness and sensitivity on the part of educators and students.

It is critical to include the student body and the teaching staff in the planning of an event such as this. Soliciting the help of the student council in recruiting simulation volunteers ensures that student leaders will be involved in sufficient numbers to support one another and legitimize the event. Teachers must be given enough advance notice to plan the necessary accommodations on simulation day.

Although the simulation volunteers did their job superbly and gained valuable insights from their experience, they were somewhat hesitant to share these reactions at the assembly. Despite the fact that the assembly took place in a small auditorium, students' voices are often soft and do not carry well. Therefore it is recommended that a microphone be used during the volunteer reaction segment of the assembly. The teacher volunteers must also be well aware of their importance in sharing their own thoughts and soliciting reactions from the student volunteers.

Equipment used in the simulations must be chosen with care. Wheelchair size must be matched closely with the size of each volunteer. Eye patches that block out virtually all light may not be necessary. Allowing participants to have limited vision would make them less dependent

---

"I felt alone when everyone around me was talking and I had to sit there alone."

a student simulating a hearing impairment

---

on helpers and allow them more opportunity to compensate. Finally, earphones become uncomfortable after several hours of wear; a combination of ear plugs and cotton might be a better alternative if this simulation activity is replicated.

References

Bookbinder, S. R. (1978). *Mainstreaming: What every child needs to know about disabilities*. Boston: The Exceptional Parent Press.

Dewar, R. L. (1982). Peer acceptance of handicapped students. *TEACHING Exceptional Children, 14,* 188–193.

Fiedler, C. R., & Simpson, R. L. (1987). Modifying the attitudes of nonhandicapped high school students toward handicapped peers. *Exceptional Children, 53,* 342–349.

Fox, C. L. (1982). *Handicapped...How does it feel?* Rolling Hills Estates, CA: B. L. Winch.

Kids on the Block. 9385-C Gerwig Lane, Columbia, MD 21046.

Martin, J., & Cashdollar, P. (1980). *Kids come in special flavors* workshop. Dayton, OH: The Kids Come in Special Flavors Co.

Riester, A. E., & Bessette, K. M. (1986). Preparing the peer group for mainstreaming exceptional children. *The Pointer, 31,* 12–20.

Simpson, R. L. (1980). Modifying the attitudes of regular class students toward the handicapped. *Focus on Exceptional Children, 13,* 1–11.

Early Childhood Special Education

Early childhood special educational services are relatively new. Head Start, Home Start, Project Follow-Through, and many other early childhood education programs were initiated in the United States in the 1960s as part of the "Great New Society" project of President Lyndon Johnson. Many of them were considered compensatory education programs. They supposedly compensated for an intellectually deprived home environment. Deprived homes usually meant poor or minority group homes. The concept of equating intellectual deprivation with poverty, or with any ethnic or racial minority group status, was controversial.

Special education in early childhood is very different philosophically from compensatory education in early childhood. Special educational services, or early intervention services, are defined as services to infants and toddlers who have a diagnosed physical or mental condition that has a high probability of resulting in a developmental delay, or has already resulted in a developmental delay. The developmental delay may be in cognitive, physical, language, speech, psychosocial, or self-help development. The early childhood intervention involves a sustained and systematic effort to assist the child with the risk of developmental delay, or the diagnosed delay, to overcome the existing problem to the greatest extent possible, and to prevent secondary problems from developing. The special educational service (early intervention) provided also assists the family of the child in multiple ways. While compensatory education programs focused on the needs of many children from the same environment (e.g., poor, minority groups), early childhood intervention programs focus on the special needs of each individual child and his or her unique family. Children at risk for, or with, developmental delays are found in all types of environments and backgrounds.

Early intervention for children with developmental delays or disabilities is considered vitally important. The central nervous system has more plasticity (ability to change) in infancy and early childhood. While therapy cannot always cure existing disabilities and delays, it can often reduce the impact of the problem. Children at risk for developmental delays or disabilities can sometimes be prevented from acquiring the expected problems. Additional problems that are secondary to the developmental disability or delay can also frequently be prevented from occurring. In addition, early intervention can appreciably reduce the stress on the family produced by the infant's developmental problems.

Early intervention is provided by a multidisciplinary team of professional therapists and by the affected infant's family. Family members as interventionists are crucial to the success of early childhood special education. Parents and other family members are taught how to help their infant or toddler by the professional team members. The professionals involved in each child's intervention team are determined by the child's special area of delay or disability. They may include physicians, nurses, social workers, psychologists, special educators, audiologists, speech/language pathologists, physical therapists, and/or occupational therapists.

Early childhood intervention may be provided in the infant's home, in a hospital or clinic-based program, in an early childhood special education center, or in combination programs.

Children who qualify for early childhood special education may be discovered in mass screenings. These are done routinely in hospital nurseries, well-child clinics, and the offices of pediatricians, pediatric nurse practitioners, and physician's assistants. They may also be referred for assessment by neighbors, friends, and family members. Child Find is a service that anyone can call to ask to have an infant or toddler assessed for possible developmental delays or disability.

When an infant or toddler qualifies for comprehensive multidisciplinary services under PL 99-457, program planning involves the development of an individualized family service plan (IFSP). This includes a statement about the infant's special needs, a statement about the family's strengths and needs, a list of desired goals, a list of specific services to be provided, the schedule for beginning and ending such services, the name of the case manager who will coordinate the services, and exit plans for a smooth transition from early childhood special services to services under PL 94-142, if necessary.

The first article selected for this unit on early childhood special education addresses the issue of providing special services for infants and toddlers in center-based programs that include children without disabilities or delays. Can PL 99-457 guidelines and IFSPs be followed in a mainstreamed infant day-care or preschool setting? The next article defines what kinds of assistive technology (such as computer software) might be appropriate for

special education in infancy and toddlerhood. The last article recommends toy libraries to help implement early special education and family-focused, home-based intervention.

Looking Ahead: Challenge Questions

Can the multidisciplinary early intervention team and the family provide high-quality special education services to a child with a developmental delay or disability in a center-based, mainstreamed, day-care or preschool program?

What are the ethical considerations of using assistive technology for infants and toddlers with delays or disabilities?

How important is play in early childhood special education? Can a toy library assure that more children, even those with disabilities, engage in play?

Mainstreaming During the Early Childhood Years

ABSTRACT: *Issues surrounding the implementation of the integration imperative during infancy and early childhood present formidable challenges to education and community providers. Key among these issues is how professionals provide high-quality services to young children with disabilities in mainstream environments. This article explores current issues related to integration and reexamines the concept of "best practices" as it applies to mainstreaming during the early childhood years. The author recommends an integrated set of indicators for high-quality programs and describes an outcomes-based process for making administrative and pedagogical decisions.*

CHRISTINE L. SALISBURY

CHRISTINE L. SALISBURY (CEC Chapter #0004) is an Associate Professor of Special Education in the School of Education and Human Development at the State University of New York at Binghamton.

When asked by a visitor what it was like having a child with disabilities in her kindergarten class, young Andrea looked puzzled. The visitor rephrased the question by asking whether the child with disabilities belonged in Andrea's class. Andrea answered, "Of course. He's five, isn't he?"

Andrea's implicit understanding of equity, entitlement, and accommodation have been fostered in an inclusive school context where children without disabilities assume that all classes contain friends with a range of abilities and needs. Why are some programs able to achieve a greater degree of integration than others? The answer lies, in part, in their commitment to the value of inclusion and their ability to incorporate desirable organizational and programmatic practices into complex education contexts.

Many programs across the United States are successfully mainstreaming young children with mild to profound disabilities in typical day-care, preschool, and early elementary settings (Guralnick, 1981; Hanline, 1990; Hoyson, Jamieson, & Strain, 1984; McLean & Hanline, 1990; Odom & Strain, 1984; Templeman, Fredericks, & Udell, 1989; Salisbury, 1989; Salisbury & Syryca, 1990; Strain, 1985). Others, however, face opposition, inaction, and frustration as they attempt to develop integrated school placement options at the local level (Gartner & Lipsky,

1987; Peck, Hayden, Wandschneider, Peterson, & Richarz, 1989).

One reason for these problems may be that although there are considerable data on the outcomes of specific interventions in integrated early childhood programs, remarkably little is known about how to apply this information to mainstreamed settings (Guralnick, 1990). This article focuses on integration during the early childhood years, with specific attention devoted to the notion of how predictors of high-quality programs themselves become integrated into service delivery systems.

INCLUSIVE PRACTICES, SUPPORTIVE SETTINGS

There is an essential, conceptual difference between inclusion and integration that has important implications for pedagogical practice and programmatic reform. Integration is the process by which physical, social, and academic opportunities are created for the child with a disability to participate with others in typical school or community environments (Taylor, Biklen, Lehr, & Searle, 1987). It is assumed that contextual supports are provided to maximize the probability of the child's success in the mainstream environment.

The social-cultural realities of integration are such that one group is viewed as the "mainstream" and one group is not; where one group must "push in" to the activities and settings occupied by the other. When students with disabilities are based in nonmainstream classrooms and are "allowed" to be incorporated into specific activities or lessons in mainstream environments, we implicitly endorse a value that says it is permissible to exclude them from age-appropriate placements. While integration is considered to be philosophically and educationally superior to segregation, such "push in" arrangements remain inherently hierarchical and unequal.

Inclusion, on the other hand, is a value that is manifested in the way we plan, promote, and conceptualize the education and development of young children. The underlying supposition in inclusive programs is that all children will be based in the classrooms they would attend if they did not have a disability. Teachers, students, parents, and administrators (in fact all stakeholders) define the school and classroom culture as including children with diverse backgrounds, abilities, and contributions.

In inclusive programs, the diverse needs of *all* children are accommodated to the maximum extent possible within the general education curriculum. Collaborative teaming and teaching, shared planning, transformational leadership, and an outcomes base provide the intentional framework for stakeholder success. Driven by a vision of schools as a place where all children learn well what we want them to learn, schools become creative and successful environments for adults and the children they serve (Chambers, Salisbury, Palombaro, & Cole, 1990; Salisbury, Pennington, Veech, & Palombaro, 1990; Salisbury & Syryca, 1990; Thousand & Villa, 1990).

Preliminary data from the Collaborative Education Project (Salisbury, 1991; Salisbury, Evans, Palombaro, & Veech, 1990) suggest that positive social and academic outcomes accrue to children with and without disabilities enrolled in an inclusive elementary school. The collaborative culture of such a school fosters a heightened sense of equity among peers without disabilities wherein they advocate for the inclusion of their classmates with disabilities and identify solutions to integration obstacles. In addition, building-level leadership is a critical factor in the success of programmatic reform. These data suggest that with proper philosophical, administrative, and instructional supports, young children with mild to profound disabilities can be appropriately based and served in classrooms they would attend if they did not have a disability.

Program policies, structures, and practices must be designed to support the inclusion of young children with disabilities in settings designed for their age peers without disabilities. Whether attending a program full- or part-time, young children with disabilities *should be included in, not integrated into,* age-appropriate mainstream environments. When supplementary aides and supports have been tried and found to be insufficient, then and only then should alternative service delivery options be considered. To maximize the likelihood of success, educators should employ those practices determined to be most directly linked to positive child and family outcomes in mainstream school and nonschool environments.

RE-THINKING THE NOTION OF "BEST PRACTICES"

Professionals in the field of special education often suggest that the way to optimize the likelihood of successful performance in mainstream environments is to implement generally acknowledged "best practices." At least three issues surface with such a proposition. First, use of the term *best* implies no need to get better and gives the impression that a well-defined, rather static corpus of information is accepted by the profession. Although an apparent consensus on a core of quality indicators has been reached by colleagues in early childhood education (Bredekamp, 1987), there is little indication that the same is true in the field of early childhood intervention.

Second, whether commonly cited practices are, in fact, "best" can only be answered on a relative basis and with an empirical grounding. Though convincing data exist to support the efficacy of specific strategies in mainstream environments, the data are insufficient to clearly identify any particular set of practices as "best."

Third, "best practices" in the field of special education have traditionally been generated from the special education perspective (e.g., McDonnell & Hardman, 1988; Meyer, Eichinger, & Park-Lee, 1987). The nature and language of these special education practices communicate a message that what we do is somehow very different from the rest of the early childhood profession. The inadvertent effect may be to create obstacles to collaboration with colleagues in general education where none were intended.

Fourth, perhaps an even more important question is, From which knowledge base or bases should we derive our "best practices"? Researchers have presented arguments in favor of creating one system of education for all children (Gartner & Lipsky, 1987; Stainback, Stainback, & Bunch, 1989; Will, 1986). Others have emphasized the importance of basing interventions on the routines, schedules, and activities of typical home and school settings (e.g., Bredekamp, 1987; Bricker & Cripe, 1990; Powell, 1989; Rainforth & Salisbury, 1988; Salisbury & Vincent, 1990). These two initiatives provide a useful benchmark for examining validated practices from mainstream settings at both administrative and instructional levels.

We can no longer assume that "best special education practices" are sufficient for ensuring the meaningful inclusion of young children with disabilities in mainstream contexts. Rather, it seems important that we examine validated practices found to be most directly linked to positive child outcomes in the general education and early childhood literatures and assess their applicability to children with special needs. Only then will we be able to determine what additional, specialized supports will be needed to maximize the probability of the child's success in a mainstream context. Adaptations embedded in the main-stream environment should be only as special as necessary to support children with and without disabilities and ensure educational benefit (Biklen, 1985). One essential question for parents, practitioners, administrators, and policy-makers becomes, What does the child, any child, need to succeed?

INDICATORS OF PROGRAM QUALITY

Given the importance of understanding the main-stream environment as a context for integration, it seems appropriate to ask: What are valid and useful indicators of program quality?

Indicators from General Education

Recently, two cogent analyses in the general education literature have addressed this question. Stedman (1987) analyzed the effective schools literature and concluded that the formula typically used for program evaluation could not be substantiated by the research. Using stringent selection criteria, he generated nine broad categories of practices that could be empirically supported by the effective schools research literature. These nine categories and their key indicators included school and classroom practices that were directly related to positive learner outcomes. Each of Stedman's key indicators was supported in a recent, large-scale analysis of the elementary and secondary schooling literature (e.g., Oakes, 1989).

Contending that indicators of school context are as necessary as indexes of student outcomes, Oakes (1989) analyzed the elementary and secondary schooling research literature and identified three global school conditions that were empirically related to student outcomes. Viewed as enabling conditions related to the attainment of high-quality teaching and learning, these three conditions and their key indicators (practices) reflect concrete decisions by schools about how to "distribute resources, what structures to create, and what processes, norms, and relationships to establish at the school" (Oakes, 1989, p. 186). Table 1 represents an integration of Stedman and Oakes' indicators.

These practices may well provide an important benchmark against which we can assess various practices recommended for infants, toddlers, and preschool age children with and without disabilities. The conceptual and developmental underpinnings among these three literatures will clearly vary. However, if we are able to ascertain where significant pedagogical differences do exist, we may then be able to address attitudes and practices that hinder efforts to integrate and include young children with disabilities in typical settings.

Indicators from Early Childhood Education

Guidelines for developmentally appropriate practice in early childhood settings were recently generated by the National Association for Education of Young Children (NAEYC) (Bredekamp, 1987). These guidelines are a blend of empirical and conceptual literatures that provide information on pedagogical practices related to infants, toddlers, and preschool age children without disabilities. Despite the comprehensive nature of these guidelines, the author(s) devoted little attention to the organizational issues included in the Stedman and Oakes analyses. The comparison in Table 1 provides a preliminary index of the commonalities among the two literatures on children without disabilities.

Indicators from Early Childhood Special Education

Because there has been limited research on the applicability of early childhood practices to children with disabilities, comparisons are limited to the form, rather than function, of these school practices. Given this limitation, what is the relationship of this information to typically cited "best practices" in the field of early childhood intervention? Researchers have described correlates of high-quality, integrated special education (e.g., Gaylord-Ross, 1989; Stainback et al., 1989) and early childhood intervention programs (e.g., Bricker & Veltman, 1990; McDonnell & Hardman, 1988; McCollum & McCartan, 1986). Table 1 depicts these indicators and their relationship to the recommended practices from the early childhood and general education literatures.

Reflections on Quality Indicators

Three observations can be made of these comparisons:

- Recommended practices in early childhood education appear generally consistent with many of the indicators from general education. While the practices related to positive child outcomes underlying these two research bases may be enacted differently, their intent may well be similar.

- Early childhood intervention practices share a general concordance with those in early childhood education. Despite differing theoretical foundations (Odom & McEvoy, 1990), there may be greater consonance in actual practice than typically assumed. Our work, in an inclusive elementary school (see next section) indicates that teaming structures, shared planning time, and a consensus on desired outcomes provides sufficient basis for the resolution of pedagogical differences.

- There were numerous areas of consistency between the early childhood intervention and general education practices.

TABLE 1
Comparison of Quality Indicators From General and Special Education

General Education	Early Childhood Education	Early Childhood Special Education
Curriculum		
Rich program content	Concrete, real, and relevant materials and activities	Functional
Appropriate materials and equipment	Developmentally appropriate	Age-appropriate
		Attuned to current and future needs
Applied, enrichment activities	Integrated content	Integrated content and setting
Cultural pluralism	Values/respects diversity	Values uniqueness of individual
Adult-Child Interactions		
Success-focused teaching	Facilitates child success	Intentional, concurrent instruction
Teaching to prevent learning problems		Prevention and remediation of learning difficulties
Accepting environment	Accepting and responsive environment	Responsive to learner needs
Engaged time	Facilitated engagement	Optimize engaged time
Student centered	Child initiated and directed	Child and family centered
Integrated supports	Meet diverse needs	Individualized, integrated teaching and therapy
Grouping practices	Age-based groupings	Heterogeneous grouping; role of peers
Clear program goals	Assess for program planning	Assess for program planning
Evaluation of student program progress	Evaluate for curriculum effectiveness	Programming changes based on formative evaluation
	Multiple sources of information	Variety of outcome measures
Home and School Relationships		
Community and parent participation	Family involvement	Family focus
	Regular communication	Systematic communication
Shared governance among parents and teachers	Role in decisions and planning	Full partners in planning and decision making
	Support to family	
	Coordinated sharing of information	Support to family
		Transition planning
Structure, Staffing, and Organization		
Strong leadership		
Well-trained teachers	Properly trained staff	Integrated preparation and experiences
Use of staff and resources	Adequate staff-child ratios	Individualized instruction
Program improvement, professional renewal	Continuing professional development	Professional development required and promoted
Collaborative staff planning, sharing, teamwork	Coordinated sharing of information	Comprehensive, collaborative teaming and decision making
		Parent and professional team membership
Clear building, program, and student goals		Outcome focused; integrated setting
Administrative support		Administrative support
Faculty beliefs about teaching and learning	Staff beliefs about children, families, and learning	Beliefs about children, families, teaching and learning
Positive, supporting school climate	Respect, accept, and value children's actions	Educative approaches; naturalistic teaching

Note: Where no entries are noted, specific reference to indicator was not evident in material reviewed.
Sources: For general education, Stedman (1987) and Oakes (1989); for early childhood education, Bredekamp (1987); for early childhood special education, Gaylord-Ross (1989), Stainback, Stainback, and Bunch (1989), Bricker and Veltman (1990), McDonnell and Hardman (1988), and McCollum and McCartan (1986).

FIGURE 1
Components and Organization of the Outcomes-Driven Developmental Model

OUTCOMES-DRIVEN DEVELOPMENTAL MODEL

MISSION: ALL STUDENTS WILL LEARN WELL

STUDENT OUTCOMES

SELF-ESTEEM • THINKING • SELF-DIRECTED LEARNER • PROCESS SKILLS • CONCERN FOR OTHERS

ADMINISTRATIVE SUPPORTS	COMMUNITY SUPPORTS	CLASSROOM SUPPORTS
STAFF DEVELOPMENT MODEL	BOARD POLICY	INSTRUCTIONAL PROCESS
COMMUNICATIONS NETWORK	BOARD SUPPORT	CURRICULUM ORGANIZATION
PROBLEM-SOLVING MODEL	COMMUNITIES	SCHOOL PRACTICES
CHANGE PROCESS	NETWORKING	CLASSROOM PRACTICES
CLIMATE IMPROVEMENT MODEL		ORGANIZATIONAL STRUCTURES
PHILOSOPHICAL BASE	**PSYCHOLOGICAL BASE**	**TRANSFORMATIONAL LEADERSHIP**

RESEARCH LITERATURE

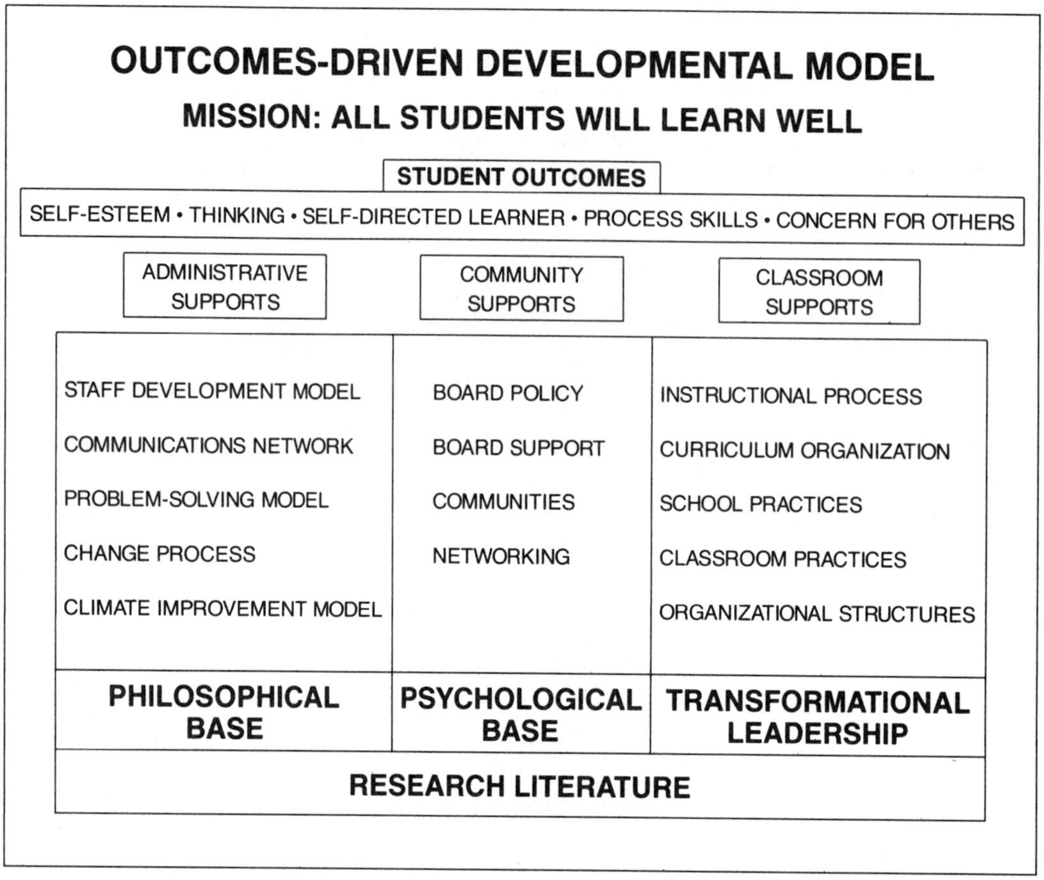

Insofar as these similarities exist, there appears to be at least a preliminary basis for considering a merger of desirable program practices from general and special education.

ASSIMILATING INDICATORS INTO SYSTEMS

Identifying discrete contextual indicators is an important policy, program development, and research issue (Oakes, 1989), but educators also need to identify effective processes for assimilating this information into programs. Practices, as well as children, must be integrated if we are to effectively meet the needs of all learners in mainstream contexts. The identification of discrete integration strategies is necessary, but not sufficient, for the development of an inclusive school and classroom climate. These validated strategies must be integrated into a framework that provides both process and outcome guidance for those wishing to initiate educational reform. Such a framework exists in outcome-based education programs.

Outcomes-Driven Developmental Model

For the past 5 years, the Johnson City Central School District in New York has provided administrative and school supports to ensure the "rein-

tegration" and inclusion of students with mild to profound disabilities in age-appropriate, elementary school classrooms (Salisbury, 1989; Salisbury & Syryca, 1990; Salisbury, Pennington, Veech, & Palombaro, 1990). The district's nationally validated Outcomes-Driven Developmental Model (ODDM) (Mamary, 1985) incorporates many practices endorsed in the effective schools literature, yet embeds these practices within an organizational framework of outcomes-based education (Blum, 1985; Purkey & Smith, 1983). Figure 1 shows this model and the breadth of contextual supports available for all faculty and students in the district.

A key feature of ODDM is the decision-making model used at the classroom, building, and district levels. The model presumes that only when staff and administrators have reached consensus on the outcomes they want for all children can they examine enabling practices, beliefs, and knowledge for their role in helping to attain those outcomes. At the heart of this model is the consensually derived vision to which all stakeholders in the school aspire. Figure 2 shows the components of the decision-making model.

Application to Integration

The following is a summary of how this model

FIGURE 2
Vision-Based Decision-Making Model

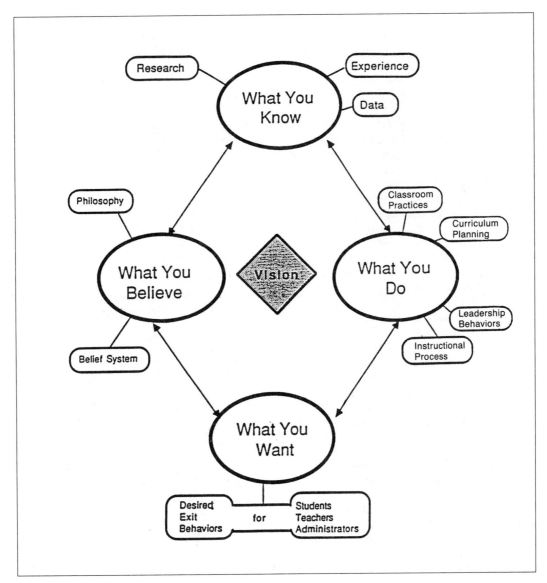

may be applied to the development of high-quality practices in mainstream settings.

What do we want? Yogi Berra once said, "If you don't know where you're going, you probably won't get there." Sound planning is predicated on what one wishes to achieve. At the Harry L. Johnson Elementary School, teachers, aides, parents, children, and building support staff have achieved consensus on a vision of inclusive education (Chambers, et al., 1990). The vision is the beckoning target to which all staff dedicate their efforts; it serves as a source of motivation, guidance, and renewal. Specific, measurable outcomes help index progress toward the attainment of that vision. The outcomes agreed to by staff in this district (see Figure 1) are among those described as quality indicators by Oakes (1989) and others.

Collaboration at the district, school, and class-room level helps ensure that actions are directed toward the attainment of shared goals. The processes for collaborative decision making are available in the leadership (e.g., Bennis & Nanus, 1985) and general education (e.g., Purkey & Smith, 1983) literatures and have recently emerged in special education (e.g., Bauwens, Hourcade, & Friend, 1989; Pearpoint, 1989; Pugach & Johnson, 1989; Thousand & Villa, 1990).

What do we know? This information is used to assess the validity of current policies and practices and serves as a source of information for developing the belief base. If, for example, staff believe that individualized instruction or family-focuses practices are important for attaining desired outcomes, then literatures from a variety of disciplines may need to be reviewed to ascertain what specific practices will most likely promote desired child and family outcomes. Knowledge of validated practices can then be used to evaluate current program practices. In the process, policies that constrain and/or foster the use of desirable practices will also become evident. In some cases, staffing patterns will need to be changed to support the attainment of desired outcomes.

What do we believe? The staff in the district developed consensus around 10 beliefs related to excellence in teaching and learning. Among these beliefs were a commitment to cooperative teaching and learning, inclusive programs, and criterion-referenced learning. Because there is an interaction between values and beliefs grounded in knowledge, staff members arrived at consensus using many sources of information (e.g., experience, research literature, and philosophy). Once faculty commit themselves to a set of beliefs, it is easier to distinguish future criticisms of practice from faltering beliefs.

Reaching consensus on accommodations for children with disabilities sometimes raises philosophical, as well as logistical, issues (Salisbury, & Syryca, 1990; Salisbury et al., 1990). Individualized instruction in mainstream settings necessitates joint planning and a shared commitment to the inclusion of children with special needs. It is unlikely that all staff will share an equal level of commitment to inclusion or integration, but all should have shared in the process of reaching consensus on outcomes and beliefs. It is, therefore, appropriate and reasonable to expect that all staff will support the implementation of program practices to promote those outcomes. Salisbury and Bricker (1991) suggested that only when administrators and staff move from action based on compliance to action grounded in commitment will current barriers to program quality be substantively addressed.

What do we do? In other words, is what you are doing getting you what you want? It may be that some practices must be abandoned, others improved, while still others have yet to be incorporated. The teaming structures, master schedule, and nature of instructional activities have changed at Harry L. Johnson Elementary School as we have assessed these practices and supports against the outcomes (e.g., inclusion, concern for others) we want for all children in this school.

CONCLUSION

Program quality is largely based on the extent to which knowledge, beliefs, and practices are aligned to produce desired outcomes. Collaborative research and program models are needed to ensure that all children benefit from integrated opportunities in their neighborhood communities. The decision-making model described here

builds on many factors that are empirically linked to positive child outcomes and has been effective in developing internally consistent program practices. As such, it may well prove useful to those who are facing the challenges of developing and implementing integrated and inclusive programs in community-based, early childhood setting.

REFERENCES

Bauwens, J., Hourcase, J. J., & Friend, M. (1989). Cooperative teaching: A model for general and special education integration. *Remedial and Special Education, 10*(2), 17-24.

Bennis, W., & Nanus, B. (1985). *Leaders: Strategies for taking charge.* New York: Harper & Row.

Biklen, D. (1985). *Achieving the complete school.* New York: Teachers College Press.

Blum, R. E. (1985). Outcome-based schools: A definition. *Outcomes, 5*(1), 1-5.

Bredekamp, S. (Ed.). (1987). *Developmentally appropriate practice in early childhood programs serving children from birth through age 8.* Washington, DC: National Association for the Education of Young Children.

Bricker, D. D., & Cripe, J. (1990). Activity-based intervention. In D. Bricker (Ed.), *Early intervention for at-risk and handicapped infants, toddlers, and preschool children* (pp. 251-274). Palo Alto, CA: VORT.

Bricker, D. D., & Veltman, M. (1990). Early intervention programs: Child focused approaches. In J. Shonkoff & S. Meisels (Eds.), *Handbook of early intervention* (pp. 373-399). London: Cambridge University Press.

Chambers, A., Salisbury, C., Palombaro, M., & Cole, G. (1990). *Developing commitment to inclusive educational practices.* Manuscript in preparation.

Gartner, A., & Lipsky, D. K. (1987). Beyond special education: Toward a quality system for all students. *Harvard Education Review, 57*(4), 367-395.

Gaylord-Ross, R. (1989). *Integration strategies for students with handicaps.* Baltimore: Paul H. Brookes.

Guralnick, M. J., (1981). The efficacy of integrating handicapped children in early education settings: Research implications. *Topics in Early Childhood Special Education, 1*(1), 57-72.

Guralnick, M. J. (1990). Major accomplishments and future directions in early childhood mainstreaming, *Topics in Early Childhood Special Education, 10*(2), 1-17.

Hanline, M. F. (1990). A consulting model for providing integration opportunities for preschool children with disabilities. *Journal of Early Intervention, 14*(4), 360-366.

Hoyson, M., Jamieson, B., & Strain, P. S. (1984). Individualized group instruction for normally developing and autistic-like children: The LEAP curriculum. *Journal of the Division for Early Childhood, 8,* 157-172.

Mamary, A. (1985). *The Outcomes-Driven Developmental Model.* Johnson City, NY: Johnson City Central School District.

McCollum, J., & McCartan, K. (1986). Research in teacher education: Issues and future directions for early childhood special education. In S. Odom & M. Karnes (Eds.), *Early intervention for infants and children with handicaps* (pp. 269-286). Baltimore: Paul H. Brookes.

McDonnell, A., & Hardman, M. (1988). A synthesis of "best practice" guidelines for early childhood services. *Journal of the Division for Early Childhood, 12*(4), 328-341.

McLean, M. B., & Hanline, M. F. (1990). Providing early intervention services in integrated environments: Challenges and opportunities for the future. *Topics in Early Childhood Special Education, 10*(2), 62-77.

Meyer, L. H., Eichinger, J., & Park-Lee, S. (1987). A validation of program quality indicators in educational services for students with severe disabilities. *Journal of the Association for Persons with Severe Handicaps, 12*(4), 251-263.

Oakes, J. (1989). What educational indicators? The case for assessing the school context. *Educational Evaluation and Policy Analysis, 11*(2), 181-199.

Odom, S. L., & McEvoy, M. A. (1990). Mainstreaming at the preschool level: Potential barriers and tasks for the field. *Topics in Early Childhood Special Education, 10*(2), 48-61.

Odom, S. L., and Strain, P. S. (1984). Peer mediated approaches to increasing children's social interaction: A review. *American Journal of Orthopsychiatry, 54,* 544-557.

Pearpoint, J. (1989). Reflections on a quality education for all students. In S. Stainback, W. Stainback, & M. Forest (Eds.), *Educating all students in the mainstream of regular education* (pp. 249-254). Baltimore: Paul H. Brookes.

Peck, C. A., Hayden, L., Wandschnieder, M., Peterson, K., & Richarz, S. (1989). Development of integrated preschools: A qualitative inquiry into sources of resistance among parents, administrators, and teachers. *Journal of Early Intervention, 13*(4), 353-363.

Powell, D. R. (1989). *Families and early childhood programs.* Washington, DC: National Association for the Education of Young Children.

Pugach, M. & Johnson, L. J. (1989). The challenge of implementing collaboration between general and special education. *Exceptional Children, 56,* 232-235.

Purkey, S. D., & Smith, M. S. (1983). Effective schools: A review. *Elementary School Journal, 83*(4), 427-452.

Rainforth, B., & Salisbury, C. L. (1988). Functional home programs: A model for therapists. *Topics in Early Childhood Special Education, 7*(4), 33-45.

Salisbury, C. L. (1989). *Translating commitment into practice: Evolution of the SUNY Binghamton-Johnson City Collaborative Education Project.* Paper presented at the Office of Special Education Programs Project Officer's meeting topical session on Integration Education: State of Implementation and Future Directions, Washington, DC.

Salisbury, C. L. (1991, May). *Empirical evidence in support of inclusion.* Presentation at the Maryland State Education Department Conference on Inclusive Education, Baltimore.

Salisbury, C. L., & Bricker, D. D. (1991). Preface—Special issue on implementation of PL 99-457, Part H. *Journal of Early Intervention, 15*(1), 3-4.

Salisbury, C. L., Evans, I. M., Palombaro, M. M., & Veech, G. (1990). *Classroom ecology in an inclusive elementary school: Focus on instructional and social interactions.* Paper presented at the national conference of The Association for Persons with Severe Handicaps, Chicago.

Salisbury, C. L., Pennington, J., Veech, G., & Palombaro, M. M. (1990). *Teaming and teaching in an inclusive school: The perspectives of regular education.* Paper presented at the national conference of The Association for Persons with Severe Handicaps, Chicago.

Salisbury, C. L., & Syryca, S. (1990). *Social and instructional interactions in kindergarten classrooms serving students with severe disabilities.* Presentation at the International Division for Early Childhood conference, Albuquerque, NM.

Salisbury, C. L., & Vincent, L. J. (1990). Criterion of the next environment and best practices: Mainstreaming and integration 10 years later. *Topics in Early Childhood Special Education, 10*(2), 78-89.

Stainback, W., Stainback, S., & Bunch, G. (1989). A rationale for the merger of regular and special education. In S. Stainback, W. Stainback, & M. Forest (Eds.), *Educating all students in the mainstream of regular education* (pp. 15-28). Baltimore: Paul H. Brookes.

Stedman, L. C. (1987, November). It's time we changed the effective schools formula. *Phi Delta Kappan,* 215-224.

Strain, P. S. (1985). Social and nonsocial determinants of acceptability in handicapped preschool children. *Topics in Early Childhood Special Education, 4,* 47-58.

Taylor, S., Biklen, D., Lehr, S., & Searle, S. (1987). *Purposeful integration . . . Inherently equal.* Syracuse, NY: Center on Human Policy, Syracuse University.

Templeman, T. P., Fredericks, H. D., & Udell, T. (1989). Integration of children with moderate and severe handicaps into a daycare center. *Journal of Early Intervention, 13*(4), 315-328.

Thousand, J. S., & Villa, R. A. (1990). Strategies for educating learners with severe disabilities within their local home schools and communities. *Focus on Exceptional Children, 23*(3), 1-24.

Will, M. (1986). *Educating students with learning problems—A shared responsibility.* Washington, DC: U.S. Department of Education, Office of Special Education and Rehabilitation Services.

Preparation of the article was supported in part by Grant 86D-00009 from the U. S. Department of Education, Special Education Programs, to the State University of New York-Binghamton. The opinions expressed herein do not necessarily reflect those of the U. S. Department of Education, and no official endorsement should be inferred. I thank Drs. Samuel Odom and Beverly Rainforth, as well as colleagues Art Chambers and Mary Palombaro, for helpful comments on an earlier draft.

Children With Disabilities Who Use Assistive Technology: Ethical Considerations

Loreta Holder-Brown and Howard P. Parette, Jr.

Loreta Holder-Brown, Ph.D., has been a leader in personnel preparation, training teachers and related service professionals. Loreta is a professor of special education at the University of Alabama, where she chairs the Program for Orthopedically Handicapped and Other Health Impaired in the Area of Special Education.

Howard P. Parette, Jr., Ph.D., has given national and international presentations and has published extensively in the area of technology service delivery for young children with disabilities.

Loreta Holder-Brown

Technology is increasingly being used by all children in our society to enhance educational opportunities and quality of life. Interactive computer programs and self-correcting/programmed learning games are commonplace in many classrooms for young children. Velcro fasteners on shoes and jackets enable children to successfully dress themselves. Tape recorders and listening stations allow teachers to individualize instruction for one child while working with other children in group activities. Such inexpensive technologies that do not require sophisticated skills to use are readily available.

Although technology is important for all children, it is especially critical for children with disabilities who depend on assistive technology for mobility, communication, and learning. The impetus for the use of technology with these children evolves from the passage of Public Law (P.L.) 101–476, the *Individuals with Disabilities Education Amendments of 1990.* This legislation amends P.L. 99–457, the *Education of the Handicapped Amendments of 1986,* through which states could provide early intervention services to children who have developmental disabilities, children who are at risk, and their families. This legislation expands the scope of services that may be provided to young children with disabilities and identifies assistive technology as a specific service that is provided to young children. The law also mandates that these children be served in the least restrictive environment. These mandates have implications not only specific to the implementation of programs serving young children who have disabilities but also for regular child care and education programs, such as Head Start (which for many years required that children with disabilities compose 10% of the service population).

Definition of assistive technology

"Assistive technology" may be defined as any item, device, or piece of equipment that is used to increase, maintain, or improve the functional abilities of persons with disabilities [P.L. 100–407, *Technology Related Assistance for Individu-*

als with Disabilities Act of 1988, 29 U.S.C. 2202, Section 3(1)]. Assistive technologies for children with disabilities range from such simple devices as adapted spoons and switch-adapted, battery-operated toys to complex devices such as computerized environmental control systems. These items, devices, or equipment may be commercially made, acquired off the shelf, or customized. The definition of assistive technology in P.L. 101–476 is consistent with that in P.L.

ethical considerations emerge that should be of concern.

Ethics and technology

As personnel in child care, Head Start, kindergarten, and other preschool settings provide services to young children with disabilities, these personnel will be involved with occupational therapists, physical therapists, speech/language pathologists, nurses, and

ment of other professionals (e.g., the occupational therapist, physical therapist, or speech/language pathologist) (Parette, Hourcade, & VanBiervliet, in press). These professionals may see the child and her needs from a different and more limited perspective than do early childhood educators who are trained to view the "whole child."

Like all areas of human endeavor, the use of technology in preschool and other early childhood settings must be guided by values and philosophies (Cavalier, 1986; Weinrich & Gerstein, 1987). Many important ethical considerations should guide early childhood professionals as they identify or adapt technologies for young children with disabilities such as cerebral palsy, spina bifida, visual impairment, or hearing impairment. These considerations are described below.

Increasingly, young children with disabilities will be afforded opportunities to participate in early childhood education settings. Dissemination of information relating to the use of assistive technologies is expected to increase, too.

100–407. The concepts found in these mandates not only open new vistas for children with disabilities but present new challenges for all professionals who provide services to preschool children.

Emerging challenge to early childhood professionals

Day care providers and other professionals will frequently be required to participate in the development and implementation of programs for preschoolers who are disabled (see "DEC Position Statement on Goal One of America 2000" on next page). Familiarity with assistive technologies will be of considerable importance to these providers as they participate in team decision-making processes (Parette, Hourcade, & VanBiervliet, in press). As caregivers and other teachers begin to acquire an expanded information base regarding assistive technologies, they must, in turn, use this information to aid in selecting and using equipment in their settings. In this process, certain

parents. Part of the team's assignment is to ensure that all dimensions of the child's present levels of performance are considered. This team approach is most effective when persons having expertise in instructional programming, including technology and its applications, work cooperatively with parents and early childhood professionals who provide the children's day-to-day care and education.

Serving as part of a team

Personnel in early childhood programs for the nondisabled will be required by law to participate in multidisciplinary team processes and may be expected to assume important responsibilities as team members. Unfortunately, many professionals have had inadequate training and/or experience with technology and its applications. When professionals are not prepared for the responsibility of selecting devices for children and using them in service settings, they may rely too heavily on the judg-

Selection of appropriate technology

"Appropriateness" has several dimensions. P.L. 99–457 was defined to encompass any need the child has relating to learning and/or development, including the need to learn basic self-help skills and to develop appropriate social interaction, cognitive, and language skills. Assistive technologies can play critical roles in assuring not only the provision of appropriate learning experiences in these areas but also the child's mobility or ability to communicate.

From a more traditional perspective, a technology is appropriate for all children when its application meets one of three criteria.

First, a technology should respond to (or anticipate) specific, clearly defined goals that result in enhanced skills for the child.

Second, a technology should be compatible with practical constraints, such as available resources or the amount of training required to enable the child, his family, and the early childhood educator to use the technology.

Third, a technology should result in desirable and sufficient outcomes (Office of Technology Assessment, 1982).

Some basic considerations for children with disabilities are related to (1) ease of training the child and his family to use and care for the technology; (2) reasonable maintenance and repair, with regard to time and expense; and (3) monitoring of the technology's effectiveness.

Maintenance of a child focus. During the process of identifying the child's needs, developing a plan, and securing funding for assistive technology, professionals sometimes have a tendency to let the interesting technology, rather than the child and her educational needs, become the focus of attention. For example, a talking computer with a colorful display could capture the attention of team members and be recommended for use even if a less sophisticated approach might be more effective. Technology is not an end in itself; it is a means to provide increased experiences, opportunities, and independence for children who have disabilities. When used in early childhood settings, technology should generally facilitate gradual behavior changes in the child that are observable and have social validity (Evans & Meyer, 1985; Snell & Bowden, 1986).

Limited knowledge of the technology. Given the many types of technology that are available, it is difficult, if not impossible, for any one person to remain informed of all new technological developments that might potentially be appropriate for a child. This may result in the professional's recommendation of a familiar technology that may not be the most appropriate to meet the child's needs. It is

---

DEC Position Statement on Goal One of America 2000

The Division for Early Childhood (DEC) of the Council for Exceptional Children (CEC) developed a position statement on America 2000 and the first goal: "All children will start school ready to learn." They requested NAEYC support for this position statement, and it was given after staff review that confirmed that the statement is congruent with existing NAEYC position statements. The position statement is reproduced below.

"Schools should be ready to accept and effectively educate all children. Schooling will succeed or fail, not children.

When we say *all* children, we do mean all—including children with disabilities, children placed at-risk for school failure, children of poverty, children who are non-English speaking, children with gifts and talents.

Reaching Goal One requires healthy and competent parents, wanted and healthy babies, decent housing, and adequate nutrition.

Quality early education and child care should be a birth right for all children. These services must be comprehensive, coordinated, focused on individual family and child needs, and available to all families that need and choose to use them.

It is not appropriate to screen children into or out of early education programs. All children must be given a legitimate opportunity to learn.

Education in the 21st century must attend to children's social and emotional growth and development, not merely focus on academic outcomes.

Early educators must be schooled in and encouraged to use a wide variety of developmentally appropriate curricula, materials, and procedures to maximize each child's growth and development.

Achieving long-term academic goals does not imply that young children be drilled in English, science, and math. These academic goals are best achieved when young children are provided with environments that encourage their eager participation, exploration, and curiosity about the world.

No important social aims are ever achieved by rhetoric. Reaching this goal will require strong and continuing leadership, a wise investment in human and related capital, and collaboration between families, service providers, government, and business."

---

crucial to explore all reasonable technology options before recommending an approach. Because a large number of human and environmental factors exist that can affect technology selection and usage, and given the wide range of assistive technologies available, it is important to use a multidisciplinary approach. The strengths of each discipline's knowledge base can then be used to increase the probability that the most effective educational or early intervention solution will be developed for each child. It is important for personnel and parents to use technical assistance centers that provide information and training with regard to the use of technology for children with disabilities, as well as vendors and professionals (e.g., orthotists, prosthetists, and computer consultants) to gain more information about appropriate and available technology.

Developmental relevance. Although attitudes toward technology are changing, personnel working in early childhood programs may view a particular kind of technology as a means of entertaining a child (Childers & Podemski, 1984; Griffin, Gillis, & Brown, 1986). The use of computers is an excellent example. Many times computers are not incorporated into the curriculum for the child but instead are used merely to keep the child occupied. Educators of the nondisabled often face the same problems with technology. Computers, televisions, and other technology can be and often are used inappropriately with nondisabled children as well as with disabled children. Early childhood educators are continually faced with making optimal use of technology to provide appropriate programming on the developmental level of young children. The same rigorous standards of developmental appropriateness applied to other strategies and materials must be applied to the use of assistive technologies not only for children who have disabilities but for all children.

Often education for children with disabilities may be as simple as enabling a child who has cerebral palsy to write by modifying a pencil. One trap to avoid with children with disabilities involves the recommendation of an assistive device that does little to promote long-term increased independence. For example, encouraging the use of a wheelchair because transporting a child using a wheelchair is easier than teaching the child to use a walker or other support devices may be detrimental. Extended inappropriate use of a wheelchair may result in atrophy of leg muscles and perhaps prevent the child from learning less restrictive means of mobility in the future.

Self-perception and the perception of others. In our society people have had a tendency to focus on children's disabilities rather than on their abilities, thus contributing to the belief that these children are abnormal or deviant and have less worth than able-bodied persons. It is important that assistive technologies do not unnecessarily draw attention to disabilities but rather assist the child to more fully participate in friendships and activities. In some instances this will mean selecting an assistive technology that will be most accepted in the child's environment, rather than the technology that best performs the task. For example, a head pointer (i.e., a rod attached to a headband or helmet) might be technically the best approach for a child to access a computer keyboard; however, it may make the child look different and subject him to ridicule. The child could use a keyguard, touch screen, light pen, or scanner to serve the same purpose and be accepted more readily by peers, family, and the public.

Dignity of choice. Efforts must be made to select and apply technology in a manner that acknowledges and promotes individual dignity and the opportunity for personal choice (Pfrommer, 1984; Guess, Benson, & Siegel-Causey, 1985; Cavalier, 1988). Children and their families have a right and a responsibility to actively participate in the educational planning process. Some people think that only specialists—for example, occupational and physical therapists—have the necessary knowledge and experience to make decisions about which technology to use, but the desires of the child and his family are also relevant. The child and his family have unique expertise concerning their activities, their goals, and the environment in which they live. Failure to use this expertise may result in the failure of the assistive technology to meet the needs of the child and his family. For example, failure to provide the child and his family the opportunity to choose the "voice" characteristics of a communication system may result in the child's reluctance or refusal to independently use the device (Parette & VanBiervliet, 1990). In addition, ignoring child and parental desires or failing to even ask them questions conveys the message that they are unimportant in the educational process. Encouraging participation in the decision-making process does not mean presenting the child and her parents with a plan and asking for their consent; encouraging participation implies sharing assessment information, information relating to strengths and weaknesses of all of the alternatives, and encouraging and facilitating the family's active participation in the creation of a plan.

Charity. Since the nineteenth century, when schools for the deaf and the blind were founded, many people have considered children with disabilities as burdens of public charity (Wolfensberger, 1969); hence, some people believe that these children should be grateful for the charity they receive. Any technology that is then prescribed is viewed as being better than nothing. This may result in the use, or attempted use, of a technology because it is available (e.g., donated by a local vendor) rather than appropriate. Basing decisions regarding assistive technologies primarily on the child's need for that technology to improve or maintain her functional abilities across environments is critical.

Limitations imposed on the technology. Unfortunately, many technologies that are acquired for children with disabilities are viewed as school property instead of technology that increases the independence and functioning of the child *across environments.* Augmentative communication systems are an excellent example and are often purchased for use only in the early childhood program setting. The use of the technology may be further limited to specific times (e.g., the child may be able to use the technology only when she is working on language skills with the speech pathologist). The child is then unable to communicate except in those settings at specified times. When the child enters another environment or returns home, she has no means of expressing her needs, wants, or ideas. Limiting the child's access to assistive technologies that are crucial to functioning across environments will disrupt learning and severely limit learning opportunities. Personnel working in early childhood settings must consider the child's total needs when developing and implementing program plans involving assistive technology and ensure easy access to the assistive technology in all environments.

Individual rights and social equity. Problems in obtaining full funding of P.L. 99–457 and other service initiatives may result in administrators' reluctance to embrace the idea of providing expensive technologies to young children with disabilities (Mendelsohn, 1989). Because most preschool and early childhood programs have limited funds, resources must be used in an efficient manner. This implies the need to examine a range of technologies that might be appropriate for a particular child, and to give the cost factor careful consideration. The most expensive technologies are not always the best ones to meet the needs of young children with disabilities. Frequently, the most appropriate

choice is a low-tech solution requiring minimal training and low maintenance. It is crucial to remember, however, that the first priority in the selection of assistive technologies for all children must be the technology's appropriateness for meeting the child's educational and life goals.

Conclusions

Increasingly, young children with disabilities will be afforded opportunities to participate in early childhood education settings. Dissemination of information relating to the use of assistive technologies is expected to increase, too. This suggests that early childhood professionals will be called upon to assume new competencies enabling them to effectively participate in team processes and ethical decision making regarding the selection and use of assistive technology for preschool children. If we work together on this, we will be able to increase children's abilities to interact with others and to exercise control over their environment.

Plans that are developed and appropriate assistive technology that is provided will shape the early experiences of these children and provide the foundation upon which much future learning will occur. It is critical that careful consideration be given to the ethical implications of technologies. Unquestionably, these decisions will have a far-reaching impact on the lives of children with disabilities.

References

Cavalier, A. (1986). The application of technology in the classroom and workplace: Unvoiced premises and ethical issues. In A. Gartner & T. Joe (Eds.), *Images of the disabled-disabling images* (pp. 129–142). New York: Praeger.

Cavalier, A. (1988). *Technology assistance: Devices, techniques, and services for people with cognitive impairments. Testimony to the Select Subcommittee on Education of the Committee on Education and Labor of the U.S. House of Representatives.* Arlington, TX: Association for Retarded Citizens.

Childers, J.H., Jr., & Podemski, R.S. (1984). Removing barriers to the adoption of microcomputer technology by school counselors. *The School Counselor, 31,* 229–233.

Evans, I., & Meyer, L. (1985). *An educative approach to behavior problems: A practical decision model for interventions with severely handicapped learners.* Baltimore: Paul H. Brookes.

Griffin, B.L., Gillis, M.K., & Brown, M. (1986). The counselor as a computer consultant: Understanding children's attitudes toward computers. *Elementary School Guidance and Counseling, 20,* 146–149.

Guess, D., Benson, H., & Siegel-Causey, E. (1985). Behavior control and education of severely handicapped students: Who's doing what to whom? And why? In D. Bricker & J. Filler (Eds.), *Severe mental retardation: From theory to practice* (pp. 230–244). Reston, VA: Council for Exceptional Children.

Mendelsohn, S. (1989, March). *Payment issues and options in the utilization of assistive technology.* Paper presented to the National Workshop on Implementing Technology Utilization, Washington, DC.

Office of Technology Assessment. (1982). *Technology and handicapped people.* Washington, DC: U.S. Government Printing Office.

Parette, H.P., & VanBiervliet, A. (1990). *Assistive technology guide for young children with disabilities.* Little Rock, AR: UALR Press.

Parette, H.P., Hourcade, J.J., & VanBiervliet, A. (in press). Technology teams and the exceptional child: Teacher guidelines for the evaluation of assistive devices. *Teaching Exceptional Children.*

Pfrommer, M.C. (1984). Utilization of technology: Consumer perspective. In M. Gergen & D. Hagen (Eds.), *Discover '84: Technology for disabled persons. Conference papers* (pp. 237–343). Menomonie, WI: Stout Vocational Rehabilitation Center.

Snell, M., & Bowden, D. (1986). Community-referenced instruction: Research and issues. *Journal of the Association for Persons with Severe Handicaps, 11*(1), 1–11.

Weinrich, S.G., & Gerstein, M. (1987). Guidelines for counselors in the selection and use of computer software. *Elementary School Guidance and Counseling, 22*(1), 53–61.

Wolfensberger, W. (1969). The origin and nature of our institutional models. In R. Kugel & W. Wolfensberger (Eds.), *Changing patterns in residential services for the mentally retarded* (pp. 59–171). Washington, DC: President's Committee on Mental Retardation.

Play for ALL Children
The Toy Library Solution

Sara C. Jackson
Linda Robey
Martha Watjus
Elizabeth Chadwick

Sara C. Jackson is Assistant Professor, Department of Special Education, University of Southern Mississippi—Gulf Coast, and Director of Toy Library—Coast, funded by the Hasbro Children's Foundation of New York. Linda Robey, Martha Watjus and Elizabeth Chadwick have been Research Assistants, Education Department, University of Southern Mississippi—Gulf Coast.

Affirming its importance in infant and child development, play is a central theme of most early childhood programs. Play "provides children with opportunities for developing mastery and competence in cognitive, social and physical skills" (ACEI/Isenberg & Quisenberry, 1988, p. 142). Yet, its value seems to have eluded many educators of young children with disabilities, as well as their parents.

There are several reasons for this phenomenon. Educational programs for young disabled children have traditionally emphasized direct instruction of specific skills, in many cases leaving little time for play. Also, parents sometimes find it difficult to engage in playful interaction with their disabled children. More paramount, yet related to the first two reasons, is the serious shortage of appropriate toys available to the child with special needs.

PLAY FOR CHILDREN WITH DISABILITIES—A PROBLEM

Lack of Play Opportunities

Although play has always been an integral part of the regular preschool curriculum, this has not been true for the child with disabilities (Widerstrom, 1983). Many preschool programs for the disabled still emphasize teaching specific skills, especially self-help skills, resulting in limited opportunities for the disabled youngster to simply "play" (Sinker, 1990). According to Thurman and Widerstrom (1990), "the traditional nursery school emphasis on play has been rejected as too nondirective and too haphazard" (p. 120). The benefits of play for optimal child development are well discussed in the research literature, yet neither spontaneous nor structured play as a method of enhancing cognitive, physical and social growth is generally stressed in programs for children with disabilities.

Playtime at home also may be less available for the child who has special needs. Parents of disabled children often have difficulty playing with their infants and toddlers. Their anxiety about the fragile condition of a disabled youngster can inhibit a spontaneous playful attitude. Also, many disabled children are less responsive than nondisabled children to their parents' attempts at play. In fact, some infants with disabilities are extremely irritable, cry incessantly and do not appear to enjoy being held (Ainsworth, 1973).

Another barrier to playful interaction between parent and disabled child is the added stress experienced in caring for the child (Bailey & Wolery, 1984). Unfortunately, with extra demands on their time and emotions, little energy is left over for quality playtime with their child. Sometimes parents feel so much pressure to teach their special child certain skills that they forget to relax and have ordinary playful interaction with the youngster (Gerlock, 1982).

Parents may be unaware that, while play is the spontaneous activity of most children, their disabled child may need to be "taught" how to play with toys or other children. Moreover, parents generally have not been encouraged to emphasize play in their relationship with their child. Even the editors of *Exceptional Parent* (October 1990) acknowledge that play has been low on their editorial priority list over the last 20 years (Schleifer & Klein, 1990).

Lack of Appropriate Toys

In addition to lack of adequate school and home playtime, ordinary toys themselves present profound difficulties. Many commercial toys are unsuitable for a significant percentage of children

From *Childhood Education,* Fall 1991, pp. 27-31. Reprinted by permission of the authors and the Association for Childhood Education International, 11501 Georgia Avenue, Suite 315, Wheaton, MD. Copyright © 1991 by the Association.

with special needs; their disabilities make it physically difficult or impossible to play with ordinary toys. To overcome this obstacle to play, appropriate new toys and specially adapted toys have been developed (Domroese, 1985). Unfortunately, these toys are not widely marketed, making them expensive and often difficult to obtain. Furthermore, parents may have to purchase several expensive adaptive switches before finding one their child is able to activate.

THE TOY LIBRARY SOLUTION—AN EXCITING CONCEPT

Attempting to solve these problems, some communities have established toy lending or play libraries. People are beginning to recognize play's value in nurturing the cognitive, physical and social development of all children—especially those with disabilities (Juul, 1987). Additionally, growing emphasis on the importance of the family experience for the disabled child has led to the development of specialized toys and adaptive switches.

Both educators and lawmakers now affirm that the best interventions must involve the entire family unit (Swick, 1989). As primary caretaker, a parent is the child's first teacher and greatest motivator. This essential role of the family has been emphasized in recent legislation, the Education of the Disabled Act Amendments of 1986 or Public Law 99-457. The law focuses on training and support for the child within the context of the family. Unlike P.L. 94-142, which requires an Individual Education Plan (IEP), P.L. 99-457 mandates an Individual Family Service Plan (IFSP) for infants and toddlers. This realization of the vital role of parents and family in early intervention is consistent with the philosophy and procedures of toy libraries.

Toy libraries for disabled youngsters and their families support both the spirit and the intent of P.L. 99-457. Through the loan of specially adapted toys and parent training in appropriate play techniques, these libraries promote family involvement in early intervention efforts for youngsters with special needs. The toy library is an ideal way to expand children's play opportunities as well as accommodate the family in its early intervention efforts.

Development of Adapted Toys

Recent technological advancements have greatly increased the availability of useful toys for children with special needs. Steven Kanor, pioneer in the field of toy adaptation, has used his expertise as a biomedical engineer to design capability switches that activate toys with minimal pressure or movement (Cole, 1982). For those with severe disabilities, he has even designed voice-responsive and light-activated switches. By enabling them to enjoy ordinary toys, he has both enriched their lives and increased their opportunities for individual growth and development.

These "special" toys are adapted by taking an ordinary battery-operated toy and bypassing the usual means of turning it on by using a new switch to activate the toy, one that can be operated by disabled children. Many types of switches have been engineered to match the needs of an individual child. The plate switches are operated by minimal pressure, using any part of the body. Other switches are voice-activated or require merely a puff of breath or a tilt of the head. All switches and toys are interchangeable. This enables the child to play with the entire inventory of toys, using the one switch that best suits his/her needs.

While computer technology provides the means to modify ordinary commercial toys for use by children with special needs, the toys may never be widely marketed. The toy library is currently the best way to make these adapted toys available to large numbers of children.

Toy Library History

Two basic types of toy libraries now operate in the United States. Lekotek, a toy library first developed in Scandinavia and specifically designed for youngsters with disabilities (Juul, 1988), stresses integration of the special needs youngster into family and community. With a primary focus on family support, Lekoteks emphasize play techniques, schedule monthly family visits and lend specially adapted toys. They are generally staffed by professionals and funded by the local community.

Another type of toy library is based on the British model. Unlike the Lekotek, it is usually staffed by nonprofessional volunteers and is often privately funded. In both Britain and America, this type of library has expanded its mission to serve not only disabled children, but other groups of needy or at-risk youngsters (Domroese, 1985)—children whose access to toys is limited due to poverty and/or chaotic home environments.

The toy library movement in the United States has followed both the Scandinavian and the British models. First formed in the early 1980s in Illinois, Lekoteks have since spread to other states (Domroese, 1985). Besides lending toys to children with disabilities, the Lekotek now offers a leader training course, publishes materials on play and toys and encourages computer use.

Toy libraries similar to the more informal British models have also increased in the U.S. Many were initially linked to public libraries, such as the Learning Games Libraries in Illinois and the ToyBrary Project in Nebraska. Some have expanded their mission to include the economically disadvantaged, children in shelters and those in hospitals. Many operate mobile units, providing door-to-door service and lending educational toys to families with special needs children (Stone, 1983). Funding has

Photos courtesy of author

Toy libraries promote family involvement by training parents in play techniques and lending specially adapted toys.

often been provided by state education agencies.

Toy Libraries in the U.S. —A Growing Movement

The state of Illinois has established a network of Learning Games Libraries in various communities, the first opening in Oak Park in 1976. This library, a project of the Illinois Council for Exceptional Children and the Illinois Library Association, provides developmental learning materials (games and toys) to children with learning problems or physical disabilities. The additional 12 libraries that have grown out of this pilot project now operate under the auspices of the Learning Games Libraries Association in Oak Park.

In Nebraska, the State Department of Education (Special Education Branch) and the Nebraska Regional Library System have collaborated to form the ToyBrary, a toy lending library for parents and children. Begun in 1977, ToyBraries now number 15 throughout the state, enabling children in rural areas to benefit from the materials offered. Primarily geared to the child with special needs, the toys and games available for loan emphasize parental involvement.

Three Florida agencies provide assistance to disabled children through the use of specially designed toys and adaptive switches. The Communications Systems Evaluation Center is administered by the Orange County School System. Valencia Community College in Orlando operates the CITE Program (Center for Independence Training and Evaluation), while the Florida Diagnostic and Learning Resources System directs 18 centers throughout the state. The Miami center houses a toy lending library; several others are directly involved in play training programs for disabled children and their families.

These agencies utilize recent advances in science and technology to evaluate and help exceptional children realize their full potential. Children who play with special toys and switches can eventually succeed in using more sophisticated tools such as computers.

Several other states have opened toy libraries, often through their public library systems. In Los Angeles County alone, more than 30 toy libraries reach 15,000 children annually. A $25,000 grant has been given to the Wisconsin Public Libraries to establish circulating toy collections. In Maryland, the Howard County Library Children's Department circulates 1,300 toys each month. Staff members are trained to advise parents on how to use the toys effectively with their children.

Between 1985 and 1988, the number of toy libraries in the United States doubled, from 125 to 250. The National Lekotek Center reports that currently 52 certified Lekoteks operate throughout the

United States. More than a million children and families are served annually by toy libraries nationwide (Myers, 1988).

How To Begin

To determine the feasibility of establishing a toy lending or play library in your community, it is advisable to explore existing facilities in your state. A personal on-site visit is preferable; calling or writing for information is certainly recommended. Contacting other state agencies or national organizations may also prove helpful (see Resources). In brief, before starting a toy library consider the following: funding (state sponsored, private or part of state library system), library space, cataloging system, staff (volunteer or paid) and effective publicity (see Suggested Readings and Toy Sources).

Conclusion

Much has been written about learning and socializing through play and its vital role in both child development and early childhood education. Fortunately, its importance in the development of the exceptional child is also becoming more broadly acknowledged. The growing number of toy libraries in the U.S. has enabled more teachers and parents to use play and toys as invaluable learning tools for youngsters with special needs.

As Isenberg and Quisenberry (1988) state in a position paper of the Association for Childhood Education International (ACEI), "The time has come to advocate strongly in support of play for all children" (p. 138). Thanks to the toy library, *all* children can now engage in play, including those with disabilities.

References

Ainsworth, M. D. S. (1973). The development of infant-mother attachment. In B. M. Caldwell & H. Riciutti (Eds.), *Review of Child Development Research* (1-94).

Association for Childhood Education International. J. Isenberg & N. Quisenberry. (1988). Position paper. Play: A necessity for all children. *Childhood Education, 64,* 138-145.

Bailey, D. B., & Worley, M. (1984). *Teaching infants and preschoolers with handicaps.* Columbus: Charles E. Merrill.

Cole, L. (1982, December 19). Toys: Not only playthings. *Daily News,* p. w-3.

Domroese, C. (1985, October). *Learning games libraries: Help for the at-risk child—A growing movement in Illinois.* Paper presented at the Council for Exceptional Children/ Division on Early Childhood, National Early Childhood Conference on the Child with Special Needs, Denver, CO.

Gerlock, E. (1982). *Parent group guide: Topics for families of young children with handicaps.* Nashville, TN: John F. Kennedy Center for Research on Education and Human Development, Families, Infant, and Toddler Project.

Juul, K. D. (1987, Winter). Toy libraries for children with special needs. *Learning Games Libraries Association Newsletter.* (Available from Learning Games Libraries Association, P.O. Box 4002, Oak Park, IL 60303)

Juul, K. D. (1988, Spring). Lekoteks in Norway. *Learning Games Libraries Association Newsletter.*

Myers, S. M. (1988, January). *U. S. A. Toy Library Association Newsletter.* (Available from U. S. A. Toy Library Association, 2719 Broadway, Evanston, IL 60201)

Schleifer, M. J., & Klein, S. D. (1990, October). Recreation and play. The time is now. *Exceptional Parent,* p. 20.

Sinker, M. (1990). Play is play— Whether or not you can walk or talk. *Child's Play, 7*(1), 3.

Stone, M. (1983, Winter). Toy libraries. *Day Care and Early Education,* pp. 19-21.

Swick, K. J. (1989, November). Working with parents of children with special needs. *An Exceptional Student Education Newsletter, 11*(3), 11-13. (Available from Florida Diagnostic and Learning Resources System/South, Dade County Public Schools, Miami, FL)

Thurman, S. K., & Widerstrom, A. (1990). *Infants and young children with special needs* (2nd ed.). Baltimore, MD: Paul H. Brooks.

Widerstrom, A. (1983). How important is play for disabled children? *Childhood Education, 60,* 39-49.

Suggested Readings

Adaptive Play for Special Needs Children by C. R. Musslewhite. College Hill Press, San Diego, CA, 1986.

An Invitation to Play: Teacher's Guide by C. Zieher. Wisconsin Department of Public Instruction, Madison, WI, 1986.

Early Childhood Special Education: Birth to Three by J. B. Jordan, J. J. Gallagher, P. L. Huntinger & M. B. Karnes (Eds.). Council for Exceptional Children, Reston, VA, 1988.

Helping the Mentally Retarded Acquire Play Skills by P. Wehman. Charles C. Thomas, Springfield, IL, 1977.

Learning Materials Catalog. Learning Games Libraries Association, Oak Park, IL, 1986.

Learning Through Play by P. Chance. Gardner Press, New York, 1979.

Looking at Children's Play: A Bridge Between Theory and Practice by P. Monigham-Nourot, B. Scales, J. Van Hoorn & M. Almy. Columbia University, New York, 1987.

Play and Education: The Basic Tool for Early Childhood Learning by O. Weininger. Charles C. Thomas, Springfield, IL, 1979.

Play as a Medium for Learning and Development: A Handbook of Theory and Practice by D. Bergen (Ed.). Heinemann, Portsmouth, NH, 1988.

Toys for Growing: A Guide to Toys That Develop Skills by M. Sinker. Yearbook Medical Publishers, Chicago, 1986.

"Developmental Toys" by J. T. Neisworth (Ed.) *Topics in Early Childhood Special Education, 5*(3), 1985.

"They Too Should Play" by C. C. Hirst & E. Y. Shelley. *Teaching Exceptional Children, 21*(4), 26-28, 1989.

Resources

Florida Diagnostic & Learning Resources System/South, 9220 S.W. 52nd Terrace, Miami, FL 33165 (305-274-3501).

Learning Games Libraries Association, P.O. Box 4002, Oak Park, IL 60303 (312-386-1687).

Lekotek of Georgia, Inc., 3035 N. Druid Hills Rd., Atlanta, GA 30329 (404-633-3430).

Los Angeles County Toy Loan Program, 2200 N. Humbolt St., Los Angeles, CA 90031 (213-586-6615).

National Lekotek Center, 2100 Ridge Ave., Evanston, IL 60204 (708-328-0001).

Nebraska ToyBrary Project, 301 Centennial Mall S., Lincoln, NE 68509 (402-471-2471).

Toy Library-Coast, USM—Gulf Park, Long Beach, MS 39560 (601-867-2636).

United Cerebral Palsy of Westchester, Mobile Toy Library for Disabled Individuals, King St. & Lincoln Ave., Rye Brook, NY 10706 (914-937-3800).

USA Toy Library Association, 2719 Broadway Ave., Evanston, IL 60201 (708-864-8240).

Toy Sources

Able Net, Inc., 1081 10th Ave. S.E., Minneapolis, MN 55414 (800-322-0956).

Crestwood Co., P.O. Box 04606, Milwaukee, WI 53204 (414-461-9876).

Jesana, Ltd., P.O. Box 17, Irvington, NY 10533 (800-443-4728).

Kapable Kids, P.O. Box 250, Bohemia, NY 11716 (800-356-1564).

Kaye's Kids, Division of KAYE Products, Inc., 1010 E. Pettigrew St., Durham, NC 27701-4299 (919-683-1051).

Rifton—For People with Disabilities, Rt. 213, Rifton, NY 12471 (914-658-3141).

Steven J. Kanor, Inc., 385 Warburton Ave., Hastings, NY 10706 (914-478-0960).

Switch Works, P.O. Box 64764, Baton Rouge, LA 70896 (504-925-8926).

The Capable Child, 8 Herkimer Ave., Hewlett, NY 11557 (516-872-1603).

Therapeutic Toys, Inc., P.O. Box 418, Moodus, CT 06469 (800-638-0676).

Children With Learning Disabilities

Learning disabilities (LDs) are often defined by what they are not. They are not due to mental retardation, environmental deprivation, emotional disturbance, or any sensory (vision, hearing, taste, smell, touch) impairment. They may, however, occur concurrently with another condition of exceptionality; for example, specific learning disability plus motor handicap, or specific learning disability plus emotional and behavioral disorder. Some children can be both intellectually gifted and learning disabled.

A specific learning disability is defined as a disorder in one or more of the basic processes involved in understanding or in using language—spoken or written. This may be manifested as an imperfect ability to listen, think,

speak, read, write, spell, or do mathematical calculations. A specific learning disability may be a perceptual handicap, but it is clearly not a sensory handicap. It may range from mild to severe and may be short-lived or permanent. Close to one hundred different characteristics of specific LDs have been described. Not every expert agrees about what is and what is not an LD. About four percent of students in public schools have been classified as having some specific learning disability. The majority of these students are enrolled in regular education classes.

Specific learning disabilities and difficulty in learning due to some of the exclusionary conditions (sensory impairment, mental retardation, giftedness, emotional dis-

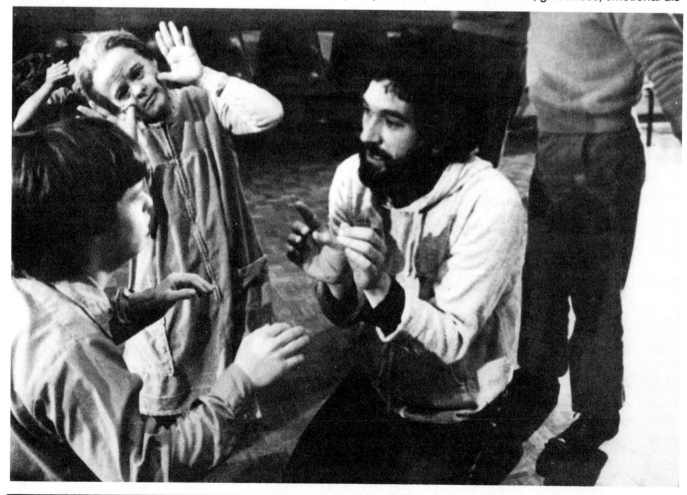

turbance, or socioeconomic disadvantage) are not always easy to differentiate. The assessment of true learning disabilities is fraught with difficulties. Mislabeling is common. Assessment usually combines the use of a standardized test of intelligence plus several achievement tests. A student with an LD usually has a discrepancy between his or her ability to learn and what has actually been learned. However, it is often a formidable task to determine either ability level or achievement with children with specific LDs.

Many persons have very little understanding of the nature of learning disabilities. Some forms of LD, such as dyslexia (difficulty in reading) and attention deficit (often referred to as hyperactivity), are fairly common. They are thus more readily comprehended and accepted by the lay public. However, because these terms are more acceptable as labels, they have become umbrella labels. They are often overused to cover a multitude of conditions that are neither dyslexia nor attention deficit disorders. In order for each child with an LD to receive an appropriate individualized education program and tailored special services, his or her unique area(s) of difficulty must be correctly assessed. Special services should be based on genuine areas of difficulty and should meet unique needs.

Two broad categories of LD are developmental learning disabilities and academic learning disabilities. Developmental disabilities are usually identified at the preschool level. They affect the prerequisite skills that a child needs to learn (attention, eye-hand coordination, memory sequencing, visual-auditory perception). Academic disabilities are usually not identified until the school-age level. They affect the ability to perform a skill (spell, calculate, read, write).

Preschool programs are very effective for children with developmental disabilities. Individualized family service plans (IFSPs) are useful in getting services provided to parents as well as children. The earlier intervention begins both at home and in a program, the less difficulty the child will have learning later.

No one method of teaching has been demonstrated to be the best way to assist children with academic disabilities. Each child must have an annually updated individualized education plan to meet his or her constantly changing needs. Teachers have a responsibility to foster acceptance and understanding of each child with an LD among classmates.

Understanding the nature of a learning disability is complicated by the fact that even within a narrow category of an LD two children may be very different from each other. One dyscalculic child, for example, may be intellectually gifted while a second dyscalculic child may be of average intelligence and have a chronic debilitating health problem. Children may have only one type of LD, or may have two or more LDs in any possible combination. Some children are very motivated to learn despite the LD; other children give up easily when asked to achieve any challenging task. Some highly motivated students appear to be resisting efforts to teach them because of the nature of their LD. It is not surprising that persons faced with the task of assessing or explaining LDs, or teaching LD students, are often confused about what to say or do.

In the first article included in this unit, "The Masks Students Wear," Sally Smith helps the reader recognize certain behaviors that LD children use to hide their problems. It lists behavioral characteristics that teachers can anticipate and handle more successfully. The effects of LDs on several famous adults are described. The next article selected for this unit examines the instructional contexts of students with LDs. The following selection outlines many ways to adapt textbooks in order to enhance the instructional contexts of students with LDs. Finally, the last article in this section discusses the need to teach study skills to students who have learning disabilities, especially at the secondary level. It is much easier for a regular education teacher to facilitate continued academic success for students with LDs if they know how to study.

Looking Ahead: Challenge Questions

Can teachers recognize characteristics of LDs? How do LD students hide their disabilities from adults? Why would they want to mask their difficulties?

What does a classroom with a student with an LD mainstreamed in it look like? How do the teacher and students behave and interact?

Can textbooks be adapted for students with LDs who are mainstreamed into regular classes? How?

Will secondary school teachers with mainstreamed classes containing students with LDs waste their time if they teach study skills before they teach academic subjects?

THE MASKS STUDENTS WEAR

Recognizing the behaviors learning disabled students use to hide their problems helps you to help them

Sally L. Smith

Sally L. Smith is the founder/director of The Lab School of Washington, a full professor and director of the graduate program in learning disabilities at The American University in Washington, D.C. and the author of the book, No Easy Answers: The Learning Disabled Child at Home and at School.

Learning disabled adults are telling educators what learning disabled children can't. What we learn from these adults can improve the teaching of children and the training of teachers.

There are many types of learning disabilities including auditory, vision and language disabilities. And students can have combinations of different learning disabilities.

One of the most important messages learning disabled adults are giving is that the greatest challenge learning disabled children face is the battle for self-esteem. These adults say they felt stupid and were treated in school as though they were. They felt defeated, worthless and "dumb." Over the years, these adults learned to mask their hurts.

"I learned to act a certain way so I couldn't be teased. I would appear bored, tired, eager to be of help, all-knowing or funny, depending upon what was going on. In other words, I would do anything but let them know I couldn't read the material," confesses one learning disabled adult.

"I faked my way all through school," says another. "I had the gift of gab and an excellent memory."

Unfortunately, many dyslexic and learning disabled adults started to develop masks in first or second grade when they could not read what others could. Few ever received special education. They were not identified as learning disabled or dyslexic. Instead, their teachers often labeled them "lazy," "willful," "poorly disciplined" and "spoiled" when actually they were trying their hardest.

These students were called "retarded" if they had any speech and language problems and "disturbed" if they were hyperactive, impulsive or had any of the behavioral manifestations of a learning disabled child. Often these children were gifted, above average in intelligence, and unable to bear their inability to accomplish the simplest academic task.

Think of the energy many learning disabled students spend hiding their disabilities and masking the feeling of being stupid. The masks are an elaborate subterfuge that make students feel worse about themselves. The masks protect the students from being thought of as "stupid," but isolate them from others. Often the masks interfere with students' ability to learn.

Recognizing the masks learning disabled students sometimes wear to hide their inabilities will help you take action to have the problem treated. Masking behavior comes in many variations. The following types are among the most common masks students wear.

The mask of super competence

"Easy!" "Oh, sure! Everyone knows that!"

With a great deal of bravado, this student tries to make everything look simple. He knows he can talk his way

Characteristics of a learning disabled child

- Looks typical but doesn't learn typically.
- Is intelligent, often gifted.
- Has reading, spelling, writing and/or math achievements that are significantly below child's capability level.
- Has a short attention span.
- Is easily distracted.
- Has poor listening skills.
- Has trouble following directions.
- Doesn't seem to be trying, acts lazy or is defiant.
- Sometimes uses immature speech and language.
- Confuses left and right.
- Sometimes uses immature movements, is awkward, clumsy. Shows poor motor coordination (i.e., reaches one hand out and the other hand follows).
- Exhibits immature behavior.
- Displays general disorganization, poor organization of time and space.
- Often has difficulty with tasks employing paper and pencil.
- Produces many reversals (i.e., "b" instead of "d") and rotations (i.e., "b" instead of "q") in written work.
- Is inconsistent in behavior and work.
- Frequently displays exceptional ability in the arts, sports, science and verbalization.

Steps you can take if you suspect a student is learning disabled

1. List the child's personal and academic strengths and areas of weakness. Back up the list with anecdotal records after a week of careful observation and listening.
2. Check student's recent eye and hearing test records as well as general physical health records to rule out physical problems.
3. Confer with parents to discuss the list; ask them if they see similar strengths and weaknesses at home.
4. Recommend an evaluation by a school psychologist. In some schools, initial referral is to the pupil personnel worker; in others it is to the interdisciplinary team or principal.
5. Inform parents about Public Law 94–142, the *Education for All Handicapped Children Act*. Specify parents' rights to have their child evaluated, and if not satisfied with the evaluation results to seek a second evaluation.

If a child is diagnosed as being learning disabled, the child is entitled by law to appropriate services.

These range from support in the classroom to resource assistance to placement in self-contained classrooms. These services may or may not include speech and language therapy, occupational therapy and adaptive physical education.

Resources

Organizations

Association for Children with Learning Disabilities (ACLD)
This grassroots organization serves parents, teachers and other professionals. It provides needed support and information to help follow the latest educational and medical research and supports legislation for special education classes and teachers in the field. To find the organization nearest you, write the National ACLD, 4156 Library Road, Pittsburgh, PA 15234, or call (412) 341–1515.

Council for Exceptional Children (CEC)
This organization for professionals publishes books, media, journals, periodicals and research findings. Low-cost informational flyers are available. For a catalog or more information, write to CEC, 1920 Association Drive, Reston, VA 22091, or call (703) 620–3660.

Foundation for Children with Learning Disabilities (FCLD)
This organization for parents and professionals is a source of information for publications concerning the learning disabled child. It also provides grants. For more information, write to FCLD, 99 Park Ave., New York, NY 10016, or call (212) 687–7211.

The Orton Society
This organization for professionals is also open to parents. It studies preventive measures and treatment for children with specific language disabilities, sponsors research, and shares its findings. For more information, write to The Orton Society, 724 York Road, Baltimore, MD 21204, or call (301) 296–0232.

Books
Smith, Sally L. *No Easy Answers: The Learning Disabled Child at Home and at School*, Bantam Books, New York, 1981.
Stevens, Suzanne. *Classroom Success for the Learning Disabled*, John Blair Publisher, 1984.

through anything. His logic is impeccable. He's good with people, numbers, problem solving and trouble shooting.

Gen. George S. Patton, a dyslexic, assured his daughter that Napoleon couldn't spell, either, and quoted Jefferson Davis as saying, "A man must have a pretty poor mind not to be able to think of several ways to spell a word."

The mask of helplessness

"I don't know." "I don't understand." "I can't do anything."

Through pity, this person gets everyone around to help her do her work and assume responsibilities so she never fails. She refuses to risk failure, but feels even worse because she knows she didn't do any of the work.

The mask of invisibility

"I would hide in my shell, hold my neck in like a turtle, almost pleading with the teacher not to call upon me."

By looking frightened, whispering to teachers and acting terrified with peers, this person gets everyone else to do his work for him.

The student realizes he can get through school by not talking, just repeating when necessary, taking a low profile, and making no waves. With his head down and sitting quietly for a long time, nobody bothers him. He has the talent of melting into the crowd. Teachers and supervisors later realize they never got to know this student or acknowledge he was there.

The mask of the clown

"Isn't that a riot!" "Ha, ha, ha." "What a joke!"

Everything is funny when this student is around. Laughter, however, hides the real issue—a learning disability.

Cher, the Academy Award-winning actress/singer, admits she was the "class clown" to divert attention from her inability to read, write or do arithmetic in school. Despite her problems, she was exceedingly verbal and outstanding in the arts. A teacher proclaimed that she was not working hard enough. Feeling stupid, she dropped out of school at 16 and wasn't tested for learning disabilities until after she was 30.

The mask of the victim

"It's not fair." "Everyone picks on me." "There's no justice anywhere."

Injustice is a basic theme with this person. Often called a "jailhouse lawyer" because he has an argument for everything, this student feels victimized and takes on a "poor me" attitude. He assumes no responsibility for anything. He angers others around him.

The mask of not caring

"I don't care." "Nothing matters." With this mask, the student is never vulnerable, and risks no failure. If she tries to succeed and fails, she says she never tried and it doesn't matter. The mask is a way of keeping others at a distance, making her feel woefully inadequate. If nothing matters, it's very difficult to change or motivate this person.

The mask of boredom

"This is boring!" *Yawn.* "What time is it now?" *Yawn.*

With big yawns, loud sighs, tapping fingers and toes, this person lets the teacher know how bored he is. This behavior puts the teacher on the defensive. Usually this person is not bored, but frustrated, and can't do what he's been asked to do.

Thomas Edison was kicked out of schools for not following instructions. He probably did not understand the instructions due to his auditory problems. Severe learning disabilities prevented him from being able to write what he was told.

The mask of activity

"Gotta run." "Sorry, I'm in a hurry, I can't talk." "I'm busy now, I'll do whatever you want later."

This student is always on the move. Standing still may bring her close to others, and she precludes any intimacy. Constant activity wards away others and keeps her from having to perform.

The mask of outrageousness

"I'm way out." "I don't like being a conformist." "I believe in individualism to the extreme." Through wild clothing, hair style and color, wigs, extraordinary glasses, stockings, boots, and so on, this student projects eccentricity and hides his problems.

Robert Rauschenberg, a famous artist who had extreme difficulty with math and spelling, did outrageous, unheard of things in school and in his career. Many artists feel he expanded the definition of art for a generation of Americans by daring to innovate.

The mask of the Good Samaritan

"Let me help you." "What can I do for you?"

This student wants to please at any cost. Frequently, she is too nice and too accommodating. She will echo what you say, work longer hours than necessary and be overly helpful to get out of doing what she can't do.

The mask of contempt

"They don't know how to teach." "This whole place sucks."

Negativity encompasses this mask. This joyless student has a negative word for everything. If it's sunny out, it could be sunnier. He wears out the people around him because nothing is ever good enough. He takes no pleasure in small successes. He's angry at the world for making him feel stupid and believes the world owes him something. He puts everyone around him on the defensive.

The mask of the strong silent type

"I'm Joe Cool." "Nobody comes too close to me, but they follow me everywhere." "Get out of my face. Nobody moves on me." "Every sport is for me. I live for sports."

Personified by a sleek body and prowess in sports, this student is revered by many and endowed, in her own mind, with every fine feature.

Bruce Jenner, Olympic decathlon champion who is dyslexic, says sports gave him his self-esteem. Jenner says reading aloud in the classroom was much harder and more frightening for him than competing in the decathlon.

The mask of perfection

"If they don't recognize my talents, that's their problem." "Good artists don't have to read really well, anyhow."

Proclaiming loudly that there are machines to spell and write, secretaries to take dictation and lawyers to read for him, this student presents himself as perfection. He tolerates no mistakes in himself or others. He often carries an impressive book or magazine he can't read and saunters into a room looking completely pleased with life. He makes everyone around him miserable.

The mask of illness, frail health and vulnerability

"My head." "My stomach." "My side." "My bladder." "My migraine."

To receive extra attention and get out of the work she can't do, this student calls in sick, leaves sick, constantly pretends to be sick and talks about her frailties.

Given something to read, she uses her illnesses and frailties as an excuse or cries if necessary. Expecting special attention, special privileges, while avoiding what she can't do, this student confuses everyone around her and usually gets by with this behavior.

The mask of seduction

"Hey, woman, write this down for me. Men don't write." The "macho man" often gets a female to do for him what he can't do. He hides behind his macho mask, making himself appear sexy.

"Math is men's work, girls can't do it." The "helpless female" asks a "macho man" to do what she can't do and hides behind her female mask to make it appear sexy.

The mask of being bad

"Don't mess with me. You'll be sorry." "I threw the book at him, so what?" "I'd rather be thought of as bad than dumb."

Losers at school often become winners on the street.

This student feels stupid, powerless and useless at school and often directs his frustration and anger towards his teachers. His peers enjoy his bad behavior and encourage more of it.

Billionaire Dallas real estate manager Rick Strauss changed schools several times, always suffering the humiliation of not learning to read or write due to his severe dyslexia. He compounded his problems by cutting up. Doing so diverted his teachers' attention away from his poor work. It wasn't until he was a high school senior that he learned that his inability to read and write resulted from his learning disabilities.

The mask of fantasy

"I'm going to be a millionaire by the time I'm 30!" "The world will understand me soon." "I'll have a Ph.D. once I learn to read."

Characterized by a fertile imagination and a great deal of creativity, this student tends to live more in her hopes and fantasies than in reality, which is filled with daily frustrations.

Hans Christian Andersen didn't learn to read and write, even with the help of 10 royal tutors of the Danish Court. He dictated his wonderful fairy tales to a scribe. His mask of fantasy protected him from the pain of facing reality, even though glimpses of his suffering appear in some of his stories, such as "The Ugly Duckling."

Removing the masks

The masks can be removed when students reach a certain comfort level. This usually happens when a student realizes he is not stupid, but suffers from a learning disability. The student experiences enormous relief when he discovers why he has been having difficulties learning.

What learning disabled adults have to say about the masks they wore in school alerts educators to the need to reach children in their early years, identify those children who have trouble learning before they begin to wear the masks, and teach them in ways that will help them succeed.

Examining the Instructional Contexts of Students with Learning Disabilities

ABSTRACT: *This review of the literature examines how instructional contexts for elementary and secondary level students with learning disabilities have been studied in the past 10 years through a variety of methodological approaches and observation instruments. These studies employed some direct measure of classroom ecology, as well as some measure of the teacher or students' classroom behavior. Information included the time that students were engaged in different activities in different settings, interactions between teachers and students, and students' classroom behavior.*

JANIS A. BULGREN

JUDITH J. CARTA

JANIS A. BULGREN is an Assistant Scientist and courtesy Assistant Professor in the Department of Special Education at the University of Kansas Institute for Research in Learning Disabilities, Lawrence. JUDITH J. CARTA (CEC #436) is an Associate Scientist at the Juniper Gardens Children's Project, Kansas City, Schiefelbusch Institute for Life Span Studies, at the University of Kansas, Lawrence.

Several factors contribute to the need to study the instructional contexts of students with learning disabilities. Among these factors are the variety of classroom environments in which these students receive instruction, the need for teaching practices that allow these students to learn more effectively and efficiently, and student characteristics that create challenges for both the student and the teacher if student potential is to be realized.

A primary reason for examining the educational contexts for students with learning disabilities is the variety of classroom environments in which these students receive instruction. Recent educational movements make it probable that many of these students will have to adjust to a variety of different settings each day. This movement has partly resulted from the least restrictive environment philosophy expressed in Public Law 94-142 and from the recent regular education initiative, which seeks the placement of students with disabilities in the regular classroom for at least part of their instruction (National Joint Committee on Learning Disabilities, 1983; Pugach & Lilly, 1984; Reynolds, Wang, & Walberg, 1987; Stainback & Stainback, 1984;

Will, 1986). The variety of instructional contexts encountered each day by students with learning disabilities is, in itself, challenging. This challenge is complicated by other factors, such as the need for effective teaching practices for all students, but especially for those with learning disabilities.

Therefore, a second area of interest is that of teacher behavior that is directed toward students with learning disabilities. A teacher's behavior, as part of the instructional context, has the potential of affecting students' academic time on task, critical to student performance. Indeed, research has demonstrated that with effective teaching practices, students with learning disabilities can exhibit academic behavior that looks much like that of their peers without disabilities (Idol, 1987; Short & Ryan, 1984; Sindelar, Monda, & O'Shea, 1990). Effective teaching practices have positively affected the learning of students with learning disabilities by increasing the amount of time during which students are actively engaged in academic responding.

Another consideration in the complex analysis of instructional contexts is the actual behavior shown by students with learning disabilities. These students need to increase the time devoted to active learning and the number of interactions with teachers. Students with learning disabilities have been characterized as "inactive learners" (Torgeson, 1977, 1982) or "disassociated learners" (Kavale & Forness, 1986) who do not participate actively in the learning process. Recalling the work of Carroll (1963), Kavale and Forness pointed out that when academic learning time (i.e., the proportion of engaged time in which the student is experiencing a high degree of success) is inadequate, a student can disassociate from school learning.

Therefore, enhancing students' opportunities to respond actively in the educational process could result in increased and cumulative gains for students with learning disabilities. Analysis of instructional contexts, including different settings and teacher and student behavior, contributes to the identification of specific areas of educational need.

This article reviews studies over the past 10 years of instructional contexts for students with learning disabilities—methodologies, instruments, and findings. The review highlights major research questions about instructional contexts, delineates the current questions, and discusses the most important questions that still remain. The overriding purpose of this article is to show how research has examined the educational contexts of students with learning disabilities and has laid the foundations for more effective and efficient instructional practices for this group of students.

METHODOLOGY FOR THIS REVIEW

We chose research-based articles that focused on some aspect of the instructional context of students with learning disabilities at the elementary or high school level. Studies we included used some direct measure of the classroom ecology, as well as a measure of the teacher or students' classroom behavior. Ecological measures included variables such as tasks, activities, or the level of structure employed in the classroom.

We undertook the following literature search procedures: First, we reviewed journals related to special education and learning disabilities (e.g., *Exceptional Children, Journal of Learning Disabilities, Journal of Special Education, Learning Disability Quarterly*, and *Remedial and Special Education*). Second, we conducted an ancestral search that traced relevant studies that were referenced in articles obtained in the journals reviewed in Step 1. Finally, we undertook a computer search of the Educational Resources Information Center (ERIC) database from 1981 to the present. We located a total of 16 studies meeting the stated criteria.

CLASSROOM ENVIRONMENTS FOR STUDENTS WITH LEARNING DISABILITIES

The student with learning disabilities is commonly placed in some combination of settings that may include a regular classroom, a self-contained classroom, a consulting-teacher classroom, or a resource room setting for a variable part of the school day (Carlberg & Kavale, 1980; Greenwood, 1985; Madden & Slavin, 1983). As a means of responding to this complexity of settings, researchers have asked ecological questions that arise from the placement of students in

these various instructional environments. One important set of ecological questions regards how students in various types of settings spend their time engaged in different activities and instructional structures. These variables have been defined as "ecological events" (Greenwood, Delquadri, Stanley, Terry, & Hall, 1985). Studies suggest that, although class structure in special education classrooms often differs from that in regular education classrooms, teachers in both settings often allocate similar amounts of time to various instructional activities.

One focus of researchers from the University of Minnesota's Institute for Research on Learning Disabilities was a comparison of students with learning disabilities across different settings, such as the regular classroom and the special education classroom. One study by Ysseldyke, Thurlow, Mecklenburg, Graden, and Algozzine (1984) was designed to discover whether students with learning disabilities received more time devoted to instruction after referral out of the regular class and placement in a special classroom. These researchers used the *Code for Instructional Structure and Student Academic Response* (CISSAR) (Stanley & Greenwood, 1981), a momentary time-sampling observation system that allows the recording of students' opportunities to engage in active academic responses as a function of different features in their instructional environments. Ysseldyke and his colleagues found that for three out of four students in their study, time allocated to instruction and time engaged in academic responding were only marginally affected by placement in the special program. Academic instructional time increased shortly after placement in the special education program, but the average gain was reduced almost to the level before placement when students were observed 2 months after placement.

In a similar study, Thurlow, Ysseldyke, Graden, and Algozzine (1984) asked whether students with learning disabilities were exposed to different instructional ecologies in service levels that ranged in their amount of restrictiveness. Using the CISSAR system, they observed students in service levels ranging from full-time placement in the regular classroom to full-time placement in the special education classroom. The authors reported finding minimal ecological differences across the five service levels and no differences across service levels in students' opportunities to learn through active academic responding. For example, though more time was allocated in less restrictive settings to academic activities such as reading and math, no differences were found in these settings in time allocated to nonacademic activities, arts and crafts, transition, free time, and management activities. In addition, no differences were found in less restrictive settings in the amounts of time allocated to any specific task, such as working with readers or notebooks. Students in these settings were allocated more time for whole-group teaching structures than were students within more restrictive settings. Students within more restrictive settings were allocated more time for individual teaching structures. No differences were found across these five settings in time allocated to small-group structures.

More recent studies by the Minnesota group have examined classroom ecological differences for students with learning disabilities, as compared with students with other types of disabilities (such as those with mental retardation or emotional disturbance) or as compared with students without disabilities. In one such study using the CISSAR code, Ysseldyke, Thurlow, Christenson, and Weiss (1987) compared the amount of time allocated to instruction in specific subject-matter areas for students with and without disabilities in elementary school classrooms. The authors also examined the amount of time that students with various disabilities spent in special education and regular classes and also examined the differences in the proportion of time allocated to specific subject-matter instruction in special education or regular settings. They failed to find many differences in the amount of time allocated to instruction in various activities for students in different categories at the elementary level. Students with learning disabilities spent less than 3 hr a day in regular education settings and less than 1 hr per day in special education settings. (In addition, the authors determined that a greater proportion of time was allocated to academic activities in special education than in regular classes.)

In a similar study, Ysseldyke, Christenson, Thurlow, and Bakewell (1987) compared the instructional tasks presented to students with learning disabilities, students with two other types of disabilities, and students without disabilities. Again, just as they found minimal differences in the allocation of time in different subject areas, here they found minimal differences in instructional tasks, that is, the curriculum materials or the stimuli provided by the teacher as a function of disability category or as a function of instructional setting.

Finally, other researchers have used ecobehavioral analysis to study the effectiveness of various interventions in enhancing the performance of students with learning disabilities. Greenwood, Carta, Arreaga-Mayer, and Rager (1991) used the Mainstream version of the CISSAR code (MS-CISSAR) to identify a set of potentially effective procedures in naturalistic classroom instruction. They used students' gains in academic achievement and observed academic behavior to identify effective versus ineffective instructional procedures in language arts classes containing students with learning disabilities.

The authors found that direct instruction was effective both in a resource room setting and a regular education classroom. They pointed out the utility of a search-and-validate approach to development and evaluation of effective instruction. They contended that it is an approach consistent with current school improvement goals because it focuses on student achievement, analysis of classroom behavior, and features of classroom instruction.

In summary, research on the classroom environments of students with learning disabilities has revealed some differences in classroom structure across regular and special education settings, but few differences in time devoted to various subjects or tasks in these settings. These findings raise critical questions regarding how each setting should be configured to respond to the needs of students with learning disabilities. An important use of instructional analysis has also been to link information gained from analysis of these instructional contexts to achievement gains.

TEACHING BEHAVIOR DIRECTED AT STUDENTS WITH LEARNING DISABILITIES

Another important aspect of the instructional context is the types of teaching behavior that are directed toward students with learning disabilities. Several studies have explored the quantity as well as the quality of teachers' interactions with these students. Examinations were conducted for students with learning disabilities in the regular classroom, for such students who move from the regular to special classrooms, and for students who remain in special classrooms. These analyses have provided information regarding differences in the type and quality of interactions of regular classroom teachers toward students with and without learning disabilities. Further comparisons have been made between treatments received by students with learning disabilities and students with other disabilities in special education classrooms. Details of these studies are provided as follows.

Observations in Regular Classes

Several researchers have studied students with learning disabilities in the environment of the regular classroom. One set of studies found differences in *quality* but not the *quantity* of types of teacher behavior toward these students in the regular classroom. For example, Slate and Saudargas (1986) examined whether regular teachers' behavior was different when directed at boys without learning disabilities. These researchers employed the *State-Event Classroom Observation System* (SECOS) (Saudargas &

Creed, 1980), a system that uses a 15-s momentary time-sampling procedure to capture the state of student behavior (e.g., schoolwork) and specific events, such as hand raising or calling out. Slate and Saudargas found that although the regular teachers engaged in contacts with all boys for an equivalent amount of time, the teachers provided the boys with disabilities with a disproportionate amount of attention when these boys were engaged in an activity other than the prescribed academic assignment. This was true even though the boys with disabilities may have engaged in similar amounts of inappropriately engaged behavior as had the boys without disabilities.

Similarly, Fellers and Saudargas (1987), also using the SECOS code, attempted to determine any major differences in teacher behavior toward elementary school girls with learning disabilities and those without disabilities in the regular classroom. They found that teachers did not spend more time interacting with girls with disabilities, but they ignored call-outs from girls with disabilities more than from girls without disabilities. This finding is apparently inconsistent with the previous finding (Slate & Saudargas, 1986) concerning boys with learning disabilities. According to Fellers and Saudargas, teachers may perceive boys with learning disabilities as having more behavioral problems than girls with the same disabilities. Consequently, teachers may find it necessary to monitor the behavior of these boys more closely than the behavior of girls with learning disabilities.

In another variation of this study, Slate and Saudargas (1987) examined how teachers responded to the specific behavior of students with different types of disabilities and of students without disabilities using the SECOS and a lag sequential analysis. Lag sequential analysis is a nonparametric statistic that permits quantitative descriptions of temporal relationships among individual behaviors that occur in sequences (Sackett, 1978). They found that the teachers seemed to respond differently to students with disabilities depending on the behavior in which the students were engaged. On one hand, the teacher was more likely to leave the students with learning disabilities alone when they were working on schoolwork, than when they were engaged in other types of behavior. On the other hand, the teacher was more likely to interact with them when the students with learning disabilities were out of seat or interacting with other children, than when they were not engaging in those types of behavior. When interactions between teachers and students with learning disabilities occurred, they lasted longer than interactions with students without disabilities. This differential attention to the off-task behavior of students with learning disabilities was not found toward students without disabilities.

Another set of studies using a different observation system found differences in both the quantity and the quality of teacher behavior toward students with and without learning disabilities in the regular classroom. Studies by Alves and Gottlieb (1986) and Siperstein and Goding (1985), using the Brophy-Good Teacher-Child Dyadic Interaction System (Brophy & Good 1972) to record the interactions between a child and his or her teacher, often reported greater frequencies of interaction between teachers and students with learning disabilities than between teachers and students without disabilities. The Brophy-Good Teacher-Child Dyadic Interaction System is an interval-based, time-sampling system that records five categories of teacher-student interactions. Using this system, Siperstein and Goding found that teachers initiated more interactions, responded with greater frequency of corrective behavior, and used more nonsupportive verbal and negative nonverbal behavior with students with learning disabilities than with other children. An intervention designed to make elementary school teachers aware of their behavior did not affect the quantity of interactions between teachers and students with learning disabilities, but it significantly reduced the negative quality of these interactions.

Alves and Gottlieb (1986) also found differences in the quantity of time teachers spent with students with disabilities, but they provided additional information regarding differences in the quality of academic time for different groups. Using an adaptation of the Brophy-Good system, Alves and Gottlieb found that teachers' academic questions and extended feedback to students were the main variables that discriminated between two groups of students: students with mild disabilities and those without disabilities. Although the students with disabilities interacted with teachers more frequently than with the students without disabilities, teachers directed fewer academic questions and provided less extended feedback to students with disabilities than to their peers without disabilities. As a result, students with disabilities had fewer opportunities for active academic involvement. Alves and Gottlieb raised serious concerns that regular teachers may not have provided as much academic input to their students with disabilities because they considered socialization and not academic learning to be the primary goal of mainstreaming for these students. Alves and Gottlieb hypothesized that if the teachers believed their primary role was to promote these students' socialization and emotional adjustment, then they may have placed these goals above that of teaching content. In addition, if these teachers attributed those students' achievement problems to inherent limitations in ability, they may have treated these pupils in ways that ultimately hampered their achievement.

Observations Across Classrooms

Other researchers have examined the types of behavior that teachers direct toward students with learning disabilities throughout the day in both the regular classroom and the resource room. These researchers have found differences in the quantity as well as the quality of time that teachers spend with students with learning disabilities. For example, in the study described earlier using the CISSAR code, Thurlow and her colleagues (Thurlow, Graden, Greener, & Ysseldyke, 1983) found that students with learning disabilities received significantly more teacher approval than did the students without disabilities. In addition, the students with disabilities received more individual instruction with the teacher at their side than did the other students. Because this study observed students with learning disabilities in both the regular classroom and the resource room, further analysis may be warranted to determine how teacher behavior differs in each setting.

Observations in Special Classes

Other studies have compared the teaching behavior directed toward students with learning disabilities, with that directed to other special populations. In a study using the Classroom Observations Keyed for Effective Research (COKER) (Coker, & Coker, 1982), Algozzine, Morsink, and Algozzine (1988) compared the nature of instruction provided in self-contained special education classrooms for students with different types of disabilities. The authors found few differences in the instructional behavior of special education teachers relative to the type of student in their self-contained classrooms. In general, instructional activities and communication patterns were similar for classes containing students with learning disabilities, emotional disturbance, or mild mental retardation.

In another study using the CISSAR code, O'Sullivan, Marston, and Magnusson (1987) explored the differences in behavior of special educators who held differing teacher licensure in the areas of learning disabilities and mild mental retardation. They found no differences in the instructional behavior of teachers in these areas of special education. Furthermore, they found that the classroom behavior of groups of students with learning disabilities and mild mental retardation did not differ. Finally, pupil behavior did not differ as a function of teacher licensure. Therefore, placement in different categorical classrooms appears to have provided little difference in the instruction received by students in various special education classes.

In summary, research presents somewhat mixed results regarding the quantity of time that regular classroom teachers spend with students with learning disabilities as compared with other students. Researchers have, however, found several differences in the quality of interactions between regular classroom teachers and students with and without learning disabilities and have begun to compile a composite picture of the types of teacher behavior often directed toward these students. This picture often reveals less interaction with these students on academic matters, and more frequent, longer, and corrective interactions on nonacademic matters, especially for boys with learning disabilities in the regular classroom. The quality of teacher behavior may vary from setting to setting. Within special education classrooms, however, students with learning disabilities do not appear to be treated differently from students with other disabilities.

A major question is, of course, whether the different quality of interactions experienced by students with learning disabilities and their teachers has an effect on those students' academic responding and achievement. It would appear that this could be the case; if so, research could well pinpoint problem areas, identify successful adjustments, and suggest optimal learning conditions in teacher interactions with students with learning disabilities.

CLASSROOM BEHAVIOR OF STUDENTS WITH LEARNING DISABILITIES

The analysis of the behavior of students with learning disabilities within their instructional contexts has been instructive in describing those students' learning characteristics within specific educational settings. In the literature reviewed, student responses were typically categorized as academic responses, task-management responses, or competing-behavior responses (Greenwood et al., 1985). These were most often considered with the student as the focal point because within the context of the classroom, a given student may or may not be responding in a manner envisioned by the teacher. The studies described below focus on the following areas of student behavior: inappropriate behavior of students with learning disabilities in the regular classroom, differing academic behavior of students with and without learning disabilities, and differing academic behavior of students with learning disabilities in different educational settings.

Inappropriate Student Behavior

First, some researchers have focused on differences between students with and without learning disabilities in the regular classroom. Ecological studies have produced results suggesting that students with learning disabilities may behave differently from other students, especially in their relative levels of inappropriate responses. McKinney and Feagans (1984) observed elementary school students with learning disabilities in the regular classroom during academic activities. These researchers used the *Schedule for Classroom Activity Norms* (SCAN), a time-sampling system that records task-oriented, social, and affective behavior as well as the settings in which the behavior occurs. The researchers found that the students with learning disabilities tended to be less on-task and to exhibit more off-task behavior than their classmates without disabilities. They were also more distractible and dependent/aggressive. McKinney and Feagans noted that this was particularly significant in that off-task behavior is negatively correlated with academic progress.

Fellers and Saudargas (1987) attempted to determine differences in the levels of academic behavior of a group of female elementary school students with disabilities and a similar group of female students without disabilities. Again, the SECOS observation system described earlier was used. The most significant difference between the two groups of students was that the girls with learning disabilities spent less time engaged in schoolwork than did girls without disabilities. In yet another study, comparing the classroom behavior of elementary school students with and without learning disabilities, Slate and Saudargas (1987) found that after interacting with the teacher, children with disabilities took longer to return to their school work than did their peers without disabilities. As a result, at the elementary school level, students with learning disabilities appeared to behave differently than students without disabilities in regular classrooms, by exhibiting more types of inappropriate behavior.

Studies have also been conducted regarding the behavior of adolescents in mainstream secondary-level classes. Bender (1985) found that the students with learning disabilities demonstrated more passive off-task behavior than did their low-achieving peers, although during whole-group instruction, both groups were more likely to be off-task in a passive manner than they were during seatwork. A study by Zigmond, Kerr, and Schaeffer (1988) supported the description of the adolescent with learning disabilities in the secondary mainstream classrooms as a passive learner who does not come to class with appropriate materials, who attends to instruction only about 60% of the time, who generally does not give information or ask questions, but who generally follows the teacher's procedural directions. Using a special observation system (Harris, Brown, Kerr, & Zigmond, 1983), their study found that such performance was not significantly different from that of students in a contrast group of adolescents without disabilities. The authors pointed out the need to collect information on students without disabilities to provide a perspective on normal adolescent behavior, particularly if the behavior of students with learning disabilities becomes more like that of other students as they progress from the elementary to the secondary level.

Academic Behavior of Students with and Without Learning Disabilities

In addition to studies that focus on appropriate versus inappropriate behavior in the regular classroom, other studies have produced results regarding specific student academic responses. Researchers using the CISSAR code have examined the nature of instruction and academic responding time for students with and without learning disabilities. Thurlow et al. (1983) explored the active academic responses (in addition to the time allocated to various activities and tasks discussed earlier) of students with and without learning disabilities and found that the two groups did not differ in total active academic responding times overall, in task management responses overall, or in inappropriate responses overall. The two groups of students differed in the time they spent engaged in specific types of academic responses. For example, students without learning disabilities spent more time writing than did students with disabilities, whereas the latter students spent more time playing academic games, reading aloud, talking about academics, answering academic questions, and asking academic questions. However, these authors found that, in general, the total academic responding time for both groups of students with and without learning disabilities was extremely small and variable.

Academic Behavior of Students with Learning Disabilities Across Settings

In another investigation, the academic responding level of students with learning disabilities was observed and contrasted in different educational settings. Thurlow et al. (1984), again using the CISSAR code, observed five different instructional levels for students with learning disabilities, ranging from full-time placement in the regular classroom to full-time placement in resource rooms, and found no significant differences across the five levels in the time students with learning disabilities spent in various responses. In addition, no significant differences across the levels were found in the proportion of time that the students with disabilities were engaged in academic responses overall, task management responses overall, or inappropriate responses overall. Students were engaged in task management for the greatest amount of time; followed by academic responses, for less than half the time spent in task management; and then by inappropriate responses, for approximately a third of the time spent in task management. Variability among students was great, even within the same type of placement. On the whole, academic responding time was low for all students, averaging less than 45 min per day.

In summary, research that focuses on students with learning disabilities in the mainstream classroom yields a picture of students who, according to some researchers (specifically those using the SCAN, the SECOS, and Bender's technique), may differ in behavior from students without disabilities in that they may be less on-task. Studies across a variety of educational settings (particularly studies using the CISSAR code) suggest that students with learning disabilities often appeared to respond somewhat differently than did other students, in terms of time spent in specific types of academic response even though total academic responding time was not different. However, students with learning disabilities do not appear to behave differently in different educational settings.

CONCLUSION

This review of the literature, focusing on the instructional contexts of students with learning disabilities, has answered some descriptive questions regarding this population but has also raised other questions. At issue is the apparent lack of significant differences found by some researchers in instruction for students with learning disabilities in special and regular education settings. We suggest future research in the following areas: quality and quantity of student and teacher interactions, effects of teacher training programs, behavior of students with learning disabilities across occasions and settings, and effective interventions for these students.

Specifically, questions about teachers in special education classrooms include the following: Does different teacher licensure lead to different teacher behavior in classrooms? Do teachers in special education classrooms treat all special education students similarly, regardless of special education classification? If so, what are the educational implications? Further questions regarding student behavior include the following: Do students with learning disabilities behave more like students with disabilities or like students without disabilities? How do instructional settings affect their behavior? Do students with learning disabilities behave more like students without disabilities as they progress from the elementary to secondary level?

Studies examining instructional contexts of students with learning disabilities have advanced our knowledge base by providing specificity regarding these students' interactions with subject matter, curriculum, tasks, and group structure or arrangements across various settings. The results of such studies lay the foundations for further exploration regarding the ecological settings in which students with learning disabilities can best

be provided with effective instructional procedures. In addition, such data may suggest ways to structure instruction to best meet the needs of various individuals through ongoing manipulation and exploration of educational techniques. As Carta and Greenwood (1985) pointed out, the data produced in ecological assessment are immediately sensitive to the effects of relatively small adjustments made in instructional methods and materials. Therefore, these analyses can guide the manipulations of classroom variables to determine the precise configurations within a setting that will enhance academic gains for students with learning disabilities.

Of course, the ultimate question is the identification of the academic procedures and classroom structures that will increase the academic gains of students with learning disabilities. Given the characteristics of students with learning disabilities, the variety of settings in which they are placed, the numerous setting demands to which they must respond, and the importance of time engaged in the learning process, careful research into quality teaching procedures is critical to this group of students.

REFERENCES

Algozzine, B., Morsink, C. V., & Algozzine, K. M. (1988). What's happening in self-contained special education classrooms? *Exceptional Children, 55,* 259-265.

Alves, A. J., & Gottlieb, J. (1986). Teacher interactions with mainstreamed handicapped students and their nonhandicapped peers. *Learning Disability Quarterly, 8,* 77-83.

Bender, W. N. (1985). Differential diagnoses based on the task-related behavior of learning disabled and low-achieving adolescents. *Learning Disability Quarterly, 8,* 261-266.

Brophy, J., & Good, T. (1972). Brophy-Good System (Teacher-Child Dyadic interaction). In A. Simon & E. Boyer (Eds.), *Mirrors for behavior: An anthology of observation instruments continued* (Vol. A, pp. 191-197). Philadelphia: Research for Better Schools.

Carlberg, C., & Kavale, K. (1980). The efficacy of special versus regular class placement for exceptional children: A meta-analysis. *Journal of Special Education, 14,* 295-306.

Carroll, J. B. (1963). A model of school learning. *Teachers' College Record, 64,* 723-733.

Carta, J. J., & Greenwood, C. R. (1985). Ecobehavioral assessment: A methodology for expanding the evaluation of early intervention programs. *Topics in Early Childhood Special Education, 5,* 88-104.

Coker, J. G., & Coker, H. (1982). *Classroom observations keyed for effective research: User's manual.* Carrolton, GA: Author.

Fellers, G., & Saudargas, R. A. (1987). Classroom behaviors of LD and nonhandicapped girls. *Learning Disability Quarterly, 10,* 231-236.

Greenwood, C. R. (1985). Settings or setting events as treatment in special education: A review of mainstreaming. In M. L. Wolraich (Ed.), *Advances in developmental and behavioral pediatrics* (Vol. 6, pp. 205-239). Greenwich, CT: JAI Press.

Greenwood, C. R., Carta, J. J., Arreaga-Mayer, C., & Rager, A. (1991) The behavior analysis consulting model: Identifying and validating naturally effective instructional models. *Journal of Behavioral Education, 1,* 165-191.

Greenwood, C.R., Delquadri, J., Stanley, S. O., Terry, B., & Hall, R. V. (1985). Assessment of ecobehavioral interaction in school settings. *Behavioral Assessment, 7,* 331-347.

Harris, A., Brown, G., Kerr, M. M., & Zigmond, N. (1983). *Training manual for research assistants* (Tech. Rep. No. 6). Pittsburgh: University of Pittsburgh.

Idol, L. (1987). Group story mapping: A comprehension strategy for both skilled and unskilled readers. *Journal of Learning Disabilities, 20,* 196-205.

Kavale, K. A., & Forness, S. R. (1986). School learning, time and learning disabilities: The disassociated learner. *Journal of Learning Disabilities, 19,* 130-138.

Madden, N. A., & Slavin, R. E. (1983). Mainstreaming students with mild handicaps: Academic and social outcomes. *Review of Educational Research, 53,* 519-569.

McKinney, J. D., & Feagans, L. (1984). Academic and behavioral characteristics of learning disabled children and average achievers: Longitudinal studies. *Learning Disability Quarterly, 7,* 251-265.

National Joint Committee on Learning Disabilities. (1983). Learning disabilities: Issues on definition (position paper). *Learning Disability Quarterly, 6,* 42-44.

O'Sullivan, P. J., Marston, D., & Magnusson, D. (1987). Categorical special education teacher certification: Does it affect instruction of mildly handicapped pupils? *Remedial and Special Education, 8*(5), 13-18.

Pugach, M., & Lilly, M. S. (1984). Reconceptualizing support services for classroom teachers: Implications for teacher education. *Journal of Teacher Education, 35*(5), 48-55.

Reynolds, M. C., Wang, M. C., & Walberg, H. J. (1987). The necessary restructuring of special and regular education. *Exceptional Children, 3,* 391-398.

Sackett, G. (1978) *Observing Behavior, Vol. 2. Data collection and analysis.* Baltimore, MD: University Park Press.

Saudargas, R., & Creed, V. (1980). *State event classroom observation system.* Unpublished observation manual. Knoxville:University of Tennessee.

Short, E. J., & Ryan, E. B. (1984). Metacognitive differences between skilled and less skilled readers: Remediating deficits through story grammar and attribution training. *Journal of Educational Psychology, 76,* 225-235.

Sindelar, P. T., Monda, L. E., & O'Shea, L. J. (1990). The effects of repeated readings on instructional and mastery level readers. *Journal of Educational Research, 83,* 220-226.

Siperstein, G. N., & Goding, M. J. (1985). Teachers' behavior toward LD and non-LD children: A strategy for change. *Journal of Learning Disabilities, 18*(3), 139-144.

Slate, J. R., & Saudargas, R. A. (1986). Differences in learning disabled and average students' classroom behaviors. *Learning Disability Quarterly, 9,* 61-67.

Slate, J. R., & Saudargas, R. A. (1987). Classroom behaviors of LD, seriously emotionally disturbed, and average children: A sequential analysis. *Learning Disability Quarterly, 10, 125-134.*

Stainback, W., & Stainback, S. (1984). A rationale for the merger of special and regular education. *Exceptional Children, 51,* 102-111.

Stanley, S. O., & Greenwood, C. R. (1981). *CISSAR: Code for Instructional Structure and Student Academic Response: Observer's Manual.* Kansas City: University of Kansas Juniper Gardens Children's Project, Bureau of Child Research.

Thurlow, M., Graden, J., Greener, J., & Ysseldyke, J. (1983). LD and non-LD students' opportunities to learn. *Learning Disability Quarterly, 6,* 172-183.

Thurlow, M. L., Ysseldyke, J. E., Graden, J., & Algozzine, B. (1984). Opportunity to learn for LD students receiving different levels of special education services. *Learning Disability Quarterly, 7,* 55-67.

Torgeson, J. K. (1977). The role of nonspecific factors in the task performance of learning disabled children: A theoretical assessment. *Journal of Learning Disabilities, 10,* 27-34.

Torgeson, J.K. (1982). The learning-disabled child as an inactive learner: Educational implications. *Topics in Learning and Learning Disabilities, 2,* 45-52.

Will, M. C. (1986). Educating children with learning problems: A shared responsibility. *Exceptional Children, 52,* 411-415.

Ysseldyke, J. E., Christenson, S. L., Thurlow, M. L., & Bakewell, D. (1987). *Instructional tasks used by mentally retarded, learning disabled, emotionally disturbed and nonhandicapped elementary students* (Research Report No. 2). Minneapolis: Instructional Alternatives Project, University of Minnesota.

Ysseldyke, J. E., Thurlow, M. L., Christenson, L. L., & Weiss, J. (1987). *Time allocated to instruction of mentally retarded, learning disabled, emotionally disturbed, and nonhandicapped elementary students* (Report No. 1). Minneapolis: University of Minnesota.

Ysseldyke, J. E., Thurlow, M. L., Mecklenburg, C., Graden, J., & Algozzine, B. (1984). Changes in academic engaged time as a function of assessment and special education intervention. *Special Services in The Schools, 1*(2), 31-43.

Zigmond, N., Kerr, M. M., & Schaeffer, A. (1988). Behavior patterns of learning-disabled and non-learning-disabled adolescents in high school academic classes. *Remedial and Special Education, 9*(2), 6-11.

This project was supported by a grant from the U. S. Department of Education (G008630071).

The authors wish to thank Carmen Arreaga-Mayer, Charles Greenwood, and Mary Todd, Juniper Gardens Children's Project, at the University of Kansas, Kansas City.

Manuscript received December 1989; revision accepted October 1991.

Adapting Textbooks for Children with Learning Disabilities in Mainstreamed Classrooms

Ruth Lyn Meese

Ruth Lyn Meese *(CEC Chapter #955) is an Assistant Professor of Special Education, Department of Education, Special Education, and Social Work, Longwood College, Farmville, Virginia.*

Cooperative efforts between special education and regular education teachers are vital if students with learning disabilities are to be successful in mainstreamed classes in which the textbook is the primary means for disseminating information.

Adapting textbooks to meet the needs of these students can be a complex task. For example, some children with learning disabilities have attentional deficits affecting their ability to differentiate what information they should attend to (Hallahan & Kauffman, 1988). The cluttered appearance of many textbooks complicates the decision as to what does or does not warrant attention. Other children are reading at a level far below that of the textbook. Their reading problems are compounded by the complex sentence and organizational structures, difficult vocabulary, and concept density typically found in expository text material (Carnine, Silbert, & Kameenui, 1990). Still other students may lack efficient strategies to comprehend and remember textbook reading assignments (Seidenberg, 1989).

Special education teachers do not have the time to rewrite textbooks. They can, however, provide adaptations based on the needs of the individual student, the demands of the textbook, and the needs of the regular classroom teacher (Margolis & McGettigan, 1988; Martens, Peterson, Witt, & Cirone, 1986).

A student listens to tape-recorded text in which the teacher has stopped periodically to summarize important information.

This article describes ways in which special educators can help students get the most from content area textbooks.

Modifying the Textbook

Modification usually involves highlighting information in the textbook, tape recording the textbook, or providing the student with a high-interest/low-vocab-ulary alternative—all of which can be both time consuming and costly. Since little research exists to document the effectiveness of highlighting, the focus here is on the other two alternatives.

Tape Recording the Text

Teachers can ask student or adult volunteer groups to prepare tape-recorded versions of textbooks (Smith &

From *Teaching Exceptional Children*, Vol. 24, No. 3, Spring 1992, pp. 49-51. Copyright © 1992 by The Council for Exceptional Children. Reprinted by permission.

Smith, 1985). Recorded text segments should be kept clear and short. On the tape, a teacher may also provide an overview of the selection before reading begins (Bos & Vaughn, 1988); give clear signals to the reader for page location; and stop periodically in order to summarize important information or ask the student to respond to questions (Salend, 1990). Tapes of textbooks commonly used in content classes are available free of charge, or for a small fee, from organizations such as Recordings for the Blind, 214 East 58th, New York, NY 10022.

Using High-Interest/ Low-Vocabulary Materials

Special educators occasionally must provide students who have extremely poor reading skills with high-interest/low-vocabulary alternatives to their assigned reading selections. Care must be taken to discuss possible alternatives with the regular classroom teacher so that proper content coverage and mastery can be ensured. Excellent lists of commercially available materials can be found in Mercer and Mercer (1989) and Wood (1989).

Altering Instructional Procedures

Many students with learning disabilities can be helped to comprehend textbook materials by relatively minor changes in the teacher's instructional procedures. Usually, these alterations increase the level of teacher-directed instruction and/or the level of active student involvement with the text.

Teaching Textbook Structure

Students must use expository text and organizational structure to find and recall information from their textbooks (Seidenberg, 1989). Unfortunately, this is often problematic for a student with learning disabilities. Therefore, the special educator must directly teach these structures (e.g., "cues" for important information such as headings, subheadings, differing print, or introductory and summary paragraphs), particularly when the information is complex and the textbooks or concepts are new (Carnine et al., 1990). The teacher can focus attention on important features of the text by beginning each reading

assignment with a systematic overview of the material. Archer and Gleason (1989) have suggested the following teacher-directed chapter warm-up procedure:

1. Read the chapter title and introduction.
2. Read the headings and subheadings.
3. Read the chapter summary.
4. Read any questions at the end of the chapter.
5. Tell what the chapter will talk about.

Previewing

To preview a reading selection before independent study, the teacher or a peer simply reads aloud the assigned passages (Salend & Nowak, 1988). Previewing is a simple procedure that can readily be combined with other techniques to increase active student involvement during reading. Examples of such techniques are guided questioning by the teacher after short textbook segments are read aloud and reciprocal teaching, in which students take turns assuming the role of teacher (see Palincsar & Brown, 1986).

Providing Advance Organizers

Advance organizers alert students to important information in the reading assignment (Darch & Gersten, 1986). For example, *graphic organizers* are diagrams depicting superordinate and subordinate relationships from the text and can provide students with a visual overview of the reading material before actual reading begins (Horton, Lovitt, & Bergerud, 1990). Similarly, teachers may provide students with a sequential partial outline of critical information, to be completed during the reading process (Bos & Vaughn, 1988). Pairing question numbers from a study guide or from blanks on a partial outline with page numbers on which the information can be found may also help students locate essential information (Wood, 1989).

In order to demonstrate the relationship between textbook questions and the structure of the text, students may be taught to rephrase headings, subheadings, or vocabulary words as questions to be answered during reading. For example, from the heading "The Greek Peninsula," numerous "What," "Where," "How," and "Why" questions might be generated (e.g., "What did the Greek Peninsula look like?"). After students

generate their questions, the teacher asks them to state what types of information the answers will contain (e.g., name, date, location, event, cause, etc.). Archer and Gleason (1989) provided a similar technique for helping students understand the relationship between textbook questions and answers:

1. Read each question carefully.
2. Change the question into a part of the answer (e.g., "How did the location of the Greek Peninsula affect the daily lives of its citizens?" becomes "The Greek Peninsula affected the daily lives of its citizens by...").
3. Find the part of the chapter that talks about the topic.
4. Read the section to find the answer.
5. Complete the answer to the question.

Having students generate questions to be answered during reading improves their comprehension of the material (Swicegood & Parsons, 1989; Wong, 1985). Providing them with a structured overview in combination with self-generated questions is even more effective in facilitating comprehension (Billingsley & Wildman, 1988).

Preteaching Critical Vocabulary

Some teachers set up rotating committees of students to seek out and define words that are likely to be troublesome to classmates. Others suggest the use of mnemonic devices to aid students in recalling important vocabulary and concepts (Mastropieri & Scruggs, 1987).

Teaching Textbook Reading Strategies

The following strategies can help students with learning disabilities become active participants in the learning process (Schumaker, Deshler, & Ellis, 1986). Instead of passively reading textbooks, students are taught ways to ask questions, formulate answers, verbally rehearse important information, and monitor their comprehension.

Self-Questioning

Wong, Perry, and Sawatsky (1986, pp. 25–40) described a self-questioning strategy used in social studies by students with learning disabilities. In this strategy, students are taught to ask themselves the following questions:

1. In this paragraph, is there anything I don't understand?
2. In this paragraph, what's the main idea sentence? Let me underline it.
3. Let me summarize the paragraph. To summarize I rewrite the main idea sentence and add important details.
4. Does my summary statement link up with the subheading?
5. When I have summary statements for a whole subsection (paragraphs under a subheading):
   a. Let me review my summary statements for the whole subsection.
   b. Do my summary statements link up with one another?
   c. Do they all link up with the subheading?
6. At the end of a reading assignment, can I see all the themes here? If yes, let me predict the teacher's test question. If no, go back to step 4 (Wong et al., 1986).

Active Reading

Archer and Gleason (1989) have presented a simple strategy, called *active reading*, to involve students in verbally rehearsing and monitoring their comprehension of textbook passages. During active reading, the student proceeds paragraph by paragraph using the following steps:

1. Read a paragraph. Think about the topic and about the important details.
2. Cover the material.
3. Recite. Tell yourself what you have read. Say the topic and the important details in your own words.
4. Check yourself. If you forgot something important, start again.

Study Cards

Students can place each important new vocabulary word on one side of an index card, with the definition and page number on the reverse (Wood, 1989). The cards are filed by chapter for continuing review and study.

Rooney (1988) detailed an excellent system for producing study cards. Students are asked to:

1. Read the subtitle and the paragraphs under the subtitle. Write on separate index cards all names of people or places, and important numbers or terms.
2. Go back to the subtitle and turn it into a test question. Write the question on one side of an index card and the answer on the other side.
3. Repeat this procedure to produce a set of study cards containing all the main ideas and important details from the reading.
4. Look at each card. Ask yourself, "How are the details related to the material?" Try to answer the main idea questions from memory.

Conclusion

Adapting a textbook does not mean rewriting the text. Altering instructional procedures and/or teaching students strategies to help themselves become more involved participants in the reading process are effective ways to help them use content area textbooks. The following common-sense guidelines can be useful to special educators collaborating with regular classroom teachers in this endeavor:

1. Examine the textbook for vocabulary and concept density and difficulty and for clear organizational structures.
2. Talk to the student regarding his or her perceived difficulties and needs. Ask the student to locate parts of the textbook, to read aloud from the text, and to answer questions about the passage.
3. Talk with the regular classroom teacher regarding his or her perceived needs. Discuss critical knowledge and skills to be mastered.
4. Choose the simplest adaptation that is most likely to meet the needs of both the student and the teacher.
5. Monitor carefully and make changes as necessary.

References

Archer, A., & Gleason, M. (1989). *Skills for school success*. Boston: Curriculum Associates.

Billingsley, B. S., & Wildman, T. M. (1988). The effects of prereading activities on the comprehension monitoring of learning disabled adolescents. *Learning Disabilities Research, 4*, 36-44.

Bos, C. S., & Vaughn, S. (1988). *Strategies for teaching students with learning and behavior problems*. Boston: Allyn and Bacon.

Carnine, D., Silbert, J., & Kameenui, E. J. (1990). *Direct instruction reading* (2nd ed.). Columbus, OH: Merrill.

Darch, C., & Gersten, R. (1986). Direction setting activities in reading comprehension: A comparison of two approaches. *Learning Disability Quarterly, 9*, 235-243.

Hallahan, D. P., & Kauffman, J. M. (1988). *Exceptional children*. Englewood Cliffs, NJ: Prentice-Hall.

Horton, S. V., Lovitt, T. C., & Bergerud, D. (1990). The effectiveness of graphic organizers for three classifications of secondary students in content area classes. *Journal of Learning Disabilities, 23*, 12-22.

Margolis, H., & McGettigan, J. (1988). Managing resistance to instructional modifications in mainstreamed environments. *Remedial and Special Education, 9*, 15-21.

Martens, B. K., Peterson, R. L., Witt, J. C., & Cirone, S. (1986). Teacher perceptions of school-based interventions. *Exceptional Children, 53*, 213-223.

Mastropieri, M. A., & Scruggs, T. E. (1987). *Effective instruction for special education*. Boston: College-Hill.

Mercer, C. D., & Mercer, A. R. (1989). *Teaching students with learning problems* (3rd ed.). Columbus, OH: Merrill.

Palincsar, A., & Brown, A. (1986). Interactive teaching to promote independent learning from text. *The Reading Teacher, 39*, 771-777.

Rooney, K. (1988). *Independent strategies for efficient study*. Richmond, VA: J. R. Enterprises.

Salend, S. J. (1990). *Effective mainstreaming*. New York: Macmillan.

Salend, S. J., & Nowak, M. R. (1988). Effects of peer previewing on LD students oral reading skills. *Learning Disability Quarterly, 11*, 47-54.

Schumaker, J. B., Deshler, D. D., & Ellis, E. S. (1986). Intervention issues related to the education of LD adolescents. In B. K. Wong & J. Torgeson (Eds.), *Psychological and educational perspectives in learning disabilities*. New York: Academic Press.

Seidenberg, P. L. (1989). Relating text-processing research to reading and writing instruction for learning disabled students. *Learning Disabilities Focus, 5*, 4-12.

Smith, G., & Smith, D. (1985). A mainstreaming program that really works. *Journal of Learning Disabilities, 18*, 369-372.

Swicegood, P. R., & Parsons, J. L. (1989). Better questions and answers equal success. *TEACHING Exceptional Children, 21*(3), 4-8.

Wong, B. Y. L. (1985). Self-questioning instructional research: A review. *Review of Educational Research, 55*, 227-268.

Wong, B. Y. L., Wong, R., Perry, N., & Sawatsky, D. (1986). The efficacy of a self-questioning summarization strategy for use by underachievers and learning disabled adolescents in social studies. *Learning Disabilities Focus, 2*, 20-35.

Wood, J. W. (1989). *Mainstreaming: A practical approach for teachers*. Columbus, OH: Merrill.

Teaching Study Skills to Students with Mild Handicaps: The Role of the Classroom Teacher

KAREN DECKER, SUSAN SPECTOR,

and STAN SHAW

Karen Decker and Susan Spector are special education teachers at South Windsor High School, South Windsor, Connecticut. Stan Shaw is a professor and the coordinator of special education, Department of Educational Psychology, The University of Connecticut, Storrs.

Secondary school teachers increasingly find themselves faced with a conundrum for which there seems to be no solution. On one hand, politicians and education reports bombard them with demands to prepare students for the international economic and technological challenges that face our nation (Felt 1985; Hagerty and Abramson 1987). They are encouraged to implement standardized tests based on performance objectives, to increase curriculum coursework and content expectations, and to establish rigid graduation requirements (Shaw et al. 1990). At the same time, special educators, parents of the handicapped, and governmental agencies are expecting schools to educate students with disabilities in the least restrictive environment. Madeline Hill (1986), former assistant secretary for the Office of Special Education and Rehabilitative Services, developed the Regular Education Initiative (REI) in which students with learning problems (i.e., learning disabled, slow learners, educationally disadvantaged, behavior problems) would be educated in the regular classroom. In addition to the special education population, classroom teachers are also expected to meet the needs of the burgeoning population of diverse and at-risk students, almost 30 percent of whom are black, Hispanic, or Asian and one-quarter of whom live in poverty (Ramirez 1990).

Can teachers possibly meet the educational needs of all these students—from those with special learning needs to those with exceptional abilities? These issues are even more pronounced and difficult to resolve at the secondary level. Schumaker and Deshler (1988) have identified barriers to implementing REI with mildly handicapped adolescents in secondary schools. They noted that secondary schools pose particular problems because of the gap between student skill level and increasing demands of the curriculum, the intensive instruction required to ameliorate skill/strategy deficits, and the teacher-centered instruction typical in secondary schools as opposed to the student-centered instruction espoused by the research on effective teaching.

Although there are no simple solutions, research and experience show us that the regular classroom teacher has a significant impact on the success of mildly handicapped students in the regular class (Algozzine and Maheady 1986). To facilitate continuing academic success for these students, regular educators need to have an understanding and awareness of the classroom changes that can make a difference. Special educators need to take the lead in helping regular education teachers incorporate these changes into both their everyday lesson plans as well as their classroom management techniques. One of the classroom changes that can greatly benefit mildly handicapped students is the inclusion of study skills into the teaching of content material.

Study skills is a very broad term that encompasses a multitude of skills that enhance the effectiveness and efficiency of learning. They are often considered to be mainly instructional strategies such as note-taking skills, memory techniques, or test-taking procedures. Just as important to learning, however, are organizational strategies, time management skills, and self-awareness skills (Shaw et al. 1991).

The purpose of study skills is to teach students how to learn. The development of skills that are transferable to all academic areas makes the teaching of study skills indispensable to education (Schumaker and Deshler 1988).

As special education teachers, we have observed these

techniques implemented within the regular class. We have also been fortunate to team-teach in both a biology and pre-algebra class. The skills and ideas related in this article were developed by regular education teachers, not by special educators. It is important to credit these teachers for having insight into the needs of their students and for cultivating these skills within the curriculum.

This article will focus on the skills of organization, learning strategies, and the development of self-awareness as prerequisites for teaching students how to be independent and responsible learners. It will give specific suggestions that can be easily adapted and used in all classes, regardless of subject. We are not in favor of developing separate courses to teach study skills; the place to teach these skills is within the regular classroom content material.

Organization

Lack of organization is cited as a deficit of many students with mild disabilities. The need to teach students to organize springs from the premise that a student must be consistently prepared to meet fundamental daily academic demands (Alley et al. 1983; Schumaker et al. 1983). Training students in good organizational skill practices takes time, but the benefits of doing so can be impressive. Although organizational skills in themselves are not difficult, the self-discipline to use them consistently is. Thus teachers must consistently reinforce organizational skills so that students automatically know when and how to use them.

Time Analysis

A typical deficiency of students with mild disabilities is the inability to structure their time and adapt their schedules to provide time for completion of assignments, studying for tests and quizzes, or completion of a paper or project.

To overcome this deficit, teachers can help their students plan ahead by either passing out or writing on the board a list of weekly or bimonthly assignments that include the dates of upcoming quizzes, tests, or papers. We saw examples of this approach in the various classrooms we visited. For example, in math class, a computer-generated monthly calendar of all assignments helps immensely by alerting students to the pace and expectations of the teacher. In a social studies class, assignments are given by units and include all the necessary work and due dates for the given unit, regardless of the time frame. Some time frames may reflect a month while others only a couple of weeks. In an English class, the teacher supplies a weekly handout of assignments with a cartoon as well as a listing of upcoming "attractions."

Whatever the method, this practice encourages students to take responsibility for their classwork. Even if a student is absent, everyone is well aware of what is due and when. This eliminates the excuses for incomplete work.

In addition, teachers find this practice an excellent opportunity to teach students that studying for a test is an ongoing process. Daily discussions of how to break up the material for studying can be quickly accomplished.

Daily Check

At the secondary level, students must show up to class prepared to participate. They must have the essentials of success: (1) writing instrument, (2) book, (3) assignment sheet filled out with the next day's assignment, and (4) notebook. Anything less and the student is considered "unprepared."

Teachers can do a "daily check" in short order. In the team-taught high school biology class of twenty-four, students are trained to have assembled the "essentials" on their desks by the time class begins. Once the routine is established, it takes the teacher about a minute to walk up and down the rows and conduct daily check and record who is prepared and who is not. Many teachers compile this information and then count the results as one or two quiz grades at the end of the quarter. Others require students to stay after school if they come to class unprepared. In order for this technique to be successful, it must be done consistently.

Notebook Check

Students need to realize that their notebook is their best friend. The goal is to show students how to use their notebooks to their best advantage. A notebook must be up-to-date and have a logical order.

Often teachers include notebook requirements in their classroom rules and regulations at the beginning of the year. Here they explain in detail that a notebook for their class should have (1) a section for class notes, (2) an area to keep returned tests and quizzes, and (3) a location for current and completed homework. Some classes also require space for handouts. The actual requirements are solely dependent on individual class needs.

Once established, it is imperative that regular notebook checks be conducted. Just how this is done is up to the teacher. In several social studies classes, a thorough check is undertaken at the end of each unit. Teachers require each student to keep a folder of everything done in class. It is arranged in the order in which each assignment or activity was completed. Several days before the folder is due, a listing is passed out with the order and date of each assignment listed. Missing work must be represented in the folder by a blank piece of paper. With this folder in order, students have all the necessary material to study for the unit test. In addition, the teachers have dramatically shown students the connection between organization and test-taking strategies. Furthermore, students are no longer surprised by their unit grades. Thus a notebook-check activity yields lessons in organization and test-taking preparation, as well as self-awareness. Although this is an ambitious undertaking, it is highly effective.

In the team-taught biology class, a quick weekly check of notes is done to make sure that students are complying with basic procedures. In other classes, a spot check, where the teacher may simply ask students to open their notebooks and locate a particular item, is conducted. Still another possibility occurs when the teacher asks students a question from previous work and then directs students to the section of their notebooks where the material can be found. Typically, this is a time-limited activity for which one or two minutes are allocated.

Once notebook guidelines are established, it is up to the regular classroom teacher to reinforce the need for organization of class material. Again, teachers often count these activities anywhere from a quiz grade to a major test grade, depending upon the need of the class to master this skill.

The ultimate goal of both daily check and notebook check is to establish good habits that eventually replace the poor ones. As the class becomes progressively more proficient in this area, there comes a point when it is no longer necessary to check organizational skills as often.

Learning Strategies

Most students—and especially students with disabilities—have great difficulty in generalizing a skill taught in isolation. It is, therefore, most effective to teach learning strategies within the regular classroom. Such basic skills as note taking, outlining, memory techniques, and test-taking skills can be incorporated into daily instruction (deBettencourt and Zigmong 1990; Lock and Abbey 1989). Here are some ideas that have been successfully used by secondary classroom teachers.

Notetaking and Outlining

Using guided notes has been effective in low-level social studies classes. Teachers begin the year putting all necessary information on the board. As the year progresses, specific information is left out, and students are required to add the information on their own. Prior to this, signal words and phrases (e.g., *first, importantly, don't forget, next*) are introduced. Either at the end of class or the following day, the teacher reviews the "missing" information to make sure everyone has it.

For some students, the conventional outline approach is very difficult. Yet these same students can learn to use alternative note-taking methods. For example, clustering, mind-maps, and concept trees, intertwined with color cueing, provide a whole new way to learn note-taking skills. Not all students learn the same way. Not all note taking should be taught the same way.

Two social studies teachers teach alternative techniques with great success. They purposely introduce different methods and then reinforce them throughout the school year, allowing students to better understand the benefits of each method. By the end of the school year, within any particular class, there are students using a myriad of techniques to take notes. Because these teachers are comfortable with note-taking methods, all students can find the best way for themselves.

Memory Techniques

Memory is an area where mildly handicapped students consistently experience difficulties. Classroom reinforcement of these skills is crucial. Some of the most effective are discussed below.

• Flashcards. In both biology and social studies classes, flashcards are required as a way to practice and learn new vocabulary. Index cards, cut in half, are passed out to all students. Class time is given to begin the exercise. Flashcards are collected and checked for spelling and definition accuracy. Some teachers consider this part of notebook check, while others collect and grade them separately.

• Color Cueing. For this, packets of highlighters are kept in the class. A different color is used to represent ideas. For example, in social studies, an economics issue might be highlighted in blue while a political concern is represented in green. A math teacher uses colored chalk for boardwork to alert students to remember what is important and what should be in their notes.

• Mnemonics. Teachers in all departments use mnemonics to help students prepare for quizzes and tests. Asking students how they would go about memorizing a certain diagram, map, or list is an exercise that takes very little time but can greatly benefit all members of the class.

Test Taking

Many students simply do not know how to study for a test, and they erroneously conclude that they are poor test takers. This is especially true of students with mild disabilities. Most of what has already been discussed in this article is all part of test taking. For example, notebook organization and use, time analysis skills, and note taking, outlining, and memory techniques all are indispensable for test-taking success. Students need to understand that studying for a test is an ongoing process and not something that a student can leave for the night before and still expect to do well.

Another important aspect of test taking is anticipating what will be on the test. A math teacher requires students to submit a practice test, complete with written directions and an answer sheet. Grading is dependent on how well students anticipate the actual test. The closer a student comes to anticipating the test questions, the better the grade.

Alternative Delivery Methods

A secondary social studies teacher believes that students need to practice learning in different ways. The traditional pencil and paper activities need variety to help students obtain information. In every unit taught, there are exercises that are written, oral, visual, and auditory. For example, a written assignment might be a worksheet or a drawing; an oral activity might be a debate, reading aloud, a skit, or having a discussion; a visual presentation could be the use of slides, pictures with no captions, moveable pieces (maps, time lines, etc.) or the use of a VCR without the sound; an audio assignment could be recording a lesson on tape instead of writing it.

None of the above learning strategies requires extensive changes in lesson plans—only a clearer understanding of what the mildly handicapped student in the classroom requires to be successful.

Self-Awareness

If students have unrealistic views, either negative or positive, of themselves or how they function it is difficult and frustrating for them to make substantive progress in school or in any other aspect of their lives. To deal with this issue, several teachers have woven self-awareness activities into their regular lesson plans to assist students to function more realistically and independently.

Pre-Test

Before the class begins a new topic, a math teacher has the students complete a checklist of specific skills that they will be addressing in the new unit. The students read a simple statement and then write yes or no depending on whether or not they feel they know how to do that skill. For example, a statement might read, "I know how to multiply with decimals," or "I know how to use ratios to solve problems." This exercise is never graded, but it allows students to preview upcoming work and lets them see that there are sections that they already know. It also lets the teacher know how realistically a student assesses his or her own abilities.

Study Skills Checklist

In a team-taught biology class and a team-taught pre-algebra class, students are asked to take a few minutes to complete a self-assessment of their study habits for that class. Questions include, "I usually receive 80 or above on my homework," or "I correct old quizzes and tests to study from." Again, the activity is not graded, but the teacher takes the time to meet individually with each student and briefly discusses his or her perceptions. No class time is lost as this is done just before class started or at the end of class if there are a few minutes left.

Quarterly Assessment

At the end of each quarter in a high school science class, students are asked to write a brief response to questions such as, "What part of the course did you do best in?" and "What do you plan to continue or plan to change during the next quarter?" Again the teacher

meets individually with each student as time permits. This activity gives the teacher excellent insight into how the students view the class and what areas individuals or the class as a whole perceive as weaknesses.

Grade Sheets

Several teachers require that students keep track of their grades on a sheet they pass out. Students must record homework assignments, quizzes, and tests, as well as grades on any papers or projects. At the end of a unit or quarter, students compute their grade averages with a formula given by the teacher. They are graded on how close they come to matching the average computed by the teacher. With this method, the students stay in touch with their grades and become aware of how their teacher actually arrives at their individual grades.

Course Self-Evaluation

At the end of each unit in an American history class, the student, teacher, and parent complete a form that evaluates the student's progress. The teacher puts the average the student earned on the top of the sheet. Then the student explains what was done to earn that grade. Next, the teacher writes his or her view of the earned grade. Finally the form is sent home and parents are asked to write their perceptions of the student's work. The parent-signed form is then returned to school. Instead of the traditional school-generated progress report, this exercise gives everyone involved tremendous amounts of shared information.

Class Evaluations

A U.S. history teacher has her students evaluate the methods used in teaching a chapter or unit of material. With this activity, the students are not evaluating the teacher, only the particular way in which the material was taught. Comments need to be specific, not general. What did they like? What would they change? What would they keep the same? This input helps the teacher evaluate the class reaction to different learning presentations. More important, it allows the students to express their feelings and to know that they do indeed have input into future assignments.

The many aspects of self-awareness, although simple on the surface, require a good deal of maturity and insight. These undertakings require students to evaluate themselves critically and not blame others for their shortcomings. It forces students to better understand where their strengths and weaknesses are and how they can adjust.

Conclusion

The teachers we talked with concur that the integration of study skills into the regular curriculum helps students to do better academically because they are better organized and have a clearer sense of what is expected of them. A social studies teacher noted that students' performance has improved 80 to 90 percent in her classes in which study skills are continually reinforced. In a team-taught biology class in which a study skills approach was integrated into the daily lessons, there was a seven- to eight-point increase in grades when compared to other biology classes using the same curriculum without the study skills approach.

A math teacher coming from a team-taught pre-algebra class commented, "There is an obvious difference between those students who 'buy-in' to the study skills. Without exception, they get better grades. They are more prepared for tests and quizzes and become more active participants." A social studies teacher observed that teaching students study skills improves their self-confidence and self-esteem. Those who actively use the techniques know that they can do well and recognize that learning and good grades are not accidents. For special education students, who traditionally feel academically inadequate, the study skills provide the structure and develop the self-confidence that students need to be more successful.

The teaching of study skills is a two-way street. Not only do students benefit, but teachers say that they find themselves more receptive to new techniques and methods. Teachers also remark that this approach helps them be more organized, which in turn allows them to present a clearer set of expectations to their students. Most important, teaching study skills shows students how to learn rather than merely how to memorize the material. These skills need to be taught and reinforced with all students in all classes. Failing to teach these skills in the regular classroom will make success elusive for the mildly handicapped student who is especially weak in the essential skills of organization, learning strategies, and self-awareness.

ACKNOWLEDGMENT

The authors would like to thank Cynthia Burroughs (social studies), MaryLou Grabowski (social studies) and James O'Loughlin (math) for sharing and teaching us the methods that make them successful teachers.

Also, the authors are indebted to Lawrence Bojarski (math) and John Longo (science) for opening their classrooms to team-teaching where many new ideas were implemented.

REFERENCES

Algozzine, B., and L. Maheady. 1986. When all else fails, teach! *Exceptional Children* 52:487–88.

Alley, G. R., D. D. Deshler, F. L. Clark, J. B. Schumaker, and M. M. Warner. 1983. Learning disabilities in adolescent and adult populations: Research implications (Part II). *Focus on Exceptional Children* 15:1–16.

deBettencourt, L. U., and N. Zigmond. 1990. The learning disabled secondary school dropout. *Teacher Education and Special Education* 13:17–20.

Felt, M. C. 1985. *Improving our schools.* Newton, Mass.: Educational Development Center.

Hagerty, G. J., and M. Abramson. 1987. Impediments to implementing national policy change for mildly handicapped student. *Exceptional Children* 53:315–23.

Locke, E. T., and D. E. Abbey. 1989. A unique equation: Learning strategies + generalization = success. *Academic Therapy* 24: 569–75.

Ramirez, B. A. 1990. Preparing special education and related services personnel to serve culturally and linguistically diverse children with handicaps: Needs and future directions. In *Critical issues in special education: Implications for personnel preparation,* edited by L. M. Bullock and R. L. Simpson, 92–96. Denton: University of North Texas.

Schumaker, J. B., and D. D. Deshler. 1988. Implementing the regular education initiative in secondary schools: A different ball game. *Journal of Learning Disabilities* 21:36–42.

Schumaker, J. B., D. D. Deshler, G. R. Alley, and M. M. Warner. 1983. Toward the development of an intervention model for learning disabled adolescents. *Exceptional Education Quarterly* 4:295–304.

Shaw, S. F., D. Biklen, S. Conlon, J. Dunn, J. Kramer, and V. DeRoma-Wagner. 1990. Special education and school reform. In *Critical issues in special education: Implications for personnel preparation,* edited by L. M. Bullock and R. L. Simpson, 12–25. Denton: University of North Texas.

Shaw, S. F., L. C. Brinckerhoff, J. K. Kistler, and J. M. McGuire. 1991. Preparing students with learning disabilities for postsecondary education: Issues and future needs. *Learning Disabilities* 2: 23–28.

Will, M. 1986. *Educating students with learning problems: A shared responsibility.* Washington, D.C.: Office of Special Education and Rehabilitative Services, U.S. Department of Education.

Children With Mental Retardation

The definition of mental retardation (MR) has three components: significantly subaverage IQ (below 70), deficits in adaptive behaviors, and a manifestation during the developmental period (before the end of puberty). Classification of a person as mentally retarded can only be done after thorough assessment of both an analysis of intelligence and an analysis of adaptive behaviors. It is desirable to make other assessments as well.

Many professionals feel that IQ tests are not valid measures of intelligence. They can be inaccurate, unreliable, and detrimental in some situations. A 1979 court case in California concluded that the IQ tests used in that state for the purpose of placing students in special classes were racially and culturally biased. Disproportionate numbers of minority children were mislabeled as retarded and maintained in MR classes in violation of PL 94-142. The judge ruled that California children must be assessed for intelligence without the use of the existing IQ tests, and any future IQ tests were to be submitted to the court for approval before use. California's ban on IQ tests has had enormous nationwide repercussions in regard to the assessment of mental retardation. While most states still use IQ tests, they also emphasize cognitive processes and problem-solving strategies. Developmental histories and health histories are reviewed, and more weight is placed on measures and observations of adaptive abilities and behaviors.

Many professionals feel that the adaptive scales now in use are also invalid and unreliable. Experts differ in how they define adaptive skills. Are they synonymous with social skills? self-care? what? The adaptive scales now in use measure such things as communication, independence, number and time concepts, the ability to handle money, self-direction, manners, and responsibility.

Due in large part to changes in the definition of mental retardation, the number of students with mental retardation in public schools in the United States has dropped 20 percent since 1980. Children with IQs above 70 and/or who pass an adaptive ability test cannot be classified as mentally retarded.

There are vast differences among children with legitimately classified mental retardation. Those with mild retardation can usually learn sufficient self-help skills and social skills to live independently or semi-independently after they finish their formal education. Children once considered the educable mentally retarded (EMR) and children once labeled the trainable mentally retarded (TMR) are not all considered mildly retarded. Some of them can read, write, and find skilled vocational jobs. Some of them drop out of school with functional illiteracy as soon as they reach age sixteen and have difficulty completing even unskilled tasks.

Individuals with severe mental retardation need custodial care for life. They are usually not placed in the public school system for education. Even within the category of severe mental retardation, however, there are wide variations in abilities.

What causes mental retardation? For the majority of persons with mental retardation, experts cannot clearly establish the origin of their mental problems. Many circumstances and conditions, singly or in combination, may be responsible. These include lack of prenatal neuron development due to drugs, viruses, radiation, chromosomal defects, genetic mutations, or lack of nutrients; neonatal destruction of neurons due to malnutrition, neglect, poisoning, head injuries, or infections; or misfiring of neurons due to some psychiatric disturbance such as a pervasive developmental disorder. Other causes may also be implicated; this is not an inclusive list of etiologic factors. It is usually impossible to pinpoint exactly why any unique individual with mental retardation has his or her degree of retarded intelligence.

The Amendment to the Education for All Handicapped Act (PL 99-457) mandated comprehensive multidisciplinary services for infants and toddlers and their families as soon as a condition of disability is diagnosed. Early childhood intervention for children with mental retardation, and for their families, has made it easier to include them in regular education classes by public schools. The children learn social skills, fundamental living skills, and appropriate behaviors. Their families can be helped to organize their lives to better meet the needs of a child with intellectual retardation, to make the home environment more intellectually stimulating, and to improve the child's nutritional status. Early intervention can enhance the lives of children with mental retardation but should not be expected to cure the disability.

Educators debate the wisdom of the regular education

initiative for children with mental retardation. The way in which they are instructed is more crucial than where they are instructed. Children with mild mental retardation should learn to read and write, to communicate effectively, to follow social conventions, and to develop some vocational skills. In order to help students with mental retardation make the transition from the world of school to the world of work, vocational education should begin early. A regular education class with supportive services offered by consultants and itinerant teachers may provide an appropriate education. In some cases a resource room pull-out, part-time special education, may provide a more appropriate education. Each child with MR should have an annually updated individualized education program to assure that his or her unique needs are being served.

In the first unit article, R. Brett Nelson, Jack Cummings, and Heidi Boltman focus on the need to teach basic concepts to retarded children. In order for children to communicate effectively, they must understand concepts, the fundamental building blocks of intelligence. The second selection suggests strategies for teaching sex education to students with mental retardation. The next article presents an effective model for group teaching of students with MR that increases their correct responses and holds their attention.

Looking Ahead: Challenge Questions

What basic concepts compromise the fundamental building blocks of intelligence? Can retarded children grasp basic concepts?

What strategies work best when teaching sex education to students with mental retardation?

Will a task demonstration model enhance the education of groups of students with mental retardation?

Teaching Basic Concepts to Students Who Are Educable Mentally Handicapped

R. Brett Nelson
Jack A. Cummings
Heidi Boltman

R. Brett Nelson *(CEC Chapter #381) is School Psychologist, Greeley Public Schools, Greeley, CO.* **Jack A. Cummings** *(CEC Chapter #280) is Associate Professor, School of Education and Institute of Child Study, Indiana University, Bloomington.* **Heidi Boltman** *(CEC Chapter #381) is Resource Teacher, Greeley Public Schools.*

C oncepts are the fundamental building blocks of intelligence (Kagan, 1966). In order for a young child to communicate effectively, the most basic concepts must be understood. Bracken (1984) defined a basic concept as a word in its most elementary sense, that is, a label representing an idea. A concept is basic if there exists no other term that means the same thing, yet is stated more simply. Examples include "in order," "least," "pair," "equal," "above," and "next to." The importance of basic concepts as they relate to classroom instruction was first recognized by Boehm (1967). She reviewed preschool and primary curriculum materials and identified concepts that occurred frequently. These concepts were seldom explained, or they were explained in the simplest form and then used in a more complex manner. After testing kindergarten, first-, second-, and third-grade children for their understanding of various concepts, she included the most difficult and frequently misunderstood concepts in the Boehm Test of Basic Concepts (BTBC) (1971).

Delayed language development is often noted as a characteristic of children who are educable mentally handicapped (EMH) (Dunn, 1973; Jordan, 1966; Robinson & Robinson, 1965; Wyne & O'Connor, 1979). Nelson and Cummings (1981, 1984) administered the BTBC to primary children with this disability. Of the 50 concepts tested, 4 were missed by more than 75% of the children, including "in order," "least," "pair," and "third." Between 25% and 49% of the children tested missed 17 concepts. A total of 29 concepts were misunderstood by more than one-fourth of the sample, among them such concepts as "above," "always," "beginning," "between," "different," "other," and "separated." These results should be contrasted to the performance of the standardization sample, nondisabled second-graders tested at midyear. Only 3 of the 50 concepts were missed by more than 25% of the standardization group.

The value of these studies was their documentation that primary children who are educable mentally handicapped have significant deficits in their understanding of the basic concepts identified by Boehm. These concepts occur frequently, and most teachers assume that children understand them.

Special education teachers are skilled at providing experiences that promote attainment of vocabulary and general concepts. However, teachers must not assume that certain concepts are understood when they are not. If children misunderstand the concepts presented in the teacher's written or oral directions, the instructions will confuse rather than orient them to the task demands.

Understanding basic concepts is a prerequisite for many educational activities and experiences, as well as for successful communication in and outside of school. Since these concepts are frequently used in both regular and special education classes, it is logical to teach them systematically. This article outlines a method for doing so.

Instructional Guidelines

Instruction in basic concepts can be enhanced by the teacher's knowledge of learning difficulties that are specifically related to children with EMH. These children often have difficulty attending to the relevant attributes of a stimulus and organizing and categorizing incoming information (Wyne & O'Connor, 1979). Deficient short-term memory processing (Ellis, 1970) and an expectancy for failure (Dunn, 1973) are also characteristics of children with EMH. These specific attributes should be considered in formulating a method for instruction in basic concepts.

Boehm (1977) described three major learning processes, including concrete and represented application, productive use in the child's own speech, and application at more abstract levels. In the concrete and represented application, as the concept is heard it is connected to its meaning in relation to the child's own body, concrete objects in the environment, photographs, or pictures of objects and the printed page. In the process of producing the concept in speech, the child is asked to use the term in everyday conversation. Alternative labels for the concept are used, and mental pictures relevant to the concept are formed and described. When applied at a more abstract level, the concept is used in making comparisons, sequencing, classifying, and in combination with other concepts. The following general guidelines represent a method for teaching basic concepts in a systematic way, based on Boehm's conceptualization of the learning process and considering the learning characteristics of children with EMH. The guidelines also take into consideration the theories of Bruner, (1973); Klausmeier (1976); and Owen, Blount, and Moscow (1978) as they relate to general concept development.

Concrete and Represented Application

In presenting the concepts at a concrete level, simple objects such as toys and clothing, as well as the children themselves, should be used so that the children are not distracted by a need to learn about unfamiliar objects. Using the concepts "top," "bottom," "above," "below," "over," and "under" in relation to the children, have them place their hands on top of their heads, on the bottom of their feet, above their belts, below their belts, over their hands, and under their hands. Repeat the exercise with the children using each other as models. Have the children place their hands on top of their partners' feet, on the bottom of their legs, above and below their knees, over their shoulders, and under their arms. Assess their understanding by having them play "Simon Says" before moving on to teaching the concepts in relation to objects in the environment.

Using the same concepts as examples in relation to their environment, have the children sit on top of their chairs and place their hands on the bottom of their desks. Ask them whether or not they can sit on the bottom of a chair. Have the children sit on top of a box and above the floor. Ask them whether or not they can be below the floor. Have them stoop under a desk and point to the bottom of it. Use the chalkboard to display the concepts, first by drawing a simple picture on the chalkboard and having the children draw an X to mark the concept and then in relation to the chalkboard itself. Do the same with other objects such as blocks, books, clothing, and writing utensils.

It is also important to provide "nonexamples" for children so that they clearly differentiate the concepts being studied from similar terms. This allows children with EMH to attend to the critical attributes that define the concept. In a matching/pairing exercise, an example and a nonexample of a concept are presented. For instance, to teach the concept of "top" in relation to the child's environment, use two desks and two balls. Placing a ball on one of the desks, be definite in saying, "The ball is on top of the desk." For the nonexample, place the ball next to the desk and point out that this is *not* an example of the concept "top." Divergent pairing involves the use of two or more examples of the same concept and again helps children attend to the critical attributes of the concept rather than the attributes of the objects used to define the concept. Have a child place the ball on top of the desk and indicate that this represents the concept of "top." Have another child place a stuffed animal on top of a box and indicate that this also represents the concept.

In using photographs and pictures, show the children examples of "top," "bottom," "above," "below," "over," and "under." Have them point to objects in a picture and ask them, "Is the chimney above or below the house?" or "Is the window at the top of the house or the bottom?" Use coloring books to have children indicate where objects appear. Again, provide nonexamples and assess understanding informally.

Repetition with distributed practice and overlearning should be used to compensate for problems with short-term memory processing that are characteristic of children with EMH. Concepts should be presented for short periods of time and frequently, with repetitions occurring daily and opportunities for review weeks later.

Concept Production in Everyday Speech

To facilitate the use of concepts in their own speech, ask the children to set up a group of objects in the room that represent the concepts. Have the children describe the concepts in their own words to their peers. Encourage them to use alternative and interchangeable labels for the concepts. Examples include "lid" for the concept "top" and "across" for the concept "over." When encouraging the use of alternative labels, provide opportunities for the children to practice (e.g., describing an object submersed in water that is both under the water and surrounded by water).

Abstract Application

In applying the concepts at more abstract levels, have the children begin reversing the concepts (e.g., by holding a ball above the table, then below the table). The same objects can be used to reverse the concepts "over" and "under" and "top" and "bottom." Other objects in the children's environment such as books, pencils, blocks, and boxes can also be used to help them reverse concepts. When comparing concepts, ask the children to grasp balloons that are not at the bottom or the top of a net. This can be applied to pictures by asking the children to show objects in the picture that are not above or below a designated object. In sequencing, have them place dolls on the various rungs of a ladder. Ask them to describe the dolls from top to bottom, then from bottom to top. In classifying, use containers of buttons and ask the children to point to the containers with white buttons at the top. Use pictures from a magazine and ask the children to identify the ones with shadows below the objects pictured. When combining concepts, use commands that provide for the use of several concepts at once (e.g., "place the top of the jar beside the chair under the window").

Implementation and Evaluation

The guidelines just described are intended to be general in application and can be used in a variety of learning situations. Basic concepts can be taught in conjunction with other instructional programs such as other language skills, mathematical skills, or orientation skills designed to help children with EMH function more successfully in the learning environment. Since it cannot be taken for granted that children with EMH grasp the meaning of basic concepts, it is important to assess their understanding of the concepts and teach them directly. By testing the entire class, either with the

Boehm Test of Basic Concepts or the Bracken Basic Concept Scale, a teacher gains a clear understanding of the needs of the individual children. In addition to the concepts measured by these two tests, teachers can add terms they feel are important conceptual statements for primary-age children.

After assessment, children may be grouped according to their instructional needs, with three to five students in a group. Needs may be dictated by age, behavior, or general range of functioning, as well as the specific concepts to be taught. To facilitate overlearning and accommodate distributed rather than massed practice, group instruction should occur more than once daily for short periods of time (i.e., 20–30 minutes). In addition to providing instructional periods for systematic teaching of basic concepts, teachers should take advantage of other opportunities for concept attainment and generalization (Vaughn, Bos, & Lund, 1986). Examples include lining up, lunch time, cooking, playground activities, and field trips.

Materials used to teach the concepts can be gathered from a variety of sources. They are already a part of any well-stocked classroom. The Boehm (1977) *Resource Guide* also provides comprehensive materials for instructional purposes. Curriculum kits developed for general language instruction also can be used. Examples include the *Cup Concept Understanding Program* developed by Blum, Irwin, Kavaloski, Sanderson, and Schippits (1974); *Systems 80*, promoted by Durrell (1973); and *Word Relationships: Cut and Paste*, developed by Nakumo (1978).

Evaluation of concept attainment should be ongoing and occur both for-mally and informally. A list of concepts should be maintained for both groups and individuals to keep track of concepts successfully mastered and those needing more practice. Formal evaluation could take the form of a posttest conducted at an appropriate time (e.g., year's end). Due to the special learning needs of the group, not all targeted concepts may be taught in a school year; some may require an extension to the following year. Informal evaluation on an ongoing basis will dictate the speed of instruction. Such evaluation might include teacher observation of the group's progress, "Simon Says" games, and having individual students indicate mastery by both showing and verbalizing their understanding of the concept.

Conclusion

Basic concepts are important building blocks for the attainment of general information and success in an instructional environment. Children who are educable mentally handicapped need direct and systematic instruction in these concepts. Basic concept instruction should become an integral part of their curriculum, and the attainment of such concepts should not be taken for granted. By using the methods described, teachers can enhance the achievement of children who have difficulty understanding basic concepts.

References

Blum, P., Irwin, S., Kavaloski, R., Sanderson, J., & Schippits, S. (1974). *Cup: A concept understanding program*. Minneapolis: Amidon & Associates.

Boehm, A. E. (1967). The development of comparative concepts in primary school children. *Dissertation Abstracts International, 27B*, 4109. (University Microfilms No. 67-5767).

Boehm, A. E. (1971). *Boehm Test of Basic Concepts manual*. New York: Psychological Corporation.

Boehm, A. E. (1977). *Boehm resource guide for basic concept teaching*. New York: Psychological Corporation.

Bracken, B. A. (1984). *Bracken Basic Concept Scale*. Columbus, OH: Charles E. Merrill.

Bruner, J. E. (1973). *Beyond the information given*. New York: Norton.

Dunn, L. A. (1973). *Exceptional children in the schools: Special education in transition* (2nd ed). New York: Holt, Rinehart, & Winston.

Durrell, D. D. (1973). *Systems 80*. Niles, IL: Borg/Warner Educational Systems.

Ellis, N. R. (1970). Memory processes in retardates and normals. In N. R. Ellis (Ed.), *International review of research in mental retardation* (pp. 1–31). New York: Academic Press.

Jordan, T. E. (1966). *The mentally retarded* (2nd ed.). Columbus, OH: Charles E. Merrill.

Kagan, J. (1966). A development approach to conceptual growth. In H. J. Klausmeier & C. W. Harris (Eds.), *Analysis of concept learning* (pp. 97–116). New York: Academic Press.

Klausmeier, H. J. (1976). Instructional design and the teaching of concepts. In J. R. Levin & L. L. Allen (Eds.), *Cognitive learning in children*. New York: Academic Press.

Nakumo, K. (1978). *Word relationships: Cut and paste*. Palos Verdes Peninsula, CA: Frank Schaffer Publications.

Nelson, R. B., & Cummings, J. A. (1981). Basic concept attainment of educable mentally handicapped children: Implications for teaching concepts. *Education and Training of the Mentally Retarded, 16*, 303–306.

Nelson, R. B., & Cummings, J. A. (1984). Educable mentally retarded children's understanding of Boehm Basic Concepts. *Psychological Reports, 154*, 81–82.

Owen, S. V., Blount, H. P., & Moscow, H. (1978). *Educational psychology*. Boston: Little, Brown.

Robinson, N., & Robinson, M. (1965). *The mentally retarded child: A psychological approach*. New York: McGraw-Hill.

Vaughn, S., Bos, C. S., & Lund, A. R. (1986). But they can do it in my classroom: Strategies for promoting generalization. *TEACHING Exceptional Children, 18*, 176–180.

Wyne, M. P., & O'Connor, P. D. (1979). *Exceptional children: A developmental view*. Lexington, MA: D.C. Heath.

Sex Education for Students with High-Incidence Special Needs

Greg M. Romaneck and Robert Kuehl

Greg M. Romaneck (CEC Chapter #466) is Director of Special Education, DeKalb CUSD #428, DeKalb, IL. Robert Kuehl is a Principal, Alturas Junior High School, Alturas, CA.

The ability to express, understand, and fulfill socially appropriate sexual needs is a basic human right. However, sexual identity is not an innate personality trait; to understand sexuality an individual must be educated. Both instruction and experience allow an individual to expand his or her behavioral repertoire and attain a satisfactory sexual self-image. Sex education programs in public schools should be one source of information for young people searching for their sexual identity.

Despite public opposition from a variety of sources, the need for adequate school-based sex education programs is pressing. This need is especially relevant for high-incidence students with special needs. This group of students includes individuals with learning disabilities, educable levels of mental disability, and moderate behavior disorders. They may have even less knowledge of their own sexual identity than their nondisabled peers (Smigielski & Steinmann, 1981). As psychologist and sex educator Sol Gordon (1973) has noted,

> Handicapped children, with the same emotions and sexual drives as their normal counterparts but with less knowledge, as well as the disadvantaged, with all their "experience," are by far the most vulnerable segment of our youth in regard to sexual exploitation and pathology. (p. 351)

Students classified as having learning disabilities, behavior disorders, and mild mental disabilities experience the same emerging sexual curiosities as those of their nondisabled peers. However, due to their disabling conditions, these learners face social problems that are not typically encountered by the majority of young people (White, 1985). Among the commonly reported obstacles in the paths of these students are social skills shortfalls (Gresham & Reschly, 1986), low peer status ratings (Dudly-Maring & Edmiaston, 1985), faulty conceptualizations of health issues (Noland, Riggs, & Hall, 1985), and rejection by regular educators (Baugh, 1984).

In the face of growing initiatives to integrate students in special education into mainstream programs, these obstacles assume an even greater significance. Students with high-incidence special needs will have to cope with their social goals in a more public fashion than previously. The provision of adequate sex education to these learners should be a part of a general education effort to acclimatize them to full social integration. As one writer stated,

> Sex education can help handicapped individuals understand their own responsibility in finding sexual satisfaction and may foster self-responsibility, maturity, and positive actions toward rehabilitation goals. Through this process they can reject the idea that they are not capable of being loved or sexual, and initiate the process of doing something about it. Sexual health is but one aspect of total health which is necessary in preparing all young people for life. (McNab, 1978, p. 301)

Thus, sex education should be part of a broad effort to provide students in special education with the skills needed to cope with their natural developmental requirements. In order to accomplish this goal, teachers must become familiar with typical strategies associated with sex education.

Teaching Strategies

In providing sex education to students with disabilities, teachers enter into a curricular world far different from mathematics, reading, or other content areas. Teachers are required to examine their own value systems and be able to present material in a nonjudgmental fashion (Reed & Munson, 1976). In many instances the attitudes conveyed to students about sex have more impact than the actual content (Gordon, 1973). The American Association of Health, Physical Education, and Recreation (AAHPER), in cooperation with the Sex Information and Education Council for the U.S. (SIECUS), have outlined the following key considerations for prospective teachers of sex education:

1. Chronological age is the best predictor of sexual concerns for learners with disabilities.

While preparing a sex education program, it is imperative to recognize student needs, interests, and questions. The goals and objectives of a sex education curriculum must be founded upon student concerns. If these criteria are not met, student interest will wane and the program will fail. To help achieve success, teachers should build in ample opportunities for student input, involvement, and feedback (Reich & Harshman, 1975). This collaborative learning environment can be established in a number of ways.

Interest inventories, needs assessments, social services, student drop boxes, group and individual counseling, and formal classroom presentations are all examples of potential program components (Payne et al., 1981). In selecting specific materials, special educators must be aware of differing student abilities. Students with mental disabilities will require slower pacing and more concrete presentations than their potentially more sophisticated peers with learning disorders or behavior disorders (Sbindell, 1975).

2. Instructional materials should be carefully assessed and, if necessary, modified prior to implementation with children and youth with disabilities.
3. The values of students with special needs, which may be different from those of the teacher, should be considered.
4. Teachers should be good listeners and not merely dispensers of information.
5. Teachers should be prepared to modify content to meet specific concerns and needs of individual students.
6. Teachers should avoid judgments and expressions of personal biases.

Research has shown that students in the high-incidence categories of disability are inquisitive, have a need to know, and can best be served by a caring person who can provide accurate information (Block, 1972). Like their nondisabled peers, these students go through a natural sexual growth and development process. Although they may differ in learning styles from individuals who have no disabilities, they experience similar affective needs.

When developing a sex education curriculum, special educators should address the following four basic issues (Payne, Polloway, Smith, & Payne, 1981, p. 315):

1. What to teach. Provide accurate, developmentally appropriate information to students. Resource guides developed by Fischer, Krajicek, and Borthnick (1974) and published by AAHPER and SIECUS (1971) are helpful. Commercially produced materials such as *About Your Sexuality* (Calderwood, 1979), or *The Coping With* series (Wrenn & Schwarzrock, 1980) may be of value.
2. When to teach it. Instruction should commence before difficulties arise, in the prepuberty period. This can be achieved by integrating sex education information into regular instruction and addressing spontaneously occurring issues appropriately.
3. Where to teach. Except for issues dealing with specific anatomical details and functions, which may be difficult to cope with, the classroom is the appropriate place for instruction. Most miseducation about sex occurs when it is ignored in the schools or home.
4. How to teach. The essential point is to be honest, direct, specific, information-based, and nonproselytize in responding to questions and comments.

Whatever methods or materials are selected, the teacher should remember that the curriculum must remain student-centered, provide a content-to learner match, and provide information of vital concern to children and youth.

The following personal traits are associated with successful teachers of sex education:

1. Credibility: the ability to win the confidence and respect of the students as well as maintain their attention.
2. Knowledge: an awareness of the subject matter and confidence in the ability to present the material in an open and straightforward manner.
3. Trust: engendering in students the feeling that they can communicate freely and openly with an authority figure.
4. Acceptingness: the ability to accept individual differences.
5. Approachability: communicating to students that they can express highly sensitive or private feelings to an authority figure.
6. Flexibility: the capability of deal-

ing with student input in a nonrigid fashion.
7. Authenticity: the ability to maintain an honest and sincere posture toward students.

Conclusion

At present, there is opposition to sex education for students with and without disabilities. However, despite the absence of empirical studies determining either the success or failure of sex education efforts, there is a general understanding within our society that a need for public school sex education exists.

The additional stresses associated with the AIDS virus and the likelihood that students with special needs may stand at greater risk (Black, 1986) make the provision of sex education to these individuals a major concern. An instructional system geared toward helping learners with disabilities achieve appropriate sexuality will require close cooperation among special educators, regular teachers, administrators, parents, and other school personnel (Smigielski & Steinmann, 1981). This type of cooperative programming will help students in special education attain satisfying and socially productive adulthoods. Sex education should be cornerstone in a relevant, developmental, and functional curriculum. As one researcher has put it,

Traditionally, the teaching of sexuality to handicapped persons has run into objections resulting from society's negative attitude toward the handicapped and parental apprehension regarding the decision-making skills of their children in relation to acceptable and unacceptable sexual behaviors. However, the Education for All Handicapped Children Act of 1975 has provided a way for parents and health professionals to put pressure on local, state, and federal programs to allocate funds for the development of a sound sex education program. As professionals in education, it is our challenge and responsibility to see that the sexual

needs of the handicapped are not forgotten. (McNab, 1978, p. 301)

REFERENCES

AAHPER. (1971). *A resource guide in sex education for the mentally retarded.* New York: SIECUS.

Baugh, R. J. (1984). Sexuality education for the visually and hearing impaired child in the regular classroom. *Journal of School Health, 54,* 407–409.

Black, J. (1986). AIDS: Preschool and school issues. *Journal of School Health, 56,* 93–96.

Block, W. A. (1972). *What your child really wants to know about sex and why.* Englewood Cliffs, NJ: Prentice-Hall.

Calderwood, D. (1979). *About your sexuality.* Boston: Beacon.

Dudly-Maring, C. C., & Edmiaston, R. (1985). Social status of learning disabled children and adolescents: A review. *Learning Disabilities Quarterly, 8,* 189–204.

Fischer, H. L., Krajicek, M. J., & Borthnick, W. A. (1974). *Sex education for the developmentally disabled: A guide for parents, teachers, and professionals.* Baltimore: University Park Press.

Gordon, S. (1973). Missing in special education: Sex. *Journal of Special Education, 5*(4), 351–354.

Gresham, F. M., & Reschly, D. S. (1986). Social skill deficits and low peer acceptance of mainstreamed learning disabled children. *Learning Disabilities Quarterly, 9,* 23–32.

McNab, W. L. (1978). The sexual needs of the handicapped. *Journal of School Health, 48,* 301–306.

Noland, M. P., Riggs, R. S., & Hall, J. W. (1985). Relationships among health knowledge, health locus of control, and health status in secondary special education students: A review. *Journal of Special Education, 19,* 177–187.

Payne, J. S., Polloway, E. A., Smith, J. E., & Payne, R. A. (1981). *Strategies for teaching the mentally retarded.* Columbus, OH: Merrill.

Reed, A. R., & Munson, H. E. (1976). Resolution of one's sexual self: An important first step for sexuality educators, *Journal of School Health, 56*(1), 31–34.

Reich, M. L., & Harshman, H. W. (1975). Sex education for handicapped children: Reality or repression? *Journal of Special Education, 5,* 373–377.

Smigielski, P. A., & Steinmann, M. J. (1981). Teaching sex education to multiply handicapped adolescents. *Journal of School Health, 51,* 238–241.

Sbindell, P. E. (1975). Sex education programs and the mentally retarded. *Journal of School Health, 45,* 88–90.

White, W. S. (1985). Perspectives on the education and training of learning disabled adults. *Learning Disabilities Quarterly, 8,* 231–236.

Wrenn, C., & Schwarzrock, S. (1980). *Coping With* series. Circle Pines, MN: American Guidance Service.

The Task Demonstration Model: A Concurrent Model for Teaching Groups of Students with Severe Disabilities

ABSTRACT: This study investigated the use of the Task Demonstration Model (TDM) of group instruction for students with severe or moderate retardation. This model and the Standard Prompting Hierarchy (SPH) were tested against each other (and baseline) across three teachers and groups of students. Results on teacher variables showed that demands and praise were roughly equivalent for both procedures, but prompts were 12 times higher in SPH than in TDM. Data on student variables showed task engagement to be the same for SPH and TDM, percent correct to be 10% higher in TDM, but rate correct to be twice as much in TDM as in SPH.

KATHRYN G. KARSH

ALAN C. REPP

KATHRYN G. KARSH (CEC #154) is a Research Associate at the Educational Research & Services Center, DeKalb, Illinois. ALAN C. REPP (CEC #336) is a Professor at Northern Illinois University, DeKalb, and a Research Associate at the Educational Research & Services Center.

Significant progress has been made in the past 10 years in implementing functional, community-based educational programs for people with severe mental retardation. However, there are many questions about the best procedures for teaching these students in their classrooms. The challenge is to identify teaching strategies that are both effective for students and practical for staff.

One of the more frequent debates has been whether these students should be taught individually or in groups (Reid & Favell, 1984). Traditionally, students with severe disabilities have been taught in one-to-one situations. Because of the finite amount of teacher time available, however, this approach has meant that students received relatively small amounts of instruction per day. Indeed, in observations of 30 classrooms, we have found direct instruction to occur less than 10% of the school day.

Group instruction involving a small number of students may significantly increase instructional

time for each student. Several investigators have compared one-to-one teaching with group instruction and found no deficit in skill acquisition when students were taught in groups (Bourland, Jablonski, & Lockhart, 1988; Favell, Favell, & McGimsey, 1978; Fink & Sandall, 1980; Storm & Willis, 1978). Moreover, group instruction has been found to be superior in efficient use of teacher time (Favell et al., 1978; Fink & Sandall, 1980), opportunities for social contact (Storm & Willis, 1978), incidental learning (Biberdorf & Pear, 1977), and decreased rates of inappropriate behavior (Ranieri, Ford, Vincent, & Brown, 1984).

Although there are many advantages to group instruction, some concerns remain regarding its use. These include the difficulty of training students with heterogeneous skills (Westling, Ferrell, & Swenson, 1982), the type and difficulty of tasks appropriate for group instruction (Alberto, Jobes, Sizemore, & Duran, 1980; Favell et al., 1978), the decreased opportunities for individual students to respond during group instruction (Bourland et al., 1988), the question of whether the students should be taught the same or different tasks (Oliver, 1983), and the selection of an appropriate group instruction model (Storm & Willis, 1978).

With respect to the latter, Reid and Favell (1984) have identified three general models of group instruction. In the *sequential* model, each student is taught individually in a sequential order while the other students in the group wait for their instructions. This is the most common alternative for persons with severe or moderate retardation, but it is in effect a series of one-to-

From *Exceptional Children*, Vol. 59, No. 1, September 1992, pp. 54-67. Copyright © 1992 by The Council for Exceptional Children. Reprinted by permission.

one teaching situations. In the combination *concurrent/sequential* model, some instruction is provided to all the students concurrently while other instruction is provided to individual students in sequential order. In the third model, the *tandem individual-to-group* model, the instruction begins with a one-to-one format and is systematically extended to include more students.

For each of these models, there is considerable time during group instruction in which the nontarget student does not have an opportunity to respond. The teacher may be requesting a response from another student, prompting another student's response, or correcting errors. During these periods, the nontarget student may decrease contact with the learning environment and increase problem behavior (Repp & Karsh, 1991; Repp and Karsh, in press). Since the major problem of students with severe disabilities is, by definition, that they take longer to learn tasks, *unnecessary* periods without instruction would seem counterproductive.

One group instruction model that has not been investigated with these students is a *concurrent* model in which all the students in the group respond concurrently on the same tasks throughout the teaching session. An advantage of a concurrent model is that each student receives many more opportunities to respond than in the previous models. In addition, there are the added benefits of socialization for the students and time management for the teacher. The implication inherent in this model, however, is that each student must exhibit a high rate of correct responding in order for all in the group to respond concurrently as the task progresses. Because students with severe disabilities are usually quite diverse in their skill levels, implementing a concurrent group instruction procedure can be problematic. The key to the success of such a model may be the incorporation of teaching procedures that result in few errors.

The purpose of this investigation was to determine whether a teaching procedure (the Task Demonstration Model) which had resulted in high rates of correct responding and few errors in one-to-one instruction (Karsh, Repp, & Lenz, 1990; Repp, Karsh, & Lenz, 1990) could be used effectively in a concurrent group instruction model. The critical features of the Task Demonstration Model (TDM) are fading (Terrace, 1963a, 1963b), general case programming (Horner, Bellamy, & Colvin, 1984), and a hierarchy of skills from matching to sample to identification to naming. In the present study, classroom teachers received training not only in the Task Demonstration Model but also in the characteristics of effective instruction based on recent stimulus control research. Teachers were trained to maintain a rapid pace of instruction, to use a signal for unison responding (Cowart, Carnine, & Becker, 1976), to present multiple examples of the stimuli to be learned, and to differentially reinforce correct responding. The research purpose

was addressed by comparing TDM with a more traditional method of group instruction, the Standard Prompting Hierarchy (SPH), which used a system of least-to-most intrusive prompts. Comparisons were made on (a) the students' percentage of correct responses, rate of correct responses, and task engagement; and (b) the teachers' rate of demands, praise, and prompts.

METHOD

Participants

Students. Three groups of students, ranging from 16 to 21 years of age, participated in the study. All three groups were part of a functional, community-based training program for students with severe to moderate disabilities in a school located in a large suburban area.

Group 1 included 2 males and 2 females whose mean chronological age was 20 years, 2 months (range, 19 years, 7 months to 20 years, 4 months). The mean score on the Stanford-Binet Intelligence Scale-Revised was 35 (range, 32-36). Group 2 was composed of 1 male and 3 female students. The mean chronological age was 19 years, 6 months (range, 19 years, 10 months to 21 years), and the mean score on the Stanford-Binet was 38 (range, 30-49). Group 3 included 1 male and 2 female students. The mean chronological age was 17 years, 8 months (range, 16 years, 7 months to 18 years, 8 months), and the mean score on the Stanford-Binet was 40 (range, 30-45).

All the students were able to attend to a task and remain seated for 20 min. Each student was able to respond to commands such as "Look at ____" and "Touch the ____" as the result of a program used to train compliance (Repp & Karsh, 1991). None of the students possessed significant sensory or motor disabilities that could interfere with the responses required during instruction.

Teachers. Three teachers participated in the study. All were certified to teach students with severe and moderate retardation and had taught this population for an average of 13 years (range, 10-15 years). Teachers 1 and 2 had earned master's degrees, and Teacher 3 had earned a baccalaureate degree with additional graduate hours in special education.

Settings

Observations took place in the students' homeroom classrooms, where functional academic tasks were taught in preparation for community activities. Classroom and community activities were alternated during the week so that students received classroom instruction an average of twice a week. In each classroom, group instruction was conducted at a kidney-shaped table with the teacher facing the students.

TABLE 1
Components of the Teacher Training Program

Component	References
1. Task Dimension	
A. The *activity analysis* determines the learner demands placed on the student by the environment. Analysis allows the instructor to design interventions that will bring student responding under the control of relevant stimuli.	A. Albin, McDonnell, & Wilcox, 1987; Horner, McDonnell, & Bellamy, 1986
B. *Stimulus presentations* are based on errorless discrimination training. The teacher arranges a sequence of stimuli to increase the probability that only correct responses occur.	B. Dietz, Rose, & Repp, 1986; Terrace, 1963a, 1963b; Sidman & Stoddard, 1966, 1967
C. *Task variation* involves interspersing items that have already been taught with new items during instruction.	C. Dunlap & Koegel, 1980; Rowan & Pear, 1985
D. *Within-stimulus prompting* consists of exaggerating the relevant component or the critical dimension of the positive stimulus.	D. Mosk & Bucher, 1984; Schreibman, 1975; Wolfe & Cuvo, 1978
2. Stimulus Modality	
E. *Stimulus modality* (i.e., real objects, photos, pictures). When two modes are to be used (e.g., student is to locate cereal in a grocery store when given a picture of a certain brand), teach picture-to-picture and item-to-item matching to sample and identification before teaching student to match the picture to the real item.	E. Dixon, 1981; Welch & Pear, 1980
3. Teacher Presentation	
F. Presentation with *short intertrial intervals* produces higher levels of correct responding and increased learning rate.	F. Dunlap, Dyer, & Koegel, 1983; Koegel, Dunlap, & Dyer, 1980
G. *Stimulus delay* requires the teacher to provide increasingly longer delays between the discriminative stimulus and the artificial prompt.	G. Snell & Gast, 1981; Touchette & Howard, 1984; Walls, Haught, & Dowler, 1982
H. In *response delay*, the teacher does not allow the student to make a response until after some designated period of time has elapsed, increasing attention to the discriminative stimulus. Response delay is used for students who respond too quickly, often without looking at stimuli.	H. Dyer, Christian, & Luce, 1982; Charlop, Schreibman, & Thibodeau, 1985
I. *Differential reinforcement* increases the likelihood that the response will occur again in the presence of the antecedent stimulus. Reinforcement can be based on a functional relationship between response and reinforcer (e.g., correct discrimination of a cup is reinforced with a drink of water from a cup).	I. Halle, Baer, & Spradlin, 1981; Williams, Koegel, & Egel, 1981
4. Environmental Arrangements	
J. *Environmental arrangements,* including schedules for instruction, management of transition times, and organization of work areas, can increase student-engaged time.	J. Hooper & Reid, 1985; Orelove, 1982
K. *Group instruction* provides more teacher direction, reinforcement, correction, and repeated practice.	K. Favell, Favell, & McGimsey, 1978
L. *Incidental teaching* uses time not allocated for direct instruction of the target skill to provide a greater number of examples for "loose training" and maintenance.	L. Campbell & Stremel-Campbell, 1982; Horner, Williams, & Knobbe, 1985; McGee, Krantz, Mason, & McClannahan, 1983

(Continued)

Experimental Design and Conditions

The study used a multiple baseline design (Baer, Wolf, & Risley, 1968) across the three teacher/student groups with an embedded alternating-treatments phase (Barlow & Hayes, 1979; Barlow & Hersen, 1984) for comparing the effectiveness of the two group teaching procedures.

Baseline. After an initial period of adjustment to allow students and teachers to become accustomed to the observers, probe sessions were randomly conducted for 5, 6, and 7 of the baseline teaching days for Groups 1, 2, and 3, respectively. Teachers were asked to instruct the target group of students as they normally would. They were not aware of the specific nature of the observations. The pri-

TABLE 1
(Continued)

Component	References
M. *Transenvironmental programming* requires the teacher to bring natural, relevant cues from the environment systematically into the classroom and then to assess (and teach if needed) the student in the natural setting.	M. Nietupski, Clancy, Wehrmacker, & Parmer, 1985; McDonnell, Horner, & Williams, 1984
5. Generalization	
N. *Delayed reinforcement* provides gradual delays between the response and the delivery of the reinforcer to increase maintenance of the skill in the natural environment.	N. Baer, R. A., Williams, Osnes, & Stokes, 1984; Fowler & Baer, 1981
O. *Generalization across instructional settings* is accomplished by systematically varying teachers and the location of instruction, by using multiple settings for instruction, and by providing instruction at various times of the day.	O. Dunlap, Koegel, & Koegel, 1984; Handelman & Harris, 1983; Horner & Budd, 1985; Richmond & Lewallen, 1983

mary and reliability observers were seated behind the students. All other activities that were a regular part of the classroom routine were continued.

Following baseline, the three teachers participated in three workshops conducted by the experimenters. The purposes of the workshops were (a) to describe teaching procedures, based on recent stimulus control research, that had resulted in more effective instruction for students with severe and moderate disabilities (see Table 1); (b) to demonstrate how these procedures could be integrated into group instruction in the classroom; and (c) to train teachers to use the TDM, which had been shown to be effective in teaching functional discriminations during one-to-one instruction (Karsh et al., 1990; Repp et al., 1990). After the workshops were conducted, the teachers were observed with target students twice a week for 5 weeks and given feedback on their use of the stimulus control instructional procedures with both the TDM and the SPH. This training period ended when the teachers had demonstrated 100% procedural reliability for three consecutive teaching sessions for both TDM and SPH.

Alternating Treatment Conditions. Three probe sessions were conducted randomly for both TDM and SPH during the intervention phase. Each group of students was taught six tasks; three tasks were randomly assigned to the TDM, and three to the SPH. All six tasks were part of a single ongoing curricular activity (e.g., shopping), similar in type and difficulty, and not known by the students, according to baseline probes. The items were judged to be of equal difficulty by a panel of three other teachers. Group 1 was taught to match to a sample and to identify six department signs for shopping at stores such as K-Mart (e.g., "Service," "Cosmetics," "Pharmacy," "Records," "Sportswear," and "Jewelry"). Group 2 was taught to match to a sample and to identify six minute-hand positions for reading analog clock times (e.g., o'clock, :15, :20, :30, :45, and

:50) that were part of the student's daily schedule, and Group 3 was taught to match to a sample and to identify six words related to mobility in the community (e.g., "Enter," "Exit," "Men," "Women," "Open," and "Closed"). All words or times selected came from the activity analysis (see Table 1) used to determine elements of community environments students should be able to identify to participate in the activity. Preintervention probes, which included 10 two-choice trials for each task for both matching to sample and identification, were administered individually to each student. These probes established that none of the students had mastered matching to sample or identification of the teaching stimuli before intervention. When all students in a group scored less than 60% on the matching to sample and identification probes for a given task, it was assigned to their group. During intervention, TDM, rather than SPH, was chosen as the first session for two of the three groups. This was an effort to control for the students' previous long-term exposure to a least-to-most prompting hierarchy taught in a one-to-one manner. Because the TDM condition was the first time these students had been taught in a group, we presumed its effects might suffer and that the data, therefore, would not be prejudiced in its favor.

Task Demonstration Model. The Task Demonstration Model (Karsh et al., 1990; Repp & Karsh, 1991; Repp & Karsh, in press; Repp et al., 1990) is a teaching procedure that incorporates elements of fading (Sidman & Stoddard, 1966, 1967; Terrace, 1963a, 1963b), general case programming (Horner, Bellamy, & Colvin, 1984), and a hierarchy of skills in which people learn to match to a sample before learning to identify a stimulus without a sample present. During both the matching-to-sample and identification phases of instruction, students were presented with correct (S+) and incorrect (S−) stimuli with the S− (i.e., the incorrect word or clock face) faded to become more like the S+ over trials. In addition, the irrelevant features of the S+ and S– examples varied across trials. This procedure reduced the probability that the student would respond to an irrelevant dimension (e.g., color, size) instead of the relevant dimension (i.e., shape of letters or position of clock hands).

Students were taught in a hierarchy that required them to match the S+ to a sample S+ before they were taught to identify the S+. In both matching to sample (MTS) and identification (ID), stimuli were presented in three hierarchical groups. These groups were roughly defined by the degree to which S– differed from S+: (a) very different S–'s, (b) moderately different S–'s, and (c) slightly different S–'s. This systematic progression from very different to moderately different to slightly different examples provided both a reduction in errors and exposure to many examples of the S+ and S– so that the student could not learn to associate the same irrelevant aspect of S+ with reinforcement across trials.

During group instruction trials, depending on whether the students were in the MTS or ID phase, each student was presented with either (a) a sample S+, a matching S+, and an S– (in MTS); or (b) an S+ and S– (in ID). The teacher gave a direction (e.g., "Everybody, touch ____"), paused 1 s, and then auditorily signaled (e.g., a hand clap) the students to respond. Students then made a unison response to the instruction. For any given trial, each student in the group had a different example of S+ and S–. After a trial was completed, students passed the stimulus materials to their left so that no one ever had the same materials across successive trials.

Incorrect responses were followed by an error-correction procedure (Karsh et al., 1990; Repp et al., 1990) during which the remaining students observed the procedure. When a student made an error, the teacher (a) physically guided the student's hand to the correct stimulus and said "No, this is ____," and repeated the trial, leaving the stimuli in place; (b) then removed the stimuli, returned them to their original positions on the table, and repeated the trial; and (c) removed the stimuli, returned them to the table in different positions, and repeated the trial. For each group of S–'s (i.e., very different, moderately different, and slightly different), each student was required to make 9 out of 10 correct responses before the group proceeded to the next step (i.e., from very different to moderately different to slightly different S–'s).

For each task taught through TDM, there were two sets of training stimuli constructed from index cards (5 × 7 in). One set represented the S+ stimuli, and one represented the S–. The S+ was always presented in its criterion form, but the irrelevant dimensions varied across the multiple examples. In the tasks requiring word identification, the following irrelevant dimensions were varied: letter style, letter size, color of letters, and color of the background card. In the tasks requiring time-telling, the following irrelevant dimensions were varied: the size and color of the clock face; the size, color, and script of the numerals; and the width and design of the hour and minute hands.

For the word identification tasks, the S–'s were words found in stores that were inventoried for this purpose. The S–'s were either functionally or structurally similar to the S+ and were put into the three categories (very different S–'s, moderately different S–'s, and slightly different S–'s) of 10-15 words each. For the time-telling task, the S–'s were analog clock times similar to the S+ and were put into the three categories according to how much the hour and minute hands of the S– differed from that of the S+.

The teachers were asked to follow the implementation steps for TDM that were outlined during training (i.e., teaching MTS before ID and programming from very different to moderately different to slightly different S–'s). During the TDM sessions, the teachers were asked to incorporate the stimulus control procedures they had learned during the workshops. The teachers were particularly encouraged to maintain a rapid pace of instruction, to use a signal for unison responding, and to praise correct responses.

Standard Prompting Hierarchy. The Standard Prompting Hierarchy is a traditional procedure for teaching identification (Steege, Wacker, & McMahon, 1987; Wolery & Gast, 1984). This procedure used a hierarchy of prompts in combination with a trial-and-error (i.e., no fading) approach to teach matching to sample and identification of the S+. During group instruction with SPH, the teacher used flashcards, picture cards (representing the words or time of day), and worksheets. Students were asked to respond to instructions such as "Touch ____," "Show me the word that goes with this picture," "Draw a circle around ____," and so forth. Students did not pass the materials as in TDM; instead, each student used the same materials throughout the session.

If the student made an error or did not respond within 10 s, a least-to-most prompting hierarchy was used in the following sequence: (a) repeated instruction, (b) instruction plus pointing to the S+, (c) instruction plus modeling (the teacher touched the S+), (d) instruction plus physical prompt (the teacher touched the back of the student's hand), and finally, (e) instruction plus full physical guidance. The students were required to make 9 out of 10 correct responses on matching to sample before proceeding to identification on each task.

There were also two sets of SPH stimuli, one for S+ and one for S–. Because this procedure did not involve fading or multiple examples, the S+ and S– stimuli did not vary as in TDM. For each task taught by SPH, two examples of the S+ were used, a flashcard (a word or clock face drawn with a black marker on a white card) and an 8 1/2- × 11-in teacher-made worksheet (a word or clockface drawn with pen on white paper and duplicated on a copy machine). No more than four examples of S– were presented on individual flashcards, and no more than four examples of S– were presented on the worksheet. The teachers were asked to adhere to the prompting hierarchy, moving from least intrusive (pointing) to most intrusive (physical guidance) when prompting student responses.

Teachers were asked to follow the steps for SPH that were outlined during training. As in the TDM implementation, the teachers were asked to incorporate the stimulus control procedures they had learned during the workshops and practiced in their classrooms. They were trained to maintain a rapid pace of instruction, to use a signal for unison responding, and to differentially reinforce correct responding.

Observational Procedures

Each teacher and group of students were observed during the three instructional conditions (baseline, TDM, and SPH), and data were collected on both teacher and student behaviors.

Response Definitions. Data were collected on three teacher and four student behaviors, defined as follows:

1. *Teacher demand*: Any verbal or gestural behavior that required an immediate task-related response from the student. Demands included questions; directions to manipulate instructional materials; or requests to make verbal, written, gestural, or physical responses.
2. *Teacher prompt*: Any verbal, gestural, or physical behavior that assisted the student in making an immediate task-related response. Such behaviors included verbal cues, visual cues, modeling, and physical guidance.
3. *Teacher praise*: Any verbal statement, gesture, or touch that indicated the student responded correctly.
4. *Student correct response*: An unprompted correct response that occurred within 10 s of the teacher's instruction.
5. *Student incorrect response*: An incorrect response or failure to make a response within 10 s of the teacher's instruction.
6. *Student prompted response*: Any correct response to the targeted instructional task that was preceded by verbal or visual cues, modeling, or physical guidance.
7. *Student engagement*: Any active or passive response that suggested attention to instruction. Active responses included verbal, gestural, or written responses according to teacher questions, or manipulation of the instructional materials. Passive responses included looking at the teacher, looking at the materials, or observing another student making a task-related response.

Data Collection. Data were not collected every day because the students received classroom instruction an average of twice a week on a schedule that varied from week to week. Therefore, an observation schedule was developed before the intervention phase, and probe sessions were randomly assigned to each condition. A sequential recording system (Thomson, Holmberg, & Baer, 1974) was used for both teacher and student behaviors. The teacher was observed throughout the whole session, but each minute a different student was observed. The average teaching session was 25 min (range, 21-35 min); thus, each of the four students was observed 5 to 8 times within a given session. The order of the sequential observations was randomly determined and changed for each teaching session.

The Epson HX-20, a portable microcomputer that had been programmed to collect data in real time (Repp, Harman, Felce, Van Acker, & Karsh, 1989; Repp, Karsh, Van Acker, Felce, & Harman, 1989), was used for recording the response codes. Before each session began, the observer entered a code to identify the teacher, the student, group, location, instructional task, and session. The observer then began the session by depressing a key that activated the computer's timer, as well as its recording mode. The computer was programmed to signal the observer to move from one student to another each minute, and the data for these 1-min subsessions were stored separately. During the session, each subject and each response code was allocated a key on the computer keyboard. During the 1-min subsessions, the observer depressed the appropriate key once for the onset of each teacher or student response code and a second time for its offset. The computer stored the response codes in the order of occurrence as well as the beginning and ending times in seconds. The computer was programmed to accept multiple entries so that responses occurring in combination with each other (e.g., engagement and correct responses) could be recorded simultaneously.

At the end of each session, the computer printed the sequence in which each 1-min observation session and each response code occurred, as well as the beginning and ending second for each code. In addition, it aggregated all the 1-min samples for each student. A data analysis program (Karsh, Repp, & Ludewig, 1989) was then used to calculate and print the following data for the teacher and each student: (a) the number of occurrences of each response code, (b) the rate of occurrence for each code, (c) the total duration of each code, and (d) the percentage of the session each code occurred. For each of these measures, the group data for each session were derived by calculating the mean of the individual student's data.

Interobserver Agreement

Observers were trained *in vivo* in classrooms until they reached a mean agreement level of 80% on each response code. Reliability checks were conducted during 33% of the sessions.

Interobserver agreement was computed for the start and finish times for each response category for the teachers and students. The method used for estimating reliability of real-time data has been described elsewhere (MacLean, Tapp, & Johnson, 1985; Repp, Harman, et al., 1989; Repp, Karsh, et al., 1989). Interobserver agreement means and ranges for each category were: (a) teacher demand: $M = 95\%$, range = 83%–100%; (b) teacher prompt: $M = 93\%$, range = 80%–100%; (c) teacher praise: $M = 94\%$, range = 83%–100%; (d) student correct response: $M = 96\%$, range = 91%–100%; (e) student incorrect response: $M = 86\%$, range = 77%–100%; (f) student prompted response: $M = 93\%$, range = 75%–100%; and (g) student engagement: $M = 92\%$, range = 80%–100%.

Interobserver agreement on the independent variable was assessed in a different manner. Each day, another observer wrote a description of the stimulus materials used for TDM and SPH, the prompting hierarchy for SPH, and whether the teacher was using matching to sample or identification. This information was also recorded by the senior author. A comparison of these data showed a reliability score of 100% for the use of the two independent variables, TDM and SPH.

RESULTS

The results of the two teaching procedures for mean student task engagement, mean percent unprompted correct responses, and mean rate of unprompted correct response by group are shown in Figures 1, 2, and 3, respectively. Each data point represents mean responding on a new task during instruction. Figure 1 shows that engagement was similar across the baseline, TDM, and SPH conditions for the subjects within Group 1 ($Ms = 76\%$, 72%, and 79%), Group 2 ($Ms = 81\%$, 80%, and 84%), and Group 3 ($Ms = 74\%$, 88%, and 76%).

Figure 2 shows that the mean percent of unprompted correct responses improved substantially from baseline ($M = 47\%$) for both the TDM ($M = 92\%$) and SPH ($M = 82\%$) conditions, although responding was 10% higher in TDM than in SPH. Group 1's correct responding improved from 47% in baseline to 94% (TDM) and 90% (SPH) during intervention. Group 2 improved from 55% (baseline) to 86% (TDM) and 71% (SPH), and Group 3 improved from 40% (baseline) to 96% (TDM) and 83% (SPH). The results for individual students in Table 2 suggest that for Groups 2 and 3, SPH produced more variability within a group than did TDM.

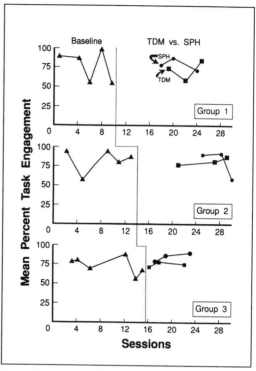

Note: The circle (●) represents the Standard Prompting Hierarchy (SPH); the square (■) represents the Task Demonstration Model (TDM). Each data point in Phase 2 represents a new task.

The mean rate of unprompted correct responses per minute (rpm), shown in Figure 3, showed substantial differences between TDM and SPH. Though both procedures resulted in higher rates than in baseline, the rate of unprompted correct responses in TDM was twice that in SPH for all three groups. The means for this measure under baseline, TDM, and SPH were 0.26, 1.93, and 0.90 rpm for Group 1; 0.39, 1.50, and 0.74 rpm for Group 2; and 0.39, 3.45, and 1.70 rpm for Group 3. The rates for the students in Group 2 were lower than those in the other two groups because these students' activity level during all educational activities was considerably lower. Individual data, presented in Table 2, show that TDM produced almost equal rates of correct responding for all students *within* each particular group, whereas SPH led to considerable variability for students within each group.

The results for teacher demands, praise, and prompts are presented in Figures 4, 5, and 6, respectively. All three teachers increased their rates of demands or instructions over baseline with no consistent differences between TDM and SPH (Figure 4). Similarly, teacher praise increased from baseline conditions for all three teachers and was roughly the same for TDM and SPH (Figure 5).

FIGURE 2
Percentage of Unprompted Correct Responses Across Conditions During Probe Sessions

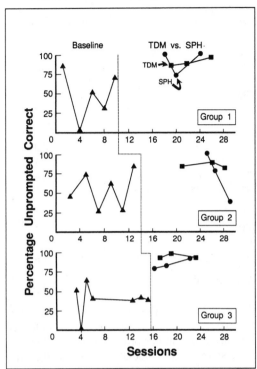

Note: The circle (●) represents the Standard Prompting Hierarchy (SPH); the square (■) represents the Task Demonstration Model (TDM). Each data point in Phase 2 represents a new task.

FIGURE 3
Mean Unprompted Correct Responses Per Minute Across Conditions During Probe Sessions

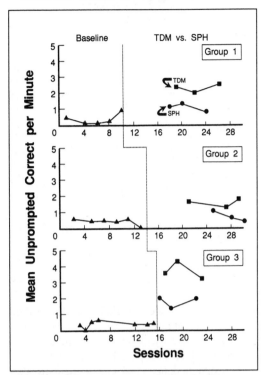

Note: The circle (●) represents the Standard Prompting Hierarchy (SPH); the square (■) represents the Task Demonstration Model (TDM). Each data point in Phase 2 represents a new task.

Data on prompts (Figure 6) show them to have been two to three times as frequent in SPH as in baseline for two of the three teachers. In TDM, the rates decreased significantly from baseline. Since prompts are a function of errors, these data are consistent with the differences in rate of correct responses found under the two conditions. The rates of prompts for baseline, TDM, and SPH for the three groups were 0.48, 0, and 1.66 rpm (Group 1); 1.22, 0.38, and 2.7 rpm (Group 2); and 1.41, 0.07, and 1.45 rpm (Group 3).

DISCUSSION

Prior research has shown that TDM could be much more effective than SPH in one-to-one teaching situations (Karsh et al., 1990; Repp et al., 1990). The present results demonstrate that the effectiveness of the TDM is not restricted to one-to-one instruction; instead, they show that TDM can also be more effective in a concurrent model of group instruction. This finding is important for teaching students with severe disabilities because they often require many trials to learn a task. TDM allowed the teacher to provide an equally high number of trials to all of the students during group instruction and to facilitate relatively rapid acquisition of skills with few errors. The procedure also allowed the teacher to moni-

tor, reinforce, and correct students and maintain a rapid pace because (a) students were attending better in TDM than in baseline, (b) reinforcement was given while the students were passing the materials, (c) error corrections were less frequently needed than during baseline, and (d) the error correction procedure was used simultaneously with the students who made errors on any given trial.

Data were collected on two sets of variables, one for students and one for teachers. The student data show, for both TDM and SPH, a substantial improvement in the students' percentage and rate of unprompted correct responding. These results validate the effectiveness of the teacher training program. In comparing TDM with SPH, one finds that while the data on *percentage* unprompted correct favored TDM slightly (by 10%), the data on *rate* unprompted correct favored TDM considerably (2 times the rate). TDM greatly increased a student's rate of contact with the learning environment, an objective we believe is essential in teaching students with severe disabilities. This effect is particularly evident when baseline and TDM are compared, showing an improvement by a factor of 6.5 (0.35 rpm vs. 2.29 rpm). The consistency of the relative relationship of the data is also interesting. Although the rate differed across the three groups, as one would expect, the TDM rate for each group was

TABLE 2
Individual Student Means Across Three Conditions

Group	% Task Engagement			% Unprompted Correct Responses			Unprompted Correct Responses Per Minute		
	Baseline	TDM	SPH	Baseline	TDM	SPH	Baseline	TDM	SPH
Group 1									
S1	75	71	84	66	100	94	0.27	1.88	0.83
S2	77	66	72	31	80	89	0.13	1.97	0.07
S3	82	72	73	75	100	89	0.58	1.94	1.18
S4	68	78	86	17	94	89	0.06	1.93	1.53
Group 2									
S1	69	71	64	73	98	75	0.49	1.37	0.41
S2	75	85	95	79	100	96	0.58	1.32	1.17
S3	98	84	87	57	77	67	0.32	1.74	0.61
S4	83	80	90	9	67	45	0.15	1.58	0.75
Group 3									
S1	75	88	76	69	100	96	0.77	3.24	1.33
S2	69	83	78	18	93	78	0.11	3.58	2.16
S3	78	92	73	32	96	75	0.29	3.52	1.62

Note: TDM = Task Demonstration Model; SPH = Standard Prompting Hierarchy; S = student.

almost exactly twice the SPH rate. These data also suggest that rate is a far more sensitive measure of the differences between some teaching procedures than is the percentage correct.

The student data on task engagement are also informative. Engagement is a variable that has been used to measure the effectiveness of instruction in classrooms for students with severe disabilities (e.g., Green, Canipe, Way, & Reid, 1986; Green, Reid, McCarn, Schepis, Phillips, & Parsons, 1986). Our data on engagement show few differences among baseline, TDM, and SPH; the rate correct data, however, show considerable differences. If engagement had been selected as the only measure by which the three conditions were compared, one might have drawn the conclusion that there were no differences among the three conditions. Our suggestion is that although task engagement can be a valuable measure, additional variables should be measured to determine the effectiveness of classroom instruction.

The second set of data, on teacher behaviors, also provides interesting results. Teacher demands and praise showed significant increases over baseline conditions, although no differences were found between TDM and SPH. These changes from baseline indicate that the teacher training program led to significant changes in teacher behavior and serve to validate the program for training in both TDM and SPH procedures. The data also suggest that these teacher-demand-and-praise behaviors cannot account for the differences between TDM and SPH in the student data. Our conclusion is that the differences may be due to variables of the TDM package other than rate of demand and praise.

One of these variables may be teacher prompts. The rate in SPH (1.94 rpm) was more than 12 times the rate in TDM (0.15 rpm). This difference in rate of teacher prompts is important for two reasons. Learning research has indicated that an extra-stimulus prompt by the teacher may "overshadow" the student's attention to the stimulus and, as a result, may prevent functional control from being transferred from the extraneous cue or prompt to the teaching stimulus (Schreibman, 1975; Schreibman, Charlop, & Koegel, 1982; Sidman & Stoddard, 1966, 1967). In SPH, students may attend more to the teacher's prompt than to the stimuli they are supposed to be discriminating. In addition, the delivery of extra-stimulus prompts to individual students during group instruction greatly reduces the number of trials that all the students in the group may receive.

The results of this study suggest that a fading procedure, when used in a concurrent group instruction model, may be an effective and efficient method for classroom instruction. Observer notes provide anecdotal data that the students appeared happier during TDM instruction, praised other students for correct responding, and asked if the teachers could use TDM more often. Observers also noted that students not included in these groups asked to be included and that teachers enjoyed the TDM procedure. For example, the teachers reported that they were able to observe and record their students' responses more accurately. Teachers either recorded each student's responses on a recording sheet as the students passed the materials, or directed students to record their own correct responses by placing a token in a small container placed in front of each student.

Further research is needed to confirm these anecdotal data, as well as to identify the types of tasks for which the TDM procedure is appropriate. Thus far, this procedure has been used to teach identification of common items that are part

FIGURE 4
Number of Demands/Questions Per Minute
Across Conditions During Probe Sessions

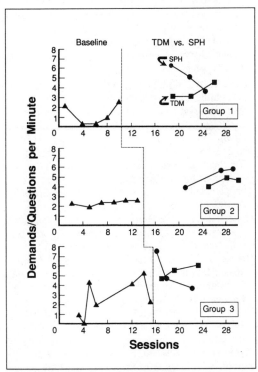

Note: The circle (●) represents the Standard Prompting Hierarchy (SPH); the square (■) represents the Task Demonstration Model (TDM).

of daily routines (e.g., eating utensils, self-care items, clothing items), coins and bills, functional words and symbols, and equipment for vocational tasks (e.g., cleaning products, cooking utensils, assembly parts). Further information is required regarding the effect of TDM on maladaptive student behaviors, the ways in which teacher training can be best conducted, and how to select students most likely to benefit. A reasonable expectation would be that students must be relatively homogeneous to participate in a group. Yet, although the data in Table 2 show a difference in baseline of as much as 70% in correct responding, students in this group performed well together. Certainly, group teaching cannot be used for all tasks with students who have severe disabilities. With TDM, however, it might be used for students previously considered too disparate to function as a group.

REFERENCES

Alberto, P., Jobes, N., Sizemore, A., & Duran, D. (1980). A comparison of individual and group instruction across response tasks. *The Journal of the Association for Persons with Severe Handicaps, 5,* 285-293.

Albin, R. W., McDonnell, J. J., & Wilcox, B. (1987). Designing interventions to meet activity goals. In B. Wilcox & G. T. Bellamy (Eds.), *A comprehensive guide to the activities catalogue: An alternative cur-*

FIGURE 5
Praises Per Minute Across Conditions During
Probe Sessions

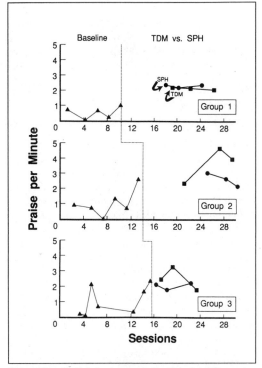

Note: The circle (●) represents the Standard Prompting Hierarchy (SPH); the square (■) represents the Task Demonstration Model (TDM).

FIGURE 6
Number of Prompts Per Minute Across
Conditions During Probe Sessions

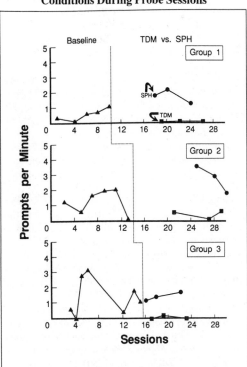

Note: The circle (●) represents the Standard Prompting Hierarchy (SPH); the square (■) represents the Task Demonstration Model (TDM).

riculum for youth and adults with severe disabilities (pp. 62-88). Baltimore: Paul H. Brookes.

Baer, D. M., Wolf, M. M., & Risley, J. R. (1968). Some current dimensions of applied behavior analysis. *Journal of Applied Behavior Analysis, 1,* 91-97.

Baer, R. A., Williams, T. A., Osnes, P. E., & Stokes, T. F. (1984). Delayed reinforcement as an indiscriminable contingency in verbal/nonverbal correspondence training. *Journal of Applied Behavior Analysis, 17,* 429-440.

Barlow, D. H., & Hayes, S. C. (1979). Alternating treatments design: One strategy for comparing the effects of two treatments in a single subject. *Journal of Applied Behavior Analysis, 12,* 199-210.

Barlow D. H., & Hersen, M. (1984). *Single case experimental design: Strategies for studying behavior change* (2nd ed.). New York: Pergamon Press.

Biberdorf, J. R., & Pear, J. J. (1977). Two-to-one vs. one-to-one student-teacher ratios in the operant verbal training of retarded children. *Journal of Applied Behavior Analysis, 10,* 506.

Bourland, G., Jablonski, E. M., & Lockhart, D. L. (1988). Multiple-behavior comparisons of group and individual instruction of persons with mental retardation. *Mental Retardation, 26,* 39-46.

Campbell, C. R., & Stremel-Campbell, K. (1982). Programming "loose training" as a strategy to facilitate language generalization. *Journal of Applied Behavior Analysis, 15,* 295-301.

Charlop, M. H., Shriebman, L., & Thibodeau, M. G. (1985). Increasing spontaneous verbal responding in autistic children using a time delay procedure. *Journal of Applied Behavior Analysis, 14,* 465-478.

Cowart, J., Carnine, D. W., & Becker, W. C. (1976). The effects of a signal on attending, responding, and following in direct instruction. In W. C. Becker & S. E. Engelmann (Eds.), *Technical report 1976-1* (Appendix B). Eugene: University of Oregon.

Deitz, D. E. D., Rose, E., & Repp, A. (1986). *The task demonstration model for teaching persons with severe handicaps.* DeKalb, IL: Educational Research & Services Center.

Dixon, L. S. (1981). A functional analysis of photo-object matching skills of severely retarded adolescents. *Journal of Applied Behavior Analysis, 14,* 465-478.

Dunlap, G., Dyer, K., & Koegel, R. L. (1983). Autistic self-stimulation and intertrial interval duration. *American Journal of Mental Deficiency, 88,* 194-202.

Dunlap, G., & Koegel, R. L. (1980). Motivating autistic children through stimulus variation. *Journal of Applied Behavior Analysis, 13,* 619-627.

Dunlap, G., Koegel, R. L., & Koegel, L. K. (1984). Continuity of treatment: Toilet training in multiple community settings. *Journal of the Association for Persons with Severe Handicaps, 9,* 134-141.

Dyer, K., Christian, W. D., & Luce, S. C. (1982). The role of response delay in improving the discrimination performance of autistic children. *Journal of Applied Behavior Analysis, 15,* 231-240.

Favell, J. E., Favell, J. E., & McGimsey, J. F. (1978). Relative effectiveness and efficiency of group vs. individual training of severely retarded persons. *American Journal of Mental Deficiency, 83,* 104-109.

Fink, W. T., & Sandall, J. R. (1980). A comparison of one-to-one and small group instructional strategies with developmentally disabled preschoolers. *Mental Retardation, 18,* 34-35.

Fowler, S. A., & Baer, D. M. (1981). "Do I have to be good all day?" The timing of delayed reinforcement as a factor in generalization. *Journal of Applied Behavior Analysis, 14,* 13-24.

Green, C. W., Canipe, V. W., Way, P. J., & Reid, D. H. (1986). Improving the functional utility and effectiveness of classroom services for students with profound multiple handicaps. *The Journal of the Association for Persons with Severe Handicaps, 11,* 162-170.

Green, C. W., Reid, D. H., McCarn, J. E. Schepis, M. M., Phillips, J. F., & Parsons, M. B. (1986). Naturalistic observations of classrooms serving severely handicapped persons: Establishing evaluative norms. *Applied Research in Mental Retardation, 7,* 37-50.

Halle, J. W., Baer, D. M., & Spradlin, J. E. (1981). Teacher's generalized use of delay as a stimulus control procedure to increase language use in handicapped children. *Journal of Applied Behavior Analysis, 14,* 389-409.

Handelman, J. S., & Harris, S. L. (1983). Generalization across instructional settings by autistic children. *Child and Family Behavior Therapy, 5,* 73-83.

Hooper, J., & Reid, D. H. (1985). A simple environmental design for improving classroom performance of profoundly retarded students. *Education and Treatment of Children, 8,* 25-39.

Horner, R. H., Bellamy, G. T., & Colvin, G. T. (1984). Responding in the presence of nontrained stimuli: An applied analysis of generalization. *The Journal of the Association for Persons with Severe Handicaps, 9,* 287-296.

Horner, R. H., & Budd, C. M. (1985). Teaching manual sign language to a nonverbal student: Generalization of sign use and collateral reduction of maladaptive behavior. *Education and Training of the Mentally Retarded, 20,* 39-47.

Horner, R. H., McDonnell, J. J., & Bellamy, G. T. (1986). Teaching generalized skills: General case instruction in simulation and community settings. In R. H. Horner, L. H. Meyer, & H. D. Fredricks (Eds.). *Education of learners with severe handicaps: Exemplary service strategies* (pp. 61-80). Baltimore: Paul H. Brookes.

Horner, R. H., Williams, J. A., & Knobbe, C. A. (1985). The effect of "opportunity to perform" on the maintenance of skills learned by high school students with severe handicaps. *Journal of the Association for Persons with Severe Handicaps, 10,* 172-175.

Karsh, K. G., Repp, A. C., & Lenz, M. (1990). A comparison of two procedures for teaching word identification to moderately retarded persons. *Research in Developmental Disabilities, 11,* 395-410.

Karsh, K. G., Repp, A. C., & Ludewig, D. (1989). *PCS: Portable computer systems for observational research.* DeKalb, IL: Communitech.

Koegel, R. L., Dunlap, G., & Dyer, K. (1980). Intertrial interval duration and learning in autistic children. *Journal of Applied Behavior Analysis, 13,* 91-99.

MacLean, W. E., Tapp, J. T., & Johnson, W. L. (1985). Alternative methods and software for calculating interobserver agreement for continuous observation data. *Journal of Psychopathology and Behavioral Assessment, 7,* 65-73.

McDonnell, J. J., Horner, R. H., & Williams, J. A. (1984). Comparison of three strategies for teaching generalized grocery purchasing to high school students with severe handicaps. *Journal of the Association for Persons with Severe Handicaps, 9,* 123-133.

McGee, G. G., Krantz, J., Mason, D., & McClannahan,

L. E. (1983). A modified incidental-teaching procedure for autistic youth: Acquisition and generalization of receptive object labels. *Journal of Applied Behavior Analysis, 16,* 329-338.

Mosk, M. D., & Bucher, B. (1984). Prompting and stimulus shaping procedures for teaching visual-motor skills to retarded children. *Journal of Applied Behavior Analysis, 17,* 23-34.

Nietupski, J., Clancy, P., Wehrmacker, L., & Parmer, C. (1985). Effects of minimal versus lengthy delay between simulated and in vivo instruction on community performance. *Education and Training of the Mentally Retarded, 20,* 190-195.

Oliver, P. (1983). Effect of teaching different tasks in group vs. individual training formats with severely handicapped individuals. *Journal of the Association for Persons with Severe Handicaps, 8,* 79-91.

Orelove, F. P. (1982). Developing daily schedules for classrooms of severely handicapped students. *Education and Treatment of Children, 5,* 59-68.

Ranieri, L., Ford, A., Vincent, L., & Brown, L. (1984). 1:1 vs. 1:3 instruction of severely multihandicapped students. *Remedial and Special Education, 5,* 23-28.

Reid, D. H., & Favell, J. E. (1984). Group instruction with persons who have severe disabilities: A critical review. *Journal of the Association for Persons with Severe Handicaps, 9,* 167-177.

Repp, A. C., Harman, M. L., Felce, D., Van Acker, R., & Karsh, K. G. (1989). Conducting behavioral assessments on computer-collected data. *Behavioral Assessment, 11,* 249-268.

Repp, A. C., & Karsh, K. G. (in press). An analysis of a group teaching procedure for persons with developmental disabilities. *Journal of Applied Behavior Analysis.*

Repp, A. C., & Karsh, K. G. (1991). The task demonstration model: A program for teaching persons with severe handicaps. In R. Remington (Ed.), *Severe mental retardation and applied behaviour analysis* (pp. 263-283).Chichester, England: John Wiley & Sons.

Repp, A. C., Karsh, K. G., & Lenz, M. (1990). A comparison of two teaching procedures on acquisition and generalization of severely handicapped persons. *Journal of Applied Behavior Analysis, 23,* 43-52.

Repp, A. C., Karsh, K. G., Van Acker, R., Felce, D., & Harman, M. (1989). A computer-based system for collecting and analyzing observational data. *Journal of Special Education Technology, 9,* 207-217.

Richmond, G., & Lewallen, J. (1983). Facilitating transfer for stimulus control when teaching verbal labels. *Education and Training of the Mentally Retarded, 18,* 111-116.

Rowan, V., & Pear, J. J. (1985). A comparison of the effects of interspersal and concurrent training sequences on acquisition, retention, and generalization of picture names. *Applied Research in Mental Retardation, 6,* 127-145.

Schriebman, L. (1975). Effects of within-stimulus and extra-stimulus prompting on discrimination learning in autistic children. *Journal of Applied Behavior Analysis, 8,* 91-112.

Schriebman, L., Charlop, M. H., & Koegel, R. L. (1982). Teaching autistic children to use extra-stimulus prompts. *Journal of Experimental Child Psychology, 33,* 475-491.

Sidman, M., & Stoddard, L. I. (1966). Programming, perception, and learning for retarded children. In N. R. Ellis (Ed.), *International review of research in mental retardation: Vol. 2* (pp. 151-208). New York: Academic Press.

Sidman, M., & Stoddard, L. I. (1967). The effectivness of fading in programming a simultaneous form discrimination for retarded children. *Journal of the Experimental Analysis of Behavior, 10,* 3-15.

Snell, M. E., & Gast, D. L. (1981). Applying delay procedures to the instruction of the severely handicapped. *Journal of the Association for Persons with Severe Handicaps, 5,* 3-14.

Steege, M. W., Wacker, D. P., & McMahon, C. M. (1987). Evaluation of the effectiveness and efficiency of two stimulus prompt strategies with severely handicapped students. *Journal of Applied Behavior Analysis, 20,* 293-299.

Storm, R. H., & Willis, J. H. (1978). Small-group training as an alternative to individual programs for profoundly retarded persons. *American Journal of Mental Deficiency, 83,* 283-288.

Terrace, H. (1963a). Discrimination learning with and without errors. *Journal of the Experimental Analysis of Behavior, 6,* 1-27.

Terrace, H. (1963b). Errorless transfer of a discrimination across two continua. *Journal of the Experimental Analysis of Behavior, 6,* 223-232.

Thomson, C., Holberg, M., & Baer, D. M. (1974). A brief report on a comparison of time-sampling procedures. *Journal of Applied Behavior Analysis, 7,* 623-626.

Touchette, P. E., & Howard, J. S. (1984). Errorless learning: Reinforcement contingencies and stimulus control transfer in delayed prompting. *Journal of Applied Behavior Analysis, 17,* 175-188.

Walls, R. J., Haught, P., & Dowler, D. L. (1982). Moments of transfer of stimulus control in practical assembly tasks. *American Journal of Mental Deficiency, 87,* 309-315.

Welch, S. J., & Pear, J. J. (1980). Generalization of naming responses to objects in the natural environment as a function of training stimulus modality with retarded children. *Journal of Applied Behavior Analysis, 13,* 629-643.

Westling, D. L., Ferrell, K., & Swenson, K. (1982). Intraclassroom comparison of two arrangements for teaching profoundly mentally retarded children. *American Journal of Mental Deficiency, 86,* 601-608.

Williams, J. A., Koegel, R. L., & Egel, A. L. (1981). Response-reinforcer relationships and improved learning in autistic children. *Journal of Applied Behavior Analysis, 14,* 53-60.

Wolery, M., & Gast, D. L. (1984). Effective and efficient procedures for the transfer of stimulus control. *Topics in Early Childhood Special Education, 4,* 52-77.

Wolfe, V. F., & Cuvo, A. J. (1978). Effects of within-stimulus and extra stimulus prompting on letter discrimination by mentally retarded persons. *American Journal of Mental Deficiency, 83,* 297-303.

This work was supported in part by Grant G008730035 and Grant H023C00090 from the U. S. Department of Education.

Manuscript received March 1990; revision accepted May 1991.

Children With Special Gifts and Talents

Children with intellectual giftedness are sickly and pale. They spend most of their free time and half the night poring over computer programs. They have no friends. Such are the myths about very bright children. The truth is far from the myth. Children with special gifts and talents are usually healthy, popular, well-coordinated, emotionally well-adjusted, and have a well-developed sense of humor.

Should children with special gifts and talents be provided with special educational services? They are not included in the categories of handicapped children for which PL 94-142 mandates free and appropriate public education. The Omnibus Education Bill of 1987 provided modest support for research on giftedness, development of special projects for the gifted, and preparation of staff to educate the gifted. States, however, must pay the lion's share of any gifted programming. Some states will foot the bills; most will not.

A child who scores 130 or above on a standardized IQ test is usually defined as intellectually gifted. Many professionals question both the validity and the reliability of IQ tests as accurate measures of intelligence. Today a multi-criteria assessment of special gifts and talents is preferred to one measure: the above-average IQ score. Standardized tests of intelligence, aptitude, achievement, and creativity are supplemented with work samples judged by unbiased professionals and classroom observations by the same.

Children with special gifts and talents may fall into several sub-categories. Not only are children with high overall intellectual ability considered gifted but also giftedness is assessed when children have high performance in any specific academic area, creative or productive thinking, high performance in the visual or performing arts, outstanding psychomotor abilities, or leadership abilities.

Many people still feel that money spent on gifted education is wasted money. Adults often cling to myths about children with special gifts and talents. One myth debunked in the opening paragraph is that they are sickly, pale, and lonely. Another myth is that they all have rich parents who can afford to buy them whatever special services they require. In fact, a large majority of children with special gifts and talents have uneducated and/or undistinguished parents. There are children with special gifts and talents from every economic level of society, from every ethnic and racial group, from every religion, and from both sexes. Children with special gifts and talents who are frequently overlooked in assessment screenings are girls, members of minority groups, children whose families are poor and/or uneducated, and children with other areas of exceptionality (e.g., learning disabled, emotionally and behaviorally disordered, communication disordered, hearing impaired, visually impaired, or physically or health impaired).

Another pervasive myth about children with special gifts and talents is that they are the "way they are" because of the environmental stimulations they received from "pushy parents." The truth is that many families are embarrassed by the child with special gifts and talents. They often apologize for, and downplay, the child's special aptitudes. Many children with special gifts and talents learn to hide their own special abilities in order to be more socially acceptable. It is not unusual to find students with special gifts and talents who are academic underachievers.

All children in the public education system of the United States are guaranteed a free and appropriate education in the least restrictive environment. Is the regular education classroom least restrictive or more restrictive for a child with special gifts and talents? Many special education experts feel that the regular education classroom is very restrictive for children with special gifts and talents. The most appropriate educational setting for them would be one in which their special gifts and talents could be encouraged. Special services that enhance their education include resource room pull-out, community mentors, independent studies, special classes, special schools, and academic acceleration. Each student with a special gift or talent should be individually assessed and provided with the special services that meet his or her needs. Each individualized education program (IEP) should be annually updated to accommodate the child's changing needs.

The first article in this section addresses the debate over special educational services for children with special gifts and talents. Do we want equity or excellence? The second article points out the unevenness in the process of selecting children for existing gifted and talented programs. Mary Frasier provides several suggestions for improving nomination methods. She believes schools

should provide more social and emotional support for children who lack confidence in their own special abilities. The last article in this section looks at the need for more freedom within the regular education classroom to enhance and encourage creativity. Selma Wassermann describes the world of play of Nobel Prize winners. She argues that learning about the world requires more play and less quiet, "on-task," pencil-and-paper worksheets in school.

Looking Ahead: Challenge Questions

Do we want all students educated equally? Do we want to challenge the excellence of our most creative, talented, and thoughtful children? What are the goals of education in the United States?

How can we improve the assessment of children with special gifts and talents?

How can we enhance the creativity of students in the regular education classroom? Is play the answer?

TURNING ON
THE
BRIGHT LIGHTS

The debate over how to educate gifted children cuts right to the heart of a larger conflict in American education: equity versus excellence. Is it fair to give special treatment to some children and not to others?

Jeff Meade

"I always associated the term 'gifted' with kids who were 5 years old and could play classical music," says Anne Marie Griffin. But nothing in that stereotypical definition prepared her for life with her son, Larry. At age 3, he could read and pronounce the polysyllabic names of preservatives on cookie boxes, and he could page through electrical manuals and learn enough to help his grandfather figure out why a new ceiling fan wouldn't turn.

By age 8, the Springfield, Mass., boy had been recognized for what he was: gifted. On standardized tests, he scored in the highly gifted range, with an IQ of 144.

Yet, in the fall of 1989, as Larry begin 2nd grade, his parents found themselves locking horns with the Springfield public schools over Larry's right to an appropriate education, a quarrel that has spilled over into this school year. On one level, the Griffins are challenging established school policy. They want Larry transferred to a nearby private school for the gifted, at an expense to the district of $6,500 a year. As Anne Marie Griffin explains, "They'll never be able to give him what he needs at his present school."

But on another level, Larry's education is symbolic of something far more fundamental. It is the question of fairness, pitting the needs of one little boy against the needs of all children in the Springfield schools. Is it fair to give special treatment to one child and not to others? No, says Springfield Superintendent Peter Negorni. "All children deserve something special and something different," he says.

The conflict over gifted education goes right to the heart of a larger conflict in American public education, a conflict as old as the republic itself: equity vs. excellence. On the one hand, we want every child to have the same opportunities to achieve and succeed. On the other hand, we want to nurture the gifted—students who rank in the top 1 percent to 3 percent of their classes—because these students possess the potential talent of future Rhodes scholars, Guggenheim fellows, and Nobel Prize winners.

We worry about writing off an entire generation of the urban poor through benign neglect, and, at the same time, we worry that America is losing its technological edge through inattention to the needs of our brightest. The

From *Teacher Magazine*, Vol. 2, No. 5, February 1991, pp. 36-43. Reprinted by permission.

debate is often passionate. And the future of gifted education hangs in the balance.

Teachers, like it or not, are

often caught in the middle of school systems' conflicting desires concerning gifted students. Most want to do right by the Larry Griffins of the world, but they have classrooms full of children who have equal, if not greater, needs. In some cities, teachers must devote enormous amounts of time and energy to keep half their students from falling behind and dropping out. They know that the bright students in their classrooms may not be challenged—but they assume they'll make it.

The issue runs deep among teachers.

Sally Reis, former coordinator of gifted programs in the Torrington, Conn., public schools, tells of the day she asked other teachers to fill out a questionnaire at the end of an after-school inservice session.

Many teachers see in gifted programs a challenge to their competence, an unspoken criticism that what they've been doing hasn't been enough.

One of the questions read: How should we deal with bright students? "Ten out of 40 answered, 'Wear sunglasses,'" recalls Reis, who is now an assistant professor of educational psychology at the University of Connecticut.

In fairness, 10 out of 40 is far from a majority. Yet, the snippy response reflects a sense of hostility and mistrust many teachers feel toward gifted programs. Many don't like the notion that there should be an educational elite of students or teachers.

"In my district, teachers didn't always love us," Reis says. "We'd take some of their best and brightest kids, and we'd do things with them that the teachers would have liked to have been able to do."

What's more, Reis says, many teachers see in gifted programs a challenge to their competence, an unspoken criticism that what they've been doing hasn't been good enough. And some of that hostility may be directed at gifted students themselves, who are, by definition, precocious.

Take, for example, J.C. Stewart of Jericho, Vt. In the beginning of 5th grade, J.C. was given a standardized test much like the one taken by Larry Griffin. J.C.'s IQ also topped out in the highly gifted range. And like Larry, J.C.'s talents were obvious from an early age: He spoke in complete sentences before he blew out his first birthday candle. And yet, J.C. spent much of 5th grade in the detention room. In addition to his gift, J.C. had a liability: an attention deficit, which affected the way he learned. Unless he was learning one on one, it was difficult for him to pay attention for very long.

"J.C. can give you the right answer to a math problem, but he can't always put it down on paper," says Maureen Stewart, his mother. "It's a conceptual problem. Once he's got it, he isn't going to lose it. But you have to lay it all out for him and go slowly."

Because of his attention deficit, J.C. found himself falling further and further behind on his math homework. He requested extra help from his teachers, but, his mother claims, "They ignored him."

Finally, as punishment for his failure to complete homework assignments, J.C.'s teachers sent him down the hall for detention. One of his worst punishments, he says, was being singled out to stand up and eat his lunch alone at a shelf near the lunchroom. "It was humiliating," he says.

Maureen Stewart says she was unable to get the school to comply with her frequent requests for additional help for her son. So, at the end of 5th grade, a time J.C. now recalls as a "total waste," he was placed in a private Roman Catholic school, where his grades improved and he received individual tutoring.

After spending 6th through 8th grade in private school and part of 9th grade being tutored at home, J.C. is now back in the public schools. He's hoping to zip through most of his curriculum in six months, a practice called curriculum compacting. And he hopes to do it on his own terms, one on one, the way he believes he learns best.

Making such exceptions for a single student doesn't always sit well with teachers, says Linda Tammi, who, until last year, was supervisor for the gifted and talented programs in the Springfield schools—the district where Larry Griffin found himself fitting in like a square peg.

"Often, if a child in a regular classroom was not performing well, and we saw that the student had a high IQ or test score, we'd want to pull the student out into another class," says Tammi, now an English teacher at the district's Bridge Academy, an alternative junior and senior high school for pregnant girls and other students teetering on the edge of academic disaster. "Sometimes the regular classroom teacher would buck this and say that until this child performs within the basic curriculum at a high level, she's not going to earn the privilege of being in a special classroom."

Many teachers harbor deep

concerns about the exclusionary nature of many gifted programs.

Historically, gifted children have been set apart from other children in two ways. In elementary school, they are often enrolled in enrichment programs, "pullout" classes, or resource rooms. In secondary schools, the preferred practice is acceleration—allowing a mathematically precocious 7th grader, for example, to take 9th grade algebra.

But one thing these approaches have in common is ability grouping, the practice of lumping children together according to their talents. On the elementary level, the divisions sound harmless enough: Kids are divided into the Bluebirds and Redbirds. But in the secondary schools, the stratification often becomes more obvious—some say insidious—as students assume their places in the tracking system.

Of all the practices common to gifted education,

Nerds Need Not Apply

In a big room, not far from the summertime fun of frisbee and tennis, Tom Hunt asks a class of adolescents, "Is botany under the 'aegis,' or umbrella, of physics?"

A girl, perhaps 14, answers: "Physics is, like, the general laws about nature, like why something happens, why, if I drop my pen, it falls."

She tosses her pen onto the floor, where it bounces and rolls over to Hunt's sneakers.

"And, like, why I pick it up?" he asks, as he reaches down and hands it back to her.

"Yeah, and botany is just the structures of cells themselves, and it doesn't have to tell you why the structures are doing what they're doing."

And so it goes, Hunt tossing out Latin and Germanic roots, the kids climbing over each other like spaniel puppies to answer his inquiries.

Such dialogue is common on the Franklin & Marshall College campus of the Center for Talented Youth, a program for the highly gifted run by the Center for the Advancement of Academically Talented Youth at Johns Hopkins University. The rural Pennsylvania campus of Franklin & Marshall—along with six other CTY sites, including one in Geneva, Switzerland—is where students identified as the brightest spend their summer vacations.

The Hopkins center annually recruits about 4,000 children between the ages of 12 and 16½ to attend these pullout classes to end all pullout classes. The students represent the top 1 percent of children in this age group, as measured by SAT scores: 930 is the minimum requirement for 13-year-olds, 430 verbal and 500 math. Not bad for kids who haven't even taken algebra I.

Once accepted, the students compete fiercely for placement in etymology, ancient Greek, and fast-paced physics with calculus. They hunger for the chance to take a year or two of high school math in three weeks. Some opt to stay for two sessions, six weeks in all.

They spend three hours a day, five days a week, with their noses buried in abstract algebra texts or racing through a chemistry course. And then there is homework—from one-and-a-half to three hours of it every day. The first classes meet at 9 in the morning; afternoon instruction starts at 1. But the kids are free—that is, when they aren't doing homework—from 3 to 10:30 p.m. It's a rigorous schedule, but most of the kids welcome the challenge.

And no, they don't walk around campus with calculators strapped to their belts. Even with all the demands made on them, they're normal, happy kids. Never more normal or happy, perhaps, than when they are on this campus, among children very much like themselves.

"Each one, individually, is the best in his or her class," says Luciano Carazza, director of academic programs at CTY. "When they come here, they're not. They form relationships and friendships, and they live for a whole year to come back here and be with their friends. If you listen to them talk, well, it's not necessarily what you hear on high school campuses."

The classes aren't what you'd find on your average high school campus, either. Many are self-paced. For example, students in the precalculus mathematics classes work their way through a textbook, reading each chapter and then taking a test, which is checked by teachers or teaching assistants. The TAs are also around to walk students through any material they don't understand. In other courses, there are regular quizzes, tests, and assignments.

At the end of the three- or six-week period, each student is mailed a written evaluation of his or her performance. Instructors are expected to make them as content-centered as possible, with a detailed assessment of the student's abilities and accomplishments—enough hard information so teachers back home will be able to compare those achievements with local standards.

For Tom Hunt, a teacher at North Yarmouth Academy near Portland, Maine, keeping ahead of the class is his ultimate challenge. "But at the same time," he says, "it's such a natural high to see the light go on quickly and to see their enthusiasm and their spark."

Given such enthusiasm, advocates of gifted education often cite CTY as definitive evidence that enrichment programs do work. Hopkins studies suggest that gifted students in these advanced classes are stimulated by competition from other students who can actually give them a run for their money. They also work at their own pace, not having to sit and twiddle their thumbs as the teacher reviews what they already know.

"One day at CTY is like a week or two of school," explains Nannette Belt, 15, of Indianapolis. "We're in our own little world."

—J.M.

Critics of gifted education oppose the practice of ability grouping because students most favorably grouped are typically white and comparatively well-off.

enrichment and ability grouping most frequently draw the brickbats.

That's because the children so enriched and most favorably grouped are typically white and comparatively well-off. Poor children traditionally have been placed in low-ability groups, often because they enter school already academically disadvantaged. This process becomes a self-fulfilling disaster. Once placed in a "slow" group, according to a recent report by the National Governors' Association, most children stay there, never rising above their labels.

"It's a vicious cycle," charges Stephanie Robinson, director of education and career development for the National Urban League. "Some students are labeled early, given watered-down content, and therefore, their skills are never developed. Students constantly exposed to the 'dumbed-down' curricula do not have the opportunity for full academic growth and development."

Studies show that what separates gifted from non-gifted students is not race, but economic class. According to a 1986 study by the U.S. Office of Civil Rights, 80.6 percent of all gifted students are white, 8.4 percent black, 5.5 percent Asian, 5.1 percent Hispanic, and 0.4 percent American Indian. A more recent, as yet unreleased, study conducted by the new federal Office of Gifted and Talented Education shows that poor children of all races are "severely underrepresented in gifted programs."

The newest numbers are still under wraps, but Patricia O'Connell Ross, director of the OGTE, says she has seen enough to know that these historical inequities cut across the color lines. "It's not just racial minorities," she says.

In a quest to redress the

longstanding racial and economic inequities, many school systems are eliminating ability grouping in favor of cooperative learning. No one knows exactly how many schools are making the switch, but one recent survey conducted for the National Educational Association found that 35 of 61 elementary schools polled were moving away from ability grouping and toward alternatives such as cooperative learning. Researchers who are studying gifted education see the practice as the most serious threat to the education of high-ability children. Few doubt the benefits of cooperative learning for low- and average-ability students, but they believe the practice holds high-ability children back.

In a nutshell, cooperative learning means taking children of mixed abilities and having them work together in small learning teams, each at his or her own pace. Students handle all of the so-called

management functions, like scoring tests and recording grades. A central feature of cooperative learning is peer assistance, in which students counsel each other, trying to resolve problems before calling in the teacher. (Cooperative learning also has been shown to improve race relations among students. . . .)

One of cooperative learning's foremost advocates is Robert Slavin, director of the elementary school program at Johns Hopkins University's Center for Research on Elementary and Middle Schools. Not coincidentally, Slavin questions the effectiveness of enrichment programs. Despite all the studies that claim they benefit high-ability students, Slavin frankly suggests that the available evidence fails to support such conclusions. "Effectiveness comes first," says Slavin. "If there were evidence of the effectiveness of separate programs for the gifted, that would be a different discussion. But when you don't have evidence, it comes down to a question of fairness."

A number of studies, conducted by Slavin and others, suggest that children in cooperative learning programs earn significantly higher test scores in math and reading than do children in traditional classes. In one form of cooperative learning used by Slavin, called team-assisted individualization, classes progressed twice as fast as would be expected—kids in a 3rd grade reading group learned to read at a 5th grade level. Further, one Slavin study notes, the effects are "equally positive for high, average, and low achievers."

What's more, many researchers—Slavin included—claim that high-ability students in cooperative learning classes learn and remember better. As Slavin has written: "High achievers gain in particular . . . because of the routine opportunity to explain to group mates what they have just learned, which as any teacher knows builds deeper understanding in the explainer."

Moreover, some cooperative learning models do

Some researchers see cooperative learning as the most serious threat to the education of gifted children because they believe it holds such students back.

offer teachers the flexibility to allow some ability grouping. Two of Slavin's models, for example, permit some grouping within mixed-ability classes, accommodating differences within the class.

"We don't want to get cooperative learning associated with one side or the other," says researcher Roger Johnson, professor of curriculum and instruction at the University of Minnesota. "Cooperative learning is not an alternative to tracking. The only alternative to tracking is not tracking."

Cooperative learning, Johnson notes, could work just as well in a homogeneously grouped gifted class because its real strength lies in diversity. Shy kids, athletic kids, minority kids, and disabled kids, regardless of the range of their abilities, all bring different perspectives to a classroom. "It's the things that we do differently that make us powerful," Johnson says.

Regardless of the dramatic

claims made for cooperative learning, researchers who study gifted programs remain equally adamant in their defense of separate programs for the gifted.

Backing up that point of view is a comprehensive review of statistical studies going back 50 years conducted by University of Michigan researchers James and Chen-Lin Kulik. In 19 of 25 studies, they found that talented students "achieved more when they were taught in homogeneous classrooms." About 63 percent of gifted students in these special classes outperformed their counterparts in mixed-ability classes, according to the Kuliks.

And although learning may improve for low- and average-ability students in cooperative learning classrooms, the benefits to gifted students are subject to debate. Researchers who study the gifted say cooperative learning has a kind of "Robin Hood" effect: It takes from the rich and gives to the poor.

But advocates of gifted education don't necessarily see this long-simmering debate as a choice between the haves and the have-nots. "It's not a black or white, yes or no, privileged or underprivileged proposition," explains Valerie Seaberg, president of the Council of State Directors of Programs for the Gifted, herself a former classroom teacher. "There are high-ability kids in all groups. Where we need to start is in learning to deal with high ability."

Some school districts—no

one really knows how many—are making an effort to redefine giftedness to embrace many children who have traditionally been excluded: girls, minorities, and non-English-speaking immigrants, for example.

One of the more popular ways of identifying giftedness in the new system is a three-ringed model devised by Joseph Renzulli of the University of Connecticut. While most gifted students have been identified by IQ or standardized-test scores, Renzulli's method involves a combination of attributes: above-average ability, task commitment, and creativity.

Renzulli, working with Sally Reis, also developed what is called the schoolwide enrichment model, which opens up many enrichment activities to the entire school, including guest speakers, concerts, and field trips.

Most researchers, however, still insist that some separate programs will always be necessary to meet the needs of pupils who are, by definition, exceptional. On this, Reis speaks with particular expertise.

"I got into gifted education because of classroom experiences I had [as a student] in elementary school," says Reis. "I used to get into trouble because I had a lot of books tucked away with my basal reader. I used to stay home pretending to be sick just so I could read. We're getting right back into a situation like that."

In the absence of separate programs, she says, bright students will be content to coast. They will surrender to boredom.

"For many of the kids I've worked with, the gifted program is a lifesaver, literally the only time of the week when they feel challenged, working alongside kids who share their interests," Reis says. "Without these programs, we will wind up with kids who learn only to put out minimal effort. They'll never learn to work in school because they'll never have to."

Sixteen-year-old Michael Nimchek, ranked third in his class of 250 at Torrington (Conn.) High School, attests to that: "If I hadn't been in the TAG [talented and gifted] program in elementary school, I would have been bored. I would have had nothing to do. I would have had to sit through six hours of school for no reason."

Michael's exceptional ability was already evident in kindergarten.

"I was so excited about going to school," he says.

'For many of the kids I've worked with,' says one educational researcher, 'the gifted program is a lifesaver, the only time when they feel challenged.'

"My parents had already taught me the alphabet, and I could read. And my dad had given me a calculator. I learned a lot of math on that. I already knew my multiplication tables up to 12. By the end of my first week, I could see that there was going to be a problem. The only thing we learned was what the color red looked like. Well, my parents were pretty good. They had already taught me that."

For Michael and other gifted students, the regular classroom literally might be a waste of time. As early as 1937, researcher Leta Hollingworth suggested that "bright children need only one-half of their time for school work."

Some argue that the same thing might be said for average students, given the amount of review and redundancy built into the curriculum. As evidence, Reis often points to a 1980 study by the Educational Products Information Exchange. In the study, beginning 4th grade students were given math tests based on the text that would guide them through the coming school year. Not one of them had even seen the book at that point, and yet 60 percent of the 4th graders scored 80 or higher.

If the regular classroom is no challenge for average students, for gifted children it may be the academic equivalent of slow death.

"We should be asking, 'What happens to gifted students in a regular classroom?'" Reis says. "What are the ramifications of that?"

For teacher Valerie Seaberg, the answer is obvious. She remembers, in particular, a student at the Maine high school where she taught who, by age 14, was already a gifted musician. "It's one of those

Dropped Out Or Pushed Out?

Margaret LeCompte remembers a girl who was very smart—in all ways, perhaps, except one. On standardized tests, the girl scored in the 99th percentile. But during her junior year in high school, she became pregnant. District policy required that she be removed from her advanced classes and placed, along with all the other pregnant teens, in a remedial program. "The girl dropped out," LeCompte says, "because she felt totally offended by what had happened."

This bright young woman is one of many students singled out for study by LeCompte, a former director of research and evaluation in the Houston Independent School District, where this incident took place. The case stands out as an example of a little-studied, poorly understood phenomenon: the gifted dropout.

Most of what is known about gifted dropouts is purely anecdotal. But if the observations of LeCompte and others are any indication, there may be more dropouts among students of high ability than most people assume. According to LeCompte's survey of students who dropped out of the Houston schools during the 1983–84 school year, 25 percent had test scores above the 75th percentile and fully 10 percent scored in the 90th percentile and above.

Clearly, not all children in the 75th percentile range are gifted, but, says LeCompte, many undoubtedly are high-ability students. "They certainly aren't remedial," she says. "They're above average."

Houston, of course, is a large, culturally diverse urban district. But the trend, if it truly is one, seems to cut across demographic lines.

For example, a team of researchers at Texas A&M University recently examined dropout rates in six suburban school districts, where the majority of students—and most of the dropouts—are white. A surprising 29 percent of students in regular and honors programs—students not considered at risk—dropped out during the 1988-89 school year. Although honors students, on average, constituted one of the smallest groups of dropouts, in one school district—College Station—8.5 percent of all dropouts were in the honors program.

The phenomenon also has been observed far north of Texas in Chicago, where one out of every five high-ability students leaves school before graduation.

Why? According to John Easton, director of monitoring and research for the Chicago Panel on School Policy and Finance, there are several reasons, including, not surprisingly, boredom. "The schools just aren't very good," he says. Additionally, many bright and talented minority students feel pressured by their peers to drop out. "The culture is anti-achievement, anti-success," he says.

And sometimes, says LeCompte, now associate professor of psychology and education at the University of Colorado, high-ability students become victims of school policy, like the pregnant teen.

"One student at our performing arts magnet school had taken first-year algebra and flunked," recalls LeCompte, coauthor, with A. Gary Dworkin, of the forthcoming book *Giving Up in School*. Under a Texas school law that requires students to pass all their subjects or forfeit extracurricular activities, including studying art in a magnet school, the boy was forced out of the special program. "He could have been allowed to enroll in consumer math, and easily passed," she says, "but they wouldn't let him do that. So he dropped out."

In this case at least, LeCompte says, there is a happy ending: "He got his high school equivalency, and now he's in college, enrolled in a fine-arts program."

—J.M.

classic stories," she says. "A neighbor had an old upright piano in a barn, and the kid had taught himself to play. We had him audition with some professional musicians at the Bowdoin College School of Music. Their assessment of him was that he was remarkable."

But the young musician had one serious handicap that effectively barred him from the big time. Since he was a small child, he had worked on his family's farm, pitching hay. As a result, the muscles of his hands and arms were horribly outsized for an aspiring artist.

"You can't do that to your hands for so long and still hit an octave," says Seaberg. "For him, it was already too late. They should have known about him when he was 6."

Poor and Minority Students Can Be Gifted, Too!

Our daily practices must reflect the recognition that gifted students come from all walks of life.

MARY M. FRASIER

Mary M. Frasier is President, National Association for Gifted Children, and Associate Professor, Educational Psychology Coordinator, and Program for the Gifted Director, Torrance Center for Creative Studies, 422 Aderhold Hall, University of Georgia, Athens, GA, 30602.

Despite all efforts toward equity in schools, minority and poor students remain noticeably absent from gifted programs. The most frequent explanation for their low representation in such programs is performance on an IQ test below the cutoff score set by a state department, school district, or school system. Other explanations describe the limitations of a low socioeconomic environment to stimulate and support the development of higher intellectual capacities. Finally, there is the persistent attitude that giftedness simply cannot be found in some groups (Frasier 1987).

Improving Nomination Methods

Such negative attitudes are reinforced by narrow nomination and screening methods that limit the access of under-involved populations to these programs. As Gallagher (1983) noted, "if you don't get a chance to come to bat, you don't get a chance to hit." To give these students their chance, we can expand the methods used to appraise children's potential.

We can create nomination forms that incorporate behavioral traits, such as the 15 indicators of giftedness delin-

eated by Hagen (1980, pp. 23-26). The use of these dynamic (rather than static) traits requires nominators to observe, for example, a student's use of language rather than just to rely on appraisal of language in a test situation.

Second, parents and other representatives of the underinvolved groups can help educators reword items on rating scales (such as the Scale for Rating Behavioral Characteristics of Superior Students, Renzulli and Hartman 1971), so

Sternberg's Triarchic Theory of Intelligence and Gardner's Theory of Multiple Intelligences became major breakthroughs in expanding the definition of *intelligence*.

that the ratings more accurately reveal the manifestations of giftedness within a cultural group.

Third, teachers can develop vignettes of poor and minority students they have taught to serve as prototypes of

successful students. Nominators can then use these vignettes as examples to help others recognize students who are demonstrating potential for achievement. The development of vignettes is enhanced by incorporating behavioral traits of successful students from disadvantaged backgrounds. (See Ross and Glaser 1973 for a particularly useful source of such traits.)

The intent of these approaches is to broaden concepts of what giftedness looks like in minority and low socioeconomic populations. Then, as teachers and parents become aware of the varied manifestations of giftedness, they are better prepared to recognize—and nominate for programs—many more poor and minority students.

Expanding The Definition of *Intelligence*

Another barrier to equity in gifted programs is the continuing but outmoded emphasis on the IQ as the *sine qua non* of giftedness. When program acceptance is based solely on this limited criterion, minority and poor students do not fare well. Thus, a more nearly complete definition of *intelligence* is part of the solution to eliminating barriers.

A few years ago, Torrance (1979) demonstrated that we can learn much about children's potential by examining indicators of intelligence that do not depend on prelearned solutions to problems. He developed the Torrance Tests of Creative Thinking, figural and verbal, to assess children's responses to open-ended problem-solving situations. Corroborating this concept, Sternberg (1982) advocated that ability be evaluated not only through the measurement of one's manipulation of *entrenched concepts* (familiar) but also one's ability to deal with *nonentrenched concepts* (unfamiliar).

Recently, Sternberg's (1981) Triarchic Theory of Intelligence and Gardner's (1983) Theory of Multiple Intelligences became major breakthroughs in expanding the definition of *intelligence*, foretelling the end of reliance on factor-analytic, psychometric measures such as IQ. Clark's (1988) research on brain/mind functioning has further supported a broad concept of giftedness, one that includes talent other than academic.

These developments, combined with the findings of other researchers (Baldwin 1984, Renzulli 1978, Treffinger and Renzulli 1986, and Tannenbaum 1983), have led to a more sophisticated array of best practices in identifying potential for gifted performance. These practices include:

● seeking nominations from a variety of persons, professional and non-professional, inside and outside school;

● applying knowledge of the behavioral indicators by which children from different cultures dynamically exhibit giftedness in the development of nomination forms;

● collecting data from multiple sources, objective and subjective, including performances and products;

New information is causing us to reconsider the misconception that poor homes are necessarily illiterate or incapable of supporting intellectual development.

● delaying decision making until *all* pertinent data can be collected in a case study (Frasier 1987).

Also noteworthy are the productive efforts of Tonemah (1987) and of the American Indian Research and Development Center in Norman, Oklahoma, in identifying gifted and talented American Indian students using creativity indicators. These and other developments are helping us to make headway, but there is more that we can do.

What Else Needs to Be Done?

As efforts continue to break down barriers to equity, we are encountering other challenges in serving poor and minority students well. We often fear that their deprived backgrounds will put them at a loss in a program that assumes familiarity with certain content and experiences. Thus, we typically *adapt* curriculum to try to fit or adjust the students to the curriculum. For example, minority and poor children are placed in pre-gifted programs designed to remediate language and performance deficiencies. Upon successful completion, they may then be certified for placement in a gifted program. What is more promising is to emphasize *accommodation* by changing the structure, function, or form that produces an enhanced learning environment. Examples of curriculum accommodations would be to emphasize high expectations for achievement, establish clear standards of excellence, and provide assistance in securing mentors.

Second, new information is causing us to reconsider the misconception that poor homes are necessarily illiterate or incapable of supporting intellectual development. Recent findings indicate that the qualities of home life that promote achievement are similar, regardless of income level (Bradley et al. 1987, Coleman 1969, Murphy 1986, Rosenbaum et al. 1987, Scott-Jones 1987, Slaughter and Epps 1987). For example, the entire August 1988 issue of *Ebony* magazine—in particular, the article "Model Youths: Excelling Despite the Odds" (Brown 1988)—compels us to reexamine notions and expand realities regarding the extent of support for intellectual development in the black community. As we reconceptualize the role of families in promoting intellectual achievement, we can better recognize their strengths and resources and work in partnership with them.

Third, we must strengthen counseling options to provide the social and emotional support these students need to gain confidence in their abilities (Exxum 1979, 1983; Colangelo 1985; and Frasier 1979). With adequate support, they can manage the conflict inherent in being identified gifted, gain access to the information they need to make good academic and vocational decisions, and resolve the problems of social interaction within their culture and the culture of the larger society. See Comer (1987) for an excellent program that defines the total academic, social, and psychological support needed to enhance the achievement of minority and poor students.

The Reality of Diversity

An encompassing perspective of giftedness and improved assessment methods will help us to remove the barriers that so often keep poor and minority students out of programs for the gifted. The gifted in our schools are a diverse group, made up of children from all racial groups, at all ages, and at all socioeconomic levels.

References

Baldwin, A.Y. (1984). *The Baldwin Identification Matrix 2 for the Identification of the Gifted and Talented: A Handbook for Its Use*. New York: Trillium Press.

Bradley, R.H., S.L. Rock, B.M. Caldwell, P.T. Harris, and H.M. Hamrick. (1987). "Home Environment and School Performance among Black Elementary School Children." *Journal of Negro Education* 56, 4: 499-509.

Brown, R. (1988). "Model Youth: Excelling Despite the Odds." *Ebony* 43, 10: 40-48.

Clark, B. (1988). *Growing Up Gifted*. Columbus, Ohio: Merrill Publishing Company.

Colangelo, N. (September 1985). "Counseling Needs of Culturally Diverse Students." *Roeper Review* 8, 1: 33-35.

Coleman, A.B. (November 1969). "The Disadvantaged Child Who Is Successful in School." *The Educational Forum* 32, 1: 95-97.

Comer, J.P. (March 1987). "New Haven's School-Community Connection." *Educational Leadership* 42: 13-16.

Exxum, H.A. (1979). "Facilitating Psychological and Emotional Development of Gifted Black Students." In *New Voices in Counseling the Gifted*, edited by N. Colangelo and R.T. Zaffran. Dubuque, Iowa: Kendall/Hunt Publishing Co.

Exxum, H.A. (February 1983). "Key Issues in Family Counseling with Gifted and Talented Black Students." *Roeper Review* 5, 3: 28-31.

Frasier, M.M. (1979). "Counseling the Culturally Diverse Gifted." In *New Voices in Counseling the Gifted*, edited by N. Colangelo and R.T. Zaffran. Dubuque, Iowa: Kendall/Hunt Publishing Co.

Frasier, M.M. (Spring 1987). "The Identification of Gifted Black Students: Developing New Perspectives." *Journal for the Education of the Gifted* 10, 3: 155-180.

Gallagher, J.J. (May 22, 1983). "Keynote Speech." *International Conference on Gifted Students*. Ontario, Canada: Sheridan College.

Gardner, H. (1983). *Frames of Mind: The Theory of Multiple Intelligences*. New York: Basic Books.

Hagen, E. (1980). *Identification of the Gifted*. New York: Teachers College Press.

Murphy, D.M. (1986). "Educational Disadvantagement: Associated Factors, Current Interventions, and Implications." *Journal of Negro Education* 55, 4: 495-507.

Renzulli, J.S. (1978). "What Makes Giftedness? Reexamining a Definition." *Phi Delta Kappan* 60: 180-184, 261.

Renzulli, J., and R. Hartman. (1971). "Scale for Rating Behavioral Characteristics of Superior Students." *Exceptional Children* 38, 1: 243-248.

Rosenbaum, J.E., M.J. Kulieke, and L.S. Rubinowitz. (1987). "Low-Income Black Children in White Suburban Schools: A Study of School and Student Responses." *Journal of Negro Education* 56, 1: 35-52.

Ross, H.L., and E.M. Glaser. (1973). "Making It Out of the Ghetto." *Professional Psychology* 4, 3: 347-356.

Scott-Jones, D. (1987). "Mother-as-Teacher in the Families of High- and Low-Achieving Low-Income Black First-Graders." *Journal of Negro Education* 56, 1: 21-34.

Slaughter, D.T., and E.G. Epps. (1987). "The Home Environment and Academic Achievement of Black American Children and Youth: An Overview." *Journal of Negro Education* 56, 1: 3-20.

Sternberg, R. (1981). "A Componential Theory of Intellectual Giftedness." *Gifted Child Quarterly* 25, 2: 86-93.

Sternberg, R. (1982). "Nonentrenchment in the Assessment of Intellectual Giftedness." *Gifted Child Quarterly* 26, 2: 63-67.

Tannenbaum, A.J. (1983). *Gifted Children: Psychological and Educational Perspectives*. New York: Macmillan Publishing Co.

Tonemah, S. (1987). "Assessing American Indian Gifted and Talented Students' Abilities." *Journal for the Education of the Gifted* 10, 3: 181-194.

Torrance, E.P. (1979). *Torrance Tests of Creative Thinking: Norm-Technical Manual*. Bensenville, Ill.: Scholastic Testing Service.

Treffinger, D., and J.S. Renzulli. (February 1986). "Giftedness as Potential for Creative Productivity: Transcending IQ Scores." *Roeper Review* 8, 3: 150-154.

Serious Play in the Classroom

How Messing Around Can Win You the Nobel Prize

Selma Wassermann

Selma Wassermann is Professor of Education, Simon Fraser University, Burnaby, British Columbia. This article is based on her keynote address at the ACEI Study Conference in San Diego, California, April 20, 1991.

The 3rd-graders sat quietly, politely, as the teacher went from table to table, giving each group of children a bundle of fabrics to examine. They were to talk with each other and make some observations of the fabric. The teacher had expected that their playful investigations would lead to further awareness of how fabric was made, particularly examinations of texture, thread, color, print and elasticity. Although this was the first time they had been involved in investigative play, and the experience of carrying on this self-directed examination to gather data was new, they went right to the task —examining the pieces of fabric, pulling, stretching, looking through the fabric at the light, scrutinizing texture, print, color. They played with the fabrics for a long time before the teacher asked them to give her their attention, since she wanted to hear about their observations. In the first few responses, the children talked about texture, thread and design. Then, Andre said, "My fabrics make different sounds."

When he was asked to tell more about what he meant, he demon-strated that when he put the fabric down on his desk and scratched along the woof or the warp, sounds of a certain pitch were produced. He also showed that when he scratched more quickly, the pitch was higher; when he scratched more slowly, the pitch was lower. Now clearly this has implications for music, pitch, sound and how music is made on stringed instruments; and this 8-year-old boy had come up with this discovery during his play with fabrics.

This is but one example of how play allows children to make discoveries that go far beyond the realm of what we adults think is important to know. But that is only one of the benefits of play. I believe that with play, we teachers can have it all: the development of knowledge, of a spirit of inquiry, of creativity, of conceptual understanding—all contributing to the true empowerment of children. Is it possible that serious play is, in fact, the primary vehicle through which serious learning occurs? If that is the case, might we consider introducing serious play at all stages of a student's learning, from kindergarten through graduate school? Given the present climate in education, such a proposal is tantamount to heresy. But what the heck? If you're sailing on the Titanic, you might as well go first class.

The Case for Play

Arguments to support serious play are found in many learned sources. Victor and Mildred Goertzel, whose seminal work investigating eminent adults resulted in *Cradles of Eminence* (1962), set out to see if they could find some common threads in the early childhood experiences of people who grew to eminence as adults. In their studies of the childhood of 400 eminent adults—writers, composers, inventors, statesmen and women, scientists, artists and others—they looked for keys to understand what factors contributed substantially to their later development as our "heroes." One of the common threads these researchers found was that, "by conventional standards, the attitude of the family toward normal schooling was negative. In many instances, some of the children were never sent to school at all" (p. 267).

To substantiate this point, the Goertzels use the example of the Wright brothers. As youths, these boys were tinkerers who enjoyed messing around. When they asked their mother for permission to stay out of school for several years, to "tinker around in the backyard," their mother agreed. What might have occurred if Mother Wright believed that school was the only place where serious learning could occur and what might that have meant for the later development of the airplane?

Another example of a tinkerer is Thomas Edison. He, too, was allowed to spend hours messing around and once again, it is interesting to speculate the future of his discoveries if he had been admonished to "get serious and get back to work and stop that messing around!"

Frank Lloyd Wright was another serious player. He was encouraged by his mother, from his very early years, to play with colored papers and cubes of wood. Mrs. Wright, in fact, actively cultivated Frank's play with these forms and believed that through such play, the boy's intellectual development would be advanced (Goertzel, pp. 85-86).

Another common thread found by the Goertzels in the families of the 400 eminent adults was that most mothers were quite permissive with their children, allowing them great degrees of freedom to make choices about what they wanted and did not want to do. Goertzels' data also reveal that for many of these adults, school was a place where creativity was stifled, rather than encouraged. It was to be avoided at all costs. These children liked best "those teachers who let them go ahead at their own pace and who gave them permission to work unimpeded in the area of their own special interests" (Goertzel, p. 267). Torrance, in his early research on giftedness, also observed that teachers considered highly creative elementary school children to be a source of great nuisance.

They seem to be playing around when they should be working at assigned tasks. They engage in manipulative and/or exploratory activities, many of which are discouraged or even forbidden. They enjoy learning, and this looks to teachers like play, rather than work. (Torrance, 1961)

Teachers preferred the high IQ student over the creative one. The creative children wanted to go off in new directions, producing new forms. Because they insisted on invention, rather than quietly submitting to what teachers asked of them, they were thought of as "obnoxious" and troublesome. The high IQ students were low risk-takers and teachers regarded them as "se-

rious, ambitious, and promising."

The Goertzels concluded that:

If a potential Edison or Einstein or Picasso or Churchill or Clemens had been in school in California in these days, he would surely not have been chosen to be screened for inclusion in the Stanford study of genius. (p. 279)

The creation of new ideas does not come from minds trained to follow doggedly what is already known. Creation comes from tinkering and playing around, from which new forms emerge. Composers play with sounds in their heads to make new music. Visual artists play with images, form and color to create art. Architects play with design and form. Poets and novelists play with words, literally and figuratively, in their literary creations. Although we may think of William Shakespeare's work as sacrosanct—the epitome of polished language usage—it helps to remember that he invented at least 1,700 words, which became part of our common language usage only after he introduced them into the language (Bryson, 1990). From all of this play, this messing around, serious and new creative forms are brought to life.

The freedom to create and invent appears to be closely connected with the development of creative, inventive, innovative adults. What about the benefits of play for cognitive development? Is play only for the gifted and talented potential artists, inventors, writers, architects—the creative geniuses? What can play do for all the other children for whom teachers wish to further conceptual development and extend knowledge?

Research of the renowned cognitive psychologist from Harvard, Jerome Bruner, supports the potential of play for cognitive development. Bruner's experiments on play reveal that not only does play promote concept development, but also that this occurs much more substantially through play than

through direct instruction. Bruner set up three learning groups and found that those children who had the opportunity to engage in previous free play with the creative materials were better prepared to solve the subsequent problems presented to them, than were the groups of children who were a) allowed to handle but not play with the materials and b) only shown the principles underlying the solutions by an adult (Bruner, 1985). Bruner has written that:

There is evidence that by getting children to play with materials that they must later use in a problem solving task, one gets superior performance from them in comparison with those children who spend time familiarizing themselves with the materials in other ways. Players generate more hypotheses and they reject wrong ones more quickly. Players seem to become frustrated less, and fixated less. They are more interested in finding out and learning from their explorations than they are in obtaining rewards. (p. 603)

Bruner further speculates that playful, flexible, mindful interaction early in a child's life may become a model later for what adults do when encountering problems. Having learned the habits of playing around, adults are more likely to feel encouraged to play around in their own heads.

There is another point worth making about the value of play in children's lives today. Authors like Elkind (1982), Postman (1982) and Winn (1981) have written powerfully about what they call "the disappearance of childhood." Children today have far fewer opportunities to live in the life of the mind, to be playful, to behave as children. In place of traditional childhood games that were still popular a generation ago, in place of fantasy and make-believe, in place of messing around, today's children have substituted television. Today, children play computer games in the amusement arcade and Nintendo at home, instead of messing around with colored paper and junk. They choose computer camps for holiday fun and ask for Apples for Christmas. If TV is contributing to the disappearance of childhood, how is the computer affecting the play of children? Such new "toys" may have very grave implications for the kinds of adults that today's children are likely to become and for the kinds of worlds they are likely to create. Perhaps we educators need to spend more time reflecting on these issues as we speculate about the future of this planet.

How Does Play Work To Produce These Results?

When we examine play more closely, we are able to see how it allows for the cognitive and creative development of children.

■ Play is generative. Anyone who is playing is creating something new, something that has not been created before. In play, we are not locked into conforming to a set standard of what is *right*. When children do worksheets or other pencil-and-paper exercises, they are expected to conform to an existing standard. What would have happened if, for example, little Billy Shakespeare had given his Grade 6 teacher a paper with the words *majestic* or *hurry* or *lonely* or *radiance*— all words that he had invented? The likelihood is great that his paper would have been returned slashed with red *X*'s and an admonition to go to the dictionary and use proper vocabulary! It is play that sanctions what is different.

■ Play allows for risks to be taken, and the taking of risks is a normal part of play. This does not mean life-threatening risks. It means risks of invention, trying something that has not been tried before, thinking ideas that have never been thought before, conceptualizing something that has not been conceived before. In play, we risk and we do so within margins of safety, because we know it is not only all right to risk in play but that

The creation of new ideas does not come from minds trained to follow doggedly what is already known. Creation comes from tinkering and playing around, from which new forms emerge.

play demands we risk. Inventions of the new do not come from duplicating what is already there. They come from minds that are unafraid to take risks to try. Worksheets or pencil-and-paper exercises make risk a terrible threat. Nothing new or imaginative is dared to be written. Children must write what is acceptable, what has been written before, what has been decided as "correct."

■ In play, there is no fear of failure, because there is no failure. Failure occurs when children have not measured up to another's preconceived notion of what they should have done. No standards of right and wrong are articulated in play, and the absence of such standards is what allows for innovation. Play invites learning to value error as a means of learning more. In play, we really *do* learn from mistakes. On the other hand, in schoolwork, teachers may say to students that "we learn from our errors," but no child has ever been thus deceived. Children learn early in school that making errors or getting it wrong involves heavy penalties, of both the academic and psychological kind, carrying long-range and painful consequences. While in work we may be encouraged to try, we learn *not* to take chances, for fear of failure, for fear we may be wrong.

■ Play builds autonomy. Through play, self-initiating behaviors are developed. It encourages children to do their own creations, to build their own castles. In fact, children want the autonomy that play gives, and they enjoy the feel-

ing of control that play gives them. Children who are serious players are the most autonomous. They don't need direction from others to tell them what to do now and what to do next. They enjoy making choices for themselves. In that way, play is ego-affirming as well.

■ Play gives the hands something to do. And when the hands are active, the mind engages. Ironically, this is the opposite of what most of us were taught when we went to teachers college. In those days, we were taught that children should not "fiddle." New data about fiddling around suggest that when hands are engaged, students pay closer attention to what is going on. Those of us who doodle during a meeting will immediately understand that doodling does not distract; it helps to keep attention riveted on the events of the meeting. Active involvement requires pumping adrenalin. Passive sitting and listening to talk that is largely boring do not lead to the pumping of adrenalin; therefore, there is very little mind engagement. When the hands are actively engaged in play, adrenalin is being pumped, and learning is more substantive.

These five principles are part of a larger theory of learning: experiential learning. Rooted in the work of Dewey, Lewin and Piaget, this theory—unlike other, more abstract learning theories— is teacher-friendly. It confirms and legitimizes what most teachers already know to be true: knowledge is not a fixed commodity. It is formed and reformed through experience. Each time we experience, we reshape and reform our ideas. Ideas are continually being sifted through the lens of new experiences.

This knowledge does not refer merely to names, dates and labels associated with the single, correct answers being sought on worksheets. Instead, it refers to the knowledge involved in being able to make meaning from information—the knowledge that means to *understand*. If students were studying the Civil Rights Movement in the United States, for example, all new student experiences—reading, looking at photographs, seeing films, listening to people who had played active roles in the movement—would cause a reshaping and reforming of their knowledge about the movement. The more powerful the experience, the more significant the reforming of the knowledge. This is part of the process of cognition, of thinking.

Active learning experience, or serious play, is the first step in advancing knowledge, in allowing learners to reach beyond names, dates and labels to deeper meanings. Active experience builds understanding. This is, of course, what schooling and education are really about. Not just to know the names, but to understand the meanings.

Learner experiences are enriched through a second stage of experience—the process of reflective observation. In this stage, learners are asked to think back on the experience; through certain questioning strategies, they are helped to see more, to look more deeply, to find important meanings.

Experiential learning, starting with active engagement with concrete materials and enriched by reflective observation, allows learners to build concepts and reach for theoretical understandings that lead, in turn, to students' ability to make more thoughtful decisions and solve more difficult problems.

Experiential learning, or serious play, builds habits of thinking.

Making Play Work in the Classroom

There are two kinds of play that I have observed in classrooms. One is more open and the other more focused. These are my definitions, and while others may see play differently, they at least serve to illuminate the paragraphs that follow.

In more open play, the teacher sets out materials so that children may mess around without any specific goal. The children use the materials to create their own inventions. These materials may include items that allow for creative opportunities, like blocks, paints, dress-up clothes, clay, wood and hardware, musical instruments, scraps of paper for collages. They may also include scraps of fabric, pine cones, seashells, buttons, mathematical counters, cuisenaire rods, attribute blocks, rulers and other measuring instruments that allow for creative investigations. Virtually any kind of material involving hands-on creations or investigations may be used for this more open type of play. The instruction to students is something like this: "Use these materials to make a design that you like." Or, "Here are some materials for you to play with." Or, sometimes, the materials are laid out with no instruction from the teacher about how they are to be used. With more open play, there is no predetermined idea or topic being investigated through these activities. In fact, the children themselves invent their own focus for the investigations.

In this more open play, children have lots of choices about what they are going to do with the materials. More open play has much greater potential for creation and invention, for risk-taking.

There's a down side to more open play. By later grades, some children have lost considerable autonomy as players; more open play,

where they have to create their own structures, defeats them. Consequently, they engage in what teachers call "behavior"—and their play may become, at worst, destructive or silly. More open play is for those children who are more autonomous, who can create structures to play from within themselves. For children who have lost the ability to play productively, teachers might prefer more focused play. In this type of play, teachers provide a specific focus to the play that sets some guidelines and gives children a structure for the activity. The structure may be quite open, but having a structure is security-giving for children who have lost the autonomy that very open play requires. Focused play results in far less "behavior."

In focused play, a teacher who wanted students to study clothing might gather about 100 photographs of different styles of men's and women's clothing over the last 100 years and focus the play by asking children to study the pictures and make some observations of how clothing has changed in the last 100 years. Even with that focus, much room remains for open investigation. It is important that a focus not be too narrow, lest the play be inhibited. In focusing the play, the teacher learns to be aware of the difference between guidelines that constrain and those that enable more productive plays.

The ideas behind serious play have taken root in primary and intermediate classrooms in British Columbia as part of the Ministry of Education's comprehensive education plan, *Year 2000* (Ministry of Education, 1990). In these classrooms, it is gratifying to see just how much curriculum content can be learned through investigative play. Far and beyond what is normally done in the arts and crafts, play is effectively and happily used as a vehicle to enable students to learn more about what is important in the "hard line" curriculum areas of math, science, social studies and language arts. Serious play is also emerging as a teaching strategy in "teaching with cases" in B.C. secondary schools as well (Wassermann, in press).

Building Curriculum Based on Serious Play

Developing curriculum experiences that are rooted in play is not difficult. A successful program, however, requires that certain conditions be met to ensure that students develop knowledge and conceptual understanding.

1. *The teacher must be able to design and orchestrate a curriculum rooted in play. This includes:*

- Visualizing how important curriculum concepts can be learned through play and being clear about the big ideas that are being studied in the curriculum
- Gathering the materials needed for the plays
- Organizing the class for cooperative group work on the plays and orienting students to this more student-centered, active learning format
- Allowing students time for play
- Trusting play to do the job of teaching the concepts
- Using classroom discussion skills that call for students' reflective observations on their play, or "debriefing" the play
- Providing for follow-up plays that enable students to develop their knowledge of principles as their learning is formed and reformed through added experience. (Wassermann, 1990)

The label *Play-Debrief-Replay* describes this curriculum design. It is a way of looking at how curriculum experiences may be organized. Recent classroom research carried out in Vancouver schools suggests that not only is such a way of organizing the curriculum productive

and exciting for teachers and students, but it is also enabling and empowering. When students are given the power to have control over their actions and their decisions, they are empowered (Wassermann & Ivany, 1988).

Virtually every important concept to be taught—whether it be at the primary, intermediate or graduate school level or whether it be in science, math, economics or business management—can be taught through the medium of serious play. Play may be either "minds on" or "hands on." Both experiences actively engage students in the examination of the concept or the big idea. Big ideas are the more important issues and concepts in the curriculum; for example: machines work for us, time and speed can be measured mathematically, living things grow and change, language is a means of communicating ideas, sound can be created and manipulated in a variety of ways, certain sounds in certain words provide clues to decoding those words.

Small ideas, on the other hand, reflect content that is considerably less substantive, that deals with acquisition of specific facts. Because small ideas are narrower in scope, they do not yield to productive, serious play. Some examples of small ideas are: buttons come in different shapes and sizes, bottles are used to hold liquid, mittens keep your hands warm, ducks quack and lions roar, some houses are made of wood, 3 + 4 = 7.

A play that is rooted in the big ideas gives direction to what is being learned. When teachers are clear about the substantive issues they want students to study, they are in a better position to develop investigative play experiences that lead to more sophisticated understanding.

2. *The second, and equally critical dimension of effective play programs, is the teacher's belief that play can, in fact, deliver the learning goals considered important for that grade.* Without the teacher's belief in serious

play as the road to important learning, these ideas will never be realized in that teacher's classroom.

Obviously, this is not an approach for all teachers. Before considering such a program, teachers ought best consider the implications of children working as serious players and measure these in juxtaposition with their own beliefs about children's learning. In making such choices, teachers will be protecting their own right to decide how they will teach in their own classrooms. There are many ways to teach children and the way a teacher chooses must reflect that teacher's beliefs. If choice is taken away from teachers, and teachers are coerced into putting into practice an instructional plan that is abhorrent to them, teachers are disempowered. And disempowered teachers cannot empower children. Teachers who are thinking seriously about the implementation of a Play-Debrief-Replay program will want to consider, first, the "goodness of fit" between this methodology and their own educational goals for children. The "comfort zone" of teachers can be assessed by considering the following:

- Play activities involve learning that is open ended. They do not lead students to the right answers. *How comfortable are you with this?*
- Play experiences call for generation of ideas, rather than recall of specific pieces of information. *How comfortable are you with this?*
- Play experiences are messy. Children are, in fact, playing around. *How comfortable are you with this?*
- Play tasks focus on the big ideas, rather than on details and specifics. *How comfortable are you with this?*
- Children are actively involved in learning. They talk to each other, share ideas, speculate, laugh, get excited. In short, they are noisy. *How comfortable are you with this?*
- Children work together in co-

Virtually every important concept to be taught—whether it be at the primary, intermediate or graduate school level—can be taught through the medium of serious play.

operative learning groups. Cooperation rather than competitive individual work is stressed. *How comfortable are you with this?*

■ The content of the curriculum is not covered in a linear, sequential way. *How comfortable are you with this?*

■ Control over student learning is largely in the students' domain. *How comfortable are you with this?*

■ As children become more empowered, they become more independent, more assertive, more challenging themselves. *How comfortable are you with a class of assertive, independent thinkers?*

These questions are best examined before teachers climb aboard yet another educational scheme that promises much, but is likely to deliver little if teachers are discontent about the operating conditions in the play. If teachers do choose to work in these ways, however, the plan will deliver what it promises: the empowerment of children. Don't take my word for it. Try it and see for yourself. And look to the children for the answers. If you see your students growing in their autonomy, self-confidence, sense of *can do*, personal power, love for learning, then what you are doing in the classroom is clearly working to their benefit. If, on the other hand, you see the entrenchment of behaviors you find repugnant— passive, submissively obedient children who are afraid to take risks or rise to challenge, who shy away from new problems, content that once the answer has been found, there's no need to learn any further—that ought to signal that more, much more work needs to be done.

But the Nobel Prize?
But the Nobel Prize? Isn't that going a little far, in promising what serious play can deliver? Richard Feynman, Nobel Laureate in physics, is at least one eminent adult who makes the case for the relationship between childhood play and the Nobel Prize. In his wonderful book, *Surely You're Joking Mr. Feynman* (1985), Feynman writes about his childhood—messing around with stuff in the basement of his home and encouraged to do so by a wise and caring father. At age 10, Feynman started to play around in a lab he set up in the basement, playing with switches and wires, making his own fuses. With his own heater, so that he could cook French-fried potatoes, Feynman set up his own crystal set, invented a burglar alarm, experimented with electric motors, built an amplifier for a photo cell that could make a bell ring when he put his hand in front of the cell, repaired his own and the neighbor's radios.

As a child, Feynman developed habits of play, and he held onto these habits of play throughout his adult life. He also attributed his love for physics and his ability to be creative in theoretical physics to his ability to play:

Why did I enjoy doing it (physics)? I used to play with it. I used to do whatever I felt like doing. It didn't have to do with whether it was important for the development of nuclear physics, but instead whether it was interesting and amusing for me to play with. When I was in high school, I'd see water running out of a faucet growing narrower, and wonder if I could figure out what determines that curve. I found it was

rather easy to do. I didn't have to do it; it wasn't important for the future of science; somebody else had already done it. That didn't make any difference. I'd invent things and play with things for my own entertainment.

When Feynman felt he was growing bored with physics, he turned to play to revitalize his interest:

So I got this new attitude. Now that I'm burned out and I'll never accomplish anything, and I've got this nice position at the university teaching classes which I rather enjoy, and just like I read the *Arabian Nights* for pleasure, I'm going to PLAY with physics, whenever I want to, without worrying about any importance whatsoever.

He attributes his habits of play to the discovery that led to his Nobel Prize:

Within a week, I was in the cafeteria, and some guy, fooling around, throws me a plate in the air. As the plate went up in the air, I saw it wobble, and I noticed the red medallion of Cornell (University) on the plate going around. It was pretty obvious to me that the medallion went around faster than the wobbling.

I had nothing to do, so I started to figure out the motion of the rotating plate. I discover that when the angle is very slight, the medallion rotates twice as fast as the wobble rate: two to one. It came out as a complicated equation!

I don't remember how I did it, but I ultimately worked out what the motion of the mass particles is, and how all the accelerations balance to make it come out two to one. I still remember Hans Bethe saying to me, "Hey, Feynman. That's pretty interesting, but what's the importance of it? Why are you doing it?" Hah, I say. There's no importance whatsoever. I'm just doing it for the fun of it. His reaction didn't discourage me. I had made up my mind. I was going to enjoy physics and do whatever I liked.

I went on to work out equations of wobbles. And before I knew it, I was playing, and it was effortless. It was easy to play with these things. It was like uncorking a bottle. Everything flowed out effortlessly. I almost tried to resist it! There was no importance to what I was doing, but ultimately there was. The diagrams and the whole business that I got the Nobel Prize for came from that messing around with the wobbling plate.

If we teachers can free ourselves from the need to keep students quiet and "on task" with pencil-and-paper worksheets, filling in correct answers, following correct procedures, learning all the names and places, in all the subjects, and recalling them correctly so that they may pass examinations—the "safe and secure" road—we may open our classrooms to the more messy, the more generative, the more original, the more delightful world of play as a means of learn-ing about the world. And in the process, who knows what future Nobel Prize winners we may be cultivating.

References

Bruner, J. (1985). On teaching think-ing: An afterthought. In S. F. Chipman, J. W. Segan, & R. Glasser (Eds.), *Thinking and learning skills: Vol. 1* (pp. 603-605). Hillsdale, NJ: Lawrence Earlbaum Associates.

Bryson, B. (1990). *The mother tongue: English and how it got that way.* New York: Morrow.

Elkind, D. (1982). *The hurried child.* Boston: Allyn & Bacon.

Feynman, R. (1985). *Surely you're jok-ing Mr. Feynman.* New York: Norton.

Goertzel, M., & Goertzel, R. (1962). *Cradles of eminence.* Boston: Little Brown.

Ministry of Education. (1990). *Year 2000: A framework for learning.* Victoria, British Columbia: Ministry of Education.

Postman, N. (1982). *The disappearance of childhood.* New York: Delacorte.

Torrance, P. (1961). *Status of knowledge concerning education and creative sci-entific talent.* Salt Lake City: Uni-versity of Utah Press.

Wassermann, S. (1990). *Serious players in the primary classroom.* New York: Teachers College Press.

Wassermann, S. (in press). A case for social studies. *Phi Delta Kappan.*

Wassermann, S., & Ivany, J.W.G. (1988). *Teaching elementary science: Who's afraid of spiders?* New York: Harper & Row.

Winn, M. (1981). *Children without child-hood.* New York: Pantheon.

Children With Emotional and Behavioral Disorders

Controversy continues to surround the issues of mainstreaming students with emotional and behavioral disorders in regular education classrooms. PL 94-142 mandates that students who are emotionally disruptive and disturbed be given an appropriate free public school education in the least restrictive environment. Imagine yourself the teacher of a regular classroom. How would you cope if one of your students was a violent, assaultive boy that used language dotted with four-letter words? Add to your class another boy who steals, extorts money from his peers, and makes lewd sexual overtures towards you. How would you manage if a suicidal female was admitted to your class? How would you handle a victim of incest? or physical abuse? or neglect?

Children or adolescents with emotional and behavioral disorders (EBDs) are those whose behaviors are so atypical that the behaviors adversely affect their social relationships, their self-concept and self-esteem, their academic

work, their self-care, and their deportment at home, school, work, and play. This category of children or adolescents with EBDs may include problems as diverse as psychoses (autism and other pervasive developmental disorders); attention deficits with hyperactivity; or physical problems such as eating or movement disorders. Four patterns of atypical behaviors generally used to classify EBDs that are relevant to the education of exceptional children are conduct disorders, anxiety-withdrawal disorders, immaturity, and socialized-aggressive disorders. Conduct disorders include aggression and defiance of authority. Anxiety-withdrawal disorders include shyness, phobias, and depression. Immaturity disorders include attention deficits and daydreaming. Socialized aggressive disorders include gang participation, truancy, and stealing. Children with psychotic disorders may sometimes also be mainstreamed into regular education classes.

While a majority of school children have occasional emotional problems, only a minority have serious emotional and behavioral disorders. Some exceptional children in other classifications (learning disabled, mentally retarded, gifted, hearing impaired, vision impaired, physically impaired) have concurrent severe emotional and behavioral disorders. The individual education programs (IEPs) on these children must include recommendations for appropriate services for each area in which a handicapping condition exists.

When a student is assessed as having an emotional or behavioral disorder, the school administrator, teacher, guidance counselor, school psychologist, special education specialist, parent(s), and other significant personnel must meet to develop an appropriate IEP for the student's school progress. The school system must "show cause" if the disturbed child is to be moved from a least restrictive to a more restrictive environment for educational purposes. The IEP must be updated annually with the goal of returning the child with the disorder to the least restrictive environment. While the law does not mandate mainstreaming of children with serious emotional and behavioral disorders, it does suggest that related supportive psychological counseling services should be utilized to achieve the least restrictive environment possible.

Teachers who have mainstreamed children with emotional or behavioral disorders in their classes must use caution to reinforce only the child's more appropriate behaviors. If other children observe atypical behaviors receiving positive reinforcement from teachers and/or other adults, they are apt to model their behaviors in order to receive similar attention. Teachers must also be alert to signs of frustration, anxiety, and distress in their students with emotional or behavioral disorders. When warnings are observed, the wise teacher can alter the lesson plan to avoid exacerbation to the emotional upheaval.

The first selection in this unit discusses the controversy surrounding the issue of mainstreaming children with emotional and behavioral disorders. Where does social maladjustment end and emotional disturbance begin? Which children are entitled to special services and IEPs under PL 94-142? The second article addresses the teacher's responsibilities for students who are seriously depressed and/or at risk for suicide. It stresses both recognition and changes in the curriculum aimed at suicide prevention. The next article was selected to include the important topic of values in children with EBDs. Brian Abrams argues that values clarification and affective education can change behaviors, but they must be individualized to match each student's needs. The last article of this unit also addresses the practical side of helping teachers find ways to work with students with emotional and behavioral disorders. Stanley Diamond has several suggestions for "what to do when you can't do anything." The article discusses relationship enhancement, sharing, changing student expectations, humor, and nonjudgmental conversations.

Looking Ahead: Challenge Questions

How can public schools fulfill their obligation to serve troubled children and youth and also provide appropriate educational services to nontroubled children simultaneously?

Can teachers recognize the symptoms of severe depression and suicide risk in children and adolescents? Can preventive measures be implemented in schools?

How can teachers assist students with emotional and behavioral disorders to clarify their values?

What kinds of interventions work with students with emotional and behavioral disorders? Is there just one more thing to try when it seems that there is nothing left to do?

Do Public Schools Have an Obligation to Serve Troubled Children And Youth?

ABSTRACT: The exclusion of pupils considered socially maladjusted in the Public Law 94-142 definition of seriously emotionally disturbed has led to gaps in services to a population of schoolchildren having significant educational needs. Issues related to this exclusionary clause are discussed in light of current research evidence and school practices. Considerable support exists for the position that the exclusion of these students from special education and related services is neither logical nor valid. A broader perspective is advocated, in which the needs of antisocial students (and their families) are addressed through early intervention for at-risk pupils, as well as in appropriate special education programs.

C. MICHAEL NELSON

ROBERT B. RUTHERFORD, JR.

DAVID B. CENTER

HILL M. WALKER

C. MICHAEL NELSON (CEC Chapter #83) is a Professor in the Department of Special Education at the University of Kentucky. ROBERT B. RUTHERFORD, JR. (CEC Chapter #455) is a Professor in the Special Education Program at Arizona State University, Tempe. DAVID B. CENTER (CEC Chapter #685) is a Professor in the Department of Special Education at Georgia State University, Atlanta. HILL M. WALKER (CEC Chapter #375) is the Associate Dean of the College of Education at University of Oregon, Eugene.

☐ The responsibility of America's schools for providing special services to socially maladjusted pupils has been debated for many years. Much of this debate has focused on the exclusion of youths considered to be socially maladjusted, antisocial, or conduct disordered from services available to those classified as seriously emotionally disturbed (SED). Public Law (P.L.) 94-142 and its recent amendments (P.L. 99-457) specifically excluded "children who are socially maladjusted, unless it is determined that they are seriously emotionally disturbed" (U.S. Department of Health, Education, and Welfare, 1977, p. 42478). However, research, scholarly opinion, and professional practices consistently have indicated that this exclusionary clause is ill founded

(Kauffman, 1989). The purpose of this article is to explore problems and issues associated with the exclusion of youth identified as socially maladjusted (SM) from special education programs in the public schools (see Nelson & Rutherford, 1990, for a more extensive discussion).

Although the *Eleventh Annual Report to Congress on the Education of the Handicapped Act* (U.S. Department of Education, 1989) indicated that 9.1% of handicapped students being served in special education programs are SED, this population continues to be significantly underserved. Federal prevalence estimates of SED pupils have ranged between 1.2% and 2.0% of the school population, but 3%-6% is regarded as a more accurate estimate by authorities (Institute of Medicine, 1989). However, less than 1% of public school students have been identified and served in SED programs (Knitzer, Steinberg, & Fleisch, 1990). Aside from the severe shortage of qualified teachers for these pupils, the basis for this serious lack of services appears to be a chain of interrelated circumstances. First, schools are antagonized by and often resist providing services for students whose social behavior deviates considerably from expected norms, especially when their behavior patterns include acts of defiance, aggression, or extreme disruption of the school environment. Second, the exclusionary clause in

P.L. 94-142 provides a rationale for excluding students from special education whose behavior is aversive, unless they also have other identifiable disabilities. As Bower (1982) observed, part of the motivation behind the SM exclusion may have been to minimize the costs of serving the SED population. Third, the *Honig v. Doe* (1988) decision by the U.S. Supreme Court established that pupils with disabilities may not be suspended for over 10 days or expelled for actions that are related to their disabilities. Furthermore, the burden of proof is on the school district to demonstrate that the student's behavior pattern *is not* related to his or her disability when such disciplinary actions are considered (Center & McKittrick, 1987; Yell, 1989). However, if the school district *does not* identify the pupil as having a disability, then suspension and explusion are viable disciplinary options. Thus, given their reluctance to deal positively with social behavior problems considered aversive to others and the court-imposed restriction on their disciplinary options, it may appear in the schools' best interests not to identify and serve students with antisocial, acting-out behavior patterns.

We contend that this exclusionary clause has the effect of denying needed educational and related services to a group of pupils who are seriously disabled by their behavior. Although there is some evidence that antisocial pupils are more often recipients of special education services than other students (Walker, Shinn, O'Neill, & Ramsey, 1987), these actions are reactive (i.e., a response to behavior patterns that have been manifest for some time and are repugnant to school personnel) rather than proactive (i.e., services aimed at preventing the development of extremely deviant behavior patterns). We will support our position through an analysis of (a) definitions of SED and SM populations, (b) the characteristics of persons exhibiting antisocial behavior, (c) identification practices, and (d) the politics of public education.

DEFINITIONS

Seriously Emotionally Disturbed

P.L. 94-142 defines SED as:

> (i) A condition exhibiting one or more of the following characteristics over a long period of time and to a marked degree, which adversely affects educational performance; a. An inability to learn which cannot be explained by intellectual, sensory, or health factors; b. An inability to build or maintain satisfactory interpersonal relationships with peers and teachers; c. Inappropriate types of behavior or feelings under normal circumstances; d. A general pervasive mood of unhappiness or depression; or e. A tendency to develop physical symptoms or fears associated with personal or school problems.

> (ii) The term includes children who are schizophrenic or autistic. The term does not include children who are socially maladjusted, unless it is determined that they are seriously emotionally disturbed (Department of Health, Education, and Welfare, Office of Education, 1977, p. 42478). The federal definition was revised to exclude autistic children. Autism was included in the category "Other Health Impaired" because of lobbying efforts by the National Society for Autistic Citizens.

This federal SED definition has come under widespread attack from the professional community, including criticisms from the author of the original definition that was adopted, with relatively few changes, by the federal government (Bower, 1982). As Bower indicated, section (ii) appears to have been added to his original definition as "a codicil to reassure traditional psychopathologists and budget personnel that schizophrenia and autism are indeed serious emotional disturbances on the one hand, and that just plain bad boys and girls, predelinquents, and sociopaths will not skyrocket the costs on the other hand" (p. 56). Whereas proponents of efforts to separate a population of students whose behavior has a purely emotional basis from those with other disorders (e.g., Clarizio, 1987; Kelly, 1986; Slenkovitch, 1983) have favored an exclusionary definition of SED, others (e.g., Center, 1989a, 1989b; Kauffman, 1989) have pointed out that research has failed to show that disorders having a purely emotional basis can be discriminated from other types of disabilities with behavioral manifestations. Center (1989a, 1989b) argued that the SED label and definition were intended to be inclusive of a wide range of disorders spanning affective, cognitive, functional, and social domains. He noted a logical fallacy inherent in excluding pupils who have problems in the social domain (especially antisocial children and youth) from the larger SED population because "an inability to build or maintain satisfactory interpersonal relationships" is a defining characteristic. Further, such children often have extreme interpersonal problems of a very long duration. Longitudinal research (Kazdin, 1987; Robins, 1966, 1979) has indicated that children with serious antisocial behavior face a greater risk for adult mental problems than any other nonpsychotic population.

Socially Maladjusted

It is noteworthy that over two-thirds of the states fail to mention the exclusion of SM in their state definitions of emotional disturbance or behavioral disorders (Mack, 1985). One factor that may be responsible for the absence of SM exclusionary clauses in state definitions is the lack of a generally accepted definition of social maladjustment. No such definition appears in P.L. 94-142, its amendments, or in the implementing regulations. The term appears to be based on the belief that certain youths are socialized in a deviant cultural group; that is, their behavior and attitudes are shaped by a social context that encourages them to act in ways that violate the standards and mores of the mainstream culture. However, it is assumed that these individuals are not SED because their behavior is in accordance with the norms of their immediate reference group. The behavior patterns considered "normative" of this deviant culture have been termed "delinquent" or "antisocial" by educators, sociologists, psychologists, and criminologists.

Delinquency is a legal term applied by the criminal justice system to indicate that a youth has been adjudicated by the courts and found guilty of criminal behavior or a "status offense" (defined as behavior judged to be deviant in a minor, such as alcohol consumption, which would not be illegal if performed by an adult). On the other hand, *delinquent behavior* is a term used to describe any illegal act, regardless of whether the perpetrator is apprehended, performed by a person under the age of majority (i.e., 18 in most states). The term *antisocial behavior* is less restrictive than delinquency, because it includes behaviors that are norm violating but not necessarily delinquent. Simcha-Fagan, Langner, Gersten, and Eisenberg (1975; cited in Walker et al., 1987, p.7) define antisocial behavior as "the recurrent violation of socially prescribed patterns of action." *Conduct disorder* is another term used to describe students who exhibit antisocial behavior, referring to overt, aggressive, disruptive behavior or covert antisocial acts (Kauffman, 1989). Youths who behave in accordance with the norms of a delinquent peer group appear to be the target of the exclusionary clause in the federal definition of SED (Center, 1989a, 1989b; Cline, 1990). This group has been labeled as *socialized-subcultural delinquents* (Achenbach, 1982; Quay, 1975), and they are characterized as participating in peer-oriented, group delinquent activities, defying adult authority, and having a delinquent value orientation (Quay).

If the exclusionary clause of the federal SED definition was directed at subcultural delinquents, a major issue in defining behavior representative of SM, but not of SED, is whether the norms of the individual's immediate reference group are deviant relative to the mainstream culture. Criteria that may be used to identity SM youth include the standards and values of the peer group, as well as whether the individual is a member of an identifiable, deviant social group, such as a delinquent gang. However, Kerr, Nelson, and Lambert (1987) emphasized that even if the behavior of SM youth conforms to the standards of their deviant reference group, it is difficult to see how they can be logically separated from the population of SED students because their behavior

does violate the norms of the larger social order and is not considered normative or tolerable by the schools. Moreover, a number of factors may be associated with an increased probability that a youth will engage in antisocial or delinquent behavior, including: (a) problems in school; (b) low verbal intelligence; (c) parents who are alcoholic or who have frequent arrests; (d) family reliance on welfare, or poor management of income; (e) homes that are broken, crowded, or chaotic; (f) erratic parental supervision and inadequate discipline; (g) parental and sibling indifference or hostility toward the youth; and (h) substance abuse (Kauffman, 1989). These factors also are strongly associated with SED.

Although the most objective method of defining delinquency and identifying delinquent individuals is in terms of "official" delinquency (commission of more serious crimes that result in arrest or adjudication; Kauffman, 1989), this is a very restrictive definition that fails to identify many youths whose antisocial behavior does not result in arrest. Furthermore, many youths classified as SED for educational purposes engage in delinquent behavior that leads to arrest or incarceration (Knitzer et al., 1990), and nearly 60% of the incarcerated population with disabilities are classified as SED (U.S. Department of Education, 1989). Thus, if separate SED and SM populations exist, they are extremely difficult to discriminate from one another.

CHARACTERISTICS OF ANTISOCIAL BEHAVIOR

Research has established two basic dimensions of disordered behavior: externalizing (overt acting-out behaviors) and internalizing (withdrawn, anxious behaviors) (Walker & Fabré, 1987). Most of the students identified as SED in the public schools are characterized as externalizing. By definition, antisocial behavior involves acting-out behavior patterns. Therefore, it is understandable that researchers studying antisocial youth find considerable overlap between SM and SED populations. Walker and his colleagues have conducted a series of longitudinal investigations of the development of antisocial behavior among middle school boys in school settings (Shinn, Ramsey, Walker, Stieber, & O'Neill, 1987; Walker et al., 1987; Walker, Stieber, & O'Neill, 1990). Pupils in their antisocial cohort exhibited significantly less academic engaged time in instructional settings, initiated and were involved in significantly more negative interactions with peers, were rated by their teachers as substantially less socially competent and adjusted, and had much greater exposure to special education services or placements than students in an at-risk control group. Differences between antisocial youth and control subjects remained consistent across grades 5, 6, and 7. The characteristics of antisocial youth derived from the research literature closely match those of pupils at risk for placement in SED programs—that is, academic deficiencies reflected in low measured achievement, poor grades, and basic skill deficits; little interest in school; careless work; lack of enthusiasm toward academic pursuits; truancy; fighting; theft; temper tantrums; destroying property; and defying or threatening others (Walker et al., 1987).

These behavior patterns bode ill for future adjustment. Walker et al. (1987) have predicted that the continuation of antisocial behavior in school will lead to increased risk of school failure, membership in deviant peer groups, school dropout, and eventual delinquency. Robins' (1966) classic follow-up study of deviant children bears out this prediction. She found that juvenile antisocial behavior was the single most powerful predictor of adult psychiatric status. The extremely high prevalence rates of learning disabilities among incarcerated juvenile offenders (Morgan, 1979; Murphy, 1986; Rutherford, Nelson, & Wolford, 1985) adds further support to the contention that school failure and social acting out are common denominators in the profiles of delinquent youth. Wolf, Braukmann, and Ramp (1987) provided convincing evidence that antisocial behavior, especially when persistent and serious, is a profoundly limiting social disability to those who exhibit it. Furthermore, they argue that long-term supportive environments are a necessary component of treatment for individuals with these behavior patterns.

Research investigating the characteristics and long-term consequences of antisocial behavior thus supports the conclusion that SM is an identifiable disability. Furthermore, antisocial behavior appears to be a frequent characteristic of pupils identified as SED. For example, Wagner (1989) found that nearly 50% of students who had been identified as SED were arrested within 2 years of leaving school. The following discussion explores the question of whether SM and SED pupils can or should be separated for educational purposes.

IDENTIFICATION PRACTICES

Although a number of states are developing standardized, objective procedures and instruments for identifying SED pupils, the final determination regarding whether a pupil is or is not SED, according to the federal definition, rests upon subjective judgment regarding each of the five P.L. 94-142 characteristics, as well as an interpretation as to what constitutes *to a marked degree* and *over a long period of time* (Kauffman, 1989). Likewise, the identification of youths as antisocial is impeded by the lack of objective criteria for defining this condition (Council for Children with Behavioral Dis-

orders, 1990). As we pointed out earlier, because delinquency is defined by actions of the criminal justice system, the tendency exists to use adjudication as a criterion for defining youth considered to be SM. However, even a cursory knowledge of the juvenile justice system will inform one that the identification of individuals as delinquent is neither standardized nor objective. In addition, delinquents constitute a heterogeneous population, with at least three recognized subtypes: socialized-subcultural, unsocialized-psychopathic, and neurotic-disturbed (Achenbach, 1982). Furthermore, far more children engage in antisocial and delinquent behavior than are adjudicated and identified; and even if adjudication were an accurate measure of delinquency, it has no relevance for educational programming.

Attempts to discriminate between SED and SM populations have relied on two sets of procedures: DSM III (American Psychiatric Association, 1980), and child behavior rating scales. (The *Diagnostic and Statistical Manual* (American Psychiatric Association, 1976) has undergone two subsequent revisions: DSM III (1980) and DSM III-R (1987). DSM III constituted a major revision, whereas the majority of changes in DSM III-R involve relatively minor adjustments in terminology.) DSM III-R is a diagnostic and classification system based on a medical model of mental disorders. This was neither designed nor intended for making educational decisions (Center, 1989). Nevertheless, several states and many local education agencies rely on DSM III-R in making SED diagnoses. An attorney has made a career of interpreting the SED definition in terms of diagnostic categories contained in the *Diagnostic and Statistical Manual*. The exclusiveness of her perception of SED is apparent in the following quotation:

> Students may not be placed in special education by virtue of being socially maladjusted, may not be found to be seriously emotionally disturbed because they are antisocial, may not be found to be seriously emotionally disturbed because they have conduct disorders. The law does not allow it. Social maladjustment is not an EHA serious emotional disturbance. (Slenkovitch, 1984, p. 293)

Slenkovitch further asserts that the DSM III diagnostic categories of Conduct Disorder, Antisocial Personality Disorder, and Oppositional Disorder are excluded from the SED definition. According to Slenkovitch, students given one of these diagnoses are not eligible for special education unless they also have been assigned another diagnosis that does qualify them. Through her workshops, Slenkovitch has influenced many school districts and several state education agencies to declare students ineligible for special education services if they do not meet her rigid definition of SED.

Several behavior rating scales have been used to identify both SED and SM pupils. *The Behavior Problem Checklist—Revised* (Quay & Peterson, 1983) contains a socialized aggression scale, and the *Child Behavior Checklist* (Achenbach, 1981) includes a delinquency scale. A third instrument, the *Differential Problem Sorter* (Kelly, 1988) lacks the standardization of the first two checklists, but contains items that, according to the author, discriminate between pupils who are SED ("emotionally disturbed") and SM ("conduct problem"). Rating scales are quick and convenient devices, they usually have face validity, and some (e.g., the *Behavior Problem Checklist—Revised*, the *Child Behavior Checklist*) have been developed through extensive factor analytic studies that established reliable and valid behavioral dimensions. However, behavior rating scales have insufficient breadth and interrater reliability to be used for diagnostic purposes (Salvia & Ysseldyke, 1988). They are useful as *screening* instruments, that is, to identify from a large pool of individuals those who *may* possess characteristics important for making differential educational decisions. They should never be used by themselves to identify or assess pupils (McMahon, 1984). However, some school districts in one state use the *Differential Problem Sorter* to initially classify students as potentially emotionally disturbed or conduct disordered. If an emotional disturbance is indicated a full evaluation is performed, but no further evaluation is conducted if the scale indicates a conduct disorder (Cheney & Sampson, 1990). The use of behavior rating scales for diagnostic classification purposes violates the assumptions upon which these instruments are based. In fact, the American Psychological Association recently adopted a resolution opposing the efforts of some states to exclude conduct-disordered students from special education and related services (Council of Representatives, American Psychological Association, 1989).

The only appropriate procedure for identifying SED and SM pupils is a systematic, comprehensive, multidisciplinary assessment process. This process must include a variety of relevant domains (i.e., cognitive, social, academic, medical, affective, and functional) sampled across the ecological settings and perspectives relevant to the pupil's functioning in school (Wood, Smith, & Grimes, 1985). Reducing decisions regarding whether students are SED or SM down to a matter of which DSM III diagnostic label has been assigned or reliance on scores on a single rating scale is an unacceptable practice. Furthermore, it violates federal law, which requires a multidisciplinary approach to diagnosis.

THE POLITICS OF EDUCATIONAL PROGRAMMING

The evidence we have presented thus far suggests that attempting to exclude SM pupils from special education appears to have no justification that can be attributed to valid distinctions between these populations. The question, then, is why is this done? We have already indicated two possible explanations: the fear that declaring SM pupils eligible for special education will open a floodgate (similar to the phenomenon that occurred when eligibility definitions of learning disabilities based on discrepancies between potential and achievement were established), and avoidance of the suspension/expulsion ban for students protected under *Honig v. Doe* (1988). The expenditure of monies and threats of litigation are powerful disincentives for school districts. Neel and Rutherford (1981) discussed three additional explanations based on prevailing attitudes and practices in the schools, including: (a) SM pupils are not truly disabled; (b) many of these students will be better served under programs for other existing disabilities where the social maladjustment is merely a secondary condition resulting from another, more readily identifiable, disability; and (c) these pupil's needs are better served either in the general school population, with its own treatment and discipline options, or through the juvenile justice system.

The classification of students into categories according to their disabilities is influenced by a host of political, social, and judgmental factors. The identification of a pupil as having a disability is guided by what the school wishes to do with that student and what (if any) special education programs are available. Distinctions between mild, moderate, and severe degrees of some recognized disabilities (e.g., SED) are very hard to make, and school officials have not been trained to recognize antisocial behavior per se as a disability. The absence of clearly articulated identification criteria, as well as the repugnance most educators have for pupils who act out socially, decreases the probability that schools will recognize or provide for their educational needs. As Long (1983, p. 53) observed, "The key issue is not whether all troublesome children should be labeled emotionally disturbed, but rather, whether the schools, and in the final analysis society, would be better served if all children who represent aggressive, disruptive behavior, regardless of how they were labeled, received special attention and help early in their lives."

We believe that efforts to identify, diagnose, or differentiate various categories of pupils in terms of who is and who is not eligible for special education services on the basis of such elusive and unreliable criteria as SED versus SM, conduct disorder, and the like, are misplaced. It is true that not all students should qualify for services that are expensive and in short supply. The right of each pupil to be educated in the least restrictive environment also must be recognized; educators should determine that the regular education program cannot meet pupils' needs before more restrictive placements are considered. However, the practice of sorting students who are disabled by their behavior into one group that receives services and another group that does not is indefensible. It must be recognized that the behavior of antisocial students (i.e., academic deficits, low rates of academic engagement, poor peer relationships, lack of social competence) places them at risk for special education intervention or placement. The needs of at-risk pupils should be addressed, in least-restrictive settings, through prereferral interventions as a prior condition to determining their eligibility for special education programs. Unfortunately, such practices are rare in most public schools, the regular education initiative notwithstanding (Braaten et al., 1988).

The majority of students exhibiting undesirable behavior in school settings generally receive no services, inadequate services under the auspices of regular education programs, or special education services applied piecemeal or too late to be beneficial. If they are unlucky enough to reside in a state or school district in which they have been labeled as antisocial but not disabled, they may be suspended, expelled, or shunted into a variety of "alternative" placements. After years of failure and exclusion, some drop out or are pushed out of school. Others find their way into institutions and programs for delinquents by virtue of their behavior in the community. In either case, schools usually fail to recognize and appropriately meet the special education needs of students with antisocial behavior patterns.

The appalling underidentification of pupils who meet the criteria in the current SED definition is sufficient evidence that the educational system is falling short of its charge to provide a "free and appropriate" education to students who are disabled by their behavior. But we would be remiss in recommending merely that more students be certified and served under the existing definition, given its many inadequacies. In addition to extending special education services to all who need them—regardless of whether they are considered emotionally disturbed, behaviorally disordered, or socially maladjusted—the *process* of identifying and serving students also needs to be changed.

We recommend two major operational changes. First, schools should adopt systematic procedures for screening and identifying pupils who are at risk for emotional or behavioral difficulties early in their school careers. Of course, procedures to identify at-risk students must be accompanied by appropriate interventions if such activities are to be meaningful. The developing

technology of early intervention through teacher consultation offers strategies for mobilizing the resources of the regular education system to meet the needs of pupils before more intrusive and stigmatizing special education interventions are considered. Johnson, Pugach, and Hammitte (1988) have observed that special education consultation models have not been widely adopted because such models are incompatible with the use of available school resources. Therefore, the development of teacher assistance teams, comprised of school staff identified with the general education program, may be a more effective strategy (see Fuchs & Fuchs, 1988; Phillips, McCullough, Nelson, & Walker, in press).

The second operational change we recommend is to revise the federal definition of SED. This definition has been widely criticized by the professional community (see our previous discussion). Moreover, the Council for Children with Behavioral Disorders (1987), the professional organization of special educators serving the SED population, has called for a change in both the federal definition and the label SED. The specific changes we suggest include eliminating the exclusion of the socially maladjusted and changing the definition's emphasis on interference with academic performance as a primary criterion. A more accurate conceptualization of the nature of behavioral disorders recognizes it as a condition that interferes with the development and maintenance of appropriate social relationships, regardless of whether academic progress is impaired. It should be noted, however, that the subjectivity inherent in defining behavior that is considered deviant from the norm cannot be eliminated completely. As Kauffman (1989) emphasized, the definition of behavior as disordered is inescapably judgmental, regardless of how objectively the behaviors in question are measured.

Again, we are not suggesting that special education labeling and placement necessarily will solve the problems of SM pupils. The lack of long-term impact of special education on the lives of students with disabilities, particularly those identified as SED, is well documented (Edgar, 1987; Neel, Meadows, Levine, & Edgar, 1988; U.S. Department of Education, 1990). Instead of merely attempting to identify and place more students in special education programs for students with emotional or behavioral disabilities, we should increase our efforts to identify and provide early intervention for students who are at risk due to their antisocial behavior patterns. Systematic school-based screening, identification, and prereferral intervention procedures (McConaughy & Achenbach, 1989; Walker, et al. 1988) must be adopted as routine school practices. Students whose needs cannot be met through this level of intervention should be referred for comprehensive assessments of their eligibility for special education programs. Programming for certified students should be orchestrated through individual educational plans that are multidisciplinary in the sense that each pupil's full range of needs is addressed, not just those needs that exist within school walls. P.L. 99-660 (the Mental Health Services Comprehensive Planning Act) is a step toward the mandate to provide appropriate community-based mental health services to children and adults in need. School and community resources should be coordinated to identify families that are at risk in terms of having at least one child who has a high probability of developing behavioral difficulties in the school or the community. Data from programs that focus on helping parents develop more effective child-rearing practices with preschool children at risk for behavioral disorders demonstrate the wisdom of early family interventions (Johnson, 1988). The national special education/mental health coalition (Forness, 1988) has added impetus to efforts for more comprehensive human services to at-risk populations.

CONCLUSION

The position taken in this article is that similarities in demographic and personal characteristics, the subjectivity inherent in identifying pupils as SED (Benson, Edwards, Rosell, & White, 1986; Kauffman, 1987, 1989), and the absence of any valid evidence or thought which justifies differentiating between SM and SED (Grosenick & Huntze, 1980) invalidate attempts to discriminate between these groups for the purpose of delivering educational services. Thus, the exclusion of SM from the federal definition is unfounded. Further, there are no instruments or methodology that can be used to differentially diagnose SED from SM either validly or reliably. In our view, the problem of delivering effective services to troubled youth supercedes that of differentially diagnosing a student as emotionally disturbed or socially maladjusted. The time spent in such attempts at differential diagnosis seldom results in more effective treatment, and the label resulting from this process may allow school personnel to abrogate responsibility by claiming that SM youth do not qualify for "special" educational provisions or program modifications.

The problem of troubled youth in the schools cannot be addressed in a piecemeal fashion, through services that are fragmented by the several bureaucracies of human service agencies. Differences among agencies in terms of definitions of their service populations and their eligibility criteria have been major factors in the failure to provide effective and cost-efficient services; attempting to make such distinctions within an agency (the public schools) is an invitation to even greater failure. Refusal to provide appropriate services to any pupil is an indictment of the educational system, just as the inability to solve the problem of antisocial behavior is an indictment of our society. The needs of troubled youth and their families across settings and time must be addressed through interdisciplinary planning and intervention, not through exclusionary practices.

REFERENCES

Achenbach, T. M. (1981). *Child Behavior Checklist.* Burlington, VT: University Associates in Psychiatry.

Achenbach, T. M. (1982). *Developmental psychotherapy* (2nd ed.). New York: Ronald Press.

American Psychiatric Association. (1976). *Diagnostic and statistical manual of mental disorders* (2nd ed.). Washington, DC: Author.

American Psychiatric Association. (1980). *Diagnostic and statistical manual of mental disorders* (3rd ed.). Washington, DC: Author.

American Psychiatric Association. (1987). *Diagnostic and statistical manual of mental disorders* (3rd ed., revised). Washington, DC: Author.

Benson, D., Edwards, L., Rosell, J., & White, M. (1986). Inclusion of socially maladjusted children and youth in the legal definition of the behaviorally disordered population: A debate. *Behavioral Disorders, 11,* 213-222.

Bower, E. M. (1982). Defining emotional disturbances: Public policy and research. *Psychology in the Schools, 19,* 55-60.

Braaten, S. R., Kauffman, J. M., Braaten, B., Polsgrove, L., & Nelson, C. M. (1988). The regular education initiative: Patent medicine for behavioral disorders. *Exceptional Children, 55,* 21-27.

Center, D. B. (April 1989a). *Social maladjustment: An interpretation.* Paper presented at the 67th Annual International Convention of the Council for Exceptional Children, San Francisco.

Center, D. B. (1989b). Social maladjustment: Definition, identification, and programing. *Focus on Exceptional Children, 22*(1), 1-12.

Center, D. B., & McKittrick, S. (1987). Disciplinary removal of special education students. *Focus on Exceptional Children, 20*(2), 1-10.

Cheney, C. O., & Sampson, K. (1990). Issues in identification and service delivery for students with conduct disorders: The "Nevada solution." *Behavioral Disorders, 15,* 174-179.

Clarizio, H. (1987). Differentiating emotionally impaired from socially maladjusted students. *Psychology in the Schools, 24,* 237-243.

Cline, D. H. (1990). A legal analysis of policy initiatives to exclude handicapped/disruptive students from special education. *Behavioral Disorders, 15,* 159-173.

Council for Children with Behavioral Disorders. (1987). *Position paper on definition and identification of students with behavioral disorders.* Reston, VA: Author.

Council for Children with Behavioral Disorders. (1990). Position paper on the provision of service to children with conduct disorders. *Behavioral Disorders, 15,* 180-189.

Council of Representatives, American Psychological Association. (1989, August 10). *APA resolution on* special education for children with conduct disorders. Arlington, VA: Author.

Edgar, E. B. (1987). Secondary programs in special education: Are many of them justifiable? *Exceptional Children, 53*, 555-561.

Forness, S. R. (1988). Planning for the needs of children with serious emotional disturbance: The National Special Education and Mental Health Coalition. *Behavioral Disorders, 13*, 127-132.

Fuchs, D., & Fuchs, L. S. (1988). Mainstream assistance teams to accommodate difficult-to-teach students in general education. In J. L. Graden, J. E. Zins, & M. J. Curtis (Eds.), *Alternative educational delivery systems: Enhancing instructional options for all students* (pp. 49-70). Washington, DC: National Association of School Psychologists.

Grosenick, J. K., & Huntze, S. L. (1980). *National needs analysis in behavior disorders: Severe behavior disorders.* Columbia: University of Missouri.

Honig v. Doe. (1988). 56 S. Ct. 27.

Institute of Medicine. (1989). *Research on children and adolescents with mental, behavioral, and developmental disorders.* Washington, DC: National Academy Press.

Johnson, D. L. (1988). Primary prevention of behavior problems in young children: The Houston parent-child development center. In R. H. Price, E. L. Cowen, R. P. Lorion, & J. Ramos-McKay (Eds.), *Fourteen ounces of prevention: A casebook for practitioners.* (pp.44-52) Washington, DC: American Psychological Association.

Johnson, L. J., Pugach, M. C., & Hammitte, D. J. (1988). Barriers to effective special education consultation. *Remedial and Special Education, 9*(6), 41-47.

Kauffman, J. M. (1987). Social policy issues in special education and related services for emotionally disturbed children and youth. In N. G. Haring (Ed.), *Measuring and managing behavior disorders* (pp. x-xx). Seattle: University of Washington Press.

Kauffman, J. M. (1989). *Characteristics of behavior disorders of children and youth* (4th ed.). Columbus, OH: Merrill.

Kazdin, A. E. (1987). *Conduct disorders in childhood and adolescence.* Beverly Hills, CA: Sage.

Kelly, E. J. (1988). *The Differential Problem Sorter manual: Rationale and procedures distinguishing between conduct problem and emotionally disturbed students and populations.* Las Vegas: University of Nevada—Las Vegas.

Kerr, M. M., Nelson, C. M., & Lambert, D. L. (1987). *Helping adolescents with learning and behavior problems.* Columbus, OH: Merrill.

Knitzer, J., Steinberg, Z., & Fleisch, B. (1990). *At the schoolhouse door: An examination of programs and policies for children with behavioral and emotional problems.* New York: Bank Street College of Education.

Long, K. A. (1983). Emotionally disturbed children as the underdetected and underserved public school population: Reasons and recommendations. *Behavioral Disorders, 9*, 46-54.

Mack, J. H. (1985). An analysis of state definitions of severely emotionally disturbed children. *Policy Options Report.* Reston, VA: Council for Exceptional Children.

McConaughy, S. M., & Achenbach, T. M. (1989). Empirically based assessment of serious emotional disturbance. *Journal of School Psychology, 27*, 91-117.

McMahon, R. J. (1984). Behavioral checklists and rating scales. In T. H. Ollendick & M. Hersen (Eds.), *Child behavioral assessment: Principles and procedures* (pp. 80-105). New York: Pergamon.

Morgan, D. J. (1979). Prevalence and types of handicapped conditions found in juvenile correctional institutions: A national survey. *Journal of Special Education, 13*, 283-295.

Murphy, D. M. (1986). The prevalence of handicapping conditions among juvenile delinquents. *Remedial and Special Education, 7*(3), 7-17.

Neel, R. S., Meadows, N., Levine, P., & Edgar, E. B. (1988). What happens after special education: A statewide follow-up study of secondary students who have behavioral disorders. *Behavioral Disorders, 13,* 209-216.

Neel, R. S., & Rutherford, R. B. (1981). Exclusion of the socially maladjusted from services under P.L. 94-142. In F. H. Wood (Ed.), *Perspectives for a new decade: Education's responsibility for seriously emotionally disturbed and behaviorally disordered youth* (pp. 79-84). Reston, VA: Council for Exceptional Children.

Nelson, C. M., & Rutherford, R. B. (1990). Troubled youth in the public schools: Emotionally disturbed or socially maladjusted? In P. E. Leone (Ed.), *Understanding troubled and troubling youth* (pp. 39-60). Newbury Park, CA: Sage.

Phillips, V., McCullough, L., Nelson, C. M., & Walker, H. M. (in press). Teamwork among teachers: Promoting a statewide agenda for students at risk for school failure. *Special Services in the Schools.*

Quay, H. C. (1975). Classification in the treatment of delinquency and antisocial behavior. In N. Hobbs (Ed.), *Issues in the classification of children* (Vol. l, pp. 377-389). San Francisco: Jossey-Bass.

Quay, H. C., & Peterson, D. R. (1983). *Revised Behavior Problem Checklist.* Coral Gables, FL: University of Miami.

Robins, L. N. (1966). *Deviant children grown up.* Baltimore: Williams and Wilkins.

Robins, L. N. (1979). Follow-up studies. In H. C. Quay & J. S. Werry (Eds.), *Psychopathological disorders of childhood* (2nd ed., pp. 483-513). New York: Wiley.

Rutherford, R. B., Nelson, C. M., & Wolford, B. I. (1985). Special education in the most restrictive environment: Correctional special education. *Journal of Special Education, 19*, 59-71.

Salvia, J., & Ysseldyke, J. E. (1988). *Assessment in special and remedial education* (4th ed.). Boston: Houghton Mifflin.

Shinn, M. R., Ramsey, E., Walker, H. M., Stieber, S., & O'Neill, R. (1987). Antisocial behavior in school settings: Initial differences in an at risk and normal population. *Journal of Special Education, 21*, 69-84.

Simcha-Fagan, O., Langner, T., Gersten, J., & Eisenberg, J. (1975). *Violent and antisocial behavior: A longitudinal study of urban youth.* Unpublished report of the Office of Child Development, OCD-CB-480.

Slenkovitch, J. E. (1983). *P. L. 94-142 as applied to DSM III diagnoses: An analysis of DSM III diagnoses vis-a-vis special education law.* Cupertino, CA: Kinghorn Press.

Slenkovitch, J. E. (1984). *Understanding special education law* (Vol. 1). Cupertino, CA: Kinghorn Press.

U. S. Department of Education, Office of Special Education and Rehabilitative Services. (1989). *Annual report to Congress on the implementation of the Education of the Handicapped Act.* Washington, DC: Author.

U. S. Department of Education, Office of Special Education and Rehabilitative Services. (1990). *Twelfth annual report to Congress on the implementation of the Education of Public Law 94-142.* Washington, DC: U. S. Government Printing Office.

U. S. Department of Health, Education, and Welfare, Office of Education. (1977, Tuesday, 23 August). Education of handicapped children: Implementation of Part B of the Education of the Handicapped Act. *Federal Register, 42,* (163).

Wagner, M. (1989). *The national longitudinal transition study.* Palo Alto, CA: Stanford Research Institute.

Walker, H. M., & Fabré, T. R. (1987). Assessment of behavior disorders in the school setting: Issues, problems, and strategies revisited. In N. G. Haring (Ed.), *Measuring and managing behavior disorders* (pp. 198-243). Seattle: University of Washington Press.

Walker, H. M., Severson, H., Stiller, B., Williams, G., Haring, N. G., Shinn, M. R., & Todis, B. (1988). Systematic screening of pupils in the elementary age range at risk for behavior disorders: Development and trial testing of a multiple gating model. *Remedial and Special Education, 9*(3), 8-14.

Walker, H. M., Shinn, M. R., O'Neill, R. E., & Ramsey, E. (1987). A longitudinal assessment of the development of antisocial behavior in boys: Rationale, methodology, and first year results. *Remedial and Special Education, 8*(4), 7-16.

Walker, H. M., Stieber, S., & O'Neill, R. E. (1990). Middle school behavioral profiles of antisocial and at risk control boys: Descriptive and predictive outcomes. *Exceptionality, 1,* 61-77.

Wolf, M. M., Braukmann, C. J., & Ramp, K. A. (1987). Serious delinquent behavior as part of a significantly handicapping condition: Cures and supportive environments. *Journal of Applied Behavior Analysis, 20,* 347-359.

Wood, F. H., Smith, C. R., & Grimes, J. (Eds.). (1985). *The Iowa assessment model in behavioral disorders: A training manual.* Des Moines, IA: Department of Public Instruction.

Yell, M. L. (1989). *Honig v. Doe*: The suspension and expulsion of handicapped students. *Exceptional Children, 56,* 60-69.

Suicide and Depression: Special Education's Responsibility

Eleanor Guetzloe

Eleanor Guetzloe *(CEC Chapter #176) is Associate Professor, The College of Education, University of South Florida, St. Petersburg.*

■Within the past decade, suicide among young people has become a major concern of parents, educators, mental health professionals, and public officials in both the United States and Canada. Public and private agencies have developed plans for promoting public awareness of this tragic phenomenon. In response to increased public concern, suicide prevention has been added to the ever-lengthening list of education's responsibilities, often mandated by legislative action or district policy. Most school-based suicide prevention programs provide primarily for detection of signs of depression and/or suicidal intent and referral to mental health professionals for diagnosis, as well as procedures to follow in the aftermath of a suicide. Some provide for additional interventions in the school setting for children at risk for suicidal behavior. These include crisis intervention; counseling; discussion groups; modifications in courses of study, schedules, and curriculum; and referral to special education for assessment.

Although many exceptional children may be at risk for suicidal behavior, not all suicidal children qualify for special education services. This article focuses on special education's responsibility in planning and implementing suicide prevention programs in the schools.

Why Are Children Killing Themselves?

Despite the efforts of a great number of researchers, the exact causes of suicide remain a mystery. Authorities generally agree that suicidal behavior results from a complex interaction of a number of factors and that there is no single cause (Hawton, 1986; Pfeffer, 1986). Any problem that contributes to feelings of depression, worthlessness, helplessness, or hopelessness has the potential to trigger suicidal behavior in a vulnerable individual. Among the many factors that have been cited as contributing to youth suicide are isolation, alienation, loss, physical or psychological abuse, disturbances in peer relationships, substance abuse, rejection, incarceration, family disorganization, availability of weapons, fear of punishment, fear of failure, knowledge of suicide, and humiliation (Guetzloe, 1987; Pfeffer, 1986; Strother, 1986).

At Risk for Suicide?

Exceptional children are often vulnerable to emotional trauma, which may lead to stress, feelings of low self-esteem, and suicidal behavior. Studies of children who have committed suicide have often revealed disproportionate numbers of exceptional children among the victims (Jan-Tausch, 1964; Peck, 1985; Shaffer, 1974).

Several authorities have observed that children with learning problems may be at high risk for both depression and suicidal behavior. Researchers have noted relationships between depression and cognitive deficits (Brumback, Staton, & Wilson, 1980) and between suicidal behavior and diminished problem-solving abilities (Levenson & Neuringer, 1971).

In a pilot study of all children under the age of 15 who had committed suicide in Los Angeles County during a 3-year period, it was found that 50% had been diagnosed as having learning disabilities (cited in Peck, 1985). Pfeffer (1986) has cited depression and suicidal behavior as special problems of learning disabled children who are excessively stressed by the demands of school. According to Pfeffer (1981), the most important issue seems to be the degree of the child's worry about academic achievement, rather than actual school performance. Feelings of low self-esteem are a contributing factor.

Gifted children are not immune to problems of stress, depression, and suicide. The director for gifted and talented on the National Education Association's Caucus for Educators of Exceptional Children has described the suicide rate of gifted students as "among the highest" (Innis, cited in "Educating the Gifted," p. 5). Other authorities have also noted suicidal behavior in gifted and talented youth (Delisle, 1986; Leroux, 1986; Willings & Arseneault, 1986).

Severe behavioral disorders are by far the most prevalent handicapping conditions associated with suicidal behavior. Many studies have confirmed the link between suicidal behavior and emotional instability (Cosand, Bourque, & Kraus, 1982; Garfinkel & Golumbek, 1974; Jan Tausch, 1964; Pfeffer, 1986; Shaffer, 1974; Toolan, 1962). According to Garfinkel (cited in Strother, 1986), young people rarely kill themselves without having some kind of psychiatric disorder. In a report to the U.S. Senate Subcommittee on Juvenile Justice, researchers from the National Institute of Mental Health estimated that 60%

of American teenagers who kill themselves are suffering from some mental disorder (Blumenthal, 1985). These authorities further noted that many of these troubled youth fail to seek professional help because they do not want to be considered mentally ill.

Depression and Suicidal Behavior

The prevalence of depression in children is reported to range from 1.8% in the general population (Kashani et al., 1983) to 23% in orthopedic inpatients (Kashani, Venske, & Millar, 1981). Depression also has been found to be associated with a variety of other long-lasting problems such as impaired peer relationships, poor communication, high irritability, lack of warmth, and parent-child hostility (Lukens et al., 1983). A significant relationship between depression and suicidal behavior in children and adolescents has been confirmed by recent studies (Kazdin, French, Unis, Esveldt-Dawson, & Sherick, 1983; Robbins & Alessi, 1985). Children who are suffering from depression are therefore considered to be at high risk for suicidal behavior (Pfeffer, 1986). Teachers, parents, and other caregivers should become aware of the symptoms of depression in children in order to make appropriate referrals for assessment and treatment.

Diagnosis of Depression

In the rules and regulations governing the implementation of Public Law 94-142, a "general pervasive mood of unhappiness or depression" is listed as a characteristic of seriously emotionally disturbed children (*Federal Register*, August 23, 1977, p. 42478.) However, the depression must be exhibited to a marked degree over a long period of time and must adversely affect educational performance in order to qualify a child for special education services. Because the definition is imprecise and the accompanying conditions are subject to interpretation, children who exhibit symptoms of depression may not be diagnosed as seriously emotionally disturbed.

More explicit criteria for the diagnosis of depressive disorders are included in the *Diagnostic and Statistical Manual of the American Psychiatric Association*, Third Edition, Revised (DSM-III-R, American Psychiatric Association, 1987). For a diagnosis of *major depressive episode*, at least five of the following nine symptoms must have been evident nearly everyday for at least 2 weeks and must represent a change from previous functioning. (One of the symptons must be either depressed mood or loss of interest or pleasure.):

1. Depressed or irritable mood.
2. Loss of enjoyment or interest in normally pleasurable activities (apathy in young children).
3. Change in weight, appetite, or eating habits.
4. Problems with sleeping (insomnia or hypersomnia).
5. Psychomotor agitation or retardation (hyperactivity in children).
6. Loss of energy, feeling of fatigue.
7. Feelings of worthlessness, inadequacy, self-reproach, self-depreciation, loss of self-esteem.
8. Diminished ability to attend, think, or concentrate.
9. Recurrent thoughts of death or suicide.

For a diagnosis of *dysthymic disorder*, symptoms of depression that are not of sufficient severity and duration to meet the criteria for major depressive disorder may have been present for a period of 1 year. There could be occasional periods of normal mood for no more than 2 months at a time.

Special Education's Responsibility

Special education personnel should participate in the development and implementation of the school or district plan for suicide prevention. While not all suicidal children will be placed in special education, special educators, who are not strangers to the problem of suicidal behavior, can be valuable resources. They are trained to observe children, assist in the diagnostic process, work closely with parents, plan appropriate interventions, and evaluate outcomes. Special educators usually have established working relationships with mental health professionals and representatives from other community agencies that are vital to the success of a suicide prevention program. They are also attuned to the need for a positive school environment, which is prerequisite to effective suicide prevention. In some communities, the special educator may be the only trained professional available to work with a suicidal child. As one teacher commented during a workshop, "In my town, I *am* Mental Health!"

The knowledge and abilities of special educators have not gone unnoticed by experts in the field of suicide prevention. Berkovitz (1985) has listed special education as an important resource for prevention of suicidal behavior, and a report from the U.S. Department of Health and Human Services stated the following:

> Many programs that are not directly aimed at suicide prevention—such as special education programs or family counseling services for adolescents with behavioral problems—may have an effect on the suicide rate. In any particular location, these indirect programs may be more important than programs designed to prevent suicide. (Centers for Disease Control, 1986, p. 6)

The Minneapolis Public School Guidelines

The Minneapolis Public Schools have developed exemplary guidelines for suicide prevention that reflect the collaborative planning of district personnel in both regular and special education along with representatives of community mental health agencies. While the guidelines clearly state that the special education assessment process should not be used in lieu of immediate parental notification or as the initial resource in assessing risk when more immediate steps are obviously indicated, provisions are made for the referral of a suicidal student for special education assessment.

> The E/BD (Emotional/Behavioral Disorders) teaming process can be helpful in determining which staff and resources in the building are available to intervene with a student, who, while not determined to be immediately at risk, may evidence behaviors that suggest a high-risk profile for suicide. (Minneapolis Public Schools, 1986, p. 5)

The Minneapolis guidelines also suggest that during the assessment process interventions should be implemented that lessen suicidal risk, for example, "parental contact or involvement, use of school staff who offer a safe and supportive environment, and disciplinary approaches that do not increase the student's sense of failure" (p. 5). It is extremely important to secure the cooperation of family, friends, school personnel, neighbors, and others who will assist in providing support and supervision for the student. Parents must be warned that a suicidal student should not be left alone.

Another important suggestion that is included in the Minneapolis guidelines (and that should be standard practice for any special education program) is to secure written parent permission for the school to communicate directly with treatment providers. The treatment plan and the school intervention plan must not work at cross purposes.

Emotional First Aid

According to Frederick (1985), suicidal individuals suffer from the Three H's: "haplessness, helplessness, and hopelessness" (p. 15). For example, suicidal youngsters may often have suffered a series of misfortunes over which they had little or no control. Following these events, they do not have the internal or external resources to deal with the problems, and, finally, feelings of hopelessness ensue and suicide seems to be the only answer. The immediate tasks of a potential rescuer are to provide relief from feelings of helplessness or hopelessness, explore alternatives to suicidal behavior, and instill in the student some feeling of being in control.

A "Just Noticeable Difference"

Some positive change, no matter how small, should be effected to prove to the student that the situation is not hopeless. Shneidman (1985) has called this a "Just Noticeable Difference," or "J.N.D." (p. 228). According to Shneidman, the focus in intervention should not be on why suicide is a choice, but rather on solving problems so that suicide is no longer necessary. "The way to save a suicidal person is to cater to that individual's infantile and realistic idiosyncratic needs" (1985,

p. 228). A suicidal student's overwhelming problems may be in one or more of several areas—the home, school, or community. The major stresses that triggered the suicidal behavior should be identified, and steps should be taken to reduce the pressures from those sources. This may require intervention from other agencies as well as from school services.

Dropping a class, providing a tutor, or removing a threat of punishment may provide a ray of hope for a student who is encountering problems in school. Exceptional children may need a change in their individualized education programs, so that specific risk factors are addressed. With appropriate intervention, depressed and/or suicidal youngsters often show considerable improvement, often within a few weeks (Peck, 1985), but depressive symptoms can recur. Plans must be made for long-term intervention and follow-up, because a suicidal child may be at risk for several years after the initial threat or attempt.

A Preventive Curriculum

Among the prerequisites for an effective suicide prevention program is the provision of a positive school climate (Berkovitz, 1985). Pfeffer (1986), in discussing the development of sense of self-preservation, has suggested that both the home and school environment must provide structure, protection from injury, opportunity to play and explore, and freedom to express emotions without fear of punishment. Any feature of a student's program that enhances feelings of security, self-worth, or self-control has the potential for preventing suicidal behavior. Many programs that are already in place in the schools, although aimed specifically at preventing other problems such as teenage pregnancy, dropouts, or drug abuse, can also be regarded as suicide prevention activities.

The "If . . ., Then . . ." Approach

Although some risk factors and precipitating events may appear to be beyond the school's control, many can be directly addressed in the curriculum—in the IEP for an exceptional student or in an individualized plan for a suicidal student in regular education. Educators can

use a very practical "If . . ., then . . ." approach to planning for a suicidal child (Guetzloe, 1988; Guetzloe & Rhodes, 1988). If a certain problem appears to be contributing to suicidal behavior, then a certain intervention is appropriate.

A teacher or counselor who has already established a positive relationship with the student is in the best position to determine, with the aid of the student and others with helpful information, the risk factors and precipitating events that may have contributed to the suicidal behavior. If a child suffers from unrealistic expectations or overprogramming, then goal setting, self-evaluation, and self-monitoring are logical inclusions in the program. If social isolation is a problem, then training in assertiveness, social skills, and communication is indicated. Problems of stress can be alleviated by learning coping skills, problem solving, time management, and relaxation exercises. A student's interest in and preparation for the future can be reinforced by studying career and vocational education, civics, government and law, home economics, marriage and family living, and use of leisure time. Problems of low self-esteem can be addressed through art, music, dance, hygiene, clothing selection, weight training, individual sports, or classroom materials such as those developed by Reasoner (1982). A number of curricula and guidelines are available that can be used in dealing with other specific areas related to suicidal risk such as alienation (Bronfenbrenner, 1986; Gerler, 1986) or lack of self-control (Fagen, Long, & Stevens, 1975).

There are several new directions in research that may have future implications for school suicide prevention programs, such as the effects of color, full-spectrum light, exercise, role playing, and metacognitive approaches on the emotions of a child (Guetzloe & Rhodes, 1986; Rhodes & Guetzloe, 1987). Any positive approach that is suitable for the school setting should be explored (Guetzloe, 1988; Guetzloe & Rhodes, 1988).

Conclusion

Suicide prevention, once the responsibility of the field of mental health, has now become a function of the school. Although not all suicidal students will become the responsibility of the special education program, special education personnel and services are important to the effectiveness of a school suicide prevention program. For exceptional students, an appropriate special education program may be an important contribution to suicide prevention.

References

American Psychiatric Association. (1987). *Diagnostic and statistical manual of mental disorders* (3rd rev. ed.). Washington, DC: Author.

Berkovitz I. H. (1985). The role of schools in child, adolescent, and youth suicide prevention. In M. L. Peck, N. L. Farberow, & R. E. Litman (Eds.), *Youth suicide* (pp. 170-190). New York: Springer.

Blumenthal, S. (1985, April 30). *Testimony before the United States Senate Subcommittee on Juvenile Justice.* Washington, DC: U.S. Department of Health and Human Services.

Bronfenbrenner, U. (1986, February). Alienation and the four worlds of childhood. *Phi Delta Kappan, 67* (6), 430-436.

Brumback, R. A., Staton, R. D., & Wilson, H. (1980). Neuropsychological study of children during and after remission of endogenous depressive episodes. *Perceptual and Motor Skills, 50,* 1163-1167.

Centers for Disease Control. (1986, November). *Youth suicide in the United States, 1970-1980.* Atlanta, GA: U.S. Department of Health and Human Services.

Cosand, B. J., Bourque, L. B., & Kraus, J. F. (1982). Suicide among adolescents in Sacramento County, California 1950-1979. *Adolescence, 17,* 917-930.

Delisle, J. R. (1986). Death with honors: Suicide among gifted adolescents. *Journal of Counseling and Development, 64* (a), 558-560.

Educating the gifted and talented. (1987, June). *Advocate,* p. 5.

Fagen, S., Long, N., & Stevens, D. (1975). *Teaching children self-control.* Columbus, OH: Merrill.

Federal Register (1977, August 23). Washington, DC: U. S. Government Printing Office.

Frederick, C. J. (1985). An introduction and overview of youth suicide. In M. L. Peck, N.

L. Farberow, & R. E. Litman (Eds.), *Youth suicide* (pp. 1-16). New York: Springer.

Garfinkel, B. D., & Golumbek, H. (1974). Suicide and depression in children and adolescents. *Canadian Medical Association Journal, 110,* 1278-1281.

Gerler, E. R. (1986, February). Skills for adolescence: A new program for young teenagers. *Phi Delta Kappan, 67* (6), 436-439.

Guetzloe, E. C. (1987). *Suicide and depression, the adolescent epidemic: Education's responsibility.* Orlando, FL: Advantage Consultants.

Guetzloe, E. C. (1988). *Youth suicide: What the educator should know.* Reston, VA: The Council for Exceptional Children.

Guetzloe, E. C., & Rhodes, W. C. (1986, November). *Suicide prevention in the schools: Current trends and promising practices.* Paper presented at the 10th Annual Conference on Severe Behavior Disorders of Children and Youth, Tempe, AZ.

Guetzloe, E. C., & Rhodes, W. C. (1988). Prevention of youth suicide: Current trends and promising practices. In R. Rutherford, C. M. Nelson, & S. R. Forness (Eds.), *Bases of severe behavior disorders in children and youth* (pp. 231-250). San Diego: College-Hill Press.

Hawton, K. (1986). *Suicide and attempted suicide among children and adolescents.* Beverly Hills, CA: Sage Publications.

Jan-Tausch, J. (1964). *Suicide of children 1960-63.* Trenton, NJ: New Jersey Public Schools, Division of Curriculum and Instruction, Office of Special Education Services, Department of Education.

Kashani, J. H., McGee, R. O., Clarkson, S. E., Anderson, J. C., Walton, L. A., Williams, S., Silva, P. A., Robins, A. J., Cytryn, L., & McKnew, D. H. (1983). Depression in a sample of 9 year old children. *Archives of General Psychiatry, 50,* 1217-1223.

Kashani, J. H., Venske, R., & Millar, E. A. (1981). Depression in children admitted to hospital for orthopedic procedures. *British Journal of Psychiatry, 183,* 21-25.

Kazdin, A. E., French, A. S., Unis, A. S., Esveldt-Dawson, K., & Sherick, R. B. (1983). Hopelessness, depression, and suicidal intent among psychiatrically disturbed inpatient children. *Journal of Consulting and Clinical Psychology, 51,* 504-510.

Leroux, J. A. (1986). Suicidal behavior and gifted adolescents. *Roeper Review, 9* (2), 77-79.

Levenson, M., & Neuringer, C, (1971). Problem-solving behavior in suicidal adolescents. *Journal of Consulting and Clinical Psychology, 37,* 433-436.

Lukens, E., Puig-Antich, J., Behn, J., Goetz, R., Tabrizi, M. A., & Davies, M. (1983). Reliability of the psychosocial schedule for school-age children. *Journal of the American Academy of Child Psychiatry, 22,* 29-39.

Minneapolis Public Schools (1986, February 12). *Student suicide prevention guidelines.* (Available from Minneapolis Public Schools, School Social Work Services, Minneapolis, MN.)

Peck, M. L. (1985). Crisis intervention treatment with chronically and acutely suicidal adolescents. In M. L. Peck, N. L. Farberow, & R. E. Litman (Eds.), *Youth Suicide* (pp. 112-122). New York: Springer.

Pfeffer, C. R. (1981). The distinctive features of children who threaten and commit suicide. In C. F. Wells & I. R. Stuart (Eds.), *Self-destructive behavior in children and adolescents* (pp. 106-120). New York: Van Nostrand Reinhold.

Pfeffer, C. R. (1986). *The suicidal chiald.* New York: Guilford.

Reasoner, R. W. (1982). *Building self-esteem.* Palo Alto, CA: Consulting Psychologists Press.

Rhodes, W. C., & Guetzloe, E. C. (1987, November). *Consciousness construction and the changing curriculum paradigm.* Paper presented at the 11th Annual Conference on Severe Behavior Disorders of Children and Youth, Tempe, AZ.

Robbins, D. R., & Alessi, N. E. (1985). Depressive symptoms and suicidal behavior in adolescents. *American Journal of Psychiatry, 142* (5), 588-592.

Shaffer, D. (1974). Suicide in childhood and early adolescence. *Journal of Childhood Psychology and Psychiatry, 15,* 275-291.

Shneidman, E. S. (1985). *Definition of suicide.* New York: Wiley.

Strother, D. B. (1986, June). Practical applications of research: Suicide among the young. *Phi Delta Kappan, 67,* 756-759.

Toolan, J. M. (1962). Depression in children and adolescents. *American Journal of Orthopsychiatry, 32,* 404-415.

Willings, D., & Arseneault M. (1986). Attempted suicide and creative promise. *Gifted Educaiton International, 4* (1), 10-13.

Values Clarification for Students with Emotional Disabilities

Brian J. Abrams

Brian J. Abrams *(CEC Chapter #248) is a Special Education Teacher, Career Development Center, Nassau County BOCES, Baldwin, New York.*

Affective education programs seek to promote students' emotional and social development by helping them develop an awareness and understanding of their feelings, attitudes, beliefs, and values (Epanchin & Monson, 1982). Morse, Ardizzone, Macdonald, and Pasick (1980) have identified three goals of affective education: (1) to develop an adequate self-concept combined with self-esteem; (2) to maximize the prosocial potential of the student; and (3) to promote positive emotional expression.

Students with emotional disabilities may exhibit a variety of maladaptive behaviors and emotional problems, many of which indicate a need for affective growth. Many writers believe that affective education is important for *all* children with exceptionalities but that it is essential for students with emotional disabilities (Epanchin & Monson, 1982; Morse et al., 1980; Werth & Sindelar, 1987). Miller (1976) discussed 17 affective teaching models; one of the most widely researched of these is values clarification. This article discusses how values clarification can be used by special education teachers to meet the affective needs of students with emotional disabilities.

Background

The classic work in values clarification is *Values and Teaching* by Raths, Harmin, and Simon (1966, 1978), which discusses the basic theory and methods of values clarification. In it, the authors express their belief that a number of student behavior problems such as apathy, inconsistency, uncertainty, flightiness, and overdissension may be the result of confusion and disturbance in their values.

Values are beliefs that have cognitive, affective, and behavioral components; they are principles people use to choose between alternatives, resolve conflicts, and make decisions (Rokeach, 1973). Values provide a stable frame of reference, give meaning and order to our lives, and are fundamental to our sense of identity (Blaker, 1982). Students suffering from value confusion lack goals and direction; their behavior is often inconsistent and aimless.

The assumptions behind the valuing theory of Raths and colleagues are that (a) human beings can arrive at values by an intelligent process of choosing, prizing, and behaving, and (b) values should relate to one's world and serve as a guide to a satisfying and intelligent

way of life. The major focus of the theory is that children who are given help in using the valuing process will behave in ways that are less apathetic, confused, and irrational and more positive, purposeful, and enthusiastic than those of their peers who do not receive this help (Raths et al., 1966).

Proponents have written many books dealing with methods, strategies, and activities for using values clarification in the classroom (see Hawley & Hawley, 1975; Howe & Howe, 1975; Simon, Howe, & Kirschenbaum, 1972; Smith, 1977). These activities encourage students to examine their attitudes, beliefs, interests, and feelings (e.g., "List 10 things you love to do"; "Describe a personal hero and the qualities you admire in that person"). The activities can be used with individuals, small groups, or an entire class. A key element of many of these strategies is the *clarifying* response (Raths et al., 1966)—a way of responding to a student's comment or behavior that encourages the student to reflect on his or her feelings, choices, beliefs, or values (e.g., "How does that idea affect your life?" "Is that important to you?" What alternatives have you considered?").

Values clarification can also be integrated into the curriculum, whether the subject is social studies, science, reading, health, or something else. Several authors have discussed how subject matter can be taught on three levels: facts (e.g., "Who wrote the Gettysburg Address in 1863?"); concepts (e.g., "What are the main ideas or themes of the Gettysburg Address?"); and values (e.g., "If you had been the mother of a slain Union soldier or slain Confederate soldier, what would your reaction have been to the speech?" or "The Gettysburg Address was given at the dedication of a cemetery. What words would you like spoken about you at your eulogy?") (Curwin & Curwin, 1974; Harmin, Kirschenbaum, & Simon, 1973).

Benefits of Values Clarification

The goal of values clarification is to have students explore their beliefs and values and become more aware of how these beliefs and values influence their choices and behavior. The teacher does not attempt to transmit the "right" values, but provides a safe, nonthreatening, nonjudgmental environment.

One activity that encourages students to examine their own interests and feelings is to ask them to "list 10 things you love to do."

Values clarification is concerned more with the valuing process than with specific values. Table 1 shows the skills involved in the valuing process according to three different authors. Values clarification seeks to develop student skills in all of these areas of development, which should result in student behavior that is more purposeful and satisfying. These areas of skill development are important to most students with emotional disabilities.

Researchers have examined the effects of values clarification interventions on a wide range of dependent variables including academic achievement, attitudes toward school, level of self-esteem, value clarity, personal adjustment, and others. They have studied student populations ranging from elementary school through college. Although many of these studies have been criticized for lacking adequate control groups, a majority of the research has shown that values clarification is effective in improving student achievement on many cognitive and affective measures (see

Kirschenbaum, 1977; Lockwood, 1978; Swisher, Vicary, & Nadenichek, 1983).

Working with Students with Emotional Disabilities

There has been little research on the effects of values clarification on students with emotional disabilities. One study of the values of students with emotional disabilities compared the value rankings and value stability (a measure of value confusion) of two groups of adolescents with emotional disabilities (conduct disorder and anxiety-withdrawal) and normal adolescents. The findings suggest that both types of adolescents with emotional disabilities are similar to normal adolescents in their stated values and the stability of those values (Abrams, 1988).

To benefit from values clarification, students need to have reached a stage of readiness for the skills listed in Table 1. In an attempt to determine which affective interventions are most effective for specific students, McKinnon and Kiraly (1984) have developed the Affective Education Continuum Model. This model matches specific affective education strategies with the students' level of socio-emotional development and management needs. At Level 1 (e.g., behavior modification and the engineered classroom), students need maximum structure for learning and strategies are teacher directed. At Level 2 (e.g., cognitive behavior modification and contracting), students show some self-control skills and strategies are mutually directed by teacher and student. At Level 3 (e.g., values clarification and peer tutoring), students exhibit appropriate self-management skills and strategies are more student directed, reflecting students' interests, goals, needs, and feelings). At this level, students can usually control their behavior and begin to focus on attitudes, feelings, and beliefs.

McKinnon and Kiraly believe that values clarification is most effective for students at Level 3 since the three goals of Level 3 are consistent with those of values clarification to increase self-esteem, develop a higher sense of self-awareness in relation to others, and improve interpersonal skills. Values clarification is clearly appropriate for students at Level 3, and it may benefit students at the later stages of Level 2.

Although only one book of values clarification activities has been written for students with emotional and learning disabilities (Simon & O'Rourke, 1977), most of the other publications on values clarification can be adapted for use with these students. Epanchin and Monson (1982) have offered the following guidelines:

1. Match the objectives and activities to the students' developmental needs and the level of trust and support in the class.
2. Evaluate the appropriateness of each activity for each child.
3. Elicit feedback from students.
4. Use outside resources for assistance.

Simon and Olds (1976) have identified several rules for using values clarification:

1. Accept other points of view.
2. There are no right or wrong answers.
3. Anyone can "pass" (each student has the right of privacy and is not pressured to reveal information that he or she may feel uncomfortable about).

A key element of any successful values clarification program is how effective the teacher is at creating a classroom climate of trust, openness, and cohesiveness. For students to examine their attitudes, beliefs, and values, they must feel that they are valued members of a group in a safe, nonthreatening, nonjudgmental environment. Establishing such an environment is a difficult task for teachers working with students with emotional disabilities, who are often extremely critical of themselves and others. Teaching students to respect other points of view, listen to other students' feelings and beliefs, and communicate their own feelings and beliefs in front of peers and the teacher is a slow, gradual process, but an important one.

To evaluate the effectiveness of values clarification some observable behavior must be measured. Teachers should have a clear idea of their goals so that they can define the goals and specific behavioral objectives operationally (e.g., "George will display an increased tolerance for the ideas of others as evidenced by his listening to the ideas of others, without any critical comments, 3 out of 5 days a week"). Some long-term effects of values clarification may take years to become evident, but teachers can measure the short-term effects by writing objectives that refer to the specific skills that their programs are aimed at.

As students feel more trusting and comfortable, they enjoy sharing parts of their inner self.

Table 1

Three Views of Values Clarification: Skills Involved in the Valuing Process

1. The Valuing Process: Criteria for a Full Value (Raths et al., 1966).

  A. Choosing: 1. Freely.

                  2. From alternatives.

                  3. After thoughtful consideration of the consequences of each alternative.

  B. Prizing: 1. Cherishing, being happy with choice.

              2. Willing to affirm choice publicly.

  C. Acting: 1. Acting upon the choice.

              2. Acting repeatedly with a pattern or consistency.

2. The Valuing Process (Kirschenbaum, 1973).

  A. Feeling: 1. Being open to one's inner experience.

              (a) Awareness of one's inner experience.

              (b) Acceptance of one's inner experience.

  B. Thinking: 1. Thinking on all seven levels (memory, translation, application, interpretation, analysis, synthesis, and evaluation.)

              2. Employing critical thinking skills.

              (a) Distinguishing fact from opinion.

              (b) Distinguishing supported from unsupported arguments.

              (c) Analyzing propaganda, stereotypes, etc.

              3. Employing logical thinking (logic).

              4. Employing creative thinking.

      5. Employing fundamental cognitive skills.

           (a) Language use.

           (b) Mathematical skills.

           (c) Research skills.

  C. Communicating (verbally and nonverbally):

           1. Sending clear messages.

           2. Listening empathetically.

           3. Drawing out.

           4. Asking clarifying questions.

           5. Giving and receiving feedback.

           6. Engaging in conflict resolution.

  D. Choosing: 1. Generating and considering alternatives.

              2. Thoughtfully considering consequences, pros and cons.

              3. Choosing strategically.

              (a) Setting goals.

              (b) Gathering data.

              (c) Solving problems.

              (d) Planning.

              4. Choosing freely.

  E. Acting: 1. Acting with repetition.

              2. Acting with a pattern and consistency.

              3. Acting skillfully, competently.

3. Values Clarification as Development of Student Interaction Skills (Casteel & Stahl, 1975).

  A. Communicating

  B. Empathizing

  C. Problem Solving

  D. Assenting and Dissenting

  E. Decision Making

  F. Personal Consistency

Getting Started

When values clarification is first introduced into a special education classroom, some students are excited and see this as an opportunity to examine and discuss issues that are relevant to their lives and interests. Other students are suspicious and fearful of disclosing personal information; they will spend most of the initial classes observing and listening. As they feel more comfortable and trusting, they will begin to enjoy sharing parts of their inner selves with the group. Teachers must be accepting of each student's right to privacy and of student responses that are in opposition to their own. When a teacher models respect and acceptance for each student, the students will begin to show respect and acceptance for each other.

Initially, the value-clarifying activities should be of high interest and low risk, requiring little self-disclosure. As the group develops a level of trust and cohesiveness, the teacher can introduce activities that seek more openness, examination, and sharing of feelings, attitudes, beliefs, and values.

Following are several suggestions for special education teachers who wish to implement values clarification programs in their classes:

1. Increase your knowledge of the theory and methods behind this approach through readings, workshops, and classes.
2. Assess the developmental needs and interests of each student as part of your planning. Before you begin your program, determine each student's level of self-control and proficiency at skills involved in the valuing process (e.g., Do you need to focus on developing listening skills? Does one student need extra assistance in generating alternatives, or learning to accept his or her feelings?). Get to know each student and learn his or her value indicators (goals, interests, feelings, needs, beliefs, attitudes and worries). This will aid you in selecting activities that are relevant to your students' lives.
3. Know where you want to go; be able to state clearly what your goals and objectives are.
4. Discuss your program activities and objectives with your supervisors and secure their approval.
5. Introduce your program slowly (perhaps one 30-minute activity per week); be patient with yourself and your new program.
6. Evaluate each activity either formally (through a questionnaire or form) or informally (by eliciting comments from students and writing down your observations): Did the topic gain the interest of students? Did the activity require too much self-disclosure? Was the task too difficult for the class? Did the students understand the rules? Were they able to follow the rules?
7. Avoid moralizing and preaching; practice acceptance. Listen carefully to your comments about your students' ideas, beliefs, and feelings. Try to practice acceptance during the values clarification class, and as you become more accepting, extend this attitude throughout the school day. You are accepting of feelings and ideas, but not behavior. You still have class rules and cannot allow students to hurt themselves and others or prevent other students from learning.
8. As you become more skillful and comfortable using this approach, begin to integrate values clarification into the curriculum. Begin by periodically asking clarifying questions about characters from literature or history, and then include clarifying questions when you are teaching other subjects.

Conclusion

Special education teachers can use values clarification to help students increase their awareness of the relationships among their choices, values, and behavior. Increasing each student's awareness and value clarity can result in more positive, purposeful, and prosocial behavior. Remember, values clarification is a life-long process for everyone.

References

Abrams, B. J. (1988). The values and value stability of emotionally handicapped and normal adolescents. *Adolescence, 23,* 721-739.

Blaker, K. (1982). Values and the counselor. In B. Hall, J. Kalvan, L. Rosen, & B. Taylor (Eds.), *Readings in value development* (pp. 117-123). Ramsey, NJ: Paulist Press.

Casteel, J. D., & Stahl, R. J. (1975). *Value clarification in the classroom: A primer.* Pacific Palisades, CA: Goodyear.

Curwin, R., & Curwin, G. (1974). *Developing individual values in the classroom.* Palo Alto, CA: Learning Handbooks.

Epanchin, B. C., & Monson, L. B. (1982). Affective education. In J. L. Paul & B. C. Epanchin (Eds.), *Emotional disturbance in children* (pp. 405-426). Columbus, OH: Charles E. Merrill.

Harmin, M., Kirschenbaum, H., & Simon, S. (1973). *Clarifying values through subject matter: Applications for the classroom.* Minneapolis: Winston.

Hawley, R., & Hawley, I. (1975). *Human values in the classroom: A handbook for teachers.* New York: Hart.

Howe, L., & Howe, M. M. (1975). *Personalizing education: Values clarification and beyond.* New York: Hart.

Kirschenbaum, H. (1973). Beyond values clarification. In H. Kirschenbaum & S. B. Simon (Eds.), *Readings in values clarification* (pp. 92-110). Minneapolis: Winston.

Kirschenbaum, H. (1977). *Advanced value clarification.* La Jolla, CA: University Associates.

Lockwood, A. (1978). The effects of values clarification and moral development curricula on school age subjects: A critical review of recent research. *Review of Educational Research, 48*(3), 325-364.

McKinnon, A. J., & Kiraly, J. (1984). *Pupil behavior, self-control and social skills in the classroom.* Springfield, IL: Charles C Thomas.

Miller, J. (1976). *Humanizing the classroom: Models of teaching in affective education.* New York: Praeger.

Morse, W. C., Ardizzone, J., Macdonald, C., & Pasick, P. (1980). *Affective education for special children and youth.* Reston, VA: The Council for Exceptional Children.

Raths, L., Harmin, M., & Simon, S. (1966). *Values and teaching.* Columbus, OH: Charles E. Merrill.

Raths, L., Harmin, M., & Simon, S. (1978). *Values and teaching* (2nd ed.). Columbus, OH: Charles E. Merrill.

Rokeach, M. (1973). *The nature of human values.* New York: Free Press.

Simon, S., Howe, L., & Kirschenbaum, H. (1972). *Values clarification: A handbook of practical strategies for teachers and students.* New York: Hart.

Simon, S., & Olds, S. W. (1976). *Helping your child learn right from wrong: A guide to values clarification.* New York: McGraw-Hill.

Simon, S., & O'Rourke, R. (1977). *Developing values with exceptional children.* Englewood Cliffs, NJ: Prentice-Hall.

Smith, M. (1977). *A practical guide to value clarification.* La Jolla, CA: University Associates.

Swisher, J. D., Vicary, J. R., & Nadenichek, P. (1983). Humanistic education: A review of research. *Journal of Humanistic Education and Development, 22,* 8-15.

Werth, L. H., & Sindelar, P. T. (1987). Affective education. In C. R. Reynolds & L. Mann (Eds.), *Encyclopedia of special education* (Vol. 1, pp. 55-56). New York: Wiley.

What to Do When You Can't Do Anything

Working with Disturbed Adolescents

STANLEY C. DIAMOND

Stanley C. Diamond is director of the Mill Creek School, Philadelphia, Pennsylvania, and a consulting editor for The Clearing House.

"There is really no one around to help out."

"There is no place to send students to let them just calm down."

"There is no chance to see them afterward to explain things or to hear from them."

"There are just too many kids in the class (school)."

"I don't have training to work with these kids. We don't know much about them or their lives; we don't meet their parents."

"I can't be a counselor and a teacher; there is just no time for that kind of involvement."

These are some comments made by teachers in large city high schools during discussions about emotionally disturbed students. The teachers readily admit that there are plenty of such youngsters in their classes, or at least they assume that to be the case. They also know that these students will either drop out or self-destruct without proper attention to their needs. They know, too, that the capacity for evaluating and servicing such students in their schools is limited and that a referral to the counselor or special education team is likely to result in long delays at best or total neglect at worst. Most school systems are stressed to their very limits in this respect. Abstract and mysterious solutions such as providing the least restrictive environment or a "regular education initiative" seem to be imposed upon the schools and teachers by near-sighted and unrealistic educators miles from the everyday classroom experience.

However true the teachers' observations may be and however well grounded their expressions of frustration and confusion are, there are practical limits to the range of choices and interventions available in the classroom for students who exhibit disturbed behaviors. Teachers become concerned about the youngster who falls asleep in the middle of the day or expresses deep hostility in the absence of provocation, the child who displays bizarre behavior or dramatically withdraws, the one who changes a behavior pattern in a significant and obvious manner or talks or acts in a regressed fashion. There seems to be little that can be done. That is often the reality of the daily experience for teachers; those who care may have to make peace with the limitations of their power. To a great extent, they do face an unsatisfying level of helplessness. Many of the students who come to their attention will not be properly served; most will not be responded to at all.

Yet it is possible for a teacher to open opportunities for such students, to be helpful to them or, at the very least, less harmful. Some of the interventions that are possible are independent of the world outside of the classroom; nothing in the school system prevents such efforts from being made. Having limited power is not the same thing as helplessness. Here are some notions about what teachers can do when there seems to be little that can be done.

Relationship Enhancement

We always make a choice about how close or how available we are to our students. All too often the most disturbed of our pupils have few productive or caring relationships to draw upon. The presence of an adult who is perceived as interested in them is potentially valuable in itself. Should they feel self-destructive or especially needy in some way, they may recognize that there exists at least one alternative to total isolation. Merely noticing the students who are feeling bad or looking stressed or worried is a validation of their importance, something that may not happen to them in any other setting. A comment such as "How are you doing today? You look a little tired" may well be more than they receive from others during their daily activities. A question about how a student did in a particular situation you are aware of is a still stronger statement of caring and can make a difference in how that youngster feels about himself. It can "make his day" in a substantive and meaningful manner.

Sharing Yourself

The classroom is a more intimate and more comfortable place when a teacher is willing to be him- or herself. By simply sharing feelings or experiences or personal anecdotes, we bring our students closer and let them know that personal sharing is welcome. This opportunity may not be present in other aspects of their lives and can enable students to offer the kind of communication that will be helpful to them. People need to be known. The process of making oneself known is a step toward better mental health, a deeper sense of connectedness, and an enhancement of one's self-esteem. Setting an example for our students may involve more personal risk than we have been accustomed to taking, but the result can be a classroom where students are freer to be themselves and where we can enjoy one another more fully as people.

Changing Student Expectations

The youngster who drifts into class a bit after the bell has rung—or who has to tweak another student's ear in passing, or who slams a book on the desk—is behaving in a disruptive and unacceptable manner in a classroom. Understandably, our tendency is to respond with discipline, usually with a counterforce at least equal to the offense committed. All teachers know the variety of options available in their school for coping with such disruptive behavior.

But what happens if we don't give the anticipated response? What if we do not perpetuate the cycle? We do need to respond in some way to unacceptable behavior; yet our response does not have to be the one the student elicits repeatedly and predictably at home and in school. In fact, the usual responses have not solved the problem, or the behavior would not still be present. Thus dancing to that old tune holds little promise for change. Just trying new responses is a useful intervention in itself. It offers the possibility that an approach can be found that will help the student to learn new, more productive behaviors.

Suppose the late arrival were greeted with humor—"I see the matinee crowd has arrived"—rather than force—"This is your third tardy this month. Go to the office." Or how about making a statement to that student that you wish to talk with him or her after class and trying a problem-solving conversation in which you and the student come together to make arrival on time a project that you are both invested in. Or how about sharing how the late arrival makes you feel about your role with the class or about your ability to be the kind of teacher you want to be. Or can you make an encouraging statement designed to let the student know that you care about his or her achievement and performance?

In other words, try for a personal exchange that is not a struggle for power. The chances are the student is used to the struggle and has difficulty finding a way out of it. We can occasionally help in that process and teach ways of resolving conflict without losing face.

Humor as a Classroom Tool

Students with emotional problems rarely come from homes where people play and have fun together. Life just is not very funny for them; nor are the people with whom they associate inclined to see and enjoy the lighter side of things. We can help to change that by allowing humor to become part of our classroom life. Not everyone is a comedian, but we all have the ability to respond to a comical setting. Many teachers fear that such relaxation threatens control in the classroom, and perhaps there is a limit beyond which each person will experience anxiety about classroom order. So be it. However, we can work within our individual limits.

A teacher I know threatens her unruly sixth-grade class of inner-city, below-average-ability students with her singing if they do not settle down. The thought of her singing to them is a source of comic distress. When she starts, they plead for silence and immediately become orderly. How refreshing for all concerned! Their fun has replaced power issues with a more salutary result than could otherwise be attained. How much easier it is for students to be part of that classroom. No wonder they love and respect that teacher!

How about a five-foot woman sidling up to a six-foot, husky, eighth-grade male student and whispering to him, "If I see that comic book on your desk again, I am going to take you outside, strangle you to death, call your mother to tell her to come pick up the body, and then I am going to collect the reward." This kind of overstatement is both private and preposterous. The book inevitably disappears, and the teacher's remedy is never tested. Two people have communicated with affection and with humor. No confiscation, no argument, no shame, and no repetition of the behavior. Those are the usual results. If humor doesn't work, some other intervention needs to be used. At any rate, it is fun to try.

Nonjudgmental Conversation

We can make another contribution by simply listening without judgment to a student's feelings, ideas, opinions, or struggles. Allowing a young person to talk with us, to select us for sharing something of him- or herself that is personal, perhaps even private, is a validation of that person. We too easily assume that what the student wants is "guidance." But that is not necessarily the case. If we are given the chance to listen, that may well be the service needed. Our interest may help the youngster to articulate whatever is bothersome in a way that causes productive reexamination. Or it may just be an answer to the need to be heard, to be respected, to be cared about. In any event, it is important not to rush to offer judgments about important things that are shared with us by our students. We may well serve them better by just being available to them.

Doing Just One Extra Thing

All the teachers with whom I have spoken know that they cannot do everything. In fact, they rarely feel they can do anything to make things better for their disturbed students. But the truth is that we can all do some little thing that has the potential to make a little difference. The warm greeting that we go out of our way to remember to give to the withdrawn student, the word of encouragement that we make sure the acting-out youngster receives after some small success, the welcome to the student who has been out sick, the phone call or note to a parent to commend a youngster's achievement, the few words after school on our "free" time, the offer of help that communicates sincerity and interest—these are all useful interventions, however minor they may seem. Each of them has the potential to make a student feel more accepted and to open up a relationship that need not be burdensome for the teacher at the same time that it is helpful to a student whose life is otherwise empty. One small action can be a start toward helping the troubled student, and each class setting offers the possibility of finding a way to fit such an effort into the daily events.

There are two levels at which caring teachers can work for the good of their neediest students. We can all be political and active within our school and our school systems. We can participate in committees, speak up at meetings where educational issues are discussed, and stand forcefully for what we believe in wherever our voice may count. In the meantime, however, we must never give in to helplessness no matter how great our odds for success may be.

Children With Communication Disorders

Children with a communication disorder may have either a delay in speech and/or language or a disordered form of speech and/or language. Delays are quite common and are usually easily resolved with proper treatment. Disorders are less common and usually require more treatment.

Children with communication problems (delays or disorders) make up the second largest group of children in the United States receiving special educational services, after children with learning disabilities. Many of them have other problems that contribute to the communication problem (e.g., autism, mental retardation, cerebral palsy, hearing loss). When children's problems are communication delays or disorders uncomplicated by other areas of exceptionality (e.g., behavioral, mental, physical, auditory), they have the highest cure rate and the shortest time in need of special services of any of the handicapping conditions.

Language is a set of oral or written symbols used by a society, following an agreed-upon set of rules, to represent thoughts, emotions, and the environment. Speech is the physical process involved in producing the oral (or sound) combinations of the language. Speech is a subsystem of language. Language (symbols used according to rules) may be delayed due to lack of language stimulation, lack of hearing of language, or bilingual or multilingual stimulation. Language disorders may involve aphasia (no language) or dysphagia (difficulty with language). Both aphasia and dysphagia may be acquired after brain injury or may be due to anatomical defects such as cleft lip and palate or loss of vocal cords.

Speech delays may be due to overresponsiveness to nonverbal language; underresponsiveness to, or criticism of, speech attempts; or any of the factors causing language delays. Speech disorders may take the form of problems with articulation, voice, or fluency. Articulation disorders include vowel or consonant substitutions, distortions, omissions, or additions. Voice disorders include problems with pitch, loudness, or nasality. Fluency disorders include stuttering or cluttering.

Speech-language pathologists are therapists who are prepared to help alleviate all delays or disorders of language or speech. They work in both public schools and in private practice. In order for children with communication disorders to qualify for special educational services and free therapeutic assistance from a speech-language pathologist, they must first be identified as having a communication disorder. Family members do not always recognize that their child has a communication problem. A teacher may be the first person to ask to have a child's language or speech assessed for possible delay or disorder. Speech that calls attention to itself, interferes with relaying an appropriate message, or which distresses either the speaker or the listener should be assessed.

When a child with a communication disorder qualifies for special educational services, the therapy will be shorter and the cure more assured when parents, teachers, and other school personnel work closely with the speech-language pathologist as an interdisciplinary team. The classroom teacher has a major role to help the peers of the child with the communication disorder understand reasons for the delayed or disordered communication. Peers can enhance the progress of speech-language therapy with empathy and encouragement. Each child can be expected to have his or her own unique differences in motivation, information-processing, speech coordination, and personality. These differences make individualized family service plans (IFSPs) and individualized education programs (IEPs) very important. The earlier the child begins therapy, the higher the cure rate.

When a child with a communication disorder has a severe speech and/or language disorder that speech-language therapy cannot cure or substantially alleviate, some form of augmentation of communication may be provided. There are many new forms of augmentative and alternate communications. These include sign language, keyboards for typing words, computers with synthetic voices, talking picture boards, and talking beams. Which form or forms of augmented communication are used with each child are ideally determined by a multidisciplinary team including parent, child (if old enough), teacher, and speech-language pathologist.

The first article selected for this unit addresses the need for early identification, assessment, and alleviation of language and/or speech delays. PL 99-457 provides services for infants and toddlers and their families if the problem is diagnosed early. The authors suggest ways to implement such services. The second unit article discusses the subtle nonverbal set of symbols that are used as language to communicate thoughts, emotions, and information about the environment. Nonverbal language is frequently used by school children in place of speech. Teachers need to learn the types of body positions, eye movements, and gestures that communicate different

messages without speech. The third selection, by Edward Carr and V. Mark Durand, alerts the reader to the problems of mislabeling children with communication disorders. "See Me, Help Me" points out that bizarre behaviors may serve as a form of communication in children who hesitate to, or cannot, use normal speech and language. It is a mistake to judge bizarre behavior as an invariant sign of emotional disorder. If one tries to analyze the message behind the strange behavior, one can often help the child find a better way to communicate the same message using speech or language. The final article focuses on one of many forms of augmentative communication: a picture task analysis. This enables students to learn meaningful skills that might be otherwise beyond their comprehension.

Looking Ahead: Challenge Questions

How can early childhood educators promote appropriate speech and language?

Can teachers understand the language of nonverbal behavior?

Can bizarre nonverbal communications be changed into more appropriate speech-language communications?

How can a picture task be used to augment speech?

Preschool Classroom Environments That Promote Communication

Michaelene M. Ostrosky

Ann P. Kaiser

Michaelene M. Ostrosky *(CEC Chapter #46) is a Doctoral Student and* **Ann P. Kaiser** *(CEC Chapter #69) is Professor, Department of Special Education, Peabody College of Vanderbilt University, Nashville, Tennessee.*

C hildren learn what language *is* by learning what language can *do* (Bates, 1976; Hart, 1985). The function of language depends upon it's effects on the environment. An environment that contains few reinforcers and few objects of interest or meets children's needs without requiring language is *not* a functional environment for learning or teaching language.

Recent research suggests that environmental arrangement is an important strategy for teachers who want to promote communication in classrooms (Alpert, Kaiser, Ostrosky, & Hemmeter, 1987; Haring, Neetz, Lovinger, Peck, & Semmell, 1987). To encourage use of language, classrooms should be arranged so that there are materials and activities of interest to the children. In addition, teachers must mediate the environment by presenting materials in response to children's requests and other uses of language (Hart & Rogers-Warren, 1978). Creating such opportunities and consequences for language use through environmental arrangement can play a critical role in a child's language acquisition (Hart, 1985).

Both social and physical aspects of the environment set the occasion for communication (Rogers-Warren, Warren, & Baer, 1983). The physical environment includes the selection and arrangement of materials, the arrangement of the setting to encourage children's engagement, and scheduling of activities to enhance children's participation and appropriate behavior. The social environment includes the presence of responsive adults and children and the verbal and nonverbal social interactions that occur among the people in the environment. In addition, contingencies for language use, the availability of a communication partner, the degree to which adults preempt children's communicative attempts, and the affective style of the listener have an impact on children's language acquisition and production (Hemmeter, 1988).

As shown in Figure 1, the social and physical aspects of the environment are linked to communication when an adult mediates the physical environment in response to children's use of language. The adult links the child's language to the environment by ensuring that the child's communication attempts are functional and reinforced. As a mediator, the adult can use an incidental teaching process to model and prompt elaborated language in order to expand the child's current skills (Hart, 1985).

Environmental arrangement can en-courage children to initiate language as a means of gaining access to materials and getting help. By providing the materials requested by a child, the adult serves the important function of specifically reinforcing that child's use of language. In addition, the environmental arrangement supports the adult in attending to the child's interest and communication attempts, thereby increasing the likelihood that the adult will respond to the child's interest and provide materials contingently (Haring et al., 1987).

Seven Strategies for Arranging the Environment

The basic goal of environmental arrangement is to increase children's interest in the environment as an occasion for communication. The environment is managed and arranged to promote requests and comments by children and to support language teaching efforts by adults. Using the environment to prompt language includes the following steps:

1. Focusing on making language a part of children's routines.
2. Providing access to interesting materials and activities.
3. Providing adult and peer models who will encourage children to use

From *Teaching Exceptional Children*, Summer 1991, pp. 6-10. Copyright © 1991 by The Council for Exceptional Children.

language and respond to their attempts to do so.

4. Establishing a contingent relationship between access to materials or assistance and use of language.

The seven environmental strategies described here are designed to (a) increase the likelihood that children will show an interest in the environment and make communicative attempts and (b) increase the likelihood that the adult will prompt the use of language about things of interest to the children by providing clear and obvious *nonverbal* prompts for them to communicate. When the environment is arranged in this way, attractive materials and activities function as both discriminative stimuli and reinforcers for language use.

Interesting Materials

Materials and activities that children enjoy should be available in the environment. Young children are most likely to initiate communication about the things that interest them. Thus, increasing the likelihood of children's interest in the environment increases the opportunities for language use and teaching. Teachers usually know which toys and materials individual children prefer. However, a simple inventory of preferences can be taken at staff meetings or by systematically observing children's choices during free play. Parents often can provide information regarding their children's preferred toys and activities. Once toy preference has been determined, teachers can enhance interest in the environment by making such toys or materials available. For example, if a child enjoys bead stringing, various shaped and colored beads, noodles, and sewing spools could be made available. Identifying preferred activities and materials is especially important for a young child with severe disabilities. Variations in activities and materials must be carefully monitored to ensure that the child remains interested. For example, a child with severe disabilities who likes squeak toys may enjoy a variety of these toys but not like a Jack-in-the-box that makes a similar sound. Rotating the toys available at any given time is also a good way to make old toys more interesting; when they reappear they seem brand new!

Out of Reach

Placing *some* desirable materials within view but out of reach will prompt children to make requests in order to secure the materials. Materials may be placed on the shelves, in clear plastic bins, or simply across the table during a group activity to increase the likelihood that the children will request access to them either verbally or nonverbally. These requests create opportunities for language teaching, since when children request a specific material they are also specifying their reinforcers (Hart & Rogers-Warren, 1978). Thus, a teacher who prompts language and provides the requested material contingent on the child's response effectively reinforces that response. The effectiveness of this strategy can be enhanced by showing the children materials, naming the materials, and then waiting attentively for the children to make requests. During snack time or before a cooking activity, a teacher can prompt children to make requests by placing the cooking materials across the table from them. Children with severe disabilities might gain access to these materials by point-

Figure 1. Social and physical aspects of the environment set the occasion for communication as the adult serves as the mediator in response to children's use of language.

ing or eye gazing, whereas more skilled children might be encouraged to use signs, words, or even complete sentences. Teachers must be careful not to frustrate students by placing too many communicative demands on them. A balance of requesting materials and playing independently is important in every activity.

Inadequate Portions

Providing small or inadequate portions of preferred materials such as blocks, crayons, or crackers is another way to arrange the environment to promote communication. During an activity the children enjoy, an adult can control the amount of materials available so that the children have only some of the parts that are needed to complete the activity. When the children use the materials initially provided, they are likely to request more. Providing inadequate portions of an interesting and desirable material creates a situation in which children are encouraged by the arrangement of the physical environment to communicate their needs for additional materials. For example, during snack time, an adult can encourage requests by presenting small servings of juice or pieces of a cookie rather than a whole cookie. A child who enjoys watching the teacher blow bubbles can be encouraged to make requests if the teacher blows one or two bubbles and then waits for the child to request more.

When children initiate language with requests for more, the teacher has the opportunity to model and prompt more elaborate language as well as to provide functional consequences for the children's communicative attempts. For example:

Teacher: (Blows two bubbles and stops.)
Child: "More"
Teacher: "Blow more bubbles?"
Child: "Blow more."
Teacher: (Blows more bubbles)

Choice Making

There are many occasions when two or more options for activities or materials can be presented to children. In order to encourage children to initiate language, the choice should be presented nonverbally. Children may be most encouraged to make a choice when one of the items is preferred and the other is disliked. For example, the adult may hold two different toys (e.g., a big yellow dump truck and a small red block) and wait for the child to make a verbal or nonverbal request. If the child requests nonverbally, the adult has the option of prompting the child to verbalize ("Tell me what you want") or simply modeling a response for the child ("Yellow truck"). Children's verbal requests can be followed with expansions of their language ("You wanted the yellow truck") or models of alternative forms for requesting ("Yellow truck, please").

Assistance

Creating a situation in which children are likely to need assistance increases the likelihood that they will communicate about that need. The presence of attractive materials that require assistance to operate may encourage children to request help from adults or peers. A wind-up toy, a swing that a child needs help getting into, or an unopened bottle of bubbles are all examples of materials that can provide a nonverbal prompt to ask for help.

Sabotage

Setting up a "sabotage" by not providing all of the materials the children will need to complete a task (e.g., paints and water but no paintbrush following an instruction to paint), or by otherwise preventing them from carrying out an instruction, also will encourage them to make requests. This environmental strategy requires children to problem solve and indicate that something is wrong or missing. They must first determine what is needed, and this initial discovery may require prompts from an adult. The missing materials are cues for the children to communicate that something is not right or that additional materials are needed. Sabotage is an effective prompt for language when the cues are obvious and children's cognitive skills are sufficiently developed to make detection of the missing material easy and rapid. Sabotage should be carried out in a warm, engaging manner by the teacher; the episode should be brief and never frustrating to the child.

Silly Situations

The final environmental strategy is to create a need for children to communicate by setting up absurd or silly situations that violate their expectations. For example, an adult who playfully attempts to put a child's shoes on the adult's feet may encourage the child to comment on the absurd situation. During snack time, an adult can set up an absurd situation by placing a large piece of modeling clay or a colored block on a child's plate instead of a cracker, then waiting expectantly for the child to initiate a verbal or nonverbal request.

Children develop expectations for the ways things should be in everyday environments. They learn routines and expect that things will happen in a particular order. When something unexpected happens, they may be prompted to communicate. Of course, children must *have* expectations before the expectations can be violated. Thus, use of this strategy must be tailored to the individual skills of the children and to their familiar routines. For example, a child who always stores articles of clothing and materials in a specific "cubbie" will probably notice when an adult places a silly picture over it; a child who does not consistently use a specified "cubbie" would be unlikely to notice and respond to such a change in the environment.

Making the Strategies Effective

To make these seven environmental strategies work, the teacher must follow the student's lead. The teacher must notice what the child is interested in, establish joint attention on the topic of interest, and encourage the child to make communicative attempts. By monitoring the child's interest and identifying which materials and activities the child enjoys, an adult can select the ones that will best serve as reinforcers for language.

The nonverbal cues that accompany the environmental arrangement strategies should be faded over time so the child is responding more to things of interest in the environment and less to the adult's cues (Halle, Marshall, & Spradlin, 1979). For example, it may be necessary at first for teachers to shrug their shoulders, raise their eyebrows, and tilt their heads, while extending their hands containing different toys, in order to direct children's attention to the environment and to the opportunity for choice making. As children become more skilled at initiating requests, fewer and less obvious nonverbal prompts should be given.

The use of environmental strategies must be tailored to each child's cognitive level and responsiveness to the environment. For example, putting a coat on a child backward and waiting for the child to communicate that something is wrong may require additional prompts if the child is unable to problem solve at this level. For environmental strategies to be effective, they must be geared to each child's level and they must cue communicative responses that are emergent in the child's repertoire.

Conclusion

How adults respond to children's communication attempts when they are elicited by environmental arrangement is extremely important. Immediate feed-back and access to the desired material or requested assistance, as well as a positive affective response, are essential consequences for communication attempts. As in all applications of naturalistic teaching processes, these episodes should be brief, positive, successful for the children, and designed to reinforce the children's use of language and their social engagement with adults (Hart & Rogers-Warren, 1978).

References

Alpert, C. L., Kaiser, A. P., Ostrosky, M. M., & Hemmeter, M. L. (1987, November). *Using environmental arrangement and milieu language teaching as interventions for improving the communication skills of nonvocal preschool children.* Paper presented at the National Early Childhood Conference on Children with Special Needs, Denver, CO.

Bates, E. (1976). Pragmatics and sociolinguistics in child language. In O. M. Moorehead & A. E. Moorehead (Eds.), *Normal and deficient child language* (pp. 411–463). Baltimore: University Park Press.

Halle, J., Marshall, A., & Spradlin, J. (1979). Time delay: A technique to increase language use and facilitate generalization in retarded children. *Journal of Applied Behavior Analysis, 12,* 431–439.

Haring, T. G., Neetz, J. A., Lovinger, L., Peck, C., & Semmell, M. I. (1987). Effects of four modified incidental teaching procedures to create opportunities for communication. *The Journal of the Association for Persons with Severe Handicaps, 12,*(3), 218–226.

Hart, B. M. (1985). Naturalistic language training strategies. In S. F. Warren & A. Rogers-Warren (Eds.), *Teaching functional language.* Baltimore: University Park Press.

Hart, B. M., & Rogers-Warren, A. K. (1978). Milieu language training. In R. L. Schiefelbusch (Ed.), *Language intervention strategies* (Vol. 2, pp. 193–235). Baltimore: University Park Press.

Hemmeter, M. L. (1988). *The effect of environmental arrangement on parent-child language interactions.* Unpublished master's thesis, Vanderbilt University, Nashville, TN.

Rogers-Warren, A. K., Warren, S. F., & Baer, D. M. (1983). Interactional bases of language learning. In K. Kernan, M. Begab, & R. Edgarton (Eds.), *Environments and behavior: The adaptation of mentally retarded persons.* Baltimore: University Park Press.

The development and dissemination of this paper were partially supported by Grant No. G008400663 from the Office of Special Education and Grant No. G008720107 from the National Institute for Disability and Rehabilitation Research. The authors are grateful to Cathy Alpert and Mary Louise Hemmeter for their contributions in the development of these environmental arrangement strategies.

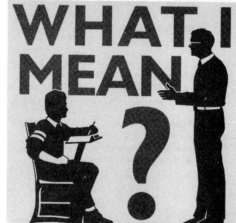

DO YOU SEE WHAT I MEAN ?

BODY LANGUAGE IN CLASSROOM INTERACTIONS

Mary M. Banbury
Constance R. Hebert

Mary M. Banbury *(CEC Chapter #514) is Associate Professor, Department of Special Education and Habilitative Services, University of New Orleans, Louisiana.* **Constance R. Hebert** *is Psychiatric Social Worker, Orleans Parish School System, New Orleans.*

Photographs by Russ Thames.

The teacher uttering the mixed metaphor "Don't look at me in that tone of voice" to a student is intuitively aware of the impact of the student's nonverbal message. All teachers should be aware of nonverbal communication in the classroom in order to enhance their ability to (a) receive students' messages more accurately; (b) send congruent and positive signals to denote expectations, convey attitudes, regulate interactions, and reinforce learning; and (c) avoid incongruent and negative cues that confuse students and stifle learning (Miller, 1986; Woolfolk & Brooks, 1985). Nonverbal communication plays a significant role in all classroom interactions. According to Smith (1979), "Whether teachers are talking or not, they are always communicating" (p. 633). In fact, studies have revealed

that 82% of teacher messages are nonverbal; only 18% are verbal (Grant & Hennings, 1971). Several studies have shown that the nonverbal component of classroom communication is more influential than the verbal component (Keith, Tornatzky, & Pettigrew, 1974; Woolfolk & Brooks, 1985).

In recent years investigators have examined commonly used nonverbal signals in educational settings. They have studied frequency and intensity of direct eye contact (Brooks, 1984), interpersonal distance (Brooks & Wilson, 1978), teacher-approval gestures (Nafpaktitis, Mayer, & Butterworth, 1985), and nonverbal criticisms (Simpson & Erickson, 1983). While teachers know about these nonverbal communication indexes, many are unaware of the influential role of nonverbal behaviors. They need to

realize, for instance, that if there is incongruity or discrepancy between words and body language, the nonverbal message will dominate (Miller, 1986).

This article explains how teachers can analyze their own communication styles so that there is harmony between what they say and how they say it and they can learn to interpret selected nonverbal signals frequently used by students. In particular, it focuses on *proximics*, a person's use and perception of space, and *kinesics*, a person's facial and body cues. It should be noted that individual nonverbal behaviors do not have implicit meaning; they should be considered in context. As Bates, Johnson, and Blaker (1982) stated, "Nonverbal messages cannot be read with certainty. To suggest that they can is irresponsible, but to ignore them is equally irresponsible" (p. 129).

Physical Distance and Personal Space

The amount of space people maintain between themselves and others provides information about relationships, regulates interactions, and affects the impressions they develop about each other. According to Hall (1966), space tolerances range from the intimate zone,

Scenario 1

Susan, a 16-year-old with mild learning and behavior problems, is sitting in the back of the room putting on makeup during her mainstreamed English class. Her teacher considers this to be unacceptable behavior and decides to correct her. He gives the assertive verbal message, "When you put makeup on during class discussion, I feel frustrated because my time is wasted while I wait for you to participate."

Don't		Do

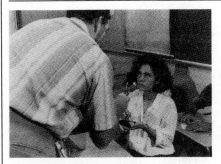  

Figure 1. Hostile Body Language. *The teacher has clearly invaded the student's personal zone. His body positioning signals confrontation since his shoulders are squared with those of the student. He is using his height to dominate and possibly to intimidate. Finally, the pen pointing is not only a further intrusion into her space, but also a threatening and intimidating gesture. These aggressive nonverbal signals defeat the purpose of an assertive message.*

Figure 2. Passive Body Language. *Equally ineffective is the opposite approach pictured above. Here the teacher appears to be intimidated and fearful of confrontation. He approaches from the rear and does not enter the student's personal distance zone. His arms are drawn up over his chest in a protective manner. His chin is retracted inwardly and hidden behind his fists. His lips are taut, and there is no eye contact. With such submissive body language, it is unlikely that his message will be taken seriously.*

Figure 3. Assertive Body Language. *The teacher gives himself a chance for a successful intervention by considering space, positioning, and body language. In this case he has approached the student from a nonthreatening lateral position, near enough to be effective but not invasive. His hands and arms are in a "open" position; his facial expression is relaxed, and his eyes are gazing at the student. Since his verbal message is congruent with his nonverbal one, he has increased the likelihood that the student will put away her makeup.*

with actual physical contact, to "personal distance," (approximately 1.5-3 feet), to "social or public distance" (more than 3 feet). Typically, people tend to get closer to those they like. They maintain more distance from those they dislike or fear; they also stand farther away from people who have disabilities or who are from different racial backgrounds (Miller, 1986).

By adjusting the distance at which they position themselves, teachers and students suggest desired levels of involvement and convey impressions about whether they are intimate, aloof, intrusive, or neutral. In certain situations a person may use close physical proximity to influence, intimidate, or warn another person. Generally, however, teachers and students use closeness to signal acceptance, concern, and approval (Richey & Richey, 1978). Conversely, they employ distance to indicate indifference, rejection, and disapproval (Brooks & Wilson, 1978).

The meaning of a given distance depends on the situation, the intentions of the individual, and the congruency between the verbal and nonverbal messages. For example, an assertive teacher sets limits by combining touch with a verbal message, eye contact, and the student's name (Canter & Canter, 1976). Likewise, a teacher who wants to increase positive communications and reinforce acceptable behaviors in the classroom says, "I like what you are doing," while making a conscious effort to move within the personal space zone of all the students, not only the favorite ones or high achievers (Miller, 1986).

Eye Contact and Facial Expressions

Eyes transmit the most expressive nonverbal messages (Marsh, 1988). They indicate mood, emotion, and feelings; they can also warn, challenge, or reassure. Although there are exceptions, most students associate wide open eyes, raised brows, and frequency of eye contact with approval, acceptance, and concern. Research demonstrates that direct and frequent teacher eye contact can improve attention, intensify participation, increase the amount of information students retain, and boost self-esteem (Woolfolk & Brooks, 1985).

Direct teacher eye contact can also express domination, disapproval, or dis-

like. Prolonged neutral eye contact with raised eyebrows serves as a powerful restraining or corrective measure. Students commonly refer to this as the "evil eye" or the "teacher look." Richey and Richey (1978) have warned teachers to keep their stares passive to avoid sending a message of dislike. Lowered eyebrows and eyes that squint or glare evoke feelings of antagonism, aggression, or denunciation.

Teachers can also use their eyes to guide discussions, promote or reward student participation, and regulate and monitor verbal exchanges. Open eyes and lifted brows signal the beginning of an activity or a request for an explanation; the brief glance serves as a conversational signal or a comprehension check. The actual amount of eye contact controls listening and speaking roles and signals information about personality, status, and culture (Marsh, 1988).

Other facial features combine with the eyes to communicate basic emotions. For example, smiles coupled with wrinkles around the eyes best predict happiness and transmit feelings of approval. (A smile is the teacher's most powerful social reinforcer; some refer to it as a "visual hug.") Lowered eyes and a downturned mouth reveal sadness or disappointment. Indicators of anger or disapproval include pursed or tightly closed lips, clenched teeth, and frowns or scowls (Hargrave, 1988).

Not all students are adept at discriminating facial affect or using social perceptual cues. In particular, students who have developmental delays, learning disabilities, or cultural differences or are inexperienced may have difficulty in describing affective states, judging nonverbal reactions, inferring information, and using body language (Wiig & Harris, 1974; Woolfolk & Brooks, 1985). Exacerbating this problem, some people may voluntarily control their facial expressions because of social dictates or cultural teachings. Therefore, the context in which they occur, as well as the accompanying verbal messages, play important roles in determining the meaning of nonverbal behaviors.

Gestures and Body Movements

Body motions or positions do not have specific meanings in and of themselves. The accompanying verbal message must be considered, as well as the individual's kinesic motions. Even then, there are times when the verbal message is not congruent with the nonverbal one. This occurs when an individual is purposely trying to mislead his or her audience or is actually unaware of the underlying emotion. For example, a young female may deny that she is angry while tightly clenching her teeth and rapidly tapping her foot; a teenage male with listless posture, overall passivity, and general drooping may refuse to acknowledge that he is depressed or, perhaps, suicidal; a teacher with fists clenched, arms crossed, and lips pursed may profess to be open to differences of opinions or other perspectives.

There are no universal clear-cut rules for interpreting body language. While it is relatively easy to read individual expressions, gestures, and movements, definitive conclusions should not be based on the observation of isolated kinetic movements. Since each element of body language can be controlled, simulated, amplified, or suppressed, it is important to observe the composite picture: the clusters of facial expressions and body movements and the congruency of verbal and nonverbal messages.

Table 1

Congruency of Verbal and Nonverbal Messages

	Approving/ Accepting	Disapproving/ Critical	Assertive/ Confident	Passive/ Indifferent
Verbal message	"I like what you are doing."	"I don't like what you are doing."	"I mean what I say."	"I don't care."
Physical distance	Sit or stand in close proximity to other person.	Distance self from other person; encroach uninvited into other's personal space.	Physically elevate self; move slowly into personal space of other person.	Distance self from other person.
Facial expressions	Engage in frequent eye contact; open eyes wide; raise brows; smile.	Engage in too much or too little eye contact; open eyes wide in fixed, frozen expression; squint or glare; turn corners of eyebrows down; purse or tightly close lips; frown; tighten jaw muscle.	Engage in prolonged, neutral eye contact; lift eyebrows; drop head and raise eyebrow.	Avert gaze; stare blankly; cast eyes down or let them wander; let eyes droop.
Body movements	Nod affirmatively; "open" posture; uncross arms/legs; place arms at side; show palms; lean forward; lean head and trunk to one side; orient body toward other person; grasp or pat shoulder or arm; place hand to chest.	Shake head slowly; "close" posture; fold arms across chest; lean away from person; hold head/trunk straight; square shoulders; thrust chin out; use gestures of negation, e.g., finger shaking, hand held up like a stop signal.	Place hands on hips; lean forward; touch shoulder; tap on desk; drop hand on desk; join fingers at tips and make a steeple.	Lean away from other person; place head in palm of hand; fold hands behind back or upward in front; drum fingers on table; tap with feet; swing crossed leg or foot; sit with leg over chair.

Table 1 is designed to assist teachers in interpreting and conveying congruent nonverbal messages; it depicts selected behavioral indexes and their verbal and nonverbal behavioral correlates. Classroom teachers who are able to recognize nonverbal signals can enhance their management techniques by curbing hostile or passive gestures and movements, matching verbal and nonverbal messages, and providing reliable and effective cues to their students.

Analysis of Nonverbal Behaviors

Teachers should examine the photographs shown here, analyze the nonverbal interactions of the teacher and the students, and match their interpretations with those of the authors. Since behavior is related to its context, there

may be more than one way to interpret the nonverbal behaviors. The purpose of this activity is to heighten teachers' awareness of nonverbal interactions during specific management and instructional activities. Scenario 1 shows how a teacher's body language can detract from or enhance his or her verbal language. Scenario 2 describes two students' nonverbal signals and suggests teacher responses.

Conclusion

The distance at which individuals position themselves, their eye focusing, facial expressions, gestures, and body movements all consciously or unconsciously complement, supplement, or supplant verbal communication. The individual significance of isolated nonverbal cues, however, is subject to as many

Scenario 2

John and Carol spend a portion of each day in a resource room for students with behavior disorders. They have been instructed to work on an in-class assignment.

Figure 4. *John is exhibiting a nonreceptive posture. His intense gaze suggests that he would like to engage in the "stare-down" game. His crossed arms and legs, indicative of a "closed" position, could be a sign of insecurity or defensiveness. This student, however, does not appear to be intimidated. His body position, in general, is one of reclining. A person interested in protecting himself generally does not recline. The shoulders are squared, not rounded, and he is turned away from his desk, not "hiding" behind it. In this case there may even be an unconscious attempt to hold back from physical aggression. This student is actually holding his left arm tightly into his chest rather than simply crossing his arms in resistance.*

A person who was aware of nonverbal signals would not openly confront this student. There should be no prolonged looks, sudden moves, aggressive gestures, or threatening comments. With arms at his or her side, a teacher would approach the student slowly from a lateral position, using nonthreatening comments to open a dialogue.

Figure 5. *At first glance, Carol, the student pictured above appears to be bored or uninterested. Upon closer examination, however, she is exhibiting several body signals for depression. Her shoulders are drooped and rounded; her torso is retracted; and her affect is flat. Her eyes are downcast; her jaw is slack and lowered; and her lower lip is in a pouting position. The twisting of the lock of hair, especially if it is done incessantly, could be a sign of anxiety. If her teacher observes a pattern or ongoing series of symptoms such as these, the student should be referred for further assessment.*

interpretations and intentions as there are people who receive or send messages. Therefore, observers of body language should concentrate on interpreting the total congruent picture, including context, verbal and nonverbal behaviors, and prior and subsequent events, before they reach conclusions based on observation and comprehension of isolated signals. Likewise, people who desire to use proximics and kinesics to enhance their communication style should verify that their body language is indeed communicating their intended messages and their nonverbal behaviors are congruent with their verbal ones.

To improve their communication styles, teachers could videotape their classroom performance, identify intended messages, and solicit structured feedback regarding the congruency of their verbal and nonverbal behaviors from students or colleagues by using a chart, checklist, or rating sheet. They could role play selected events or simulate interactions with peers to assure that they are sending congruent messages while responding to the expected defensiveness of certain students and parents. To develop and enhance their ability to interpret the nonverbal messages of other people, teachers could set aside 10 minutes a day to consciously

notice and interpret proximic and kinesic signals sent by students, friends, and family members. They could focus on academic or social interactions, using a videotape without the audio portion to read the body language and replaying the scene with sound to check their perceptions. Alternatively, they could examine photographs, especially family albums, paying particular attention to the body language and what it indicates about personal and interpersonal relationships, attitudes, and emotions. Taking the time to study ways of interpreting and conveying nonverbal messages can help teachers enhance the teaching and learning process.

References

Bates, M., Johnson, C., & Blaker, K. E. (1982). *Group leadership: A manual for group counseling leaders.* Denver: Love.

Brooks, D. M. (1984, April). *Communicating competence: Junior high teacher behavioral expression during the first day of school.* Paper presented at the annual meeting of the American Educational Research Association, New Orleans.

Brookes, D. M., & Wilson, B. J. (1978). Teacher verbal and nonverbal expression toward selected students. *Journal of Educational Psychology, 70,* 147-153.

Canter, L., & Canter, M. (1976). *Assertive discipline: A take charge approach for today's educator.* Los Angeles: Lee Canter.

Grant, B. W., & Hennings, D. G. (1971). *The teacher moves: An analysis of nonverbal activity.* New York: Teachers College Press.

Hall, E. T. (1966). *The hidden dimension.* Garden City, NY: Doubleday.

Hargrave, J. (1988, March). Actions speak louder than words. *OEA Communique,* pp. 28-31.

Keith, L. T., Tornatzky, L. G., & Pettigrew, L. E. (1974). An analysis of verbal and nonverbal classroom teaching behaviors. *Journal of Experimental Education, 42,* 30-38.

Marsh, P. (Ed.). (1988). *Eye to eye: How people interact.* Topsfield, MA: Salem House.

Miller, P. W. (1986). *Nonverbal communication* (2nd ed.). Washington, DC: National Education Association.

Nafpaktitis, M., Mayer, G. R., & Butterworth, T. (1985). Natural rates of teacher approval and disapproval and their relation to student behavior in intermediate school classrooms. *Journal of Educational Psychology, 77,* 362-367.

Richey, H. W., & Richey, M. H. (1978). Nonverbal behavior in the classroom. *Psychology in the Schools, 15,* 571-576.

Simpson, A. W., & Erickson, M. T. (1983). Nonverbal communication patterns as a function of teacher race, student gender, and student race. *American Educational Research Journal, 20,* 183-189.

Smith, H. (1979). Nonverbal communication in teaching. *Review of Educational Research, 49,* 631-672.

Wiig, E., & Harris, S. (1974). Perception and interpretation of nonverbally expressed emotions by adolescents with learning disabilities. *Perceptual and Motor Skills, 38,* 239-245.

Woolfolk, A. E., & Brooks, D. M. (1985). The influence of teachers' nonverbal behaviors on students' perceptions and performance. *The Elementary School Journal, 85,* 513-528.

SEE ME, HELP ME

In some children, bizarre behavior is a way of communicating. Understanding the message helps.

EDWARD G. CARR
AND V. MARK DURAND

Edward G. Carr, Ph.D., is a professor of psychology at the State University of New York at Stony Brook and a research psychologist at the Suffolk Child Development Center in Smithtown, Long Island, New York. V. Mark Durand, Ph.D., is an assistant professor of psychology at the State University of New York at Albany.

BOB IS A 14-YEAR-OLD autistic boy. As part of his therapy, he attends lessons to learn how to dress himself, but he gets little from this instruction. He repeatedly throws tantrums and tries to kick, scratch and bite his teacher. The attacks are so violent that the teacher has to wear protective clothing, including gloves and a heavy coat. After 10 minutes the teacher usually gives up, puts away the lesson materials and moves the work desk aside. Within seconds, Bob calms down and begins softly humming to himself.

Jim is a 10-year-old mildly retarded child who scratches himself so badly that he has ugly sores all over his body. Other students in his school shun him and call him names. The family physician can find no medical reason for the scratching, so the boy's parents conscientiously nag at him whenever they see him scratching. But, oddly enough, when they are absorbed in other matters and say nothing about his scratching, Jim hardly ever scratches himself.

For the past 11 years, these and other puzzling cases have fueled our research at the Suffolk Child Development Center in Long Island. That research has convinced us that severe behavior problems are often not senseless acts but primitive attempts to communicate. Indeed, aggression, self-injury and tantrums are often the only effective ways some children have of making their needs known.

The notion that bizarre behavior may be a form of communication has a long history. Over 2,300 years ago, Plato suggested that newborns communicated with their caregivers by crying and screaming. The 18th-century French philosopher Jean Rousseau wrote that "When children begin to speak, they cry less. This is a natural progression. One language is substituted for another."

The ideas of these philosophers are supported by recent studies of normal child development. Harvard psychiatrist Peter Wolff, for example, found that infants cry in different ways for different purposes. They cry one way if they are hungry, another way if they are uncomfortable, yet another if they merely crave company. The differences are subtle, but by the time a baby is a few weeks old, many mothers can tell one kind of cry from another. When babies are older, they will fuss and cry when given foods they don't like; withdraw the foods and the crying stops. In a sense the baby is saying, "Take that stuff away. I don't want it." In a related study, psychologists Silvia Bell and Mary Ainsworth found that the more skillful a 1-year-old was at communicating by means of facial expression, gesture and speech, the less the baby cried.

Although most of the children we study are autistic or retarded, their behavior problems also seem to be means of communicating. We have found that these children are most likely to be aggressive or injure themselves when seeking adult attention or attempting to escape from unpleasant situations. Their strange behavior is a way of saying, "Please pay attention to me" or "Please don't ask me to do this."

Our ideas owe much to an important study conducted in 1965 by Ivar Lovaas, a psychologist at the University of California, Los Angeles, and his colleagues. The 9-year-old schizophrenic girl with whom they worked banged her head against objects such as the edge of a desk top or a wall. The more adults pleaded with her to stop, the harder she hit her head. Apparently, she had learned that hurting herself was an effective way of getting attention. (Most adults find it very difficult to ignore a child who is deliberately injuring herself.) When the adults paid no attention to her self-destructive behavior, however, but attended to her when she played in a normal way, she rarely hurt herself.

Lovaas's work showed that self-destructive behavior is often simply an abnormal way of getting something that all children normally crave: attention. Since 1965, researchers have found that many forms of bizarre behavior are often ways of asking for attention. Jim, the retarded boy who constantly scratched himself, is an example.

A chance observation in 1975 led to the conclusion that attention-seeking is not the only reason children behave abnormally. In collaboration with psychologists Crighton Newsom and Jody Binkoff, one of us (Carr) studied an 8-year-old schizophrenic boy named Tim who screamed and punched himself in the face whenever anyone tried to teach him anything. At the end of each lesson the teacher would say, "Tim, that's it for today." The boy would immediately stop hitting himself and say, "That's it, that's it," as he ran smiling for the exit. In a matter of minutes, the rate at which he punched himself fell from 30 times a minute to zero. This sudden change in behavior made us realize that bizarre behavior sometimes expresses a desire to escape an unpleasant situation. It is a way of saying, "I don't want to do this. If you try to make me do this, I'll act crazy until you stop."

In the 11 years of research that followed this discovery, we came across many children who behaved oddly as a way of escaping unpleasant situations. These situations were often those in which demands were placed upon the children. Asked to practice a speech lesson or learn how to dress themselves, for example, they would punch, bite, kick or scratch themselves—or their teacher—or scream and throw tantrums. Under these circumstances, children can often force adults to let them have their way. Bob, the autistic boy who attacked his teacher, is an example.

It now seems so obvious that bizarre behavior can be a way of communicating that it may be hard to see why this wasn't understood long ago. There are three reasons. First, such behavior used to be (and

in some quarters still is) attributed to things going on inside of the person. It is only when you look to events in the environment that the communicative function of the behavior becomes clear.

Second, until 1975 most disturbed children languished in institutions where they received little more than custodial care. Since few demands were placed on them, there were few opportunities to notice that demands triggered bizarre behavior. Then, in 1975, Congress passed a law requiring that all handicapped children must be educated. This meant that the children were required to do things, and some expressed their displeasure by behaving strangely.

The third reason that we did not see the message in abnormal behavior is that the relationship between bizarre behavior and things going on in the environment is often

Scratching, hitting, screaming, throwing things— all can be different ways of saying the same thing.

more complex and subtle than our examples suggest. For instance, the same behavior may mean different things in different situations. One moment a child may bang his head against a wall because he objects to a demand someone has made, but in another moment he may do the same thing to get attention. And a child may have a number of different ways of "saying" the same thing—scratching or hitting, screaming, throwing objects around a room. Often the purpose of the behavior becomes clear only when the circumstances under which it occurs are carefully studied.

The notion that abnormal behavior is a form of communication has important implications. For one thing, it means that we must understand the meaning of the behavior to treat it successfully. For example, when a child misbehaves, we sometimes use "time out" as a form of punishment. We isolate the child in an area from which he or she can't see or hear others. Usually 10 minutes is enough to discourage attention-seeking behavior. But if the misbehavior is a way of asking to get out of a demanding situation, time out can backfire. When we used time out to punish aggressive behavior in one boy, for example, he became more aggressive when he returned

to his lesson. We realized that what we were asking him to do was too difficult for him. When we simplified the task, aggression practically disappeared.

Another implication of the communication approach to bizarre behavior is that if we teach children normal ways of conveying their needs, they might give up their abnormal behavior. This idea is supported by the research of psychologists Margaret Shodell and Henry Reiter with autistic children. Some of these children had good language skills and some of them did not. Their parents and teachers were asked how often the children bit themselves, banged their heads or scratched themselves during a 10-day period. The results showed that while only 19 percent of the good communicators engaged in such self-injurious acts, 47 percent of the poor communicators did so.

A second study, this one by L.W. Talkington and colleagues, compared institutionalized retarded children who had language skills with similar children who lacked such skills. Adults who worked with these children rated their tendency to behave aggressively by, for example, destroying property. On several categories, those who lacked linguistic skills were rated more aggressive than those who could communicate more or less normally.

For the past five years, we have conducted studies to see if teaching disturbed children how to communicate their needs reduces their bizarre behavior. We work with children in educational settings, since bizarre behavior is particularly troublesome there. Our first step is to determine whether the behavior is an effort to receive attention or to escape an unpleasant situation. We do this by instructing the disturbed child and one other child at the same time. At first, the teacher interacts exclusively with the problem child and then, after a few minutes, begins directing attention to the other child. If the bizarre behavior suddenly increases, we know that attention is what the child is after.

If we suspect that the behavior is a way of objecting to frustrating demands, then we ask the child to perform a series of tasks. The first is something easy, such as naming the animals in a series of pictures. Then we try something harder, such as asking the child to say how many animals are shown in a picture. If abnormal behavior suddenly increases, then we know the child is telling us the task is too difficult.

Once we understand the message in the behavior, we attempt to teach the child better ways of communicating. Children who seek attention are taught various ways of asking for praise. For example, they learn to show their teacher a completed assignment and ask, "Am I doing good work?" or "Look at what I've done!" We teach children frustrated by difficult tasks to say, "Help me" or "I don't understand." This way the children can avoid repeated failure by speaking to the teacher rather than by, for example, hitting the teacher. We teach sign language to children who are unable to speak, and signing can be just as effective as speech in getting a message across.

Teaching children new ways of communicating is more difficult than it sounds. For instance, the teacher who is working with a child who screams when frustrated must be alert to the first signs of frustration, which may be only a slightly wrinkled brow or a faint whimper. If the teacher acts too quickly, the child may be annoyed by the assistance. If the teacher waits too long, the child may progress to a full-scale tantrum.

The teacher's role is made more difficult by the fact that the children sometimes appear indifferent or confused at first. Gradually, however, the children learn that the new methods work better than the old ones.

We have worked with several dozen children in this way and all have shown marked reductions in, or the elimination of, severe behavior problems. The children appear eager to use their new communication skills, perhaps because for the first time they can reliably influence another person.

The benefits seem to persist long after the training is over. We studied three children for two years and found that two of them continued to use their new linguistic skills throughout the period. Their behavior problems during this period were also negligible. In the case of the third child, however, the teacher did not respond to normal requests for attention and the child reverted to the face slapping and hand biting he

had used earlier. Once the teacher learned to respond to normal requests, the problem behavior diminished.

So long as adults are sensitive to attempts to communicate normally, the children use those methods. They do not abandon their new techniques even when faced with a substitute teacher or other stranger. Perhaps we should not be surprised by this. After all, most adults know how to respond when a child says, "Help me."

For many years psychologists considered the bizarre behavior of disturbed children to be either meaningless or the expression of mysterious unconscious conflicts. We believe instead that such behavior is often a primitive way of communicating needs. By carefully analyzing the message behind the behavior, therapists, parents and teachers can help the children in their care to find better ways of communicating what they want to say.

Using a Picture Task Analysis

to Teach Students with Multiple Disabilities

Wynelle H. Roberson
Jane S. Gravel
Gregory C. Valcante
Ralph G. Maurer

Wynelle H. Roberson *is Lead Teacher at the Multi-disciplinary Training Project Diagnostic Classroom;* **Jane S. Gravel** *is formerly with the Department of Psychiatry, College of Medicine;* **Gregory C. Valcante** *(CEC Chapter #1024) is Special Educator at the Children's Mental Health Unit, Department of Psychiatry, College of Medicine; and* **Ralph G. Maurer** *is Chief, Children's Mental Health Unit, Department of Psychiatry, College of Medicine, University of Florida, Gainesville.*

The task analysis approach to teaching multiple-step skills to students with disabilities has been used for many years (Brown, 1987). Teachers of students with moderate and severe disabilities provide instruction across domains by (a) breaking the skill into component steps; (b) prompting students through forward, backward, or total task chains; and (c) recording step-by-step progress toward skill acquisition. Likewise, the use of pictures to augment communication for

persons with speech and language disabilities now is commonplace (ASHA, 1981). In addition to this use as a method of expressive communication, pictorial symbols are used in advertising, transportation, and public facilities.

Increasingly, educators and researchers have combined task analysis and augmentative communication procedures to produce sequences of pictures that represent the steps an individual must perform to carry out domestic, community, vocational, and leisure tasks. A *picture task analysis* is a pictorial representation of the critical steps in a task analysis sequenced and displayed for the learner to follow. Picture task analyses enable learners with moderate and severe disabilities to gain meaningful skills that previously were beyond their grasp.

Benefits of Picture Task Analyses

One of the earliest studies of sequenced pictures (Robinson-Wilson, 1977) was conducted with picture recipes based

on previously published cookbooks. Since then, the use of sequenced pictures has been validated for instruction in cooking (Johnson & Cuvo, 1981), grooming (Thinesen & Bryan, 1981), and vocational skills (Connis, 1979; Wilson, Schepis, & Mason-Main, 1987). Wiggins and Behrmann (1988) used sequenced pictures for community instruction in grocery stores and restaurants. In fact, picture task analyses can be used to teach any skill that can be analyzed into component steps (e.g., operating a tape player, using a calculator, making coffee, emptying trash).

All of the advantages of using traditional task analytic instructional strategies (e.g., size and number of steps tailored to student ability levels) are maintained with the picture task analysis format. Furthermore, picture task analyses may be integrated into existing educational methods. For example, they may be used in conjunction with other prompting strategies for students who need more than just the visual cue, and a time delay procedure may be incorporated if desired. Picture task analyses

By use of a picture task analysis, this student is shown a skill broken down into component steps.

enhance receptive communication, serve as a memory aid, and are cost and time efficient.

Receptive Communication Strategy

Effective communication between teacher and student is essential for effective teaching. One of the limitations of a traditional task analysis is its accessibility. A task analysis typically is written by the teacher for a student with little, if any, reading ability. The teacher must then communicate these steps to the learner, usually by modeling and by employing numerous verbal, physical, and gestural prompts. The picture task analysis provides additional input and increases the likelihood that the message will be understood. The pictures communicate that the task to be performed

requires a sequence of steps to be carried out and that there are specific starting and stopping points.

Memory Aid

While verbal prompts and cues last only momentarily, the visual format of the picture task analysis endures to serve as a constant reminder of the steps to be completed. Students may refer back to the pictures as often as necessary to ensure that they are performing the steps accurately. This enduring nature of the pictorial representation holds a great advantage over other prompting and cueing strategies.

The ultimate goal of a picture task analysis is to enable the student to perform meaningful tasks independently. However, in some cases, complete independence may not be possible due to the nature of the individual's disabilities or the complexity of the task. In these

cases, a picture task analysis can serve as an adaptive device or memory aid, allowing the student to progress from partial participation to further levels of independence.

Efficiency

An additional benefit of picture task analyses is their time and cost effectiveness. They are easy to develop and implement. They are portable and allow other personnel (e.g., job supervisors, paraprofessionals, volunteers) to supervise or aid in instruction. Although modeling provides a living, three-dimensional cue, it does not endure over time like the picture task analysis does, and it requires the instructor's presence. The visual representation of the picture task analysis, on the other hand, allows the instructor to spend time with other students and to fade direct supervision. Once created, all or part of a picture task analysis may be used for several students if it is appropriate to their individual needs and ability levels. It lends itself not only to teacher data recording but also to students' producing data-based documentation of their own progress (Connis, 1979).

At the University of Florida, we have used picture task analyses with students who have multiple disabilities, including moderate and severe intellectual disabilities, language impairments, and behavior problems. This article presents an easy method of constructing picture task analyses and steps for integrating their use into community environments based on our experience.

Developing and Implementing a Picture Task Analysis

Our procedure for constructing picture task analyses requires only (a) photographs (which may be taken with an instant camera and film); (b) manila folders, posterboard, or another medium on which to mount the photo; (c) glue; and (d) clear contact paper or lamination to protect the photographs. The following steps are taken:

1. An appropriate skill is selected from the student's individualized education program (IEP) and broken down into component steps suitable for the student's abilities.

2. A symbol system is selected. At the

University of Florida, instant photographs are used to represent component steps. Line drawings or other symbols may be appropriate for other students.

3. The necessary materials are gathered.

4. A photograph is taken of each step in the task analysis.

5. The photos are arranged in sequential order on a manila folder and secured with glue.

6. Numbers depicting the sequence of steps are written beneath the photos and arrows are drawn to direct the learner's attention from one step to the next step in the sequence.

7. A description of the behavior in each photograph is written below the photograph.

8. The picture task analysis is laminated to preserve the photographs.

Instructional Procedure

The instructional procedure follows five steps. The duration of each step depends on the abilities, disabilities, and learning patterns of individual students.

1. The teacher presents the picture task analysis and reviews it with the student by pointing to each photo and reading the sentence accompanying it.

2. The teacher models the behaviors while the student watches and follows along with the picture task analysis. Students who read should read the description of each step as the teacher performs it.

3. The student guides the teacher through the task using the picture task analysis as a guide. The teacher may prompt the student by asking "What do I do next?" Students with reading ability read the description of each step aloud. Nonreaders and nonverbal students may respond by pointing to the appropriate photograph.

4. The student begins performing parts of the task one step or group of steps at a time, using the picture task analysis as a guide. The teacher completes the steps not yet attempted by the student and provides feedback and supervision. The number of steps attempted at one time depends on the student, the difficulty of the task, and whether a forward chaining, backward chaining, or total task procedure is used.

5. The teacher gradually fades his or her presence so that the student eventually performs the task, using the picture task analysis as a guide without direct supervision.

A Collaboration Success Story

In one of our classes, an adolescent with multiple disabilities was taught to make coffee using a standard automatic coffeemaker. Initially, the teacher consulted with the speech/language pathologist to determine the appropriateness of photographs as symbols for the student and the skill of coffeemaking. The speech/language pathologist then wrote the task analysis and provided written descriptions of the steps for making coffee in language appropriate for the student's ability level. An audiovisual technician took photographs of the teacher performing each step, and the teacher prepared the picture task analysis. After demonstrating the use of the folder and modeling the correct performance of coffeemaking, the teacher assisted and supervised the student as she began to prepare coffee.

The acquisition phase of the 13-step task began on October 5, with a paraprofessional implementing the instruction following the instructional procedure just outlined. The following chronology illustrates this student's progress, the fading of prompts, and the fading of the instructor as supervisor:

- October 14: Performed one step without referring to pictures.
- October 21: Performed three steps without referring to pictures.
- November 5: Corrected own mistake.
- November 17: Checked own work using pictures.
- November 21: Performed four steps without referring to pictures.
- December 8: Began by saying "Wash hands," the directions for step one.
- January 14: Only one prompt (verbal) given.
- January 20: Paraprofessional proximity faded to outside the office door.
- February 18: Performed with only natural job supervisor.

As can be seen from this chronology, within the first month and a half this adolescent began performing some steps without referring to the picture task analysis. Furthermore, after 3½ months the student was able to prepare

coffee without any teacher supervision. The picture task analysis facilitated this student's learning and allowed her to gain independence more quickly than if she had to rely on teacher prompts. An additional benefit of this learning experience was seen in April, when a revised picture task analysis was introduced briefly for the student to learn to prepare coffee in a different environment, with a different coffeemaker, as part of her vocational program. As expected, she used the picture task analysis to learn the new steps required with different equipment and quickly progressed from teacher supervision to natural job-site supervision.

Conclusion

Picture task analyses are adaptive devices that are easily constructed by classroom teachers. They may be used in a variety of natural community and vocational environments. As a supplement to other instructional strategies, picture task analyses can provide access to independence from teacher supervision for learners with severe disabilities.

References

American Speech-Language-Hearing Association (ASHA). (1981). Position statement on non-speech communication. *Asha, 23,* 577-581.

Brown, F. (1987). Meaningful assessment of people with severe and profound handicaps. In M. E. Snell (Ed.), *Systematic instruction of persons with severe handicaps* (pp. 39-63). Columbus, OH: Merrill.

Connis, R. T. (1979). The effects of sequential pictorial cues, self-recording, and praise on the job task sequencing of retarded adults. *Journal of Applied Behavior Analysis, 12,* 355-361.

Johnson, B. F., & Cuvo, A. J. (1981). Teaching mentally retarded adults to cook. *Behavior Modification, 5,* 187-202.

Robinson-Wilson, M. A. (1977). Picture recipe cards as an approach to teaching severely and profoundly retarded adults to cook. *Education and Training of the Mentally Retarded, 12,* 69-73.

Thinesen, P. J., & Bryan, J. A. (1981). The use of sequential picture cues in the initiation and maintenance of grooming behaviors with mentally retarded adults. *Mental Retardation, 19,* 246-250.

Wiggins, S. B., & Behrmann, M. M. (1988). Increasing independence through community learning. *TEACHING Exceptional Children, 21*(1), 20-24.

Wilson, P. G., Schepis, M. M. & Mason-Main, M. (1987). In vivo use of picture prompt training to increase independent work at a restaurant. *Journal of the Association for Persons with Severe Handicaps, 12,* 145-150.

Children With Hearing Impairments

While 8 to 10 percent of school-age children may have some hearing loss, less than 1 percent qualify for special educational services as children with significant hearing impairments. Hearing may be impaired due to a conductive disorder (the problem originates in the outer or the middle ear) or a sensorineural disorder (the problem originates in the inner ear). On rare occasions, hearing may be impaired due to central auditory processing in the brain. Conductive disorders can be treated with sound amplification. Sensorineural and processing disorders cannot. In addition, hearing impairments can be congenital (child is born with impaired hearing) or adventitious (child loses hearing due to accident or illness). If a child has learned language before acquiring a hearing impairment, that would have profound implications for the type and degree of special educational services needed to continue learning. A third means of classifying a hearing impairment is by the degree of loss in terms of intensity of sound. A child with a loss of more than 55 decibels in the better ear has a moderate hearing impairment and requires some special services. A child with a loss of more than 70 decibels in the better ear has a severe hearing loss and requires special speech, hearing, language, and educational assistance.

About half of all children with hearing impairments have congenital losses or losses acquired during infancy. They are thus prevented from hearing normal speech and learning language. It is very important to assess hearing in infancy. PL 99-457 mandates comprehensive multidisciplinary services for infants and toddlers and their families. Once a hearing impairment is assessed, services should begin immediately. If the loss is conductive, the infant or toddler should be fitted with a sound amplification device (hearing aid). If the loss is sensorineural, the infant or toddler and the parents should begin learning sign language. Special educational services should also begin. Both receptive language (understanding what is said) and expressive language (speaking) are fostered with the earliest possible intervention. Cognitive processes and socialization processes are also dependent on early comprehension of some form of language.

While PL 94-142 mandates a least restrictive environment for all children with disabilities, the education of hearing impaired children often progresses more rapidly in a more restrictive setting. Decisions about educational placement of children depend on many factors: age of onset of hearing loss, degree of hearing loss, language ability, cognitive factors, social factors, whether the parents are hearing impaired, whether the parents learn manual (signing) communication, and presence or absence of other educational disabilities. Even children with only moderate hearing impairments need some special services. The National Technical Institute for the Deaf takes the position that teaching children with hearing impairments in regular education classrooms without providing appropriate supportive services is tantamount to child abuse.

Teachers have a responsibility to provide an environment in which the child with a hearing impairment can maximize his or her learning. Many regular education teachers need supportive services to help develop the skills they need to teach such a child. This can include learning how to use an FM auditory training device and microphone, checking hearing aids on a daily basis, keeping mouth movements visible for lip reading, sharing notes or providing a note-taker, allowing an interpreter to sign to the child, learning to use sign language, making sure classroom films, videos, or television programs are captioned, and selecting and using appropriate computer software for each child with a hearing impairment.

Each child with a hearing loss should be motivated to do all he or she is capable of doing both in educational and in social activities of the school. The teacher has a major responsibility to help the nonhearing impaired peers understand the special needs of the child with a hearing loss. Teachers, peers, and all ancillary school personnel should encourage the child to participate to the fullest extent possible. The hearing impairment should not be allowed to become an excuse for nonparticipation. Children with hearing losses should be reinforced for their efforts but not praised for inaction. Understimulation and/or pity are detrimental both to educational progress and to socialization and self-esteem.

The first unit selection addresses the issue of providing special services to children who choose a private school education over a public school education. How far will government go in paying for special services for a child with hearing loss to be educated in a nonsecular (religious, philosophic) setting? The next article discusses the negative attitudes displayed by hearing peers towards children with hearing impairments in the regular classroom. Teachers can help reduce ethnocentrism and prejudice, whether it is directed at age, sex, race, religion, social class, or a handicapping condition. The final article

in this unit provides information about the uses of a frequency modulation (FM) auditory training device in a regular classroom. These technological aids are increasingly being used by children with hearing losses mainstreamed into regular education classrooms.

Looking Ahead: Challenge Questions

Should tax dollars pay for an interpreter for a student with a hearing loss who attends a private school? Should the interpreter be limited to interpreting only academic subjects or should spiritual, philosophic, and/or religious subjects be interpreted as well?

Can teachers recognize prejudice against students with hearing impairments? What classroom strategies can be used to promote acceptance and understanding of the child with a hearing loss?

What is an FM auditory training device? What must a classroom teacher know about wearing a microphone and checking the receiver worn by the student?

Public Aid for Handicapped and Educationally Deprived Students

The Establishment Clause As Antiremedy

Steven Huefner

STEVEN HUEFNER is a judicial clerk for Justice Christine M. Durham of the Supreme Court of Utah, Salt Lake City.

Mr. Huefner critiques the reasoning in Aguilar v. Felton *and in a later case involving Jimmy Zobrest, a deaf student — and he proposes some alternative means of addressing similar issues in the future.*

SCHOOLS, a fundamental institution of American culture and society, have historically failed to meet the needs of significant groups of students, including students with disabilities, minorities, and impoverished youths. In recent decades the U.S. Congress has sought to remedy some of these failures by establishing various assistance programs targeted at specific groups. Predictably, however, many obstacles stand in the way of the full success of such programs. For instance, the Education for All Handicapped Children Act (P.L. 94-142) and

its successor require all public school districts in the United States to provide appropriate educational services to all special education students within their district boundaries.[1] Yet, although this requirement extends to *all* special education students, whether or not they are enrolled in a public school, the establishment clause of the First Amendment to the Constitution prevents the government from providing many sorts of assistance to sectarian institutions. Thus when a deaf student who attends a parochial school seeks, under P.L. 94-142, to obtain from the local public school district the services of a sign language interpreter, the establishment clause may preclude the desired injunctive relief. But should it?

Precisely this controversy arose in a federal district court case brought in Arizona in 1989 by deaf student Jimmy Zobrest. Using Jimmy's case as a means of framing the issues, I will examine the broader relationship of the establishment clause to supplementary educational programs that may have an incidental impact on sectarian institutions. First, I will examine the background and central issues of Jimmy's case — issues that resemble

those in the much more widely reported 1985 Supreme Court decision, *Aguilar* v. *Felton*.[2] Next I discuss the decisions in both Jimmy's case and in *Felton*, considering how their implications for the remedial goals of supplementary education may lead us to view them as instances of "antiremedy" — a term coined by Kellis Parker of Columbia University. I then offer a final critique of the reasoning in these cases and propose some alternative means of addressing similar issues in the future.

P.L. 94-142

Congress passed P.L. 94-142 in the wake of growing concern over the treatment that students with disabilities were receiving in the public schools. Sometimes these students were relegated to "special" programs, in which all they really learned was to withdraw further from their nondisabled peers; at other times they were left in the regular classroom entirely unassisted.[3] P.L. 94-142 sought to improve the education of students with disabilities by keeping them in the regular classroom when appropriate while providing them with whatever

From *Phi Delta Kappan*, September 1991, pp. 72-77. Reprinted by permission of *Phi Delta Kappan* and Steven Huefner.

support services they needed, such as wheelchair ramps,[4] braille texts and other instructional materials,[5] sign language interpreters, or other special tutors. P.L. 94-142 also stipulated that any state receiving federal education funds had to show that all of its school districts were providing "all handicapped children the right to a free appropriate public education" in the least restrictive environment.[6] Theoretically, states can refuse to comply and thereby simply lose their federal funding, but the states are currently too dependent on federal aid to do so. Hence, the statute is effectively compulsory.

Although P.L. 94-142 required little in the way of specific progams, its broad mandate to the states required them to demonstrate that, "to the maximum extent appropriate, handicapped children, including children in public or private institutions or other care facilities, are educated with children who are not handicapped, and that . . . removal . . . from the regular classroom occurs only when . . . education in regular classes with the use of supplementary aides and services cannot be achieved satisfactorily."[7] Subsequent court decisions have established that schools are required to enable students with disabilities to receive special education instruction in the regular classroom to the maximum extent appropriate, using whatever related services may be required in the process — a form of "mainstreaming."

THE *LEMON* TEST

Jimmy Zobrest was a deaf high school student who required "the services of a sign language interpreter" to assist him in his schooling.[8] He resides within the Catalina Foothills public school district in Arizona, and, had he wished to attend the local public high school, he would have been entitled to the assistance of a sign language interpreter at school at public expense, according to the provisions of P.L. 94-142. But Jimmy wished to attend a religiously affiliated school, the Salpointe Catholic High School, where his entitlement to an interpreter under P.L. 94-142 was less certain. In the summer of 1989 Jimmy and his father brought suit against the Catalina Foothills School District, seeking an injunction mandating that the school district provide a sign language interpreter for him at Salpointe.[9]

At first blush it may seem hard to imagine how a court could compel a public school district to provide support for the educational programs of *any* private school. Yet this aspect of Jimmy's case is not an issue. P.L. 94-142 requires each state to establish procedures that will ensure that all children with disabilities who are in need of special education have access to appropriate special educational services, even if they attend private schools.[10] The Supreme Court has held that publicly employed teachers may provide instruction in special programs at private schools if instruction comparable to that which public school students are receiving is not otherwise available.[11] School districts already routinely include private and parochial school students in many of their programs, although this mixing is most easily accomplished when the supplemental programs occur on public (or at least nonsectarian) property. Therefore, Jimmy's problem was not that he wished to attend a private school and still obtain a state-sponsored interpreter. Rather, his problem was that the private school he desired to attend was a *religiously affiliated* school and that the assistance he needed had to be provided on the school grounds. He thus encountered problems with the establishment clause.

The establishment clause is of primary importance whenever the relationship between government and sectarian schools is at issue; any public aid granted to a private institution having a religious affiliation is likely to receive careful scrutiny to ensure that it does not constitute "an establishment of religion." The principal judicial standard used today for assessing whether an educational program violates the establishment clause is the test articulated by the Supreme Court in 1971 in *Lemon* v. *Kurtzman*.[12] This three-part "*Lemon* test" structures the analysis of a congressional or state statute with respect to the establishment clause as follows:

> First, the statute must have a secular legislative purpose; second, its principal or primary effect must be one that neither advances nor inhibits religion; finally, the statute must not foster "an excessive government entanglement with religion."[13]

When Jimmy sought to have an interpreter from the public schools assist him at Salpointe as part of his entitlement to "a free appropriate public education," the second and third parts of this test stood in his way. The first part of the test was easily satisfied: the statute's clear and sin-

gular purpose was to provide better education for *all* students with disabilities. But satisfying the second and third parts of the test — neither advancing or inhibiting religion nor fostering excessive government entanglement — was much harder.

Central to Jimmy's difficulty was the district court's reliance on the 1985 Supreme Court decision in *Aguilar* v. *Felton*. This case involved a challenge to New York City's administration of a congressional program designed to provide supplemental education in local schools to "educationally deprived children" from low-income families.[14] The program, now part of Chapter 1 of the Education Consolidation and Improvement Act of 1981, sought to improve the education of *all* children whose opportunities had been limited by their economic background. It mandated that students attending private schools also receive supplemental educational services comparable to those they would receive if they were in a public school. Some 13% of the students eligible for the assistance in New York City in 1982 were enrolled in parochial schools, and federal funds were being used to pay public employees to work at these parochial schools, where they taught courses in remedial reading, reading skills, remedial mathematics, and English as a second language.

In *Felton*, six taxpayers had successfully challenged these expenditures as a violation of the establishment clause, thus creating a precedent that boded unfavorably for Jimmy.

ANTIREMEDY RULES THE DAY

In *Zobrest* v. *Catalina Foothills School District*, the U.S. District Court for the District of Arizona, following *Felton* with almost no discussion, denied Jimmy the interpreter he needed.[15] Although superficially the reasoning in *Felton* — and by extension in Jimmy's case — is well within the normal bounds of establishment clause reasoning and thus seems to advance the legitimate ends of separation of church and state, the apparent logic of the analysis only masks the deeper remedial failures that it causes.

In *Zobrest* the district court stated that the interpreter would "act as a conduit for the religious inculcation of James — thereby, promoting James's religious development at government expense." Such entanglement of church and state is not allowed, the court said, citing *Aguilar* v.

Felton. The majority opinion in *Felton* first considered the religious character of the schools in question, noting that their substantial purpose was "the inculcation of religious values." Although New York City carefully supervised the Chapter 1 remedial classes being taught in the schools to ensure that no inculcation of religious beliefs actually occurred in these special courses, the Court determined that this day-to-day supervision created an excessive entanglement between "pervasively sectarian" institutions and the state. Although the classes all took place in classrooms free of any religious icons and were taught by public school personnel who had complete control over both the curriculum and the students in their classes and who used only materials provided by the government, the Court was still troubled by the symbolic link between government and religion.[16]

Implicit in the *Felton* and *Zobrest* analyses is a concern for the purpose of the Court's recent establishment clause reasoning, which has been to preserve religious freedom and independence. This important end must not be overlooked. Fearing that state-supported indoctrination of religious beliefs "would have devastating effects on the right of each individual voluntarily to determine what to believe (and what not to believe) free of any coercive pressures from the State,"[17] the Court has nullified a wide variety of practices deemed to constitute state support of religion.

In terms of the theory of judicial remedies, such decisions have usually served both a declaratory function (delineating the acceptable scope of state/church behavior) and an expectation function (ensuring citizens that their religious protections are being safeguarded). Yet an overly cautious decision under the establishment clause may go beyond what is needed either to create legitimate expectations regarding these protections or to declare their proper scope. Meanwhile, such caution may abrogate other legitimate interests. Such a result could properly be labeled an *antiremedy*.

Antiremedy refers to the result that occurs when the success of one "remedy" actually creates or exacerbates another problem, sometimes leaving everyone worse off or even destroying "the possibility of a better future."[18] Antiremedy is almost always present to some extent in every legal controversy, since the prevailing party's remedy will be an anti-

remedy to the losing party. But the concept of antiremedy takes on added meaning when it is used to describe a remedy gone wrong, a form of relief no longer functioning as it should. A misapplication of the establishment clause in a way that fails to advance its intended remedial end will thus be antiremedy to society at large — and doubly so if, in the process, it also frustrates important remedial aims of other statutes. In addition, even a proper invocation of the establishment clause will function as antiremedy to those particular individuals who are challenging its invocation.

The *Felton* opinion describes the intended end of the establishment clause as preventing the government from "promot[ing] or hinder[ing] a particular faith or faith generally."[19] Whether the decisions in these cases actually advanced this end will depend on how "promote" or "hinder" are interpreted, but the interpretation implicit in *Felton* is hard to defend. If, as *Felton* holds, the teaching of secular material by public employees is a promotion of religion when it occurs at a parochial school, then the fire marshal's visit to instruct students about fire safety or a public health nurse's visit to advise students about hygiene would also be a promotion of religion. Yet these are matters of routine. We expect public employees to become "entangled" with parochial institutions to a certain extent, to ensure that legitimate secular ends are also being advanced in the sectarian setting. Therefore, preventing remedial education teachers from fulfilling their secular role in a sectarian setting can be seen as an anomalous result — an antiremedy to the community they serve.

A sign language interpreter is arguably different from a fire marshal or a remedial education teacher, however, because in a parochial school the interpreter will actually be conveying religious content to the student. Yet the interpreter is merely a tool of communication, much as eyeglasses or hearing aids are tools that facilitate communication. It would be absurd to think that public funds could not be used to purchase glasses or hearing aids for needy students who intended to use them in a parochial school on the theory that providing such devices would "further the religious inculcation" of the students. Rather, establishment clause problems would arise only if this assistance were being provided *exclusively* to parochial students.

Similarly, if P.L. 94-142 provided in-

terpreters only for deaf students attending parochial schools, it would immediately violate the establishment clause. But the services are available to all students who need them to receive an appropriate education, in whatever educational setting they have chosen. The only proper restriction on the availability of these educational services should be that they be used in a setting approved by the state as providing an appropriate education. When the state accredits an educational setting — be it a private, parochial, or home school — the state expresses its conclusion that the school provides a satisfactory alternative to the public schools. When Congress then asks states to provide special services to all students with disabilities, the aid should be available to students in all such accredited schools, just as hearing aids might be provided to all hearing-impaired students. Yet because Jimmy's needs could not be satisfied by a simple mechanical tool, the district court denied him access to public assistance as long as he remains a parochial school student.

Thus, to Jimmy Zobrest, the establishment clause must surely feel like antiremedy. Paradoxically, it has operated to constrain his religious freedom, which is explicitly protected by the free exercise clause of the First Amendment, because he is effectively being told that, in exercising his religious freedom by attending his parochial school, he will become ineligible for a government benefit, the sign language interpreter. Although the statute frames this entitlement as a benefit available to all students with disabilities, in fact, Jimmy must forsake his religious education if he is to qualify for this service.

Likewise, the hundreds of thousands of students across the country who were adversely affected by the *Felton* decision initially had to choose between remaining in their parochial schools or obtaining access to government-sponsored remedial education; they could not do both. As a result, immediately after *Felton*, participation of private school students in Chapter 1 programs dropped 98% in Los Angeles and dropped significantly in all other urban areas as well.[20] Surely, to the thousands of students no longer receiving the supplementary services, as well as to the sponsors of the remedial programs of Chapter 1, this invocation of the establishment clause was an antiremedy.

Slowly, however, the states have come up with alternative ways of providing remedial educational services to parochial students. The most common means has been to purchase portable classrooms, place them on property leased from the parochial schools or on adjoining land, and use them for the remedial instruction. Alternatively, some districts have begun to make extensive use of computer-assisted instruction.

Yet participation is still well below the pre-*Felton* levels. More important, these "solutions" adopted by the school districts to circumvent the *Felton* decision have only increased the cost of the remedial programs, while not furthering the goals of the establishment clause. When a publicly employed teacher conducts remedial instruction in a mobile trailer parked next to a parochial school, the risk that religion is thereby being impermissibly promoted or that the state is thereby excessively entangled with a sectarian institution is practically the same as if the instruction took place within the school under carefully controlled conditions. Even admitting that there could be some small difference, this marginal difference comes at great cost: the expense and inconvenience of using a fleet of trailers and leased land rather than freely available space. Thus, even to the taxpayers who brought the suit, the decision in *Felton* may be an antiremedy.

The four dissenting opinions in *Felton* also support the idea that in cases like *Felton* and *Zobrest* the establishment clause has become an antiremedy, with one dissenter, Justice Byron White, claiming that such decisions are even "contrary to the long-range interests of the country."[21] Besides arguing that no legitimate establishment clause interest was served, Chief Justice Warren Burger's dissenting opinion expressed dismay about the significant educational needs that were being frustrated: "Under the guise of protecting Americans from the evils of an Established Church such as those of the 18th century and earlier times, today's decision will deny countless schoolchildren desperately needed remedial teaching services funded under [Chapter 1]."[22]

The establishment clause is a critical protection in our pluralistic society, but it can be misconstrued. Both P.L. 94-142 and Chapter 1 also have important goals. When a true conflict arises between the establishment clause and one of these statutory programs, the establishment clause must prevail. But courts should not go out of their way to find such conflicts when no legitimate infraction of the establishment clause needs to be remedied. In the two supplemental educational programs considered above, the establishment clause was invoked to deny the relief Congress intended to provide, without furthering any of the proper concerns of separation of church and state.

MAKING *LEMONADE*

How to make the best of this bad situation will depend on who one is. Jimmy Zobrest has very different concerns from those of a U.S. senator worried about the undermining of congressional intent, though both suffer from the same antiremedy problem: overzealous use of the establishment clause to limit supplementary educational programs. Possible responses may come at the individual, local, or national levels and may be directed at the schools, the legislatures, or the courts.

Jimmy must face some immediate problems. He has three obvious options: struggle on at Salpointe without an interpreter, perhaps making little educational progress but enjoying the social and spiritual community there; transfer to the public high school, where he will have to foreclose his religious training and adjust to a new environment (a particularly difficult task for a student with a disability); or use his family's funds to pay for a private interpreter to assist him at Salpointe. This last option may seem most attractive, but a full-time private interpreter is costly. The fact that Jimmy attends a private school reveals little about his family's financial status, since parochial schools frequently provide very low-cost education to members of their faith. Jimmy may simply be unable to afford an interpreter.

A less obvious possibility would be for Jimmy to negotiate with the school district — and also with other concerned students and parents — to develop some intermediate level of assistance. Perhaps computers or other technologies could be put to use to create some sort of compromise program. If a feasible alternative were to be found, the district would be required to provide it. But it is much harder to find an intermediate solution to meet the needs of a disabled student like Jimmy, who requires assistance in his total educational program, than to find a compromise to meet the need for remedial instruction created in the wake of *Felton*, because students who require Chapter 1 services could receive them anywhere, for only a few hours a day.

Hence it seems that Jimmy may have a hard time doing anything to improve his antiremedial position by himself. He did, however, appeal the decision to the Ninth Circuit, where, as this was being written, it was still pending.[23] Although it is doubtful that the appeals court will feel any freer than did the district court to distinguish Jimmy's case from *Felton*, his case is slightly different because it involves the interests of so few students. One concern in *Felton* was that the monitoring necessary to supervise the work of dozens of teachers who were instructing hundreds of students would involve excessive government "entanglement." But in Jimmy's case a school district could monitor the work of a single interpreter without much entanglement at all. On the other hand, Jimmy's interpreter would be heavily involved in the transmission of religious material, and this was another sort of "entanglement" equally disdained by *Felton*. Thus Jimmy seems to stand little chance of succeeding at the appellate level as long as *Felton* is good law.

Also worth thinking about, however, is an ultimate petition to the Supreme Court, urging a reversal of *Felton*. Several intervening events since *Felton* suggest that such a petition could prove successful. First, the experiment with mobile trailers following the decision may have shown the Court the arbitrary nature of the way in which it has been drawing the "excessive entanglement" line. Second, in 1986 the Court itself, in *Witters* v. *Washington Department of Services for the Blind*, concluded that state aid available through a vocational rehabilitation program could be used to finance one student's preparation for the ministry at a Bible college without violating the establishment clause.[24] If rehabilitation funds may be used to support religious instruction, thus allowing a student who would not otherwise even be in the sectarian environment to receive such instruction, it seems arbitrary to prevent funds for the education of students with disabilities from being used to help a deaf student receive an appropriate education in a sectarian setting *in which he is already enrolled*.[25] The final intervening event is that Justices Antonin Scalia, Anthony Kennedy, and David Souter are now on the bench, and what had been a 5-4 decision could be ripe for reversal.

Furthermore, the reasoning within the

Felton decision is widely recognized as weak. Hence it deserves to be reconsidered. The decision's treatment of the second and third parts of the *Lemon* test curiously turned them into a sort of Catch-22. *Felton* first held that extensive monitoring would be necessary to ensure that the New York City Chapter 1 program did not violate the second part of the *Lemon* test by impermissibly advancing religion. But then the Court held that any such monitoring sufficient to prevent the impermissible advancement of religion would inevitably involve the state in "excessive government entanglement" with the sectarian schools, thus creating a violation of the third part of the *Lemon* test.[26] The school districts were stuck, unable to satisfy both parts. This kind of reasoning from the *Lemon* test makes it worthy of its sour name.

The problem lies in the entanglement component of the *Lemon* test. The Court now makes an entanglement inquiry regardless of whether or not it has identified any real threat to religious liberty.[27] Dissenters in *Felton* made it clear that they were ready to abandon this use of the entanglement component and to rely only on the first two parts of the *Lemon* test in most circumstances. The Court has never attempted to eliminate all contact between church and state; indeed, it has approved such indirect aid to parochial schools as subsidizing bus fares and providing textbooks. As a result, the Court must continually face the vague question of what constitutes excessive entanglement. Answering this question as a separate inquiry, independent of what direct impact on religious institutions is likely to occur, produces antiremedies by disqualifying programs that have only an incidental impact on the religious institution.

Thus there are several reasons why a reversal of *Felton* is conceivable. Nevertheless, waiting and hoping for this to happen is not a particularly promising response to the problem created by the *Felton* and *Zobrest* decisions. Unfortunately, none of the other responses yet discussed is particularly promising either. However, one alternative holds potential: basing the provision of various supplemental educational services on a system of vouchers.

A voucher system would first identify the types of services to be provided, e.g., sign language interpretation for deaf students or remedial reading for impoverished students performing below grade level. Vouchers entitling the bearer to procure such services at government expense would then be prepared, and individuals who qualified for the vouchers would be identified. The identified students would be given the vouchers, in appropriate quantity. Individuals and their families would make their own determination about where to use the aid, redeeming the vouchers at their pleasure for government-funded instruction or assistance. The assistance could be "purchased" for use at any educational institution, just as a tutor could be hired with private funds for tutoring at any location.

No impermissible entanglement is deemed to have occurred when the choice of where to use the aid is a private one, just as no impermissible entanglement was involved when a vocational rehabilitation participant made an independent decision to use the rehabilitation benefits to pursue religious studies. Under this system, the vouchers authorize payment, while individuals determine where to use them. Such a system could be adopted either on a national level or on a local level, but either would require significant lobbying of legislators.

That the current interpretation of the establishment clause could be circumvented by something like a voucher system further demonstrates the arbitrariness of the Court's currently strict application of the excessive entanglement component of the *Lemon* test.

Both *Zobrest* and *Felton* saw the establishment clause trump important congressional programs because of perceived "entanglement." Yet, as the federal government becomes more involved in public education generally, it also inevitably becomes more entangled with private and parochial schools. According to former Justice Lewis Powell, such schools provide "an educational alternative . . . , afford wholesome competition with our public schools; and in some States they relieve substantially the tax burden incident to the operation of public schools."[28] Hence the government must be able to deal with these schools as well as with the public schools in order to accomplish its educational objectives. Unfortunately, the vague notion of "entanglement" has proved to be an antiremedy in this area, increasing the cost and complexity required to achieve the public goals.

When life gives you lemons, make lemonade. The best response here would be to rethink (and abandon) the "entan-

glement" criterion of establishment clause jurisprudence as articulated in the *Lemon* test — at least for cases like *Zobrest*. In the meantime, school districts and students will need to employ a little creativity in applying federal programs, and legislators may be able to make use of a voucher system to further many of the same desirable ends.

---

1. Codified at 20 U.S.C. Sections 1232, 1401-2, 1405, 1406, 1411-20, 1453 (1988). (In 1990 the Education for All Handicapped Children Act became the Individuals with Disabilities Education Act.)
2. 473 U.S. 402 (1985).
3. See S. Rept. 168, 94th Cong., 1st sess., 8 (1975).
4. 20 U.S.C. Section 1406 (1988).
5. Ibid. at Sections 1452-53.
6. Ibid. at Section 1412(1).
7. Ibid. at Section 1412(5). P.L. 94-142 also authorized an administrative agency to oversee the statute, which predictably produced extensive interpretive regulations.
8. *Zobrest* v. *Catalina Foothills School District*, No. Civ.-88-516-TUC-RMB, at 1 (D. Ariz. 18 July 1989).
9. Ibid.
10. 20 U.S.C. Section 1413(a)(4)(A)(1988).
11. See *Wheeler* v. *Barrera*, 417 U.S. 402, 420-21 (1974).
12. 403 U.S. 602 (1971).
13. Ibid. at 612-13.
14. 473 U.S. 402, 404 (1985).
15. The complete opinion (cited above) is barely over one page long.
16. See *Grand Rapids School District* v. *Ball*, 473 U.S. 373, 385 (1985). (This was the companion case to *Felton*.)
17. Ibid. at 385.
18. Kellis Parker, "Remodeling Remedies," unpublished paper, 1990.
19. 473 U.S. at 414.
20. Mark Walsh, "Study Finds *Felton* Led to a Drop in Private Students in Chapter 1," *Education Week*, 11 October 1989, p. 7.
21. *Felton*, 473 U.S. 402, at 400 (Justice White, dissenting in both *Ball* and *Felton* in single opinion reported with the majority opinion in *Ball*).
22. *Felton*, 473 U.S. at 419 (Chief Justice Burger, dissenting).
23. In a case with very similar facts, the Fourth Circuit recently ruled that aid could not be provided for the student without violating the establishment clause. *Goodall* v. *Stafford County School Board*, 17 EHLR 745 (4th Cir. 1991). However, in 1990 the Office of Special Education and Rehabilitative Services reaffirmed the position of former Secretary of Education William Bennett that the Department of Education would not interpret *Felton* to preclude the provision of services to students in parochial schools under statutes such as P.L. 94-142.
24. 474 U.S. 481 (1986).
25. *Witters* is distinguishable, however, in that it concerned a higher education setting, while *Zobrest* involved secondary education. But this distinction may prove more form than substance.
26. 473 U.S. at 412-14.
27. Ibid. at 419 (Chief Justice Burger, dissenting).
28. 473 U.S. at 415 (Justice Powell, concurring).

REDUCING ETHNOCENTRISM

David S. Martin

David S. Martin (CEC Chapter #264) is Associate Professor of Education and Dean of the School of Education and Human Services, Gallaudet University, Washington, DC.

■Misunderstanding, miscommunication, and negative attitudes—problems of *ethnocentrism*—are common in the day-to-day contact between any two different cultures. They can occur regularly when deaf and hearing children interact in schools.

What is classroom ethnocentrism? It includes negative attitudes exhibited toward other culture groups being studied in the classroom or toward groups represented in the school itself. How will a teacher recognize ethnocentrism when it is expressed? There are two kinds of ethnocentrism, which anthropologists label *cultural absolutism* and *cultural relativism* (Guggenheim, 1970):

1. Cultural absolutism: When children respond to some foreign cultural behavior with a statement such as, "How awful—how could anyone do that?", they are looking at their own culture as superior.
2. Cultural relativism: If the same children look at the same foreign behavior and say, "Well, we have our ways, and they have theirs," they are missing the idea of the unity that underlies all human behavior.

The problem of reducing ethnocentric behavior in educational settings is complex because it involves both thinking and feeling. For example, a hearing person who looks down on a deaf peer's sign language may be expressing ethnocentrism toward the deaf population rather than merely judging their method of communication.

The Deaf Population and Ethnocentrism

How can we be sure that the misunderstandings between deaf and hearing people are forms of ethnocentrism? We know that there is a deaf "subculture." Meadow (1975) has explained its characteristics as (a) intermarriage among deaf people, (b) membership in certain voluntary organizations, (c) membership in special religious organizations, (d) special opportunities in the arts for deaf people, (e) traditional residential schooling, and (f) use of American Sign Language.

Other research has found that people who are deaf believe that hearing people are more negative toward them than they really are (Schroedel & Schiff, 1972) and that hearing students' attitudes toward deaf students can become more negative after a period of months of going to school together (Emerton & Rothman, 1978).

Methods for Reducing Ethnocentrism

Researchers have found some ways to reduce ethnocentrism between different cultural groups. We can apply some of these findings to the specific goal of increasing understanding, positive attitudes, and clear communication among both deaf and hearing children in mainstreamed school settings and adults in the workplace. The following six areas of research can be helpful in revealing ways to accomplish this goal.

Prejudice Reduction

Pate (1981) has reported that facts alone are not enough to reduce prejudice toward another group, so teachers need to focus on attitudes, too, by asking children to openly discuss how they *feel* toward another group.

People who have high self-image tend to have a low degree of prejudice. Therefore, teachers need to help *all* children feel positive about themselves so that they will feel positive toward those who are different from them.

The thinking, feeling, and behavioral components of prejudice are not necessarily related. Therefore, teachers may see children expressing kind *words* but prejudiced *feelings* toward children of different groups. To uncover their true attitudes, teachers should confront children individually when their behavior does not match their expressed words. The first step toward changing attitudes is for individuals to *admit* what they feel *now*.

Films and other media also tend to improve intergroup attitudes. In schools, multimedia lessons on deafness may go further than books and discussion to help improve attitudes of hearing students.

Social contacts among members of different groups may reduce prejudice, whereas isolation of deaf children may foster prejudice toward them. Therefore, the more direct contact between deaf and hearing children, the better. Classes of hearing children should experiment with joint field trips and other activities with special classes of deaf children.

Expression of Negativism and Cultural Contact

Another study looked at attitude changes between deaf and hearing people after an 8-week period in which deaf student teachers taught full-time classes of hearing public school students (Martin, 1983). The study showed a clear improvement in attitudes of the hearing children toward the deaf teachers, supporting the idea that regular contact between the two cultures can reduce ethnocentrism.

If a regular public school has a special day-class of deaf children, those children need to have regular, supervised interaction with hearing children. Recess is not enough; lunch periods, joint projects, and paired reading activities could help develop more positive attitudes.

But what do these studies mean for hearing learners who have *no* opportunity to interact with deaf learners and vice versa? The data suggest two other instructional conditions for reducing ethnocentrism: (a) providing sufficient time for in-depth study of both deaf and hearing cultures in social studies and (b) a classroom climate that allows open expression and discussion of students' initial negativism toward other cultures. Teachers need to encourage students to express their negative attitudes so that they can be discussed openly.

Process of Stereotyping

The work of Glock, Wuthnow, Pilievin, and Spencer (1975) showed that "cognitive sophistication" is also important in reducing negative attitudes toward other groups. This sophistication requires that children understand the mental process of stereotyping and labeling as well as the other culture's life experience and history. Therefore, teachers should teach both deaf and hearing children about how stereotypes are formed. Activities could include showing how a picture of one poor beggar in tattered clothes in New Delhi could make us wrongly generalize that *all* Indians are poor if we do not know all the facts.

Countering Stereotypes

Freedman, Gotti, and Holtz (1981)

built on Glock's work by teaching elementary students about this stereotyping process and then showing them some examples of "counter-stereotypic" behavior by members of ethnic groups (e.g., Puerto Rican celebrities in the United States). Students demonstrated reduced stereotypic attitudes after the use of these two techniques.

Pecoraro (1970) also found that exposing children to the positive contributions to the American heritage by an ethnic subgroup (Native Americans) could improve their attitudes toward that subgroup. In this vein, teachers of hearing and deaf students could teach about the contributions of famous deaf persons to American society, both now and in the past.

Three books that would be useful for this purpose are *Fastest Woman on Earth* by A. M. Thacher (1980); *Works of James O'Connor, the Deaf Poet* by J. O'Connor (1882); and *Representative Deaf Persons of the United States of America*, edited by J. E. Gallagher (1898).

Simulating the Other Culture

The Hawaii State Department of Education (1981) developed a framework for studying another culture that included the following activities:

* exploring an "arranged" or artificial cultural environment in the classroom,
* raising questions about that culture, and
* observing and analyzing each other's behaviors.

Thus, the classroom could become a kind of anthropology "lab." Teachers could set up a "deaf" environment for hearing children by having them carefully insert cotton in their ears and list their feelings and sensations for a period of 5 minutes. They would then remove the cotton and share the insights they gained about being "deaf."

Some teachers have also taught hearing children some basic sign language and helped them to understand how the use of a manual language assists some deaf persons to distinguish between sounds that take similar shapes on the lips (e.g., "m" and "b"). Without some visual cue, a deaf person cannot distinguish such pairs.

Teaching Logical Categorization

Still another method may be worth testing: teaching children how to find underlying *similarities* as well as the more obvious differences among peoples. The program *Instrumental Enrichment* (Feuerstein, 1980) teaches students how to compare and categorize on a logical basis. Teachers can also teach children better categorization skills by having them look at a randomly organized collection of pictures of objects, such as tools arranged on a flannelboard, then listing the criteria for sorting them (color, size, shape, number, etc.), sorting them into categories, and labeling the categories. Then, teachers can ask, "What is the same about all the pictures, even though they are in separate labeled groups?" (They are all still tools.) These same categorization skills can be applied to pictures of people. No matter how many separate groups and labels one might invent (skin color, eye shape, face shape, hair color, etc.), they are all still people, and people are all similar in needing food, shelter, clothing, beliefs, and love.

Summary

These research studies suggest the following classroom strategies for the teacher who wants to reduce ethnocentrism among deaf and hearing students:

1. Provide multiple opportunities for deaf and hearing students to interact on a regular basis, preferably on joint projects or activities.

2. Give deaf and hearing children the opportunity to discuss openly why they react positively or negatively toward each other.

3. Encourage children to express in what ways their own culture might appear strange to a person from the other group. For example, hearing children should imagine which aspects of spoken language might appear bizarre to a deaf person.

4. Discuss the fundamental ways in which *all* human groups are similar (kinship, division of tasks, language, prolonged childhood dependency, belief system, use of symbols, tool systems, etc.). Deaf and hearing people are equally "human" because each group has

established its own specific responses to those *same* needs.

5. Teach children about the processes by which humans develop stereotypes and have them list the ways in which they have seen themselves follow those processes in judging or misjudging deaf or hearing children.

6. Teach students that there is a wide variation of behavior *within* any culture; thus, stereotyping is bound to be false (e.g., some deaf people use sign language, while others do not).

7. Point out some nonstereotypic behaviors of both groups. For example, numerous deaf persons today have earned Ph.D.'s and teach in universities.

8. Teach about the positive contributions to human life by both groups. For example, focus on well-known deaf actors or athletes.

9. Help students to create and analyze a written description of a model culture in order to develop their thinking tools for understanding the deaf or hearing culture.

The teacher's yearly plan for using these methods would include the following activities:

1. Working at the beginning of the school year with the principal and other teachers to plan joint activities for deaf and hearing children.
2. Working with the Parent-Teacher Association to schedule their fall meeting around the topic "Improving Children's Attitudes Toward Handicaps," in which parents of handicapped and nonhandicapped children would share their own experiences and positive suggestions.
3. Inviting a guest speaker into the classroom to tell about deafness, teach some sign language, and describe the problems of being deaf.
4. Planning at least one social studies unit on deaf culture to teach children about the traditions of the deaf community and sign language in America. This would be the place for multimedia presentations and teaching about the stereotyping process.

5. Incorporating into the reading program some biographies of famous deaf persons in history.

6. Inviting deaf and hearing children to tell each other, in pairs, about experiences, problems, and solutions they have in communication. This could take place once a week, perhaps on Friday afternoons during a special activity period. A sign language interpreter would be important in ensuring communication among these children.

7. Invite a skilled parent to visit the classroom twice a week throughout the year to teach the hearing children basic sign language, which they could use during the regular interaction times with deaf children.

A local teacher of deaf children can also serve the regular classroom-teacher as a valuable resource and support person in learning to employ these and other ideas and in solving problems that may arise between deaf and hearing students.

Conclusion

Teachers have a responsibility to take advantage of what is known about ways to intervene in the tendency toward ethnocentrism. If teachers and administrators truly believe that positive interaction between handicapped and nonhandicapped persons can lead to a better world for everyone, then they must employ the techniques available to them for fostering such interaction on a regular basis.

Only as educators take advantage of these useful procedures can they hope to promote a world where the word "handicap" will lose its original negative connotation and instead be seen as merely another manifestation of the amazing variation in human characteristics. It is not *bad* to be different; it is only *interesting* to be different. At the core, we are all human.

References

Emerton, R. G., & Rothman, G. (1978). Attitudes toward deafness: Hearing students at a hearing and deaf college. *American Annals of the Deaf, 123*, 588-593.

Feuerstein, R. (1980). *Instrumental enrichment.* Baltimore, MD: University Park Press.

Freedman, P. I., Gotti, M., & Holtz, G. (1981, February). In support of direct teaching to counter ethnic stereotypes. *Phi Delta Kappan*, p.456.

Gallagher, J. E. (Ed.). (1898). *Representative deaf persons of the United States of America.* Chicago: J. E. Gallagher.

Glock, C. Y., Wuthnow, R., Pilievin, J. A., & Spencer, M. (1975). *Adolescent prejudice.* New York: Harper & Row.

Guggenheim, H. (1970). The concept of culture: Talks to teachers. In *Man: A course of study.* Washington, DC: Curriculum Development Associates.

Hawaii State Department of Education. (1981, June). A framework for culture study with special focus on the study of Hawaii. *Resources in Education.* (ERIC Document Reproduction Service No. ED 198 031).

Martin, D. S. (1983). Preparing hearing-impaired teachers of hearing children. *Teacher Education and Special Education, 6*, 143-150.

Meadow, K. (1975, July-August). The deaf subculture. *Hearing and Speech Action.*

O'Connor, J. (1882). *Works of James O'Connor, the deaf poet.* New York: N. Tibbals.

Pate, G. S. (1981, January). Research on prejudice reduction. *Educational Leadership*, 288-291.

Pecoraro, J. (1970). *The effect of a series of special lessons in Indian history and culture upon the attitudes of Indian and non-Indian students.* (ERIC Document Reproduction Service No. ED 043 556).

Schroedel, J. G., & Schiff, W. (1972). Attitudes toward deafness among several deaf and hearing populations. *Rehabilitation Psychology, 19*(2), 59-70.

Thacher, A. M. (1980). *Fastest woman on earth.* Milwaukee: Raintree Publishers.

HEARING FOR Success IN THE C·L·A·S·S·R·O·O·M

JoAnn C. Ireland
Denise Wray
Carol Flexer

JoAnn C. Ireland *is Communication Specialist/ Audiologist, Special Education Regional Resource Center, Cuyahoga Falls, Ohio.* **Denise Wray** *is Assistant Professor of Speech Pathology, Department of Communicative Disorders, University of Akron, Ohio.* **Carol Flexer** *is Associate Professor of Audiology, Department of Communicative Disorders, University of Akron, Ohio.*

■Increasing numbers of hearing-impaired children are being mainstreamed, causing educators to express legitimate and realistic concerns. Many of these concerns are in regard to the assistive listening devices needed by hearing-impaired children. Although this equipment can be intimidating, it is essential; hearing-impaired children cannot function in the classroom setting without it (Berg, 1986; Ross, Brackett, & Maxon, 1982). This article answers questions that are typically asked about the technology necessary for children with any degree of hearing loss, from mild to profound, to participate actively in *any* educational environment.

A Prerequisite for Achievement

Hearing is pivotal to academic achievement. Hearing loss is an initial step in a detrimental progression of cause and effect. Loss of hearing sensitivity acts as an acoustic filter that hinders a child's normal language development due to inappropriate sensory input (Ling, 1976). The hearing loss subsequently impacts expressive language as well as reading, writing, attending skills, social interaction, and, ultimately, overall academic achievement (Ross, Brackett, & Maxon, 1982). Since reading and writing are built on verbal language skills, they suffer as a direct result of hearing loss. Until the problem of auditory reception is addressed, the pervasive effects of hearing loss will persist and escalate. Therefore, anything that can be done to maximize hearing will have a positive impact on the child's academic performance.

Hearing aids are typically worn to augment auditory reception. Unfortunately, however, the problems of distance, room reverberation, and background noise can greatly interfere with the wearer's ability to discriminate a preferred auditory signal such as a teacher's voice (Berg, 1986; Bess & McConnell, 1981). In fact, speech discrimination is significantly reduced, even when the child is only 1 foot away. A signal must be 10 times louder than the background noise in order to have a signal-to-noise ratio that will allow for intelligibility of speech (Hawkins, 1984; Ross & Giolas, 1978). A typical classroom could not possibly provide a preference signal (teacher's voice) that is loud enough to be intelligible over the background noise (Berg, 1986).

When the signal-to-noise ratio is poor, an auditory signal may be audible to a hearing-impaired child, but not necessarily "intelligible" (Boothroyd, 1978). In other words, the child may respond in a seemingly appropriate way but not really understand what he or she has heard. The child may actually be responding only to intonation patterns and not truly comprehending the specifics of the utterance.

Lipreading is an ineffective substitute for hearing, because visual cues do not provide enough information for identifying the many homophenous words in the English language, for example, "pan," "man," and "ban" (Jeffers & Barley, 1971). These words look alike on the lips and cannot be discriminated without the addition of some auditory information. Therefore, lipreading is considered important, but only as a complement to auditory reception (Boothroyd, 1978).

Preferential seating, even with the use of hearing aids, is not enough! Neither lipreading skills nor hearing aids can substitute for a learning strategy that incorporates the use of an optimal auditory signal.

FM Assistive Listening Devices

Frequency Modulation (FM) auditory training devices are one of the many systems available as personal listening devices. According to Zelski and Zelski (1985), assistive listening devices are products designed to solve the problems of noise, distance, and reverberation that cannot be solved with a hearing aid alone. They do not replace hearing aids, but augment them to more fully meet the needs of hearing-impaired individuals in group listening situations.

An FM auditory trainer is comprised of a microphone, which is placed near the desired sound source (e.g., teacher, loudspeaker, etc.), and a receiver worn by the listener, who can be situated anywhere within approximately 200 feet. These devices can often be coupled to the child's own hearing aid for appropriate individual amplification. There are many models of FM equipment on the market (Van-Tasell, Mallinger, & Crump, 1986). It is important to obtain a model that can be worn by both the teacher and the child in an inconspicuous fashion (Flexer & Wood, 1984). The multiple FM fitting and setting options require visits to the audiologist for appropriate selection and adjustments.

The FM device creates a listening situation that is comparable to the teacher's being only 6 inches away from the child's ear at all times. Ideally, if the unit is fitted and adjusted correctly by an audiologist, its use promotes speech intelligibility and not simply audibility. For example, a child might hear the teacher's voice through a hearing aid alone, but might not be able to distinguish the differences between words such as "wade/wait," "can't/can," "invitation/vacation," and "kite/kites." Such confusions are detrimental to the child's concept and vocabulary development, and they influence the child's potential for success in a regular classroom.

Unfortunately, the FM system is not a panacea for classroom management of hearing-impaired students (Ross, Brackett, & Maxon, 1982). One successful supplement to the regular class curriculum with FM use is to provide tutoring, which can be offered on a pre- and postlesson basis. Teachers can also employ other facilitating strategies such as repeating and rephrasing information and using the cue word "listen" prior to presenting instructions.

Incorporating FM into the Classroom

The Ling Five Sound Test offers a quick and easy way to check, on a daily basis, whether or not a hearing-impaired child can detect the necessary speech sounds (Ling, 1976). This information is vital for instruction. The test can be administered with the child at the far end of the classroom, wearing the FM device and facing away from the teacher. The child repeats each sound as the teacher says it 6 inches from the microphone. The sounds used are /a/, /oo/, /e/, /sh/, and /s/ and are representative of the speech energy contained in every English phoneme. If the child can detect these five sounds, he or she can detect every English speech sound (Ling, 1976). Responding to the sounds may take some practice for children who have not been encouraged to use their residual hearing to its fullest extent.

If the Ling Five Sound Test reveals absent or abnormal FM function, the teacher should always check the battery first. Some 90% of breakdowns reportedly are due to problems with the battery (Ross, 1981). The charge should be checked with a battery tester, because even a new battery or one that has been plugged in may not be fully charged. The teacher should make sure the battery is in the compartment properly and check to see that the poles match. A contact person should be available to take care of quick repairs. Many repairs such as replacing cords or receivers can be done inhouse by an audiologist, speech-language pathologist, or other trained personnel.

As soon as a hearing-impaired child enters any kind of classroom situation, even preschool, an FM device is necessary and appropriate. The child will need to wear the FM unit throughout the school day, since it provides vital assistance any time instructions or information are presented (e.g. gym rules, art, lunch, speech therapy, etc.).

Children never outgrow their need for FM units; even college students find them invaluable. Hearing-impaired people use the devices any time they wish to hear in public or group situations such as lectures, movies, or church services (Leavitt, 1985).

Summary

It is evident that FM auditory trainers are an integral part of educating hearing-impaired students. These units improve speech intelligibility by reducing the effects of background noise and reverberation and providing an adequate signal-to-noise ratio. There are no substitutes for the efficient use of residual hearing. Therefore, all hearing-impaired children mainstreamed into regular classrooms need FM units. If such a device is not provided, both teacher and child are made to function at an unnecessary disadvantage. The classroom teacher may need to serve as the child's advocate in order to maximize his or her potential for academic success and minimize the frustration often encountered when hearing-impaired pupils are mainstreamed.

References

Berg, F. S. (1986). Classroom acoustics and signal transmission. In F. J. Berg, K. C. Blair, S. H. Viehweg, & J. A. Wilson-Vlotman (Eds.), *Educational audiology for the hard of hearing child* (pp. 157-180). New York: Grune & Stratton.

Bess, F. H., & McConnell, F. E. (1981). *Audiology, education, and the hearing-impaired child.* St. Louis: C. V. Mosby.

Boothroyd, A. (1978). Speech perception and severe hearing loss. In M. Ross & T. G. Giolas (Eds.), *Auditory management of hearing-impaired children* (pp. 117-144). Baltimore: University Park Press.

Flexer, C., & Wood, L. A. (1984). The hearing aid: Facilitator or inhibitor of auditory interaction? *Volta Review, 86,* 354-355.

Hawkins, D. B. (1984). Comparisons of speech recognition in noise by mildly-to-moderately hearing-impaired children using hearing aids and FM systems. *Journal of Speech and Hearing Disorders, 49,* 409-418.

Jeffers, J., & Barley, M. (1971). *Speechreading (lipreading).* Springfield, IL: Charles C Thomas.

Leavitt, R. (1985). Counseling to encourage use of SNR enhancing systems. *Hearing Instruments, 36,* 8-9.

Ling, D. (1976). *Speech and the hearing-impaired child: Theory and practice.* Washington, DC: The Alexander Graham Bell Association for the Deaf.

Ross, M. (1981). Classroom amplification. In W. R. Hodgson and R. H. Skinna (Eds.), *Hearing aid assessment and use in audiologic habilitation* (2nd ed., pp. 234-257). Baltimore: Williams & Wilkins.

Ross, M., Brackett, D., & Maxon, A. (1982). *Hard-of-hearing children in regular schools.* Englewood Cliffs, NJ: Prentice-Hall.

Ross, M. & Giolas, T. G. (1978). *Auditory management of hearing-impaired children.* Baltimore: University Park Press.

VanTasell, D. J., Mallinger, C. A., & Crump, E. S. (1986). Functional gain and speech recognition with two types of FM amplification. *Language, Speech and Hearing Services in Schools, 17,* 28-37.

Zelski, R. F. K., & Zelski, T. (1985). What are assistive devices? *Hearing Instruments, 36,* 12.

Children With Visual Impairments

Visual impairment is legally defined as from 20/70 to 20/180 vision in the best eye after correction. Blindness is legally defined as 20/200 vision or less in the best eye after correction. These legal definitions are useful in the education of children with visual impairments for purposes of funding and allotment of resources. However, the degree of vision available for use is more important for individualized education programs. One must consider the amount of vision in the worst eye as well as in the best eye. One must also consider the field of peripheral vision (from 180 degrees to 20 degrees or less). A field of vision restricted to 20 degrees or less is assessed as legal blindness. Most children with visual impairments are more correctly termed low vision students because they have some useful vision. However, some of them may be assessed as legally blind for administrative purposes. Most legally blind persons have at least some perception of light, some degree of visual acuity, and some field of vision.

Students with visual impairments are the smallest group of children with disabilities being served under the mandates of the Education for All Handicapped Children Act (PL 94-142). Many of them are being educated in mainstreamed classrooms complying with the regular education initiative. Many mainstreamed children with low vision benefit from teacher-consultant services, itinerant teacher services, pull-out time in resource rooms, or cooperative class plans. Some mainstreamed children with visual impairments do not receive as many special services as they need to function in the regular classroom. Some children with low vision or legal blindness prefer education in a special class, a special day school, or a residential school designed for the visually impaired. It is important that parents, teachers, and vision specialists consider each individual child's age social skills, cognitive skills, communication skills, and self-concept as well as vision when assessing the environment in which the child will learn best. Each visually impaired student is entitled to an annually updated individualized education program (IEP). Flexibility should be available so that a child can move from a more restrictive environment to a less restrictive environment, or vice versa, depending on how well he or she is learning and developing.

Depending on the nature and the degree of the visual impairment, a teacher may need to become acquainted with a variety of technological equipment to assist the child with low vision to learn in the classroom. These aids may include talking books (books on tape), speech plus talking hand-held calculators, closed-circuit television, magnifiers, large-type books, special typewriters, braille writers, books in braille, an Optacon scanner, personal computers with special software, sonic guides, sonic pathfinders, and/or laser canes. The teacher should have enough knowledge about each piece of technological equipment to assure that the student with the visual impairment is using it correctly and appropriately. Each child with a disability should be challenged and motivated to learn while in school. The teacher should respond to legitimate requests for assistance. The teacher should not, however, give unwanted help, nor do the work for the student.

Each child with low vision needs to feel accepted by his or her more visually abled peers. The teacher plays a major role in encouraging positive interactions between children with and without visual impairments. The teacher should discuss each child's special visual needs with the class. Having one's very own personal computer, television, talking calculator, or other intriguing piece of technological equipment may be viewed as favoritism. The need for the equipment should be explained fully at the beginning of the school year and whenever questioned during the remainder of the school year. As each child with a visual handicap grows, develops, and learns, the special educational services required in the classroom will change. Therefore, with each new school year, and with each technological change, more explanations are required to help children without visual impairments understand the special child's needs.

Each child with low vision needs self-acceptance as well as peer acceptance. The teacher can enhance self-concept and self-esteem by encouraging the impaired child to be as active and independent as possible. Too often sympathetic teachers encourage passivity and dependence in blind or low vision students as a means of keeping them "safe." They will be safer, in fact, if they learn to take care of themselves in any situation and develop as many self-help skills as possible.

The first article selected for this unit addresses the need for early detection of visual handicaps. Children born with visual impairments should receive comprehensive multidisciplinary services as early as possible in infancy. Children who acquire visual impairments may have more social unresponsiveness while adjusting to low vision than children who are born visually impaired. Fam-

ily reactions to visual handicaps are generally negative. This article describes a parent and toddler training program that focuses not only on vision but also on parenting skills, the quality of family life, and the social responsiveness of the visually impaired child. The last two articles deal with classroom applications of services for visually impaired children. Geraldine Scholl discusses the development of individualized education programs (IEPs) for each unique child. She also addresses the issues of placement and the uses of technological equipment. The efficacy of classroom services for low vision students is examined in the last article. The use of technological equipment lags behind the need for low vision technological aids in most classrooms.

Looking Ahead: Challenge Questions

Can parents of visually impaired infants and toddlers provide intervention services for their children? Do they need intervention services themselves?

What constitutes appropriate education for children with visual impairments? What special technologies can be incorporated into their educational programs?

How many low vision students who qualify for special education services are actually receiving them?

The Parent and Toddler Training Project for Visually Impaired and Blind Multihandicapped Children

Abstract: Numerous clinical reports have shown that many families with visually impaired or blind multihandicapped children have problems of social and emotional adjustment and that the development of seriously handicapped children is enhanced by early intervention. This article describes the Parent and Toddler Training (PATT) Project—research-based early intervention program—that serves visually impaired and blind multihandicapped infants and toddlers and their families. The purpose of this project is to 1) increase the social responsiveness of handicapped infants, 2) implement a psychoeducational intervention program to develop adequate parenting skills, 3) initiate specific treatment approaches with parents to reduce psychological distress and improve the quality of family life, and 4) collect quantifiable data that permit the assessment of the progress of all participants.

B. Klein; V.B. Van Hasselt; M. Trefelner; D.J. Sandstrom; P. Brandt-Snyder

Barbara Klein, M.S.W., former project coordinator and social worker (PATT Project), Western Pennsylvania School for Blind Children, 201 North Bellefield Avenue, Pittsburgh, PA 15213; Vincent B. Van Hasselt, Ph.D., former project director (PATT Project), and presently assistant professor of psychiatry, Department of Psychiatry and Human Behavior at the University of California-Irvine Medical Center, 101 City Drive South, Orange, CA 92668; Mary Trefelner, child development specialist (PATT Project); Dorothy Sandstrom, M.S., senior child development specialist (PATT Project); and Patrice Brandt-Snyder, M.S., former senior child specialist (PATT Project).

In recent years, special educators, psychologists, and child development specialists have directed increased attention to social functioning in young children (see reviews by Gresham, 1981; Strain & Kerr, 1981; Van Hasselt, Hersen, Whitehill, & Bellack, 1979). The heightened activity in this area is attributable, in part, to research that has found that problems in social adaptation

Preparation of this article was facilitated by Grant No. G008302245 from the Handicapped Children's Early Education Program, U.S. Department of Education. The authors thank Judith A. Lorenzetty and Mary Jo Horgan for their assistance in preparing the manuscript.

may be associated with the quality of interpersonal relationships formed as early as infancy. A major developmental task for the first two years of life is to establish effective social interactions with others. This process is facilitated by the formation of a strong attachment (reciprocal relationship) between infants and their caregivers, usually their mothers (see the review by Campos, et al., 1983). The social interactions of handicapped infants, however, may be severely impaired (Odom, 1983). As Walker (1982) posited, ''the handicapped infant may have qualities that affect his [or her] abilities as initiator, elicitor, responder, and maintainer of synchrony in the interactive bout. He or she may be less reinforcing,

Journal of Visual Impairment & Blindness, Vol. 82, No. 2, February 1988, pp. 59-64, is reproduced with kind permission from American Foundation for the Blind. © 1988 by American Foundation for the Blind, 15 West 16th Street, New York, NY 10011.

less interesting, and more difficult as a social partner.''

The potential for the disruption of the social relationships of handicapped infants and their caretakers is perhaps more clearly illustrated by the behavior of blind children. For example, smiling is regarded as potent behavior for promoting infant-adult interactions (Odom, 1983) and is considered an "indicator of the infant's participation in a social relationship. . . and of the strength of the developing attachment bond" (Warren, 1977). However, blind infants, in comparison to their sighted counterparts, have a low rate of smiling and the quality of their smiles is different (Fraiberg, 1970, 1977). Another elicitor of infant-adult interactions is the ability of infants to establish eye contact and then a gaze. The role of eye contact as a "releaser of appropriate and personal maternal responses" has been discussed in the developmental literature for many years (Bakeman & Brown, 1977; Robson, 1967). Although empirical data regarding the amount of eye contact established by blind infants is limited (see Als, 1985; Als, Tronick, & Brazelton, 1980a; 1980b). Warren (1977) suggested that this response is also deficient in blind infants. Moreover, Fraiberg (1974) found that mothers were disturbed by the absence of gaze in their blind infants. Thus, the blind infants' minimal smiling, eye contact, and absent gaze may affect their ability to engage in social interactions.

In addition, parental behaviors and difficulties in adjustment have a direct impact on the quality and quantity of infant-adult social exchanges and, hence, may adversely affect the parent-child relationship (Lowenfeld, 1971; Sommers, 1944). For example, parents who feel angry, sad, guilty, or depressed about their handicapped child may not be able to identify and appropriately interpret their blind infant's signals. Their difficulties in adjustment are underscored by early case studies that found psychiatric symptomatology (primarily maternal depression) in some parents of blind children (see, for example, Catena, 1961; Fraiberg & Freedman, 1964).

To prevent problems in the social and emotional adjustment of visually impaired and blind multihandicapped infants and their families, the Parent and Toddler Training (PATT) Project was developed in October of 1983 at the Western Pennsylvania School for Blind Children in Pittsburgh. PATT was initiated through a grant from the Handicapped Children's Early Education Program of the U.S. Department of Education. The purpose of the project is to 1) enhance the social responsivity of visually impaired and blind multihandicapped infants and toddlers; 2) provide a psychoeducational training program that develops adequate parenting skills in families with a handicapped infant; 3) initiate specific interventions with distressed parents to improve their overall psychological adjustment and the quality of family life; and 4) conduct comprehensive assessments that yield quantifiable data regarding patterns of interaction and adjustment in participating families.

Population served
The population served by PATT includes newborn to 3-year-old visually impaired and blind multihandicapped infants and toddlers from Western Pennsylvania and the surrounding tri-state area. The major criterion for eligibility is legal blindness or suspected legal blindness, as determined by ophthalmological evaluations. In addition to legal blindness, the multihandicapped population served by PATT includes infants with neurological conditions, cerebral palsy, and metabolic or endocrine diseases. Referrals to PATT are made by ophthalmologists, pediatricians, health care agencies, friends, or parents. Direct involvement by at least one significant caregiver (the mother, father, or foster parent) is required. When families are intact, efforts are made to include both parents; when the parents have separated or divorced, a significant other (a relative or close friend) is recruited as a support person. The project consists of four phases: assessment, training, booster sessions, and follow-up.

Assessment
Assessments of infants and families are carried out using a variety of procedures. First, parents complete a number of self-report measures to evaluate their level of social and emotional functioning, including the Beck Depression Inventory (Beck, 1967), Minnesota Multiphasic Personality Inventory (Dahlstrom & Welsh, 1960), Questionnaire on Resources and Stress (Holroyd, 1974), and the Hopkins Symptoms Checklist (Derogatis, et al., 1974). In addition, parents answer questions about their level of marital satisfaction on the Locke-Wallace Marital Satisfaction Scale (Locke & Wallace, 1957) and of family support on the Family Support Scale (Dunst & Jenkins, 1983). Their perceptions of their handicapped child are evaluated by their answers on the Infant Temperament Scale (Carey & McDevitt, 1978), the Toddler Temperament Scale (Fullard, McDevitt, & Carey, in press), Vision-Up (Wright, 1980), and their perceptions of any nonhandicapped children in the family are evaluated by the Child Behavior Checklist-Parent Form (Achenbach, 1978). When age-appropriate, the handicapped child's siblings complete the Youth Self-Report Inventory (Achenbach & Edelbrock, 1979) to determine possible behavioral problems. The handicapped infant is assessed via the Adaptive Performance Instrument (Consortium on Adaptive Performance Evaluation, 1978).

Second, behavioral observations of parent-child interactions (mother-infant, father-infant, and mother-father-infant combinations) in play- and task-oriented situations are conducted for each family. These interactions are videotaped and retrospectively rated using guidelines developed by Wilcox and Campbell (1986) to examine such factors as the type of behavioral cues exhibited by infants during interactions, the consistency of responding, reciprocity, and the engagement of the infants.

Third, both physical and occupational therapy consultants complete an evaluation of each infant to examine gross and fine motor development, respectively. During these assessments, parents are encouraged to ask questions about their child's gross or fine motor development and are instructed by the therapists in specific remedial activities.

Fourth, the social worker and the assessment specialist make a home visit to observe the infant in a natural environment. At this time, the mother is administered the Home Inventory (Caldwell & Bradley, 1978), for additional information about the child's home life.

All assessment data are reviewed by PATT staff and utilized to design an appropriate individualized treatment plan for each family. Families are reevaluated after they complete the training program and at a six-month follow-up. This information allows PATT staff to monitor any significant changes that may occur in the infant and the family and to address them accordingly.

Training
The PATT curriculum is implemented after reviewing the assessment data. PATT cotrainers (a social worker and a senior child development specialist) sequentially address the following topics: 1) early childhood development, 2) social development, 3) the family members' reactions, 4) behavioral management, 5) enhancing

the infant's development, and 6) family communication and problem-solving. The components of the curriculum were selected on the basis of our previous clinical work and areas of need that have been identified in recent investigative efforts involving handicapped infants and their families (see Bricker, 1982). The project's curriculum offers parents information, training in a number of skills, and support to help them cope with current problems, as well as those that may arise.

Families participate in two-hour weekly sessions over a six-month period. They generally spend three to four two-hour sessions on each topic in the curriculum. Training includes a variety of components: didactic presentations, direct instruction, behavior rehearsal, feedback on performance, modeling, and role playing. In addition, homework assignments, in the form of self-monitoring and record-keeping of specific areas targeted in training, are used to monitor the progress of the infants and parents and to provide ongoing feedback to parents and staff.

The curriculum

As was noted, the PATT curriculum includes six topic areas designed to address the unique needs and difficulties of families with visually impaired or blind multihandicapped infants. These are outlined in the following sections.

Early child development
Visually impaired or blind multihandicapped infants may differ from non-impaired infants in that they often exhibit significant, albeit not necessarily permanent, delays in most areas of development (Adelson & Fraiberg, 1974; Fraiberg, 1968, 1977; Scholl, 1986; Warren, 1977, 1984). Such delays may produce considerable stress in parents. Providing parents with adequate knowledge about development and responding to their questions and concerns, therefore, are important initial steps in diminishing their distress. This topic area presents an overview of the 1) normal sequence of development, 2) nature of developmental delays typically found in visually impaired or blind multihandicapped infants, and 3) similarities and differences between handicapped and nonhandicapped infants in attaining developmental milestones. Parents are encouraged to assist their infants to maximize their potential for development. When developmental delays occur, parents come to understand that with practice and adapted environmental experiences, their baby can make progress. Parents of multihandicapped infants are helped to understand the nature of the handicapping conditions, their synergistic effects, and their possible impact on their infants' overall development.

Social development
Parents' early interactions with their baby, their attitudes toward his or her disability, and the opportunities they provide are crucial to their child's short- and long-term adaptive functioning. As was previously noted, certain interactions foster the attachment between infants and their parents. When these behaviors are absent, deficient, or misunderstood, attachment may be delayed or seriously disrupted. This topic provides information on the social development of infants, the relationship of synchrony and reciprocity as they relate to parent-infant interactions, atypical or alternative cues that the visually handicapped infant may provide to parents, the types of decreased social responsiveness demonstrated in many visually handicapped infants (such as the lack of eye contact, delayed smiling, the tendency to be quiet and less mobile at the approach of a parent), and the impact of blindness on an infant's social development. To promote a healthy and reciprocal social relationship, parents are taught to identify their baby's interactive cues and to respond appropriately and consistently with the same (or even greater) quantity and quality of attention as they would give to a nonhandicapped infant.

Family reactions
As was mentioned earlier, numerous reports have described negative reactions, including stress, grief, anxiety, and depression, of parents to the diagnosis of a handicapping condition in their child (Beckman, 1983; Breslau, Staruch, & Mortimer, 1982; Catena; 1961; Fraiberg & Freedman, 1964; Froyd, 1973). The acknowledgement of these reactions and the realization of their commonality in many families can be of considerable therapeutic value to parents. Furthermore, a conceptualization of each member of the parental dyad as the primary support for the other helps to underscore the vital role of reciprocity in their relationship. In this topic, these issues are discussed to facilitate the couple's examination of their feelings, reactions, and attitudes and to help them begin to explore new ways of perceiving their infant and their relationship.

The reactions of the extended family can also have a significant impact on the family. For example, siblings of the handicapped child are a group that has received surprisingly little attention (see review by Skritic, Summers, Brotherson, & Turnbull, 1984). According to Clay (1961) and Bentovim (1972), the time and energy directed to the handicapped child often results in the neglect of other children in the family. The social isolation of the families also has a limiting effect on the breadth and scope of siblings' interpersonal behavior. Bentovim (1972) argued that the presence of a handicapped child may lead to the following responses of siblings: 1) aggressive, attention-seeking behavior, 2) anxiety, 3) depression, and 4) jealousy. These problems are discussed to help parents understand the various reasons for the reactions of siblings and extended family members and to encourage parents to seek alternative ways to elicit more understanding and support.

Behavioral management
Most parents use some techniques (for instance, positive reinforcement and punishment) that are based on learning principles in dealing with their children. However, such approaches often are ineffective because they are applied incorrectly or unsystematically. An understanding of fundamental learning principles and the use of behavioral interventions enables parents to manage problems related to their infants, as well as other children in the family, more effectively. In this topic, parents are trained to use specific behavioral management strategies and to implement behavioral intervention programs at home. In one case, parents were taught to plan and execute a behavioral management program for their visually impaired toddler who displayed high rates of eye pressing. They were asked to keep a record for two weeks of the number of times the problem behavior occurred. The staff charted these baseline (pretreatment) data (Figure 1), and then directed the parents to begin a program of positive reinforcement and contingent hands restraint in the following manner. First, each time the toddler pressed his eyes, the parent was to give a loud verbal cue ("Stop!") and restrain the toddler's hands in front of him for 30 seconds. At the end of this interval, the parent released the toddler's hands and continued with regular activities. The parents were also instructed to provide positive reinforcement in the form of verbal praise when the toddler was engaged in appropriate motor activities. As Figure 1 shows, one week of this treatment procedure resulted in a significant suppression of eye-pressing behavior. The parents reported that when the child's hands started in the direction

of his eyes, all they eventually had to do was use the verbal cue and he would immediately put his hands down.

Enhancing the infant's development
Mothers often report feeling stressed and overwhelmed by the increased burden and responsibilities of caring for their handicapped infants. Although the role of fathers in these families has only recently been the focus of investigation, the research has indicated that the level of the father's involvement may have a significant effect on 1) the infant's overall development, 2) effectiveness and satisfaction of both the father and the mother, and 3) the quality of the marital relationship (Meyer, 1986; Meyer, Vadasy, Fewell, & Schell, 1982; Vadasy, Fewell, Meyer, & Greenberg, 1985; Vadasy, et al., 1986). This topic provides strategies for increasing the father's role in care giving activities with the handicapped child. A skills-training format is used to enhance the fathers' ability to perform certian daily routines, such as bathing and feeding, with their handicapped child.

A second aspect of this topic involves instructing parents in a variety of infant-stimulation techniques and play skills that are relevant to their handicapped infants. Some of these procedures involve showing parents how to use 1) hand-over-hand skills to teach visually impaired children to wind up a toy, drink from a cup, or feed themselves, 2) objects to elicit motor and verbal responses from their infants, and 3) tactile and kinesthetic stimulation to compensate for diminished sensory input. Parents are taught that play stimulation activities should include practice in movement, communication, and a variety of sensory experiences. They then begin to identify appropriate skills that can be shaped to become part of the handicapped children's behavioral repertoire.

Family communication and problem solving
The birth of any baby requires the devotion of substantial time and energy to the tasks and demands of caregiving. In the case of handicapped infants in general and the visually impaired infants in particular, the commitments of time, energy, and responsibilities are even greater and often place a tremendous strain on the marital relationship (Blacher, 1984; Gath, 1977; Jan, Freeman, & Scott, 1977; Tavormina, et al., 1981). Studies have found that parents of handicapped children spend less time together and often decrease the extent of their individual social activities. The well-documented association between marital

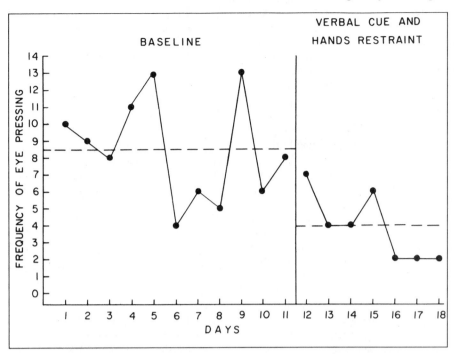

Figure 1. Baseline and treatment phases of a behavior modification program implemented to reduce eye pressing in a visually impaired toddler.

satisfaction and parental effectiveness underscores the need for intervention in this area (Emery, 1982; Long, Forehand, Fauber, & Brody, 1987; Margolin, 1981).

The concept of marital partners as mutual support persons is emphasized in this topic. Parents are trained in specific skills to increase the efficacy of their efforts to effect changes in their relationships. The primary aim is to resolve conflicts through behavioral and cognitive changes. Role-play and problem-solving tasks are utilized to give parents the opportunity to practice requisite skills. Parents are provided with guidelines for simplifying the process of decision-making and then assigned the task of solving relevant family or marital problems. When parents return for their next session, they discuss the specific steps taken at home to resolve conflicts or diminish distress.

Booster sessions and follow-up
Booster sessions are reviews of areas in which the parents were trained. They take place after the families' participation in the PATT program has formally ended. In this phase, parents meet monthly with staff for about three to six months. The topics that are covered in the booster sessions depend on the problems, deficits, concerns, and questions that have arisen in the preceding period. The purposes of booster sessions are to 1) consolidate the gains made during the project's training phase, 2) facilitate the maintenance and

generalization of intervention effects, and 3) provide parents with continued support, information, and feedback.

During the next six months, booster sessions are faded to bimonthly meetings. During this follow-up period, the PATT staff provides ongoing coordination and consultation with community-based agencies in an effort to maintain a consistent overall program.

Other parental activities
With the multitudinous tasks that are inherent in the care of a visually impaired or multihandicapped infant, it is not unusual for parents to feel isolated from the mainstream of normal life. Throughout the course of the PATT project, various social activities (for example, birthday parties for infants, holiday celebrations, and visits to the zoo) are scheduled for families. Siblings are always included and grandparents often participate as well. Opportunities are also provided for parents to meet and network with other parents of visually impaired or multihandicapped children through their participation in such voluntary activities as a parent support group that meets once a month. In the group, the parents are responsible for planning and conducting their own meetings, and guest speakers are invited to discuss pertinent issues concerning handicapped children and their families.

Conclusion
By providing efficacious early intervention

to families with visually impaired or blind multihandicapped infants and toddlers, PATT is attempting to prevent possible social and emotional difficulties in these children later in life. A more immediate goal is to decrease the stress of and improve adaptation in families. A major impetus for PATT is the realization that few such models are available to address the complexities of parenting a young blind or multihandicapped child.

Observational and self-report data are providing important information about the deficits and strengths of families who have visually impaired and multihandicapped infants. We believe that the evaluation and training components developed in this project will be of considerable value to families with such infants or toddlers. Furthermore, the PATT project is replicable and compatible with a variety of special education systems. Indeed, PATT already is being replicated in a rural setting to contrast the experiences of an urban-based program with that of a less densely populated area in which services are scarce.

The impact of PATT on participating children and families has yet to be empirically determined. However, preliminary analyses and anecdotal reports from families seem to suggest the utility of this effort. Data pertaining to the assessment of infant and family functioning and treatment outcome will be disseminated soon.

References

Achenbach, T. (1978). The child behavior profile: I. Boys age 6–11. *Journal of Consulting & Clinical Psychology,* **46,** 478–488.

Achenbach, T., & Edelbrock, C. (1979). The child behavior profile: II. Boys age 12–16 and girls age 6–11 12–16. *Journal of Consulting & Clinical Child Psychology,* **47,** 223–233.

Adelson, E., & Fraiberg, S. (1974). Gross motor development in infants blind from birth. *Child Development, 45,* 114–126.

Als, H. (1985). Reciprocity and autonomy: Parenting a blind infant. *Zero to Three,* **5,** 8–10.

Als, H., Tronick, E., & Brazelton, T.B. (1980a). Affective reciprocity and the development of autonomy. *Journal of the American Academy of Child Psychiatry, 19,* 22–40.

Als, H., Tronick, E., & Brazelton, T.B. (1980b). Stages of early behavioral organization: The study of a sighted infant and a blind infant in interaction with their mothers. In T.M. Field, D. Stern, A. Sostek, & S. Goldberg (eds.). *High-risk infants and children: Adult and peer interactions.* New York: Academic Press.

Bakeman, R., & Brown, J.V. (1977). Behavioral dialogues: An approach to the assessment of mother-infant interaction. *Child Development,* **48,** 195–208.

Beck, A.T. (1967). *Depression: Causes and treatment.* Philadelphia: University of Pennsylvania Press.

Beckman, P.J. (1983). Influence of selected child characteristics on stress in families of handicapped infants. *American Journal of Mental Deficiency,* **88,** 150–156.

Bentovim, A. (1972). Handicapped pre-school children and their families: Effects on child's early emotional development. *British Medical Journal, 9,* 634–637.

Blacher, J. (ed.) (1984). *Severely handicapped young children and their families: Research in review.* New York: Academic Press.

Breslau, N., Staruch, K.S., & Mortimer, E.A. (1982). Psychological distress in mothers of disabled children. *American Journal of Diseases of Children,* **136,** 682–686.

Bricker, D.D. (ed.) (1982). *Intervention with at-risk and handicapped infants: From research to application.* Baltimore: University Park Press.

Caldwell, B., & Bradley, R. (1978). *Home observation of the environment.* Unpublished manuscript, University of Arkansas at Little Rock

Campos, J., Barrett, K., Lamb, M., Goldsmith, H., & Stenberg, C. (1983). Socioemotional development. In P. Mussen (ed.). *Handbook of Child Psychology, 4th ed., Vol. 2: Infancy.* New York: John Wiley & Sons.

Consortium on Adaptive Performance Evaluation (1978). *Adaptive assessment for evaluating the progress of severely profoundly handicapped children functioning between birth and 2 years.* Annual report of a field-initiated research project funded by the Bureau of Education for the Handicapped.

Carey, W.B., & McDevitt, S.C. (1978). Revision of the Infant Temperament Questionnaire. *Pediatrics, 61,* 735–739.

Catena, J. (1961). Pre-adolescence: The caseworker and the family. *New Outlook for the Blind, 55,* 297–299.

Clay, F. (1961). Social work and the blind child. *New Outlook for the Blind, 55,* 321–325.

Dahlstrom, W.G., & Welsh, G.S. (1960). *MMPI handbook.* Minneapolis: University of Minnesota Press.

Dunst, C.J., & Jenkins, V. (1983). *The family support scale: Reliability and validity.* Morganton, NC: Family, Infant and Preschool Program, Western Carolina Center.

Derogatis, L.R., Lipman, R.S., Rickels, D., Uhlenhuth, E.H., & Covi, L. (1974). The Hopkins Symptom Checklist (HSCL): A self-report symptom inventory. *Behavioral Science, 19,* 1–15.

Emery, R.E. (1982). Interparental conflict and the children of discord and divorce. *Psychological Bulletin,* **92,** 310–330.

Fraiberg, S. (1968). Parallel and divergent patterns in blind and sighted infants. *Psychoanalytic Study of the Child, 23,* 264–300.

Fraiberg, S. (1970). Smiling and stranger reaction in blind infants. In J. Hellmuth (ed.). *Exceptional infant.* New York: Brunner-Mazel.

Fraiberg, S. (1974). Blind infants and their mothers: An examination of the sign system. In M. Lewis & L. Rosenblum (eds.). *The effect of the infant on its caregiver.* New York: John Wiley & Sons.

Fraiberg, S. (1977). *Insights from the blind.* New York: Basic Books.

Fraiberg, S., & Freedman, D. (1964). Studies in the ego-development of the congenitally blind child. *Psychoanalytic Study of the Child, 19,* 155–169.

Froyd, H.E. (1973). Counseling families of severely visually handicapped children. *New Outlook for the Blind, 67,* 251–257.

Fullard, W., McDevitt, S.C., Carey, W.B. (in press). Assessing temperament in one to three year old children. *Journal of Pediatric Psychology.*

Gath, A. (1977). The impact of an abnormal child upon the parents. *British Journal of Psychiatry, 130,* 405–410.

Gresham, F.M. (1981). Social skills training with handicapped children: A review. *Review of Educational Research,* **51,** 139–176.

Holroyd, J. (1974). The Questionnaire on Resources and Stress: An instrument to measure family response to a handicapped member. *Journal of Community Psychology, 2,* 92–94.

Jan, J.E., Freeman, R.D., & Scott, E.P. (eds.) (1977). *Visual impairment in children and adolescents.* New York: Grune & Stratton.

Locke, H.J., & Wallace, K.M. (1957). Short marital adjustment and prediction tests: Their reliability and validity. *Marriage & Family Living, 42,* 118–123.

Long, N., Forehand, R., Fauber, R., & Brody, G.H. (1987). Self-perceived and independently observed competence of young adolescents as a function of parental marital conflict and recent divorce. *Journal of Abnormal Child Psychology, 15,* 15–28.

Lowenfeld, B. (1971). *Our blind children: Growing and learning with them.* Springfield, IL: Charles C Thomas

Margolin, G. (1981). The reciprocal relationship between marital and child problems. In J.P. Vincent (ed.). *Advances in family intervention, assessment and theory: An annual compilation of research* (Vol. 2). Greenwich, CT: JAI Press.

Meyer, D.J. (1986). Fathers of children with mental handicaps. In M.E. Lamb (ed.). *The father's role: Applied perspectives.* New York: John Wiley & Sons.

Meyer, D.J., Vadasy, P.F., Fewell, R.R., & Schell, G. (1982). Involving fathers of handicapped infants: Translating research into program goals. *Journal of the Division for Early Childhood, 5,* 64–72.

Odom, S. (1983). The development of social interchanges. In S. Garwood & R. Fewell (eds.). *Educating handicapped infants: Issues in development and intervention.* Rockville, MD: Aspen.

Robson, K.S. (1967). The role of eye-to-eye contact in maternal-infant attachment. *Journal of Clinical Psychiatry,* **8,** 13.

Scholl, G.T. (1986). Growth and development. In G.T. Scholl (ed.). *Foundations of education for blind and visually handicapped children and youth: Theory and practice.* New York: American Foundation for the Blind.

Skritic, T.M., Summers, J.A., Brotherson, M.J., & Turnbull, A.P. (1984). Severely handicapped children and their brothers and sisters. In J. Blacher (ed.). *Severely handicapped young children and their families: Research in review.* New York: Academic Press.

Sommers, V.S. (1944). *The influence of parental attitudes and social environment on the personality development of the adolescent blind.* New York: American Foundation for the Blind.

Strain, P.S., & Kerr, M.M. (1981). Modifying children's social withdrawal: Issues in assessment and clinical intervention. In M. Hersen, R.M. Eisler, & P.M. Miller (eds). *Progress in behavior modification* (Vol. 2). New York: Academic Press.

Tavormina, J.B., Boll, T.J., Dunn, N.J., Luscomb, R.L., & Taylor, J.R. (1981). Psychosocial effects on parents of raising a physically handicapped child. *Journal of Abnormal Child Psychology,* **9,** 121–131.

Vadasy, P.F., Fewell, R.R., Meyer, D.J., & Greenberg, M.T. (1985). Supporting fathers of handicapped young children: Preliminary findings of program effects. *Analysis and Intervention in Developmental Disabilities,* **5,** 151–163.

Vadasy, P.F., Fewell, R.R., Greenberg, M.T., Dermond, N.L., & Meyer, D.J. (1986). Follow-up evaluation of the effects of involvement in the fathers program. *Topics in Early Childhood Special Education,* **2,** 16–31.

Van Hasselt, V.B., Hersen, M., Whitehill, M.B., & Bellack, A.B. (1979). Social skill assessment and training for children: An evaluative review. *Behaviour Research and Therapy,* **17,** 413–437.

Walker, J. (1982). Social interactions of handicapped infants. In D.D. Bricker (ed.). *Intervention with at-risk and handicapped infants: From research to application.* Baltimore: University Park Press.

Warren, D.H. (1977). *Blindness and early childhood development.* New York: American Foundation for the Blind.

Warren, D.H. (1984). *Blindness and early childhood development* (rev. ed.). New York: American Foundation for the Blind.

Wilcox, M.J., & Campbell, P.H. (1986). Interaction patterns of mothers and their infants with severe handicaps. Paper presented to Division of Early Childhood Conference on Children with Special Needs, Louisville.

Wright, F.J., (1980). Project Vision-Up Assessment, validity and reliability. Unpublished doctoral dissertation, Brigham Young University, Provo, UT.

Appropriate Education for
VISUALLY HANDICAPPED STUDENTS

Geraldine T. Scholl

Geraldine T. Scholl *(CEC Chapter #551) is Professor of Education at the School of Education, The University of Michigan, Ann Arbor.*

■ The provisions of Public Law 94-142 (Education for All Handicapped Children Act of 1975) present many challenges to school administrators and teachers as they strive to implement appropriate educational programs for visually handicapped pupils. Three major challenges are assessment, placement in the least restrictive environment, and planning an appropriate program. Who are visually handicapped pupils? What special educational needs do they have that are unique to them because of their visual impairment? Finally, what should be included in their individualized education programs (IEP's) to assure them equal educational opportunities? This article will explore these questions, focusing on pupils whose only special education needs are those that accompany a visual impairment. (Additional adaptations are necessary when other handicapping conditions are present.)

Who Is Visually Handicapped?

Pupils with visual impairments constitute a relatively small portion of the total school population—approximately 1 in 1000—and they make up only about 1% of all handicapped pupils served in special education programs and services (Kirchner, 1985). Thus, a school district with 20,000 pupils might expect about 20 to have moderate to severe visual impairments that will require special educational programs and services. However, because of the heterogeneity of this population, it might not be possible to group those 20 pupils for educational purposes. Some of the reasons are as follows:

- They might represent the entire age span from birth through high school.
- They are very likely to have other impairments that may be more educationally handicapping than their visual impairments.
- They have a broad range of visual abilities.
- They have a broad range of intellectual abilities.
- They have educational needs that might require different service delivery systems.
- They may come from families with a wide variety of socioeconomic and cultural characteristics.
- They may have a minimal support system provided by their families.
- They may reside in geographical locations that preclude having a full continuum of services available to them.

Thus, teachers typically have limited opportunities to become familiar with the special educational needs of this small but heterogeneous population. A commitment by school administrators to provide appropriate educational programs for *all* children is required to assure equal educational opportunities.

Special Educational Needs

A visual impairment can modify the normal patterns of growth and development, creating barriers to learning. Visually handicapped students may have delayed concept development, must learn through other sensory channels, (e.g., touch and hearing), need specialized skills and equipment for learning, are limited in learning through observation and incidental learning, often require individualized instruction to learn specialized skills, and require unique strategies or adaptations to acquire necessary skills (California Leadership Action Team for the Visually Impaired, 1985).

The impact of these barriers will differ for each individual pupil, depending on the variables associated with the visual impairment (age of onset, degree of vision, etiology of the visual impairment); the presence of other educationally handicapping conditions such as mental retardation or emotional disturbance; attitudes of family, school, and community; and the social and cultural characteristics of the family.

From birth onward visual impairments limit or deprive pupils of a valuable source of sensory input. This may have an impact on cognitive development, causing delays and deficiencies that interfere with social, emotional, psychomotor, academic, and vocational development. Learning by visual imitation often is not possible and incidental learning is limited. Some concepts, for example, color and three dimensions, may never be acquired. To compensate for these deficits, pupils must be provided with specialized media, materi-

A partially sighted volunteer (l) helps a totally blind student (r) develop her manual dexterity in the Work Activity Center.

als, equipment, and instruction in compensatory skills to learn to use their limited vision effectively and efficiently and to maximize the use of other sensory channels in the learning process, primarily hearing and touch. In implementing such a compensatory education program, school and family must cooperate to teach skills that other pupils learn naturally by visual observation.

The Educational Program

Modifications in assessment procedures, creative placement practices, and IEP's specifically designed to meet their unique educational needs are essential ingredients of educational programs designed to assist visually handicapped pupils overcome barriers to learning.

Modifications in Assessment

Identification of these pupils presents the first challenge to school personnel. Young children have no frame of reference to let the adults in their environment know that they have a vision problem. Routine vision screening programs may not be adequate since most screen only for distance vision. Therefore, parents and teachers must be aware of the signs of possible eye trouble, as shown in Figure 1. Teachers of pupils with other handicapping conditions especially must be aware of possible unidentified visual impairments that may hinder the progress of their pupils.

After visual impairment has been identified, the next step is to assess whether or not the impairment is educationally handicapping. Eligibility for special education programs and services usually is based on an eye examination by an ophthalmologist or optometrist. While this is a necessary component of a comprehensive assessment, the results often have little relevance for educational planning. A qualified teacher of visually handicapped pupils should be requested to administer a functional vision assessment.

Instruments designed for this purpose usually consist of checklists based on observation of the pupils performing visual tasks (see Jose, 1983; Swallow, Mangold, & Mangold, 1978). Functional vision assessments coupled with medical eye examinations are helpful in determining what pupils see and how well they are using the vision they have. For pupils who retain some vision, an optometrist may be consulted to determine whether or not a low-vision aid might be useful.

Although an assessment of the visual impairment is the critical component for determining eligibility for services, other areas such as intellectual functioning, emotional-social skills, and career-vocational skills should also be assessed in order to develop the IEP. Tests specifically designed for pupils with visual impairments are few in number; yet they are critical since the use of instruments standardized on other populations is questionable (Warren, 1984). (See Bauman & Knopf, 1979; Hall, Scholl, & Swallow, 1986; Scholl & Schnur, 1976; Swallow, 1981 for lists.)

Teachers of visually handicapped pupils should participate in planning the assessment and should function as consultants to school psychologists so that the comprehensive assessment of the pupil's abilities can lead to an appropriate IEP (Morse, 1975; Spungin & Swallow, 1977). Informal or nonstandardized assessment procedures such as observation, interviews, and curriculum-based approaches may yield more meaningful educational information. (See Hall et al., 1986; Oka & Scholl, 1985; Swallow et al., 1978; and Tucker, 1981 for descriptions of these alternatives.)

Creative Placement Practices

Selecting an appropriate placement probably presents the greatest challenge to administrators. A full continuum of services for pupils with visual impairments as required by P.L. 94-142 is not likely to be available in the typical school district, resulting in school administrators sometimes considering placement in another special class or program in the school district or in a residential school. However, these options may not be appropriate for many pupils. The decision should be based on what is most appropriate for each student, and this often requires creative planning.

Education of visually handicapped pupils in integrated settings can be successful only with the specialized help of professionals qualified to understand and interpret the educational needs unique to the visual impairment and regular teachers who are provided with the support they need to work effectively in meeting those needs. Cooperation with local agencies and organizations, making use of all available community resources, pooling resources to encompass a wider geographical area, and professional development for all regular school personnel may help the school district with few visually handicapped pupils create the multiple program options necessary for appropriate placements. Several states use the intermediate school district organizational structure effectively to serve low-prevalence groups with, for example, one district operating the program for hearing impaired students and another for the visually impaired populations of both districts.

Individualized Education Programs

All components of the regular curriculum offered to nonhandicapped pupils should also be available to visually handicapped pupils, even including the classroom activities that accompany driver education. The IEP should detail which of these instructional areas a particular pupil should study with nonhandicapped peers.

To meet their special education needs, visually handicapped pupils require instruction from specialists and use of special techniques in certain areas. In the communication skills area, they need instruction in the following:

- Reading-tactile forms (braille and Optacon).
- Reading-auditory forms (readers, talking books, Kurzweil Machine, and cassettes).
- Reading-print forms (large type and low-vision aids).
- Writing (Braillewriter, slate and stylus, handwriting, and typewriter).
- Computer literacy.

Visual efficiency training should include nonverbal communication, science/mathematics, social studies, map reading, and reference skills. Additional instructional areas include concept development, orientation and mobility, and independent living skills.

Substitutes for the typical visual materials used in classrooms are essential, including textbooks—in braille for some, in large print for others—and recorded materials. The Optacon should be provided for tactile readers. The Optacon is a device that enables blind students to read regular print; images on the retina of a miniature camera activate tiny pins to vibrate in the shape of the letters so that they can be perceived by the finger. Volunteer readers can be recruited from local agencies or the nonhandicapped student population to help out when materials in these media are not accessible. For some pupils with very limited vision, low-vision aids can provide access to visual materials. These aids may include hand-held magnifiers, telescopes, or closed-circuit televisions.

Teachers of the visually handicapped or the state department of education consultant for the visually handicapped are the best resources for locating such materials. Some instructional materials resource centers provide valuable assistance in procuring needed materials. Additional teaching suggestions include the following:

- Braillewriters, slates, and styli to facilitate written communication for pupils who are tactile learners.
- Felt tip pens and wide lined paper for those who are visual learners.
- Cassettes for pupils with physical disabilities that inhibit the use of their hands or whose vision loss is recent.
- Typewriters for all visually handicapped pupils.
- Microcomputers with large print, braille, and voice output options.

Pupils with visual impairments often are limited in their ability to move about safely, gracefully, and easily. Qualified teachers can provide instruction in orientation and mobility skills. Additional work in physical education is helpful to improve posture, fitness, orientation, and mobility skills.

Because visual impairment may prohibit students from learning by visual imitation, their independent living and social skills such as self-care in dressing and eating are often limited and must be taught, frequently through individualized instruction. Social skills areas such as getting along with peers, engaging in turn taking in conversation, and other social graces often require direct

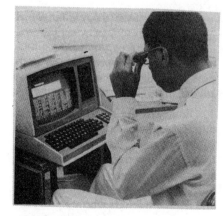

A student uses a prescription telescopic lens to help him read the screen of a computer.

instruction. These areas are the joint responsibility of parents and both regular and special education teachers.

Except for those who have no vision, all pupils with visual impairments should be instructed in techniques that will help them use their vision more effectively and efficiently. This includes special instruction in visual efficiency as well as the proper use of specialized materials and equipment and appropriate low-vision aids. Again, teachers of visually handicapped pupils are the best suited to help pupils in these areas.

Nonacademic or extracurricular experiences, including clubs, recess, and athletics, should not be neglected. Play is an important part in the life of all pupils and provides experiences in social learning. Visually handicapped pupils may need help in joining into games and other physical activities on the playground. Skill in indoor games should also be developed to provide future leisure activities. When age-appropriate, participation in community activities such as Scouts should be introduced.

Conclusion

Visually handicapped pupils are a small group of handicapped pupils who are more similar to than different from their nonhandicapped peers. Their visual impairment is, in general, little known and understood, so that they are often considered more different than they actually are.

They have the same educational needs as all other pupils. The major difference lies in their need for compensatory education to meet their unique educational requirements. School administrators and teachers must work in concert with parents and other professional personnel qualified in the area of visual impairments to ensure that the IEP includes the full range of instructional areas: those studied with their nonhandicapped peers, those that require special instruction, and those outside of the school curriculum that are essential to enable them to compete with their nonhandicapped peers when they move into the adult world.

References

Bauman, M. K., & Knopf, C. A. (1979). Psychological tests used with blind and visually handicapped persons. *School Psychology Digest, 8,* 257-270.

California Leadership Action Team for the Visually Impaired. (1985). *Statement of educational needs of visually impaired students in California.* San Francisco, CA: American Foundation for the Blind.

Hall, A., Scholl, G. T., & Swallow, R. M. (1986). Assessment. In G. T. Scholl (Ed.), *Foundation of education for blind and visually handicapped children and youth: Theory and practice* (pp.187-214). New York: American Foundation for the Blind.

Jose, R. T. (1983). *Understanding low vision.* New York: American Foundation for the blind.

Kirchner, C. (1985). *Data on blindness and visual impairment in the U.S.* New York: American Foundation for the Blind.

Morse, J. L. (1975). Answering the questions of the psychologist assessing the visually handicapped child. *The New Outlook for the Blind, 69,* 350-353.

National Society to Prevent Blindness (NSPB). (1978). *Signs of possible eye trouble in children.* (Pub. G-102.) New York: Author.

Oka, E., & Scholl, G. T. (1985). Non-test-based approaches to assessment. In G. T. Scholl (Ed.), *The school psychologist and the exceptional child* (pp. 39-59). Reston, VA: The Council for Exceptional Children.

Scholl, G. T., & Schnur, R. (1976). *Measures of psychological, vocational, & educational functioning in the blind and visually handicapped.* New York: American Foundation for the Blind.

Spungin, S. J., & Swallow, R.-M. (1977). Psychological assessment: Role of psychologist to teacher of the visually handicapped. In Swallow, R.-M. (Ed.) *Assessment for visually handicapped children and youth* (pp. 67-82). New York: American Foundation for the Blind.

Swallow, R.-M. (Ed.). (1977). *Assessment for visually handicapped children and youth.* New York: American Foundation for the Blind.

Swallow, R.-M. (1981). Fifty assessment instruments commonly used with blind and partially seeing individuals. *Journal of Visual Impairment and Blindness, 75,* 65-72.

Swallow, R.-M., Mangold, S., & Mangold, P. (1978). *Informal assessment of developmental skills for visually handicapped students.* New York: American Foundation for the Blind.

Tucker, J. A. (1981). *Non test-based assessment: A training module.* Minneapolis, MN: National School Psychology In-service Training Network, University of Minnesota.

Warren, D. (1984). *Blindness and early childhood development* (2nd ed.). New York: American Foundation for the Blind.

Efficacy of Low Vision Services for Visually Impaired Children

Abstract: Though it is known that visually impaired children can be helped by low vision aids, little research has been done on the use of such aids by children. In this study of 137 children, subjects were screened for visual capacity. Where appropriate, recommendations were made that they be examined further, in most cases by low vision specialists and in others by general optometrists. Follow-up was made on many of the children who received aids as a result of these examinations to determine whether the aids were being used effectively.

H.W Hofstetter

Henry W Hofstetter, O.D., Ph.D., professor emeritus of optometry, Indiana University, 2615 Windermere Woods Drive, Bloomington, IN 47401.

Several studies of adults classified as visually impaired have demonstrated that a majority, whether or not they routinely receive conventional vision care services, can be significantly helped by specialized ophthalmic analyses, low vision aids, and supportive rehabilitation services (Mayer, 1927; Feinbloom, 1935; Freeman, 1954; IHB Optical Aids Survey, 1957). However, the studies included few if any children, because the frequency of visual impairments uncorrectable by conventional eyewear is highly correlated with aging.

In addition to the lack of studies, a well-known physiological factor points to the need for a separate study of children who are visually impaired. It is the phenomenon of accommodation: the ability of the normal or optically corrected eye to focus clearly on objects at various distances. This physiological function is greatest in infancy and gradually declines to zero by about age 58. In contrast, an 18-year-old can normally see clearly from infinity to within 5 inches of the face, and a 6-year-old can see clearly up to about 3 inches.

This ability enables the school-age child to get an image on his or her retina that is double, triple, or even quadruple its normal size, merely by holding an object extremely close to the face. Therefore, a child is less likely than an older person to utilize a low vision aid for reading, even though it might have been recommended. Differences in the frequency of successful utilization by children and adults justify a separate investigation of children.

Another reason study is needed is to determine how schools follow up with low vision children. It has been too readily assumed that because a child has been certified as visually impaired, there is continuous follow-up with rehabilitation measures that will enable him or her to utilize residual vision more effectively (Hofstetter, 1983). On the contrary, there seems to be an "abandoning attitude," held by general eye professionals as well as others, that the low vision child should simply be taught how best to live with the handicap. Study is essential to clarify the attitudes and presumptions of adults.

Final considerations for undertaking the study are the explosion in low vision aid technology and the emergence of low vision care as a professional specialty. These developments raise the question of whether the successes reported in the earlier surveys indicate the rehabilitative potentials today.

The study described here and elsewhere (Hofstetter 1985, 1988) was designed to screen a sample of low vision children from all grade levels, determine their visual capability, prescribe the most effective low vision aids, and in cooperation with teachers, evaluate the degree of successful utilization of aids.

Procedure

This study was carried out from 1985 to 1988. Personnel included a coordinator from the Indiana Department of Education, seven optometrist members of the Indiana Low Vision Rehabilitation Society, teachers of the visually impaired, and directors of special education. The low vision children were identified by interdisciplinary committees (administrative, teaching, nursing, and/or medical personnel) as having visual defects which, even with conventional eyewear, necessitated special education. The interdisciplinary committee relied on information provided by whatever local optometrist or ophthalmologist each child had consulted, plus whatever other criteria might have indicated the advisability of special teaching procedures.

Team members contacted teachers of the visually impaired to enlist their cooperation in identifying eligible children and in arranging for screening dates and working space. The parents or guardians of 137 children—almost all of whom were invited to let their visually impaired children participate—signed the consent form. Although three of the children did not show up for screening, all 137, approximately 25 percent of Indiana students classified as visually impaired, were included in the study.

Geographically, the participants represented communities in 15 counties. No single school provided more than 13 percent of the participants, and no single low vision examiner was clinically involved with more than 28 percent of them.

As described in the original report (Hofstetter, 1985), the screening procedure was an abridgement of the complex examining procedures employed by low vision specialists, but it included several trials with optical magnifiers for distant and near viewing. After processing, the records for each child included information provided by the child's responses, the parent or guardian, the teacher, the optometrist performing the tests, and in cases referred for clinical evaluation, by the optometrist or an associate low vision specialist. With input from so many sources, there were numerous omissions in isolated categories of data, necessitating selective analyses of data to include for each inference only the paired correlation factors for which reliable entries had been made. For example, in several instances funds were unavailable to purchase prescribed low vision aids, so utilization could not be computed.

One particular shortcoming of the procedure was the lack of rehabilitative services as a follow-up to the prescription of low vision aids. To some extent, the children who had teachers of the visually impaired may have had some rehabilitative services, but such services were not formally programmed into this study. Thus, the success rates obtained in utilization may be considered statistically conservative.

Traits of the sample

Sex

Figure 1 shows the number of males and females at each age level. There is a rather puzzling mean ratio of three males to two females, with the males predominating in all but 3 of the 16 age groups represented. A statistical evaluation of the male minus the female frequencies for each age shows a mean value significantly different from zero at the chance probability of only 0.003.

There was a similar imbalance in the first of the two research reports (Hofstetter, 1985) from which this article is adapted. In that report, the names of the 60 screened children indicated 40 males and only 14 females. Six names were undifferentiable in terms of sex. Males predominated in all but one of the 13 age levels, and the statistical evaluation of male minus female frequencies at each age showed a mean value even more significantly different from zero than that of the present group. It is not known whether these lopsided ratios are the result of biology or a social bias in designating participants for study.

of 132 of the subjects with the conventional correction each was wearing at the time of screening and the best attainable acuity for the better eye of 116.

Table 1. Frequency distribution of visual acuities of the better eye.

Snellen acuity of the better eye	As previously corrected N=132	Best attainable N=116
20/20 to 20/49	17.4%	23.3%
20/50 to 20/124	35.6%	32.7%
20/125 to 20/319	22.7%	25.9%
20/320 to 20/799	15.2%	9.5%
20/800 to 20/1999	3.0%	2.6%
20/2000 to under	6.1%	6.0%

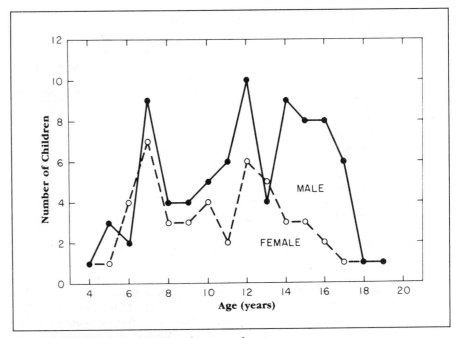

Figure 1. Distribution of children by sex and age.

Causes of low vision

Classifying the 137 children according to their most impairing etiology, 62 percent had receptor system or muscular control defects, 10 percent had opacities in the media, 22 percent had optical or refractive deformities, and 6 percent had undetermined etiologies. The proportions of defects were almost identical for both sexes and did not differ significantly from the proportions in the prior study (Hofstetter, 1985).

Vision correction

Although loss of Snellen visual acuity, which relates to the perception of small details, is only one type of visual impairment, it is the single most frequently used criterion of reference. Table 1 shows the habitual acuity recorded for the better eye

(The fact that the table shows only a modest improvement with the best possible spectacle correction points up the relatively greater significance of magnification, brightness, contrast, illumination, field enhancement, and color in the application of special aids for the visually impaired.)

The table also makes it clear that virtually all the children had been examined earlier and when substantial refractive errors were found, conventional corrective glasses had been appropriately prescribed.

Of the 137 subjects, three (2%) wore contact lenses and 82 (60%) wore glasses. The latter percentage is at least four times greater than that of the general school population.

Fifty-one of the 82 pairs of glasses were

evaluated. Forty-two were judged to be in satisfactory physical condition and only nine (18%) in poor condition (e.g., damaged or undersized frames, scratched lenses). The low percentage of glasses in poor condition indicates that most were new as compared with those of other children, since children outgrow frames and scratch lenses at a fast rate.

Academic standing

Teachers were asked to indicate on a checklist whether the student's academic progress was average, above average, or below average. Of the 110 youngsters for whom these evaluations were made, 52

ophthalmologists or optometrists to obtain new lenses, update their eyewear, or receive other services. The remaining 31 (23%) were deemed to have received or to be receiving all the ophthalmic services that could currently be of benefit.

The actions, dispositions, and evaluations that followed the screening are listed in Table 2.

The first column of figures in Table 2 relates to the 82 children for whom comprehensive clinical evaluations were recommended. For reasons such as limited funding, the unavailability of transportation, parental neglect, or unwillingness on the part of the child, 23

indicated successful utilization. No follow-up information was pursued for the other child who received an aid or for the 19 who had routine optometric services.

The third column of figures in Table 2 shows that 1 of the 31 children who had not been referred for vision care was brought to one of the low vision specialists by his parents for the full evaluation. A special visual aid was provided and a subsequent report indicated that it was being utilized moderately.

One more point on utilization: Some of the children who were given special aids didn't use them for near visual tasks. This may mean that they preferred to bring the visual task extremely close to the eye for retinal magnification, as many young children do.

Table 2. Interrelated results of screening and subsequent examinations.

	Low vision examination recommended for 82 children	General optometric examination recommended for 21 children	Referral not indicated for 31 children
Low vision examination not made	23	19	30
Special low vision aid not recommended	1	0	0
Special low vision aid recommended	58	2	1
Prescribed aids were not ordered	3	0	0
Prescribed aids were provided	56	2	1
Prescribed aids not used	5	0	0
Moderate success indicated by subsequent use	13	0	1
Significant success indicated by subsequent use	30	1	0
Follow-up information lacking	34	20	30

(47.3%) were rated average, 19 (17.3%) above average, and 39 (35.4%) below average.

That so few of the visually impaired children were below average is even more remarkable when one realizes that quite a few were also additionally handicapped. For example, 14 percent were partially or totally immobilized without physical assistance. Another 12 percent were unable to read print at all and 11 percent could read only with difficulty. Sixty-two percent were utilizing no other low vision aids than conventional eyewear. It seems reasonable to conclude that the visually impaired students had all the academic potential of the general school population.

Clinical evaluations

Of the 134 children screened in school by the low vision specialists, it was recommended that 82 (61%) have comprehensive clinical evaluations in an adequately equipped office or clinic. An additional 21 (16%) were advised to contact their

subjects were not clinically examined. Of the 59 who were, 56 were provided with low vision aids. (One was advised that aids were not presently justified and two others, for whom aids were prescribed, declined to accept them for cosmetic reasons.)

Follow-up information on 48 of the 56 children who received aids was obtained from visitations and from teachers' reports. It was learned that five (10%) were neglecting to use their aids, 13 (27%) were using them less than they should have for maximum benefit, and 30 (63%) were utilizing them successfully. No follow-up information was sought for the 23 children referred for clinical evaluations who did not receive them.

In Table 2, the second column of figures, which reports on the 21 children who had been referred only for routine optometric services, shows that two were given full low vision evaluations anyway, at the request of their parents. Both were provided with special low vision aids. Follow-up information on one of the two

Summary

Screening by specialists indicated that 61 percent of the children studied could benefit significantly from low vision care by specially qualified eye practitioners and another 16 percent could benefit from services generally available in the community. Follow-up showed high confirmation of the screening accuracy, with clinical evaluations determining that 60 percent of the children could benefit from special services and 14 percent from general care.

Subsequent surveillance showed that the recommendations were satisfactorily utilized by 53 percent of the children classified as needing low vision services and 13 percent of the children classified as needing general ophthalmic care. Thus, 66 percent benefited appreciably from appropriately applied vision care.

Even allowing for test reliability limitations, one can safely conclude that a majority of the impaired vision children in Indiana could be made more competent by the vision care now available.

A number of additional observations emerged from the study:
• A predominance of frequency of males over females at all age levels suggests a sexually related difference in visual impairment or that there was a social bias in the identification of participants.

• More than three-fourths of the children had attainable central visual acuity of only 20/50 or less in the better eye.

• Central visual acuity without magnification aids was only moderately improved by changes of conventional eyewear, but even modest improvements are extremely important for low vision persons.

• Sixty percent of the children were wearing glasses at the time of screening and 82 percent of the glasses were rated to be in satisfactory condition.

• Academic progress ratings of the visually impaired children by their teachers showed 47 percent to be average, 35 percent below average, and 18 percent above average.

• The fact that visually impaired children are officially classified for special education does not seem to provide any added incentive to seek or provide appropriate, periodically needed vision care.

Further research is needed to explore the implications of these suggestions.

References

Feinbloom, W. (1935). Report of 500 cases of sub-normal vision. *American Journal of Optometry,* **12**(6) 238–249.

Freeman, E. (1954). Optometric rehabilitation of the partially blind: A report of 175 cases. *American Journal of Optometry and Archives of American Academy of Optometry,* **31**(5) 230–239.

Hofstetter, H.W (1983). *Unmet vision care needs in Indiana.* Indianapolis: Indiana Chapter of the American Academy of Optometry, Suite 1920, 201 N. Illinois Street, Indianapolis, IN 46204.

Hofstetter, H.W (1985). *The unmet vision care needs of the visually handicapped of Indiana.* Indianapolis: Indiana Chapter of the American Academy of Optometry, Suite 1920, 201 N. Illinois Street, Indianapolis, IN 46204.

Hofstetter, H.W (1988). *Efficacy of low vision services for visually impaired children.* Indianapolis: Indiana Chapter of the American Academy of Optometry, Suite 1920, 201 N. Illinois Street, Indianapolis, IN 46204.

IHB optical aids service survey (1957). Brooklyn, New York: The Industrial Home for the Blind.

Mayer, L. (1927). Visual results with telescopic spectacles. *American Journal of Ophthalmology,* **10**, 256–260.

Children With Physical or Health Impairments

Judicial rulings and legislative actions have made dramatic changes in the ways in which children with physical or health impairments are educated today. Intervention begins as soon as the impairment is diagnosed. Special educational services, as well as medical services, may be initiated at birth. Preschools now provide multidisciplinary services to children with physical or health impairments. Public schools must provide access to all facilities. They must also supply equal opportunities for children with disabilities to participate in school activities, transitional services, and free and appropriate education. The reform and restructuring of special education, mandated by the courts, has opened public school doors to many physically and/or health impaired children who were formerly taught at home, in hospitals, in residential institutions, in special schools, or in special classes.

Children with physical (or orthopedic) impairments are those with muscle, skeletal, or neurological problems that affect their mobility. They may need wheelchairs, crutches, or other special orthopedic equipment or prosthetic devices. Examples of such conditions are cerebral palsy, muscular dystrophy, brittle bone disease, paraplegia, hemiplegia, and quadriplegia. Children with health impairments are those who need special medical attention, treatment, or medications to help them maintain their vitality. Examples of such conditions are asthma, heart defects, anemia, cancer, AIDS, epilepsy, diabetes, arthritis, anorexia nervosa, and pregnancy.

The prevalence figures for children with physical and health impairments appear lower than they actually are. Many children with such impairments are well enough with medical attention, treatment, or medications so that they are not in need of special educational services. Many children with such impairment are concurrently disabled in one of the other categories of exceptionality (e.g., learning disabled, speech impaired) and are either assessed in that category or are considered multihandicapped.

Children born with physical or health impairments should receive comprehensive multidisciplinary services as early as possible in infancy. Early intervention can help these children develop social, cognitive, and language skills that will enhance their participation in public school regular education as they reach middle childhood and adolescence.

Children who acquire physical or health impairments in early, middle, or late childhood or adolescence usually have special problems adjusting to the acquired disability. They may go through periods of denial and mourning before they accept the impairments of their condition. They usually need to be motivated to comply with the special care requirements imposed on them by their conditions. School teachers and ancillary school personnel can give invaluable assistance to parents and medical specialists. Working together, they have more chance of helping the students accept their disabilities and adapt to their changed circumstances.

A major role for teachers of children with physical or health impairments is to help establish positive interactions between the children with disabilities and their more abled peers. It is important that the teachers and other school personnel become acquainted with the special situations of each physically or health impaired child. They should understand limitations, needs, treatments, and/or medications. In addition, they should discuss each special child's condition openly with his or her classmates. Peers are more willing to accept special arrangements of classroom furniture and special attention or time given to children with physical or health impairments if the need for them has been made clear from the beginning.

A second major role for teachers of children with physical or health impairments is to challenge them to work up to their highest level of competency despite the condition of their disability. The teacher has a responsibility to be honest in evaluations as well. Sympathy grades are detrimental to the self-concept and self-esteem of all children with disabilities. Children with diseases such as epilepsy, asthma, and diabetes must be watched carefully. Work on assignments or examinations must be postponed if symptoms of an abnormal state develop. Seizures, bronchial spasms, hypoglycemia, and other such abnormal states require emergency care and assistance. When the normal condition is reestablished, the school work can be resumed.

Teachers of children with physical or health impairments may be called on to do some extraordinary procedures above and beyond emergency care. Judicial rulings have established life support services as legitimate duties of schools with regular education classes. For example, if a child with spina bifida needs urinary catheterization during the school day in order to benefit from mainstreamed education, the school staff must provide

this service. If a school nurse is not available, a teacher may be asked to learn to provide catheterization. Teachers may be asked to supervise ambulatory kidney dialysis, oxygen administration, intravenous feedings, ventilators, and other services that allow the child with a physical or health impairment to benefit from education in the least restrictive environment.

In the first article of this unit, Nettie Bartel and S. Kenneth Thurman discuss three early childhood physical and health impairments: cancer, at-risk birth status, and medical fragility. Educators, in conjunction with parents and medical personnel, should initiate special services as soon as the condition is diagnosed and continue them as long as necessary. In the second article, Thomas Zirpoli asks and answers the question, "Are children with disabilities at greater risk of physical abuse?" Educators should be aware of the implications of research in this area as they work with physically and health impaired children. The third selection provides strategies for integrating students with disabilities into regular education classes giving both challenges and solutions. Finally, Jennifer York and Terri Vandercook discuss teamwork in developing individualized education programs (IEPs) for children with severe physical impairments.

Looking Ahead: Challenge Questions

What modifications of school curriculum should be made for children who survive life-threatening illnesses?

How can we help prevent the abuse of children with physical or health impairments? How can we help support their families?

What solutions have been successfully pursued to meet the challenges of integrating students with disabilities into supported regular classes?

Where can a regular education teacher get help to develop appropriate individualized education plans for children with physical or health impairments?

Medical Treatment and Educational Problems In Children

NETTIE R. BARTEL AND
S. KENNETH THURMAN

NETTIE R. BARTEL (Temple University Chapter) and S. KENNETH THURMAN are professors in the Special Education Program, Department of Psychological Studies in Education, Temple University, Philadelphia.

Educators, in conjunction with the medical profession and parents, must respond to the special physical and cognitive needs of children who are alive today only because of advances in medical technology, Ms. Bartel and Mr. Thurman suggest.

JANET IS a 13-year-old who attends a junior high school. She is shorter and heavier than most of her classmates, and her physical development seems more suited to an elementary school. Although she is well-motivated and has two supportive parents, Janet is barely getting by in her school program. In elementary school, she was labeled "learning disabled" and received assistance in arithmetic and reading comprehension in a resource room. Her homeroom teacher describes Janet as industrious and earnest but indecisive and easily discouraged. Her mother states that Janet needs a structured home environment to enable her to function successfully in such everyday situations as getting herself ready for the school bus in the morning or completing her homework and household chores in the evening.

Janet's functioning is like that of many other students with learning disabilities. But there is one major difference. Janet was once precocious and lively. At age 5 she suddenly became anemic and sickly. Her pediatrician administered some blood tests and diagnosed her as having acute lymphocytic leukemia. She was taken to a major children's hospital in a nearby city and given treatment that saved her life. That treatment included cranial radiation.

Janet is one of thousands of children whose lives have been saved by aggressive medical treatment. Only later was it discovered that the very treatment that saved their lives also reduced the quality of their lives. These children provide poignant evidence that the miracles of modern medical technology sometimes come with unanticipated costs — costs that often must be borne by the very children whose lives are saved. These costs include the educational difficulties that can result from treatment.

We will consider the educational implications for three groups of children whose health conditions are such that they would not survive without medical intervention. Some of these children are like Janet: after a period of normal, healthy life, they contract a disease (often cancer) that would be fatal without medical treatment; yet the side effects of the treatment may cause school problems.

Other children seem normal at conception and during fetal development but have difficulties that can be attributed to the fact that they were born "too soon" or "too small." That is, they were born prematurely or born with low birth weight. Years ago, these babies would simply have died; today, many survive, sometimes with significant developmental problems.

A third group of children are those whose difficulties apparently go back to the prenatal period. These children (sometimes referred to as "medically fragile") are born with complex medical needs and remain alive only because of intensive medical care that often continues throughout their lives. A few years ago, these children, too, would not have survived. But today they are found in significant numbers in our infant, preschool, and school programs.

CHILDREN TREATED FOR CANCER

There are a number of potentially lethal childhood diseases. However, because of their prevalence and the success with which they are being treated, we will concern ourselves here only with childhood cancers.

Nature of the condition. Cancer is a disease in which one or more cells of the body divide more rapidly than is healthy. The most common childhood cancer, acute lymphocytic leukemia (also known as acute lymphoblastic leukemia) is a cancer of the blood-forming organs of the body, including the bone marrow, the spleen, and the lymph nodes. Eighty percent of all cases of acute lymphocytic leukemia are seen in children, where it accounts for approximately one-third of total childhood cancers. In this disease, the body produces a large number of immature white blood cells that are unable to develop into normally functioning parts of the immune system. These immature cells proliferate rapidly, crowding out and interfering with the manufacture of other crucial blood cells, including red cells and platelets.

Taken together, leukemias and malignancies of the brain and nervous system account for more than half of all childhood cancers. Current statistics indicate

From *Phi Delta Kappan,* September 1992, pp. 57-61. Reprinted by permission of *Phi Delta Kappan* and the authors.

that at least one child in 800 to 1,000 is a cancer survivor. This suggests that most schools have at least one survivor of childhood cancer in the student body.

The causes of these cancers are not known. As with other cancers, a number of factors appear to trigger the disease — including viruses, a genetic propensity, and exposure to radiation or other environmental factors.

The early symptoms of cancer in children are vague and frequently include headache, fatigue, a low-grade fever, easy bruising, and pallor. Bleeding, irritability, frequent infections, lowered resistance to infections, loss of appetite, weight loss, and facial puffiness are also seen. Diagnosis of acute lymphocytic leukemia is made by a complete blood count and an examination of a blood marrow sample. In the case of brain tumors, diagnostic imaging techniques — including x-rays, CAT scans, and NMRI (nuclear magnetic resonance imaging) — are often used.

Nature of the treatment. The treatment goal for acute lymphocytic leukemia is to eliminate all leukemic cells and to induce a remission. This goal is achieved by various combinations of radiation, chemotherapy, and systemic drug therapy. Treatments are given at the time of diagnosis and as a prophylaxis following initial treatment. Cranial radiation is also given prophylactically in an effort to prevent central nervous system disease later.

Treatment for brain tumors usually includes a combination of surgery, radiation, and chemotherapy. The use of cranial radiation has been suspected as a major cause of cognitive dysfunction. Because brain-tumor therapy requires much higher doses of radiation than does leukemia therapy, children with brain tumors may be at higher risk for subsequent learning problems than children with leukemia.

As recently as the 1950s a child diagnosed as having leukemia had an average life expectancy of three months. Today, almost 90% of such children achieve initial remission, and almost 80% are symptom-free five years after diagnosis. Patients with a poorer prognosis — boys, blacks, those younger than age 2 or older than age 10, and those with complications — require more aggressive treatment. The survival rate for brain cancer and nervous system cancer is not as high, hovering just above 50%.

Families of children with cancer frequently experience a roller coaster of

> Overall, children who survive leukemia or brain tumors show a decline in cognitive functioning.

emotions in which the initial shock of the diagnosis of a life-threatening disease is followed by relief at the apparently successful medical treatment. In cases in which the diagnosis calls for cranial radiation, this feeling may be followed by increasing concern on the part of the family as it becomes apparent that the child is manifesting learning difficulties that were not present previously. Many parents, in an attempt to avoid having the child stigmatized, may try to minimize the seriousness of the child's condition to school personnel. Yet, when learning problems become more pronounced, families and schools need to work closely together to address the special learning needs of the child.

Educational implications. Overall, children who survive leukemia or brain tumors show a decline in cognitive functioning and academic ability, with more severe problems evidenced by the latter group. While it is believed that acute lymphocytic leukemia does not in and of itself cause learning problems, the situation is more complicated in the case of brain tumors. It is difficult to separate the effects of the tumors themselves from the effects of the treatment. Recent studies have attempted to delineate the exact nature, severity, and possible cause or causes of adverse aftereffects of childhood cancers. It has been proposed that children treated at an early age (4 or younger) are more vulnerable to serious effects than are children treated when they are older. This suggestion is based in part on the theory that, because it is rapidly developing, the immature brain is more susceptible to adverse influences than the mature brain.

One major study reported intellectual and neuropsychological dysfunction over time in a group of children whose acute lymphocytic leukemia had been treated with cranial radiation.[1] This study is especially significant because it evaluated children both at the time of diagnosis and every six months for three years afterward. Three years after being treated with radiation and methotrexate, this group's average I.Q. score was 89, as compared to 109 at their first evaluation. The researchers concluded that the cognitive decline was not apparent until at least three years after treatment, that the children who were younger at diagnosis suffered greater adverse effects, and that children who received radiation experienced more adverse effects than children treated with methotrexate in the absence of radiation. The results of this study are typical of a number of similar studies, most of which have found an I.Q. decline of 12 to 20 points, with specific types of intellectual and academic deficits most frequently seen.

Between one-half and two-thirds of children who survive acute lymphocytic leukemia have been found to require some kind of special academic help, as compared to 15% of their siblings (about average for the school population as a whole). Teachers and parents report that these survivors take longer to complete tasks, have difficulty following multiple commands, and learn more slowly. They also describe them as less active, less expressive, and less able to concentrate.

A higher percentage of leukemia survivors than of the general student population attend special education classes or receive some form of specialized instruction; a higher than usual percentage of these children repeat grades. The reports of teachers and parents suggest that the specific areas in which these children experience the greatest difficulties include attention/concentration, mathematics, motor speed, visual/motor integration, timed performance, comprehension, spelling, planning ability, fine motor skills, and abstract thinking.

Of children successfully treated for brain tumors, about two-thirds are found in special education programs, while many of the rest require some specialized school help. Declines of 25 I.Q. points are common, and the school achievement of children who survive brain tumors is markedly below that of the general population. Learning disabilities are common. In one study in which none of the children with brain tumors had been in special education prior to diagnosis, at six months after treatment 50% of those under age 6 and 11% of those over age 6 were in special classes.

The specific learning problems of children who have been treated for brain tumors include attention deficits, problems with arithmetic, difficulty in self-organization, and reduced speed and dexterity. In addition to cognitive dysfunction and problems with school achievement, children treated for brain tumors often exhibit problems with emotional adjustment, shortened stature, and poor peer relations that stem from hair loss and otherwise feeling "different." Factors that seem to affect cognitive and academic functioning include amount of radiation, pre- and postoperative mental status, postoperative central nervous system infection, and how much of the head is irradiated.

Current treatment protocols for children with acute lymphocytic leukemia emphasize reducing or eliminating the use of cranial radiation whenever possible without reducing the child's survival chances. And fewer children with leukemia are receiving cranial radiation today than five years ago. Nevertheless, a significant number of such children still need this treatment if they are to have a chance of surviving. This means that educators will continue to see children with the specific cognitive deficits described above. The very success of treatment for these two most common childhood cancers is creating a population of children at risk academically and is presenting educators with the unique challenge of developing and implementing interventions that may spare these children from failure in school. Improved medical interventions in the future will no doubt increase the rate of survival even more and result in the presence of more cancer survivors in our nation's schools.

LOW BIRTH WEIGHT AND PREMATURITY

Nature of the condition. Low birth weight is defined as weighing less than 2,500 grams or 5.5 pounds at birth. Very low birth weight refers to infants who weigh less than 1,500 grams or 3.3 pounds at birth, and extremely low birth weight is defined by a weight of 1,000 grams (or 2.2 pounds) or less at birth. In 1986 the National Center for Health Statistics reported that 6.8% of all infants born were classified as low birth weight.

> The ultimate prognosis for low birth weight and premature infants is most clearly mediated by environment.

Given that there are between 3.5 and four million births each year in the U. S., this means that every year about 255,000 infants are born who can be classified as low birth weight. Sixty percent of all neonatal deaths (i.e., death within the first 28 days of life) can be accounted for by low birth weight, and 20% of babies who die in the first year of life were low weight at birth.

Typically, low birth weight is the result of premature birth or of intrauterine growth retardation. Birth is deemed premature when an infant is born after less than 37 weeks of gestation. Prematurity occurs in about 11% of all births, according to 1986 data from the National Center for Health Statistics. This means that about 412,000 infants are born prematurely each year. A number of factors are related to increased risk of premature birth, including adolescent pregnancy, maternal age greater than 35 years, poverty, poor nutrition, poor prenatal care, and drug use.

Retarded intrauterine growth is the other major contributor to low birth weight. This condition often results from decreased blood flow to the fetus that may be related to incomplete placental development, the effects of drugs, high altitude, or multiple births. It may also be related to certain chromosomal abnormalities. Babies whose growth was retarded in utero are referred to as small for gestational age. Unlike babies who are premature, babies who are small for gestational age are most often carried to full term. However, babies who are born prematurely may also be considered small for gestational age if their birth weight is more than 90% below the weight

that would be expected for their particular gestational age.

Both low birth weight and prematurity place infants at increased risk of poor development. Examining the literature since the early 1970s reveals an improving prognosis for low birth weight infants, especially those weighing less than 1,500 grams. In the early 1970s only about 20% of infants weighing less than 1,000 grams survived. By the early 1980s about 40% of these infants were surviving. A recent study also suggests that these infants are surviving with a lower incidence of developmental problems.[2] The data indicate that, by age 5, 80% of children who weighed 1,000 grams or less at birth showed either slight or only minor neurodevelopmental difficulties.

The prognosis for a low birth weight or premature infant can be influenced by a number of factors. The treatment of these infants in neonatal intensive care units may require physicians to deal with such complications as brain hemorrhages, lung damage, infections, and damage to sensory systems. Multiple complications may affect one infant, while another of equal birth weight or gestational age goes unaffected. Unfortunately, there is no way to tell at the onset which infant is more likely to experience such complications and to need extraordinary treatment.

The ultimate prognosis for these infants is most clearly mediated by environment. Studies have consistently demonstrated that infants of low birth weight and premature infants who are reared in enriched environments fare better than their counterparts who are reared in poverty or without the proper types of nurturance and stimulation from caregivers.

The birth and subsequent hospitalization of a premature or low birth weight infant can have significant impact on a family. The uncertainty experienced by the family during hospitalization can create stress. As one mother recalled:

> After I got over the initial shock of Julia's appearance it got easier to visit her. . . . I couldn't feel comfortable in the NICU [neonatal intensive care unit]. . . . Hospitals are intimidating; NICUs are even more so. I felt I had no control; I was just a bystander. Meanwhile, my poor husband was run ragged. [He] would work all day, and then drive to the hospital, which was a three hour round trip. [He] was also assembling furniture, painting her room, and scouting around for very tiny baby clothes.[3]

Once the infant has been brought home, the family remains under stress since the baby's course of development is not yet clear. In addition, prematurity alters the patterns of interaction between infants and their caregivers. Premature infants tend to be more irritable, less regular in their sleeping and eating patterns, and more ambiguous in the social cues that they emit. As a result, parents of these infants may tend to feel frustrated and less than competent.

Educational implications. Infants who survive low birth weight or prematurity need early intervention. At a minimum, these infants should be evaluated periodically to help make certain that they are developing properly. Early intervention should stress cognitive, language, and motor development and should focus on providing the necessary supports to the family to reduce stress and maximize the development of the child. The passage and implementation of P.L. 99-457 and its recent reauthorization with the passage of the Individuals with Disabilities Education Act Amendments (P.L. 102-119) provide the framework within which this early intervention can take place.

The need for special education services for these children as they get older is very much a function of the individual child. It is important to keep in mind that the largest percentage of children who experience low birth weight or who are premature function well within normal limits by the time they reach school age. Thus, while many children who begin life in neonatal intensive care units do manifest developmental and learning problems when they reach school age, it would be unwise to conclude that any child whose life begins under these trying circumstances is predestined to require special educational services.

THE MEDICALLY FRAGILE

Nature of the condition. The term *medically fragile* refers to children whose medical needs are complex and encompasses a wide range of conditions that affect the health and subsequent education and development of the children. Most often, the problems experienced by these children are chronic and require ongoing — frequently daily — treatment and monitoring (sometimes in a hospital setting) if the children are to survive. These children have conditions that are "extremely disabling or life-threatening. Usually such [children] are dependent on life-

support equipment such as ventilators, feeding tubes, or apnea (i.e., breathing) monitors for survival."[4] However, children with such conditions as diabetes, sickle-cell anemia, cystic fibrosis, and hemophilia may also on occasion manifest acute symptoms and have medical needs that significantly interfere with their education.

It is difficult to determine the incidence and prevalence of medically fragile children because the term is rather broad and because those children with multiple disabilities can end up being classified under some other label. The U.S. Department of Education estimates that, during the 1988-89 school year, there were 50,349 children between the ages of 6 and 21 who were classified as health-impaired and who were being served in special education programs across the nation.[5] Keep in mind that this low figure does not include any children who fall into another classification.

Because their conditions vary greatly, the exact prognosis of children with complex medical needs is difficult to determine. Many have decreased life expectancies. Some children with complex medical needs can experience relatively long periods of stability, though constant monitoring of their conditions remains necessary. For example, a child who has a tracheostomy and is dependent on a ventilator for assistance with breathing may be able to function reasonably well from day to day with proper suctioning, cleaning, and maintenance of the tubes that connect him or her to the ventilator. However, that situation may change rapidly if the child acquires an upper respiratory infection.

Families of medically fragile children often experience stresses that go beyond those of other families. They must adapt to the special needs of their child and often must learn how to maintain the equipment and use specialized devices and therapeutic techniques. Moreover, they must cope with the uncertainty of when their child's condition may suddenly become acute, requiring emergency treatment or hospitalization. At the same time, they may need to provide additional emotional support to help the child cope more easily with the medical condition. The constant care required by children who have complex medical needs can lead to parental fatigue and can create the potential for burnout. Such effects can adversely affect the relationships in the family.

Educational implications. Children with complex medical needs can be unique challenges to the education system. On occasion, these children will require homebound or hospital-based instruction. When they are attending school, these children may tire more easily and thus need periods of rest or inactivity between instructional sessions.

Nor is it uncommon for these children to require the services of a nurse or of a physical or occupational therapist in order to render treatment or to help them gain the most benefit from their learning experiences. Frequent or prolonged periods of hospitalization can further disrupt the educational process and frustrate the teacher, the child, and the family. Finally, it may be necessary to modify classroom space and routines in order to accommodate the equipment to maintain a child with complex medical needs. The effective education of these children depends on a flexible, interdisciplinary approach that can be equally responsive to their medical, psychological, and educational needs.

Educators, in conjunction with the medical profession and parents, must respond to the issues raised by the presence in our schools of children who are alive today only because of advances in medical technology. As we learn more about the physical and cognitive needs of these children and as their numbers increase with the use of new medical procedures, we must work to see that the quality of their lives remains at the highest possible level. Only as parents and educators are trained to help children overcome the cognitive problems brought about by their medical conditions and treatments can this goal be achieved.

---

1. Ann T. Meadows et al., "Declines in I.Q. Scores and Cognitive Dysfunction in Children with Acute Lymphocytic Leukemia," *Lancet*, vol. 2, 1981, pp. 1015-18.
2. William H. Kitchen et al., "Children of Birth Weight <1,000 Grams: Changing Outcome Between Ages 2 and 5 Years," *Pediatrics*, vol. 110, 1987, pp. 283-88.
3. Jean D. Rapacki, "The Neonatal Intensive Care Experience," *Children's Health Care*, vol. 20, 1991, p. 16.
4. Beverly A. Fraser, Robert N. Hensinger, and Judith A. Phelps, *Physical Management of Multiple Handicaps: A Professional's Guide*, 2nd ed. (Baltimore: Paul H. Brookes, 1990), p. 5.
5. *Thirteenth Annual Report to Congress on the Implementation of the Individuals with Disabilities Education Act* (Washington, D.C.: Office of Special Education and Rehabilitative Services, U.S Department of Education, 1991).

PHYSICAL ABUSE:
Are Children with
Disabilities at Greater Risk?

A look at the facts.

Thomas J. Zirpoli

Thomas J. Zirpoli, PhD, is currently an assistant professor and program director for special education at the College of St. Thomas in St. Paul, Minnesota. Address: Thomas J. Zirpoli, Mail #5017, College of St. Thomas, St. Paul, MN 55105.

Child abuse, a generic term, is used to describe emotional or psychological injury, negligence, non-accidental physical injury, and sexual molestation of children by caregivers. Nonaccidental injury, or physical abuse of children with disabilities by caregivers, will be the focus of this article.

One of the more tragic elements regarding the abuse of our nation's children is the lack of accurate data concerning the scope of the problem. Estimates of the prevalence of child abuse in the United States are limited to the number of reports recorded by local agencies. Local data are submitted to national agencies where they are totaled and reported back to the public. As of 1987, the American Association for Protecting Children reported over 2 million cases of child abuse nationally. This compares to 1 million cases reported in 1980 and .5 million cases reported in 1976.

It is unclear whether the amount of child abuse is actually increasing or if the increase in documented cases reflects a greater public awareness of the problem and a greater willingness to report suspected cases (Hoffman, 1981). As previously stated, these numbers reflect only *reported* cases. It is important to keep in mind that much abuse remains unreported; some professionals believe that the number of actual cases is at least twice the number of reported cases (Straus, Gelles, & Steinmetz, 1980).

Child Abuse and Neglect Reported by Year (1976–1987)

Year	Reported Cases
1976	669,000
1977	838,000
1978	836,000
1979	988,000
1980	1,154,000
1981	1,225,000
1982	1,262,000
1983	1,477,000
1984	1,727,000
1985	1,928,000
1986	2,086,112
1987	2,178,384

Source: American Association for Protecting Children, Personal Communication, 1/16/90.

Understanding the Variables Associated with Abuse

Before discussing the issue of abuse of children with disabilities, it is important to understand the variables associated with child abuse in general. Child abuse is the result of an interaction of many variables. These variables include the characteristics of the caregiver, environmental and sociocultural factors, and the characteristics of the child or victim of abusive behavior. Each of these will be briefly discussed below.

Characteristics of the Abusive Caregiver

Child abuse research has historically focused on the characteristics of the abusive caregiver, with relatively little attention on other variables frequently associated with abusive behavior. This focus was based upon the belief that most abusive caregivers were mentally ill and that early discovery and treatment of caregiver dysfunction was the key to prevention (Gelles, 1973). Current theories of child abuse, however, view the caregiver role as a single, although significant, variable, within a model of many interacting variables that cannot be separated and understood in isolation (Pianta, Egeland, & Erickson, 1989).

Johnson and Showers (1985) found that the median age of abusers in their study was 25 years. Rogers (1978) reported 26 years and 30 years as the mean age of female and male abusers, respectively. These studies do not take into account recent significant increases in teenage pregnancies leading to adolescent parents with little or no knowledge of child development, poor parenting skills, and unrealistic expectations of child behavior. These adolescent parents frequently live within dysfunctional families, in addition to the hardships of other disadvantageous environmental circumstances (outlined below). When combined with their own immaturity and the lack of appropriate social support, adolescent parents may not be able to cope with the responsibilities of parenthood, and their children may be considered at risk for maltreatment (Meier, 1985).

Caregivers who abuse their children often are victims of abusive behavior themselves (Straus, 1983). In addition, they may have witnessed other forms of domestic violence between parents or other family members. Many abusive caregivers have only their abusive parents from whom to model and learn the skills of caring for children and how caregivers and children should interact. Egeland, Jacobvitz, and Papatola (1984) followed 47 women who had been physically abused as children and found that 70% were maltreating their children at 2 years of age.

Straus, Gelles, and Steinmetz (1980) found that many abusive caregivers believed physical punishment of children and slapping a spouse were appropriate behaviors. Female caregivers who were victims of spouse abuse tended to be more violent toward their children (Straus, 1983), and males were likely to abuse their own spouse and children after having lived in a home where spouse abuse existed (Rosenbaum & O'Leary, 1981). Unless this cycle is broken, and as long as other environmental and sociocultural factors continue to exist, the cycle of abuse is likely to continue.

Environmental Factors

Environmental conditions are frequently thought of as trigger variables in child abuse. That is, abusive behaviors are likely to occur under certain conditions that, given an already dysfunctional caregiver-child relationship, trigger inappropriate caregiver behavior. These conditions may include unemployment, household poverty, frustration, and a dysfunctional family structure (Straus, 1983).

The absence of a support system tends to aggravate the effects of the other environmental conditions. For example, extended family members may be able to assist a single caregiver who has recently become unemployed. Neighborhood support groups, social agencies, and other community organizations may also provide assistance to caregivers and reduce the burden to a tolerable level. Garbarino (1982) talked about the importance of social support systems for healthy families, and noted that, as society becomes more mobile, many couples find themselves separated from the natural support systems of their extended families and longtime friendships.

Sociocultural Factors

One cannot begin to understand the problem of child abuse without reviewing the significant sociocultural factors that foster abusive environments. Straus (1983) has referred to the culturally sanctioned violence within families where spouse abuse and child abuse are learned and acceptable forms of interaction. Zigler (1979) reviewed the acceptance of physical punishment of children within our homes and schools and stated that the willingness of caregivers to employ physical punishment is the most significant determinant of child abuse in America.

Even the United States Supreme Court, in the case of *Ingraham v. Wright* (1977), found that children are not protected from cruel and unusual punishment. This decision followed the case of a student who was severely spanked with a 2-foot paddle by three school teachers. Rose (1983) found that the majority of school administrators reported using physical punishment with students with disabilities. Violence seems to be embedded in our society, and this social acceptance of violence, found within families, on television shows, and in our schools, is directly related to the high prevalence of child abuse in America (Zirpoli, 1986).

Characteristics of the Abused Child

Abused children should never be blamed for the maltreatment they receive from caregivers. It is helpful to understand the child-variables that may place children at greater risk for abusive treatment, however.

The idea that children affect caregivers' behavior (known as *child effects*) has received considerable attention during the past two decades, beginning with Bell's (1968) review of the parent-child relationship as a *reciprocal* relationship. As professionals have begun to realize the significant contribution children make toward caregiver-child interactions, interest in the characteristics of children abused by caregivers has increased considerably (Rusch, Hall, & Griffin, 1986; Zirpoli, 1986; Zirpoli, Snell, & Loyd, 1987).

Many researchers believe that younger children are at greater risk for abusive behavior than older children. In fact, premature infants, representing less than 10% of all births, have been reported to represent up to half the cases of child abuse (Fontana, 1971). Pianta, Egeland, and Erickson (1989) reported that "there appears to be a greater chance of a maltreated woman to maltreat her toddler age child than there is for her to maltreat her school age child" (p. 203). However, in a study by Gill (1970), over three-quarters of the abused children were over 2 years of age. Rusch, Hall, and Griffin (1986) stated that there does not appear to be a consensus on the impact of age on child abuse.

Premature infants present an ex-

Factors Associated with Physical Child Abuse

Caregiver Characteristics
** Victim of child abuse, victim of spouse abuse
** Low self-esteem and feelings of isolation
** Youthful marriages and unwanted pregnancies
** Unrealistic expectations & general lack of understanding about the nature and behavior of young children
** High vulnerability to caregiving stress with little or no understanding of basic child management.
** Infrequent use of reinforcement or other positive methods of behavior management
** Frequent use of physical punishment as the primary method of behavior management

Environmental Influences
** Household poverty and general family disorganization or dysfunction
** Lack of extended family or inadequate community social support systems
** Conflict between spouses or among other family members within the home
** Conflict between caregiver and child
** Unemployment & economic hardship
** Substance abuse, especially alcohol abuse

Sociocultural Factors
** Widespread social acceptance of physical punishment
** Children not provided adequate constitutional protection

** Inadequate child protection services and resources
** Low priority given to children's issues at national, state, and local levels
** Vague and varied child abuse laws and guidelines

Victim Characteristics
** Prematurity and dysmaturity (low birth weight)
** Difficult temperament, irritable, frequent crying, poor sleeping & eating habits
** General unresponsiveness to caregiver expectations & demands
** Require special and additional caregiving and attention
** Emotional/behavioral disabilities
** Developmental disabilities

cellent example of the theory of child effects. These infants are prone to colic, irritability, and restlessness. They have irregular sleeping and eating patterns, and may be difficult to feed. The premature infant may have an annoying and irritating cry, and usually requires additional parental care and attention. Combined with some of the caregiver, environmental, and sociocultural factors outlined above, one can easily understand how the premature infant may be at greater risk for maltreatment by caregivers who are already stressed by other family and environmental challenges.

There is some debate concerning the extent or degree of child effects on adult behavior; specifically concerning the role of child effects in child abuse. Some professionals believe that child effects are short term and situational, and that child effects do not account for the quality of caregiving over time (Patterson, 1983; Starr, 1982). It is generally agreed, however, that some child characteristics have been associated with maltreatment, but that these characteristics

alone are not enough to predict future child abuse. Again, if we are to understand child abuse, we must understand the interaction of a multiple of variables. The following statement reinforces this point.

> To the extent that the child with extreme individual differences is placed in a family which may not be ready to parent, characteristics of that child may exacerbate an already difficult situation. This child may become the victim of maltreatment, not because of its own behavior, but because the child places added burdens upon an already stressed or incapable family system, resulting in a breakdown in the processes of good parenting. (Pianta et al., 1987, p. 203)

Maltreatment of Persons with Disabilities

There is documented evidence of the maltreatment of children with disabilities throughout history (Sakemiller, 1986). A review of early history outlined the legalized killing of infants born with disabilities, and

the selling of these children for slave labor and prostitution (Rogers, 1978). During the late 1800s and early 1900s, concern regarding the hereditary transmission of disabilities was followed by mass institutionalization, sterilization, and castration of persons with disabilities. As stated so well by Cranefield (cited in MacMillian, 1982) "Seldom in the history of medicine have so many intelligent and well-meaning men embarked on so vicious and brutal a program with so little scientific foundation for their actions" (p. 13).

But the general maltreatment and physical abuse of persons with disabilities continued and by the mid- and late 1900s, many investigations concerning persons in institutional settings had exposed hundreds of cases of abuse (Sakemiller, 1986). The maltreatment of persons with disabilities has not been limited to institutional settings. Zirpoli (1990) has outlined his concerns of the maltreatment of persons with disabilities in community settings where appropriate support systems are not in place, where direct care staff are in-

Child Abuse Organizations

American Humane Association
9725 East Hampden Ave.
Denver, CO 80231-4919
303/695-0811

American Association for Protecting Children
Same as American Humane Association

C. Henry Kempe National Center for the Prevention and Treatment of Child Abuse and Neglect
1205 Oneida St.
Denver, CO 80220
303/321-3963

International Society for the Prevention of Child Abuse and Neglect
Same as C. Henry Kempe National Center

National Association of Counsel for Children
Same as C. Henry Kempe National Center

National Center on Child Abuse and Neglect
Children's Bureau
Administration for Children, Youth and Families

U. S. Department of Health and Human Services
PO Box 1182
Washington, DC 20013
202/245-2840

National Child Abuse and Neglect Clinical Resource Center
University of Colorado Health Sciences Center
Same as C. Henry Kempe National Center

National Child Abuse Coalition
1125 15th St., NW
Suite 300
Washington, DC 20005
202/293-7550

National Child Abuse Hotline
800/422-4453

National Clearing House for Child Abuse and Neglect
PO Box 1182
Washington, DC 20013
703/821-2086

National Committee for Prevention of Child Abuse
332 S. Michigan Ave.
Suite 950
Chicago, IL 60604-4357
312/663-3520

National Resource Center on Child Abuse
Same as American Humane Association
800/227-5242
303/695-0811

National Resource Center for Child Sexual Abuse
11141 Georgia Ave.
Suite 310
Wheaton, MD 20902
301/949-5000 (Maryland)
205/533-KIDS (Alabama)
800/KIDS-006 (toll free)

Parents Anonymous 22330 Hawthorne Blvd.
Suite 208
Torrence, Ca 90505
800/421-0353 (outside California)
800/352-0386 (inside California)

St. Joseph Center for Abused Handicapped Children 1835 K. St., NW
Suite 700
Washington, DC 20006
202/634-9821

Source: Clearinghouse on Child Abuse and Neglect Information

---

adequately prepared, and where profit seems to be a greater priority than quality of life.

Disabilities as Antecedents to Abusive Treatment

As the debate regarding the general characteristics of children as antecedents to child abuse continues, so does the debate regarding the association between specific disabilities and abusive treatment. It is generally accepted, however, that although many caregivers cope very well with children who have disabilities (Dunlap & Hollingsworth, 1977), having a child with disabilities, in combination with environmental variables

previously outlined, may induce a greater level of stress than a caregiver can manage.

Many studies have found relationships between specific disabilities and disproportionate incidents of abuse. Martin (1972) found that 33% of the 42 physically abused children he studied had an IQ less than 80. Sandgrund, Gaines, and Green (1974) studied 120 children (60 abused, 30 neglected, and 30 nonabused). They reported that 25% of the abused group were found to be mentally retarded compared to 20% of the neglected group and 3% of the nonabused group. In a study of all (430) students referred for evaluation of learning problems from Oahu, Hawaii, during a 1-year period, it

was found that 6.7% of them had been reported as abuse victims (Frisch & Rhoads, 1982). This was 3.5 times higher than the rate of child abuse reported for all other children from Oahu during the same time period.

Bousha and Twentyman (1984) found that children who were victims of abusive behavior were significantly more aggressive than control subjects. Lorber, Felton, and Reid (1984) also found that abuse victims were more disruptive and aggressive. The research on children with physical handicaps is mixed. A study by Diamond and Jaudes (1983) found that 20% of 86 children with cerebral palsy (CP) were victims of physical abuse. However, Martin, Beezley, Conway, and Kempe (1974) found no physical disabilities among 58 abused children.

Abused Versus Nonabused Comparisons

Whether a child's disability is directly or indirectly related to abusive treatment will probably be an ongoing topic for future research. Meanwhile, two studies have explored this research question directly (Rusch, Hall, & Griffin, 1986; Zirpoli, Snell & Loyd, 1987). These two studies compared groups of abused and nonabused clients living within institutional settings and found that some disabilities were significant in differentiating the abused from the nonabused clients.

In research conducted by Rusch, Hall, and Griffin (1986), 160 clients residing in a North Carolina institution for persons with disabilities were studied. Eighty of the clients represented all of the substantiated physical abuse cases occurring within the institution between 1977 and 1982. A control group of 80 nonabused clients was randomly selected from the remaining institutional population.

Records of all 160 clients were reviewed to determine the following characteristics of each client: age, sex, IQ (as measured by the Stanford-Binet Intelligence Scale), social maturity quotient (as measured by the Vineland Social Maturity Scale), physical disabilities, communications skills, and tendency to be aggressive (defined by exhibiting two or more serious aggressive episodes during a 6-month period). The two groups, abused and control, were compared on the above seven variables.

Rusch and his colleagues found no significant differences between the two groups on the basis of sex (although there were five more males in the abused group), and no significant differences between the two groups on mean IQ levels. However, 71% of the abused group scored in the profound level of retardation compared with 60% in the control group. Also, no significant differences

were found regarding the physical disabilities variable, although more clients in the abused group (49%) had physical disabilities compared to the control group (38%).

Significant differences were found on the age variable (more abused clients were found in the youngest age category), and on the social maturity quotient, with 76% of the abused group scoring in the profound range compared with 61% of the control group. Other significant differences were found between the number of clients demonstrating self-injurious behavior (16% for the abused and 5% for the control group), the number of clients who were verbal (38% for the abused compared to 59% for the control group), the number of clients who were ambulatory (86% for the abused and 73% for the control group), and the number of clients who were aggressive (51% of the abused and 11% of the control group). The difference between the two groups on the aggression variable was very strong. In the Zirpoli, Snell, and Lloyd (1987) study, 91 victims of physical abuse from five state training centers in Virginia for individuals with disabilities were compared to 91 randomly selected control clients from the same five facilities. The abused clients represented all confirmed cases of client abuse occurring from 1980 through 1985.

Records of each of the 182 clients were reviewed to determine the following characteristics: age, sex, level of functioning, auditory, visual, ambulation, speech ability, and the frequency of four challenging behaviors (aggression, disruption, rebelliousness, and hyperactivity).

Zirpoli and his colleagues (1987) found no significant differences between the two groups on the basis of age, sex, and on the clients' auditory, visual, ambulation, and speech skills. Significant differences were found between the two groups on the level-of-functioning variable. Over twice as many clients in the abused group were labeled severely disabled (59%) compared to the control group (25%), and half as many of the clients in the

abused group were labeled profoundly disabled (18%) compared with the control group (44%). No differences were found between the two groups on the number of clients labeled mild and moderately disabled.

In the area of challenging behaviors, the abused group had twice as many clients considered frequently aggressive, disruptive, rebellious, and hyperactive compared to the control group. As in the Rusch et al. study, the differences between the two groups on the basis of challenging behaviors was particularly strong.

Summary and Recommendations

Are children with disabilities at greater risk for physical abuse than other children? The answer to this question depends upon the condition of a host of other variables concerning the child's caregivers and environment. Having a disability alone does not place a child at greater risk for abusive treatment. As previously stated, *most* parents of children with disabilities cope very well with the additional demands of a child who requires additional supports. But unless we provide caregivers with the necessary support, we place children at risk for maltreatment. Not all caregivers who were abused as children develop into abusive parents. Given the appropriate and necessary support, some are able to break the cycle of abuse and establish healthy, functional families.

Given the variables that are associated with abuse, how can we help in breaking the cycle? Some solutions require significant changes in national priorities and attitudes. Parents and educators, however, are in the best position to advocate for these changes. Four fundamental changes are outlined here. First, we must put an end to the widespread tolerance of physical punishment against children. As parents and educators, we can start in our own homes and educational settings.

Second, we must advocate for

highest priority status for our nation's children and the issues related to their protection and enrichment (physical, mental, and emotional). This means full funding for Head Start (only 30% of our nation's children who qualify for Head Start are being served), the Women, Infants and Children (WIC) program, and other effective programs that serve our nation's impoverished children.

Third, we must ensure that all caregivers, regardless of background or income, are provided with the appropriate community support necessary to provide their children with a protecting, healthy, and enriching environment. This means appropriate prenatal care for *all* women, appropriate medical care for *all* children, and quality day care and educational services for *all* children, regardless of family income or ability to pay. These are sound investments for the future of our nation's children *and* our nation.

Lastly, in direct regard to children with disabilities, families of children with disabilities must be provided the necessary support to live as a family unit and participate in all community activities. This means full inclusion of persons with disabilities into our society and an end to the isolated, segregated settings forced upon many families with a disabled member. Family isolation is a significant contributor to child abuse that can be dramatically decreased by greater societal acceptance of all people with disabilities.

How well we advocate for and achieve the above objectives may well answer our primary question. Are children with disabilities at greater risk for abuse and other forms of maltreatment? It depends. And it depends upon what we do to change the contributing variables to this national tragedy.

References

Bell, R. Q. (1968). A reinterpretation of the direction of effects in studies of socialization. *Psychological Review, 75,* 81–95.

Bousha D. M., & Twentyman, C. T. (1984). Mother-child interactional style in abuse, neglect, and control groups: Naturalistic observations in the home. *Journal of Abnormal Psychology, 93,* 106–114.

Diamond, L. J., & Jaudes, P. K. (1983). Child abuse in a cerebral-palsied population. *Developmental Medicine and Child Neurology, 25,* 169–174.

Dunlap, W. R., & Hollingsworth, J. S. (1977). How does a handicapped child affect the family? Implications for practitioners. *Family Coordinator, 26,* 286–293.

Egeland, B., Jacobvitz, D., & Papatola, K. (1984, May). *Intergenerational continuity of parental abuse.* Proceedings from the Conference on Biosocial Perspectives on Child Abuse and Neglect, Social Science Research Council, York, ME.

Fontana, V. J. (1971). *The maltreated child.* Springfield, IL: Thomas.

Frisch, L. E., & Rhoads, F. A. (1982). Child abuse and neglect in children referred for learning evaluation. *Journal of Learning Disabilities, 15,* 583–586.

Garbarino, J. (1982). *Children and families in the social environment.* New York: Aldine.

Gelles, R. (1973). Child abuse as psychopathology: A sociological critique and reformation. *American Journal of Orthopsychiatry, 43,* 611–621.

Gill, D. (1970). *Violence against children: Physical child abuse in the United States.* Cambridge, MA: Harvard University Press.

Hoffman, E. (1981). Policy and politics: The Child Abuse Prevention and Treatment Act. In R. Bourne & E. H. Newberger (Eds.), *Critical perspectives on child abuse* (pp. 157–170). Lexington, MA: Lexington Books.

Ingraham v. Wright, 498 F. 2d 248 (5 Cir. 1977).

Johnson, C. F., & Showers, J. (1985). Injury variables in child abuse. *Child Abuse and Neglect, 9,* 207–215.

Lorber, R., Felton, D. K., & Reid, J. B. (1984). A social learning approach to the reduction of coercive processes in child abusive families: A molecular analysis. *Advances in Behavior Research* and *Therapy, 6,* 29–45.

MacMillian, D. L. (1982). *Mental retardation in school and society.* Boston: Little, Brown.

Martin, H. P. (1972). The child and his development. In H. C. Kempe & R. E. Helfer (Eds.), *Helping the battered child and his family* (p. 93). Philadelphia: J. B. Lippincott.

Martin, H. P., Beezley, P., Conway, E. F., & Kempe, C. H. (1974). The development of abused children: A review of the literature and physical, neurologic, and intellectual findings. *Advances in Pediatrics, 21,* 25–73.

Meier, J. H. (1985). *Assault against children: Why it happens and how to stop it.* Austin, TX: PRO-ED.

Patterson, G. (1983). Stress: A change agent for family process in M. Rutter & N. Garmezy (Eds.), *Review of child development research* (pp. 235–264). Chicago: University of Chicago Press.

Pianta, R., Egeland, B., & Erickson, M. F. (1989). The antecedents of maltreatment: Results of the mother-child interaction research project. In D. Cicchetti & V. Carlson (Eds.), *Child maltreatment: Theory and research on the cause and consequences of child abuse and neglect* (pp. 203–253). New York: Cambridge University Press.

Rogers, D. E. (1978). *Hear the children crying.* Trenton, NJ: Fleming H. Revell.

Rose, T. L. (1983). A survey of corporal punishment of mildly handicapped students. *Exceptional Education Quarterly, 3*(4), 9–19.

Rosenbaum, A., & O'Leary, K. (1981). Children: The unintended victims of marital violence. *American Journal of Orthopsychiatry, 51,* 692–699.

Rusch, R. G., Hall, J. C., & Griffin, H. C. (1986). Abuse-provoking characteristics of institutionalized mentally retarded individuals. *American Journal of Mental Deficiency, 90,* 618–624.

Sakemiller, L. L. (1986). *Child abuse of handicapped children.* Unpublished master's thesis, Bowling Green State University, Bowling Green, OH.

Sandgrund, H., Gaines, R., & Green, A. (1974). Child abuse and mental retardation: A problem of cause and effect. *American Journal of Mental Deficiency, 79,* 327–330.

Starr, R. H., Jr. (1982). A research-based approach to the prediction of child abuse. In R. H. Starr, Jr. (Ed.), *Child abuse prediction: Policy implications* (pp.105–134). Cambridge, MA: Ballinger.

Straus, M. A. (1983). Ordinary violence, child abuse and wife beating: What do they have in common? In D. Finkelhor, R. J. Gelles, G. T. Hotaling, & M. A. Straus (Eds.), *The dark side of families: Current family violence research* (pp. 194–223). Beverly Hills, CA: Sage.

Straus, M. A., Gelles, R. J., & Steinmetz, S. K. (1980). *Behind closed doors: Violence in the American family.* New York: Anchor Press.

Zigler, E. (1979). Controlling child abuse in America: An effort doomed to failure. In R. Bourne & E. H. Newberger (Eds.), *Critical perspectives on child abuse* (pp. 171–207). Lexington, MA: Lexington Books.

Zirpoli, T. J. (1990). Problems in paradise. *TASH Newsletter, 16,* 4.

Zirpoli, T. J. (1986). Child abuse and children with handicaps. *Remedial and Special Education, 7*(2) 39–48.

Zirpoli, T. J., Snell, M. E., & Loyd, B. H. (1987). Characteristics of persons with mental retardation who have been abused by caregivers. *The Journal of Special Education, 21,* 31–41.

INTEGRATING
Elementary Students with Multiple Disabilities into Supported Regular Classes
Challenges and Solutions

Susan Hamre-Nietupski
Jennifer McDonald
John Nietupski

Susan Hamre-Nietupski *(CEC Chapter #88) is an Associate Professor, Division of Curriculum and Instruction/Special Education, The University of Iowa, Iowa City,* **Jennifer McDonald** *is a Special Educator, Adams Elementary School, Des Moines, Iowa.* **John Nietupski** *(CEC Chapter #88) is an Adjunct Associate Professor, Division of Developmental Disabilities and Division of Curriculum and Instruction, The University of Iowa, Iowa City.*

Integrated placement of students with multiple disabilities in regular classes (Strully & Strully, 1989) is being advocated by professionals and parents alike. With this model, assistance is provided in the areas of curriculum modification, participation, and social integration by special education/support teachers, paraprofessionals, integration facilitators (Ruttiman & Forest, 1987), and/or nondisabled peers (Forest & Lusthaus, 1990). Students with disabilities are offered increased opportunities for interactions with nondisabled peers as well as meaningful curricular content (Ford & Davern, 1989; Sailor et al., 1989; York, Vandercook, Caughey, & Heise-Neff, 1990).

The professional literature has described strategies for preparing regular educators and students for positive integration experiences (Certo, Haring, & York, 1984; Gaylord-Ross, 1989; Stainback & Stainback, 1985) and for teaming special educators with regular educators to promote regular class integration (Vandercook, York, & Forest, 1989; York & Vandercook, 1991). One practical concern for teachers is how they can promote both skill gains and social acceptance while involving students in regular class activities.

This article describes four potential challenges to supported education along with solutions that have been effective in meeting those challenges in an elementary school setting. Our observations are based on 4 years of experience in integrating students with multiple disabilities, including students with moderate and severe mental disabilities or autism with accompanying physical, visual, and/or behavior challenges. Our efforts focused on integrating elementary-age students into kindergarten through sixth-grade classes.

Background

The case of Stephanie, a first-grader, illustrates points in each challenge and solution. Stephanie was a student with multiple disabilities, including mental retardation in the moderate to severe range with accompanying physical disabilities and a vision impairment. She attended a 350-student elementary school in a midwestern community of 35,000 people. When Stephanie was kindergarten age, she spent half her day in a regular kindergarten class. The following year, she spent the entire school day in a regular first-grade class.

Challenges and Solutions

Challenge 1: Providing Functional Curriculum in a Regular Class

Instruction on the functional skills necessary to live, work, and participate in recreation activities in integrated community environments is a critical component of an appropriate education for students with multiple disabilities (Falvey, 1989). Since functional skills such as grooming and dressing rarely are taught in regular education, a challenge to supported education is how to teach these skills in the primarily academic environment of a regular class.

Five possible solutions might be considered to address this challenge. First, partial assistance might be provided by a peer in the context of class activities. For example, when Stephanie arrived at school in the winter, she could remove her boots easily. However, putting on her shoes was time-consuming, and she often missed out on much of the opening routine. One solution was to have Stephanie remove her boots upon arrival and take her shoes to the opening-group area. There she was taught to ask a nondisabled peer for assistance in putting on and tying her shoes. The peer was shown how to assist Stephanie with the difficult steps while encouraging her independence on the easier steps. This solution resulted in positive interactions between Stephanie and her peers, enabled her to take part in the opening routine, and allowed her to progress in this self-care skill.

A second strategy is to identify the "down times" during the school day in which functional skill instruction could be provided without disrupting the class routine. For example, Stephanie often had a runny nose and had not yet learned to blow her nose independently. The support teacher took her aside at such times as arrival, between academic activities, and prior to and after recess and lunch for brief, unobtrusive instruction. As a result, she missed very little regular class activity and she showed increased independence by the end of the school year.

A third potential solution is to provide parallel instruction on functional skills in the regular classroom while peers participate in their academic work. For example, when the nondisabled students were working on place value in mathematics, part or all of that period could be spent teaching Stephanie functional mathematics skills such as matching coins or other skills. One regular teacher reduced the possible stigma associated with parallel programming by identifying nondisabled students who needed similar instruction and rotating them through the self-care lessons with Stephanie. Since the teacher referred to this as a "health" or "hygiene" unit and involved nondisabled students, Stephanie was not singled out as different from her peers. Nondisabled children can benefit from this functional life skills instruction as well as their peers who have disabilities.

When none of the previously mentioned strategies seems feasible, brief removal of the student from the regular class for specialized instruction might be considered. For example, when nondisabled students receive instruction on academic activities clearly beyond the student's present skill level, instruction

on functional skills such as bathroom use, snack preparation, and street-crossing outside the classroom may be more appropriate.

Finally, to guarantee that instructional time is not sacrificed, districts should ensure that individualized education program (IEP) goals are drawn from an approved curriculum guide (e.g., Falvey, 1989; Ford et al., 1989). Such a guide can provide assurances that important instructional goals will not be overlooked.

Challenge 2: Providing Community-Based Instruction

Another challenge to regular class integration is including community-based instruction within the educational program. Community-based instruction is needed because of the generalization difficulties experienced by students with multiple disabilities. However, little opportunity for such instruction currently is provided to students in regular elementary education.

In addition to following an approved curriculum guide that includes community-based instruction, two strategies might be employed to address this challenge. The first is to bring the community into the classroom. An example of this strategy was implemented in conjunction with a creative writing unit in which students were required to write about turtles. In order to make this unit more meaningful to Stephanie, who had limited exposure to turtles, arrangements were made to borrow a turtle from a local pet store. After the morning visit by the turtle, Stephanie, three of her nondisabled peers, and the support teacher returned the turtle to the pet store. All four students were able to see, touch, and learn about a variety of exotic birds and animals. As Stephanie and two other students looked at the animals, another wrote down the group's favorite pets and their cost. Upon returning to school, the four wrote and shared a story about their trip and sent a thank-you note to the pet store. Thus, all four students had a community experience that was integrally related to the creative writing unit and allowed the nondisabled students to apply their skills to a meaningful situation. While use of community resources may be difficult to achieve on all units, careful consideration of such opportunities can both enhance the regular curriculum

and provide opportunities for community-based instruction.

Another possible strategy involves providing community-based instruction to the student with disabilities in an integrated manner (Ford & Davern, 1989). Small groups of nondisabled students could accompany a peer with disabilities on a rotating basis. The community experiences would allow all students to apply skills being taught in the classroom to real-world settings. For example, integrated instruction in a supermarket could be structured so that a student with multiple disabilities locates various grocery items while peers practice adding costs and comparing prices.

Challenge 3: Scheduling Staff Coverage

Special education staff can support integrated students in many ways, including (a) making adaptations when needed; (b) assisting the classroom teacher in working with a student; (c) coaching nondisabled peers; (d) providing direct instruction; and (e) facilitating positive interactions among students. The scheduling challenge lies in providing this support when it is needed for the student to participate in classroom activities.

One solution in Stephanie's situation was for the regular education and support teachers to determine cooperatively when support was most needed. The support teacher developed a flexible schedule so she could assist Stephanie during activities that were the most challenging for her and/or were most difficult to individualize.

While scheduling support during critical periods is helpful, teachers occasionally need to support several students in several classes simultaneously. In those situations, university students or parent volunteers might provide additional support. With training, these volunteers could assist in regular classrooms when the support teacher is unable to do so.

Another strategy is to empower regular teachers to assume greater instructional responsibility for students with multiple disabilities. Our experience has been that regular teachers can be as effective as special education teachers in meeting the needs of students with disabilities. Encouraging them to do so, involving them in solving instructional problems, demonstrating particular techniques, and reinforcing accomplishments are all strategies for increasing the competence and confidence of regular class teachers.

Another strategy for dealing with the coverage challenge is to work closely with the classroom teacher to identify when and how nondisabled peers might serve in a support role. For example, activities might be designed on the basis of cooperative learning (Johnson & Johnson, 1989), whereby students become responsible for working together and assisting each other.

One additional solution to providing adequate staff coverage is to reduce class size when integrating a student with multiple disabilities. Sailor and colleagues (1989) suggested that this strategy can make support from the regular classroom teacher a more realistic option.

Challenge 4: Promoting Social Integration

The final challenge addressed here is that of promoting social integration and friendships between students with and without disabilities. Strully and Strully (1989) argued that supported education is important because it facilitates the formation of friendships and long-lasting, supportive, personal relationships. Research by Guralnick (1980) has suggested that these relationships do not occur simply through integrated physical placement but must be facilitated.

Administrator Support. Administrators can facilitate friendships in several ways. First, students with multiple disabilities can be assigned to the regular school they would attend if they were not disabled, along with children from their neighborhood, making participation in after-school activities such as parties and school functions more feasible (Brown et al., 1989; Sailor et al., 1989).

Second, administrators can set the tone for integration in a school. In Stephanie's school, the principal strongly believed that all children belonged in regular classes and that promoting positive, cooperative social interactions was an important goal in each classroom. Thus, teachers had a heightened awareness of the social aspects of education and focused on promoting positive relationships among students.

Third, administrators can arrange for after-school social opportunities.

Stephanie's principal was instrumental in developing monthly recreational drop-in programs and summer recreation offerings that allowed all students to socialize.

Teacher Support. Regular class teachers, too, can address the challenge of promoting social interactions and friendships. One well-documented strategy is cooperative learning (Johnson & Johnson, 1989), in which rewards and evaluations are based on the quality of the work and student collaboration.

Regular class teachers also can promote a positive social atmosphere by treating students with multiple disabilities as normally as possible. Stephanie's teacher, for example, placed Stephanie's name on the class roster and assigned her a desk, coathook, and materials space amidst those of the other students. She expected, encouraged, and reinforced adherence to classroom rules for all students, including Stephanie. These actions communicated to all students that Stephanie was as much a member of the class as anyone else.

Finally, regular class teachers can actively promote social relationships (Stainback & Stainback, 1987). Stephanie's teacher did so by pairing children for many activities, modeling and encouraging social interactions, and reinforcing students when positive interactions occurred.

Special educators, support teachers, and integration facilitators can address the challenges of promoting social interaction in several ways. They can model and encourage social interactions. Early in the school year, nondisabled students often would ask the support teacher whether or not Stephanie would like to play and whether or not she enjoyed certain activities. The support teacher would encourage the children to ask Stephanie themselves or show them how to do so. By the end of the year, nondisabled students initiated conversation directly with Stephanie, not through her support teacher.

A second strategy is to develop sensitization sessions that focus on recognizing similarities and differences and getting along with people who are different in some way (Hamre-Nietupski & Nietupski, 1985). In Stephanie's class, her support teacher and the guidance counselor developed a six-session unit on how children are similar and different, how to be friends with those around you, and how to communicate

in different ways. Activities included having all children identify their strengths and weaknesses and likes and dislikes, generate specific ways to be friends with people in the class, and learn how to initiate and respond to social interactions. These activities were carried out in a large group that included Stephanie but did not single her out.

Support teachers can develop circles of friends to promote social interactions (Forest & Lusthaus, 1990). In Stephanie's school, a student with autism was integrated into a regular fifth-grade class. The support teacher, concerned about the lack of social integration, organized a circle of friends with nondisabled volunteer companions. This group identified in- and out-of-school interaction opportunities such as going to the library together and attending the drop-in recreation program, and they socialized with her.

Finally, support teachers can keep parents informed about interaction opportunities and encourage parental support. Stephanie's support teacher regularly kept Stephanie's parents informed about the students she interacted with and upcoming after-school events. On occasion, she even made transportation arrangements so Stephanie could participate with her peers.

Parental Support. Parental support is also necessary to promote social relationships and friendships. Parents can become active in the parent-teacher organization and in school-wide activities. They might encourage their child's participation in extracurricular activities such as Cub Scouts, Brownies, and 4-H or help in initiating play opportunities by having their child invite a nondisabled friend to spend the night or hosting or having their child attend birthday parties. Such activities are extremely important in making and maintaining friendships.

Parents also can promote social relationships through sensitivity to clothing selection and hairstyle. Nondisabled students, even in elementary schools, are keenly aware of "in" clothing. Since this a sensitive and value-laden issue, interventions may need to be quite subtle. For example, when asked, teachers might suggest holiday or birthday gift ideas for students (e.g., "I've noticed that Stephanie really likes Tracy's [name brand] sweatshirts") as a way to assist parents in facilitating social acceptance.

Conclusion

While we are encouraged by the outcomes of the strategies described here, two limitations should be noted. First, the strategies were developed for elementary-age students. Additional research and demonstration are needed to guide teachers serving older students. Second, questions have been raised about how and the degree to which students with profound, multiple disabilities might be integrated into regular classes. At this point, perhaps those questions should remain open—with practitioners and researchers encouraged to examine them through empirical demonstration activities.

Supported regular education for students with multiple disabilities is not without challenges, but potential solutions are beginning to emerge. It is our hope that, through examples such as these, increasing numbers of school systems will be encouraged to integrate elementary-age students with multiple disabilities more fully into regular education classes.

References

Brown, L., Long, E., Udarvi-Solner, A., Davis, L., VanDeventer, P., Algren, C., Johnson, F.,

Gruenewald, L., & Jorgensen, J. (1989). The home school: Why students with severe intellectual disabilities must attend the schools of their brothers, sisters, friends, and neighbors. *Journal of the Association for Persons with Severe Handicaps, 14*, 1-7.

Certo, N., Haring, N., & York, R. (1984). *Public school integration of severely handicapped students.* Baltimore: Paul H. Brookes.

Falvey, M. (1989). *Community-based curriculum: Instructional strategies for students with severe handicaps.* Baltimore: Paul H. Brookes.

Ford, A., & Davern, L. (1989). Moving forward with school integration: Strategies for involving students with severe handicaps in the life of the school. In R. Gaylord-Ross (Ed.), *Integration strategies for students with severe handicaps* (pp. 11-32). Baltimore: Paul H. Brookes.

Ford, A., Schnorr, R., Meyer, L., Davern, L., Black, J., & Dempsey, P. (1989). *The Syracuse community-referenced curriculum guide for students with moderate and severe disabilities.* Baltimore: Paul H. Brookes.

Forest, M., & Lusthaus, E. (1990). Everyone belongs with the MAPS Action Planning System. *TEACHING Exceptional Children, 22*, 32-35.

Gaylord-Ross, R. (Ed.). (1989). *Integration strategies for students with severe handicaps.* Baltimore: Paul H. Brookes.

Guralnick, M. (1980). Social interactions among preschool children. *Exceptional Children, 46*, 248-253.

Hamre-Nietupski, S., & Nietupski, J. (1985). Taking full advantage of interaction opportunities. In S. Stainback & W. Stainback (Eds.), *Integration of students with severe handicaps into regular schools* (pp. 98-112). Reston, VA: The Council for Exceptional Children.

Johnson, D., & Johnson, R. (1989). Cooperative learning and mainstreaming. In R. Gaylord-Ross (Ed.), *Integration strategies for students with handicaps* (pp. 233-248). Baltimore: Paul H. Brookes.

Ruttiman, A., & Forest, M. (1987). With a little help from my friends: The integration facilitator at work. In M. Forest (Ed.), *More education/integration* (pp. 131-142). Downsview, Ontario: Roeher Institute.

Sailor, W., Anderson, J., Halvorsen, A., Doering, K., Filler, J., & Goetz, L. (1989). *The comprehensive local school: Regular education for all students with disabilities.* Baltimore: Paul H. Brookes.

Stainback, S., & Stainback, W. (Eds.). (1985). *Integration of students with severe handicaps into regular schools.* Reston, VA: The Council for Exceptional Children.

Stainback, W., & Stainback, S. (1987). Facilitating friendships. *Education and Training in Mental Retardation, 22*, 10-25.

Strully, J., & Strully, C. (1989). Friendships as an educational goal. In S. Stainback, W. Stainback, & M. Forest (Eds.), *Educating all students in the mainstream of regular education* (pp. 59-68). Baltimore: Paul H. Brookes.

Vandercook, T., York, J., & Forest, M. (1989). The McGill Action Planning System (MAPS): A strategy for building the vision. *Journal of The Association for Persons with Severe Handicaps, 14*, 205-215.

York, J., & Vandercook, T. (1991). Designing an integrated program for learners with severe disabilities. *TEACHING Exceptional Children, 23*(1), 22-28.

York, J., Vandercook, T., Caughey, E., & Heise-Neff, C. (1990, May). Regular class integration: Beyond socialization. *The Association for Persons with Severe Handicaps Newsletter, 16*, p. 3.

Designing an Integrated Program for Learners with Severe Disabilities

Jennifer York • Terri Vandercook

Jennifer York *(CEC Chapter #298) is Assistant Professor of Special Education and* **Terri Vandercook** *(CEC Chapter #298) is Associate Director for Field-Based Training, Institute on Community Integration, University of Minnesota, MN.*

An environmentally referenced approach to curriculum development has been advocated widely as the basis for designing and implementing individualized education programs (IEPs) for students with severe disabilities (Brown et al., 1979; Falvey, 1986; Thousand, Nevin-Parta, & Fox, 1987). The primary rationale for this approach is that children with severe disabilities learn best when the skills being taught are useful in daily activities. In addition, through observation and assessment in typical daily environments, IEP team members can identify more accurately the objectives that are most relevant to individual children. For these reasons, four environmentally referenced life-space domains have been promoted as the basis for organizing curriculum content: Community, Domestic, Recreation/Leisure, and Vocational (Brown et al., 1979; Falvey, 1986).

In some instances, a life-space domain curricular organization has led educators and parents to focus predominantly on instruction in off-campus, community environments. Some of the most important age-appropriate daily environments for

children with disabilities, however, are regular education environments within the school building. In the context of regular classes, extracurricular activities, and other age-appropriate environments, students learn social competencies in addition to subject-area curriculum content. Successful participation and acceptance in home, community, and work environments depend not only on performing the steps delineated in a task analysis, but also on demonstrating appropriate social, communication, and related skills. By attending school together, both learners with disabilities and those without can gain the attitudes, values, and skills necessary to get along as interdependent members of society. One way to incorporate the school community into a life-space domain curricular organization is to simply expand the Community Domain to include both school community and general community sections.

This article presents a strategy for developing IEPs based on the assumption of age-appropriate participation in regular education classes, with special education and related services provided in regular school environments as the need arises. The strategy reflects the work of the authors in collaboration with personnel in numerous school districts who are in the process of moving from a self-contained special education classroom model of service delivery to a model in which

children are based in age-appropriate regular education homerooms and other regular classes, supplemented by community-based instruction.

IEP Team Strategies

Teamwork among regular educators, special education teachers, support personnel, parents, and peers is critical to the success of integrated education programs. As IEP teams strive to make objectives relevant and functional, they must have a clear picture of the outcomes desired for individual students—a vision of these students participating in typical school, home, community, and work environments. The strategy for IEP development presented here is intended to guide teams through a process that builds on learner strengths in planning for goals and objectives related to integrated settings.

Assumptions for an Integrated IEP Strategy

Integration. The first basic assumption underlying an integrated IEP process is that students with severe disabilities must be integrated members of their school communities. This includes regular class membership and participation in extracurricular activities and other aspects of school life. By law, children with disabilities are to be educated in the same environments as their peers without disabilities to the greatest extent possible. The assumption is that special education is a support and service, instead of a place. Although the merit of an integrated approach for children with severe disabilities is an issue of some debate, an increasing number of IEP teams are planning for elementary-age learners to receive most of their instruction in regular education classes and for secondary-age learners to receive instruction in both regular education and general community environments. Their aim is to design and implement IEPs that minimize isolation from peers and maximize the learning opportunities available to all children.

Individualization. The second assumption is that educational needs and priorities must be determined individually for each student. Given the overwhelming number of environments and activities in which an individual student could learn to participate and the variety of skills that would enhance participation, educational team members who know the student best must collaborate in making decisions about program priorities based on individual, family, school, and community characteristics. This individualization of educational priorities can help to assure the most appropriate and relevant use of instructional time.

Teamwork. The need for teamwork is becoming increasingly evident as teams plan for children with even the most severe disabilities to be included in regular school and community environments. How does a student with severe disabilities actively participate in regular classroom activities and routines? What are the educational priorities? How are interactions with classmates facilitated? What curricular, environmental, and instructional adaptations need to be made? These questions cannot be answered by one person alone. Children with severe disabilities have many varied assets and needs. Pooling the expertise, perspectives, and resources of a variety of team members is essential to the design and implementation of high-quality educational programs in integrated settings. Each learner's team should include at least the learner; the learner's parents; friends; a special educator; a regular educator; and, as needed, paraprofessionals, therapists, and others with specialized areas of expertise. The involvement of the principal or an administrative designee on the

team is also critical to success. The administrator may not attend all planned meetings, but his or her leadership and support in drawing together resources and helping to solve logistical and programmatic problems are essential. All team members share responsibility for program development and student success, and each should feel supported by the other team members in his or her efforts.

Flexibility. The need for flexibility is particularly important to keep in mind, since designing integrated education programs is a new process for most team members. An IEP is a working document that should reflect a student's current program. It should be updated and modified as student needs and abilities change and as team members learn more about student abilities in integrated settings. Before a student is integrated into regular class environments, it is difficult to predict with certainty the instructional priorities related to each class. All people modify their behavior to some extent based on the environment, and children with disabilities are no different. This is why objectives identified prior to integration may have to be changed after a student begins to participate in the actual class. Modifications in IEP objectives are not restricted to annual reviews. Instead, parents and school personnel should remain in contact throughout the school year and collaborate in decisions regarding appropriate modifications to the IEP in response to integrated experiences.

Environmental Referencing. The final assumption relates to the need to reference targeted skills to performance demands in actual environments. Skills are useful only if they can be demonstrated in typical daily environments and activities (e.g., on the playground, during reading group, at home, and in the community). Therefore, goals and objectives must communicate not only targeted skills but also the contexts in which performance outcomes are desired. By conducting an inventory of the demands and opportunities in regular classes and observing as the student functions in specific regular classes, the IEP team can identify both priority skills and the regular class contexts in which they can be demonstrated.

An Integrated IEP Strategy

Step 1: Get the big picture. Before a team can collaborate in planning an integrated

education program for an individual learner, team members should develop a common vision of the learner's educational outcomes. First, the assumptions for IEP development are discussed, with the team acknowledging that they may present a considerable deviation from the usual basis of IEP design. Team members are encouraged to ask questions and express concerns, because it is difficult to accept a new way of thinking and of providing services that is not based on personal experience. Greater commitment and confidence develop as the process is implemented successfully and the vision begins to take shape.

Second, the team identifies places or environments in which the learner should be able to participate both at present and in the future. This list of potential instructional environments is derived from several sources. In elementary school, regular education classroom teachers can outline the periods and activities in which same-age peers spend their school day. At the secondary level, where classes change every period and students are taught by several different teachers, the grade-level counselor may be the most appropriate person to outline a typical school day. The school course catalog and extracurricular activities schedule can also be used to identify specific opportunities for integration. Peers know about informal school happenings and preferred curriculum offerings. Parents assist by identifying the family's home and community environments and activities engaged in by neighborhood peers. All team members contribute to generating a list of school, home, community, and work environments that the student might encounter in the future. By identifying actual places, the team develops and shares a collective vision of the student leading an integrated life.

The worksheet shown in Figure 1 can be used to organize the lists of environments and activities generated by the team. It is intentionally labeled as a *worksheet* because each team member receives a copy of it and is free to write and revise his or her own thoughts about priority places and targets for instruction as the team discussion takes place. Notice that the Community Domain has been divided into two parts: the school community and the general community. This is done in recognition of the fact that the school is a primary community environment for school-age learners. In addition to conducting an inventory of the general community, it is equally important to conduct an inventory of the regular education curricular and extracurricular opportunities at school.

In the top set of boxes, actual environments, activities, or regular classes are specified. In the bottom set of boxes, priority skills to be addressed across environments and activities are delineated. These are referred to as *embedded skills* (Ford et al., 1989). For example, making choices, transferring in and out of a wheelchair, reaching, following a schedule, and writing all are skills that may be required in one or more environments throughout the day. The term *embedded skills* is intended to reinforce a functional approach to instruction in which skills are addressed instructionally in the contexts in which they are useful, instead of in isolation, where generalization to relevant situations can only be assumed.

Step 2: Identify initial IEP priorities. From the list of places identified on the IEP worksheet, the team selects environments and activities to be given instructional attention for the current IEP. For elementary-age students, most of the instructional environments will be located in and around the school building, in regular classes and other places used by same-age peers who do not have disabilities. For secondary-age students, an increasing number of instructional environments will be off campus, in the community, thereby making the school day a combination of regular class and community-based instruction. Figure 1a illustrates the priorities for an elementary-age student. The student (age 7) spends all of her day in typical school environments, regular classes, and other general areas of the school. As shown in Figure 1b, the secondary-age student (age 15) spends homeroom plus three periods a day in regular education classes. During the remainder of the day, instruction is provided in off-campus community environments. Two or three times a week during the school day, the student goes to two of the community environments (i.e., to an integrated work site and to the mall for exercise). He goes to the store and to the restaurant twice a week. His mother provides regular opportunities for him to engage in the identified domestic activities at home.

With the priority environments identified, team members collaborate in projecting initial goals and objectives based on their current understanding of the demands and opportunities in the regular classes (and other environments) and of the student's current abilities and future-referenced activities. It is not until after the student's abilities are assessed in the actual environments, however, that IEP goals and objectives can be finalized. Consistent with an environmentally referenced approach to curriculum development, IEP goals and objectives can be organized as follows. The annual goal identifies participation in the priority environment. Objectives related to the annual goal identify the skills targeted for instruction in the environment. Following are two examples related to participation in regular classes that specify goal and objective content areas:
Goal: Karen will participate in seventh-grade art class.

> Objective: When assisted to the correct hallway, she will locate and enter the art room independently.
> Objective: At the beginning of the class, she will initiate saying "Hi" to an adjacent peer at the table.
> Objective: When presented with a choice of paints and a gestural cue to each option, she will choose the color of paints she wishes to use.
> Objective: At the end of the class before clean up, she will tap the arm of a peer at the table and will point to her own artwork so the peer looks at her artwork.

Goal: Vicki will participate in a second-grade reading class.

> Objective: She will maintain a supported sitting position on the carpeted floor in the reading area.
> Objective: She will look at and turn the pages of the book as a peer reads out loud.
> Objective: She will select from among two audiotapes with picture cues.
> Objective: She will depress a microswitch to turn on her portable cassette player to listen to the tapes.
> Objective: She will maintain her body weight in a standing position when being helped to transfer back into her wheelchair.

Organizing goals and objectives in this manner makes it easy for the team to locate and understand which IEP objectives correspond to each period of the day. This facilitates communication of the instructional priorities related to each regular class and off-campus instructional environment to all team members, including the regular educator.

Step 3: Integrate the learner into regular class and other priority environ-

ments. The team then implements a plan for the learner to begin participation in the designated environments. Frequently, the support of a special education teacher, related services person, or paraprofessional is provided initially in the regular class. Some regular education classroom teachers, however, prefer that the student with disabilities begin attending the class without a support person so that the classroom teacher, classmates, and new student have the opportunity to learn about each other without an intermediary. A team decision is made about what initial supports are appropriate given the specific student, class, and teacher variables. If the team decides that a support person is necessary, the role of that person must be delineated clearly. It is crucial for the support person to focus on facilitating inclusion of the student in the class and not serve as a barrier to interactions.

Precise and environmentally referenced IEP goals and objectives are identified by carefully assessing learner abilities within each of the priority school and community environments, including regular classes. In some classes, this assessment may focus primarily on skills required to participate in the regular activities and routines (e.g., following class rules, sharing materials with peers, working cooperatively with peers) and on social and communication skills (e.g., interaction with peers at appropriate times, making choices, following directions) (Macdonald & York, 1989). For some students, skills related to the actual content area may be emphasized to a lesser degree, or individualized curricular adaptations or activities may be designed. For example, in a painting class, a middle school student with severe disabilities was learning to use a hand-held wood engraver. Working with wood was identified as a potential lifelong leisure interest based on previous involvement in a wood shop class. In a home economics class, another student's priorities included making drinks and snacks in the microwave oven, even though use of the oven was not part of the regular curriculum for that particular grade level. An elementary student in a regular reading class was working on depressing a microswitch to turn on a tape recording of a storybook, which she and a peer listened to with headphones. Parallel activities such as these, which can be conducted alongside classmates, are identified by the team and referenced to functional demands in current and future

Figure 1:

IEP Development Worksheet (Note: some of the items could be written in more than one column. The domains are not mutually exclusive.)

a) Example for elementary school student

Life Span Domains: Specify Places

School	Community	General	Recreation/Leisure	Domestic	Vocational
Opening (make choices)	Handwriting (use name stamp, fine motor leisure skills)	Bus stop (wave hi and bye to family/peers)	Girl Scouts	Kitchen (eat and drink independently)	
Reading (use microswitch for taped story)	Art (make requests)			Family room and bedroom (transitional movement and weight bearing)	
Language (match objects/photos)	Lunch (feed self and lunch clean-up)				
Math (1:1 correspondence, getting and passing out juice)	PE (take turns, weight bearing)				
Restroom	Health				
Social Studies	Recess (Recreation with peers)				
Storytime	Music (use microswitch)				
Science (turn-taking)					

Embedded Skills: List Priorities

Motor	Communication	Academic	Other
Transitional movement sequences from floor to chair, from chair to stand)	Making choices	Using a picture schedule	Quieting vocalizations which occur during transitional movement sequences
Weight bearing in kneeling and standing positions	Matching objects and photos	Using a microswitch	Using a spoon to feed self
Using power wheelchair (moving forward, stopping on verbal command, stopping when hits objects)	Making requests	Using a name stamp	Drinking without spilling
Active full range of motion of extremities and trunk	Waving hi and bye and giving a peer a "high five"	Holding and turning pages of a book	Taking turns

b) Example for secondary school student

Life Span Domains: Specify Places

School	Community	General	Recreation/Leisure	Domestic	Vocational
Homeroom	Bus stop (greet neighbor kids)		Rosedale Mall (wheel with "mall-walkers")	Kitchen (use microwave)	Hardware store (stock supplies and work-related skills)
Home Ec Class (meal prep and clean up)	Transportation in car (transfer in/out, wheelchair storage)			Bedroom (transfer from wheelchair to bed)	
Art Class (independent leisure, paint, wood carve)	Cub Foods (grocery shop)				
Computer Lab (play games with peer)	Hardees (eat out)				
Newspaper Club					

Embedded Skills: List Priorities

Motor	Communication	Academic	Other
Standing pivot transfers in/out of wheelchair	Making choices	Developing picture sequence of daily schedule	Keeping mouth area and hands dry and clean
Walking short distances with physical assistance	Answering yes/no questions	Using picture shopping list	
Wheeling (consecutive pushes)	Greeting (making eye contact and saying "Hi")		
	Using message cards to communicate with school and community personnel		

domestic, leisure, community, and vocational environments.

Step 4: Revise and implement IEP priorities. It is not until learners have an opportunity to participate in regular classes and other instructional environments that actual needs and specific supports can be identified and assessed accurately. This is the main reason why the initial delineation of priority IEP objectives (Step 2) is tentative. As regular class integration becomes the rule instead of the exception, IEP teams will be able to delineate objectives more accurately, because they will be based on a history of performance in regular classes. Based on the learner's actual involvement in designated environments, the team can revise the IEP to reflect more clearly defined needs, priorities, and supports. Objectives for each regular class may identify skills related to the class routine, age-appropriate social and interaction competencies, and regular or individualized curriculum content areas. Results of the assessment form the basis for team verification of objectives for instructional emphasis. With objectives delineated, instructional programs and data collection methods can be developed.

Common Questions and Possible Solutions

Developing an integrated IEP—not just the written document but the education program itself—is a new process for most team members that requires acquisition of new skills. The acquisition stage of learning is inefficient by definition, and false starts should be expected. Initially, team members may be at varying levels of agreement with and understanding of the integrated IEP assumptions and process. During initial change efforts, team members should be selected who are, at a minimum, interested in and willing to try a new way of service delivery. Over time, as team members interact and become more efficient in their new roles and as positive results of integrated education are demonstrated, the team members' operating assumptions and vision of an integrated education will become more similar, and change efforts can be extended to include greater numbers of educators and students. Following are some of the common questions that arise when teams begin to implement the integrated IEP process, along with useful strategies for addressing them.

Where Do We Start?

A team might start by initiating an integrated IEP process for one student to demonstrate the process in action. In a school district where parents are advocating for more integrated programs, the logical student of choice would be the son or daughter of one of those parents. In a district where integration pursuits are initiated by teachers, the team might start by approaching parents who they believe would be in favor of their child's being included to a greater degree in regular education activities with same-age peers.

Because one of the goals of integration is full inclusion in regular school community life, consistent presence and participation in regular classes, instead of periodic visits, is an important guiding principle. In elementary schools, regular education students spend most of their school day with the same classmates and teacher. A student with disabilities should also begin by spending the school day based in the regular class. This provides team members with the opportunity to observe the student in the class and to devise ways to increase participation. Although some educational needs may require use of environments outside the regular class (e.g., self-care skills addressed in restrooms, mobility skills addressed in hallways and on the playground), the primary base of the elementary school student is the regular class of which he or she is a member.

In secondary school programs, regular education students usually rotate classes every period and have several teachers. For a middle school or high school student with disabilities, one place to start is to assign the student to an age-appropriate regular homeroom and select two or three regular classes. The remainder of the school day is likely to be spent receiving instruction in community environments.

Perhaps the most difficult task for educational teams is to set priorities. This requires them to acknowledge that all the pieces for assuring high-quality integration cannot be put in place tomorrow and that all the problems will not be solved immediately. Focusing on facilitating inclusion, high-quality interactions, and high-quality programming in one or two classes at a time is a reasonable start. Of course, there *are* students for whom very little adaptation and problem solving are required. In some classes, students with disabilities fit in, follow the regular class

Students with disabilities must by law be integrated into the classroom so that they feel supported by the learning community.

routine, and even participate in curricular activities similar to those of their classmates with very few, if any, special arrangements. In some situations, classmates quite naturally take on a support role, and little intervention is needed. Frequently, however, peer support must be facilitated.

Who Does What?

The answer to this question depends largely on the resources available in the

district and building and the experience of the individuals involved. For example, one rural special education cooperative hired a half-time special education teacher to provide curricular and instructional expertise for three elementary-age students with severe disabilities, each of whom attended a different regular class in a different school district. In this situation, daily instruction was provided by the classroom teacher and a paraprofessional, but the education program was designed in concert with the special educator. In more urban districts, where a greater number of students with severe disabilities attend the same neighborhood school, a special education teacher might be assigned to one school, providing curricular and instructional support as well as some direct instruction on a regular basis. Addressing the question of who does what, therefore, requires careful analysis and creative solutions based on the particular situation.

In order to determine who does what, the input required from each team member is identified. The regular educator is familiar with the curricular and social expectations, instructional formats, and types of students in his or her class. This teacher's input is also important when curricular or logistical adaptations are required. The expertise of the special educator is in the area of individualized and functional design of curriculum and instruction. Therapists and other support services personnel are responsible for seeing that the student's motor, communication, and other needs are addressed as they relate to functioning in educational activities.

Where Do We Find the Time?

Again, this will depend on each situation. In elementary classes, planning frequently involves only one regular educator, the students' classroom teacher. In secondary programs, where more than one regular educator is involved, participation in frequent team meetings is more difficult, because teachers are sometimes responsible to hundreds of students each day. In deciding how and when to include regular educators, it has been helpful to view large-scale annual planning and ongoing programmatic planning separately.

At annual IEP planning meetings, a regular educator who knows the student must be present. For elementary students, this is the classroom teacher. For secondary students, the regular education participant could be the grade-level counselor or dean, a homeroom teacher, or a subject-area teacher. In some districts, administrators have been able to support regular education involvement in these planning meetings by hiring substitute teachers for part of a day or even teaching the class themselves. Ongoing meetings to discuss programming issues are more informal and may include only the special education teacher and regular educator. Smaller amounts of time are needed for these purposes, and the meet-

ings frequently occur before school, after school, or during planning periods.

Programmatic problem-solving and planning activities may occur during regular classes also. When the special educator or therapist is consulting in the class itself, information can be exchanged with the regular educator during that time. Block scheduling of consultant time, a strategy developed for therapists implementing an integrated therapy model (Rainforth & York, 1987; York, Rainforth, & Wiemann, 1988), can be used for special educators serving in a consultative and support role to regular educators. With this strategy, consulting schedules are devised that allocate larger blocks of time with individual students to special educators and therapists so that they can observe the child functioning in a variety of situations and determine appropriate curricular, instructional, and therapeutic methods to increase participation in an integrated setting.

Almost without exception, regular and special education team members have commented that during the initial stages of implementing the new process considerable time is required for planning and meeting. Over time, however, the need for such intensive collaboration decreases substantially as successful interventions are designed and implemented. Also, team members frequently remark that classmates have proved to be a tremendous resource both in helping to solve problems and, in some cases, in providing support.

In addressing the issue of finding time for planning, it is helpful to consider two points. First, it is critically important to adhere to the natural ratios of students with disabilities to peers without disabilities. Approximately 1 out of every 100 children of the same age has severe disabilities. Being involved in intensive planning for 1 child is much more manageable than planning for 3 or 5 or 10 children who have intensive needs. Unfortunately, special education systems have been designed to cluster children with similar disabilities, which results in disproportionate numbers of students with disabilities and greatly strains regular education resources. When approaching integration from a systems design standpoint, therefore, adherence to natural proportions should be a guiding principle.

Second, integration of students with severe disabilities is not just a one-way giving of time and resources. Many reg-

ular educators who have been involved in regular class integration efforts have remarked that they and their regular education students have benefited (York, Vandercook, Heise-Neff, & Caughey, 1988). Regular educators have commented that they feel more supported in their work and have learned new instructional strategies that benefit nondisabled children as well. Some classroom teachers have noted improved self-esteem and in some cases improved grades on the part of nondisabled classmates who become involved with a peer who has disabilities.

How Can Peers Be Involved?

Time and again, nondisabled peers have emerged as some of the best problem solvers and supporters for achieving the successful integration of students with disabilities. Increasingly, classmates are becoming involved in the IEP process by identifying important age-appropriate, socially valid activities in which their peers with disabilities should participate (see, for example, Forest & Lusthaus, 1987; and Vandercook, York, & Forest, 1989). Classmates have also been involved in "Circles of Friends" activities in which social support networks have been created for peers with disabilities (Mackan & Cormiere, 1987; Perske & Perske, 1988; Snow & Forest, 1988). After students with disabilities become members of regular classes, classmates and neighborhood peers who get to know and become friends with the students are asked to participate in formal planning strategies. Some of the planning sessions for elementary school students might occur during the school day. For secondary school students, planning is more likely to occur after school. On a more informal basis, classmates are encouraged to provide assistance as needed for students with disabilities to participate in regular class activities and routines. For example, peers might assist a student to locate the class, find a seat, obtain appropriate materials, and partially participate in small-group and laboratory activities.

Conclusion

When developing IEP goals and objectives, teams must think about the places and activities in which learner participation is desired, both currently and in the future. Inclusion in regular school life, including regular classes and extracurricular activities, is a primary emphasis in designing IEPs. Families, friends, and educational service providers work together to identify high-priority school and community environments and activities for each student. Both assessment and instruction occur in a variety of real environments, including regular classes, so that children learn skills required for participation and have regular opportunities to use them. IEP goals and objectives then reflect this functional, environmentally referenced approach. Providing instruction in regular education environments alongside peers without disabilities gives children with severe disabilities the opportunity to be more valued and participating members of the regular school community. Only when children learn and grow up together can the barriers to community integration be overcome.

References

Brown, L., Branston, M. B., Hamre-Nietupski, S., Pumpian, I., Certo, N., & Gruenewald, L. (1979). A strategy for developing chronological age appropriate and functional curricular content for severely handicapped adolescents and young adults. *Journal of Special Education, 13*(1), 81–90.

Falvey, M. (1986). *Community-based curriculum: Instructional strategies for students with severe handicaps.* Baltimore: Paul H. Brookes.

Ford, A., Schnorr, R., Meyer, L., Davern., L., Black, J., & Dempsey, P. (1989). *The Syracuse community-referenced curriculum guide for students with moderate and severe disabilities.* Baltimore, MD:Paul H. Brookes Publishing Company.

Forest, M., & Lusthaus, E. (1987). The kaleidoscope: A challenge to the cascade. In M. Forest (Ed.), *More education/integration: A further collection of readings on the integration of children with mental handicaps in regular school systems* (pp. 1–16). Downsview, Ontario: G. Allan Roeher Institute.

Macdonald, C., & York, J. (1989). Regular class integration: Assessment, objectives, and instructional programs. In J. York, T. Vandercook, C. Macdonald, & S. Wolff (Eds.), *Strategies for full inclusion* (pp. 83–116). Minneapolis:University of Minnesota, Institute on Community Integration.

Mackan, P., & Cormier, L. (1987). *The dynamics of support circles.* Toronto: Frontier College, Center for Integrated Education.

Perske, R., & Perske, M. (1988). *Circles of friends.* Nashville, TN: Abingdon Press.

Rainforth, B., & York, J. (1987). Related services on community-based instruction. *Journal of the Association for Persons with Severe Handicaps, 12*(3), 190–198.

Snow, J., & Forest, M. (1988). *Support circles: Building a vision.* Toronto: Frontier College, Center for Integrated Education.

Thousand, J., Nevin-Parta, A., & Fox, W. L. (1987). Inservice training to support the education of learners with severe handicaps in their local public schools. *Teacher education in special education, 10*(1), 4–13.

Vandercook, T., York, J., & Forest, M. (1989). MAPS: A strategy for building the vision. *Journal of the Association for Persons with Severe Handicaps, 14*(3), 205–215.

York, J., Rainforth, B., & Wiemann, G. (1988). An integrated approach to therapy for learners with developmental disabilities. *Totline, 14*(3), 36–40.

York, J., Vandercook, T., Heise-Neff, C., & Caughey, E. (1988). *Feedback from teachers and classmates about regular class integration.* Minneapolis: University of Minnesota, Institute on Community Integration.

This article was developed with support by Grants No. G008630347-88 and 07DD0282/04 from the Office of Special Education and Rehabilitative Services of the U.S. Department of Education, and the Minnesota Integrated Education Technical Assistance Grant. Points of view or opinions stated in this article do not necessarily represent the official position of the U.S. Department of Education or the Minnesota Department of Education, and no official endorsement should be inferred.

abuse, children with disabilities and physical, 224–229

abusive caregivers, characteristics of, 224–225, 226

accountability, outcomes-based education and, 6–19

active learning, 148

active reading, 108

acute lymphocytic leukemia, influence of treatment of, on education, 220–221

adolescents, working with emotionally disturbed, 171–173

advance organizers, 107

African Americans, culturally sensitive instructional practices for, with learning disabilities, 60–67

Aguilar v. Felton, 192, 193–194, 195, 196

America 2000: An Education Strategy, 8–9, 42, 84

American Association of Health, Physical Education, and Recreation (AAHPER), guidelines of, for teaching sex education, 119–120

American Association of School Administrators, 23

antiremedy, establishment clause of First Amendment as, 192–196

antisocial behavior, 156, 157, 159

apprentice programs, 42

appropriate technology, 83–84

assessment: outcomes-based education and, 7–8, 9, 11; teaching study skills and, 112

assistive listening devices, mainstreaming hearing impaired children and, 200, 201

assistive technology: adapting textbooks and, 106–108; computerized instructional principles and, 26–29; ethical considerations of using, 82–86; for hearing impaired children, 200, 201

authentic assessments, 8

automaticity, 27

autonomy, play and, 147

Beck Depression Inventory, 205

behavior: antisocial, 156, 158, 159; instructional contexts and teacher and student, 98–99, 100–104; problems, as type of communication, 184–186

behavior disorders, suicide among young people with, 163

"best practices," notion of, in special education, 75–76

bizarre behavior, as communication, 184–186

blacks, *see* African Americans

blind children, parent and toddler training project for, 204–209

body language, in classroom interactions, 180–183

body movements, nonverbal communication and, 182

Brophy-Good Teacher-Child Dyadic Interaction System, 101

Bruner, Jerome, 146

cancer, influence of treatment of, on education, 220–221

career education, 39–40

Career Education Implementation Incentive Act, 39

caregivers, characteristics of abusive, 224–225, 226

Center for Talented Youth, 138

child abuse, of children with disabilities, 224–229

child effect, theory of, 225–226

childrearing, among African Americans, 62

Classroom Inventory Checklist (CIC), 33–34

classroom environment, examining instructional contexts of students with learning disabilities, 98, 99–100

Code for Instructional Structure and Student Academic Response (CISSAR), 99

Collaborative Education Project, 75

color cueing, 111

communication: nonverbal, 180–183; in preschool environments, 176–179; receptive, strategy and picture task analysis, 188

community-based instruction, integrating elementary students with multiple disabilities and, 231

computerized instruction, 26–29

concepts, teaching of basic, to educable mentally handicapped, 116–118

concurrent model, of group instruction, 123

conduct disorder, 156, 158

conflict resolution, 56–57

constructivist theory, 61–62

cooperative learning: African-American children and, 63, 65–66; as alternative to gifted education, 139–140; computerized instruction and, 27, 29; play and, 149–150

cooperative work/study programs, 38–39, 40

Council for Exceptional Children (CEC), 10, 39, 66, 84

Cradles of Eminence (Goertzel and Goertzel), 145–146

daily check, teaching study skills and, 110

deaf children, classroom ethnocentrism and, 197–199

delinquencies, 156

depression: suicide and, 163–166; *see also,* emotionally disturbed children

direct instruction, 26–27

disability simulation, for regular education students, 68–71

dropouts, gifted, 141

dysthymic disorder, 164

early childhood education, mainstreaming in, 74–81

EASE (Exit Assistance for Special Educators), 32–36

Edison, Thomas, 145–146

educable mentally handicapped (EMH), guideline for teaching basic concepts to, 116–118

Education for All Handicapped Children Act of 1975; *see* Public Law 94-142

Education of the Disabled Act Amendments of 1986 (PL 99-457), 88

educational accountability, 6–19

educational reform, 41–42

emotionally disturbed children: special education for, 154–160; suicide and, 163, 164; values clarification for, 167–170; working with, 171–173

environment: classroom, and instructional contexts for students with learning disabilities, 98, 99–100; communication and preschool, 176–179; factors, and physical abuse of children with disabilities, 225, 226

establishment clause, of First Amendment, as antiremedy, 192–196

ethnocentrism, deaf children and classroom, 197–199

Etzioni, Amitai, 40

evaluations, teaching study skills and, 112

Exit Assistance for Special Educators, *see* EASE

experiential learning, 147–148

externalizing of disordered behavior, 156

eye contact, nonverbal communication and, 181–182

facial expressions, nonverbal communication and, 181–182

Feynman, Richard, 150–151

First Amendment, establishment clause of, as antiremedy, 192–196

flashcards, 111

focused play, 148

friendships, *see* peer supports; social integration

Germany, 42

gestures, nonverbal communication and, 182

gifted dropouts, 141

gifted/talented children: controversy over separate education for, 136–141; minorities as, 142–144; suicide and, 163

Goertzel, Mildred, 145–146

Goertzel, Victor, 145–146

graphic organizers, 107
Great Britain, 88
Greenberg, Paul, 43
group instruction, comparative study of Task Demonstration Model and Standard Prompting Hierarchy methods of, 122–133

health, influence of poor, on education, 220–223
hearing aids, 200, 201
Hendrick Hudson Central School District v. Rowley, 22, 23
High Success Network (HSN), 7–8
Honig v. Doe, 155, 158
humor, as classroom tool, 172

IEPs, *see* Individualized Education Programs
IFSPs, *see* Individualized Family Service Plans
Individual Family Service Plan (IFSP), 88
individualization, integration programs and, 235
Individualized Education Programs (IEPs), 32, 49–51, 210, 212, 213
Individuals with Disabilities Education Act of 1975; *see* Public Law 94-142
Individuals with Disabilities Education Amendments of 1990, 82
Ingraham v. Wright, 225
instructional contexts, examining, of students with learning disabilities, 98–105
integration, *see* mainstreaming
intelligence, changing definition of, 142–143
interaction styles, 56
internalizing, of disordered behavior, 156

Kaufman, Sandra, 37–38

Learning Games Library, 88, 89
learning strategies, teaching study skills and, 111–112
learning styles: computerized instruction and, 29; cultural differences and, 60–66
Lekotek, 88
Lemon v. Kurtzman, 193, 195, 196
leukemia, influence of treatment of, on education, 220–221
lipreading, as ineffective substitute for hearing, 200
low birth weight, influence of, on education, 222–223
low self-esteem: suicide and, 163; *see also,* values clarification
low vision services, efficacy of, for visually impaired children, 214–217

mainstreaming, 43; adapting textbooks for children with learning disabilities, 106–108; during early childhood years, 74–81; of elementary students with multiple disabilities, 230–233; encouraging peer supports and, 54–59; hearing impaired children and, 200–201; public schools and, 48–53
masking behavior, of learning disabled students, 94, 96–97
materials, preschool environment and, 176–179
McGill Action Planning System (MAPS), 17
medical treatment, influence of, on education, 220–223
memory: picture task analysis and, 188; techniques and teaching study skills, 111
Michigan Outcomes Training Project, 17
Minnesota Public Schools, suicide prevention program in, 164, 165
mnemonics, 111

National Assessment Governing Board (NAGB), 43
National Assessment of Educational Progress (NAEP), 9
National Association for Education of Young Children (NAEYC), 76
National Center on Educational Outcomes (NCEO), 6–7
National Council of Teachers of Mathematics (NCTM), 8, 9
National School Boards Association (NSBA), 23
"nonexamples," importance of, in teaching concepts, 117
nonverbal communication, in classroom interactions, 180–183
nonverbal prompts, preschool environments and, 177, 178–179
notebook checks, 110–111
notetaking, 111

Office of Special Education and Rehabilitation Services (OSERS), 40
open play, 148
Outcomes Driven Developmental Model (ODDM), 7–8, 78
Outcomes Training Project, 17
outcomes-based education, 6–19
outlining, 111
overlearning, 27

Parent and Toddler Training (PATT) project, 204–209
parents, 44–45; integrating elementary students and, 232; outcomes, 17, 18; toddler handicaps and, 204–209
Parks v. Pavkovic, 21, 22
peer supports: encouraging in integration settings, 54–59; *see also,* social integration
peer tutoring, 66

personal space, nonverbal communication and, 180–181, 182
physical abuse, of children with disabilities, 224–229
physical distance, nonverbal communication and, 180–181, 182
picture task analysis: benefits of, 187–188; developing and implementing, 188–189
P.L. 94-142, *see* Public Law 94-142
P.L. 95-207, 39
P.L. 99-457, 88
P.L. 100-407, 82–83
P.L. 101-476, 82
play: serious, 145–151; toy libraries and, 87–91
Play-Debrief-Replay, 149
premature infants: influence of, on education, 222–223; physical abuse of children and, 225–226
preschool, environments and communication, 176–179
previewing, 107
proxemics, nonverbal communication and, 180–181, 182
proximity, peer supports and, 54–55
Public Law 94-142, 164, 192–193, 210–213; controversy over responsibility to educate severely mentally disabled and, 21, 22, 23, 24
Public Law 95-207, 39
Public Law 99-457, 88
Public Law 100-407, 82–83
Public Law 101-476, 82
public schools, mainstreaming and, 48–53
"push in" arrangements, 74–75

quality indicators: assimilating, 78–80; comparison of, 77; from early childhood education, 76; from general education, 76; reflections of, 76, 78

Raspberry, William, 42
relationship enhancement, between teachers and disturbed adolescents, 171–172
residential placements, 21–22
Retarded Isn't Stupid, Mom! (Kaufman), 37–38
Royko, Mike, 44

sabotage, preschool environments and, 178
self-awareness, teaching study skills and, 112
self-esteem, 94, 163
self-questioning, 107–108
sequential model, of group instruction, 122–123
serious play, in classrooms, 145–151

seriously emotionally disturbed (SED) children and P.L. 94-142, 154–162, 164

severely disabled children, controversy over responsibility for educating, 20–25

sex education, for special education students, 119–121

Sex Information and Education Council for the U.S. (SIECUS), guidelines of, for sex education, 119–120

simulation, disability, for regular education students, 68–71

social integration: mainstreaming and, 232; public schools and, 49

socialized-subcultural delinquents, 156

socially maladjusted (SM) children, special education for, 154–162

socioeconomic status, of gifted youth, 139, 142–144

speech, concept production in, 117

Standard Prompting Hierarchy (SPH), vs. Task Demonstration Model of group instruction, 122–133

standards, 9–10, 12

student expectations, changing of, 172

study cards, 108

study skills, teaching, to students with mild handicaps, 109–113

suicide, emotionally disturbed children and, 172

Supreme Court, *see* United States Supreme Court

Surely You're Joking Mr. Feynman (Feynman), 150–151

tandem individual-to-group model, of group instruction, 123

tape recording, of textbooks, 106–107

Task Demonstration Model (TDM), as concurrent model for teaching groups of students with severe disabilities, 122–133

teacher(s): determination of appropriate education for, 210–213; disability simulations and, 68, 69; gifted education and, 137, 139; instructional contexts and behavior of, 98, 100–102; working with emotionally disturbed adolescents, 171–173

teaching, of study skills to students with mild handicaps, 109–113

teamwork, integration programs and, 234, 235, 236

technology: effect of, on play, 146–147; *see also,* assistive technology

Technology Related Assistance for Individuals with Disabilities Act of 1988, 82–83

teenagers, *see* adolescents

testing, teaching study skills for, 111

textbooks, adapting, for children with learning disabilities, 106–108

time analysis, 110

Timothy W. v. Rochester, New Hampshire, School District, 20–21, 22–23

toy libraries, 87–91

ToyBrary Project, 88, 89

tracking, 43

transition movement, 40, 42

treatment, influence of medical, on education, 220–223

United States Supreme Court, 193, 195, 196; abuse of children and, 225; on responsibility for educating severely disabled children, 20–23

values, 167

values clarification, for students with emotional disabilities, 167–170

verbal interaction, African-American children and, 63, 64

visually impaired children, 204–209, 210–213; appropriate education for, 210–213; efficacy of low vision services for, 214–217

vocational apprentice programs, 42

work/study programs, 38–39, 40

Wright, Frank Lloyd, 146

"zero-reject policy," 23

Zobrest v. Catalina Foothills School District, 193–194, 195, 196

Credits/ Acknowledgments

Cover design by Charles Vitelli

1. The Regular Education Initiative
Facing overview—United Nations photo by W. A. Graham.

2. Transition Concerns
Facing overview—United Nations photo by Yutaka Nagata.

3. Inclusionary Education: Peer Interactions
Facing overview—United Nations photo by L. Solmssen. 55-58—Photographs by Mark A. Regan.

4. Early Childhood Special Education
Facing overview—United Nations photo by L. Solmssen.

5. Children With Learning Disabilities
Facing overview—United Nations photo by Jane Hanckel.

6. Children With Mental Retardation
Facing overview—United Nations photo by J. Isaac.

7. Children With Special Gifts and Talents
Facing overview—EPA-Documerica.

8. Children With Emotional and Behavioral Problems
Facing overview—EPA-Documerica.

9. Children With Communication Disorders
Facing overview—United Nations photo by L. Solmssen. 181, 183—Photographs by Russ Thames.

10. Children With Hearing Impairments
Facing overview—WHO photo by S. Schwab.

11. Children With Visual Impairments
Facing overview—United Nations photo by S. Dimartini. 211, 212—Courtesy of J. A. Bensel, Maryland School for the Blind.

12. Children With Physical or Health Impairments
Facing overview—United Nations photo by L. Solmssen. 238—United Nations photo.

ANNUAL EDITIONS ARTICLE REVIEW FORM

■ NAME: _____ DATE: _____

■ TITLE AND NUMBER OF ARTICLE: _____

■ BRIEFLY STATE THE MAIN IDEA OF THIS ARTICLE: _____

_____

_____

_____

_____

■ LIST THREE IMPORTANT FACTS THAT THE AUTHOR USES TO SUPPORT THE MAIN IDEA:

_____

_____

_____

_____

_____

■ WHAT INFORMATION OR IDEAS DISCUSSED IN THIS ARTICLE ARE ALSO DISCUSSED IN YOUR TEXTBOOK OR OTHER READING YOU HAVE DONE? LIST THE TEXTBOOK CHAPTERS AND PAGE NUMBERS:

_____

_____

_____

_____

_____

_____

■ LIST ANY EXAMPLES OF BIAS OR FAULTY REASONING THAT YOU FOUND IN THE ARTICLE:

_____

_____

_____

_____

■ LIST ANY NEW TERMS/CONCEPTS THAT WERE DISCUSSED IN THE ARTICLE AND WRITE A SHORT DEFINITION:

_____

_____

_____

_____

*Your instructor may require you to use this Annual Editions Article Review Form in any number of ways: for articles that are assigned, for extra credit, as a tool to assist in developing assigned papers, or simply for your own reference. Even if it is not required, we encourage you to photocopy and use this page; you'll find that reflecting on the articles will greatly enhance the information from your text.

ANNUAL EDITIONS:
EDUCATING EXCEPTIONAL CHILDREN,
Seventh Edition
Article Rating Form

Here is an opportunity for you to have direct input into the next revision of this volume. We would like you to rate each of the 40 articles listed below, using the following scale:

1. **Excellent: should definitely be retained**
2. **Above average: should probably be retained**
3. **Below average: should probably be deleted**
4. **Poor: should definitely be deleted**

Your ratings will play a vital part in the next revision. So please mail this prepaid form to us just as soon as you complete it.
Thanks for your help!

We Want Your Advice

Annual Editions revisions depend on two major opinion sources: one is our Advisory Board, listed in the front of this volume, which works with us in scanning the thousands of articles published in the public press each year; the other is you—the person actually using the book. Please help us and the users of the next edition by completing the prepaid article rating form on this page and returning it to us. Thank you.

Rating	Article	Rating	Article
	1. Outcomes Are for Special Educators Too		21. Poor and Minority Students Can Be Gifted, Too!
	2. Severely Disabled Children: Who Pays?		22. Serious Play in the Classroom
	3. Instructional Principles: Behind Computerized Instruction for Students With Exceptionalities		23. Do Public Schools Have an Obligation to Serve Troubled Children and Youth?
	4. EASE: Exit Assistance for Special Educators—Helping Students Make the Transition		24. Suicide and Depression: Special Education's Responsibility
	5. Transition: Old Wine in New Bottles		25. Values Clarification for Students With Emotional Disabilities
	6. Public Schools Welcome Students With Disabilities as Full Members		26. Working With Disturbed Adolescents
	7. Encouraging Peer Supports and Friendships		27. Preschool Classroom Environments That Promote Communication
	8. Culturally Sensitive Instructional Practices for African-American Learners With Disabilities		28. Do You See What I Mean? Body Language in Classroom Interactions
	9. Disability Simulation for Regular Education Students		29. See Me, Help Me
	10. Mainstreaming During the Early Childhood Years		30. Using a Picture Task Analysis to Teach Students With Multiple Disabilities
	11. Children With Disabilities Who Use Assistive Technology: Ethical Considerations		31. The Establishment Clause as Antiremedy
	12. Play for All Children: The Toy Library Solution		32. Reducing Ethnocentrism
	13. The Masks Students Wear		33. Hearing for Success in the Classroom
	14. Examining the Instructional Contexts of Students With Learning Disabilities		34. The Parent and Toddler Training Project for Visually Impaired and Blind Multihandicapped Children
	15. Adapting Textbooks for Children With Learning Disabilities in Mainstreamed Classrooms		35. Appropriate Education for Visually Handicapped Students
	16. Teaching Study Skills to Students With Mild Handicaps: The Role of the Classroom Teacher		36. Efficacy of Low Vision Services for Visually Impaired Children
	17. Teaching Basic Concepts to Students Who Are Educable Mentally Handicapped		37. Medical Treatment and Educational Problems in Children
	18. Sex Education for Students With High-Incidence Special Needs		38. Physical Abuse: Are Children With Disabilities at Greater Risk?
	19. The Task Demonstration Model: A Concurrent Model for Teaching Groups of Students With Severe Disabilities		39. Integrating Elementary Students With Multiple Disabilities Into Supported Regular Classes
	20. Turning On the Bright Lights		40. Designing an Integrated Program for Learners With Severe Disabilities

(Continued on next page)

ABOUT YOU

Name_____ Date_____

Are you a teacher? ☐   Or student? ☐

Your School Name _____

Department _____

Address _____

City _____ State _____ Zip _____

School Telephone # _____

YOUR COMMENTS ARE IMPORTANT TO US!

Please fill in the following information:

For which course did you use this book? _____

Did you use a text with this Annual Edition?   ☐ yes   ☐ no

The title of the text? _____

What are your general reactions to the Annual Editions concept?

Have you read any particular articles recently that you think should be included in the next edition?

Are there any articles you feel should be replaced in the next edition? Why?

Are there other areas that you feel would utilize an Annual Edition?

May we contact you for editorial input?

May we quote you from above?

ANNUAL EDITIONS: EDUCATING EXCEPTIONAL CHILDREN, Seventh Edition

BUSINESS REPLY MAIL

First Class   Permit No. 84   Guilford, CT

Postage will be paid by addressee

The Dushkin Publishing Group, Inc.
Sluice Dock
DPG **Guilford, Connecticut 06437**

No Postage
Necessary
if Mailed
in the
United States